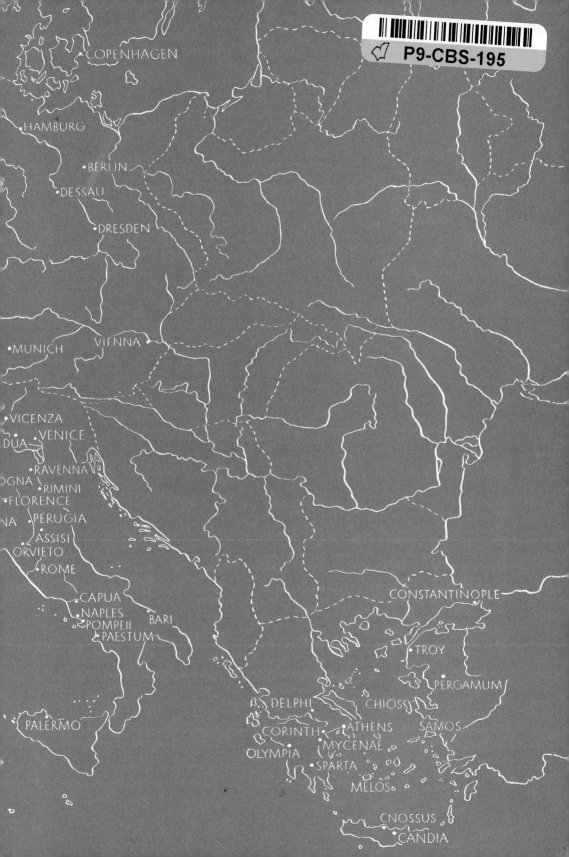

Bonnie Seymour
Long Beach '62

HISTORY OF WORLD ART

Duccio di Buoninsegna (*c.* 1255–1319) *Temptation of Christ*, Detail, Majestas,
Cathedral of Siena (1308–11) Frick Collection, New York. Tempera on wood.

HISTORY

OF

WORLD ART

EVERARD M. UPJOHN
PROFESSOR OF FINE ARTS
COLUMBIA UNIVERSITY

PAUL S. WINGERT
ASSOCIATE PROFESSOR OF FINE ARTS
COLUMBIA UNIVERSITY

JANE GASTON MAHLER
ASSOCIATE PROFESSOR OF FINE ARTS
COLUMBIA UNIVERSITY

SECOND EDITION   REVISED AND ENLARGED

NEW YORK · OXFORD UNIVERSITY PRESS · 1958

PRINTED IN THE UNITED STATES OF AMERICA

Preface

THE task of preparing this volume has not been that of a simple revision but has been rather a complete reworking and rewriting of the entire book. Encouraged by the enthusiastic reception accorded the first edition, and guided by the frank, friendly, and constructive criticisms of colleagues throughout the country, we have effected major changes in organization, content, and format.

The noticeably striking change in this edition is the revised format. In almost every case the work of art being studied is reproduced at the point of discussion. The pertinent physical data is also given, and where appropriate an architectural plan accompanies the illustration. By this scheme the student can constantly refer to the pictures and corroborate the text; he can appreciate the uses made of materials, apply the dimensions and plans given in the text to the impression of the work as it appears in the illustration.

In making the textual changes we have trimmed, reorganized, and added with careful consideration for the basic requirements of introductory courses throughout the country. We have added a chapter on the art of prehistoric man, another on the arts of the American Indians of Peru and Mexico before the Spanish conquest and of the post-Conquest tribal art of the Indians, and a third on the arts of Negro Africa and of Islands of the South Pacific. Furthermore, those chapters that deal with the arts of the twentieth century in Europe and America have been completely rewritten and greatly expanded since even the short span of a decade has brought further artistic achievement and increased historical perspective.

Finally the most dramatic addition to this revision has been the inclusion of twenty-five works of art on seventeen plates in full color. Line, mass, and space can be understood through black and white illustrations. Color cannot. These works have been chosen as representative examples from artists and periods where the element of color plays an unusually important role. It should be added that considerable care and expense has gone into the preparation of the plates to make certain a high quality of color reproduction.

It is impossible to over-emphasize our indebtedness to those colleagues and critics who have had a share in shaping this new volume. The following suggested revisions in the original edition and read portions of the revised manuscript at the request of the publisher: Mr. John R. Stafford, Professor of Art at City College of San Francisco, Mr. Richard G. Tansey, Associate Professor of Art at San Jose State College, Mr. Carl K. Hersey, Professor of Fine Arts at University of Rochester, Mr. John Galloway, Assistant Professor of Art at University of Alabama, Mr. John F. Kienitz, Professor of Art History at University of Wisconsin, Miss Eleanor P. Spencer, Professor of Fine Arts, Goucher College, Mr. Edwin C. Rae, Associate Professor of Art at University of Illinois, Mr. Frederick Hartt, Professor of History of Art at Washington University, and Mr. Francis S. Grubar, Assistant Professor of Art at University of Maryland. Nor can we forget that our thanks are due to our distinguished former colleagues Professor William B. Dinsmoor and Professor Margarete Bieber for their comments of the classical chapters, to Professor Ralph Fanning of Ohio State University and the late Mr. Peyton Boswell of the *Art Digest* for their constructive criticisms of the chapters on Western art, to Mr. John Pope and Dr. Richard Ettinghausen of the Freer Gallery in Washington, D.C., and Miss Pauline Simmons of the Metropolitan Museum in New York for their careful reading of and suggestions for the chapters on Oriental art. We want further to express our appreciation of the care and imagination taken in the design of this volume by Mr. John Begg of the Oxford University Press and of the careful editorial guidance given us by Miss Leona Capeless of that organization. Acknowledgment of the courtesy of the many museums and private individuals from whom photographs have been obtained will be found in the list of illustrations, and in this regard mention must be made of Francis G. Mayer, who furnished color Kodachromes for eighteen of the color illustrations, and of the kindness of the late Mr. Joseph Powers.

Columbia University   E.M.U.
New York, N. Y.   P.S.W.
1 October 1957   J.G.M.

Table of Contents

List of Color Plates

List of Illustrations

DECORATIONS BY JANE RANDOLPH

HISTORY OF WORLD ART

I

A fundamental human demand calls art into being. Its primary purpose is to add to the interpretation and completeness of life. It may be, and at times has been, made to serve other ends, the glorification of religion, propaganda, symbolism; but these aims, whether laudable or not, are foreign to its main goal. They may even hinder artistic achievement. This achievement does not contribute in itself to the necessities of being. Mankind cannot live without food, shelter, and clothing; it can exist without art. Under frontier conditions, since art has no immediate and practical value, it may be subordinated to more pressing needs. Nevertheless, man's craving for art is very deep-rooted; it has appeared continuously since prehistoric days throughout the world. All that we know of early man, except what may be gleaned from his bones, is learned from his handicrafts.

These reveal his desire to add something to his tools beyond pure utility. To adorn them cost him time and effort, but only under the lash of necessity has humanity been willing to forgo the pleasure it gains by seeing and handling well-made objects that not merely satisfy their practical purpose but in addition delight the hand and eye, the mind and soul.

Few activities of man offer such a variety of legitimate interpretations as his art. It has a different meaning to everyone. To an Aristotle, it suggests the formulation of an aesthetic theory; to a Spengler, the reflection of a civilization. A scientist or an engineer may be concerned only with its techniques; a poet with its personal expression as well. It is an opportunity for intellectual organization, in painting, sculpture, or architecture. Its beauty may enhance man's pleasure in the objects with which he surrounds himself. The sensitive creator or observer may find room here for emotional catharsis.

The existence of these and many other paths to the understanding of art, or any conceivable combination of them, should compel tolerance. Aesthetic creeds are like customs; each has validity in its time and place. So long as mankind is composed of individuals, each will take the way he finds most congenial. Some avenues are open to everyone, regardless of training; others require experience or information or both. But that person will receive the richest satisfaction to whom the greatest number of approaches is available.

A work of art is like a triangle whose sides are content, expression, and decoration. These three factors are interdependent, but not necessarily equal. An artist may choose to develop one phase beyond another. Since none of these elements is inherently of more value than its companions, to emphasize decoration is neither better nor worse than to stress expression or content.

The sides of our triangle are distinct from the artistic vehicles, such as line, mass, volume, space, color, and texture, which may serve the artist in developing content, expression, and decoration. Let us examine each side in turn, beginning with content. Almost all examples of painting and sculpture have a subject; they represent something, although in recent times some artists have minimized if not eliminated this factor. In Las Meninas (fig. 294), Velásquez records an incident of the Spanish court.

He draws the figures as masses existing in space; the color of the costumes is that of the cloth itself; the light is made to appear in the painting as it is in the artist's studio wherein the scene is laid. The means available to the painter are here utilized to convey to the spectator the content or representational aspects of the design. To recognize the dominance of content in this instance is not to deny other values in the work. Because the color, for example, of the Infanta's dress records that fact, we need not conclude that it has no decorative or expressive value; on the contrary, these factors amplify and reinforce the content. The Apollo and Daphne (fig. 283) by Bernini avails itself of the means of sculpture to describe an incident of classic mythology. Each contrast of texture in flesh, hair, textile, or foliage is rendered by the artist; the movement dramatizes the chase, and also contributes to the decorative or expressive possibilities.

Representation cannot exist in architecture and in many of the so-called minor arts; the corresponding element in these categories is function, the purpose the building or object is designed to meet. Architecture diverges from the representational arts in the importance of this factor. In painting and sculpture, content, as we have used the term to refer to descriptive possibilities, may be primary or it may be negligible. With very few exceptions, function is vital to architecture. Effective provision for the use of a building is a prerequisite; if the edifice is not necessarily successful because it fulfills its function, it is unsuccessful if it fails to do so.

By expression, we mean the artist's comment on, or interpretation of, his theme. Theoretically an artist may attempt a dispassionate statement in paint or stone of what he sees; a colored photograph, so to speak, of an event or object. Practically, such impersonality seldom exists. The portrait of Georg Gisze (fig. 277) by Holbein is objective, but its very strength of characterization is in effect the artist's analysis of his sitter's personality. The very selection of subject involves some comment by the artist, since it indicates what seems to him important or of aesthetic interest. Usually much more than this is involved. Two artists rarely respond to the same problem in the same way. An incident of daily life may be humorous to one artist, tragic to another, or to a third an opportunity to appraise society. Such variety of response reveals the artists' personalities. At times this response is highly individual, and therefore susceptible of complete understanding only by others of similar temperament. Since personality is unique, its extreme expression may be comprehensible only to the artist, but this is not a common occurrence.

The painters of China and Japan use line as a means of expression to a greater extent than any European artist. The fine lines of the waves and rigging and especially those in the twigs of the tree in Sesson's painting of a Boat Returning in a Storm (fig. 658) express the power of the wind. In the Italian Simone Martini's portrait of Guidoriccio da Fogliano (fig. 173), fortified towns, spears and pennons, and palisade not only represent the martial character of the man but intensify it by their spiky angularity of silhouette. The mobility of a horse intrigued Simone. Repeated curves in both horse and rider create a suggestion of motion as vivid in its conventionality as it could be in the most scientific record of a horse in movement, though the latter might reveal a more equine, less undulating action. To Maillol, the mass and weight of the Seated Woman (fig. 474) have the greatest significance and are so emphasized. Color also can be made interpretive. The color of the gaunt figures in Picasso's 'blue period' enhances their poignancy. At the time, 1901–3, this Spaniard's life intensified his feeling for the tragedies of existence. He experimented with painting in a single color, blue, which to him best conveyed depression. Evidently the prevailing tone was not chosen for representation, since the subjects would be clearer if painted with a wider palette, nor does the unity of color enhance the decorative aspect. It must be, then, an emotional mirror of Picasso's view of life.

Allied to expression is artistic character, applicable especially to architecture. The phrase describes the revelation of the purpose of an edifice in its design. We expect a church to look like a church, a bank like a bank. Function should mold the plan, which involves the size, shape, and disposition of the several spaces in a building. Since the plan in turn governs the exterior, it reveals the building's character. Thus, in theory, the character of any structure stems properly from adequate planning. In practice, character tends to become recognizability, which is conditioned by our knowledge. We expect a school to look not merely like a school, but like schools familiar to us. This is unfortunate if the buildings we identify as schools do not function well as such. Moreover, we may expect the design to express spirituality in a church, entertainment in a theater. We may find character in painting and sculpture. A carved or painted altarpiece is devotional in intent, and different in expression from a picture destined for a boudoir, or a statue designed for a hall of state.

Decoration is the third side of our triangle. The term refers to formal organization in any design beyond that which may be demanded by content or expression. It is not essential to narrative or illustrative clarity; indeed, it may act in opposition. Nor does it, of itself, extend the expressive possibilities. It may include such matters as composition, proportion, scale (at times), and other qualities which are in themselves pleasing to the eye. If it is sometimes difficult to separate content from expression, it is impossible wholly to distinguish decoration from the other two. Nevertheless, in Gauguin's painting, Mahana No Atua (Plate xi, facing p. 588), the lines limiting shapes in the water are essentially decorative. These watery lines have some illustrative value

in conveying the liquid nature of this placid sea, but their decorative rhythms predominate. It would be easy to conceive a method, even through line alone, that would more clearly depict water, as in fact Hokusai has in The Wave (fig. 670), and perhaps one that would better express its limpid surface; to find a more telling decorative passage might be hard. The rich color of medieval stained glass is highly decorative. A window in Chartres (Plate ii, facing p. 269) makes no pretense to accurate representation of objects. In the Parable of the Sower from Canterbury, the trees and plants are a golden yellow, blue, or purple, not because green was not available—it exists in the same window—nor because the designer saw purple bushes, but because those tones in their particular combination afford a rich decorative ensemble. A Persian manuscript by Bihzād (Plate xvi, facing p. 653) is magnificent as decoration.

These three factors then, content, expression, and decoration, are present in works of art. The artist may select one of them, or any combination that suits his needs; or historical formulation of the problem may determine the combination. In any case he must try to achieve such unity that his primary purpose will be impressed on the observer. Though several aims may be included, like plot and sub-plots in a novel, one usually dominates. Introduction of foreign subject matter, no matter how expressive or decorative such extraneous material may be, is apt to weaken the concentration on the main theme. To

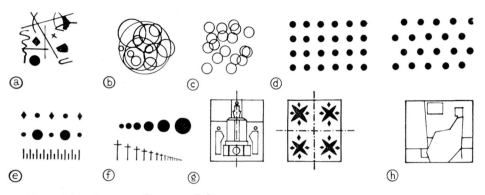

1. *Composition:* Harmony, Sequence, Balance.

take an extreme case, imagine a still life depicting a bowl of fruit on a table. A knife and fork lying beside the bowl may seem appropriate, but if the artist were to substitute a sword or an ax, one's mind would rebel. The sword might provide just the right shape, size, and color, but one would still feel it to be a disintegrating element. Conversely, pertinent material can enrich a theme. By painting Georg Gisze (fig. 277) in his office surrounded by his business equipment, Holbein helps to characterize the man. The artist may also deliberately introduce contrasting objects to heighten the effect, but in this case the material is not extraneous.

Aesthetic unity in a work of art is achieved through composition or design; that is, a visual co-ordination of its parts. Composition has three factors, though not all need be exploited in a single example. The first, *harmony*, refers to the creation of a sense of order by repetition of aesthetic motives. In figure 1, *a* illustrates lack of harmony in size, shape, value, and arrangement of the

lines or areas. With *b*, a simple motive, the circle, is adopted and a vague pattern appears. The sense of order, though minor, is due to the repetition of a series of circles. In size and arrangement, however, there is still no harmony. Make all the circles of the same size, as in *c*, and a contributory factor enhances the harmony; place them in some specific relation to one another, for example, at the corners of squares, triangles, hexagons, or in any other fundamental system, and a recognizable pattern results, *d*. Not only is the familiar polka dot design so created, but most all-over patterns of textiles and wallpapers adopt this foundation.

Sequence, or rhythm, the second element of composition, may be defined as regularity of change. While not always distinguishable from harmony, which also involves regularity, sequence is nevertheless distinct. It has two forms. In *e*, the regularity of change is that of alternation of long and short, large and small; it may be of different tones or colors, or of contrasting motives. Such schemes can be considered as two patterns illustrating harmony superposed on one another. Or a motive may show a sequence of progression, *f*. Applied to size, it results from repeated forms seen in perspective, as when one looks along a line of telegraph poles, or down a railway track. We know the distant ties are as large as those in the foreground, but they appear to diminish in size. A spiral, like a mathematical progression, shows regularity of change in direction, as in an Ionic capital (fig. 32). Or again, a sequence of direction exists in a group of curves becoming successively flatter, or a series of angles more and more acute. The anthemion motive forming a band below the capitals of the north porch on the Erechtheum in Athens (fig. 60) is an application of this device.

The third of our factors, *balance*, again has two types. Axial balance, or symmetry, refers to the duplication of motives on either side of an imaginary central line or point, *g*. One of our diagrams might apply to many late fifteenth-century or early sixteenth-century Italian paintings, such as the Castelfranco Madonna by Giorgione. What we define as asymmetrical or occult balance is the arrangement of motives unlike in shape, size, color, and so on, but whose visual sum creates a sense of equilibrium around a point. For example, *h* is based on Whistler's painting of his mother. Furthermore, diagonal lines might be made equal and regular, but a series of diagonals moving in one direction can be balanced by another series, not identical, moving in the opposite direction.

Or again, in Titian's painting called the Duke of Norfolk (fig. 245), the central line of the canvas passes through the left eye of the subject, so that the head is slightly to the left, as is the right hand. But, though small, the cuff of the left hand is placed so far to the right that a sense of equilibrium is established between the three light areas in the design. Perhaps the majority of Far Eastern paintings are based on occult balance.

These elements of composition are so broad as to admit of no exceptions, although an artist may apply them either deliberately or by instinct. Order can be analyzed in these terms, not only in the visual arts, but in other forms of artistic expression, and in nature herself. The organization of nature in general is so complex as to defy analysis, but in her component parts she affords countless illustrations of harmony, sequence, and balance. The symmetry of a pine and the balanced distribution of leaves on either side of a stem in certain plants are homely illustrations. The color sequence of a rainbow, the radial arrangement of the petals in a daisy, the progressive length of feathers in a bird's wing come to mind. Harmony is so universal that one need only cite the billowing masses of cumulus clouds or the broken wisps of cirrus to prove the point. Occasionally nature destroys her own organization; more commonly the activities of man accomplish the same result. The disorder resulting from a forest fire, a timber cutting, or a hurricane destroys the beauty of a landscape.

In the sister arts, too, these elements,

though perhaps called by other names, are present. Rhythm and meter in poetry are harmony; rhyme often shows sequence of alternation. The repetition of phrases or variations on a theme in music accomplish the same end. For the dance, as also in music, the time factor leads to an emphasis on sequence, rhythm.

Although the application of these elements will recur in the following chapters, two examples may be analyzed here as demonstrations. The Chicago Daily News Building (fig. 447), by Holabird and Root, consists of a harmony of cubical masses. Like most public buildings, it is symmetrical, the voids and solids balanced on either side of an axis. Most of the windows are identical, separate units, but at both ends of the main front two vertical rows are united in a projecting mass as continuous strips. That projection and those strips terminate the design from side to side, but the same projecting feature also includes a row of normal windows like those in the large area of the front, not tied together in bands and so repeating the motive of the central treatment. Moreover, beyond these terminal sections, the plane of the wall is recalled in a single-windowed bay. A *bay* is a unit of architectural design extending from the axis of one column or section of wall to the center of the next support. See, too, how these terminals are repeated with variations on the end of the building, so that from most points of vision the front and sides of the structure act together as parts of a single design. In themselves, the vertical strips of windows might form an element of contrast, but they are not so left. Over the main area, the windows of the second, third, and fourth floors from the top of the principal mass are again tied together in short vertical bands, serving not only to recall the vertical accents of the end pavilions but also to advertise the vertical termination. Once more the plain window form recurs in a single row above that. Then the first setback takes up the theme again. At or near the bottom of the building, the voids and solids are larger; at the top also that scheme is reintroduced as a crowning member. Such an analysis, however incomplete, takes many words; but the effect of unity is perceived instantaneously, even when the observer does not take pains to examine the way in which the unity is achieved.

In the Purification of the Temple (fig. 290), El Greco depicts Christ in the center of a compact knot of figures. That group forms a rectangle whose proportions are similar to the shape of the whole canvas. Another area of like proportions exists in the portraits of four artists in the lower right corner, a clear example of harmony of shape. In the mother and child to the right of the main characters, and in the men of the extreme background, the movement tilts to the right. The vertical standing figures limit the principal theme on its right edge, but in Christ the action causes the upper part of His figure to shift to the left. As the traders try to escape His lash, their bodies lean more and more to the left, until they reach the diagonal motive of the woman dealing in doves. El Greco recalls that diagonal in the seated man at the right corner of the group, and again in the infant lying on the steps. Such a sequence toward the diagonal needs something to terminate it; hence the strong vertical of the woman's arm, and of the man behind her.

El Greco accents Christ as the principal figure. His head centers on the opening to the piazza against the front of one of the distant palaces. For dramatic interest, Jesus, though in the center, is distinct from the group. Compact elsewhere, the group opens up in v-shaped voids to His right and left, more apparent in the original than in any reproduction because of the color. This, too, contributes its share to the compositional unity. Each major tone of red, blue, yellow, or green is echoed again and again through this design.

If one is to speak precisely about color, one must realize that the word includes three properties that together are better called *tone*. The three elements of tone have many names. The first is *color* properly speaking, its redness, blueness, or yellowness. One may produce two tones, both pure blue, but one a bright blue and one a gray blue. This vividness or dullness of tone is known as *intensity*. Finally, tone may change in lightness or darkness, that is in *value*.

This triple division offers certain opportunities to the artist. The complete range of tone is infinite, but an artist in any particular work can select his palette, limiting himself but achieving thereby possibilities of harmony. Van Gogh may prefer tones of maximum or nearly maximum intensity, and reach harmony by that means. In many of his landscapes, Corot does just the opposite, choosing to employ only low intensities, and further avoiding very high and very low values. The richness of Venetian painting is due in part to its *tonality*; that is, the sense of a general tone dominating the several colors. In this school, a transparent yellowish glaze, spread over the strong local colors, leaves them in the same relation to one another, but pulls them all toward the tone of the glaze. Thus a white dress may seem to be white in relation to a red passage next to it, whereas in actuality if we isolate the 'white' area, we shall find it to be yellow in color. A similar consequence stems from nature in Monet's painting of the mists at Giverny, where all tones are drawn toward the tone of the fog.

Egyptian artists (Plate 1, facing p. 268) accepted the fact that paintings exist in only two dimensions, and drew their figures as silhouettes with almost no indication of projection or recession in or around them. *Line* served to define the shape and form of the figures. In the three-dimensional arts of sculpture and architecture, line may play an important role, such as in the silhouette of any statue against its background. This silhouette differs with every change in the angle of vision, but the sum of the silhouettes defines the form of the statue.

Further, changes of surface in sculpture may be arranged in a system of lines, as in The Great Buddha at Kamakura (fig. 653). The façade of the Cancelleria Palace, Rome (fig. 223), is a pattern of narrow lines of shadow.

Giotto, on the other hand, feels that the solidity or *mass* of his human figures (fig. 175) is more essential than the flat surface of his wall. He therefore draws them in varied tones of light to create in them an illusion of roundness, a sense of mass or form. Similarly, Maillol emphasizes the weight, the mass, of his Seated Woman (fig. 474), as do the Pyramids at Gizeh (fig. 8). V*olume* is the antonym of mass. The shape of the Bauhaus, Dessau (fig. 480), is almost as simple as that of the Pyramids, but the observer is forced to perceive the space contained within this shape in contrast to the apparent and actual solidity in the mass of the Pyramid.

When Giotto perceived his figures as masses, it was necessary to create three-dimensional *space* for them. In his case this is limited, but Pozzo in his ceiling paintings (fig. 288) creates an illusion of vast depth. The three figures in Raphael's Madonna del Cardellino (fig. 238) form a compact pyramid, contained within itself and distinct from the unlimited space of the landscape. The figures in Watteau's Embarkation for Cythera (fig. 324) merge with space. A similar contrast is apparent in the Parthenon, Athens (fig. 52), and in Rheims Cathedral (fig. 140). The former is a prism discrete from surrounding space; but the cathedral fuses with space. The volumes of nave, aisles, and transepts in Santiago de Compostela (fig. 116) are relatively distinct; those of Chartres (fig. 142) flow into one another. In most buildings of the past, the spaces enclosed are thought of as something different from the out-of-doors; in the Tugendhat House, Brno (fig. 483), the glass walls provide a minimum separation of internal and external space.

Finally, an artist may find an interest in *texture*. Bernini in sculpture (fig. 283) or Vermeer in painting (Plate VIII, facing p. 365) simulate the texture of flesh or cloth. Seurat (fig. 401) is indifferent to this, but through his technique creates texture with the pigment itself. Richardson exploits the texture of stone in the Marshall Field Warehouse, Chicago (fig. 435). In these matters a contemporary artist finds himself remarkably free. In the past, his client decided on the subject; the Church dictated its arrangement; and often the very pigments were specified in advance. Today, the artist limits himself when he selects the problem through the demands of composition, and by the medium or material chosen.

Each substance offers only certain possibilities because of its physical properties—the strength and weight of stone, the lightness and workability of wood, the toughness of metal. Giovanni da Bologna's Flying Mercury (fig. 257), feasible in bronze, would be impossible in stone. The small cross section through the wind from the mouth of Aeolus would hardly support the weight of a stone figure. Neither could marble be carved into the flowing wings or the shape of the caduceus. This is obvious, but the sensitive designer will respect somewhat narrower limits than those imposed by the physical properties.

For example, the range of color, value, and intensity available for fresco painting is more restricted than in oil painting. The possibilities of brush work in oils are not identical with those in water color. In sculpture, the choice of stone compels some compactness of conception. The actual limits are however very wide. In his Apollo and Daphne (fig. 283), Bernini shows what technical dexterity can do with stone. But perhaps his pictorialism here exceeds the proper limits of his medium. The sculpturesque diorite portrait of Khafra (fig. 15) has more respect for stone. Its design conveys the weight of material; its compactness confines our attention within the block, instead of leading our eye out of it, as do the extended arms of the Apollo or the Daphne. A clever imitation of textures by Bernini almost convinces one that marble has ceased to be stone; their absence in the Khafra allows full expression to the texture of the stone itself.

Though the effect on design in architecture is no greater than in sculpture or painting, the results are easier to isolate. Wood, a fibrous material strong in proportion to its weight, can be cut into long members for beams or columns. Slender wood posts supporting long beams result in a rectangle longer than it is high. The Lecture Hall (fig. 620) at Tōshōdaiji, founded on wood construction, is composed of such horizontal rectangles, not only in its proportions but in its details. The weight of stone compels a different form. A stone beam as long and thin as the wood members of the Kōdō would break of its own weight and certainly could not support any additional load of a roof or floor. Therefore stone beams must be short and the supports close together. Similar factors suggest heavier proportions for stone columns. The result must be vertical rectangles, taller than they are wide.

The earliest examples of architecture, such as prehistoric Stonehenge (fig. 6), illustrate this stone aesthetic. The design of this ring of monoliths spanned by short beams is composed of repeated vertical rectangles. Most Western architecture was based on stone construction until recent times. Such styles as the eighteenth-century Georgian in America often employed wood, but both proportion and architectural vocabulary derive from styles developed in masonry. In this case, sympathetic craftsmanship adapted details to the new material; columns were attenuated to a point where they could not be executed in marble.

The bearing of material on design is not only apparent in the distinction of wood and stone, but may be narrowed to the treatments appropriate to oak or mahogany, to granite or marble. The hardness of granite suggests that its design should rely on simple proportions with little surface interruption. The Temple of the Sphinx at Gizeh (fig. 9) speaks with solemn grandeur through its prismatic blocks supporting plain beams. In the marble Parthenon, Athens (fig. 52), greater detail is possible because of the comparative ease of cutting marble. The same is true in sculpture. The diorite portrait of Khafra (fig. 15) is severe as compared with the marble figure of Michelangelo's Night (fig. 234) on the Medici Tomb.

The matters discussed so far are inherent in the artistic problem. If the artist lived in a void, only such considerations would be pertinent. Since that cannot be true, other forces bear on any specific creation. These stem from the time and place in which the work is born. They shape the problem confronting the artist; they also mold his mentality.

Geography, though its effect is often overrated, has some bearing especially on architecture. First, the site chosen for a building may determine its direction and character. Except for the prevailing incidence of sun or wind, a structure on a plain might face in any direction. A sloping plot restricts such freedom. Moreover, a design suited to the great plains may be inappropriate for wooded, mountainous terrain.

Second, where an architecture is indigenous, we might expect to find a low pitched roof in southern countries, a high pitched roof in northern. The gentle slope of the roof of the Parthenon (fig. 52) suffices to void any rainfall, but would be less suitable if snow were a serious consideration. The steep roof of the Parson Capen House in Topsfield, Massachusetts (fig. 357), implies the rigorous New England climate. Architecture in a desert exhibits a flat roof, as in the Indian pueblos of the Southwest or in Egyptian temples (fig. 10). However, so many other considerations exist, such as the wind, the type and materials of construction, or the transmission of an architectural style from one region to another, that precipitation is not a paramount factor.

A third and more important effect of geography, especially in the past with its primitive methods of transportation, is the supply of local materials. Where wood is plentiful, it will be used and so will shape the design. Greece, because of its marble quarries, developed a stone architecture. Mesopotamia, lacking both stone and wood, had to resort to clay, and a style in brick came into being. Finally, geography often accounts for the spread of artistic styles from one land to another. Trade routes as well as propinquity bear on the history of art more than is often realized.

Economic conditions are even more influential. A continued period of economic chaos can eliminate the arts. The period of the Hundred Years' War in France, which brought to an end the epoch of cathedral building, was, by comparison, artistically barren. The Thirty Years' War blighted those parts of Germany touched by it. The centuries of poverty and confusion in Western Europe following the collapse of the Roman Empire nearly extinguished the creative flame. A few insignificant buildings, some manuscripts and ivory carvings, enamels, and other small objects are all that remain in the West from this time.

It does not follow that a period of economic prosperity will be great in the arts; merely that some surplus beyond the minimum needs of man is essential for aesthetic activity. Moreover, it is almost a rule that cultural expression lags a generation or more behind an economic or political rise, since it may take years to train men to the appropriate expression.

In another sense economics impinges on art. The change from a handicraft to a machine technique in the production of building materials is one cause of the new style of twentieth-century architecture. Labor is a factor; the higher the cost of skilled labor, the less can one afford its products.

Although the form of government in itself may not be important, nevertheless by preserving order a strong state can promote conditions suited to artistic growth. When taxation was based on the number or size of windows, builders limited themselves in these respects; when levied on the number of stories in the wall of a house, it prompted the development of the mansard roof, a device to add a story within the roof. More important is patronage. The wealth and power of the Church in the Middle Ages accounts for the primarily ecclesiastical art of that time. Official support and encouragement of the Academy in France since the seventeenth century helped to give her the leadership she held in the world of art from that time almost to the present. The results achieved by the Academy were not always admirable; on the contrary, the progressive work of the nineteenth century was done in protest against the official stand. Still, though its aims were sometimes misdirected, its efforts have contributed a stimulus to the general field.

Even more vital is the broad social structure of an age, since that, in the last analysis, establishes its problems. The power of imperial Rome created a civilization, and therefore an art, to reflect itself—immense in scale, sumptuous in colored marbles, crass in effect. The aristocratic democracies of Greece nourished philosophical and aesthetic discussion, and were bound to develop balance, delicacy, and refinement in art. The emphasis on the salon in eighteenth-century France produced a boudoir art, small in scale, playful, lawless, but never crude.

Finally, religion has often taken the lead in artistic development, in part because of the common identification of religion and government. Egyptian architecture, as we know it, exists chiefly in the temple and the tomb, and the bulk of sculpture and paintings was produced for them. Most Greek sculpture is also religious in purpose. The nature of the belief calls for a specific expression. The basic contrast between Greek temples and Gothic cathedrals stems from the different conceptions of God held by these two cultures. Most directly of all, the usages of any liturgy write the programs for the artist to follow.

That the arts are produced by the spirit of an age is self-evident, but not the whole story. The arts have also done their share to shape their cultures. Just as the poems of Homer crystallized the concepts of the Olympic deities, so too the Romanesque and Gothic cathedrals, themselves in part formed by medieval ritual and faith, in turn helped to form that ritual and to clarify that faith. Subsequent to Giotto's innovations in painting, men could no longer conceive of man as they had before. Perhaps therein lies the greatest contribution that the arts have made through human history.

In so far as any period is itself a historical unit, the government, religion, and form of society act to produce a unity of expression. Hence we may speak of a Gothic age, or the epoch of the Renaissance or the Baroque, to indicate the existence of some similarities in contemporary production. But though several of these factors may hold good at any moment in history over large geographical areas, others may not, or may be of differing degrees of significance within smaller regions. Consequently, we have to take into account not only the Gothic or Renaissance styles, but also the dissimilarities of English as contrasted with French Gothic, of Flemish with Italian Baroque. Finally, any individual artist may respond differently to the same conditions of time and place. A Michelangelo and a Raphael do not react alike to their times. Both are characteristic of the High Renaissance in Italy, but as personalities their work is distinct. It is because of the interaction of time, place, and person upon the artistic problem that the history of art through the centuries is so infinite in variety.

II PREHISTORIC ART

The earliest art of man was created in the dim geological past when slowly receding glaciers still covered much of northern Europe. Remains of it have been discovered archaeologically in many sites in Europe, Africa, the Near East, and Asia. But the best-known and most spectacular examples of this art appear in caves and rock shelters in south-central France, and in northern and eastern Spain, occupied in the late Paleolithic period, which is frequently referred to as the Ice age and believed to date some twelve thousand to twenty thousand years ago. The climate, and the flora and fauna were then very different from those of today. During part of this period it was extremely cold and dry, and such animals as the mammoth, bison, reindeer, and wild horse were plentiful and provided food for these early hunters. Animal representation dominates the art, particularly in the north Spanish and French areas, where it appears largely on the walls of caves as incised and/or painted forms, although small sculptures in the round in bone, antler, ivory, stone, and clay are numerous at many sites. Paleolithic art was discovered only a century ago; but since then the gradual and often accidental discovery of more than a hundred caves has contributed to a constantly increasing knowledge of Prehistoric man and his art.

In many parts of the world early man pecked, engraved, or painted on the rock surfaces of shelters or caves. Examples have been found in south, central, and north Africa; in a number of areas of western United States; in various islands of the South Seas; and in many parts of Australia and elsewhere. Not all of this rock art was of the same antiquity; in fact, the age of much of it is still somewhat speculative; but the distribution of it indicates the appearance of an early art of comparable media and technique in many widespread areas. It is certain, too, that in some regions this art persisted until fairly recent times. The earliest and most important development of it was, however, that of the Paleolithic age in southwestern Europe.

Two areas of this ancient European art have been differentiated, that of northern Spain and southwestern France, known as the Franco-Cantabrian area; and the somewhat less ancient art of the east Spanish or Levantine area to the south. Franco-Cantabrian art may be divided into two Upper or Late Paleolithic chronological periods, the Aurignacian or earlier and the Magdalenian or later, both named after southwestern French sites. Prehistoric art of this northern area occurs often deep within caves; while that of the southern region is found on the rock walls of open shelters beneath overhanging cliffs.

Northern Paleolithic caves with decorated walls did not serve as shelters or habitations, since evidences of human occupation are found only at or near their entrances. The paintings and engravings frequently appear in almost inaccessible chambers within the caves, seemingly special areas set aside for use as sanctuaries or ceremonial centers and used again and again in this way for some millennia. It is impossible, however, to do more than speculate on what the motivating beliefs for this art may have been; but since the subjects represented are, with few exceptions, the food animals of these Ice-age peoples, it would seem that they were depicted to insure a plenitude of the animal or the actual securing of it in the hunt. Both motivations may very well have been behind the art.

Many believe that Prehistoric art began with small three-dimensional sculptures and engravings. These small sculptures have been found often deep in the debris on cave floors in association with archaeologically datable chipped and flaked stone tools. Although the majority of small sculptures represent animals or details of animals, some female figurines, complete or in fragments, are carved in a rigid, highly stylized manner with certain strongly exaggerated physical features. The best-known examples are the so-called Venus of Willendorf, a 4½ inch limestone figurine found near the Danube River in lower Austria, and the Lespugue Figure discovered in southwest France. Small animal sculptures were produced in considerable quantity in Aurignacian and later periods; but unlike the more symbolic human representations, animal figures have a remarkable vitality of pose and realization of natural form.

On the basis of style conventions apparent in many hundreds of examples, it is evident that Franco-Cantabrian cave paintings and engravings date from both the earlier and later Paleolithic periods. The earliest of this art is represented by finger tracings of geometric designs and of simple animal outlines on the damp clay walls, and by hands stenciled negatively against a red or black background.

These were followed by pecked outline engravings and paintings of animals, sometimes accompanied by geometrical, possibly symbolic, patterns. A fine example of early or Aurignacian art is the elephant in the cave of Castillo in the Pyrenees area of northern Spain (fig. 2).

2. *Elephant* (c. 16,000 B.C.) Castillo. Red outline drawing, 1'2".

It is a simple drawing in red ochre with only two legs rendered and no details given within the outlines. In contrast, a mammoth of slightly later date in the Combarelles cave in the famous Dordogne area of France shows an engraving with four legs rendered in perspective and a broken lower outline suggesting the long hair of the animal (fig. 3). The cave of Combarelles, discovered in 1901, contains only engravings; but here the styles cover almost the full range of this medium in Paleolithic times, such as continuous to broken outlines, and the use of etched lines to suggest texture.

Animal representations in Prehistoric art, whether in the round, in relief, incised, or painted, have one outstanding feature in common: they all depict or characterize the animal with a strong, direct visual reality. Momentary poses, a suggestion of varied movement, and the basic 'seen' nature of the animal, in contrast to an intellectual knowledge of its structure, typify this vibrant art; while a monumentality or largeness of scale is evident whether the animal is only inches or several feet in size.

Remains of Paleolithic pigments reveal that they were ochres, largely mineral oxides, ranging in color from red through various browns to black, with a deeper carboniferous black obtained from burned bones. The pigments were used as sticks for drawing or were ground and mixed with animal fat to produce the 'oil' paints for the great wall decorations. Monochrome color outlines or solidly painted forms and, in the great or Magdalenian period, polychrome renderings are characteristic. Not any of the paintings are realistic, since only the essentials of the form and a few details are given, a representation based on a memory image of the animal observed during the hunt.

3. *Mammoth* (c. 15,000 B.C.) Les Combarelles. Mural engraving, 2'4" wide.

4. *Animal Group* (*c.* 12,000 B.C.) Lascaux. 5'6" wide. From Maringer and Bandi, *Art in the Ice Age*, Frederick A. Praeger, Inc.

Altamira, found in 1868 near Santander in northern Spain, was the earliest of the caves discovered. It was not until 1879, however, that a little girl noticed that there were paintings on its walls and ceiling. It is a large cave, almost 1000 feet in length, containing both painted and engraved animals in its decorations, some outlined in black, some painted solidly red or black, and others rendered in polychromy. The most important and famous Altamira painting is the so-called 'great fresco' on its ceiling, a work measuring 46 feet long. More than twenty animals of late Paleolithic species, such as the deer, wild boar, and bison, are represented mostly in polychrome, some of them from four to seven feet long and incised before being colored. The reality in the pose of these animals, running, wounded, or at bay, is striking. Distinctive of the paintings at Altamira are the remarkable richness of colors and the manner in which irregular geological formations on the surface of the ceiling are utilized as relief forms within the painted rendering of the animal.

Of the many Franco-Cantabrian caves, Font-de-Gaume, discovered in 1901, and Lascaux, in 1940, both in the Dordogne district of France, are of great importance. At Lascaux practically all Prehistoric painting and engraving styles, from the early Aurignacian to the late Magdalenian periods, are represented in its many galleries and chambers; while the quality of the art of each period warrants the evaluation of this cave as one of the most significant of all Paleolithic sites so far discovered (fig. 4).

The numerous superpositions of later

figures over indistinct earlier ones, coupled with the lack of any compositional arrangement of the animals, constitute two of the most consistent and striking features of Franco-Cantabrian art. These characteristics appear in the majority of cave paintings and are readily observable in those at Lascaux, where an exceptional freshness of color has survived. The art of Lascaux, together with that of Altamira and Font-de-Gaume, represents the greatest achievements of Paleolithic artists.

East Spanish or Levantine rock painting differs in a number of respects from that to the north. In east Spain relatively small paintings are found in rock shelters or beneath overhanging cliffs, rather than deep within caves. They are painted in solid colors, mostly red, sometimes black, and represent compositional arrangements of humans and animals in which an idea or narrative is portrayed. The animals, including stag, wild horse, boar, and antelope, are usually depicted in silhouette in flat, summary fashion, in contrast to the depth, roundness, and vitality of form in the Franco-Cantabrian art. Human figures, rarely found in northern paintings, are small, solidly painted forms, often stylized almost to the point of abstraction. Since superposition is likewise common to this art, it seems likely that the east Spanish sites may also have been sanctuaries or ritual centers.

But a number of features in these southern paintings indicate a different motivation and possibly a later chronology than those of Ice-age art to the

north. For example, the presence of dancing, hunting, and fighting scenes involving both human and animal figures at once sets them apart from the animal representations in the French and Spanish caves; while in some scenes, such as the one in the rock shelter near Cogul, female figures in skirts dance around a nude male figure, perhaps symbolizing or representing an initiation or fertility dance or ritual involving only human beings. Clothed female figures also appear in the large painting in the cave or grotto of La Vieja near Alpera,

5. *Group of Archers* (*c.* 7000 B.C.) Valltorta Gorge. 3′10″ high. From Maringer and Bandi, *Art in the Ice Age*, Frederick A. Praeger, Inc.

and numerous hunters in vigorous, stylized postures and forms were painted in various east Spanish sites, particularly well represented in the shelters of the

Valltorta Gorge (fig. 5). An intense, dramatic movement is characteristic of this art, while non-naturalistic shapes indicate details of the body and costume as an intellectual interpretation rather than as a visual perception of the object. Hunters, often represented in rapid pursuit of animals, are armed with the bow and arrow, a weapon not depicted in Paleolithic Franco-Cantabrian art.

It seems likely that at least some east Spanish rock paintings are of a later date than those of the Ice age to the north, possibly from the Neolithic period. Levantine painting, a thoroughly interesting and aesthetically exciting Prehistoric art, has numerous analogies with early rock-shelter paintings in south-central Africa.

The achievements of Upper Paleolithic art have been ascribed to Cro-Magnon man, but it now appears that he was only one of a number of the species *Homo sapiens* responsible for it. Following the Paleolithic period and the further recession of glacial ice fields, the Mesolithic period, roughly eight thousand to twelve thousand years ago, slowly developed an era during which the climate, geography, and biology of the Europe of today gradually emerged. Mesolithic art was very meager, almost limited to small, water-rounded pebbles painted with geometric designs in red ochre, possibly symbolizing human figures or ritual objects.

In central and western Europe a comparatively long Neolithic period followed the Mesolithic and may be dated approximately 8000 to 2000 B.C. During this period many of the basic features of later historic civilizations were developed or invented. One of the important differences between the Paleolithic or Old Stone age and the Neolithic or New Stone age was the manufacture of more efficient tools and weapons through the process of grinding and polishing of stone. Of these New Stone age tools the most significant was the stone axe or celt, polished to a refined form and surface and ground to a strong, sharp, cutting edge, a tool vastly superior to the chipped and flaked stone blades of Paleolithic peoples.

During the Neolithic period plants, particularly grains, and animals were domesticated. These two fundamental developments led to permanent homes in villages or communities, a drastic change from the earlier seasonal nomadic hunting life based on following the migratory movements of game animals. Food storage pits indicate that there were now reserves of food, a contributing factor to a rapid rise in population, more leisure, and a greater degree of specialization. It is clear, too, that during this period fighting, aggression, and protective defense measures became pronounced. The arts of Neolithic man, aside from the aesthetically satisfying shape and finish of tools, also included pottery and megalithic stone structures. Pottery at first was handmade, coarse and undecorated, but later its manufacture was improved and engraved or imprinted geometric decorations appeared, and still later modeled pottery objects and vessels were produced.

6. *Stonehenge*, Salisbury Plain, England (*c.* 2000–1500 B.C.) 25′ high.

The megalithic stone structures are in many instances associated with burials, perhaps as memorials to the dead, but sometimes as tomb-like coverings over graves. Two main types of structures were erected, the *menhir* and the *dolmen*. The menhir is a single small or large stone monolith set up vertically in the ground at or near a burial site. Some menhirs are unshaped, slab-like stones, others are roughly formed to taper toward the top, and a few of them are crudely engraved with geometric designs. They occur in many areas in Spain, and in western France, where the menhir at Penmarch in Brittany measures almost 25 feet high; while at nearby Carnac ten avenues of small menhirs lead away from a circle of menhirs, known as a *cromlech*. The dolmen is a construction of several often large stones set vertically in two parallel rows with a large stone slab placed across their tops as a roof or lid. Beneath it one or more burials were made and afterward the entire construction was covered with a mound of earth. A good example of a dolmen has been unearthed near Bagneux in western France.

At Stonehenge, near Salisbury in England, is seen the remains of one of the most famous, complex, and, even in its present ruinous condition, impressive of early stone constructions (fig. 6). Stonehenge has been hypothetically dated between 2000 and 1500 B.C., and so falls a bit beyond the end of the Neolithic period. It consisted originally of a large circular earthwork surrounding a circle of tall stone uprights, their tops connected by stone lintels held in place by cut tenons and sockets. An inner circle of smaller menhirs paralleled this outer ring. This circle surrounded five great separated pairs of almost 25-foot-high uprights, with their connecting lintels, set in a horseshoe-shaped ground plan. This plan was repeated by an inner row of small menhirs, and within these concentric horseshoe rows was placed a large stone slab, over 16 feet long and 3 feet wide, known as the 'altar.' The purpose and significance of Stonehenge are not known; although it seems likely that it was a ceremonial center of religious and perhaps sacrificial intent. While neither the menhirs nor the dolmens, nor in fact Stonehenge, can actually be considered architecture, the presence of these constructions does reveal permanent memorials or markers and suggests a ritual centering around the dead.

Aside from its remarkable aesthetic qualities, Prehistoric art is of further value for the insight it permits us into the thoughts and life of Prehistoric man.

III

THE PRE-CLASSICAL ARTS

EGYPT

History, as we know it, starts in the eastern Mediterranean area along the valley of the Nile, or possibly that of the Tigris-Euphrates. Recent archaeology indicates that Mesopotamian civilization may have begun before the Egyptian. But there is little difference between these two regions in date, and since through large parts of its history Egypt was self-contained, one may consider its development first. To be sure, Egyptian isolation is only comparative. Egyptian pottery has been found in Crete, and through trade and war the Nile valley had some contact with neighboring countries. Nevertheless, though Egypt partly inspired such other cultures as the early Greek, she accepted little in return.

That civilization should flower early in the Nile valley was inevitable. Herod-otus described Egypt as the gift of the river. By simplifying existence in many ways and by complicating it in a few, the Nile stimulated culture as does a hot-house. Primitive methods of agriculture sufficed in a soil whose fertility the river renewed with layers of silt deposited from annual inundations. Irrigation by water wheels or by a device like a well-sweep was essential after the floods had subsided, since rain was unknown and one hot cloudless day followed another. Not only did the Nile water the land and fertilize it, but the river also served as an avenue for communication and transportation, binding the country together. The cliffs that flank the valley provided stone; if need arose this could be ferried up or down the Nile. Clay, too, was available for less permanent buildings, such as houses, and for unimportant tomb figures. Satisfactory timber was scarce; the palm was not a desirable building material. Although at the outset the Egyptians relied on reeds of the lotus or the papyrus bundled together and matted with clay, when the buildings became monumental the earlier system of construction came to be adapted to stone.

These geographical advantages were balanced by a few difficulties. The floods of the Nile obliterated landmarks and so compelled an early development of surveying to re-establish boundaries. Disputes were bound to arise, however, and a legal system must have been devised to care for them. During Egypt's long history of over three thousand years, four periods of strong government rose and fell, separated by centuries of weakness. These four periods coincide with the times of artistic activity, presumably because they imposed settled conditions in which the arts could flourish. During the third century before Christ, an Egyptian priest named Manetho listed the rulers of Egypt according to dynasties, thereby providing a convenient chronological system.

The earliest epoch of strong government is often called the Old Kingdom, comprising Dynasties III-VI, which flourished about 3000–2500 B.C. The power of the rulers, whose capital was at Memphis, declined during the VI Dynasty, and Egypt subsided into chaos and artistic inactivity after the brilliant achievements of early sculpture and the building of the Pyramids, a condition from which the strong rulers of the Middle Kingdom (2160–1785 B.C.) of the XI and XII Dynasties rescued her. Then the feudal system set up by these kings at Thebes in turn decayed. The warlike Pharaohs of the XVIII Dynasty established the Empire or New Kingdom, as it is sometimes called (1580–1100 B.C.). It grew in power through the XIX Dynasty, pushing its conquests into Nubia in the south and into Mesopotamia or the Fertile Crescent to the northeast; these were the Pharaohs who accomplished the bondage of Israel. Though still fairly strong, the XX Dynasty lacked the energy of its predecessors; its wars were defensive, and it was followed by another time of weakness and foreign domination when the Assyrian warrior kings captured the land. Finally, the XXVI Dynasty formed the Saite period (663–525 B.C.), named from its capital at Sais in the Nile delta, whose rulers drove out the Semitic invaders and returned to purely Egyptian forms of expression. Still later, the Greek Ptolemies and Rome in turn ruled Egypt, but the fact that Egyptian art clung to its native character in these later centuries as that of no other country has ever done to the same extent, demonstrated the force of tradition in the Nile valley.

On close inspection Egyptian art differed slightly in each of these eras of history; the sculpture of the Old Kingdom, for example, is realistic when compared with the conventionality of the Middle Kingdom, or with the elegant or colossal works of the Empire, but such sweeping generalizations admit of many exceptions. A broader view shows not divergence but uniformity. The art of no other country, even over a shorter span of time, displays such adherence to established forms.

This continuity was a consequence of Egyptian social and religious customs. The Pharaoh was the head of the state both in religion and politics. As priest and prince, from being the representative of the god on earth, he was soon to be himself deified, at first after death, and later even while alive. The very name Pharaoh, meaning 'great house,' indicated his sanctity by so oblique a reference to his sacred person. And yet the Pharaoh was not free; the priesthood, whose figurehead he was, controlled him. The priests and the nobility would not jeopardize their position by allowing change of any kind. Early in their civilization, the Egyptians found an expression in art so satisfactory to them that any change could only be for the worse. It is significant that the one period of experimentation and comparative freedom in Egyptian art occurred during the reign of Ikhnaton in the XVIII Dynasty, when the ruler turned from polytheism to monotheism—a departure from tradition that was reversed by the priesthood after his death.

The most important aspect of Egyptian religion in its bearing on art was the nature of its belief in the after life. Four components were present in every human being: the *ka*, or double, a dematerialized replica of the body, analogous to our conception of a ghost; the *ba*, which approximates the soul in Christianity; the *khû*, or spark of divine fire; and the body. Immortality required the preservation of all four. The *ba* and *khû*, as spiritual elements, could be sustained by prayers and did not profoundly affect art. Preservation of the body as the home of the *ka*, however, involved mummification and, what is still more important, protection of the mummy from damage. The Egyptians strained every nerve to preserve their tombs intact since the *ka* lived there. As the *ka* was identical with the deceased, save in its lack of substance, the tomb became a house for the dead, equipped to support life after death and to make it enjoyable. Foreseeing the possibility of damage to or disintegration of the mummy, the Egyptians placed one or more effigies of its owner within the tomb. As substitutes that the *ka* might inhabit in case the body were destroyed, these portrait statues were often made in hard materials. Granite might be expected to outlast wood or limestone, and was preferable in that respect, though the difficulty of working granite restricted its use, and its hardness militated against realism in portraiture.

If the *ka* could exist in the mummy, or in the portrait statues, and live in the tomb, it had to be fed. The offerings of pious descendants supplied this want, but within a few generations this duty might be neglected. Since the *ka* was itself immaterial, its food and drink could be carved or painted on the walls. From this, it was but a step to represent food in preparation, its production, and eventually all the activities of life. Thus the tomb became a picture book of Egyptian life.

Mastabas (fig. 7), the characteristic tombs of the nobility in the Old Kingdom, clustered around the Pyramids at Gizeh, the necropolis of ancient Memphis. They vary in length from 15 to 170

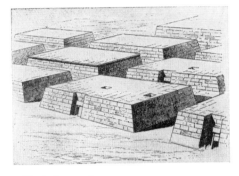

7. *Typical mastabas.*

feet, from 10 to 30 feet in height. These simple rectangular buildings are *oriented*; that is, laid out according to compass directions. The sides face north, east, south, and west. The outer walls are not vertical, but slope inward in the form called a *batter*. Such a battered wall is more stable than a vertical one, and was adopted no doubt because it promised greater permanence. From the top of the mastaba, a shaft descends through the mass into the rock below, leading to the burial chamber where the sarcophagus is placed. This shaft, which in some examples is more than 100 feet deep, is filled with rubble after the coffin receives its mummy and the opening is sealed to disguise it as part of the roof. Little of value is interred with the body. A second chamber, called the *serdab*, also is embedded in the mass without

communication from the outside. Though often undecorated, this room contains the portrait of the owner, as well as the treasure and utensils to sustain the *ka* in his ethereal existence.

The only opening in the outer walls of the mastaba leads to the chapel where the living could place offerings for the dead. On one wall of the chapel a sculptured relief of the owner sometimes comes through a false door to welcome his descendants. Perhaps above or to one side of this door, the owner appears again, this time at table, partaking of the offering. Scenes in paint or low relief cover the other walls, and show the activities of the owner, and his wife, his children, his servants, his ox, and his ass, and everything that is his. Through these decorations, the *ka* could enjoy in death what he had possessed in life.

The colossal pyramids are royal tombs. Whatever their origin, whether in a mound of stones or in a superposition of mastabas, they are the outstanding monuments of the Old Kingdom. The largest, those at Gizeh (fig. 8), are the sepulchers of the IV Dynasty Pharaohs. So precisely were they oriented that one might see Polaris from any point in the long and narrow entrance passage, which led in turn through other passages too complex to describe in detail to the burial chamber in the center of the mass. After interment, the blocks of stone slipped into these passages completely cut off the interior from the outside world. Where the entrance had been was concealed with the utmost care. It was all to no avail. Entrance to the pyra-

8. *Pyramids and Sphinx*, Gizeh (*c.* 2700–2600 B.C.) Limestone, pyramid height originally 479′; breadth 767′; sphinx total height, 66′.

mids was forced even in antiquity. Since the pyramids were closed, the chapel had to be separate, and thus developed an independent existence.

The pyramids are composed of large blocks of stone cut with metal tools, and heaped step upon step to the apex. In proportion of width at the base to height, they are almost precisely 11 to 7, which suggests that these numbers had special significance even at that time. So huge an undertaking—the base of the Great Pyramid of Khûfû is about 750 feet square—presupposes an army of slaves acting under the king's foremen. It has been calculated that ten thousand men must have worked on them for twenty years. To support, administer,

and direct such an army of laborers argues organizing ability of a high order.

These pyramids have always captured man's imagination. Although today we see them composed of flights of colossal steps, these steps were sheathed with a smooth coating of limestone, the face of each forming one unbroken plane. This strict adherence to geometry appeals to man's sense of organization, just as does a crystal ball; nothing detracts from the unity. But a small model, capable of resting on the hand, may be equally complete without stimulating awe. Surely it is the size of this simple form that makes it imposing. We measure ourselves against it and feel overwhelmed.

The shape of the pyramid is appropriate. Except perhaps for the cone, a pyramid is the most stable of geometric forms. Its immobility of mass is the essence of permanence; it comes as near to being eternal as any man-made object can. Not without reason have the Pyramids come to be associated with changelessness.

The cost in labor of the Pyramids forbade their being undertaken on so imposing a scale by any but powerful monarchs. The Middle Kingdom abandoned them in favor of the shallow rock-cut tombs in the cliffs along the Nile valley. The best preserved are at Beni Hasan. Here a small colonnaded portico gives access to the chapel. Its columns, like those within, are not constructed, but allowed to remain when the surrounding rock is cut away. The functions of the serdab seem to have been combined with those of the chapel, forming a niche or sanctuary in it. A shaft to the burial chamber might be cut through the chapel floor, or into the cliff from in front of the portico.

By the Empire period, it had become obvious that no strength of blocked passages within a tomb would avail to exclude thieves. The visibility of the tomb advertised the treasure concealed within, and the challenge was accepted by rob-

9. *Temple of the Sphinx*, Gizeh (c. 2700–2600 B.C.) Granite, monoliths 13′6″ high.

bers of Egyptian days despite severe laws against desecration. Yielding to necessity, the Pharaohs of the Empire period, who dug their tombs in the Valley of the Kings near Thebes, sacrificed the prestige of a visible tomb to security. They chose to tunnel a shaft into the foot of the cliffs. The existence of the tomb itself was concealed by broken stone, such as might have fallen from the cliffs. The tomb of Tutankhamen remained intact until the twentieth century of our era, having defied searchers for more than three thousand years. The corridor-like shaft, sometimes more than 400 feet long, led to one or more decorated chambers, furnished with models of all that the soul could desire. Although these deep, rock-cut tombs add another step in the development of sepulchral design, and although the treasures of Egyptian art preserved in them are invaluable, as architecture they are negligible. To elaborate an architectural setting not to be seen by a living eye would be absurd, at least to the modern mind. By this time the chapel was completely divorced from the tomb and was placed near the river.

However much their decoration tells us of Egyptian life, the tombs as architecture do not compare with the Egyptian temples. One of the earliest preserved is the IV Dynasty Temple of the Sphinx at Gizeh (fig. 9), which is connected with the pyramid of Khafra by a covered causeway. Exceptional in plan and in severity of design, its granite monoliths support plain granite beams, impressive through their austerity and their reliance on beauty of material. In

order to light the interior, its architect invented the *clearstory*, an architectural device that reached its apogee thousands of years later in the Christian church. The roof over the central aisle was raised above the side aisles to allow space for small windows that admit shafts of light to the interior.

While the Temple of the Sphinx is exceptional, the Temple of Khonsû at Karnak (fig. 10), from the Empire pe-

10. *Temple of Khonsû*, Karnak (*c.* 1200 B.C.) Limestone, *c.* 225' x 105'.

riod, illustrates the normal elements of the Egyptian temple. An avenue lined with sphinxes introduces the axis along which the principal units follow. The first part of the temple proper is the *pylon*, a monumental gateway composed of two tall masses of masonry flanking a door. The Pharaoh who finished the building placed his obelisks and statues to either side in front of the pylon, which was further enlivened by flagpoles set in narrow grooves. Behind the pylon is the *peristyle*, an open court bounded by colonnades on three or four sides. This leads to the *hypostyle hall*, where files of columns support a roof. The last principal component of the plan, the *sanctuary*, lies behind the hall.

These four elements, pylon, peristyle, hypostyle, and sanctuary illustrate sequence of composition. The top or roof of each part becomes lower from the entrance to the sanctuary. In answering movement, the hypostyle floor is a few steps above that of the peristyle, the sanctuary a step above the hypostyle. The height of each unit, therefore, lessens as one proceeds. Moreover, though the open peristyle is brilliantly lighted, the hypostyle hall gets its light only through the door leading from the peristyle, and is dark in consequence, while the sanctuary, lighted only from the hypostyle, is still darker. This progressive darkening must have enhanced the mystery associated with the abode of the god. The mystery was further increased by the fact that the laity had access only to the peristyle and hypostyle, whereas the sanctuary was reserved for the consecrated priests of the god and, of course, the Pharaoh as the head of the state religion. Thus the people could see but dimly the ritual performed by the awesome white-robed priests within.

The visual stability of the battered walls of the pylon, like the same device in the mastaba, reveals again the Egyptian craving for permanence that we have already noticed in the pyramid. Pier and lintel construction is almost universal, because of its stability and simplicity. Though the arch is known, its dynamic forces are contrary to the Egyptian genius and it is therefore restricted to utilitarian structures. The flat roof is inevitable in this rainless climate. The hypostyle hall in the great Temple of Amon Ra at Karnak (fig. 12), in the XIX Dynasty, is too large to be even dimly lighted from the peristyle. This required a clearstory taller than the tentative one in the Temple of the Sphinx.

Some of the most characteristic Egyptian forms seem to recollect primitive construction in mud reinforced by lotus or papyrus reeds. If a clay wall were strengthened with a surface of vertical reeds, these stems would have to be anchored to the wall near its top. A horizontal bundle of reeds could effect this. In time the weight of clay might bend outward the tips of the reeds above the anchor. Perhaps this accounts for the typical Egyptian *cornice* over the door of the Temple of Horus at Edfû (fig. 11), which curves outward in a quarter circle above a small round molding.

The *clustered column*, whose earliest examples date from the Old Kingdom, looks like a bundle of lotus or papyrus stems strapped together just below the capital. These plant forms no doubt sheathed a core of clay. The Empire period sometimes smoothed over the surfaces of the separate reeds but retained to the end the horizontal band under the capital (fig. 12). Moreover, whether clustered or round, the column bulges slightly outward just above the base, and is enriched by painted leaves, like the stems of certain plants just above the roots. The proportions of these columns were adapted to stone when that material came into use.

11. *Temple of Horus*, Edfû (237–212 B.C.) Pylon *c.* 250′ wide x *c.* 145′ high.

The *capital* is that part of the column above the shaft. Three types of Egyptian capitals derive from buds, flowers, or leaves. The first is shaped like closed buds above the several stems of clustered shafts, or as a single bud when the shaft is round. In either case, sepals are painted on it. The open flower of the lotus inspires the second, or campaniform, capital, like an inverted bell decorated with petals and sepals. The third type with leaves curling out from its surface is usually later. These types are not wholly satisfactory in either structure or design. The aesthetic purpose of a capital is to afford a transition for the eye from the vertical shaft to the horizontal beam above. The campaniform capital does this well, but the presence of a tall block above it interrupts this transition. In the bud capital, no attempt at all is made to perform this function; on the contrary, its constricting lines accentuate the change from vertical to horizontal, so that the beam appears to be impaled on the shaft. The structural purpose of the capital is to provide a larger surface than the top of the shaft to support the ends of beams. Here again the bud capital, whose bearing surface may be smaller in diameter than the shaft, fails, and although the campaniform capital and the similar palm-leaf type may seem to be satisfactory, their thin rims are too fragile to give even the appearance of adequate support. Thus neither the bell nor the bud types, the commonest forms of Egyptian capital, can be judged as entirely successful, though the bell shape is the better one.

The Egyptian temple was always adorned with sculpture and painting, sometimes so richly as to lose the value of contrast. For example, the Temple of Horus at Edfû (fig. 11) of Ptolemaic times shows the walls of the pylon covered with low-relief sculpture. This depicts the prowess of the king capturing and slaying his enemies. The Pharaoh is drawn at larger scale than the others to emphasize his superiority. Similar scenes line the walls of the peristyle in Egyptian temples, but in the hypostyle hall the action is less violent. This chamber is conceived as a microcosm of the world; around the lower walls and at the bottom of the columns luxuriant plants flourish in low relief, birds flutter above them, and gold stars sparkle on a blue ceiling. Prayers in hieroglyphics and representations of ceremonial enrich the sanctuary and the rooms around it, which Egyptologists believe were designed to house the equipment and treasure of the temple.

This type of temple constitutes the bulk of Egyptian architecture. In the hemi-speos temple, illustrated by the Mortuary Temple of Queen Hatshepsût of the XVIII Dynasty at Deir-el-Baharî, the sanctuary and hypostyle are entombed in the rock, but the open courts, corresponding to the peristyles in constructed temples, rise one above another as terraces. Here we may see employed the sixteen-sided shaft. It was developed by cutting off the corners of square piers, such as those in the Temple of the

12. *Hypostyle Hall*, Temple of Amon Ra, Karnak (*c.* 1300 B.C.) Model, Metropolitan Museum, New York. Central columns 69′ high, 12′ diameter.

Sphinx, and then again cutting the corners. The repeated vertical lines so produced dramatize the idea of support, of upward or downward movement in the column; and the simplicity of the courts surrounded by such shafts commands a respect that is hardly attained in the sumptuous architecture of the usual temple.

In the speos temples, such as that of Rameses II of the XIX Dynasty at Abù Simbel (fig. 13), not only are the sanctuary and hypostyle cut out of the living rock, but the peristyle is also. The arrangement and the architectural vocabulary are not substantially different from those already discussed. Carved figures of Osiris, god of the underworld, stand before and in part supplant the piers within the temple, but this somewhat exceptional motive is known in normal temples. Externally, the only visible unit is the pylon, with its gigantic guardian statues, cut from the face of the cliff.

The human craving for permanence, more pronounced in Egypt than elsewhere, is confined to Egypt's religious architecture. The immortality of the gods dictated this need in their homes, while a belief in the after life, immeasurably longer than man's sojourn on earth, called for a similar timelessness in the tomb. Houses for the living, even the royal palace, need be no more than temporary. Mud brick sufficed for them, and as a consequence they have vanished, though the type and method of construction have affected Egyptian building.

At its best, the scale of Egyptian architecture and its instinct for geometric mass endow it with an imposing but austere character, as in the pyramids, even if it lacks the clarity, delicacy, and sophistication of the Greek, or the complex organization of the Roman. Though some of its forms, like the clustered column and the bud capital, derive from plants, the forms themselves are well adapted to the stone medium, while other units, such as the pylons, are conceived in stone, with a monumentality rarely equaled and never surpassed by later civilizations. In the smaller temples, organization dominates the ordered sequence of one element after another. However, in some of Egypt's greatest buildings, the Pharaohs sacrificed unity to their desire to outstrip their predecessors in size, by adding to a plan already complete in itself other hypostyle halls, other peristyles, and especially other pylons. The largest temples, those of Karnak and Luxor, are the worst offenders; in consequence, they seem to sprawl. Finally, the inordinate love of decoration defeats one of its important functions: if decoration be for accent, too much of it results in equal emphasis everywhere, leaving an accent nowhere.

Naturally the same religious factors mold Egyptian sculpture that play so large a part in shaping the architecture. It is customary to speak of Egyptian sculpture of the Old Kingdom as realistic, or of the Middle Kingdom as conventional, but one must realize at the outset that these terms are relative. If by realism we understand an attempt to reproduce nature, and by conventional-

13. *Temple of Rameses II,* Abû Simbel (1257 B.C.) Façade 119′ wide, colossi 65′ high.

ism a willingness to accept certain shapes as symbolical or typical of natural forms, then we must admit that the most realistic Egyptian statue is conventional when compared with a Roman portrait (fig. 76). Moreover, statues of Pharaohs are usually idealized; that is, their individuality is minimized and their features carved in general terms to suggest their power and immortality.

Certain traits persist from dynasty to dynasty. The desire for permanence dictates the choice of materials and the dimensions of the sculpture. The love of size, apparent in the Pyramids, is obvious in the Sphinx (fig. 8). This monster's head, with an ear larger than a man, is an idealized portrait of the

Pharaoh Khafra of the IV Dynasty, with whose pyramid the Sphinx is connected. Or again, in the colossi of Rameses II at Abû Simbel (fig. 13) from the Empire period, about 65 feet high, the effectiveness results from their enormous scale. Size in itself may not ensure permanence but at least it suggests it. The selection of obdurate materials, however, is a more effective way of assuring durability. Though such soft media as limestone and sandstone, and even wood, are employed, the harder stones like granite, basalt, and diorite are common in Egyptian sculpture, in spite of the difficulties involved in working them.

The use of an effigy as a substitute for the body, in case it should be destroyed, created a demand for portraits. This required a moderate realism, most pronounced in the Old Kingdom, where it appears especially in the heads. However, such realism is apt to be present in inverse ratio to the social position of the subject. The Seated Scribe (fig. 14) from the Old Kingdom, now in the

14. *Seated Scribe* (*c.* 2500 B.C.) Louvre, Paris. Limestone, painted red, 21″ high.

Louvre, betrays his sedentary occupation by the rolls of flesh on his torso. In naïve fashion, his toes appear to have sunk into the limestone block so that only three are visible. But in the head, the artist displays his power of observation. He records the bony structure of the skull; the eyes and mouth reveal the scribe's close attention to the dictation of his master. As on most Egyptian statues, the male flesh is painted red,

the inlaid eyes are colored white with a black pupil and iris, to enhance the effect of life.

The Seated Scribe belongs to the servant class. On the other hand, Ranefer (fig. 16) in the V Dynasty represents the dominant priesthood. His pose, the commonest in Egyptian sculpture, shows him walking, the left foot forward, the weight evenly distributed between the feet, the axis of the body erect. While some concern for the details of nature is obvious in the articulated toes and knees, and in a few indications of the torso, nevertheless, the treatment of the sharp shin, narrow hips, broad shoulders, and the absence of much anatomical detail prove that for such a person a generalized appearance was preferred. By this stately pose, and above all by the head, the artist has portrayed a person independent and accustomed to command. Ranefer at once depicts an individual and the class to which he belongs. We must regard some of the conventions as expressions of the material. For instance, the slab at his back not only strengthens the statue but preserves the cubic form of the block of stone from which the figure was hewn. The body follows the original limits of this block; the shoulders extend as far as they may, the arms hang vertical, and therefore the hips are small to permit room for the arms within the prism of stone.

If statues of the lower classes are carved with moderate realism, those of the Pharaohs, because of their semidivine character, are idealized. The

15. *Khafra*, detail, from the Temple of the Sphinx (*c.* 2700–2600 B.C.) National Museum, Cairo. Diorite, complete figure 5'6" high.

regular features and absence of individuality create an ideal or even god-like personage in the diorite Khafra (fig. 15). No later age has ever surpassed the majesty and serenity of this five thousand-year-old masterpiece. It is outstanding for its related masses, its sculpturesque repose, its feeling for the material, and its detail selected with an eye to expressive and decorative value more than for representation, though that also is served to some extent. The simplified forms may be due in part to the material, but it seems probable that the idealization is an attribute of the royal sitter, and therefore deliberate.

In spite of occasional masterpieces, such as the seated Khafra or the Ranefer, and in spite of the simplification and feeling for the material, any considerable number of Egyptian figures in the round appear monotonous. This uniformity results in part from the limited number of types the sculptor was allowed to develop. The most common is the standing or walking type with one foot forward. The figure may also sit on a block, or cross-legged on the floor, or more rarely kneel on both knees. Beyond these possibilities the sculptor seldom experimented. This repetition of pose is the more pronounced since all these attitudes approximate a cubic form and respect the law of frontality: that is, a rigid verticality of the body with no deviation of its axis from side to side, no bending of the body, and but little animation. These types, established at the dawn of Egyptian history, remain unchanged through its dusk, three thousand years later. But tradition enforced uniformity in Egypt in other ways. A comparison of the Ranefer (fig. 16) and the colossi of Rameses II (fig. 13) is illuminating here. There is convention in both, but in the former the narrow hips, sharp shins, and simplified forms may be deliberate, so largely do they enhance the design. In the latter, the legs and arms, the puffy cheeks, the pharaonic headdress seem perfunctory. Absorbed by the scale at which he is working, the sculptor is content with these conventions because by the XIX Dynasty they have been sanctioned by age-old custom.

Although tradition plays a large role in sculpture in the round, it is even more obvious in sculpture in relief or in painting, two modes of expression that in Egypt are basically one, since the re-

16. *Ranefer* (*c.* 2500 B.C.) Cairo Museum. Limestone, painted red, 5′11″ high.

and cheapest method, scratch relief, engraves the outlines of its figures but makes no attempt to model them within the limits of that outline.

The exquisite bas-relief of Seti I Offering to Osiris (fig. 17), from the XIX Dynasty, in his mortuary temple at Abydos, shows the same subtlety of detail as does the figure of Khafra. No amount of convention can destroy the delicacy of the planes that indicate the light garment worn by the Pharaoh, the bodily forms seen through it, or the elegance resulting from these refinements. Such a relief bespeaks a sculptor of real sophistication, sensitive to the decorative possibilities of line and of subtle changes of surface.

Such reliefs as this adorned the temple walls and the chapels in tombs. As we have seen, these reliefs were practical in purpose, to record and glorify the exploits of the kings, to depict religious practices, or to perpetuate by representation human activities necessary to the life hereafter. As such, they become pictographs whose legibility is of cardinal importance. Their over-abundance as decoration is due to this purpose: the more recorded, the better. The Egyptian distaste for blank walls is to be explained by their desire to tell as much as possible; they often added hieroglyphics to whatever spaces were not filled by figures or other represented objects. To this need for exposition, aesthetic considerations were subordinated.

Many of the conventions of Egyptian reliefs are also traceable to this cause. The peculiar angularity of the figures re-

lief is almost flat and was regularly painted. Indeed, painting was a handmaid to relief sculpture, or a cheap substitute for it. Three methods were in common use. The first, low or bas-relief proper, consists of figures carved with a slight projection from the background. In sunk relief, the figures are also modeled but the surrounding background is not cut back to allow them to project; consequently each object is embedded behind the surfaces around it. The third

sults from each part being drawn in its most easily recognizable shape, its most characteristic attitude. The feet are drawn in profile (Plate I, facing p. 268), regardless of the pose of the figure. It is easier to achieve a shape that will be immediately recognized as a foot when drawn in profile than when drawn from the front, from which point of view the foot would have to be foreshortened or rendered in perspective. That Seti I (fig. 17) has two right feet did not bother his sculptor so long as the feet were readable, nor need it bother us. The profile view is maintained from the feet through the hips, but at the waist the body half turns so that the shoulders are represented facing front, again because they are readily identifiable in that position. For the same reason, the head is in profile, but the eye in full front. Thus, the figure consists of an alternation of the facing and profile positions, each designed to be legible, even if the result seems incongruous to eyes conditioned by realistic painting.

Such figures, and indeed all objects in the scene, are painted in a few standard tones, laid on in flat washes; that is, within an outline no change of color or value occurs. We must not expect shadows in Egyptian painting. This method is known as line and flat tone. The available palette was simple, too. A brick-red tone distinguishes the flesh of men; ochre-yellow of women. Hair and the pupil and iris of the eye are black, though the ball of the eye is white. These tones, with green, blue, and a few others, may depict details of necklaces

17. *Seti I Offering to Osiris*, Abydos (*c.* 1300 B.C.) Limestone.

or the varied tones of birds, animals, trees, and water. It is a primitive method, naïve, but clear through its conventions.

Certain other arbitrary devices must also be described. An obvious way of emphasizing one figure in a group is to enlarge that figure. The owner may be several times as large as his servants. Often the husband is drawn at a bigger scale than his wife; for example, the queen of Rameses II at Abû Simbel (fig. 13) stands between his legs. Of course, the smaller size of subordinates permits a greater number of them within any area. Rather than break up the wall into separate scenes, the Egyptian artist treats his minor figures in bands, allowing one incident to carry over into the next with nothing like a frame to separate them. A further result of the small size of minor characters is that several bands of them are possible, one above another. A modern painter, by applying perspective, may arrange one action behind another with the plane of the ground receding into the distance. The Egyptian painter, without perspective, draws a single line to represent the ground, scatters his figures along it, and then repeats another ground line above their heads.

These conventions negate any illusion of space. In perspective, a larger figure may appear to be closer to us than smaller ones, but this is not so when both sizes stand on a single ground line. Then they all appear to be in one plane, that of the wall. Only when one form overlaps another do we have any indication of its relative position in space. Perhaps as something intangible, the Egyptian painter was indifferent to space. The absence of perspective has several other consequences. If a number of persons are engaged in the same action, or if more than one identical object is to be recorded, instead of representing each one behind the other, the artist draws one of them in the required posture, and then repeats the front half of his outline as often as may be necessary. This serves well for things that stand on the ground, but what of things that parallel the plane of the ground? Two solutions are possible. A lake or a river may be painted in cross section with fish swimming in the blue water. Or it may be represented as though seen from above—fundamentally the same profile full-front device used in figures. Thus, we see a lake as though from the air, but the trees on its banks and even the figures within the pond are drawn from the side. Finally, in the details of nature, the artist reduces many things to patterns: the lotus or papyrus stems in a marsh, or the zigzag lines on a blue background to indicate water.

The bulk of Egyptian decoration consists of these formulas, established early and followed by generation after generation of artists. Rigid though they are, a wide variety of action can be indicated within them. Indeed they form a script less limited in its possibilities of expression than many languages. Moreover, this conventionality was imposed on the artist by his patrons; it is unreasonable to suppose that he adhered to it through inability to observe nature. Convention is more pronounced in the human figure than in other objects, where we may suppose conservatism was less necessary to preserve the *status quo*. Even in the figure, there are some departures from the norm. Semitic captives are distinguished from Egyptians not only by their costumes, but by their bearded faces and prominent noses; Nubians, by their color and their negroid features. Rarely the profile full-front tradition is abandoned; for example, a painting of dancing girls and the musicians who play for them is a clear attempt at naturalism, created during the reign of

Ikhnaton, when the power of priestly conservatism was momentarily broken.

A genuine love of nature impels the painter to observe and record some of her minutiae. If papyrus in a swamp tends to become a pattern, its details are precise. The famous Geese from Medum, a masterpiece dating from the Old Kingdom, repeats the colors and outlines of those fowls with great fidelity; the shrike and other birds on the walls of the tomb of Khnumhotep at Beni Hasan, from the Middle Kingdom, are no mere symbols; they are readily identifiable. In part, this naturalism may be attributed to the artist's desire to make them recognizable for what they are, but in any case he has not reduced them to a formula.

Many Egyptian reliefs and paintings, despite their conventions, are interesting for the same reason that the figurines once buried in the tombs but now displayed in museums arouse the curiosity of visitors. They provide a panorama of a rich and varied culture, and bring us close to the very existence of the past.

MESOPOTAMIA

Like the Egyptian civilization, that of Mesopotamia began in the fourth millennium before Christ. Born in the Tigris-Euphrates valley, it spread through the whole of the Fertile Crescent, which bounds the deserts of Arabia on the north and west. By 3000 B.C., the non-Semitic Sumerian tribes were already settled in city kingdoms, and had begun to make the contributions of this region to civilization. These kingdoms strug-gled with each other for survival, and also with the Semitic Akkadians, who conquered them about 2750 B.C., but through the rest of the millennium the balance of power in Babylonia shifted back and forth between Semitic and non-Semitic tribes. During the second millennium, the Semitic Assyrians were slowly rising to power and laying the foundations for their empire, which flourished under strong rulers from the ninth to the seventh centuries. Finally, at the end of the seventh century, the Assyrian capital at Nineveh was utterly destroyed by the Chaldeans from Babylonia, who were themselves in the next century to fall before the might of Persia. The Fertile Crescent gave birth to three of the great faiths of the world—Judaism, Christianity, and Mohammedanism. Our system of chronology and the source of astronomy are traceable to Mesopotamia; its cuneiform writing, by means of wedge-shaped marks, evolved into an alphabet that served as the origin of all Western written languages.

Whereas Egyptian architecture at its outset was hampered by a lack of timber suitable for building, the lower part of the Tigris-Euphrates valley provided neither wood nor stone. These materials had to be brought from a distance; on the other hand, clay pits abounded. Consequently an architecture in brick developed. The relative absence of stone hampered sculpture even more, since although clay is easily modeled, its products are neither monumental nor durable. Thus, the corpus of Mesopotamian art is limited compared to that of Egypt.

Like the Egyptians, the Sumerians believed in a life after death, but in their religion the after life did not depend on the preservation of the body, or on the sustenance of the spirit by physical objects or representations of them. Since the religious motive, which in Egypt had demanded an illustration of existence, was absent, we find no such total record of life here as we did in the Nile valley. In its place, the artists celebrate the king and his exploits in hunting and warfare; the more so since most of the sculpture preserved to us appears to have been executed at the royal command. Divinities are represented either as protectors of the king or as worshiped by him.

One consequence of the difference of religion from that of Egypt is that the tomb ceases to be an architectural problem. In its place is the palace; and of course the temple, or at least the temple tower, is prominent. The latter, a feature of the Palace of Sargon at Khorsabad (fig. 19) built during the eighth century B.C., in mass is like the Egyptian pyramid. Here it was only part of the palace chapel, but in large independent examples, the temple consisted of six or seven stages, whose vertical faces were laced by ramps that gave access to the shrine of the god on the top. This tower, called a *ziggurat*, was exactly oriented with its angles pointing to the cardinal points of the compass. Built of unbaked brick, perhaps faced with glazed brick, each section was colored. Herodotus describes the city walls at Agbatana, which was inspired by the Mesopotamian culture, as having the battlements colored white, black, scarlet, blue, orange, silver, and gold in that order, a sequence of tones rising to a climax of brilliance.

Because of their material, these ziggurats have disintegrated into mounds of clay, but they must have had a garish audacity in antiquity. However, it seems doubtful that they could ever have rivaled the pyramids in grandeur. For one thing, the material lacks the implication of permanence that stone gives us; for another, the stepped form has not the austerity of the Egyptian geometric monuments.

The palaces of the Assyrian kings were both military and domestic in purpose. The huge platform, which at Khorsabad served as a bastion in the city fortifications, raised the palace 60

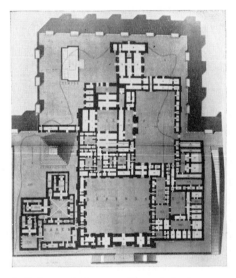

18. *Palace of Sargon,* Khorsabad (722–705 B.C.) 1050′ wide x 1140′ deep.

19. *Palace of Sargon*, Khorsabad (722–705 B.C.) Front, *c.* 1050' long.

feet above the level of the city (fig. 19). The task involved in building this mass of brick, 1140 by 1050 feet in dimensions, staggers the imagination, and could only have been accomplished by slave labor, the unwilling service of war captives. To void any moisture that might find its way into this pile, it was honeycombed with drains. These were arched to carry the weight above them. In the absence of other materials, brick was also employed for the single-story palace. Probably the roof was used as a terrace in the cool of the evening, as it certainly was in Palestine at the other end of the Fertile Crescent. Several Biblical incidents, such as the story of David and Bathsheba, refer to this use of the roof.

The plan of the Palace of Sargon at Khorsabad (fig. 18) consists of several courts surrounded by long and narrow rooms. One large court formed the nucleus of the service quarters; another, the men's portion, accommodated the king and his retainers; and a third corresponded to the harem. The presence of a ziggurat indicates that a temple was incorporated in the palace complex, like the chapels of medieval fortresses. The multiplicity of chambers and courts offered opportunities in design, which were only partly seized. In so far as the courts expressed the purposes of the palace, we may characterize the design as functional. It is less successful in the lack of relation between the parts, and the seemingly indiscriminate location of the rooms around the courts. The units of the Egyptian temple were related to one another; the rooms here are not. However, before we condemn these builders, let us remember two things. With their knowledge of the purposes of these parts, they may have had more reason for this apparent disorder than we can guess. Secondly, the problem they were facing was more complex than that offered in the Egyptian, or for that matter the Greek, temple.

The narrow shape of the rooms results from the material and the system of construction it imposed. Sunbaked brick is not strong; it does not lend itself to a columnar system, like that of the Egyptians, although remains show that brick columns were employed in rare cases. Instead, it suggests thick walls with as few openings as possible: precisely what we see in this plan. Still more important, since a brick is too small to serve as a beam, and since the region provided no adequate timber nearer than the cedars of Lebanon, the Mesopotamian builders were compelled to develop the arch and vault as a means of covering space. The drains in the platform show that several forms of vault were known. It seems certain that the long narrow rooms were so planned partly to facilitate covering them with semicylindrical, or barrel, vaults. No doubt some, if not all, of the square chambers were domed. These vaults might have been visible externally, but the evidence indicates that the roof above them was generally level, with a solid filling of brick or clay between the vaults. The weight of this form of roofing provided a further reason for the solid walls.

The description of such a palace sounds forbidding, but textile hangings and carpets, sumptuous in color, mitigated the severity of the interior. That part of the world has always been famous for its rugs. Indeed, the slab that paved the entrance to the Palace of Sennacherib at Kouyunjik was carved with a pattern derived from rugs, but transmuted into stone because of the wear to be expected in this location. Also brick, glazed and painted with patterns or figures or animal designs, accented doorways and other important features. But sculpture provided the most interesting decoration. Monsters carved in stone guarded the portals, while friezes or bands of sculpture in low relief adorned the interiors and recounted the prowess of the monarch in arms or in the hunt.

As in Egypt, so in Mesopotamia the early sculpture displayed a degree of realism absent in later work. The fragmentary figures from Tellô, carved in the twenty-fourth century B.C., especially that of Gudea, Patesi of Lagash (fig. 20), are the best known. Whether standing or seated with the hands folded in deference, these statues adhere to the law of frontality as do the Egyptian. One consideration, not present in Egypt, hampered any tendency the sculptor may have had toward anatomical realism: Egyptian men were clad only in a loin cloth; both sexes in Babylonia and Assyria encased their bodies in robes of heavy stuffs. The cylindrical mass produced by these garments adds to the

20. *Gudea, Patesi of Lagash* (*c.* 2400 B.C.) Louvre, Paris. Diorite, 30″ high.

sense of weight and of simplified form to produce a sculpturesque result. Nevertheless, the garment blocks the sculptor's opportunity to study the human form. That these artists were capable of observation and considered some accuracy of anatomy worthy of attention appears in those parts of the body that remained unclothed. The joints of the toes, the toenails, and the sinews of the foot are emphasized. The fleshy arms are fully muscled, and the bony structure of the head, missing in this example, is clearly perceived. For details, patterns replace realism, a phenomenon common in the early stages of art in many countries. The heavy eyebrows, a racial trait, form a herringbone design of lines engraved in the stone; the hair is reduced to a formula; and fringes of drapery are also abstract. Nonetheless, the squat proportions, large heads, and simplification endow these statues with a sculptural feeling that almost rivals the best of Egyptian work.

In later Assyrian times, examples of sculpture in the round are even less common. The incipient realism of the Gudea disappears in the ninth-century Ashur-nasir-pal, in the British Museum. Cut from a thin slab of stone, the linear conventions are more pronounced. Rows of artificial curls alternating with zigzag bands portray a formal beard. Heavy eyebrows join over the root of a Semitic nose. Ringed ridges accentuate the bulging eyes of the figure. Robes cover the body from shoulders to toes, and their pattern-like details absorb the sculptor's attention. The artistic impetus of the early phases of Mesopotamian art has faded into formalism.

One peculiar conception is illustrated by the creatures who guard the entrance to the Assyrian palaces. These are not cut in the round, since they do not stand free of the wall, nor are they in relief in the ordinary sense of that term, since the slab is carved at one end as well as on the side. Because of their architectural position, they are carved in the three-quarter round. These curiosities have the body and feet of a lion, or sometimes of a bull, the wings of a bird, and a human head crowned with the horned headdress peculiar to deities in Mesopotamia. The primitive love of pattern comes out here, not only in the hair and eyes, but in the pattern-like treatment of the feathers that form the wings, and in a diagrammatic indication of the muscles. One naïve detail results from their being viewed from the front as well as from the side. As one approaches the entrance the monsters appear to be standing still, their weight carried on the two forelegs, while from within the portal they seem to be walking, with all four legs visible; consequently they have five legs in all, one of the front legs being represented twice. These creatures form monumental accents in the architectural ensemble, and their sculpturesque masses which parallel the original planes of the block of stone give them an artistic integrity worthy of their prominent position in the palace.

But the largest body of Assyrian sculpture consists of friezes in low relief, which lined the lower part of the walls in the important rooms of Mesopotamian palaces. The sculptor faced the same problem here as did the Egyptian sculptor, and some of the conventions are the same, though modified by the traditions of the region. As in Egypt, a series of wavy lines represents water.

21. *Ashur-nasir-pal Storming a City*, from Palace at Nimrud (884–859 B.C.) British Museum, London. Height of frieze, 3'.

The slab of Ashur-nasir-pal Storming a City (fig. 21), of the ninth century, treats the hair and drapery in the usual Assyrian manner, but tends, as in Egypt, to alternate full-front and profile aspects for the several parts of the body. The eye, for example, is rendered full front in a profile head; the legs are in profile, but the shoulders are not always twisted around so fully as they had been along the banks of the Nile, and therefore the result is less angular. Where not hidden by drapery, the anatomy, as in the calf of the leg, is symbolic, each muscle defined as an area with rounded edges, with ridges between indicative of tendons. Thus the leg becomes the basis of a pattern as formal as the reduction of a flower to a rosette. For emphasis, the royal figure and his attendant deities are exaggerated in scale and, similarly, landscape features are introduced to explain the setting without regard for their comparative size. The defenders of the fortress can hardly be contained within it; they are too large to pass through the gates of their own city or to enter its buildings. If this discrepancy in size occurred only in the king or in the Assyrian soldiers, one might conclude that the artist imagined them to be nearer to the observer, and therefore that their size was an indication of distance, but the soldiers within the walls prove that this was not the case. It must be interpreted as a means of emphasis, to call attention to what the sculptor or his audience considered important.

Though human beings in Assyrian art are conventionalized, animals are drawn with greater freedom. The Wounded Lioness (fig. 22) from the Palace of Ashur-bani-pal, of the seventh century, is a masterpiece. Here the sculptor grapples with a problem involving representation and expression. In the solution of the former, he only half succeeds. The head and forequarters convey its appearance, but because the dragging hindquarters, paralyzed by the arrows that transfix her, are too difficult for him to represent he resorts to the

22. *Wounded Lioness*, from Palace of Ashur-bani-pal, Nineveh (668–626 B.C.) British Museum, London. 25″ x 40″.

Assyrian conventions for muscles. On the other hand, the expression is vivid. The artist feels to the limit the strength and courage of the lioness. Though wounded to the death she still drags herself forward, snarling, to the attack. A more realistic version might convey less of her spirit than this simplified design. The forward movement is not achieved by the posture alone, but more by the flowing curves, which really create it. To find a clearer example of the expressive possibilities of line in sculpture would be difficult.

Though less completely than in Egypt, these reliefs illuminate the civilization that produced them. Because the subjects are restricted to royal activity, they yield little information about ordinary life. Instead, they depict the military caste, headed by the ruler and his court, whose occupation was warfare and whose diversion the hunt. They confirm the reputation for ferocity that caste has won in literature. The heads of the king's enemies are impaled on spikes, their headless bodies strewn over the ground. When Ashur-bani-pal dines with his favorite queen—almost the only instance where a woman is represented in Assyrian sculpture—the food is served in the palace garden. His majesty, dressed in embroidered robes, half reclines on a couch and drinks from a bowl brought to him by his attendants. Perhaps his wine was the sweeter for the heads of foes impaled on a tree in his line of vision.

The civilization of this region, through conquest and trade, spread in all directions. Persia, for instance, which ultimately conquered Mesopotamia, was an artistic province, except in architecture. The same three-quarter-round monsters we have already seen in Assyria, but without the fifth leg, have been discovered at Persepolis (fig. 490); the Frieze of Archers from the Palace of Darius at Susa in glazed brick adopts a technique and a style developed in Mesopotamia. Here, and in the Frieze of Lions, also in glazed brick, the repetition of stylized forms in rich color results in a decorative magnificence derived from the art of the Fertile Crescent.

THE AEGEAN

The Aegean culture, third and last of the great cultures of the Mediterranean area previous to the classical, was unknown and its existence unsuspected until about a century ago. Even now, everything we know of this civilization is deduced from its art. Egyptian hieroglyphs, deciphered a century ago by Champollion, provide us with a mass of recorded history; the clay tablets of Babylonia and Assyria, first read by Layard, document their past; but in the Aegean, few inscriptions have come to

light, and these have yet to yield their secrets. The enthusiasm of the one-time indigo merchant Heinrich Schliemann, by his excavations at Troy, Tiryns, and Mycenae first brought proof of a pre-Greek civilization. However, when early in the present century Sir Arthur Evans discovered the Cretan remains at Cnossus, it became clear that the Aegean civilization had developed and reached its apogee in Crete, and that the Mycenaean age on the mainland was merely the afterglow, a barbaric imitation of a higher culture. This Minoan culture has been named from Minos, the mythical name of the sea kings of Crete.

Thus the island Palace of Cnossus, its present remains dated in the middle of the second millennium, outshines the

23. *Palace*, Cnossus (c. 1800–1600 B.C.) c. 400′ square.

mainland fort at Tiryns. Its plan (fig. 23) has as many rooms as a Mesopotamian palace, but in several ways is more advanced. The elements are grouped around one principal court, and although their purpose is not certain, at least some of the rooms form a suite, one chamber leading to another with a definite order in their disposition. The Cretan palace had at least two stories and perhaps three or four. Therefore, stairs were essential, and because a staircase is an element of two or more stories, its relation to the second and third floors had to be visualized before the ground story was built. In itself, this requirement postulates a more than rudimentary architectural training. Furthermore, the upper stories compelled the inclusion of courts or light wells to illumine the ground floor. The stair wells were built with columns, tapered toward the bottom as seen in paintings, and of the type adopted in tombs on the mainland of Greece. Made of wood, the columns have vanished, but the stone sockets where they rested are preserved and make it possible to restore the hall (fig. 24). The peculiar bulging capital of these columns has some resemblance to the later Greek Doric form, though any historic connection between them is conjectural. In other ways besides its advanced plan, the palace of Cnossus bespeaks a high state of civilization. Extensive piping and a flush toilet provided sanitation. The latter invention, so essential in modern life, was not destined to reappear in European civilization until the sixteenth century after Christ, a lapse of over three thousand years. Cnossus in its heyday was unfortified; evidently the sea kings of Crete relied on their navy for protection. In fact the late fortifications probably indicate that Crete lost control of the sea toward the end of her long history, and had to provide those land defenses that had been superfluous during her prime.

The Palace at Tiryns on the mainland of Greece, built somewhat later than that of Cnossus, in contrast is fortified, like a medieval castle, with thick walls of huge stones laid together without mortar, and with its gates defended by additional walls. The sequence of gates, courts, and rooms probably comes from Crete, as does the type of column used

24. *Palace at Cnossus* (*c.* 1800–1600 B.C.) Stairhall, restored.

in the entrances to the palace proper. The principal chamber, entered from the portico, is doubtless to be identified as the *megaron*, familiar to us from the Homeric poems; it has an open hearth in the center. A second suite of rooms, presumably the *thalamus*, or women's quarters, connects with the megaron by a circuitous route easy to control. The various rooms of this, as of the Cretan palace, were roofed with timber, but such contemporary tombs as the Treasury of Atreus at Mycenae adopt the so-called *corbel* vault. Built underground, its single chamber is shaped like a beehive, which looks like a true vault; but whereas in a true vault the stones are wedge-shaped and the joints between each course or layer of stone radiate from a point within the void covered by the vault, in the corbel system the stones are laid with the joints horizontal, so that each block lies flat on the

one below it, its interior surface projecting further into the void.

The discovery of Egyptian pottery in Crete proves that there had been some trade with Egypt, a conclusion corroborated by the abundant paintings of the region. The design, called the Bull Leapers, from the Palace of Cnossus (fig. 25), like Egyptian painting, is executed in line and flat tone, the several parts of the composition outlined, and each area then filled with a single tone. In Crete, however, a slight modification of the major tone may appear along the edges of each area, which mitigates the stiffness characteristic of Egyptian work. The red-brown men and the pale yellow women recall a similar color scheme in the Nile valley. Even the conventions of the body have some parallels; the eye in full front in a profile head, the hips even narrower than in Egyptian painting, and the shoulders broader; but the profile

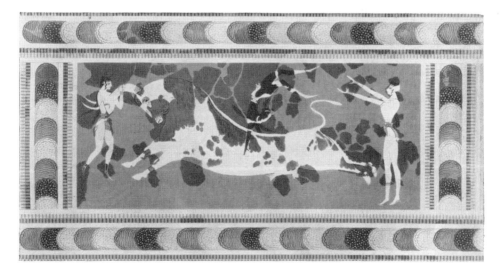

25. *Bull Leapers,* from Palace at Cnossus. Candia Museum. Fresco, 5'3" wide.

full-front alternation is not quite so regular.

In spite of these points of correspondence, Cretan painting differs from Egyptian and is more pleasing to many people today. The less precise blocking out is partly responsible, but more important is the remarkable sense of selection. Instead of crowding the composition with a host of details, the Cretan artist realizes the value of open space and stresses fundamentals, ignoring the rest. The linear rhythm of the bull and the figures is cardinal; all that is needed to dramatize action is included and nothing else. Extraneous material is so conspicuously avoided that the painting looks almost Oriental. The bull strikes an attitude that is improbable from a naturalistic point of view, but that lends itself to design and to the suggestion of movement. Curves are simplified to make them expressive. Such drawing is not the work of an amateur but of a highly sophisticated artist. These lines are swept in with consummate assurance. With such artistic success, the fact that we cannot surely interpret the scene is of small significance; whether these figures vaulting over the back of the bull are to be interpreted as acrobats, as performers of a dance, or as engaged in some religious rite, one does not know. The frequency with which the bull recurs in Aegean art colors the supposition that the animal was connected with religion, but just how is still a matter for archaeology to determine.

Painting in Crete takes the place occupied by sculpture in Egypt and Meso-

potamia. Except for the Lion Gate at Mycenae, which comes from the bitter end of this civilization, no monumental carving has been discovered. In the minor arts, sculpture on a small scale does exist. The exquisite Snake Goddess

26. *Cretan Snake Goddess* (16th cent. B.C.) Museum of Fine Arts, Boston.

(fig. 26), in the Boston Museum, has her body and dress made of ivory, but the nipples of her breasts, the flounces of her skirt, and the writhing snakes held in her hands are of gold. Though only about seven inches high, she conveys the impression of a larger figure, freely modeled and idealized with aristocratic features. This independent little lady stands with the utmost assurance, her arched back balancing her outstretched arms. The narrow waist and the elaborate costume, both of which occur in paintings, follow the fashion of the day.

27. *Gold Cup from Vaphio* (*c.* 16th–12th cent. B.C.) National Museum, Athens. 3″ high.

In the famous Gold Cups from Vaphio (fig. 27) the artist demonstrates his skill in metalwork. Bulls again form the subject; on one cup they are grazing, while on the other they are captured in nets. Though some realistic shortcomings are evident, the total result is remarkably natural. However, the artistic quality comes from the creative selection, the rhythm, and the technique with which the material is handled.

Though much remains unknown about this civilization, its general course is clear. It rose slowly through the third millennium before Christ, until the sea kings of Crete brought their culture to its apex during the second millennium, when the Palace at Cnossus with its masterpieces of painting was created. At this time, Crete controlled some of the islands in the Aegean Sea, and spread her style to them. Then, during the second millennium, barbarian Greeks from the north began to arrive in the Peloponnesus, to touch the hem of this culture and to learn its elements. These people, who form the Mycenaean civilization, catch a provincial reflection of the sophisticated Minoan art; for example, a version of the Bull Leapers in Tiryns is the same in subject as the masterpiece from Cnossus, but its technique is amateurish. Presumably, these people undermined the power of the sea kings until they forced the addition to Cnossus of the late fortifications.

That these Mycenaeans were the Greeks who fought the Trojan War, and of whom Homer wrote, seems certain. The sites of the Homeric poems, Troy, Tiryns, Mycenae 'rich in gold,' as the poet says, which yielded over a ton of gold objects to the excavations of Heinrich Schliemann, are the sites modern archaeology has found most fruitful of Mycenaean remains. Homer speaks with wonder of the walls of Tiryns, of Crete and its ninety cities. The poems mention only one statue, but describe in detail several objects of the minor arts, such as the cup of Nestor and the shield of Achilles. If one allows for poetic exaggeration, these descriptions might apply to the metalwork of Mycenaean days. But pale reflection of Crete though this be, it was yet superior in culture to anything known to the new waves of barbarian Greeks who began to arrive in the Peloponnesus toward the end of the second millennium. The Homeric Greeks had learned something from Crete, but had not had time themselves to become fully civilized; for the newcomers, Dorian, Ionian, and Aeolian tribes, overthrew the long-haired, mail-clad Achaeans of whom Homer wrote. Centuries were to elapse before these new tribes, the Greeks as we know them, were to find their own manner of artistic expression, one that was to be distinct from the Mycenaean or that of any other civilization which had preceded them.

According to tradition, the historic Greeks entered the Peloponnesus in 1100 B.C. To accept this literally is absurd; the Greeks did not arrive on schedule like a conducted tour. The process was slower and less simple, one of infiltration by successive waves of migration by these peoples from the north, like the barbarian invasions that centuries later upset the Roman Empire. Like that later and better-known movement, the Greek migration was followed by several centuries of the 'Dark Ages,' so-called partly because we know little about them, and partly because they cover the time when these peoples were taking the first toddling steps toward what would one day emerge as a glorious culture.

The land where these newcomers found themselves was very different from either Egypt or Mesopotamia. Odysseus said of his native Ithaca that it was 'a rugged land but a good nurse of men,' and the description might apply to all Greece. Life was not so easy here as in the Nile valley, but the Greeks' very struggles for existence may have stimulated their innate energy, their resourcefulness, their willingness to experiment and to adventure on untried lines of endeavor. The mountains that break up the country and the arms of the sea that penetrate it fostered small city states, often at war with their neighbors, but intensely proud of themselves. Although the Homeric poems were read throughout the Greek world and helped to give the Greeks a feeling of brotherhood distinct from the barbarian or non-Greek world of the older civilizations, still it required the danger of a Persian invasion to compel one city even partly to co-operate with another. However, the smallness of the city state, which enabled every citizen to play an active part in civic life, promoted public spirit and an atmosphere of free discussion stimulating to the individual. The artists of older civilizations knew when they were doing good work and must have been proud of it. We may assume that this was true in Mesopotamia and Egypt; in Greece, the individual, even the humblest potter, paraded his pride of creation in dozens of inscriptions, while the prominent sculptors won reputations that have lasted down to this day.

Moreover, this land supplied all the materials necessary for sculpture and architecture. Good timber could be had and was used for domestic building as well as for the roofs of temples, and at the beginning probably for the whole temple. Limestone was plentiful, varying from the coarse grained *poros*, used for some early examples of sculpture, to finer types. But above all, the quarries yielded the fine-grained marbles of Paros and Pentelicus, stones hard enough to wear well, yet workable under the sculptor's chisel. Given an intellectual people stimulated by their surroundings, with the raw materials of architecture and sculpture at hand, a brilliant artistic development was bound to occur.

The first of the visual arts to emerge was architecture. Sometime during the Dark Ages, the Greek temple and the two principal *orders* of Greek architecture developed. An order is a specific type of base, column, and entablature. The more important of the orders is the Doric (fig. 28), which, when matured in the fifth century, was to exhibit a rare balance of strength and delicacy, a perfect relation of the parts to the whole and of the parts to their purposes, which has never been surpassed. Any structural member in architecture may be classified according to function in one of three types: a base or foundation member, a supporting member, or a crowning or terminating member. In the Doric order these functions are expressed in the three principal divisions, the same triple memberships carrying through even the minor units. A base or *stereobate* serves as and expresses the foundation of the temple; the *columns* stand on it; and they in turn support an *entablature* which reflects the roof. Several steps, generally three, compose the stereobate. Since the Doric column has no individual base, the *stylobate* or top step serves a double function: it terminates the stereobate and it serves as a foundation to the colonnade. This combination of purposes in the stylobate links the stereobate and the colonnade. The *shaft* of the column, which gives the height necessary for the temple, has its essential movement emphasized by narrow vertical grooves or *flutes* (collectively, *fluting*). In the Doric order, these are shaped as elliptical curves and meet one another in an edge. The shaft is not quite cylindrical; it tapers toward the top, an expressive device in that the bottom of the shaft must support the mass of the column in addition to the weight of the entablature. This tapering is not uniform but is cut in a flat curve, called *entasis*, which gives the shaft a vigorous beauty.

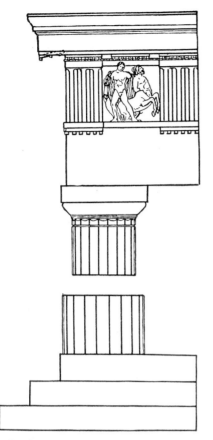

28. Greek Doric Order.

completes the transition from the circular plan of the shaft and echinus to the rectangular shapes of the entablature above, and yet is not too high to break the transition from the vertical to the horizontal line afforded by the echinus.

The abacus not only terminates the capital it also serves as a base for the lowest of the three members of the entablature, the *architrave*, a plain beam that spans the void from column to column. This, in turn, is topped by a narrow molding, which links it to the *frieze*, the middle member of the entablature. The Doric order is peculiar in that the frieze, a continuous band in the other orders, alternates triple vertical bars, called *triglyphs*, and almost square slabs, either plain or sculptured, the *metopes*. The alternation of verticals and plain areas in the frieze recalls the alternation of vertical columns and open spaces in the colonnade, though there are almost twice as many triglyphs as columns. Above the frieze, horizontal moldings compose the *cornice*, the third member of the entablature, analogous to the eaves of a wooden roof; it expresses the roof and throws rainfall away from the stonework below. The lower or bed moldings of the cornice support the upper projecting members, on which, above each triglyph and each metope, appear flat blocks, called *mutules*. These recall the divisions below, and so establish the harmony between the frieze and the cornice. Peg-like ornaments, *guttae*, decorate the under surface of the mutules. Finally, since the climate of Greece is not rainless, a low gable roof

The column terminates with a *capital*, which also consists of three parts: the fluted *necking*, separated from the shaft by a narrow groove; the bulging cushion-like molding, the *echinus*; and, at the top, a square block, the *abacus*. Through its similarity to the shaft, the necking merges that part with the capital. The strong freehand curve of the echinus creates an enlarged area to help in supporting the beams, and both in appearance and in actuality is strong enough to hold considerable weight. The abacus is necessary. The triangular ends of that roof over the front and back of the temple are called *pediments*. The entablature, except the top molding of the cornice, continues as a horizontal band below the pediments, but most of the cornice must be repeated along the slope of the roof, where it is called the *raking cornice*. Most of these terms apply to other orders besides the Doric and recur through later architectural history.

The Doric order raises two questions. First, to what extent, if at all, was this architecture influenced by previous civilizations, and second, did its forms originate in stone or wood? The vaulted architecture of Mesopotamia was foreign to the Greeks; for although they knew the principle of the arch and used it for unimportant structures and in inconspicuous positions, its dynamic nature contradicted the serenity and quietness they considered essential in monumental buildings. The colonnaded architecture of Egypt might have suggested a colonnaded style to the Greeks, but this assumption involves several difficulties. For one thing, while Egypt during the Saite period welcomed the Greeks, that period postdates the earliest steps in the formation of the temple and the Doric order. Secondly, the Egyptian temple is an internal form; its colonnades line the interior of the peristyle and support the roof of the hypostyle hall; only the pylon is enriched externally, but that member has no parallel in Greek architecture. With the Greek temple, however, the converse is true. Essentially a shrine and a monument to the god, it is designed to be seen from without rather than from within. Finally, the only type of Egyptian column at all resembling the Doric is the sixteen-sided column. Although at first glance the similarity is striking, closer examination suggests that these parallels are fortuitous. Nothing in Egypt corresponds to the entablature of the order and, although the shafts look alike, many details differ. The Egyptian column has an abacus but no true capital. Most significant, the Egyptian shaft is light in its proportions, which are like those of the Greek Doric of later days, but unlike the heavy proportions of the early Doric. Egypt could have suggested only the pier and lintel system to the Greeks. Even that seems doubtful, since so elementary a method is probably indigenous in any region, like Greece, where appropriate materials are available.

Geography implies that the Aegean area might well have influenced the early Greeks. The portico, restored as an entrance to the Palace at Tiryns, resembles the colonnaded porches of some smaller Greek temples. Moreover, the capital of Aegean columns vaguely suggests the cushion-like Doric echinus, and there are some details in Aegean architecture that may have prompted the triglyph and metope system of the Doric. On the other hand, the Minoan column tapers toward the bottom, exactly opposite to the Greek. It is conceivable that some memories of the earlier architecture of the Aegean area may have persisted in the later Doric forms, but if so, they were so slight that we may consider the Doric order as a purely Greek development.

Less difficult is the question whether the Doric order originated in wood or stone. Advocates of the latter theory maintain that its details and proportions are so expressive of stone that they could hardly have developed in wood. The massive, close-spaced columns support this argument. As we have seen in the first chapter, timber construction tends to produce a horizontal rectangle with slender, widely spaced supports. The Doric column, notably in the early examples, is heavy and squat. It could be true that the early Greeks took the trunks of trees for their first columns, but nevertheless it seems absurd to suppose that they would have chosen such large trees and spaced them so closely.

In reply to this, the proponents of a wooden origin assume that, when the order was translated from wood to stone, a complete change of proportions in the column was effected. They rest their case on the evidence of the order itself and on certain historical indications. First, it is not wise to expose the cross section of a wood beam to the weather. Moisture and consequent decay penetrate deeper into the ends of timbers than through their sides. The triglyphs look like cleats placed for protection over the ends of beams that might have supported the ceiling of the temple. Second, the guttae attached to blocks below the triglyphs resemble wooden pegs intended to hold the triglyphs in place. It is hard to imagine what else can have

suggested them. Finally, in a wooden roof the rafters must be covered with planks to support tiles, shingles, or slate. Are not the mutules the projecting ends of these planks again pegged into position with guttae?

One of the earliest large temples is the Heraeum (Temple of Hera) at Olympia. In its present form it is not earlier than about 600 B.C. In this temple, the original wood columns were replaced from time to time in the current style of stone columns. As one might expect under these circumstances, they differ from one another in their proportions and details. Pausanias, who wrote a guide book of Greece during the second century after Christ, tells us that one column in the back porch was still of wood in his day. If the columns were originally of wood, then the entablature must also have been of wood. This building, therefore, would seem to settle the argument; and so it might, if we could prove that the existing stone members were like the wooden shafts they replaced, and if we could demonstrate that the vanished wood entablature was Doric. The presumption is strong that it was, but final proof is impossible. Still, the Heraeum, coupled with the evidence of the order itself, makes so clear a case for a wooden origin of the Doric that one can only assume that the column proportions were adapted to stone when that material came into use.

The Greeks crystallized the arrangement of the temple early in their history. It is planned (fig. 29) with a rec-

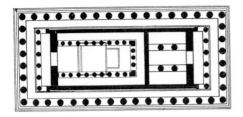

29. *Parthenon*, Athens (447–432 B.C.) 101′ x 228′.

tangular chamber, the *cella* or sanctuary, ringed by a free-standing colonnade. This scheme, sometimes with one or two additional chambers behind the cella for storage, was followed in all the larger Greek temples from the seventh or eighth century before Christ to the end of Greek history. Smaller examples, such as the Temple of Wingless Victory at

30. *Temple of Wingless Victory*, Athens (427–424 B.C.) 26′10″ x 17′9″.

Athens (fig. 30), omit the colonnade on the sides. To refine and perfect this plan, the Greeks devoted their architectural energies for the next few centuries. So long a period of experiment and adjustment alone made possible the exquisite balance of the Parthenon. In general, this development followed certain clear lines. The Heraeum is about three times as long as it is wide, with six columns in front and in back and sixteen on each side. Later examples such as the Parthenon are more compact with a length just over twice the

width. Fifth-century temples usually have on the side one column more than twice the number that they have across the front. Thus the Parthenon has eight columns in front and seventeen on the side; the contemporary Theseum in Athens has six and thirteen columns.

With the passing centuries, the entablature lightened as compared with the total height of the temple or that of the columns. In early examples, it was a crushing mass almost half as high as the column and therefore a third of the height of the building above the stylobate; but by the fifth century, the entablature became about a third as high as the column, and so a quarter of the total building height. Meanwhile, the shaft grew taller in proportion to its width at the base, referred to as its lower diameter. The early examples might be only four lower diameters in height; when the Parthenon was designed, they were almost five-and-a-half lower diameters. These figures, of course, tell us nothing of the actual height of the column, which depends on the size of the temple, but simply the proportions of the column. The last development to be mentioned is found in the echinus. In the early capitals of the Heraeum this member flared out from the shaft with a bulging curve that, as time went on, became less marked and rose at an angle of approximately 45 degrees. This flatter curve and sharper rise is both more powerful in support and more subtle in appearance than the early type.

The fifth-century Temple of Hera at

31. *Temple of Hera*, Paestum (*c.* 460 B.C.) Limestone, front 79'8" wide.

Paestum (fig. 31), formerly identified as the Temple of Poseidon, in southern Italy, while not perfected in detail, forms a fitting illustration of the type, though the emphasis still is more on robustness than on refinement. Compactness of form, held in such high esteem by the Greeks and illustrated in Greek tragedy, here has its exact architectural expression. To this form nothing is lacking, and from it nothing can be subtracted; its unity is outstanding. Furthermore, the decoration is restrained. In some examples sculpture in the round filled the pediments, the metopes were carved in high relief, and groups placed above the angles of the pediments served to accent those parts. All this decoration was restricted to the top of the temple, leaving simpler forms below. Color added a final grace; tones of bright red and blue gave contrast to the smaller moldings of the entablature, that otherwise could hardly be seen from the ground. Any patterns applied to these moldings, either in color or by carving, repeat on their surfaces the shape of the moldings in cross section. For example, a molding that is rectangular in section may be adorned with a fret, composed of straight lines and right angles, a molding whose profile forms a quarter circle, in curved shapes. Thus the pattern repeats in design the shape of the surface where it is placed.

To the Greeks, the strong Doric order was masculine; the grace of the Ionic was feminine. Developed at the same time as the Doric, the less simple and less vigorous Ionic order was popular in the islands of the Aegean and on the mainland of Asia Minor, but not so

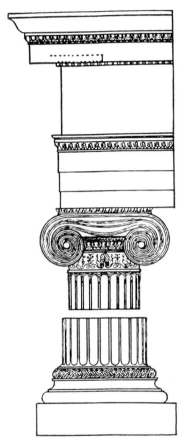

32. Greek Ionic Order.

common in the Peloponnesus and in southern Italy. Its first point of difference (fig. 32) is the individual *base* under each column. A square *plinth* or block of stone may serve as a foundation (though not in the Athenian buildings), with convex and concave moldings above combined in several ways.

The shaft, more slender than even the developed Doric shaft, tapers less than the Doric. The semicircular flutes are deeper, and are separated from one another by a narrow band. A pair of flanking *volutes* or scrolls connected by straight and curving lines compose the capital. It is as though paper had been rolled up from either end, with the edges of these scrolls visible on the front and back of the capital. Charming as the result is, it raises several problems. Since the front and side of the capital contrast, an adjustment must be made at the corner of the building, lest either the front or the side colonnade exhibit one capital different in appearance from the others in the same range. The Greek solution before Hellenistic times was to bend the volute on the corner capital outward to a 45-degree angle, and so force an approximate similarity of appearance on the neighboring faces of the capital. Though this device has been praised as showing the ingenuity of the Greeks, it is in fact awkward. A lopsided capital does not look well from any point of view; its resemblance to its neighbors is superficial, while its irregularity betrays it as a makeshift. The Hellenistic Greeks solved the problem of the corner capital of the Ionic order by changing its shape. The canted volute was repeated at all four corners of the capital; this made it symmetrical and so adapted it for use equally on the corner and in the center of a colonnade. The truth is that the earlier Greek Ionic, though graceful in itself, can be entirely successful only where the colonnade does not turn a corner.

The Ionic entablature, like the Doric, has architrave, frieze, and cornice, but the architrave is broken into three bands adorned by small moldings. The continuous frieze is sometimes adorned with sculpture. A distinguishing element in the Ionic cornice is the *dentil range*, broken into square blocks like a row of teeth, which supports the overhanging parts of the cornice.

That the Ionic order developed from wood is universally admitted. The dentil range, for instance, derived from the ends of rafters, and the earliest examples show proportions in the column hardly possible except in wood. When the order was converted to stone, these proportions became more robust, but never rivaled the massiveness of the Doric. Scrolls of early capitals seem to grow out of the shaft; only later were they connected with one another. Like the Doric, the most splendid examples of the order occur in the fifth century.

Whereas architecture begins to exhibit its characteristic, if still archaic, forms at least as early as the seventh century, sculpture becomes important only toward the end of that century. That this art reached a high level in Hellenic times is the universal testimony of ancient authors. Their comments are valuable in two ways: first, their descriptions identify some of the famous statues and connect them with sculptors whom antiquity regarded as masters; and second, their criticisms and comparisons allow us to imagine what the original beauty of the statues may have been. In this connection, much depends on how we value the judgment of ancient critics; some, like Pliny, confused fame with artistic merit and admired some statues for reasons modern critics do not consider important. Others, such as Lucian, appear to have been more sensitive to qualities other than mere verisimilitude. From the period that antiquity, including so discerning a critic as Lucian, regarded as the culmination of Greek sculpture, few, if any, of the famous originals are preserved. We know approximately what many of these statues looked like, because they were copied for the Roman market, just as photographs or casts of 'old masters' are available today.

These late Greek or Roman copies seldom warrant the praise bestowed on them by the nineteenth century. Their quality varies but often is dull and uninspired. One would not dream of trying to evaluate the painting of Titian, for example, on the basis of copies, even if they were made by men of recognized talent, since the hand of the copyist must alter the subtle relations established by the original master, and yet this is what one must do with the famous masters of Greek sculpture. Two courses, therefore, remain open today. The first is to deflate the prestige of Greek sculpture, at least during the period of its maturity, on the ground that the copies do not justify a high opinion. To accept this position is to reject the testimony of classic critics (who saw the originals) as based on the idea that art must hold the mirror up to nature. The other and fairer approach is to withhold judgment, to admit the shortcomings in extant copies, and, in the absence of other evidence, to accept the dicta of the more discerning critics of antiquity. We should test these dicta so far as possible by comparisons, but must make allowance for qualities that may have been present in the original, but which the copyist might have lost, partly through inability and partly through copying in marble a statue designed by the master in bronze—a profound modification to be remembered in most of the famous copies.

However, some original Greek work of two sorts is extant. First, archaic sculpture was not sufficiently esteemed by the Romans to be carted away by them; much of it, too, had been buried by accident, or, after it had been damaged during the Persian wars. Second, some architectural sculpture, the metopes and friezes and the figures in the pediments of Greek temples, remains to us. The marbles of the Parthenon, for example, are Greek originals of the fifth century and, in the absence of more famous statues, must establish for us the character of the period. The slightest comparison of these originals with Roman copies from other contemporary work demonstrates the vitality of the former and the dullness of the latter. But in antiquity, architectural decorations like these were secondary in importance, worth only a passing mention by critics, and often the product of less celebrated artists working under the direction of a master—what, in other epochs, are called 'school' works. If these originals are so superior to the copied masterpieces, how much more allowance we should make for the discrepancy between those copies and the lost masterpieces on which they were based.

Though not productive of monumental sculpture, the Dark Ages laid the foundations of civilization in Greece. During this time, Greece came into contact with the older cultures of the Mediterranean region. Then, too, the Homeric poems received their definite form. The poet looks back longingly from his own day to the heroic past—that is, to the Mycenaean civilization. In *The Iliad*, Homer says that Ajax picked up a large stone to cast at his adversary; no one in the poet's time could lift such a stone.

This pessimism may be an instinctive tendency to admire 'the good old times,' but comparison of the Vaphio Cups with geometric vases of the eighth century goes far to explain Homer's attitude. The Aegean proficiency of technique has vanished. Most of the surface of these large funerary vases is banded with patterns, but in a few of the wider bands the craftsman drew 'memory pictures,' extreme simplifications of human forms. The figures these contain are diagrammatic, their legs shaped like those of wasps, their torsos inverted triangles, and their heads circles. No less symbolic is the drawing of horses. In many vases of this period, and even more so in the seventh-century vases from Rhodes, Oriental animal motives testify to the contact with Egypt and particularly with

Mesopotamia. Wherever space permits among the figures, horses, and chariots, the craftsman inserted decorative motives. Nothing remains of the beauty of technique or of the sophistication of the Vaphio Cups, and yet the geometric vases have a primitive vigor. Their patterns are well adapted to the surfaces they decorate. The fact is that these vases are not crude attempts to preserve Mycenaean tradition; on the contrary, they illustrate the birth of a promising Hellenic culture.

Perhaps the most important result of the Homeric poems was to vivify the gods of the Olympic pantheon. No one, after reading *The Iliad*, can think of Zeus and Hera, Ares and Aphrodite as abstract conceptions; they are too individual and human. Unlike the deities of Egypt and Mesopotamia, these gods are envisioned in human form, though more perfect physically and more powerful than ordinary mankind. To overemphasize the importance of this anthropomorphism in religion is impossible. When the Greeks began to carve statues of their gods, they found the whole force of religion behind them, impelling them to seek a result that would incorporate this human conception. No conventionalized version could long prove satisfactory. Since gods were like men, their statues had to be reasonably realistic. But once the sculptor acquired the ability to carve a realistic figure, he had to conceive and render forms more perfect than any to be found on earth, shapes that might be at once human and superhuman. Hence

on a basis of realistic knowledge, the Greek sculptor molded his idealized conceptions of the Olympic pantheon until, a century later, he eliminated the individual, the incidental, and the accidental.

Naturally, this idealism was not reached overnight. The first century and a half of Greek sculpture, called the archaic period, extends from the late seventh century to the end of the Persian wars in 480 B.C.; it is a time of experimentation, of observation of the body and its possibilities, of struggle for mastery over stone—all calculated to reach this realistic first goal. Especially at the beginning, the sculptors were hampered by ignorance of how to present the body accurately, and how far it was safe to cut into the block of stone. In lieu of these skills, at least in part, the archaic tendency for pattern provided an outlet for the creative energies of the craftsmen. This concern with design produced masterpieces of high quality, possibly a purer expression than might have been reached had the sculptor been more sophisticated. That the trend of Greek sculpture was away from convention and toward realism is historical fact. For better or worse, the Greeks regarded these limitations, that may result in a sculptural mass and a design based upon the sense of pattern, as restrictions to be escaped as soon as possible. Consequently the Greek sculptor experimented constantly. Recognizing the realistic defects of his own or his master's works, he sought to rectify them. Unlike Egypt, tradition could be ignored.

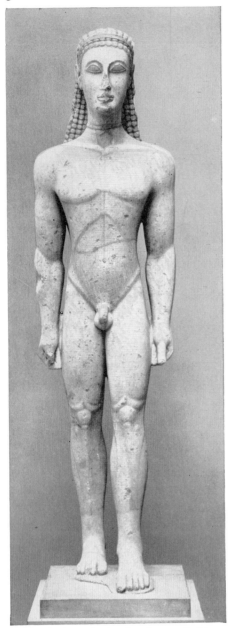

33. *Youth*, from Attica (*c.* 600 B.C.) Metropolitan Museum, New York. Island marble, 6'1" high.

The sculpture of the first seventy-five years (625–550 B.C.) exhibits a limited number of types or poses, the most important of which is the standing nude male figure. Though called the 'Apollo' type, these figures are not all identified. Some may be statues of that god, but some others are statues of athletes, victors in the Olympic games or one of the other festivals. The similarity to the Egyptian priest Ranefer (fig. 16) is obvious. Like him, the Youth or *Kouros* (fig. 33) walks forward, the weight carried on both feet; the erect body respects the law of frontality; the shoulders are broad and, since the arms are locked to the sides, the hips are narrow. Clearly the material dominates the conception. Perhaps the sculptor started with a prismatic block of stone, drew the silhouette of his figure first on the front of the block and then chiseled away the parts that were not within that outline. The procedure was repeated on the sides of the block. When the edges of this rough mass were rounded off, an approximation of the human form resulted, but the planes of such a figure tended to mirror the original planes of the block and so expressed the material. Moreover, details show that the craftsman was afraid to cut deeply into the stone. The hands are not free of the body, and indeed in the earliest examples almost the whole length of the arm is attached to the torso. The long hair falls over the shoulders to strengthen the neck at its weakest point. Instead of cutting into the stone to embed the eyes beneath the brows, the eyes bulge out to pre-

serve the ovoid mass of the head. The
compact sculpturesque result of the
early archaic figures comes in part from
these considerations.

But if the 'Apollos' parallel Egyptian
standing or walking figures, the differences are even more prophetic. The slab
of stone that served as a background for
Ranefer is gone. The Greek figure is
nude, innocent even of the loin cloth,
that almost universally appears in Egypt;
this points to the Greek concern with
the body as the primary vehicle for
sculpture. Significant is the willingness
to experiment with anatomy. The sculptor of the Youth indicates the muscular
divisions of the torso, articulates the
kneecap, and represents the bony structure of the body, as in the shoulder
blades. The characteristic archaic smile
to modern eyes creates a stilted, even
irritating, impression of complacency;
the hair is reduced to patterns, with
snail-shell curls over the forehead and
repeated wavy lines for the mass of the
hair. As a work of art, the Youth is not
equal to the Ranefer; it lacks the assurance, the competence, and the strength
of the Egyptian. The Greek sculptor
does not yet rival his predecessors in
technique. But the statue itself contains
the germs of progress.

The standing female type of the Hera
of Samos (fig. 34), dated about 550 B.C.,
is almost as common as the 'Apollo'
type. Its cylindrical mass presupposes
earlier statues in wood, images carved
from trunks of trees; and although the
sculptor is here working in stone, he preserves the familiar shape. No parts sepa-

34. *Hera of Samos* (*c.* 550 B.C.) Louvre, Paris.
Marble, 6' high.

rate themselves from the mass; the arms
join the body through their entire
length. At this time, the female figure

35. *Chares of Branchidae* (late 6th cent. B.C.) British Museum, London. Parian marble, 4′10″ high.

in Greek art is always clothed; therefore, the sculptor seizes the opportunity to use the drapery for design in pure pattern. Small parallel folds compose the skirt as though it were accordion-

36. Micciades and Archermus, *Nike of Delos* (550–520 B.C.) National Museum, Athens. Marble, 3′ high.

pleated, and contrast with the plain overskirt and with another system of lines in the upper garment that sweep down from the left shoulder and spread outward over the breast. The sequence in direction of these wider folds serves as a foil to the vertical harmony below, at once enhancing and being enriched by it. Unrealistic though she is, the compactness and the pattern make the Hera of Samos a masterpiece comparable with any.

Other early figure types are less common. If the 'Apollo' type recalls the contact Greece had with Egypt during the seventh century, the seated Chares of Branchidae (fig. 35) has Mesopotamian qualities. Like the Gudea (fig. 20), it is draped so heavily that little of the underlying body can be perceived. The folds of the garment, indicated by lines, are flattened on the surface rather than modeled with any considerable projection and recession. So block-like is this figure and so intimately connected with its chair, that it could not rise without taking the throne with it. Although compact, the result seems heavy.

The archaic Greek artist rarely essayed bolder problems. The winged Nike or Victory of Delos (fig. 36) is the oldest Greek statue ascribed, however doubtfully, to known sculptors, Micciades and Archermus of Delos. Literary evidence indicates that the Nike was carved early in the sixth century. This kneeling figure corresponds to Egyptian methods of representing the body, as though an Egyptian relief were converted into sculpture in the round. The head and shoulders are viewed from in front, but at the waist the figure half turns so that the legs are seen in profile. In short, Micciades and Archermus transferred to

37. *Seated Gods*, Frieze, Treasury of Siphnians, Delphi (550–520 B.C.) Museum, Delphi. Marble, height of frieze 25″.

sculpture in the round a convention understandable in relief. They conceived of their statue not as something the spectator may inspect from all sides, but as something to be seen from a single point of view, as relief sculpture is. If the result is not quite successful, to attempt the Nike of Delos at all took courage. These sculptors were eager to portray new poses still beyond their technical ability.

The early sculptors laid the foundations and established the traditions to be developed in the next seventy years, from 550 to 480 B.C. The frieze of the Treasury of the Siphnians at Delphi (fig. 37) represents a struggle of gods and giants; it exploits the decorative pos-

sibilities inherent in earlier work. These artists seem not to have concerned themselves with the possibilities of the body. Most of the figures are draped, and the body serves more as a frame to hold patterns of clothing than as something interesting in itself, although the drapery is often pulled so tight that it reveals the contours of the figure. The bodies are heavy in proportion, puffy rather than muscular, with the archaic smile, patterned hair, and bulging eyes still prominent. On the other hand, the draperies themselves invite rich designs. The folds are not cut deep enough to destroy the expression of mass, but they are arranged with a superb feeling for rhythm. Their variety may indicate dif-

38. Execias (active 6th cent. B.C.) *Dionysus* (*c.* 530 B.C.) Museum, Munich. Black-figured vase, diameter 12".

such as that by Execias (fig. 38). Within the bowl, Dionysus sails through a school of porpoises. The setting is symbolic, with no indication of the sea save for the presence of the fish. These and the grapevine that Dionysus brings to man approximate a scalloped pattern around the rim of the vase to echo and harmonize with its shape. Up to this time, Greek vases retained the black-figured style, wherein the motives are glazed in black, sometimes with other colors added, on the red ground of the baked clay.

ferences in the costumes, but it also displays a love of design and fertility of imagination.

The archaic decorative sense predominates in the vases of the mid-century,

However, the late sixth century reversed this technique to the red-figured style, that allowed greater freedom to the artist. This is illustrated in the vase by Euphronius, whose theme is the struggle of Heracles and Antaeus (fig. 39). Once more the omission of land-

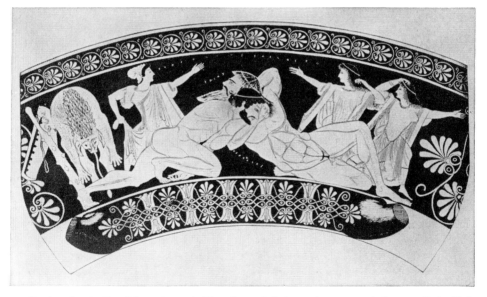

39. Euphronius (active 6th cent. B.C.) *Heracles and Antaeus* (*c.* 500 B.C.) Louvre, Paris. Red-figured vase.

scape details enables the painter to concentrate his whole attention on the
human figures. This preoccupation with
man could be explained in sculpture by
the nature of the medium, which does
not lend itself to the indication of landscape. The same omission in painting
testifies to the Greek belief in the pre-
ponderant importance of humanity as
an artistic motive. The figures, drawn
in line alone, show the same eagerness
to experiment with pose that characterizes archaic sculpture. The drapery of
the female figure on the right falls in
repeated parallel folds ending in a zigzag line.

This same motive reoccurs in the *Kore*
or Maiden from the Acropolis (fig. 40),
who looks like the artistic daughter of
the Hera of Samos (fig. 34). Many figures of this type were dedicated in
Athens in late archaic times. Some of
them were damaged when the Persians
sacked Athens, and were buried on the
Acropolis when the Athenians returned
to their city. Posed as quietly as the
Hera, the right arm extends forward
from the elbow, bearing an offering in
its hand. This part of the figure was
carved from a separate stone fitted into
a socket on the main block. Though
their pattern is still prominent, the folds
of drapery have become somewhat more
plastic or three-dimensional than on the
Hera, and have more realism of detail.
The extended right arm and the left
arm cut free of the body bespeak an
increased mastery of the material.

The use of color in these figures is
noteworthy. We have become accus-

40. *Maiden from the Acropolis* (c. 530 B.C.)
Acropolis Museum, Athens. Marble, 4' high;
complete figure 6' high.

tomed to think of sculpture as monochromatic and executed chiefly in white
marble because most of us get our first
impressions of sculpture from colorless
Roman copies of Greek statues, from
carvings by Renaissance or modern

41. *Statuette from Ligourio* (*c.* 460 B.C.) Museum, Berlin. Bronze, 5″ high.

blue, or less frequently with other hues. Perhaps they were garish, but in these Maidens only details are picked out in color, black for the hair, red lips, black eyes, and above all patterns of embroidery on the hem of the garments. These well-selected touches of color enhance the loveliness of the work and contribute to its realism. They do not conceal the texture and inherent beauty of the stone as had the more completely painted earlier examples.

The bronze Statuette from Ligourio (fig. 41) has the same relation to the 'Apollo' type as the Acropolis Maiden has to the Hera of Samos. It reflects the athletic style of Ageladas of Argos. This statue stands at ease, not at attention like the earlier figures. Surely Ageladas was dissatisfied with the formalism of his predecessors. He would discard the law of frontality, and allow one leg to carry more weight than the other. Therefore the axis of the torso need be vertical no longer, but curved so that one hip is higher than the other, balanced by raising the opposite shoulder. The right arm swings free of the body, and the head turns a little to the side. How much of this new-won freedom of movement was made possible by the tensile strength of bronze is uncertain, but it is quite certain that most famous later artists preferred bronze to marble.

If this movement helps to create a lifelike figure, so too does the anatomy. The muscles of the torso are not scratched in lines on the surfaces but modeled as plastic masses to approximate the body of a sturdy young man.

sculptors who choose uncolored marble or limestone, and from white plaster casts. In truth, most great ages of sculpture have known the value of judicious color. Many of the earliest Greek works were painted in strong tones of red and

He looks like an athlete, perhaps a weight-thrower or a wrestler. Indeed, sculpture of this type is sometimes called the school of athletic art. The athletic festivals in Greece, such as the Olympic games, and the preparations for them must account for these sculptured athletes. In the palaestra, the youth of Greece trained in the nude; constant observation of young men running, jumping, wrestling, and throwing the discus or the javelin gave the Greek artist an opportunity for study enjoyed by sculptors of no other country. He had continually before him the spectacle of the body in action. Through long familiarity, a knowledge of the figure must have become second nature to him and to his critical audience. Unlike the artists of our own day, who must base their work on a few models observed in the relatively cramped quarters of the studio, these artists had as their models the flower of Greek youth. That the Greeks should have developed their study of the male figure beyond that of the female is illuminating. Woman in sculpture remains archaic long after man has become natural. Indeed, the Greeks themselves realized the disadvantage under which the sculptor labored in representing the female figure. When, in the fourth century, the people of Croton ordered a painting of Helen by

42. *Athena and Warriors*, West Pediment, Temple of Aphaia, Aegina (*c.* 495–485 B.C.) Glyptothek, Munich. Marble, figure of Athena 5′6″ high.

Zeuxis, they tried to compensate for this deficiency by affording him as nearly parallel an opportunity as possible to observe the figures of the fairest maidens of the city.

The sculpture of the pediments from the Temple of Aphaia at Aegina (fig. 42), at the beginning of the fifth century B.C., restored by Thorvaldsen, points this contrast. The goddess Athena in the center of the group is more conservative in style than the warriors on either side. Like the Maidens from the Acropolis, her frontal figure is clothed in a patterned garment, but the male figures take advantage of the new freedom. The sculptor, possibly Onatas, who was then the leader of the school of Aegina, has posed them with extraordinary freedom: they lie wounded, on their elbows, crouch in defense behind shields, stoop forward to assist a fallen comrade or, spear in hand, to await the attack of an enemy. The action of these figures is far removed from the conventional pose of the 'Apollos.' These are athletic types too, hard muscular figures that bespeak hours of exercise. The muscles of these men are blocked out, sharp and crisp, and do not flow into one another as in later and more facile productions. The sculptor exults in his mastery of the medium, but that control has been so recently acquired that he has not forgotten the demands of stone; he knows that it is hard to carve, his new technical skill is not taken for granted, and consequently a certain stony quality lingers in his design. Only in the heads are the conventions of archaism still obtrusive. The hair on the scalp is engraved in wavy lines, with a row of curls over the forehead; the eyes, not yet sunk under the brows, do not rival the realism of the bodies; and the archaic smile still predominates. The latter contrasts with the freedom of the figures, as it did in the 'Apollos,' where it shared in the general formalization. To see a warrior

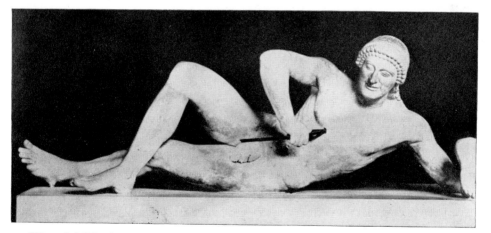

43. *Wounded Warrior*, West Pediment, Temple of Aphaia, Aegina (*c.* 495–485 B.C.) Glyptothek, Munich. Marble, height of head 18″.

(fig. 43), wounded no doubt to the death, smile while he pulls a javelin from his breast is incongruous, unless we read the smile as a grimace of pain.

The problem of design within the low triangle of the pediment offered a challenge to the artist. In the early pediments, such as that of the Treasury of the Siphnians at Delphi, the sculptor had allowed the action to progress from left to right. Since the triangle of the pediment established an axis, it demanded in sculpture a balanced design. Moreover, realism requires that figures within a single composition must all approximate the same scale; therefore, if figures stand erect to fill the center of the pediment, it follows that those designed for the outer angles cannot also be posed standing. This axiom was not grasped by the earlier designers; for example, the lateral figures of the Siphnian pediments are midgets alongside of the principal characters.

stands in the center; warrior balances warrior; each pose duplicates the figure opposite. And yet, much remains to be solved. Though the balance is complete, it is achieved by means too obvious to sustain the interest of an observer. The axis is emphasized more than necessary. Though some rhythmic relation of the figures exists, their connection is not strong enough to unite the design. The carving of each individual figure has so absorbed the artist that little creative energy remains to solve the larger problem of the whole pediment.

The century and a half that separates the earliest 'Apollos' and the Aegina pediments witnesses the sculptor's acquisition of the technical knowledge which enables him to carve stone with freedom while retaining great respect for his medium. Progressing from crude attempts at representation in the beginning, the latest works show remarkable skill. Most of the fundamental problems have been

44. *West Pediment Restored*, Temple of Aphaia, Aegina (c. 495–485 B.C.) Pediment 45′ wide.

These problems are partly solved in the Aegina pediments (fig. 44). The subject, the Trojan Wars, appears to have been arranged as two lines of battle, opened out like the leaves of a book. Athena, who directs the fortunes of war,

solved. One problem remains—that of the head. Even at Aegina, the conventions of the head obtrude themselves as archaisms in these otherwise advanced works.

To previous generations, this century

and a half had a merely archaeological interest; the absence of anatomical realism implied inability. Today we realize that while many of these statues do solve only in part the twin problems of design and representation, the best welcome comparison with the greatest productions of more sophisticated ages. Though the goal of Greek sculpture had not been reached, the sense of pattern and design, the feeling for the material and for sculpturesque mass, provide these not yet mature works with an artistic quality that needs no apology.

V GREEK ART DURING THE FIFTH AND FOURTH CENTURIES B.C.

The end of the Persian Wars in 480 B.C. loosed a surge of creative energy in Greece to flow in all directions. To have repulsed the unmeasured forces of the Achaemenid empire with their own small numbers and resources must have confirmed the Greeks' confidence in themselves. Surely the gods approved their civilization and had protected it. In literature, this date introduces the flowering of Greek drama at the hands of Aeschylus, Sophocles, and Euripides, while in the visual arts it marks the inception of that era which the later Greeks were to deem the climax of their sculptural and architectural history. The Persians had destroyed much, especially in Athens, and so had cleared the ground for new undertakings. Also, the spoils of war helped to provide the wealth for new creations: the colossal bronze Athena Promachos by Phidias was made from the spoils of the battle on the plains of Marathon. Athens in particular enjoyed a generation or more of great prosperity, partly due to the Delian League; the smaller cities of this league, which had banded together under Athenian leadership during the Persian Wars, contributed money to construct and man a navy for mutual defense. When peace returned, the Athenians assumed that, so long as protection was provided, they might use the funds of the League for their own ends. The civic works program undertaken by Pericles in Athens, an extraordinary effort considering the size of the city, could hardly have been completed without this money. However, the full effects of the new wealth and the new self-confidence did not at once reveal

45. *East Pediment Restored,* Temple of Zeus, Olympia (468–460 B.C.) Pediment 91′ wide.

themselves. About a generation had to elapse before these conditions bore fruit.

The largest corpus of sculpture from this generation is that from the Temple of Zeus at Olympia, dated about 460 B.C. It includes two pedimental groups and twelve metopes. The former (fig. 45) at once demand comparison with the earlier pediments at Aegina. In the east pediment, where we find the chariot race of Pelops and Oenomaus, the traditional origin of the Olympic games, chariots separate the principal characters from the subordinate. Consequently, some concentration on the major characters replaces the distributed interest at Aegina. In the Battle of the Centaurs and Lapiths in the west pediment, the figures are grouped in twos and threes. Here, group balances group, but only approximately, not with the duplication of figure and even of action that marked the late archaic example. However, a few matters in design remain to receive their final polish. The central group in the east pediment is monotonous because of the repeated verticals of five standing figures; in both pediments a single erect form too openly strikes the axis; and,

finally, the transitions from group to group leave something to be desired.

As regards the separate figures, a corresponding change appears. The sculptor of the Centaur and Lapith (fig. 46) is no longer so conscious of his hard material. The extra decades of experience enable him to execute in stone

46. *Centaur and Lapith,* West Pediment, Temple of Zeus, Olympia (468–460 B.C.) Museum, Olympia. Marble, 6′8″ high.

whatever he wishes. While it is not yet true that he has lost respect for his medium, he leaves his marble with less of the stony feeling than did his Aegina predecessors. Perhaps this is to say that he has become more realistic. Few statues have ever reached a finer balance between conception and execution than the Apollo (fig. 47) of the west pedi-

47. *Apollo,* West Pediment, Temple of Zeus, Olympia (468–460 B.C.) Museum, Olympia. Marble, complete figure *c.* 10′ high.

ment. This godlike figure guides the fortune of battle by his presence alone, calm and majestic, with outstretched hand and quiet glance. Muscular masses are still in evidence, but a little rounder

and less defined than hitherto; as if to emphasize their flowing contours, drapery falls over his shoulder and wrist; its plain lines and surfaces enrich, and are enriched by contrast with, the body.

48. *Head of Apollo,* West Pediment, Temple of Zeus, Olympia (468–460 B.C.) Museum, Olympia. Marble, 17″ high.

The obvious archaisms present at Aegina vanish here (fig. 48); the hair is less patterned, the eyes lose their protrusion and the mouth its archaic smile. In many figures details are suppressed. The hair, for example, is suggested by a raised surface like a skull cap, a summary treatment possible because of the height above the ground at which these figures must be seen, and because of the use of paint to distinguish such parts as were visible. A uniformity of expression in the faces tempts one to conclude that the artist was indifferent to human emotions, but

49. *Heracles and the Cretan Bull*, detail, Metope, Temple of Zeus, Olympia (468–460 B.C.) Museum, Olympia. Marble, complete metope 5′3″ high, 5′ wide.

a further glance at the Centaur and Lapith (fig. 46) proves that such a conclusion is unwarranted. The Centaur's distorted features convey his anger and excitement, his bestiality in the heat of battle as he bites the Lapith's arm, but the latter can hardly have been so stoical as this. The statue demonstrates the Greek feeling that Lapiths, the gods, and the Greeks themselves are above emotional display, though that may be permitted to inferior beings liks Centaurs. Such higher beings as Greeks and gods are uniformly serene, detached from reality; they look not at you but through you.

The metopes, placed not on the outside of the temple but over the porches front and back, within the colonnade, recount the twelve labors of Heracles. The finest in design, that of Heracles and the Cretan Bull (fig. 49), conveys the dynamic tension of action adjusted to a sense of balance. In this location, diagonals are the more desirable since they contrast with the vertical lines of the triglyphs to either side and with the horizontal direction of the other parts of the entablature. These metopes are better preserved than the pediments because of their protected situation in the temple; but after all allowances

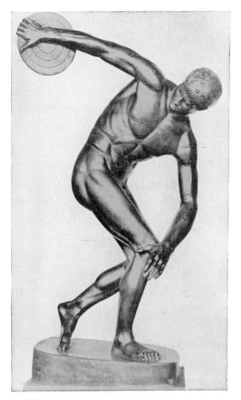

50. Myron (*c.* 490–430 B.C.) *Discobolus* (*c.* 460 B.C.) Reconstruction, *c.* 4′6″ high.

Acropolis in Athens, was so natural that cows used to low at it as they passed— or so it was said. His most famous statue today, the Discobolus or Discus Thrower (fig. 50), must have been popular in antiquity to warrant the number of copies still preserved. Since the original bronze has vanished, it is hard to judge the quality of Myron's work in most respects; but from the pose and proportions of the copies, we can recognize his preference for athletic figures in violent movement, or, more precisely, in a moment of equilibrium between two periods of action. This youth is modeled at just the moment when the backward swing of the discus has been completed and the forward revolutions of the exercise have not yet commenced. In consequence a certain poise is preserved, and the muscles are not strained to the utmost. He has the supple balance of a well-trained athlete. The free pose, with the head looking backward toward the hand that holds the discus, as Lucian describes it, consists of a series of curves that turn the spectator's attention back into the figure. Conceived in bronze, it is not block-like, as were the archaic figures, but still retains the contained or enclosed quality of the composition.

The inadequacy of Roman copies in conveying the beauty of the original may be measured by turning from the Discus Thrower to the Charioteer from Delphi (fig. 51), dated about 470 B.C. Its sculptor is unknown, though on tenuous evidence the name of Calamis of Athens has been associated with it.

have been made for weathering of the pedimental figures, it is apparent that the metopes are more carefully finished. In so large a body of sculpture, it seems probable that even if the work were designed and controlled by a single artist, more than one man must have shared in the execution. Such an assumption may account for the variation in style between the pediments and metopes at Olympia.

At about this time, Myron reached his full creative power. He was famed in antiquity for the realism of his bronzes; his Heifer, set up on the

51. *Charioteer of Delphi* (*c.* 470 B.C.) Museum, Delphi. Bronze, 5′11″ high.

That an increased realism is compatible with design is evident here; the deep folds of the garment below the waist, different one from another in depth and spacing, develop into smaller rhythmic folds over the shoulders. A compactness and sculpturesque simplification form the basis of this masterpiece. At the same time, a love of realism is evident in the modeled feet, in the lively curls escaping from the fillet with its inlaid silver fret which binds the hair over the temples, in the soft half-grown sideburns of youth untouched as yet by a razor, and in the eyes, which are inserted in white paste with a black disk to imitate pupil and iris. He looks as though at any moment he might step from his chariot or turn his head to speak to you. We must also recognize that the proportions, the crisp articulation of the features, and the broad modeling of the surfaces are elements of continuity from earlier times.

These works illustrate the final steps toward freedom taken by the Greek artist. By this time, near the middle of the fifth century, he controls his resources; his medium, whether bronze or stone, continues to influence his designs, but it no longer dominates and restricts them; his ability to conceive is not hampered by an inability to execute; and, if he chooses to avail himself of it, an accurate knowledge of the human figure is at his disposal.

When Pericles rose to power in Athens during the 460's, a time of great prosperity, he adopted a program designed to make Athens the cultural and artistic center of Greece. On the Acropolis, to replace the damage of the Persian Wars, the Parthenon, the Erechtheum, the Propylaea, and the Temple of Wingless Victory were designed anew on a grand scale and with exquisite refinement of detail. These, combined with other buildings constructed elsewhere in the city and in Athenian territory at this time, constitute a civic effort unparalleled elsewhere in history. It was the more remarkable in view of the size of this city state of 300,000 inhabitants, including slaves. Pericles entrusted the supervision of these undertakings to Phidias, then the leading sculptor in Athens; but for the architecture of the various buildings other men were responsible.

In the Parthenon, begun in 447 and completed by 432 B.C., Ictinus and Callicrates undertook to create the most splendid temple in Greece, one that should be worthy of Athena and a fit shrine for her image. Though not the largest Greek temple, its size is exceptional, approximately 228 by 101 feet, measured along the stylobate (fig. 29). Consequently, the usual six-column front is here expanded to eight columns, with seventeen along each side. Its proportions of width to length approximate the simple ratio of four to nine. Built of Pentelic marble throughout, the Parthenon marks the culmination of the Greek Doric temple. The adjustment of all its parts is the fruit of centuries of experiment by Greek architects. Where the earlier temples

52. Ictinus and Callicrates, *Parthenon*, Athens (447–432 B.C.) 101' wide, 228' long.

had emphasized weight and power in proportions, the Parthenon (fig. 52) balances strength and grace. The columns, about five and a half lower diameters in height, look sturdy but not ponderous, and require a lighter entablature, approximately one fourth the height of the building.

If the Parthenon has a completeness and perfection of form rarely found elsewhere, we must remember that the temple form is a simple problem by comparison with the complex requirements of a Roman bath on the one hand, or a medieval cathedral on the other. The form seems expressive of Greece. The deities of the Olympic pantheon, though more powerful than men, and though immortal, were subject to human passions—to anger, jealousy, and love. The scale of the Parthenon is not so large that man is insignificant in relation to it, as he is in the French cathedrals. In autocratic Egypt,

the unbroken walls of the temples seemed to repulse the common man; in democratic Greece, the steps of the base and the open colonnade on all sides invite him to enter its shade.

Greek religion was not a religion of the spirit, as Christianity is. It might be crudely described as a system of barter; if an individual respected certain customs and performed sacrifices, he might expect protection or favor from the god. Emotion, love, adoration had little place here. A rational attitude dictated its architectural expression, which seems to cling to the earth. Moreover, unlike a church, worship took place outside a Greek temple, at an altar in front of it. Within such a building, one could hardly slaughter victims or pour out libations of oil or wine. The temple was a shrine to house the statue of the god, and though people could enter it to see the statue, it was not intended to accommodate crowds. Consequently, its visual effectiveness was greater on the exterior than on the interior.

Furthermore, the care lavished on the structure shows itself not only in the larger aspects of design, but also in the processes of construction. While the columns seem to be vertical and evenly spaced, careful measurements show that the central openings are wider than those at the corners, both on the front and the sides of the temple. Moreover, the columns tilt inward. The variations in spacing and the departure from verticality are so minute as to be almost invisible, but they contribute to the impression of stability. The eye rightly demands in stone buildings some hint of greater strength at the corners—such strength being rooted in sound construction. But the most curious feature of the Parthenon lies in the curvature of its main horizontal lines; the stylobate is not a dead level but curves upward slightly, 2½ inches in a length of 101 feet on the front, and on the side 4¼ inches in 228 feet. This refinement is visible when one sights along the line of the top step. That the regular curves are due neither to accident nor time is certain; the Greeks felt it worthwhile to incur the trouble and expense of such careful construction to counteract an illusion of sagging, said to be produced when a series of vertical lines rest on a long horizontal line, or, in other words, by columns based on a stylobate. Whether such an illusion might exist or not, the refinements prevented a mechanical appearance in the building.

To the Greek, man was incomparably the subject most worthy of his study. The purpose of the Greek sculptor, in the century and a half after the Persian Wars, was to achieve a version of the figure that should be not so much like the individuals of his experience as an embodiment of their possibilities, an ideal concept worthy to represent the gods of Olympus. This goal is manifest both in what he chose to do, with the consent of his patrons, and in how he did it. With all of the new knowledge at his disposal, the sculptor still limited himself to a few age types. His males might be adolescents, boyish forms of fifteen or sixteen, slight and graceful, but without the malproportions that so often mark that stage in a man's development. A second type is the young man (fig. 63) in his early twenties, now physically developed; and beyond that in turn, the type adopted for the older gods, Zeus and Poseidon, still in the prime of life and physical vigor, full bearded, the muscles hardened by years of exercise. The young woman, such as the Athena Lemnia (fig. 53), in age and growth is a fit sister to the young man, adult and sturdy; her type also matures, as in the Demeter of the Parthenon east pediment (fig. 57), heavier but with no signs of age yet apparent. To the Greeks of this period, infancy was immature and unworthy of the sculptor's study, whereas old age, with its attendant physical decline, was also avoided. Only ideal types were suitable.

Furthermore, the artist was concerned only with the body as it might be, per-

53. *Athena Lemnia* (c. 450 B.C.) Head, Museum, Bologna; body, Museum, Dresden. Marble copy, 6′6″ high.

tellectual and objective analysis of the human figure. Through this approach both the figures and their parts involve clarity of definition, unity of structure, and a formal description that transcends reality and endows them with an Olympian detachment.

The sculpture of the Parthenon is basic today for an understanding of the art of Periclean Athens, though it would not have been so for one of Phidias' contemporaries, who could examine his huge gold and ivory Athena Parthenos and the still larger Zeus at Olympia, statues on which rested Phidias' reputation in antiquity. But the intrinsic worth of the materials of these statues invited their destruction, and the copies of them have only an archaeological interest, whereas the Parthenon sculpture is original. Although Phidias had charge of that sculpture, its quantity is too great to have been the product of a single chisel. Its harmony of design and its adaptation to the architecture exhibit a unity postulating some guiding spirit, but to carve 92 metopes, some 520 feet of frieze, and the monumental figures of the pediments called for the work of many hands. One may imagine, without proof, that the opportunities drew to Athens in these years many artists—some of them of an older generation, whose artistic style crystallized about the time of the Aegina pediments, others who grew up with the sculptors of Olympia—and there were doubtless many men, still in the formative stage of their careers, whose meth-

fect in proportions and detail, not as it ordinarily is. His treatment was generalized, selective in the extreme; he eliminated all accidentals and individualisms that might distract attention from his broad purpose. He thus created an in-

54. *Centaur and Lapith*, Metope, Parthenon, Athens (447–432 B.C.) British Museum, London. Marble, 3′11″ x 4′2″.

ods of expression might have been shaped by Phidias himself.

The metopes, completed before the frieze and pediments, confirm this supposition. Their position on the building proves that they were in place by 438 B.C., by which time the building was roofed. The best-preserved examples deal with the struggles of Centaurs and Lapiths. They exhibit striking dif- ferences of hand; some are mediocre, reminiscent of the angularity but devoid of the quality of the Aegina marbles; others seem to show the influence of Myron. A few are wholly Phidian in style (fig. 54). Here a Lapith of superb physique has pulled a Centaur back on his haunches. Surely such an incident might have occurred this way—or could it have? How could the Lapith's robe fall behind the Centaur? The sculptor has ignored the actual for the sake of design. To emphasize the broad masses of the bodies he has used the alternate lights and darks of simple folds, as he has used the thrusts of the Lapith and Centaur to left and right to create a dynamic composition suited to its position on the building. Perhaps this metope was carved by the master, since he probably executed one or two himself as models for his assistants.

The frieze illustrates the Panathenaic procession, the culmination of the quadrennial celebration in honor of Athena, which carried to her in the Parthenon the robe embroidered during the preceding four years by maidens of Athens. In this ceremony all the citizenry of Athens are represented: maidens, magistrates, and young men come to pay honor and offer sacrifices to the patron of their city. In the west frieze, youths form the procession, standing beside their horses or mounting them (fig. 55). The parade moves along each side toward the east, so that it accompanied, so to speak, the visitor to the Parthenon. As he walked along the side of the building toward the door at that end, he glimpsed it at the top of the cella wall inside the colonnade. On the east end a group of seated gods (fig. 56), guests at Athena's festival, form, as it were, a divine reviewing stand, and look backward toward the procession as it approaches around the corners of the building.

To treat without monotony a band of sculpture so long and narrow—it meas-

55. *Horsemen*, West Frieze, Parthenon, Athens (447–432 B.C.) British Museum, London. Marble, 3'4" high.

56. *Seated Gods*, East Frieze, Parthenon, Athens (447–432 B.C.) British Museum, London. Marble, 3'4" high.

ures over 520 feet in length but only 3 feet 4 inches in height—called for fertility of imagination. The clothed or nude figures vary in pose, in their relation to the horses, mounted or on foot, in front or behind, active or quiet. Chariots, sheep and cows for the sacrifices, youths on foot bearing water jars, magistrates, maidens, and gods add to the wealth of material filling the frieze without crowding it. Its location on the building under the ceiling of the porch, where light could not reach it directly but had to be reflected from the floor of the porch or the ground outside, demanded an exceptional technical scheme.

Ordinarily in low-relief sculpture, the parts of the figure project from the background in proportion to their roundness or mass in the human figure; thus, the calf of the leg would project more than the ankle, the head more than the neck. However, with the light coming from below, a normal projection of feet and legs would allow them to cast heavy shadows, and so draw overmuch attention to themselves at the expense of the head and torso. Therefore, Phidias invented a system of sloping outward the planes of relief. The boldest projection of the upper parts of the relief may reach 2¼ inches, while those in the lower part are restricted to a maximum of 1¼ inches. Also, to indicate several planes, as when a man stands behind a horse, or as in a four-horse team, he lets the planes overlap like shingles, to create more apparent depth than would ordinarily be possible with this degree of relief.

The pediments climax this sculptural scheme. In the east pediment, Phidias depicts the Birth of Athena; in the west, the Contest of Athena and Poseidon for the patronage of the land of Attica. Though the central groups of both pediments have now vanished, it is possible, through sketches made centuries ago and from descriptions, to reach some idea of their arrangement. Their composition is the culmination of the line of development in pedimental sculpture that began back in archaic times. First,

the single figure, which overstressed the axis of the pediment, is replaced here by a group of two figures to create a a dynamic contrast of action. In the west pediment, for example, Poseidon's movement to the right answers that of Athena, who draws away to the left. Second, on either side group echoes group without duplication; in any pair, Phidias varies the pose, sex, or costume without losing the larger balance. Third, a sequence of action leads the eye from the angles up to the climax in the center, and fourth, individual figures and groups alike exhibit a series of beautiful transitions from one to another. For example, in the three figures identified as Demeter, Persephone, and Iris (fig. 57), the first leans against the second, whereas Iris is more independent. However, the extended arm of

57. *Demeter, Persephone, and Iris,* East Pediment, Parthenon, Athens (447–432 B.C.) British Museum, London. Marble, Persephone, 3'4" high.

58. *Theseus*, East Pediment, Parthenon, Athens (447–432 B.C.) British Museum, London. Marble, 5′8″ long.

Persephone overlaps that of Iris to carry the eye from one to the other. Moreover, the deep fold of drapery that sweeps back from Iris's shin leads over in one direction to the lap of Persephone, and in the other develops into reversed curves to complete the action of Iris.

In the drapery of these figures, Phidias selects his detail to emphasize those folds and movements that help to explain the meaning of each character; for instance, the flowing curves of Iris's costume express her haste to spread the news of Athena's birth. Minor folds which might be accurate in a realistic sense would have no artistic validity here and are suppressed by the sculptor,

lest they destroy the effect of ideal intellectualized conceptions in godlike form. The so-called Theseus (fig. 58) illustrates the same method as that ap-

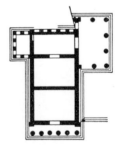

59. *Erechtheum*, Athens (421–405 B.C.) North porch 35′2″ wide.

plied to the figure. The principal masses are firmly defined; veins, wrinkles, minor changes of surface are ignored, not because Phidias and his associated artists were unaware of them, but because, in their intellectual analysis of the figure, these minutiae seemed incidental. Such elimination of detail, if carried to an extreme, may result in lifeless generali-

60. *Erechtheum*, Athens (421–405 B.C.) North porch 35'2" wide.

61. Mnesicles, *Propylaea*, Athens (437–432 B.C.) Central portico 69′ wide.

zation, as it does at the hands of Roman copyists, but judiciously employed it produces epic conceptions. As a nineteenth-century sculptor remarked on first seeing these marbles, 'They look like human beings, but where is one to find such models?' Such models do not, and never did, exist; given a thorough knowledge of the body, one must then analyze it, distinguish the important from the incidental, and give form to the significant parts. The Theseus is particularly interesting, since it alone of all the figures of the pediments has the head preserved. The broad skull and rounded cheeks appear to indicate the type of head preferred by Phidias, since

these characteristics also exist in the copies of the Athena Parthenos.

Great as is the artistic effort represented by the Parthenon and its sculpture, it was only one of the Periclean undertakings for the beautification of Athens. If, in the Parthenon, the apogee of the Greek Doric order is reached, the Ionic order comes to its peak in the Erechtheum. The asymmetrical, not to say amorphous, plan (fig. 59) of this edifice as built is unique in Greek architecture, which makes it more than probable that the conception of the architect was not completed. The north porch (fig. 60), exquisite in proportions, is graceful but has only as much strength as this lighter order permits. The Ionic never lends itself to an expression of austere power, unlike the Doric. The door of the north porch is sumptuous, the size of the jambs and of the cornice at the top proportioned to the scale of the opening. On the south front of the Erechtheum, in the

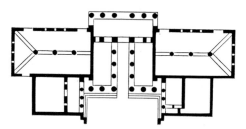

62. *Propylaea,* Athens (437-432 B.C.) Central portico 69' wide.

small Porch of the Maidens, the architect substituted six female figures for columns to support the superstructure. In theory, it is dubious whether such a motive is desirable, but one must admit that the device handled with tact on a small scale adds a charming variant to the customary portico. The sturdy figures look capable of carrying the weight above, which is lightened by the omission of the frieze from the entablature.

The Acropolis, as the ceremonial center of Athens, needed a suitable gateway. Mnesicles designed the Propylaea (fig. 61) for this purpose, and although circumstances prevented his ambitious plan (fig. 62) from being carried out in its entirety, even the part that was built exhibits a monumentality of scale fit for an entrance to this great center. The principal colonnades are Doric, but to

line the central passage Mnesicles selected the slender Ionic, which left a more open interior. This passage is accented by a large portico, flanked by smaller colonnades on either side, one of which gives access to the little Ionic Temple of Wingless Victory (fig. 30) on a bastion in front of the Acropolis. A sculptured frieze or parapet surrounded this eminence, adorned with low reliefs of Victories driving cows to sacrifice. The style is similar to but more developed than that of the Parthenon, the clinging drapery thinner and with less elimination of detail.

A second sculptor of this generation, almost as famous in antiquity as Phidias, was Polyclitus. The uninspired copies from late Greek or Roman days of his best-known statue, the Doryphorus or Spearbearer (fig. 63), give little idea of his ability. Pliny implies that much of the beauty in the bronzes of Polyclitus lay in the surface treatment, always the first quality lost in a copy. However, we see here the so-called *walking motive* of Polyclitus. Like the Statuette from Ligourio (fig. 41), the Spearbearer rests his weight on one foot, hardly touching the ground with the other. Therefore, the axis of the body assumes a slightly reversed curve, with one hip higher than the other, but the torso bent enough to balance the figure. The ease of posture realized in this way was carried further by the succeeding century. Polyclitus modeled the Doryphorus to illustrate his canon or theory of the ideal proportions of the human body. He himself said, 'Successful attainment in art is the result of minute accuracy in a multitude of arithmetic proportions.' With parts of the body as units of measurement,

63. Polyclitus (active 450–420 B.C.) *The Doryphorus*, National Museum, Naples. Roman copy, 6'6" high.

Polyclitus worked out his arithmetic of the figure. The head, for example, was one seventh the height of the figure; the foot three times the length of the palm of the hand; the lower leg to the knee-cap, six palms; from the kneecap to the middle of the abdomen, six palms; and so on. As in the proportions of the Parthenon, these are simple ratios.

Polyclitus defines each part of the figure with a clarity of shape that leaves it an integral and yet independent unit of the larger whole. Indeed this tendency is characteristic of Greek thought at this time on all matters. The column is so defined as an entity in itself that it can be and has been set up by itself as a monument, such as the column of Trajan in Rome, and yet for all its own unity, it subordinates itself to the larger unity of the temple. The singleness of purpose and expression of the temple is composed of the sum of its parts. Similarly, the choruses in Aeschylus and Euripides are poems, independent entities, and yet essential to the larger expression of the drama, as that in turn forms part of the trilogy. This craving for clarity of form was deep-rooted in the Greek mind. It is suggestive that Greek mathematics, as far as it was developed, found no place for the concept of infinity; that, by definition, is unformed, amorphous, and thus incomprehensible to the Greek mind. This clarity of form applied to sculpture derives from the linear structure of archaic figures, whose forms attain greater breadth and more idealism in the fifth century. Polyclitus gave perfect form to the ideal toward which the Greek sculptors had been moving for centuries.

By this time, vase painting also had freed itself of the last traces of archaism. Although the figures are still indicated in line, the Slaughter of the Niobids (fig. 64) on the Orvieto vase shows how free the painter is to repre-

ficed for both support and setting, the later painter feels it necessary to indicate uneven ground and to suggest by repetition of the ground line the existence of two or more planes in depth. That such an innovation is a step in the direction of realism of setting is undeniable; but this needless complication

64. *Slaughter of the Niobids* (460–450 B.C.) Louvre, Paris. Red-figured vase; height of band *c.* 10".

sent his characters in any posture he may wish. Some of the types are idealized and reminiscent of statues by Phidias; the drawing and the composition, on the other hand, reflect the manner of Polygnotus, the foremost painter of the time of Pericles. At least as significant as the new-won freedom is the irregular ground line on which Apollo and Artemis and the children of Niobe stand or lie. Whereas in archaic vases, such as the Heracles and Antaeus (fig. 39), the lower border of the scene suf-

destroys the clarity of design and the adaptation of the figures to the surface. The gain in reality hardly compensates for the decline in decorative value and the indifference to the medium. The great period of vase painting had passed; and as realism advanced, the art declined to a craft, its place being taken by the celebrated painters whose works have vanished.

Toward the end of the fifth century, the Peloponnesian War grew out of the struggle for supremacy between Athens and Sparta and, before it ended, involved and weakened most of the Greek city states. It foretells the uninspiring history of the fourth century, a dismal series of petty wars, when one city after another, singly or in coalition, rose to pre-eminence for a few years, only to fall before the jealousy of its neighbors. The spectacle was hardly edifying; it tended to lower the prestige of the state. In Pericles' time the city had been the great patron of the arts. The Parthenon and the Temple of Zeus, with their sculpture, were civic undertakings, grand in scale and public in purpose; so, too, were the gold and ivory Athena and the Olympian Zeus of Phidias, as well as Polyclitus' Hera of Argos of the same materials. In the fourth century the cities, impoverished by war, could not afford such enterprises, and the citizens, partly inspired by the philosophers, developed their own individualism, and no longer submerged their personalities as before in the collective expression of the city.

Inevitably, the artists worked more than hitherto for private individuals. At least by comparison, they began to turn from idealism to reality, although they did not yet carry that quality to an extreme. They concerned themselves with the minor gods, or with intimate aspects of the greater deities. The Olympian divinities lose their abstract grandeur, their serene dignity; within limits, they display more human emotions. The artist and his patrons began to approach the work subjectively, and substituted sentiment and prettiness for grandeur.

65. *Corinthian Capital*, Tholos, Epidaurus (*c.* 360–320 B.C.) Museum, Epidaurus.

Portraits became commoner and more literal than the generalization of fifth-century examples. None of these changes are carried to excess, but they point the new direction for art, and introduce some of the tendencies that, after the death of Alexander, became more pronounced.

In architecture, a feature of the late fifth century, seen in the Temple of Apollo Epicurius at Bassae, is the invention or development of the Corinthian order, in detail the richest of the three Greek orders. Somewhat similar to the Ionic, the column has a more elaborate base. Its capital, the easiest identification card of the order, is illustrated in the fourth-century Tholos at Epidaurus (fig. 65); its inverted bell-shaped mass is encircled with two rows of acanthus leaves, whose tips curl away from the bell; above them, paired tendrils coil like watch springs under the corners of an abacus, concave on all four sides. Such a capital, less austere and less functional than the Doric, seems analogous to the subjectivity of its contemporary sculpture. An entablature, richer than the Ionic, is characterized by a cornice, supported on *modillions*, brackets of stone whose under surface is formed by a curling acanthus leaf. However, the Greeks seem to have used this order sparingly, and mainly in small buildings, such as the Choragic Monument of Lysicrates in Athens; whereas its richness was to bring it popularity in Roman times.

Three sculptors rose to fame at this time, namely, Praxiteles, Scopas, and Lysippus. The first two were active early in the fourth century, but of Scopas little is known. Classic authors mention 25 works by him. Of these, the very fragmentary sculpture of the Temple of Athena Alea at Tegea reflects his style, and even this bears the same relation to Scopas that the Parthenon marbles do to Phidias. His most famous statue, the Meleager, was often copied. One of the best versions is that in the Fogg Museum in Cambridge, Massachusetts, but the discrepancies among existing replicas are so pronounced that few trustworthy conclusions about Scopas can be deduced from them. This wandering artist seems to have concerned himself with the stormier, more emo-

tional aspects of life, an interest suggested by the wide-open eyes, the lips parted as though the figure were breathing heavily, and the tragic implications of much of his subject matter.

Praxiteles, on the other hand, preferred the cheerful and pleasant side of existence. The number of his works cited in ancient literature exceeds that of Scopas', and testifies to his popularity. He was exceptional among the great sculptors of Greece in that he preferred

66. Praxiteles (active *c.* 390–330 B.C.) *Hermes Carrying the Infant Dionysus.* Museum, Olympia. Parian marble, 6′11″ high.

marble to bronze. Consequently the designs of his statues, such as the Hermes Carrying the Infant Dionysus (fig. 66), an original Greek work, take into account, within limits, the material. Extant marble copies of the Discus Thrower and the Doryphorus (fig. 63) derived from originals in bronze; since the cross section of stone at the ankles seemed weak, the copyist introduced the ungainly tree stump to support these athletes. But Praxiteles used the support as part of the motive, so that, no longer extraneous, it became an integral unit of the design. In this instance Hermes, at rest for a moment on his journey, lounges against the tree stump over which his drapery falls.

The pose of the figure involves a reversed curve in its axis, what is often called the *S-curve of Praxiteles*. This device developed from Polyclitus' walking motive, but is softer and more relaxed. Subtlety has replaced power; energy has given way to languor. The dreamy eyes suggest the introspective, as though Hermes' thoughts were far away. This effect comes from lids drawn half over the eyeball, the lower lid barely indicated, its edges blurred. The beauty of finish that ancient writers extol in the work of Praxiteles is illustrated in the textures of the drapery, which simulates cloth with remarkable success; of the hair, looking more like hair than the formal versions of earlier designs; and of the flesh, with its subtle sensuousness. The modeling, closer to clay modeling than to stone carving, rebels against the fifth-century sculptor's

67. Praxiteles (active *c.* 390–330 B.C.) *Aphrodite of Cnidus.* Vatican, Rome. Roman copy, marble, 6'8" high.

technique. Definition has yielded to a softer, filmier approximation of reality. No longer do we see each muscular mass separated, and the whole figure composed of the sum of its parts; instead, the parts fuse, one plane melts into another; for Praxiteles was more concerned than Polyclitus, for example, with the visual effect of the figure, and consequently less interested in an intellectualized statement of its structural parts.

These changes entail a decline in sculpturesque quality and open the path to the softness and sentiment of later times. The Hermes itself, however, retains because of its idealism much nobility of conception. The effeminacy, often observed in copies of Praxiteles' work and in statues influenced by him, resulted from an overemphasis by the later craftsmen of qualities that he himself kept under control. The wide difference in quality between the Hermes and the Aphrodite of Cnidus (fig. 67) testifies to the inadequacy of Roman copies. The former is probably unique as the only extant example carved by the chisel of an artist whom antiquity ranked among the great. The latter, far more famous than the Hermes in classic times, was according to Pliny 'the finest statue not only by Praxiteles but

in the whole world.' Today it is impossible to accept this glowing opinion of what seems to have been the first rendering of the female nude in Greek sculpture in the round. The motive, Aphrodite preparing for the bath, permits the goddess to drop her clothing on a vase beside her, which gives the same kind of support within the composition as that provided by the stump on which Hermes leans. This theme, though subjective and sensuous, avoids sensuality; the goddess is unaware of or indifferent to the presence of spectators, and is in fact as languid as the Hermes. By analogy with the Hermes, it seems only fair to conclude that the extraordinary fame in the past of this Aphrodite was partly owing to a beauty of finish in the original, and possibly in part to the sensational nature of the motive.

The death of Mausolus, Satrap of

68. *Greeks and Amazons*, Frieze, Mausoleum, Halicarnassus (*c.* 350 B.C.) British Museum, London. Marble, 2′11″ high.

Caria, in the middle of the fourth century, gave his widow Artemisia the opportunity to build the Mausoleum at Halicarnassus as his tomb and memorial. Its scale and the quantity of its sculpture made it one of the seven wonders of the ancient world. Three friezes in high relief, a chariot group, and many individual statues enriched it. One frieze showed a chariot race, with figures influenced by Scopas; another the Battle of Centaurs and Lapiths; while a third dealt with the struggle of the Greeks and Amazons (fig. 68), and at once invites comparison with the Parthenon frieze. In the Mausoleum, the characters, rendered in bolder relief, are widely spaced, thus creating an emphasis on each individual figure. The violence of action demanded by the subject permits insistence on the diagonal line, as the fighters attack or withdraw from their adversaries. The drapery of many of the Amazons is so disposed that the figures are seen virtually in the nude, another example of the fourth-century interest in the female figure previously displayed by Praxiteles.

The story of fourth-century sculpture closes with the career of Lysippus, a younger man than Praxiteles or Scopas, and one of the court portraitists of Alexander the Great. Tradition says that Lysippus worked in a bronze foundry, and, though he did not restrict himself to that medium, he seems to have preferred it to marble. The lighter proportions of the figure favored in his generation are emphasized by his new canon of proportions, wherein the head is one

eighth the height of the figure rather than the one seventh that Polyclitus deemed ideal. The Apoxyomenos, a statue of an athlete, who after exercise scrapes from his skin the dust and the oil with which young men anointed themselves, is extant only in later copies; it seems to illustrate these taller proportions. The Agias, on the other hand, is a Greek statue (fig. 69), probably produced by the workshop of Lysippus

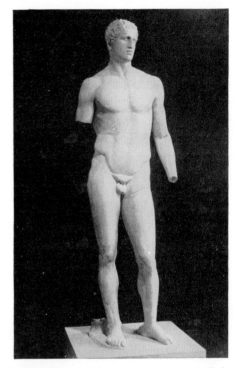

69. Lysippus (active c. 370–325 B.C.) *Agias*, Museum, Delphi. Marble, 6'5" high.

himself and, if so, under his personal supervision. The academic quality of the Apoxyomenos is less obvious here, as though Lysippus' new formula had not yet been developed, but the approach to a more visual rendering is evident. Pliny tells us that 'while others had made men as they were, he had made them as they were seen to be (*quales viderentur esse*).' The statement characterized the direction taken by fourth-century sculpture culminating in Lysippus, namely a decline in the intellectual analysis of the figure, replaced by a softer articulation of the body, less definition of its separate parts, and hence a greater naturalism. The old clarity of structure is no longer sought; in its place, there is a looser organization, paralleling the change in Greek drama between the tragedies of Euripides and the comedies of Aristophanes.

During these two centuries, the Greeks first acquired such knowledge and skill as enabled them to be realistic in their version of the figure. That information was no sooner available than they turned to an intellectual ideal. Then the austerity of that concept yielded in turn to more intimate and human conceptions, which inevitably led to a realism that was to mature only after the death of Alexander.

VI   THE CHARACTER OF LATER CLASSIC SCULPTURE

Short-lived though it was, the empire of Alexander the Great created a profound change in Greek life and ideals. For the two previous centuries, Greek culture had exhibited a completeness within itself. The archaic influences from Egypt and Mesopotamia had dissolved or had been absorbed, permitting the Greek or Hellenic civilization its purest expression. With the armies of Macedonia, Hellenic culture overflowed the geographic limits of Greece, affecting the art of other countries as remote as India; but as it spread, Hellenic culture itself was modified by the ideals of the conquered lands, thus producing a Hellenistic or Greek-like world. Some of its characteristics grew from seed already planted in the fourth century. The old confidence in the Olympic pantheon was already waning, partly under the influence of the philosophers and partly in the normal course of history, when Greece was brought into closer contact with the religions of Egypt and the Near East. Oriental cults, some of them mystic, rose to momentary or permanent consequence: for example, the Oriental conception of Artemis as the earth mother. As in modern times, many shades and varieties of belief existed simultaneously.

Moreover, the Hellenistic age gave birth to criticism and erudition, one cannot say at the expense of creative and imaginative energy, but supplementary to it and modifying it. Libraries were founded, such as that at Pergamum, and especially the one at Alexandria which contained half a million scrolls. Scholarly editions of the 'classics of literature' were compiled, just as to-day we have annotated versions of Shakespeare and Chaucer. After all, Homer was as remote from the Greeks of the third century as Chaucer is from us in the twentieth century. With schol-arship came a development of science. Aristotle, after the middle of the fourth century, tended to base his philosophy more on the world as he found it than did Plato, who early in the same cen-tury dealt with the world as he would have liked it to be. Plato's *Republic* de-scribes an ideal state; in *The Poetics*, Aristotle examines tragedy, for instance, by an analysis of the elements that ap-pear in successful tragedies. During the third century, Archimedes had diverse interests in many branches of science; he experimented with the lever, discov-ered the principle of specific gravity, and contributed also to astronomy. Euclid developed his theorems of geometry, for centuries the basis of that division of mathematics. Eratosthenes measured the earth, computed its diameter and circumference, and came remarkably close to the truth.

Such a complex background is apt to produce an art period without the con-sistency characteristic of earlier Greek epochs. Strains and counterstrains weave a diverse texture, difficult of compact treatment. An art of the connoisseur ap-pears, with the variety of delicate fig-urines from Tanagra and elsewhere— statuettes in terra cotta made from molds in which the head, the body, and perhaps other elements might be united in different combinations. A wider range is now permitted the sculp-tor; no longer is he restricted to a lim-ited series of types, but rather he may turn at his discretion to figures of old age or infancy, to genre scenes based on incidents of daily life, and even to narrative or descriptive topics handled as pictures in relief sculpture.

These tendencies gain momentum during the third century, but reach their climax only after the conquest of Greece by Rome, that is, about 146 B.C., the date of the fall of Corinth. Then the Greek cities were pillaged of their art treasures. Some generations earlier the Roman conquest of Greek cities in southern Italy and Sicily had stimu-lated Roman admiration for Greek art. But with the growth of Rome, there were not enough originals to satisfy the demand and a thriving trade in copies of famous originals sprang up, analo-gous to our production of casts and cop-ies of paintings or even photographs of masterpieces. These copies, often made by Greek craftsmen, provide much of our information about noted Greek stat-ues. However, through most of its his-tory, the Roman taste was realistic and measured the success of a work of art by its fidelity to nature; this taste helps to explain not only the naturalism of their own sculpture, but also the avid-ity with which the Romans sought cop-ies of Greek originals from the time of the Parthenon and later, but paid slight attention to the archaic period. Occa-sionally, but only occasionally, do we find artists who recognized the beauty of pattern in archaic art enough to use it for inspiration. From the more sophisticated generations the later designers borrowed freely, sometimes from one man, sometimes from another, or stole ideas from Lysippus to combine with others more likely to be found in the fifth century. This free borrowing from the past, called eclecticism, like so many other characteristics of late classic sculpture, is echoed in recent times.

One of the finest examples of Hellenistic sculpture is the Aphrodite of Melos (fig. 70), to which archaeologists have assigned many dates from the fifth century on. But so far as is known, the fifth century avoided the nude female figure in art, and while the fourth century accepted it, such statues as the Aphrodite of Cnidus (fig. 67) are completely nude. It remained for later times to try the effect of a partly draped figure. The small head exaggerates the lighter proportions instituted by Lysippus, again an indication of late work, and the cryptic motive also seems unlikely in earlier times. But although in all probability a late work, the Aphrodite of Melos has an undoubted beauty; its idealization and its sense of form rank it with the masterpieces of any epoch.

The one thread that leads through the maze of these later centuries is the emphasis on realism, the precise record of the visual, the individual, and even the accidental, in contrast to a concern with the imaginary or ideal in form. Such a purpose demanded a technical dexterity that at times approached vir-

70. *Aphrodite of Melos* (3rd–2nd cent. B.C.) Louvre, Paris. Marble, 6′8″ high.

tuosity. The Victory of Samothrace (fig. 71), reconstructed from many fragments, is conceived sensationally as she lands on the prow of a ship to sound the trumpet of victory. The whole figure is made to convey movement. A

71. *Nike of Samothrace* (*c.* 200 B.C.) Louvre, Paris. Marble, 6'6" high.

thin flowing costume, reminiscent of late fifth-century statues, gathers here and there in heavy masses, as it might have toward the middle of the fourth century. However, these eclectic features merge with the Hellenistic desire for intricacy when this drapery sweeps around from the front to the side, drawing with it the attention of the spectator. The front seems incomplete in itself; so too does the side; and only when the work is seen from several points of view can the artist's conception be fully grasped. In short, he insists that his admirer walk around the work. This attitude, at the opposite extreme from the method of archaic sculpture, had been growing steadily, until here it reached its full possibilities.

The purest realism of the time characterizes the first school of Pergamum, represented by the dedications of Atta-lus I, late in the third century. This ruler commemorated his defeat of the Gauls by sculptured groups, some dealing with the subject itself, while others, like the struggles of the Gods and Giants, of the Greek and Amazons, or of the Greeks and Persians, implied comparison of his success with the epic and historic contests of civilization and barbarism. Two and a half centuries earlier, an archaic sculptor had rejoiced in his new-won command of pose and material in the Wounded Warrior (fig. 43) from Aegina. He had carved all essentials of the athletic body freely and with understanding to create the effect he wanted. Anatomical details and peculiarities of the individual were unimportant to him. On the other hand, the sculptor of the Dying Gaul (fig. 72) enhances the impression of physical prowess with the Gaul's superb body,

72. *Dying Gaul*, Pergamum (*c.* 225 B.C.) Capitoline Museum, Rome. Marble, 3' high.

73. *Gods and Giants*, Frieze, Altar of Zeus, Pergamum (197–159 B.C.) Museum, Berlin. Marble, 7′6″ high.

whose anatomy is thoroughly observed and recorded, no part overemphasized and none neglected. The hair, matted with grease, follows the custom of the Gauls. His calloused feet are cut and scratched on the soles, as though by sharp stones. Gore drips from the wound in his side, while on the ground litter of the battlefield creates a similar reality of setting. However, it is his courage, his reluctance to accept defeat while he yet breathes, that gives vitality to the figure. These qualities are vividly in contrast to those of the Dead Persian of the same series of statues, who seems soft even in death. This latter, dressed in trousers which the Greeks considered effeminate, has crooked his arm under his head as though to welcome death as an escape from the lash of his masters. The contrast of these

figures implied that to defeat the vigorous Gauls was even more difficult than it had been two and a half centuries before to repulse the Persians.

If these dedications of Attalus I form the first school of Pergamum, the chief monument of the second school of Pergamum under Eumenes II, early in the second century before Christ, is the Altar of Zeus at Pergamum. The altar itself, surrounded on three sides with Ionic colonnades and on the fourth approached by a flight of steps, was placed on a high platform on whose walls a frieze of figures in high-relief sculpture (fig. 73) depicted the time-honored, if not hackneyed, theme of the struggle of gods and giants. The designer's concept of his subject typifies the scholarship of his own day. To represent only the well-known gods of the Olympic pantheon would not have provided enough figures to fill this length of over 400 feet. It seems as though the sculptor had read all the available sources in literature to compile as complete a catalogue of gods as possible, together with all attributes, whether objects or attendants, that could be associated with them. Many of these characters did not enter into the common knowledge of the people of his day; therefore the sculptor had to label each figure. In the Parthenon such an expedient was unnecessary, since the principal figures would be recognized instantly by any Greek and it made little difference whether the minor individuals were identified or not; their decorative and expressive bearing on the major theme was too clear to need comment. That this later sculptor felt it necessary to label his characters indicates an atmosphere of pedantry rather than of imaginative creation, as though a Shakespearian actor paused in the midst of his lines to deliver a footnote to his audience on the interpretation of 'miching mallecho.'

The many figures in the Pergamene relief are well united, partly because the legs of the giants change into serpents whose coils wind in and out among the characters to bind them together. Like the Parthenon frieze, but unlike that of the Mausoleum, figures fill the space; in other respects the contrast is marked. These figures exaggerate reality, if such be possible, and so insist on the muscular structure that each independent mass in the torso clamors for attention. Heavy though the muscles are, one feels less real strength in these gods or giants than in the Dying Gaul; in fact they look like professional strong men, muscle-bound in every part. Thus as representation they leave something to be desired; in other respects, they are even less satisfactory. Emphasis on everything results in emphasis on nothing; the protrusion of each small mass in the figures creates a monotony of small lights broken by deep shadows. A sense of strain and of striving for effect results from the exaggerated muscular structure, the agitation, and the sensational treatment. The sculptor is a remarkable technician, not to say a virtuoso, but he lacks that supreme gift of the artist, a knowledge of when to stop. In literature the concept of Zeus, king of gods and men, enthroned on Mt. Olympus and able to enforce his will by the thunderbolt that only he can wield, is grand and vivid. But a thunderbolt hardly lends itself to definition in stone; to render it as a torch, spiked at one end, that could be twirled in the hand like a tomahawk, or could project, splinter-like, from a leg, destroys that concept. Admirable in some respects, and typical of its generation, the Pergamene frieze, nevertheless, grows tiresome, whereas the beauties of the Parthenon frieze increase with familiarity.

This Hellenistic advance in realism involved a decline or disappearance of idealism. If that is true of style in the Dying Gaul and the Pergamene altar, the abandonment of idealized subjects further exemplified it. While not unknown before, genre figures—that is, characters taken from daily life whose interest lies more in their action than in their abstract implications—now acquired wide popularity. The tendency of the fourth-century sculptors toward humanization and the growth of emotion and sentiment prepared the way. In subject, these genre figures are diverse, but a passion for realism binds them together in treatment. For example, we find a Drunken Old Woman singing in her cups, her knees clasping the wine jar, her scrawny neck like that of a plucked chicken, her features haggard, her skin loose, and the physical decline of old age apparent in every detail. Such a work reaches its realistic goal. Equally literal is the Old Market Woman in the Metropolitan Museum, even to the indication of feathers on the fowl she carries to market in her basket; if she is less disgusting than the previous example, one should observe that in each case it is the subject and its associations, not sculptural considerations, which dictate one's reaction. Aside from the virtuosity of technique, the artist was content to rest his case on his subject, presented as vividly as possible. Some of these genre figures, such as the second-century Boy with a Goose (fig. 74) by Boethus, are humorous and mock-heroic. The subject stimulates in us a pleasant sensation compounded of sentiment and amusement. To be convincing in its comedy, the figure must have the proportions of infancy, the large head and the plump arms and legs.

Even when a child was a part of the subject, as in Praxiteles' Hermes Carrying the Infant Dionysus (fig. 66), the earlier artists had avoided the character of infancy. That character, inherently human, is here essential to the effect.

Reality again predominates in the pictorial reliefs, also called pastoral, Hellenistic, and Alexandrian reliefs. They correspond in spirit as well as in date with the Idylls of Theocritus and his associates. Some of them may have come from the workshops in Alexandria in Egypt; they first appear in Hellen-

74. Boethus (active 2nd cent. B.C.) *Boy with a Goose*, Museum, Munich. Marble, 2'9" high.

istic times, though they continue to be produced much later; frequently their subjects are pastoral, reflecting an urban dweller's attraction to the simplicity

75. *Farmer Driving His Bull to Market*. Museum, Munich. Marble, 11″ x 12″.

and peace of country life and nature; and there is a strong tendency to design the relief as though it were a painting. Typical is the Farmer Driving His Bull to Market (fig. 75), a pleasant bucolic scene of a peasant carrying a basket of produce; he and his bull pass a building, partly in ruins, and approach what may be an arched city gate. In the upper left-hand corner, some distance away, is a shrine housing a statue. The same technical skill is in evidence here as in the genre figures. The sculptor presents a picture in stone, remarkable as representation or narrative, even to the inclusion of landscape elements, such as buildings and trees in the background. Such details of setting may descend from the litter of the battlefield on the bases of the dedications of Attalus I (fig. 72), or from the pictorial features that helped to fill the great frieze from Pergamum. The artist keeps some of these features in very low relief, and allows others to project boldly; thus he implies depths that do not exist and prepares the way for the illusionism sometimes present in Roman sculpture.

ROMAN

With the growth of realism and individualism, an objective attitude in portraiture is inevitable. Such portraits as exist from the fifth century in Greece and many even from the fourth century are idealized and generalized. They show types, not persons, hardly to be distinguished from statues of gods. The Hellenistic sculptors, however, turned eagerly to portraiture and have left us many individualized statues of such men as Demosthenes. By Roman times, the patron demanded of his artist a description of his features as precise as an official report. The matter-of-fact, practical spirit of the Romans dwelt in reality, not in an imaginative sphere. Consequently, their architecture deals with specific problems, their sculpture records the men who for centuries ruled the Western world. The Unknown Roman (fig. 76) of the first century before Christ is a speaking likeness. One can imagine this stern individual debating in the senate, or leading the legions to fresh conquests; one cannot picture him enraptured by art or literature. For his portrait, he would expect that the individual bony structure of his skull, the worried furrows of his brow, all his facial peculiarities would be present in true proportion. He would want to compare his bust to himself. And yet this portrait reveals his character through his features.

Realism as an artistic goal is no less evident in the series of painted portraits from Fayum in Egypt, mostly from the

76. *Portrait of an Unknown Roman* (1st cent. B.C.) Museum of Fine Arts, Boston. Terra cotta.

first and second centuries of the Christian era. These paintings were made during the lifetime of their subjects. After death, these life-sized portraits were held in place over the head of the mummy by wrappings so arranged that the painting would be visible. The medium selected was *encaustic*, in which a considerable range of pigment suspended in melted wax could be applied to a surface of wood. The artist devoted his greatest attention to the head,

77. *Augustus,* from Prima Porta (*c.* 10 B.C.) Vatican, Rome. Marble, 6'8" high.

78. *Frieze*, Ara Pacis Augustae, Rome (13–9 B.C.) Uffizi, Florence. Marble, 5′3″ high.

delineated in light and shade, with unusually large eyes, and with much success in characterization. The costumes, on the other hand, are indicated in a broad or impressionist manner.

The purpose of a state portrait is different, but only slightly. The Augustus from Prima Porta (fig. 77) not only resembles Augustus as a man, but also indicates his position as emperor. Again the head is realistic; it tells us exactly how this ruler looked. His oratorical pose, as though he were addressing his troops, and his baton of command bespeak his position. Virgil traces the ancestry of the Julian line of emperors back through Aeneas to Venus, and the cupid and dolphin beside Augustus allude to this compliment. The statue represents a great man, accustomed to command, and idealizes his position.

The procession on the frieze of the Ara Pacis Augustae (fig. 78) contains a double file of portraits, including those of Augustus and Livia, and between them her son. The same individuality reigns here, though Augustus appears rather as a citizen than as a ruler. The foreground figures are in high relief, those of the background in low relief. This device, like that in the pictorial reliefs, indicates distance and reminds one of the spatial effects in Roman architecture. In this case, the sculptor restricts himself to long quiet rows of figures, with no landscape in the background to distract attention from the procession, but nevertheless the Ara Pacis Augustae looks forward to illusionism.

The panels from the Arch of Titus (fig. 79) in the Roman Forum illus-

trate that quality. The Roman legionaries in A.D. 81 carry the spoils of Jerusalem in triumph, and are about to pass
through an arch. Ignorance of perspective makes the illusion less convincing
than it might be otherwise, but the
planes of high relief for the foreground
figures, contrasted with low relief for
those in the background, and coupled
with the landscape elements beyond
them, betray a love of fact. The Romans did not trust the imagination; all
circumstance must be specific and as
descriptive as possible.

The motive in the Arch of Titus was
a single isolated event, but at times the
Romans wanted to tell a continuous
story in sculpture. A spiral band in relief winds around the shaft of the Column of Trajan. In what is called the
method of *continuous narration*, the
sculptor recounts Trajan's campaign
against the Dacians (fig. 80) early in

the second century. The incidents arrange themselves in sequence, but are
not separated by means of a frame or
any other device, though the action of
the figures, like those in Egyptian reliefs or wall paintings, serves to describe
each scene adequately. This band records the campaign: the soldiers build a
bridge or a camp, attack the enemy or
are attacked; the emperor addresses his
troops or offers sacrifices. A clearer picture of Roman military life and methods would be hard to imagine; indeed,
its fascination lies in what it depicts of
the past rather than in the sculpture
itself.

Aside from the encaustic portraits, the
largest single group of Roman paintings
are from Pompeii, though parallel work
exists elsewhere. Archaeologists establish the chronology of these murals in
four groups. The Incrustation or Architectonic Plastic style extends down to

79. *Spoils of Jerusalem*, Arch of Titus, Rome (A.D. 81) Marble, 7'10" high.

80. *Trajan's Campaign against the Dacians,* Column of Trajan, Rome (A.D. 117) Marble, band 3′4″ high.

80 B.C. Panels of unbroken color or diaper patterns divide the wall into horizontal zones, as though in imitation of marble slabs or other features of architectural decoration. The Architectural style occupies the next seventy years. Perhaps under the influence of stage design, painted columns, arches, entablatures, and pediments appear to recede to enframe landscape and figure compositions, and to obliterate the surface of the wall. Nevertheless, the scenes around which this architectural setting is disposed convey some idea of the

achievements in painting during the reign of Augustus. The Odyssey Landscapes once illustrated eight incidents, of which six are preserved, of the wandering of Ulysses as told in the tenth and eleventh books of *The Odyssey*. These panels, linked by painted red pilasters or flattened columns, contain small figures set within imaginary landscapes. The purpose of the artist seems not to attempt to render specific scenes, but to create a decorative setting. The indication of atmosphere and of perspective, and the sense of depth given by contrasting color, echo the tendency in sculpture toward illusionism in its depth and spatial sense.

The Architectural style yielded about 10 B.C. to the Ornate style. The semblance of architectural construction hitherto preserved tended to become subordinate to decoration and of minor importance. The paintings within its borders gain in prominence as though imitating easel pictures. Decorative devices, Egyptian in origin, recall the Roman conquest of that country not long before the Ornate style began. Finally, most Pompeian paintings date from the Intricate style, which commenced about A.D. 50 and came to an end with the burial of the city in A.D. 79 by the eruption of Mt. Vesuvius. The painted architectural settings become fantastic, with reed-like colonnettes and arabesques in abundance. Extensive panels of flat color, perhaps a vivid red or black, enclose diminutive scenes. Those from the House of the Vettii, such as the Cupids as Wine Dealers (fig. 81),

81. *Cupids as Wine Dealers*, House of the Vettii, Pompeii (c. A.D. 50–79) Painting, figures c. 6″ high.

are playful in character, but not inappropriate as wall decorations. Many murals from Pompeii have been preserved, but it is well to remember that that city was not a fashionable center and therefore its paintings are at best pallid reflections of the quality of Roman painting.

The estimation of late Greek and Roman art has changed radically through the centuries. During the Renaissance, when Greek art of the earlier periods was as yet unknown, the kind of sculpture reviewed in this chapter was considered supreme, the acme of skill, and the ultimate to which a sculpture might hope to approach. Even Michelangelo felt it to be the great source of inspiration, however much he might differ from it when he conceived his own sculpture. But with the discovery of the earlier phases of Greek art in the late eighteenth and early nineteenth centuries, this judgment was reversed. The new wave of enthusiasm rated the Hellenic as supreme, almost above criticism, and came to regard Roman art as degenerate Greek, to castigate its lack of taste, its want of ideals, its arrogant and vulgar realism. More recently, we have modified that estimate in turn with a saner realization that although Roman art owes much to Greek, it is the expression of a different civilization, one that is by no means inferior to the Greek in all matters. Generally, this later sculpture is weakest where most it follows or tries to follow Hellenic precedent. Less imaginative—one might almost say less creative—certainly less intellectual and abstract than Greek art of the time of Pericles, Roman sculpture has a straightforward, matter-of-fact power, developed from later Greek work but in its essence peculiarly Roman. Its realism, its interest in illusionism, and its desire to tell a story in the method of continuous narration are all fruits of the practical Roman genius, the same mentality that made their architecture the most grandly organized in space up to their time, if not indeed of all time.

VII

The character of the Romans inevitably led them to greater success in architecture than in sculpture or painting. The direct applicability of architecture to human needs brought it into accord with their factual spirit, that had called forth those realistic portraits. One thinks of the Romans as soldiers, not as imaginative poets; as ambitious and efficient administrators and statesmen, rather than as artists. Theirs was a world of affairs, not the abstract realm of the mind and spirit. Virgil himself recognized and admitted this characterization.

Others shall beat out the breathing bronze to softer lines . . . shall draw living lineaments from the marble . . . be thy charge, O Roman, to rule the nations in thine empire; this shall be thine art, to ordain the law of peace, to be merciful to the conquered and beat the haughty down.

(*Aeneid*, Book VI, J. W. Mackail translation, p. 126, Modern Library.)

Roman architecture grew from Roman needs. Its engineering accomplishments are stupendous; its sense of planning hitherto not even approached. Its weakness, as might be expected, lies on the decorative side; minor elements, such as moldings, are carved as applied decoration rather than developed as aesthetic growths; never do the Romans approximate that sensitiveness and restraint, that perfect sympathy of design and form in these details, which typifies the Parthenon and Erechtheum. They confuse the ornate with the rich. Their aim is an imperial magnificence, capable at its best of grandeur, but, when less inspired, of grandiosity or vulgarity.

To imagine that Roman architecture, any more than Roman sculpture, is degenerate Greek is to mistake its significance. Nevertheless, the admiration of the Romans for things Greek made inevitable a strong influence from Greek forms, if not from the Hellenic spirit; for example, the orders of Roman architecture derive from those of the earlier civilization, although even here changes are evident. In the first place, the three Greek orders increase to five in number; secondly, the Romans modify even those most traceable to the Greek (fig. 82). Though existing remains show that

of detail, the Roman Doric has individual bases for each column. Nine diameters are normal for the Roman Ionic, and straight lines unite the volutes of the capital, instead of the graceful curves exemplified in the Erechtheum. The Corinthian, the most popular of the orders in Rome, and the Composite order are ten diameters in height. The latter, of still more elaborate design than the Corinthian, derives its name from its capital, where the scrolls of the Ionic are superposed on

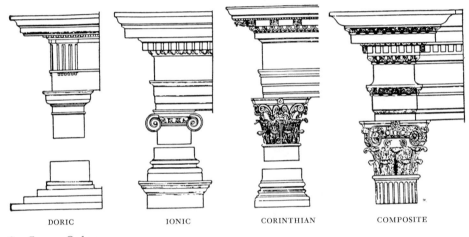

DORIC   IONIC   CORINTHIAN   COMPOSITE

82. *Roman Orders.*

no rigid system of proportions prevailed, Vitruvius, a Roman architect of the first century before Christ, codified rules of design for the several orders. He prescribed seven lower diameters for the column height of the simplest Roman order, called the Tuscan, a plainer version of the Doric. The Doric itself rises to eight lower diameters, a Roman continuation of the Greek trend to reduce its mass; in addition to other changes

the acanthus leafage of the Corinthian order. While the Romans effect dozens of modifications in smaller matters in each of these systems, in general they prefer opulence and discard the restraint of Hellenic detail.

The Romans borrowed the form of their buildings sometimes from the Greeks and sometimes from the Etruscans. The latter had already developed a civilization of their own, strongly influenced by Greece, while Rome was still a small city state. Their use of the arch and vault may well have affected Roman architecture, while Etruscan temples, many of them constructed of wood and terra cotta on a raised platform, expanded the cella to the entire width of the temple, and deepened the porch, restricted to the front, to the extent of two or three intercolumniations. The Roman rectangular temple, for example in the entablature with its carved modillions and scroll design in the frieze. The plan of the Maison Carrée is more Etruscan than Greek in derivation. The cella increases in width; therefore, although the colonnade remains, much of its length consists of *engaged columns:* that is, of columns attached to the wall rather than standing free in front of it. It is often said that the Romans used the column less as a struc-

83. *Maison Carrée,* Nîmes (16 B.C.) 49'3" x 85'4"; 55'9" high.

ample the Maison Carrée at Nîmes (fig. 83) in the south of France, dating from the age of Augustus, is an amalgam of Greek and Etruscan influences. This small building is beautifully proportioned and sumptuous in detail, especially tural member than for decoration, and it may be true that if these columns were removed, the walls and roof of the Maison Carrée would still stand, whereas no column of the typical Greek temple could be taken away without causing that part of the building to collapse. To that extent, the engaged column is not a vital structural element. Nevertheless, it stiffens and thereby strengthens any wall to which it is applied, and thus makes it possible to build a wall thinner than would be safe without it. This additional strength cannot be expressed quantitively in simple figures. The critic should recognize this, and not condemn the engaged column as though it were a form of moral turpitude.

Whereas the Greek temple with its free-standing colonnade and continuous porch may be approached on all sides, the cella of the Roman temple extends the full width of the building and rests on a pedestal or *podium*, another indication of Etruscan influence. This arrangement lacks that close connection with the ground that the Greek temple maintains through its unbroken lines of steps; instead, the Maison Carrée seems set up as a monument. The podium demands a flight of steps as wide as the front of the building, which leads to a deep porch. Since access is possible at one end only, the Maison Carrée has a more explicit direction than the Greek temple, whose ends are almost identical.

The greatness of Roman architecture, however, is not due to its debt to the Greeks or to the Etruscans; it comes in spite of it. The permanence of their roads is proverbial; built for the ages, the foundations are in some instances still in use today. Roman bridges and especially Roman aqueducts, such as the Pont du Gard at Nîmes (fig. 84), have a stark grandeur; when solving problems like these, the Romans con-

84. *Pont du Gard*, Nîmes (*c.* A.D. 150) Total length 902′3″, total height 160′9″.

centrated on their purpose, not on architectural effect, and indeed the beauty of the Pont du Gard lies in its directness. The sturdy masonry of its plain arches, their austerity not mitigated by even a molding, and the sense of scale derived from the contrast of the large arcades with the smaller arches at the top that carried the water channel to feed ancient Nîmes, are powerful as Rome itself.

The cardinal achievement of the Romans in architecture, however, is their planning of vast and complex edifices. To say that the Parthenon is not well planned would be absurd, but the Greek temple with its single chamber is a simple problem. Greek life did not call for complicated buildings, since it was lived largely out of doors. In the Roman buildings, the architects had to provide enormous spaces to shelter the crowds of such vast cities as Rome, and so relate these interior volumes to one another that the building would seem coherent.

These interiors need uninterrupted spaces. To carry the roof of a large hall by the pier and lintel system of the Greeks would mean that the supports would interrupt that space; columns could not be placed far apart, and the sense of interior volume would be lost in the forest of columns, as it is in the hypostyle hall of the Egyptian temples (fig. 12). Before the days of steel construction, such spaces could be obtained only through vaulting. The Romans early became proficient in building arches, perhaps—but by no means certainly—under Etruscan inspiration. In some instances, including most of the aqueducts, the arches are of stone, but the concrete arch and vault are commoner in the best-known Roman buildings. Vaulted architecture involves problems unknown in the pier and lintel system. An arch (fig. 85) is composed

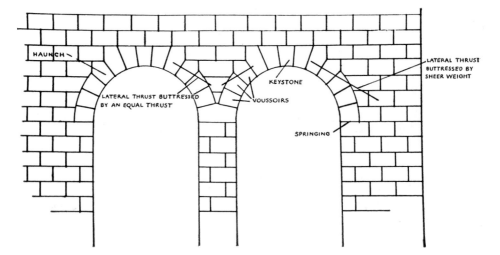

85. *Structure of an Arch.*

of wedge-shaped blocks, called *voussoirs*. The blocks near the center, though pulled downward by gravity, cannot fall unless they push their neighbors so far apart that the wider dimension of the block at the top can squeeze through the narrower space at the bottom. Therefore, the lateral pressure of the contiguous blocks holds each voussoir in position. This outward pressure of the central stones, called *thrust* or more precisely lateral thrust, must be counteracted, for clearly if it is not resisted or *buttressed*, the central blocks will push aside their neighbors and fall. Buttressing may be effected in two basic ways. Another arch of the same size may be built beside the first, as in an arcade; then, the thrust of one arch will meet and balance the thrust of the next. Secondly, a mass of material can be provided by a thick wall or otherwise so heavy that the thrust of the arch or vault cannot push it over or move it. Moreover, the weight of a masonry vault greater than that of a wooden roof necessitates heavier supports, larger walls, or bigger piers.

Finally, we must consider how an arch can be built. Once the blocks are in position and given sufficient buttressing, they will hold themselves there, but as the stones are placed upon one another, although those at the sides might be held in place by friction on the blocks below them, those nearer the center must have some temporary support, or *centering*. This is usually of timber, and calls for more or less complex carpentry. If a series of like arches

are to be erected, a single form of centering may be constructed and moved from one arch to another as each is completed. Similarly, since a vault is composed of arched surfaces, a repetition of similar shapes in vaulting will perhaps effect great economy in centering. Because the shape of the centering determines the under surface of the vault, a series of sunken panels or coffers could all be formed from a single piece of centering, and thus through using repetitive shapes in their buildings the Romans economized on skilled labor.

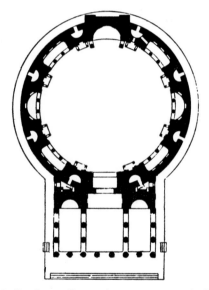

86. *Pantheon*, Rome (c. A.D. 120–124) Interior diameter, 142′.

The geometry of the Pantheon, dated A.D. 120–24, one of the most famous of Roman vaulted structures, is a sphere (fig. 86). A vast dome rests on, and its lower part is contained within, a cylinder of masonry thick enough to support and buttress its weight and thrust. At present, the thrust in the Pantheon is probably small, since the concrete of the dome appears to be monolithic; if so, as in an inverted teacup, no thrust exists. However, until the concrete had hardened, thrust would have been present. Unlike the domes of the Renaissance, the dome of the Pantheon is not a dramatic culmination of the exterior. Only the upper half of its height is visible as a low saucer-like form to crown the cylindrical mass of the walls (fig. 87). The Romans felt that concrete should be covered by some more finished surface and therefore, originally, sheathed the exterior of the Pantheon with marble, which has now vanished; but the austere cylinder of brick-faced concrete may even have gained in impressiveness thereby. Such a mass is imposing through its size and through the simplicity of its shape. The colonnaded portico, splendid though it may be in itself, seems out of place by contrast, like an excrescence on so colossal a mass.

The dome of the Pantheon, one of

87. *Pantheon*, Rome (*c.* A.D. 120–124); portico (27 B.C.) Portico 108′ wide.

88. *Colosseum*, Rome (A.D. 70–82) 157'6" high.

the largest in the world, creates an unparalleled sense of unity and space, with nothing whatever to interrupt its unbroken volume. Extensions of the interior space into the thickness of the walls produce seven niches or chapel-like areas at intervals, but always as arms of the main spatial area rather than as separate volumes. The under surface of the dome is marked off in squares, or more exactly in trapezoids, by horizontal rings crossed at regular intervals by bands radiated from a single opening, 30 feet in diameter in the center of the dome, which lights the whole building. The coffers or sunk panels within these trapezoids are repeated around the dome in every horizontal row. More than a single form was certainly constructed, but such a system might be built with a small group of centers, moved around the dome as one part after another was completed. The floors and walls of the Pantheon were originally sheathed in thin slabs of marble; that surfacing did not look structural, as did the solid marble blocks of Greek temples; it was treated frankly as a veneer, almost like wallpaper, to add the beauty of color of the veined marble to the wall surfaces. To use marble thus seems legitimate, so long as it does not suggest that the surface is doing structural work. So splendid a wall covering reflects imperial Roman power, able to draw its materials from the length and breadth of the empire and to concentrate limitless wealth and resources of labor.

The remarkable preservation of the Pantheon, in contrast to the ruins of most Roman buildings, is the result of its having been converted into a Christian church. The interior finish and a section of the exterior of the Colosseum

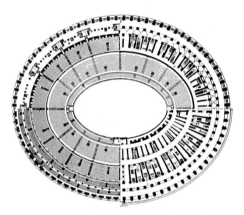

89. *Colosseum*, Rome (A.D. 70–82) 620' x 513'.

(fig. 88) have disappeared. This huge bowl (fig. 89), designed in the first century of the Christian era to accommodate some 50,000 people, served the same purpose as our football stadium does today: a setting for spectacles, gladiatorial combats, and the like, to be attended by throngs of people. The three stories of arcades, to which a fourth story was added later, by their horizontal continuity echoed the elliptical plan and supported tiers of seats rising above the arena. To permit so large a crowd readily to find their places and as easily to leave them, multiple stairways and exits were needed. The

complex arrangement of those stairs lead through the arcades on each level to the seats, and of course on the ground floor possible ingress and egress through all the arches simplified the handling of such throngs.

The Roman combination of arch and column, known as the Roman arch order, is nowhere better illustrated than in the Colosseum. The structure rests on the arches, but those are enframed by an engaged column on each pier, which supports an entablature; thus the columns and entablature create a rectangle around the arch. This use of the orders, like the engaged columns of the Maison Carrée, if not wholly decorative, is less structural than the Greek. It does, however, hold in check the visual movement created by the arches, and balances their dynamic appearance with the repose of the pier and lintel system. In the three lower stories, these orders are superposed. In such a design, the sturdiest order is placed at the bottom, the lightest at the top; thus the Tuscan serves on the ground floor, the Ionic on the second, and finally, the Corinthian terminates the series. Each order supports above its entablature a parapet, that also acts as a pedestal or base for the order above, and thus serves as a link between the stories.

Many Roman buildings exemplify this combination of arch and column, such as the triumphal arches intended to commemorate the victories of Roman emperors. Some earlier examples, like the first-century Arch of Titus in the Roman Forum, have but a single

90. *Arch of Constantine*, Rome (A.D. 312) 82' wide, 67'7" high.

opening; but the more elaborate Arch of Constantine, rebuilt in the fourth century (fig. 90), near the Colosseum, is triple; a large passage in the center is flanked by smaller ones. Though the columns in this case are free-standing, they perform the same purpose in design as if they were engaged. Here at last one really finds the decorative use of the column; they support nothing but the statues, which in turn look as though they were added to give some excuse for the columns. Since they do not touch the mass, the columns can add nothing to its stability, which, in any case, is patently sufficient. But to consider a triumphal arch as an exercise in construction is absurd. The Arch of Constantine looks imposing, thanks

to its scale and size, its bold proportions, and its decorative richness both of architectural features and of sculpture. He is dull indeed who does not perceive in such a monument the pomp and circumstance of imperial Rome.

The Roman feeling for space is nowhere more evident than in the Basilica of Constantine (fig. 91), more accurately known as the Basilica of Maxentius, since that emperor began the project between A.D. 306 and 312. What is preserved, colossal though it be, represents less than a third of the original building (fig. 92). For more complex problems like this, the simpler vault forms no longer suffice. A hemispherical dome suggests a circular building like the Pantheon. A semi-cylindrical

91. *Basilica of Constantine*, Rome (A.D. 310–313) Interior length 265'.

barrel vault covers a rectangular area like the passages through a triumphal arch, but since it requires continuous support on each long side, as well as continuous buttressing, it tends to be heavy and difficult to light, best adapted to tunnels and hence often called a

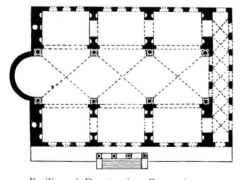

92. *Basilica of Constantine*, Rome (A.D. 310–313) Interior 265' x 195'.

tunnel vault. The *groined* or cross vault obviates these difficulties; if two equal barrel vaults intersect at right angles, their groins or lines of intersection will form a diagonal cross in the square covered by their intersection. If that square, then, be taken as a unit, it need be supported and buttressed only at the corners, and therefore may be lighted from all four sides or any combination of them, and for the same reason it can be combined with other groined vaults or barrel vaults. The three groined vaults of the central aisle in the Basilica of Maxentius covered an enormous volume, extended on each side by barrel vaults. Since each of these barrel-vaulted compartments continued the transverse axis of one of the major bays or sections of groined vault- ing, the connection between them was unmistakable, and the impression of or- ganized space was inescapable. Though the Basilica of Maxentius, like most Roman ruins, has long since lost its sur- face treatment, the pattern of octagonal coffers still enlivens the under surface of the vault; but most impressive is the scale of this fragment, which commem- orates the Roman engineering genius and the wealth and administrative power necessary to carry to completion such a project.

The Roman genius for planning might be expected to display itself in such civic centers as the forums. How- ever, the most celebrated of them all, the Forum Romanum, grew slowly through the centuries. New buildings were added from time to time with lit- tle relation to the old. Magnificent though it was, restorations of it leave an impression of confusion. As a meet- ing place, the Roman Forum satisfied the needs of the city while it was still small, but with its growth under the Empire to a population estimated at well over a million, all available space was exhausted. Therefore, emperor after emperor built his forum adjoining the old center to accommodate the over- flow, and since these imperial forums were designed as units, one can look to them for examples of the Roman abil- ity in planning. In the Forum of Trajan, dedicated in A.D. 113, a single principal axis gave unity and clarity to the whole. First, a large court, flanked by colonnades and with curved shapes,

called *exedrae,* to conclude the trans- verse axis, provided meeting places where the businessmen of Rome might conduct their activities. Doubtless small shops found room within the colon- nade. The further side of the court was blocked by the Basilica Ulpia, again a common meeting place, whose axis once more crossed the major axis at right angles, and again was terminated by exedrae. Beyond that in turn was the column of Trajan, still on axis, and finally, in the center of yet another axial court, the Temple of the Divine Trajan completed the whole coherent scheme.

Certainly the most remarkable in- stances of Roman planning are found in the great imperial bathing or thermal establishments. Bathing became a ritual under the Roman Empire, and the buildings provided not only for hot, me- dium, and cold baths, dressing rooms, and halls, but also for all sorts of con- veniences that might be associated with them; small shops around the perime- ter, libraries where the more studious patrons could relax before or after bath- ing, palaestra in which exercise might prepare the visitor for his ablutions, gar- dens where he might stroll after they had been completed, and so on. With the bath as a primary excuse, all and more than all the functions of a mod- ern country club were combined in one vast composition.

The plan of the Baths of Caracalla (fig. 93), built early in the third cen- tury, shows a characteristic organiza- tion, developed on the basis of a com- plex pattern of crossed axes. The princi-

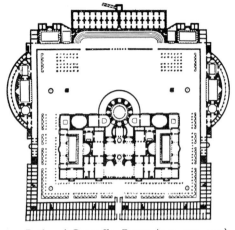

93. *Baths of Caracalla*, Rome (A.D. 211–217)
Central building, 750' x 380'.

crossed axes; it is more than a disposition of symmetrical shapes on paper.
Such a plan is fundamentally the organization of a succession of volumes; it
leaves its mark, almost subconsciously,
on the mind of the visitor. A sequence
of vistas results from the forethought
and imagination of the architect who
relates these multiple requirements to
one another. The layman is soon aware
of inconvenience in a building not adequately planned, even though he fails
to recognize the reason; but the design
of the Baths of Caracalla guides the
visitor directly to the services he wants.

pal structure is placed within a rectangle
of subsidiary buildings, on axis with an
entrance and again with the stadium at
the rear. Each major axis is adequately
terminated. Consider the long axis of
the central hall; not only are the three
bays of the hall based upon it, but it is
prolonged at either end by a vestibule-
like chamber, only partly separated
from the hall by colonnades, but
enough so to prepare the visitor for
something different beyond. Each of
these vestibules leads to colonnaded
courts, still on the same axis. On the
further side of these courts within the
colonnades, niches, intended to enframe
statues, give termination to this axis.
Moreover, it is apparent that most of
the units placed upon this axis have
secondary axes, less developed but sufficient to bring coherence and clarity to
the complex of rooms and services demanded by the bath.

The importance of this type of axial
planning does not lie in the pattern of

94. *Baths of Caracalla*, Rome (A.D. 211–217)
Central hall, restored, 183' x 79', 108' high.

The main hall of these baths (fig. 94)
was roofed by three groined vaults like
those that once covered the central aisle
of the Basilica of Maxentius. From the

lunettes or semicircular windows, at the sides as well as from either end, light streamed in to flood the space. The vaults appeared to rest on Corinthian columns supporting blocks of entablature, but these really served less to hold the weight of the vault, which was carried by the solid mass of masonry behind the columns, than to give visual intimation of that support, a declaration, so to speak, of the structural forces. The scale and impressiveness of this hall, its space and light, made it a source of inspiration to architects of much later periods. The concourse of the Pennsylvania Station in New York is inspired by it, and gains much of its impressiveness from the Roman system of design.

Roman architecture has exerted a greater direct influence than the Greek on later European and American developments. For one building that traces its ancestry to Greece today, there must be a hundred that descend from Rome. To some extent, this must be attributed to geography; aside from the vast extent of the Roman Empire, Italy lies nearer the center of the European circle than Greece, and was consequently more familiar through subsequent history. Moreover, the differences of religion between Western or Roman Catholicism and the Eastern or Orthodox Church, coupled with the centuries of domination of the Greeks by the non-European Turks, removed Greece from the main stream of Western culture to whose origins she had given so much. Such classic elements as may be discovered in Western medieval art were Roman. When, in the fifteenth century, the new energy called the Renaissance welled up in Italy, the Italians naturally sought guidance from imperial Rome, and as that movement spread north of the Alps, it carried with it the enthusiasm for Roman classic forms, which, though modified, remained the only sources of inspiration until the end of the eighteenth century. At that time, Greek art was rediscovered by Western Europe and, from then on, examples of direct Greek influence occur, but even then the restricted scope of Greek architecture could not replace the flexibility of the Roman principles of planning and their applicability to later problems. The extent of this influence of Rome on later times is a matter of historic fact. When varied problems of design arose during the nineteenth century, the academies of the European countries turned to Rome, the one previous civilization that had faced comparable problems of interior space design.

VIII

THE ARTS OF THE EARLY CHURCH

EARLY CHRISTIAN ART

The year 476, when the last of the Roman emperors in the West was displaced by his German soldiers, is merely the central point in a long economic and political decline. It used to be believed that the barbarian Goths, Franks, Vandals, and other peoples, who poured across the frontiers of the Empire during the fifth century, were responsible for its collapse. Further study has shown that the barbarians did no more than give the final push to an empire already riddled by the economic troubles of the third and fourth centuries. It is doubtful whether the disappearance of the last Roman emperor from Rome would have seemed a violent change to the people of the time. They had been accustomed for a century or more to the elevation and deposition of ruler after

ruler, and to the steady decline in power of the central government and its subservience to an unruly army. The latter was recruited from among the barbarians who exerted pressure in the West at this time, because of unsettled conditions in Asia, where the Han Empire in China was breaking up and northwest India was being sacked by Nomadic invaders.

Late in the third century, Diocletian divided the Empire for administrative convenience into halves, East and West. The step resulted in almost independent histories for the two. While the empire in the West disappeared, the Eastern branch persisted for centuries as the Byzantine Empire, and was not finally destroyed until the Turkish conquest in 1453. With the removal of the last figurehead from the imperial throne in Rome, the Christian Church was left to assume the dominance earlier exercised by the state. During its early years, Christianity had grown very slowly. At the beginning, it was merely one of many Oriental cults that led a precarious existence in Rome. Probably most scholars of the third century, if told that one of these cults would become the dominant religion of Europe, would have guessed it to be the cult of Mithras, the Persian sun-god and helper of Ahura Mazda (p. 650). However, Christianity prevailed, its triumph signalized by the conversion of the Emperor Constantine and official toleration of Christianity by the state early in the fourth century. The earlier rivalry with Mithraism is reflected and symbolized beneath the church of San Clemente in Rome, where the house of that Christian saint faces a Mithraic temple across the narrow Roman pavement.

To assume that the Christians of the fourth and fifth centuries were hostile to Roman civilization is ridiculous. They were none the less Romans because they were Christians. Their art differs from that of imperial Rome, but the changes may be traced to changed economic circumstances and new problems. The imperial magnificence of Roman baths, the Colosseum, triumphal arches, and forums presupposes a wealthy central government, able to command vast resources of labor and materials, which Rome could no longer supply during the fourth and fifth centuries. If the Christian buildings were, in some respects, plainer in design and simpler in construction than the earlier Roman monuments, so too were contemporary pagan structures.

The breakdown of the classic canons of design, so evident in the early Christian buildings, is equally clear in late Roman monuments. The systems of proportion followed by the designers of the first and second centuries, and their conception of the purpose and relationship of architectural elements gave way during the fourth century to greater liberty, especially in the combination of arch and column. The classic columns are designed to carry an entablature, whose architrave rests its ends upon them. Therefore, if the architects of the earlier Empire need to support an arch on a column, they insert an entablature between them. On the other hand, in one part of the Palace of Diocletian at Spalato, late in the third century, the whole entablature is bent into an arch; elsewhere, arches rest directly on the capitals, which are ill-adapted to support them. In other cases, the column itself is treated as a decorative device; it stands free of the wall and, since it is supported on a bracket, obviously can carry no important weight. The palace not only demonstrates the late pagan freedom in handling the classic elements of architecture; it also symbolizes the growing danger to the Empire. Planned on the lines of a Roman camp, the palace is a fortress and suggests a possible need for defense.

With the toleration of the Church, first granted by Galerius in 311, and its subsequent recognition by Constantine

in 313, the Christians could venture to
build churches of some size. In Rome
the type, already well established in the
fourth century, is known as the Early
Christian basilica. None of the many
types of Roman building would serve as
a church. Its origin is one of the most
debated matters in all the history of art.
Possibly some ideas were borrowed from
the Roman private house, where the
Christians often gathered for worship;
others may have come from the pagan
civil basilica. The solution called forth
by the Christian liturgy is simple. The
plan (fig. 95) includes first an *atrium*
or forecourt, open to the sky but surrounded by covered walks. The walk
next to the church may be developed
more than the others, to serve as a
vestibule or *narthex*. Beyond the atrium
on the same axis is the basilica proper,
divided into three *aisles*, the wider central one known as the *nave*. The nave
and aisles, designed to house the congregation, lead to a cross member, at
right angles to the main axis, which
may project beyond the aisles to each
side as *transepts*. Finally, beyond the
transepts, and usually as wide as the
nave, is a semicircular exedra known as
the *apse*. In the apse and to a lesser
extent in the transepts, the clergy performed the services of the ritual. Some
larger churches have five aisles; in some,
the transepts terminate with the walls
of the aisles, but in general these features are standardized and provide the

95. *Early Christian Basilica*, typical plan and
section.

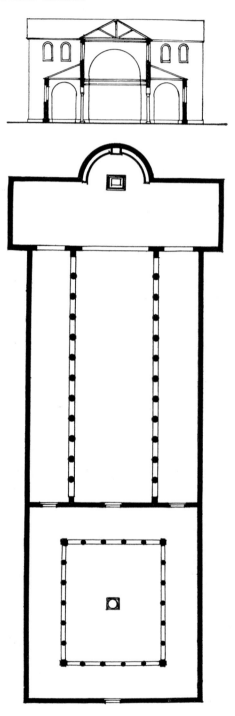

fundamental elements in plan of almost all later church architecture.

The cross section (fig. 95) is equally standard. A wooden roof supported by thin walls covers the nave, that rises above the roof of the aisles to produce a *clearstory*. These walls may then be pierced with windows to light the nave. Below the clearstory, a plain wall corresponds to the height of the lean-to over the aisles; this zone is in later architecture to be developed into the *triforium*. A colonnade permits access from nave to aisles, and supports beams in some of the early churches, or arches in the later examples. Finally, a half dome over the apse is the only vault in these churches.

At the beginning of Christian church architecture, orientation had not be-come fixed; some churches placed the altar near the west end of the building, so that the priest stood behind the altar and faced east, and therefore the congregation faced west. During the fifth century, this custom changed, so that the congregation and the priest both faced toward the east, and the priest at the altar now had to turn his back on the people at significant points in the service. Thus the altar was so regularly located at the east end and the entrance at the west that these points of the compass can be used to indicate the corresponding parts of churches throughout the later course of the Middle Ages.

The church of San Clemente (fig. 96), though not built in its present form until the twelfth century, and though without transepts, illustrates the

96. *San Clemente*, Rome (1084–1108) Nave and apse, length 129'; nave width 35'.

type. Externally, the walls are as drab as any shed. It has been suggested that this unpretentious exterior recalls the days of persecution of the Christians, when to advertise themselves was to court suppression. Probably, the need for economy dictated this plainness. At San Clemente, the atrium is the only one preserved in Early Christian basilicas. Within the church, drabness disappears. Floors patterned in marble, mosaic of colored stone or glass in the apse vault and sometimes on the walls, and marble columns produce a magnificent polychromy. Files of columns, rows of clearstory windows, and the beams of the ceiling (here replaced), all lead the attention to the altar as the focal point. Above it, the half dome of the apse forces the eye downward to that point again. Thus the architecture enhances the concentration on the ritual center.

As a corollary to the poor economic conditions of the times, the temptation arose to use materials already at hand whenever possible. The changed religion and the falling population left many Roman buildings deserted, and to them the Christians turned for materials. Fragments of entirely different design are often combined in a haphazard manner; in the church of San Clemente some columns are fluted, others plain; in the fifth-century church of San Lorenzo, the beams over the columns near the west end are carved, but the designs on neighboring stones vary from one another, making it evident that blocks were borrowed from wher-

ever they could be found. The patterns in the floor and the furniture are arranged around disks of red, green, yellow, or black marble, which probably were sliced from Roman columns, as ready sources of such costly substances. Light though its construction is, the Early Christian basilica was admirably adapted to its purpose. If its roof should be burned in the frequent fires of medieval towns, it could be replaced at slight cost. The effectiveness of the basilica is testified by its persistence in Rome from the time of Constantine in the fourth century almost to the Renaissance, a thousand years later. The changes in medieval architecture were to be rung elsewhere.

The fronts and more rarely the lids of Early Christian sarcophagi are carved with small figures in high relief. In a sense, these are examples of late Roman sculpture, but a decay in technical ability as compared to earlier Roman standards is evident throughout these works. The clumsy heads retain little of the topical realism of older Roman times. For example, the Jonah sarcophagus (fig. 97) of the third century deals with a number of incidents: Jonah thrown overboard by the sailors into the gaping mouth of a sea monster, spewed up by his host on the shore, at rest under the vine; Moses striking water from the rock; the raising of Lazarus. As in the Column of Trajan, several incidents find room in a single frame. These subjects are scriptural and symbolic in interpretation, but, except for their lack of realism, they also have some of the pic-

97. *Jonah and the Whale*, sarcophagus (3rd cent.) Lateran Museum, Rome. 7'2" x 2'3" x 2'2".

torial interest of the Farmer Driving His Bull to Market (fig. 75). The presence of such landscape features as the vine or the water, or ships and architecture, can be traced to this source.

Pagan motives are retained but given specifically Christian interpretation. During the hard times before the recognition of Christianity, to select motives that only the initiated would identify as Christian was safer, and protected the mysteries of the church. The meaning and derivation of some of these symbols are obvious, but others are more involved. The Good Shepherd in the Lateran, from the middle of the third century, one of the few large works of Early Christian sculpture, comes from the type of a man carrying a calf, sheep, or ram on his shoulders, a motive that goes back to the beginning of Greek sculpture, but here is probably derived from the bucolic genre figures similar to those in the pictorial reliefs. That the Christians should identify such a figure as Christ, the Shepherd of His flock, is easy to understand. So, too, the fisherman suggests Christ, the Fisher of Men. On the other hand, the fish itself is often used as a cryptogram of Christ, because the initial letters of the Greek words for Jesus Christ Son of God Saviour spell the Greek word for fish.

These motives are also present in mosaics. The fourth-century vault of Santa Costanza in Rome shows the vine pattern, amplified along the sides by small scenes; laborers gather the harvest in carts and bring it to the press, where men tread juice from the grapes (fig. 98). This vine theme had been common for tavern floors, but since wine plays a part in the Eucharist, the Christians did not hesitate to identify the vine with the sacrament. The art of mosaic was common in Roman times. At the outset, small cubes or *tesserae* of colored marbles were set in patterns, figures, or landscape. Though mosaic is highly architectural, to create a realistic representation in this medium is impossible; subtleties of linear expression cannot be achieved with tesserae. The color may be rich, though its scope is limited by the tones of available marbles. However, the 'palette' of the mo-

saic worker expanded in the fourth century with the substitution of tesserae
of colored glass for marble. The possibilities inherent in this substitution
were not immediately exploited. Here in
Santa Costanza, even though the mosaic is made of glass, the white back-

late fourth century, Christ is enthroned
in the center, flanked by seated apostles.
The cross above Christ marks the axis
of a semicircle composed of the four
beasts emblematic of the evangelists,
which parallels the semicircle below.
This repetition of shapes adapts the

98. *Aisle Mosaic*, Santa Costanza, Rome (4th cent.) 12′ wide.

ground, gray-green vine pattern, and
dull yellow or ochre in the figures and
other parts, all repeat tones available
in stone. Obviously the designer, accustomed to white marble backgrounds,
did not avail himself of the wider color
range.

    The climax of the mosaic scheme in
the basilica is the half-dome of the apse.
At Santa Pudenziana (fig. 99) of the

composition to the shape of the half-
dome; the motive inspired Raphael centuries later. The treatment of figures is
still classic. In spite of the limitations
of the medium, they are not conventional; on the contrary, modeling by
gradations of tone adds a classic sense
of form and mass to the apostles; a pronounced individuality distinguishes the
heads (restored in the nineteenth cen-

99. *Apse Mosaic*, Santa Pudenziana, Rome (4th cent.).

tury); and even the buildings, which doubtless symbolize the heavenly Jerusalem in terms of the earthly city, display the Roman bent toward realism.

The more hieratic Byzantine style modified this classic spirit soon after the disappearance of the Roman Empire in the West. Even in Rome itself, the sixth-century apse of SS. Cosmo and Damiano adopted the linear patterns and forsook the indication of weight in the figures obtainable through modeling. The color is equally formal: a path of reddish clouds, against which Christ stands, splits the gorgeous dark blue background of heaven. A new vigor animates the faces, as though the barbarians had infused their vitality into the weary Romans. This mosaic does not attempt the realism of the fourth- and fifth-century designs, but in decoration by simplified and powerful color, the apse of SS. Cosmo and Damiano grasps the real possibilities of the medium.

Roman tradition persisted also in manuscript illumination. The Vatican Virgil of the fourth century (fig. 100) is classic; it contains illustrations of the *Georgics* and of the *Aeneid*, enframed in bands of solid color, and extending the full width of the page. The best of these bucolic scenes retain something of Roman illusionism in their depth and naturalistic setting, in the classic style and pose of the figures, and in their rich

100. *The Vatican Virgil* (4th cent.) Vatican, Rome. Illumination, 10″ wide.

but heavy color. By the sixth century, the classic traditions had faded. The purple pages and silver lettering of the Vienna *Genesis* bespeak its East-Mediterranean origin, as do details of costume, though traces of classic tradition remain in the personification of natural phenomena. In most of the miniatures, the setting is eliminated to compel the crude but vivacious figures to tell their story without any assistance from landscape.

BYZANTINE ART

While the new social, economic, and religious conditions in Rome were destroying the imperial Roman style, Constantinople or Byzantium presented a different story. If Rome itself dwindled from a city of millions to one with a mere fraction of its former population, Byzantium retained and even increased its power. Far from being overthrown, the East Roman Empire survived for a thousand years, until its conquest by the Ottoman Turks in 1453. The civilization it produced had its religion in common with the Christians of the West, though interpreted differently in the Greek Church than in the Roman. On the other hand, the presence of the emperor with a concentration of wealth and power in the court resulted in an imperial architecture, vaster in scale and more sumptuous than the Early Christian Roman productions. This empire, because of its geographical location, became a semi-Oriental despotism, Eastern in its hieratic approach to life and art, colorful to a degree seldom approximated by the West, with a passion in art for surface patterns illustrated alike in the use of marble, in crisp undercut carving, and in the mosaics. The Byzantine style first flowered during the reign of Justinian in the sixth century, and was spread far by his conquests, and further by his prestige as successor to Rome. His general, Belisarius, conquered Sicily, to impose over the classical cultures of that island a layer of Byzantine culture that was felt for centuries. At Ravenna in the north of Italy, the Byzantine style appeared in the churches of Sant' Apollinare in Classe, and Sant' Apollinare Nuovo, both Byzantine versions of the basilica, and above all in San Vitale, with its influential architecture and mosaics.

Although the Byzantines retain, in

Ravenna and elsewhere, the unvaulted design of the Early Christian basilica, their more typical monuments are vaulted. The increased sense of space, the added monumentality, and the fire-proof nature of vaulted buildings as compared to the wooden-roofed basilicas dictated the adoption of that system of construction. The greater difficulty of vaulting and its higher cost could be overcome by the imperial wealth of Byzantium. The chief type of vault with which the Byzantines experimented was the dome; it was part of their Near Eastern heritage, used with great magnificence by the Sassanian Persians at this time. As a hemispherical shape, the dome appears to require a circular wall, or supports arranged in a circle; such a plan, as represented in the Pantheon (fig. 86), is satisfactory when the dome covers almost the whole interior space. If, however, the dome is to cover only part of the interior and is to be combined with other domes or with some different type of roof, the circular support may be inconvenient. It was necessary to contrive some method by which the dome could be carried on four piers placed at the corners of a square, and thus permit combination with other shapes.

The *pendentive* was developed to solve this problem. In shape pendentives are spherical triangles. Four of them, one of which is visible in the drawing of Hagia Sophia (fig. 101), rest their lower points on the main piers; their other angles touch the neighboring pendentives, and so produce along

101. Anthemius of Tralles and Isidorus of Miletus, *Hagia Sophia*, Constantinople (532–37) Isometric, exterior length 308', exterior width 236'.

their upper edges a circle upon which the dome can be built. The pendentive, like other Byzantine motives, existed in Roman buildings, but experiments in the fourth and fifth centuries led to the full development of the dome on pendentives in the sixth century. So adequate was this solution that the Byzantines retained it through their long subsequent history, and even after the end of medieval architecture the builders of Western Europe found it useful.

The Byzantine architects of the sixth century tried in many ways to adapt the dome to the problems of church architecture. The Church of the Holy Apostles in Constantinople, now destroyed, was laid out as a Greek cross with five domes, one in the center and the other four over the equal arms of the cross. In SS. Sergius and Bacchus in Constantinople, and in San Vitale in Ravenna, a single dome covers most of the area, but is surrounded by an aisle, so that in the one case the building is approximately square, in the other case octagonal. Such buildings are often described as the central type: that is, the composition develops around a central vertical axis rising through the dome, rather than along a horizontal axis bisecting the church lengthwise. Architecturally, this type lends itself to concentration, since it subordinates the whole building to the dome. It permits the building to be symmetrical on all four sides, which cannot be true of the Early Christian basilica. However, a small apse often projects from the eastern side of the structure without any attempt to duplicate it on the other three sides.

One flaw is inherent in the form: the dominance of the dome creates an architectural focus under it. To place the altar at that point is bad, for the Christian liturgy demands that the congregation shall be in front of the altar; it is undesirable to allow any considerable part of the congregation during a service to occupy space at the sides of the altar, or still worse behind it. Therefore, the altar is usually removed from the center to a small apse with a chancel or sanctuary to the east. But this separates the architectural and liturgical climaxes of the building. In the Early Christian basilica, on the other hand, the long horizontal lines of the building lead to the east end, where the altar is logically placed, the architecture quite properly stressing the purpose of the building.

Perhaps this prompted the experiments that produced what is called the domed basilica, whose greatest expression is found in Hagia Sophia. The earlier church of Hagia Sophia was destroyed during the Nika sedition of 532.

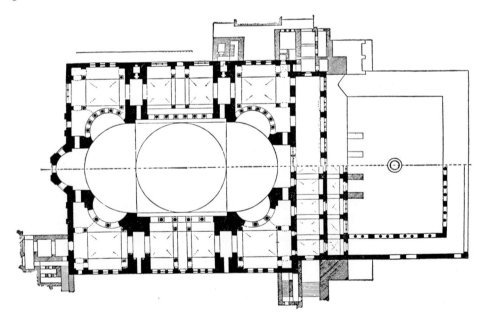

102. *Hagia Sophia*, Constantinople (532–37) 308' x 236'.

Justinian immediately directed his architects to rebuild along more magnificent lines. Except for the atrium, this great church was built with extraordinary rapidity, and dedicated in 537; and although part of the structure collapsed in 558 as the result of an earthquake, it was rebuilt on stronger buttressed supports by 563. Such an accomplishment postulates imperial backing. The plan (fig. 102), developed by Anthemius of Tralles and Isidorus of Miletus, is almost square. A single dome insures unity, but length is gained to the east and west by half-domes, lower than the main dome, but of the same diameter. Although a dome may have less outward thrust than other types of vault, because of the way in which the units are laid, still that thrust pushes out in all directions. On the east and west, the half-domes of Hagia Sophia begin to transfer the thrusts from the main dome outward and downward toward the outer walls of the building. These half-domes are in turn buttressed by domical niches and other vaulted forms. To the north and south, sections of barrel vault, or broad arches, bound the main dome. Much later, in 1317, four huge blocks of masonry were added, for further security, behind the piers that uphold the four main pendentives.

As a result of this complex system the exterior builds up to the central dome like waves of masonry around the rim

103. Anthemius of Tralles and Isidorus of Miletus, *Hagia Sophia*, Constantinople (532–37). Exterior height 183'9".

of the culminating feature (fig. 103).
One mass after another prepares the
way for the climax. Only part of the
curve of the dome is visible externally,
since the lower part is concealed behind
smaller buttresses between each of the
multiple windows that pierce its base.
While the dome of Hagia Sophia is not
embedded in the mass of the building,
like that of the Pantheon, its effect is
achieved more by the complex mass design than by a full revelation externally
of the domical form. In this respect it
is unlike the domes of the Italian Renaissance, the Cathedral of Florence or
St. Peter's in Rome, for example. However effective Hagia Sophia may be in
its mass, little or no decoration appears
on the drab masses of the exterior.

The full splendor of Hagia Sophia is
evident only in the interior (fig. 104).
The affirmation of spatial unity is apparent immediately on entrance. The
combination of domes and half-domes,
illuminated by the ring of windows at
the base of the dome, at once catches
the eye and creates an impression of
monumentality and, at the same time,
of lightness. The dome looks as though
it were suspended from heaven, not supported from earth. The sense of scale,
the result of permitting the smaller volumes to lead insensibly to the larger, is
further emphasized by the columns that
separate nave from aisles, and by the
smaller columns and arcades in the gallery. Red and green porphyry shafts
contribute to a rich polychromy, amplified by polished marble slabs on the
lower walls and a complete incrusta-

tion of mosaic on the higher surfaces.
The veined marble slabs themselves
create rich patterns. A block of stone is
cut in half and opened out like the
leaves of a book, so that the pattern
of veins is repeated in reverse; these two
in turn may be divided in half to create
the same pattern of veins in four neighboring slabs.

The carved architectural members
contribute to the richness of this design.
Extensive use of the drill, sharp undercutting, and a reliance on surface patterns relieved against deep shadows create a lacelike effect (fig. 105), contrary
to the plastic type of moldings developed by the Greeks and Romans. Such
patterns are emphasized by the shadowed incisions, sometimes picked out by
gold leaf on a ground of deep blue to
increase contrast—another indication of
the kinship between Byzantine art and
Near Eastern. The same technique
transforms the capitals of antiquity. The
modeled form of the Corinthian capital
with its projecting leafage gives way to
designs, sometimes of foliate origin,
sometimes of pure pattern, that adhere
to the cushion-like mass. The decorative possibilities of such capitals are
limitless, and if traces of the older types
of capital sometimes remain, the Byzantine fertility in design opened the
way to variety. Moreover, the capitals of
the older orders were designed to support beams; now they must often carry
an arch. This new purpose requires a
larger bearing surface, and so compels
the inclusion above the capital of an
impost block, whose function it is to

104. Anthemius of Tralles and Isidorus of Miletus, *Hagia Sophia*, Constantinople (532–37).

105. *Capital and Impost Block*, Hagia Sophia, Constantinople (532–37).

sade in 1204. During these centuries, most churches follow a plan derived from the lost church, the Nea, built by Basil I before 886. This standard plan (fig. 106) consists of a Greek cross inscribed within a square. A central dome is buttressed by four other domes in the angles of the square between the arms of the cross, which themselves are roofed with barrel vaults. This scheme is compact and logical in abutment. The barrel-vaulted arms of the cross push out sidewise against the four angle domes; to some extent their thrusts balance. These arms and the four subsidiary domes abut the central dome on all sides. The smaller size of the

gather the uneasy load of the arches and concentrate them on the capital.

The spaciousness of Hagia Sophia and its sumptuousness make it a masterpiece of world architecture. Justinian had cause to be proud, and to feel that his church outshone the temple in Jerusalem. At the dedication of the new church he exclaimed, 'Oh Solomon, I have surpassed thee.' The reign of Justinian marks the first climax of the Byzantine style in all the arts. This period, called the First Golden Age, ends with the Iconoclastic controversy of the eighth century. With the rise of the Macedonian dynasty under Basil I in 867, a new epoch of Byzantine art emerges. From this date, the Second Golden Age [1] lasts down to the capture of Constantinople by the Fourth Cru-

---

[1] Although the term 'First Golden Age' to describe Byzantine art before the Iconoclastic controversy is generally accepted, no such agreement exists for the terminology of later periods.

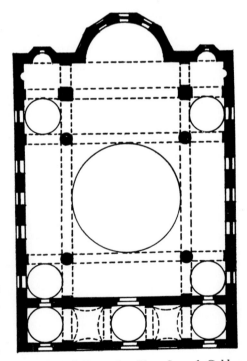

106. *Typical Byzantine Plan*, Second Golden Age.

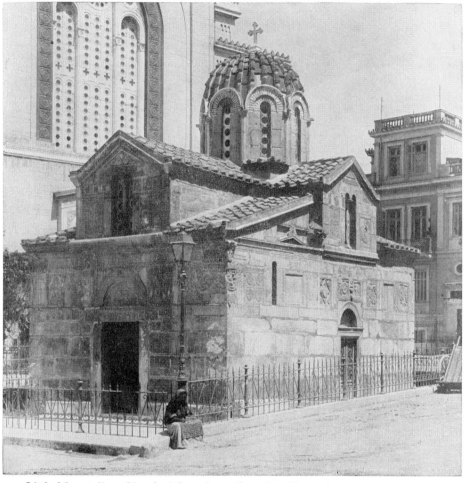

107. *Little Metropolitan Church*, Athens (*c.* 12th cent.) 38' x 25'.

churches at this period and especially the small size of the central dome minimize the liturgical loss of concentration on the altar inherent in this arrangement.

The exterior of the twelfth-century Little Metropolitan Church in Athens (fig. 107) shows greater richness of moldings and flat decorative sculpture than do churches of the First Golden Age. The angle domes are often invisible from the exterior, but the central dome, raised on a drum or cylinder of masonry, is fully visible. The small size makes this revelation of the curve possible without serious danger from thrust, such as would exist in a larger building. Though not in this case, arches often echo the barrel-vaulted arms of the cross on the exterior. Much building of this time occurred outside the capitol of the Byzantine Empire, and even in regions not under Byzantine control. The most famous Byzantine church of the period to Western Europeans is St. Mark's, Venice, built c. 1063. This design accords with its period in the polychromatic and dynamic exterior (modified later), but in plan reverts to the Church of the Holy Apostles in Constantinople.

The Fourth Crusade overthrew the Byzantine Empire in 1204, and set up a short-lived Latin kingdom in its place. After that in turn had fallen in 1261, a last epoch of the style arose, which we may call the Byzantine Renaissance or the Late Byzantine. The metropolis itself never fully recovered from the shock, so that many churches were built in the provinces, in Greece or in the northern Balkans, for example. Mostly small in size, they follow no one type of plan. Sometimes they retain the five-domed arrangement of the Second Golden Age, sometimes they return to the domed basilica, or even to the still simpler form of the unvaulted basilica. A tendency to emphasize height in these buildings is evident in the small domes raised on tower-like drums. These centuries correspond to the Gothic period in Western Europe, though it might be difficult to trace any direct connection in style between them. They prove the longevity of the Byzantine style, which is still later maintained in the architecture of Russia. Even before this, Russian architecture had been an offshoot of Byzantine, modified by local conditions and impulses. Many of the Russian churches are Byzantine in plan but their onion-shaped domes probably have their origins in Sassanian Persia. The influence from Constantinople dominated all Russian art for centuries, just as the Orthodox Church became the standard religion, and yet both were modified as the centuries passed.

The Byzantine concern with the decorative is already prominent in the ivory-covered throne of Archbishop Maximianus in Ravenna dating from the sixth century (fig. 108). Apparent in the vine pattern with peacocks and even animals in its scrolls, it also modifies the figures. If the latter are not yet fully Byzantine, they have ceased to be

108. *Throne of Maximianus*, Cathedral, Ravenna (546–56) Wood and ivory.

Roman. Though not purely linear, the drapery verges on convention, and the poses of the figures display a stylization more pronounced in later times. On the other hand, the beauty of execution and the command of the material prove that the sculpture of these panels had not suffered the technical decline that deadens most Early Christian sarcophagi.

The developed Byzantine style substitutes almost abstract design and symbolism for the classic point of view. Christ Crowning the Emperor Roman IV and Eudoxia (fig. 109) of the eleventh century is rigidly axial. The drapery of Christ has become linear, while in the human figures the sumptuous costumes have consumed so much attention that any distinction between the sexes has vanished. Reliance is placed on the decorative value of the contrasted patterns, the placement of the figures within the space, and the adaptation of the design to the material.

The Byzantines seem to have regarded sculpture as a minor art, though only in the Iconoclastic controversy did they suppress the graven image, forbidden by the Mosaic code, and then only in religious art. Even then, the monasteries took that prohibition lightly, and though such hostility was bound to react on all the arts, painting and mosaic were not strictly graven images. The Byzantine apsidal mosaic of San Vitale (Plate II, facing p. 269) of the sixth century contrasts with the fourth-century Early Christian one at Santa Pudenziana

109. *Christ Crowning the Emperor Roman IV and Eudoxia* (945–49) Cabinet des Médailles, Paris. Ivory, 9½″ x 6″.

(fig. 99). At Ravenna, Christ is seated on a globe flanked by angels and by figures of San Vitale and Archbishop Ecclesius, who carries in his hands a model of the church. Though some indication of ground remains, the background has now become pure gold with no suggestion of depth. The faces still retain some trace of individualism, but the figures are elements in a pattern. Both here and in the choir mosaics of Justinian and Theodora with their attendants, the Roman factual sense has disappeared. While some of the heads look like portraits, the artist is more

110. *Chastity*, Mosaic, St. Mark's, Venice
(11th cent.).

Pudenziana mosaic and more effective than it as decoration.

The mosaics of San Vitale turn from illustration to decoration, but that ideal becomes more deliberate in later Byzantine mosaics, such as those in St. Mark's, Venice. Here the figure of Chastity (fig. 110) has become a unit of design. The drapery symbolizes rather than represents the body beneath it; concentric dark lines surround oval or tear-drop light areas to create patterns focused over certain parts of the body. In many cases, the proportions of the figures are strikingly elongated, the attitudes sharp and angular. The artist knew that his symbol did not look like a human being, but he was not trying to present a real man; instead, his purpose was to express the superhuman nature of his subject and adapt it to its role as architectural decoration. Consequently any setting is symbolic, and often the pictographic figure is simply relieved against a pure gold field. The idea in St. Mark's is identified by lettering, by scrolls held in the hands of the characters, and by well-known emblems, such as the lion for fortitude. The more these figures are reduced to formulas, the less open they are to charges of transgressing the Mosaic code. Though foreign to the concept of art as representation, held through most Western history, one must admit their success as decoration.

Manuscript illuminations demonstrate that formalism inherent in Byzantine art. The opulent color of mosaics mingles with a strong influence from the classic tradition, to combine in turn

concerned with decoration in formal linear arrangements of drapery, one fold repeated after another with only a trace of interest in the body beneath and the merest touch of roundness in them. But what the artist sacrifices in realism, he more than replaces by his color. Against the glow of a gold background, passages of pure deep color create an impression of semi-Oriental splendor, different from the factual approach of the Santa

with the symbolic bent of the Eastern Church, with sometimes one and then another of these factors uppermost. The classical strain predominates in the Joshua Roll of the Vatican in the breadth and free movement of its figures. This manuscript has been variously dated from the seventh to the tenth centuries and may possibly have been copied from a still earlier production. However, the classic influence gives way in the late-tenth-century Menology of Basil II in the Vatican to rigid poses. A monotonous series of figures with upraised hands stand within arcades or between hills silhouetted against gold backgrounds. Still later, in the twelfth century, the Melissenda Psalter of the British Museum exaggerates the conventions of Byzantine art. The emaciated figures are clad in draperies whose folds are reduced to linear patterns analogous to the mosaic from St. Mark's, Venice.

The significance for Western art of the Byzantine style is immeasurable. Constantinople kept alive a civilization inherited from Rome, but changed the classic modes of expression. The years from about 500 to 1000, called the Dark Ages, may have been less dark than is commonly supposed; the name may reflect only our ignorance. Nevertheless, these five centuries in the West produced little in the major arts, whereas they were a time of artistic brilliance in India, in the T'ang period in China, and in Japan, where Buddhism had just been accepted and brought with it the cultural impact of the older civilizations.

111. *Initial Page of the Gospel of St. Matthew,* Book of Kells (8th cent.) Trinity College, Dublin. 10" x 7".

In the West, more has been preserved in some minor arts. Celtic manuscript illumination discarded representation, but in its place substituted a rich vocabulary of decorative ornament. Such figures as are introduced carry two-dimensional representation even farther away from nature than does Byzantine art. The initial page of the Gospel of St. Matthew from the *Book of Kells* (fig. 111) of the eighth century runs riot with spirals, rows of red dots, patterns, interlaced ribbons, and lacertines. The last named are bird or animal forms so elongated and intertwined that they are hardly distinguishable from ribbons. No other artistic tradition has ever produced such exquisite richness of linear patterns, which are related to the Scandinavian arts and to the animal style in Asia.

When a new wave of creative energy swept over Western Europe, the emerging peoples turned to the one Christian center that had maintained a high level of artistic creation. Therefore, when Charlemagne in the eighth century built a palace chapel at Aachen, his builders journeyed to Ravenna to study the Byzantine design of San Vitale; they did not understand it, but tried to reproduce it; and even later in the eleventh century, the Western churches met their need for decoration by symbolic figures, partly inspired by Byzantine manuscripts and ivories. So, too, does the Byzantine style play an important role in Carolingian manuscripts, though the latter are also influenced in decoration by Celtic patterns in line. The classic Roman sources likewise played a part in this later revival of art, but the influence of Rome is less than the influence of the symbolic style of the Eastern Empire. Not only is Byzantium important as a link between the classic civilization and the later culture of Western Europe; it is a great independent style, wherein the engineering achievements of Rome and its spatial sense are crossed with a semi-Oriental love of color, a sense of decoration, and a perfect willingness to replace realism by symbolism. No other style has ever reached such splendor without loss of the architectonic flavor.

All cultures discussed up to this point have been homogeneous. Though the styles they produced were at times influenced by outside civilizations, as in the case of the Egyptian and Mesopotamian influences on Greek art, and though each style developed within itself, still the expression of the Greek, the Roman, and the Byzantine cultures had in each instance been unified. With the Romanesque period that ceases to be true. In art, the term Romanesque refers to a group of eleventh- and twelfth-century styles in Western Europe that have some characteristics in common but many differences. Such variations reflect the breakdown of Roman unity in Europe. In the second century, one might have journeyed from Italy through Spain, France, and England and found in each town baths, aqueducts, and temples of much the same form; though a house in Britain might not have been identical with one in Italy, it would have been like enough to cause no great sense of change in passing from one to another. One language was spoken; one would encounter the same customs, the same ideals, and the same manner of living.

Roman unity broke down after the settlement of the barbarians in Western Europe. These peoples, during the so-called Dark Ages from about 500 to 1000, developed differences, reflected in the gradual emergence of Italian, French, or Spanish tongues as distinct from Latin, their common source. In art we can distinguish the German Romanesque style from the French or Italian, and we can also differentiate several styles within a country. The art of the Lombard plain contrasts with that of Tuscany to its south, while other types characterize southern Italy and Sicily. In Germany, the Rhenish buildings are not like those found elsewhere. In France, some scholars have distinguished sixteen or seventeen styles of Romanesque; others limit themselves to seven. Certainly St. Trophîme at Arles in Provence is so different from the domed churches, such as St. Front at Périgueux in Aquitaine, that to group them together would result in confusion; Cluny in Burgundy and St. Etienne at Caen in Normandy have some elements in common, but more differences. These local variations are partly the architectural consequence of feudalism. Although the great nobility in theory might hold their lands from the king and owe to him the same feudal duties that their vassals in turn owed to them, still the power wielded by the Dukes of Normandy even before the conquest of England, by the Dukes of Burgundy, or by the Counts of Toulouse, enabled them to defy the royal power at will. Under these circumstances, the provinces were virtually independent. Moreover, although pilgrimage and travel were extensive during the Romanesque period, poor roads tended to throw each region on its own resources.

The Romanesque is the great age of the Church. The papacy through the Dark Ages to some extent took the place in the West occupied earlier by the Roman Empire. Although under Charlemagne the imperial idea was partly revived as the Holy Roman Empire, the emperors concerned themselves with Germany and Italy, and it was the power of the Church more than that of the Empire that was felt throughout Western Christendom. Perhaps the summit of ecclesiastical power was reached at Canossa in 1077, when the Emperor Henry IV was forced to do penance before Pope Gregory VII. That submission, though superficially an abasement of the secular power to the ecclesiastical, in less obvious ways strengthened the lay power; but the Church seemed to have brought to its knees her only secular rival.

The religious energy of the age found a dramatic outlet in the Crusades. While the enthusiasm to free the Holy Land from the Saracens may have been reinforced by a spirit of adventure, one cannot doubt the primary importance of the religious fervor behind the Crusades. The first three, when that spirit was most prominent, all occurred before the end of the twelfth century. But, if the devotion of the people vented itself in the Crusades, the Church served the ends of civilization with greater effect through the monasteries. As centers of learning, they stand out like beacons in the intellectual night. Their role might later on be played by others, but during the Romanesque period they reached their greatest height. Though the monks themselves did not build and decorate all their churches, nevertheless artistic energies centered in and on the artistic problems of the Church.

Succinct definition of the eleventh- and twelfth-century styles is nearly impossible. De Lasteyrie, following Quicherat, defines the Romanesque as 'that architecture which, retaining many elements of the classic, has ceased to be classic, and which, anticipating many elements of the Gothic, has not yet become Gothic.' This statement tends to relegate Romanesque architecture to a mere link between two other styles. Moreover, those styles that have any substantial heritage from antiquity do not foretell the Gothic, and vice versa. Nevertheless, this definition calls attention to the genealogy of some branches of the style. To these relationships, one should also add an occasional connection with the Byzantine, as in Aquitaine; with the Saracenic wherever the Romanesque impinged on Mohammedan culture; and of course, at the beginning, with northern elements.

Some of the designers are traditionalists in the sense that they preserve in their buildings architectural ideas that had developed earlier. They may modify these ideas or arrange them in new combinations to meet new problems, but they do not propose fundamental changes in structure. They prefer to concentrate their creative energies on monumentality, grandeur, and finish. Other designers are innovators who envision new structural expedients that promise more effective solutions for church building problems than wooden roofs, barrel vaults, or domes. Their churches are rugged, vigorous, prophetic, but often smaller and less finished.

To discuss all the divisions of the Romanesque is neither possible nor necessary. A few examples illustrate the character of the movement, and some of its variety. The Tuscan Romanesque as we see it in the cathedral group at Pisa, begun in 1063, displays the reliance of that region upon tradition. Of the four structures within this group—the cathedral, the leaning tower or campanile, the baptistry, and the Campo Santo—the first two and part of the third were completed during the eleventh and twelfth centuries. The plan of the cathedral (fig. 112) looks like a development from the Early Christian

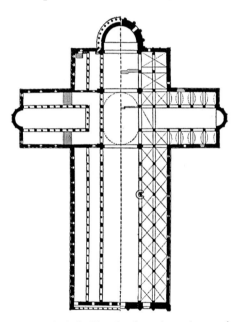

112. *Cathedral*, Pisa (1063–92). 320' x 230'.

Roman basilica (fig. 95). Divided into nave and side aisles by colonnades, and lighted by a clearstory, it expands the rudimentary transepts of its ancestor into great salient arms, and prolongs the nave of the church beyond the transepts; it thus becomes a Latin cross in

113. *Cathedral*, Pisa (1063–92) Nave, total length 320'.

plan. The thin walls and slender supports indicate that, although small vaults exist over the aisles, the nave is still covered by a plain timber roof, less heavy than a stone vault and without its lateral thrust.

Though by no means imperial Roman, the Early Christian basilica represents late classic architecture, and, in so far as Pisa follows that lead, it retains a classic flavor. The interior (fig. 113), especially in the Corinthian colonnade, follows Roman precedent to an exceptional extent. It is doubtful whether the Middle Ages ever produced elsewhere so classic a feature as this. On the other hand, the arcaded triforium gallery with its paired arches is probably inspired by contemporary work in Lombardy. The Tuscan love of color in architecture

shows itself both in the use of marble patterns in the spandrels or triangles between the arches of the nave arcade, and in the alternate bands of light and dark marble in the triforium, and to a lesser extent in other parts of the building. The violent alternation of its strident pattern may not commend itself to all modern eyes, but it suggests the vigor of the eleventh century.

The basilican mass of the church is visible on the exterior (fig. 114), although the transepts and the dome above the *crossing*, as the intersection of transepts and nave is called, complicate the mass. On the other hand, the drabness of the basilica yields to decorative arcading, some of it in the form of shallow galleries behind small columns and arches, but with a blind arcade for the lowest tier, its columns and arches engaged to the wall. Five stories of arcading reflect the divisions of the interior: the blind arcade corresponds in height to the nave arcade within, the lowest open arcade to the triforium, the next to the roof of the triforium gallery, the third to the clearstory, and the last to the pitched roof over the nave. The proportions of the several stories are almost simple ratios: the blind arcade occupies a third of the height, while one sixth is devoted to each upper gallery. The love of color, so prominent on the interior, reappears on the façade in restrained banding, and in lozenge-shaped panels enlivened with marble patterns within the arches. The rich shadows, caught by the open arcades, contribute to this sense of color, and,

114. *Cathedral*, Pisa (1063–92) Façade 115′ wide.

indeed, the marble itself has a luminous beauty.

The Middle Ages did not attempt to construct buildings of the accuracy of the Parthenon. Hardly an arch in the arcade along the sides of Pisa Cathedral rises to the same level; some of them almost touch the horizontal molding above, while others are noticeably lower. Builders capable of so large an undertaking as the cathedral were also capable of making arches within the same series rise to a uniform height. Therefore, they must have considered such regularity as either undesirable, or, more probably, as a matter of indifference. Discrepancies like these in a formal Greek temple would destroy the effect, but they enhance the free and easy medieval design.

The passion for arcades carries over from the cathedral to the campanile at Pisa, constructed a century later, where eight stories of them are superposed. The varied length of the arcades on the cathedral façade overcomes monotony, but that difference cannot occur in the cylindrical mass of the tower. The latter owes its fame to its deviation from the perpendicular, a discrepancy present in most Italian towers of the Middle Ages but rarely to the same degree. Details of construction indicate that the tower settled into the ground unequally while it was being built. The angle of inclination is slightly greater near the bottom than further up, as though the builders tried to overcome the settlement, or at least to mitigate it, as the tower rose. That angle is startling, and its implication of insecurity can be very disturbing when one visits Pisa. Though said to be structurally safe at present, the Leaning Tower must be called an architectural aberration.

Quite different from this Tuscan Romanesque is the style of Sicily. It also relies on tradition, but its past is more varied. Few regions so well demonstrate the influence on architecture of layer after layer of civilization. After the classic era, Sicily fell in turn under Byzantine, Saracenic, and during the Romanesque period, Norman domination. The twelfth-century Cathedral of Monreale, in the hills above Palermo, retains the light construction and wooden roof of the basilica for both nave and aisles, but Byzantium contributed the capitals with their impost blocks, and the mosaics. An Oriental luxuriance of polychromy also appears on the exterior; for instance, the golden stonework of the blind arcades in the apse contrasts with the plaster surface of the wall within them. Those arcades interlace as though one series of arches had been placed on another, the supports of the second arcade intermediate between those of the first. This interlacing arcade characterizes Norman architecture. On the other hand, in Sicily the arches are pointed after the Saracenic fashion rather than the round arches of the usual Romanesque styles. This use of the pointed arch, inspired by the East, has no connection with the Gothic. Indeed, the Romanesque styles adopt it wherever they come into contact with Moslem or Saracenic peoples, as, for example, in

Spain. From Normandy, however, come the twin towers that flank the façade of Monreale. For all their simplicity of structure, few Romanesque buildings display the exotic charm of the Sicilian.

These wooden-roofed styles borrow much from tradition; the barrel-vaulted styles of the period somewhat less. A notable group of churches sprang up along the routes to the shrine of St. James, Santiago de Compostela in northwestern Spain. The stream of pilgrims along these roads stimulated the exchange of ideas, and created a demand for monumental churches at intervals along the way. One function of the monasteries was to afford hospitality to all; but while the pilgrims might accept food and lodging at no charge, it was common to contribute something, and the pilgrim gifts helped in the creation of such vast churches as Santiago itself, and St. Sernin at Toulouse in southern France. The standard plan of these churches, which we see at Santiago (fig. 115), begun during the eleventh century, is repeated at least five times in large churches along the roads to Spain. A nave of great length leads to the bold transepts and to the choir to create a cruciform plan. The rich ceremonial of medieval worship, its processions, and its ritual demand this large space. The choir ends in an apse, around which the aisle is bent in a semicircle, with a series of chapels radiating from it. This aisle, called an *ambulatory*, made it possible not only for processions but, even more important, for pilgrims to visit each of the chapels and pay their devotions.

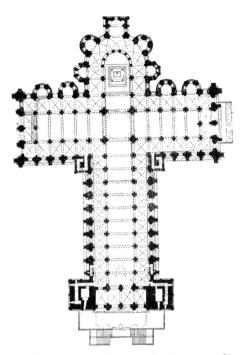

115. *Santiago de Compostela* (1075–1128) 308′ x 207′.

that demanded structures on so magnificent a scale.

The interior of Santiago (fig. 116) shows a nave roofed with a barrel vault partly carried on transverse ribs or arches below its surface. These ribs, which divide the vault into bays, were probably devised in part to reduce the amount of centering needed during construction. They dramatize the support offered by the piers, and visibly connect pier and vault. On every pier, a colonnette or shaft apparently carries to the ground the weight borne by the rib. The nave arcade also rests on shafts in the main pier, which becomes a complex of several parts, each designed to express some specific function. Those parts produce lines in the pier to em-

Each chapel had its own altar with some relic of the saint to whom the chapel was dedicated, the popularity of these relics being dependent in part on their miraculous power. Consequently, a church with a number of such objects of devotion was fortunate indeed, not merely because they attracted crowds of the devout, but also because of the gifts they might bring to the church. It is suggestive in this connection that the Cathedral of Canterbury was rebuilt and enlarged immediately after the burial there of St. Thomas à Becket. To recognize the financial value of relics is in no way to underestimate their religious significance; they were venerated with an unquestioning faith. It was this faith

116. *Santiago de Compostela* (1075–1128) Nave 164′ x 33′, 69′ high.

phasize its vertical movement and to state visibly its function as a support. A barrel vault, by definition a half-cylinder, creates thrust along its full length. In so far as the ribs carry some of the weight, more lateral thrust collects on them than along the intermediate length; even so, such a vault requires continuous abutment. Therefore, it became necessary to cover the triforium galleries with continuous half-barrel vaults, which partly counteract the thrust and partly carry it over the aisles to the outer wall of the building, where sheer weight of masonry might resist it. Though logical, this system sacrifices the clearstory. Windows may be present at the end of the nave, or in the aisle walls, but not enough light passes across the width of the aisles and through the arches of the nave arcade by modern standards. This thick gloom, through which the sonority of the Gregorian chant reverberates, hangs like a pall overhead and half conceals the vaults, but also creates a sense of religious mystery.

The heavy walls, large piers, and plain vault define the major volumes of the church. If smaller volumes exist in the aisles, they are stated rather as parallel voids than as parts of the space contained within the nave. That clear definition of space characterizes the Romanesque style, both inside and out. In St. Sernin at Toulouse (fig. 117), built chiefly in the eleventh century, each unit of the complex mass is separately conceived. Its own roof distinguishes the nave from the aisles with their lower

117. *St. Sernin,* Toulouse (1080–96) Exterior of apse, total height, 215'.

roofs; the apse protrudes above the ambulatory, where each chapel is a separate bulge. The church is designed as a collection of its parts, each related to the whole but not fused with it; every part retains its discrete individuality. This combination of apse, ambulatory, chapels, and transepts builds up to the tower over the crossing, to make the east end of St. Sernin one of the most monumental of all Romanesque buildings. In its expression of sheer power, it surpasses the Italian buildings already discussed.

Priority is not important among these styles that preserve at least some traditional forms. Many of them appeared simultaneously, and it is unnecessary to assume any direct influence of one upon another. On the other hand, the designers of Lombardy claim precedence among the innovators. Though this is

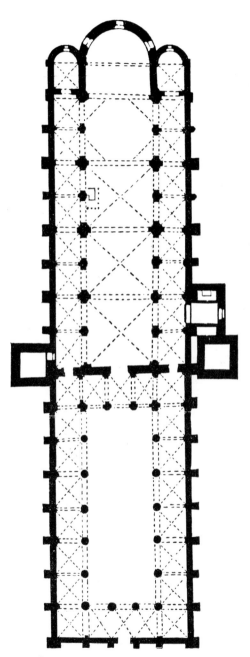

119. *Sant' Ambrogio*, Milan (1046–1196) Transverse section, nave and aisles, 92' wide.

disputed, history points to an influence of Lombardy on the Rhenish and Norman churches. Four primary structural innovations characterize Lombard work. The first is the ribbed quadripartite groined vault, present in Sant' Ambrogio in Milan (fig. 118), begun in the eleventh century. The area of the nave is divided into square bays, the sides of the square and its diagonals marked by ribs. Three pairs appear in each bay: two transverse ribs cross the nave, two wall ribs run along its sides, and two diagonal ribs divide each bay into four triangular compartments. Whether the ribs in fact support these triangles of masonry or simply effect economies in centering, at least they articulate the vault, dramatize the structural forces, and seem to concentrate them on the piers. Since all the Lombard ribs are semicircular, the diagonal ribs, longer than the wall and transverse ribs, must

118. *Sant' Ambrogio*, Milan (1046–1196) 390' x 92'.

rise to a higher point. Consequently, as one sees in the section (fig. 119), each vaulting bay is domical.

But if the ribs carry any part of the weight of the vault, as they appear to, we may expect distinct support for each rib. To effect this, the membered pier had to be developed. In its complete form this includes a pilaster or colonnette to correspond to each rib, and since each pier supports five ribs of the nave vaults, one transverse, two wall, and two diagonal ribs, five members must appear on the nave side of each pier. Moreover, the design of each colonnette indicates the direction taken by the rib it serves. The interior of Sant' Ambrogio shows that the shafts carrying the diagonal ribs face diagonally across the nave of the church.

The piers of Sant' Ambrogio (fig. 120) are not all the same size; large piers alternate with smaller ones. To see the reason for this, turn again to the plan (fig. 118). The nave is flanked by side aisles, half its width. If the aisles are also to be vaulted in square compartments (and to vault an oblong rectangle in the Lombard system would be very difficult), two bays in each aisle must correspond to one in the nave. These bays need support at their corners. Therefore, smaller intermediate piers are introduced, smaller because they carry only the aisle vaults, whereas the main piers carry both the aisle vaults and the larger nave vaults. If this intermediate pier were destroyed, theoretically nothing would happen to the nave vaults; therefore, we do not find on the

120. *Sant' Ambrogio*, Milan (1046–1196) Nave.

nave side of the intermediate piers the complex membering that characterizes the principal piers.

The ribs of these vaults bring a considerable thrust to bear against the walls of the church, but only against those points of the wall opposite the pier. If a solid masonry buttress were placed behind the main piers of the nave to resist that thrust, it would have blocked the aisles. Practically, the buttress must be located outside of the aisle, where it appears as a mass thickening the wall opposite each main pier of the interior (fig. 120). The aisle vaults also thrust outward, but just as the alternate pier is enough to support them, so a smaller buttress is sufficient to care for this thrust. The same alternation we have seen on the interior is also visible on the exterior, which thus reveals the structural system. These pier buttresses, to be effective, must be connected with the nave vaults. The Lombards placed a gallery over the aisles; as we see in the section (fig. 119), arches in these galleries support a wall, which transmits the thrust from the nave vaults over the aisles to the outside of the church. These four structural features of the Lombard style, the ribbed vault, membered pier, alternate system, and pier buttress are a milestone in architectural history. Though they raised many problems, both practical and aesthetic, they broke the ground for later development.

Such a system is more complex than the scheme of the Cathedral of Pisa, and must have been more costly to construct in proportion to the area enclosed. On the other hand, the heavy masonry of the interior has an appearance of permanence and power that the Cathedral of Pisa lacks. Most important among its advantages is that of fire protection. Wooden roofs were liable to destruction by fire; while they might be replaced without much trouble, the destruction to the interior and its contents caused by the burning timbers could not be so easily repaired. Important as such protection is, it does not follow that the presence of a vault dispenses with the necessity for a roof. The upper surface of a vault cannot be exposed to the weather; rainfall, penetrating the joints between the stones, would soon disintegrate any vault. Consequently, all vaults are covered by some form of wooden roof. The most serious defect of the Lombard system is the lack of light. The galleries and the buttress system limit windows to the outer walls of the aisles and to the end of the nave, and as a result most of the Lombard churches are very dark.

The Lombard style has a robust vigor, but not the finish and sophistication of many traditional styles. The carving of the capitals is rugged, but on the whole little decoration enlivens the church. Its effectiveness lies in the structural logic and the rhythm inherent in the alternate system, though some unity of the interior is lost because of the domical form of the vaults, which suggest separate units rather than continuity. Externally (fig. 121), Sant' Ambrogio is monochromatic, in contrast to the Tuscan and Sicilian styles. Built in brick,

121. *Sant' Ambrogio*, Milan (1046–1196) Exterior, total length, 390'.

with stone reserved for the important architectural members, it makes free use of the arched *corbel table*, a range of small arches supported on projecting blocks or corbels, as decorative bands to accent the principal divisions. Corbel tables in Sant' Ambrogio run along just under the eaves of the church, below the gallery level, and at each story of the tower beside the building. Slight as it is, this feature identifies the spread of the Lombard influence in German Romanesque architecture, in southern Italy, in Normandy, and elsewhere. No single church of the Lombard Romanesque is as distinguished in design as any of the examples of other Romanesque styles

already considered. The Lombard buildings are hardly comparable with them in scale, in complexity of mass, or in delicacy of detail. On the other hand, such distinction must not be expected. The solution of the structural problems absorbed so much creative energy that the significance of Lombard buildings is concentrated there.

The connection between Germany and Lombardy, two of the most important regions within the Holy Roman Empire, in part accounts for the spread of the Lombard style northward. During the Dark Ages, to judge from the slight remains, a preference for multiple towers, double apses (one to the west as well as one to the east), and double transepts characterizes German buildings. The resulting silhouette was complex, and the mass composition elaborate to the point of confusion. Something of this spirit remains in the twelfth-century cathedrals of Mainz and Worms. At Worms, for example, apses occur to the east and to the west, each flanked by paired towers, and a lantern rises near each end of the edifice. On the other hand, the quadripartite ribbed vault, the membered pier, the alternate system, and the rudimentary buttresses derive from Lombardy. The German churches are less logical than the Lombard, because they do not always adopt the complete system but are willing to omit one or more members of the vault or of the pier. A further indication of Lombard influence, the arched corbel table, recurs even in the more traditional buildings of the Rhineland and in other parts of Germany. But if the German style yields to the Italian in structural logic, it is ahead in monumentality. The organization of this complexity in design, the combination of vertical and horizontal masses, and the feeling for scale make this Romanesque style the finest architectural achievement of Germany, an indigenous style that commands respect through its power and dignity.

Normandy, on the English Channel, also fell under Lombard influence. The Normans were eager to learn from Lombardy, which enjoyed great intellectual prestige throughout Western Europe during the eleventh century. Prelates trained in Lombardy brought with them to Normandy a knowledge of Italian architecture. Thus Lanfranc, born in Pavia early in the eleventh century, entered the monastery of Bec in Normandy in 1042 and became prior a few years later. Subsequently he took charge as abbot of the new Abbaye aux Hommes at Caen and, as archbishop of Canterbury after the conquest of England, began the building of a magnificent cathedral. St. Anselm, from Aosta in north Italy, followed Lanfranc in each of his positions and doubtless also drew southern influence in his train.

So energetic a people as the Normans would hardly accept suggestions in architecture without trying to improve them. The plan of St. Etienne at Caen (fig. 122), called the Abbaye aux Hommes, begun in 1064, though the vaults were added seventy-five years later, reveals the ribbed vault, the membered pier, the alternate system, and the buttresses, but with some differences from the Lombard. The vault has ceased to be four-part, or quadripartite; an intermediate transverse rib bisects the square compartment, to halve the lateral triangles and so produce the six-part, or sexpartite, vault. Since this intermediate transverse rib in St. Etienne supports part of the nave vault, and since it rests on the intermediate pier, that pier now becomes vital for the support of the nave as well as the aisle. However, it carries less of the nave vault than the main piers, as indicated by the single rib resting on it, and therefore it follows that the intermediate pier may

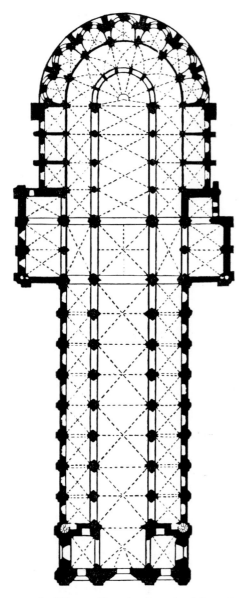

122. *St. Etienne*, Caen (1064–77) 360′ x 73′.

onal ribs, but the intermediate pier needs only one member for the intermediate transverse rib. The walls in the Norman Romanesque are so massive that they absorb, as it were, the wall rib, which is not visible in the vault or reflected in the pier. These walls are thick enough to be pierced with passages at several levels, for inspection of the building, and to facilitate repairs.

The Norman church includes a clearstory. This feature, so fundamental to adequate lighting, had been sacrificed to the buttress problem by the Lombards. But in Normandy, the thick walls probably suffice for abutment, though buttresses are often placed against the clearstory wall behind each pier. In the contemporary church of Ste. Trinité, the Abbaye aux Dames, a half arch under the roof of the aisle back of each support is designed to transfer thrust over the aisles to the outer wall, where pier buttresses resist it. This expedient affords the germ of the Gothic flying buttress. Moreover, Norman vaults are not domical as are Lombard and, occasionally, German vaults. The transverse ribs remain semicircular, but the diagonal ribs are either semi-elliptical or segmental, and thus lower than a full half-circle; they reduce the height of the diagonal arches to the same level as that attained by the transverse ribs. Therefore, the nave of the Norman church (fig. 123) does not show the same interruptions that meet the eye in Sant' Ambrogio. However, this unity has its price. Over any given

remain smaller than the main piers and thus preserve the alternate system. The main pier has members to support the main transverse rib and the two diag-

123. *St. Etienne*, Caen (1064–77), vaults (*c.* 1135) Nave 32' wide, total length 360'.

but in its gaunt proportions. Its design repeats the divisions of the interior, and so becomes a prototype of the Gothic façade. Shallow buttresses divide the façade and correspond to the nave and side aisles, while three tiers of openings express the vertical stories of nave arcade, triforium, and clearstory. The western towers, whose spires were added later, emphasize that part of the building where the principal entrances are located. Also, they give dramatic interest to the façade, as they rise above the roof in stages—the lower ones plain in design with few openings or none, and the number of windows and the richness of their treatment increased in the

span, the lower and flatter the arch, the greater is its thrust; and consequently the Norman scheme of flattened diagonal ribs results in a greater thrust than that created by semicircular members of the same size.

Austerity pervades the best of these Norman buildings. The sturdy masonry of local stone may be carved around the arches, and in horizontal bands between the stories. These do not usually attempt floral, figure, or animal designs; instead, we find the zigzag, the chevron, the billet mold like rows on a checkerboard. In Normandy itself even these are seldom employed, but they abound in the churches put up by the Normans in England after the Conquest.

The façade of St. Etienne (fig. 124) is severe, not only in its dearth of detail

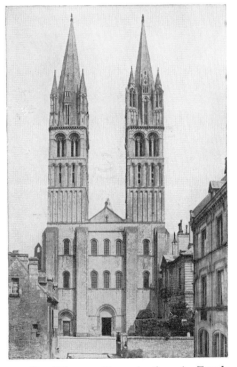

124. *St. Etienne*, Caen (1064–77) Façade 295' high.

upper stories. Otherwise, however, the Norman façade is bare, its portals and windows small, its buttresses narrow strips, and the plastic character of the Gothic nowhere visible.

When the Normans invaded England in 1066 their architecture was grander than that of the conquered Saxons. During the next century, they built cathedral after cathedral in their own style. In England they sought scale, ponderous rhythms, and an overwhelming result to impress their new subjects. The Anglo-Norman style wins its greatest architectural triumph at the end of the eleventh century in Durham Cathedral (fig. 125). A clear Romanesque definition of volumes in nave and aisles results from the vast size of round columns and alternate membered piers. Though its vaulted nave is exceptional among English Romanesque buildings, even here the Norman scheme is not complete; its diagonal arches above the intermediate piers do not continue to the ground on any colonnette or pilaster. However, Durham does not lack structural interest to the historian; certain features of its vaulting and its buttress system are amazingly advanced when one considers that the nave vaults were completed by 1133; but its sonorous architecture does not rely for effect on structure. Few styles are more imposing than the Anglo-Norman in the expression of sheer power, and among the monuments of that style none can equal Durham Cathedral,

125. *Cathedral*, Durham (1096–1133) Nave 39′ wide, 72′ high, total length nave and choir, 469′.

'half house of God, half castle 'gainst the Scot.'

The same variations in style we have reviewed in architecture occur in sculpture, and for the same reasons, but it does not follow that a region need be prominent in both arts. In general, these styles form a design woven of classic, northern, and Byzantine threads. The last named was the one living source of inspiration, and even of information in the visual arts, to which the Western artists after the Dark Ages could turn. Though Byzantium produced little monumental sculpture, her manuscripts and ivories were readily portable. By their very nature, these arts tend to represent or symbolize primarily by outline. That linearism affects much Romanesque sculpture, even when it is executed on a monumental scale. Few arts have ever attained so architectonic a flavor. To some degree, this results from carving stones already set in place in the building, and of the same material as the architecture. Also the angular forms and the distortion of the figure for the sake of design bring the sculpture into dependence on the architecture.

In many regions, the sculpture concentrates around the doorway. In St. Trophîme at Arles (fig. 126), the rich

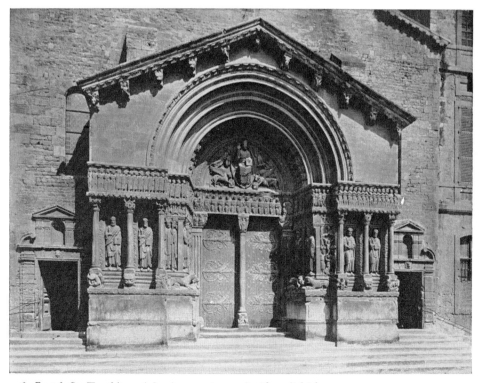

126. *Portal*, St. Trophîme, Arles (*c.* 1150) *c.* 40' wide, 46' high.

127. *Apostles*, portal, St. Trophîme, Arles (*c.* 1150).

ter, and separate the Blessed on the left, and the Damned to the right. The architecture needs a band in that position; to provide this, individual figures are elements of a pattern; each figure duplicates its neighbors in pose. The victims chained together on the right, each with his hand on the shoulder of the man in front, march off in lock step with the patterned flames of hell licking their legs. The subject is clear, and the artist free to turn to the artistic needs of the design.

A different style centers around the pilgrimage routes to Santiago de Compostela, though whether the French or Spanish workshops take precedence remains uncertain. If St. Trophîme is related to the classic Roman, the affinities in St. Pierre at Moissac of the twelfth century lie with a school of manuscript illumination, ivory carving, and metal work that flourished in Western Europe in the ninth and tenth centuries and which was remotely influenced by Byzantium. The figure of St. Peter (fig. 128) on the door jamb has as little correspondence to a human being as it well can. The proportions are attenuated, the head thrown forward at an angle with the body that is realistically impossible; the neck long; but above all the figure has now become a frame for an arrangement of drapery. The pipe-like legs, especially prominent in the angels of the tympanum above (fig. 129), afford an excuse to change the pattern, not to represent the leg. The garments fall in flat pleats. Similar patterned drapery characterized the archaic

portal contrasts with the plain façade. Provence, a once-flourishing Roman province, was littered with classic monuments bound to affect later styles. Many details in this twelfth-century portal, such as the fluted pilasters for door jambs and the fret molding above, attest this influence, as do also the senatorial figures of apostles flanking the door. These squat figures (fig. 127), heavily robed and full-bearded, are not far removed from late Roman tradition. The heads are large in proportion to the bodies. This massiveness is appropriate to the location. The multiple folds of drapery are not cut so deeply into the mass, in spite of the classic influence, as to create a plastic treatment.

A tendency to pattern, vague in the large figures, is more in evidence in the frieze, where the Apostles sit in the cen-

128. *St. Peter*, St. Pierre, Moissac (early 12th cent.) 5′ high.

129. *Tympanum*, St. Pierre, Moissac (12th cent.) 18'8" wide.

period of Greek art. This parallel is a coincidence, but the relation to the art of the Dark Ages and to Constantinople is not. Both the Byzantine ivories, and the mosaic Chastity in St. Mark's (fig. 110) show the same angularity, attenuation, and kind of design in drapery. However, the dynamic spirit and nervous energy of northern and western Europe, manifest in the cross-legged figures and the swirls of drapery, animate the sophisticated type and motives from the East.

The composition culminates in the *tympanum*, that is, in the lunette within the arch of the doorway above the openings into the church. There is carved the Christ of the Apocalypse, surrounded by the symbols of the evangelists, angels, and elders (fig. 129). The twenty-four elders, ranged in tiers, gain animation from their crossed legs and varied postures as they look upward to the Saviour. They contrast in scale with the larger central group. Christ dominates by His size, by the larger treatment of His robe, by His crossed halo, and, of course, by His central position. Still, though His figure has some mass, the sculptor refuses to cut into it. Instead, he folds the garment against the figure, and lets the edges end in a zigzag, so that the surfaces rather than the mass create the effect.

130. *Tympanum*, La Madeleine, Vézelay (*c.* 1130) Diameter of tympanum, *c.* 24'6".

Burgundy achieves still more of stylization. The tympanum of the Church of the Madeleine at Vézelay (fig. 130), also from the twelfth century, presents the Pentecost, the descent of the Holy Ghost upon the Apostles. This mystical occurrence is given curiously literal form; Christ in the pointed oval or mandorla shape in the center stretches out His hands; from His finger tips, symbolic rays descend on the head of each of the Apostles. Naïve as this may seem, it would be hard to find a more effective method of presenting this mystery. The body has become, even more than at Moissac, a frame of bent pipe to hold the drapery. In fact, because of the influence of illuminated manuscripts, the whole figure is flattened out; that Christ had a body does not concern these sculptors. Their design is magnificent and their meaning clear. To tell a Romanesque sculptor that his statue did not look like a figure would have meant nothing to him. He might have replied that his figures were not intended to be human; they portrayed spiritual characters whose actuality had no bearing on their emotional religious significance. To consider them from our realistic point of view is to miss what is important: namely, their supreme effectiveness as symbolic and didactic illustrations of church dogma and as abstract design.

A second, and yet more extreme, tympanum from Burgundy is that of St. Lazare at Autun, designed by master Gislebertus. The characters of the Last Judgment are more elongated, the figure of Christ flatter, and the whole design more diagrammatic and two-dimensional than the sculpture at Moissac. The beguiling devils provide an outlet for the exuberance of the time, but the composition is more confused and less effective than that at Moissac or at Vézelay.

The character of Italian sculpture, itself varied, is distinct from these French styles. For one thing, the sculpture is scattered around the church, not concentrated at the doors and in the cloisters. For another, the Italians carve in marble, regardless of the material of the building. Therefore, the sculpture is less integrated with the architecture than in the best northern work. Lombardy in the twelfth century borrowed from Provence, as, for example, in the treatment of drapery in the Deposition, a twelfth-century relief from the Cathedral of Modena, possibly by Benedetto of Parma. This formal design fits its rectangle, without such distortions of the figure as those in Burgundy. Southern Italy, as one might expect, turned to the Byzantine or to the Roman classic. The former, modified by the Italian love of vivacious narrative, bore fruit in a series of bronze doors, illustrated at the Cathedral of Benevento. On the other hand, the sculptors of the court of Frederick II at Capua in the early thirteenth century evolved a plastic style so classic in appearance that some of its products, such as the bust of Pier della Vigna or the head of the personified Capua, might be confused with Roman art. This school has exceptional importance as the source for the style of Nicola d'Apulia, the outstanding Tuscan sculptor of the mid-thirteenth century.

Outside of Italy, the monumental sculpture of the period is often restricted to doorways and cloisters. However, the sculptured capitals, though minor, illustrate the range of Romanesque sculpture and are themselves a fascinating study. The vast majority are plain, molded, or adorned with foliate patterns, sometimes based on Roman precedents, sometimes on Byzantine, but in the aggregate showing a remarkable fertility of invention. When the motive is foliate, the Romanesque carver pays little heed to any specific flower or leaf; instead, he reduces the suggestions from nature into elements of design, as he does in his figure sculpture. A smaller number of capitals deal with figure subjects. One from Autun (fig. 131) depicts the Temptation of Christ; a devil, winged and with clawed feet, stands before Christ on top of the temple. The barbaric vigor of the northern imagination is allowed free rein in

131. *Temptation of Christ*, Capital, Autun (12th cent.).

132. *Cain and Abel*, Capital, Moutier St. Jean (12th cent.) Fogg Museum, Cambridge, Mass. 26" high x 25" wide at top x 16" wide at bottom.

the demon, who seems unlikely to tempt anyone with success, least of all Christ. Frankly handled as a grotesque, his wrinkled face is deliberately distorted. Christ, whose head is encircled by a halo inscribed with a cross, exhibits the same angularity and linearism as the tympanum figures. From Moutier St. Jean in the twelfth century comes a naïve version of the story of Cain and Abel (fig. 132). The older brother can be recognized by his full beard as well as by the sheaf of grain in his hand, while Abel carries a lamb from his flock. The hand of God indicates His preference for the live offering by pointing to it through the cloud presented by wavy lines. Simple as is this arrangement, the story is readable, a primary aim of the sculptor in days when the lessons of the Church might be taught through illustration, since books were rare and few

but churchmen could read. These narratives filled the place of printing in modern life. For the twentieth-century observer, in addition to a knowledge of the Bible narrative some imagination is often necessary to recognize these scenes, but they may have been more easily identified by those for whom they were made. The same tendency to distortion that characterizes the monumental sculpture is evident here. The heads at Moutier St. Jean are one quarter of the total height of the figure in contrast to the one seventh of the Greek Polyclitan ideal (fig. 63). Holes drilled to catch black shadows create the eyes, while at Autun Christ is twice as high as the temple. One must further observe in these capitals that the design in spite of considerable modeling follows the surface of the capital. In this way the design accords with the structure of the capital.

As in architecture, so also in manuscript illumination the Germans retained some of the complexity of Carolingian traditions. The Gospels of Emperor Otto, at the end of the tenth century, display some Byzantine influence in the figures, with a copious use of gold. On the other hand, Byzantine influence on the eleventh-century Grimbald Gospels is slight. Distorted, symbolic, and linear though the figures are, they have a vivacity unknown to their forerunners, but common to the Winchester school. That sprightliness is apparent in the Newminster *Liber Vitae* (fig. 133) early in the eleventh century.

133. *Liber Vitae,* Newminster (1020–30) British Museum.

The figures, here sketched in brown ink, depict St. Peter welcoming the elect to heaven and rescuing a soul by force from the devil, and an angel closing the gates on the damned in hell. Some distortion remains, but this is insignificant in comparison with the freedom of pose and expression. Much the same feeling for the grotesque vitalizes the devils here that we have seen in the Romanesque capitals.

The Romanesque style used to be regarded as a crude preparation for the Gothic; its sculpture was uncouth because of the ignorance of the epoch that produced it. Even from this brief review, it should be obvious that such an attitude is unjustified. While some of its styles are less refined than the Gothic, in the expression of sheer strength it is greater. If some of its branches provide the structural experimentation preparatory to the Gothic, many Romanesque styles have no connection with the later French style. The Romanesque stands triumphant on its own feet, an inevitable expression of the new vigor of Western Europe, of its faith, and of its feudal system.

X   The Early Development of French Gothic Art

In the popular mind today and for centuries past, medieval art is Gothic art. Though this idea ignores Byzantine and Romanesque art, it has some justification: Gothic art is the most striking manifestation of the whole age; its style or group of styles has the most vivid character, at least in architecture; and in so far as any one style can represent so long and varied a period, the Gothic does so best. The judgment of its success has altered through the years, as its name, the Gothic, indicates. During the centuries when it was 'modern,' this style was known as *opus francigenum*, French work, which suggested where its principal motive force lay. With the revival of enthusiasm for antiquity, the fifteenth- and sixteenth-century Italians maintained that the Middle Ages had

been barbaric; its most striking product was the style usually characterized by the pointed arch; the Goths were the best known of the barbarians; therefore, the style was Gothic, that is, barbaric. Although for more than a century now the term has ceased to carry a stigma, it was coined in the sixteenth century as a term of contempt.

In general, Gothic art is more homogeneous than is Romanesque art. If the style differs in France, England, Spain, and Italy, and if a thorough study of the field uncovers local variations within each country, those differences are minor when compared with the contrasts in the architecture and sculpture of neighboring regions during the Romanesque period. To some extent, the greater uniformity of the Gothic may be attributed to bands of lay workmen who journeyed from town to town as opportunities for employment arose. More important, however, were the new circumstances of the late twelfth and thirteenth centuries. At this time, the royal government in France was slowly gaining power. Though the feudal system had by no means disappeared, the royal vassals were not so independent as they had been in the eleventh century. The rise of towns, fostered by the kingship, altered the structure of society. During the thirteenth century under Philip Augustus, France attained a degree of unity unknown before, and even though subsequently the English conquered large provinces of France, and in spite of the rival power of the Dukes of Burgundy, the trend was toward increased unity. Moreover, means of communication slowly improved and brought a fuller knowledge to any one region of the activities in other areas. These changes fostered a French Gothic style rather than an individual Norman style or Provençal style.

The growth of towns in particular distinguished the Gothic era from the Romanesque, which had been so largely the product of the monasteries. The cathedral was the center of the town life, many of whose activities took place in it or in front of it; it partook of the character of a civic monument. Each group in the town played a part in building and adorning its great church. The several guilds might donate stained-glass windows, or undertake the responsibility for a chapel, dedicated to the patron saint of that guild. At Chartres, the townsmen harnessed themselves to carts to draw stone to the cathedral, a contribution of personal service prompted first by religious enthusiasm, but not unmixed with civic pride. The rivalry between towns was intense. Paris built its Notre Dame first, rearing its vaults 110 feet in the clear; Amiens, a little later, raised its vault 139 feet above the pavement; then Beauvais outdid them both with its cathedral 158 feet high internally. In Beauvais, the zeal to outstrip its rivals was carried to such lengths that parts of the building collapsed and had to be replaced. Again, Siena, always jealous of Florence, built its sumptuous cathedral first. When Florence accepted the challenge, her cathedral was made much larger than the Sienese. Not to be outdone, the Sienese determined to convert their new church into merely the transepts of a tremendous structure; they never completed more than the foundations, but the intention remains clear.

This pride of the towns in the cathedrals and the active role taken by the townsfolk in their construction has led to a widespread supposition that there were no architects. It is true that the title of architect rarely appeared in the medieval records; the man who performed that function was variously described as master builder, master mason, or clerk of the works. These craftsmen differed from modern architects in their relation to the process of building, since they combined the functions of architect, contractor, and foreman. But the idea that such complicated designs could be the product of a community is absurd. There must have been some individual whose vision, whose sense of proportion, and whose knowledge of structure made him essentially the architect, in whose mind the conception of the cathedral crystallized. That such a person might allow his subordinates greater latitude than is possible today, or that the subordinates developed their own ideas in carving the capitals or other parts of the building, does not mean that there was no architect in charge. Indeed, the names of many of these master builders have been preserved. What we do not have from the Middle Ages, in contrast to later periods, is any information about the personalities of these men. They remain merely names to us. The conception of fame had not yet grown to the point where an architect or artist might take steps to ensure the preservation and dissemination of his reputation.

Even if we recognize the importance of the secular and civic backing of the cathedrals, we must still admit the spiritual force behind them. That the town should choose to make the cathedral its biggest monument is in itself significant. The soaring lines of the church, its buttresses, pinnacles, and spires express a religious enthusiasm and aspiration never reached before or since. No other style has touched that summit of mystical exaltation the Gothic so perfectly expressed.

In architecture, the Gothic style is characterized by the pointed arch. It spreads from France over Western Europe, beginning late in the twelfth century and lasting until the Renaissance—that is, through the fourteenth century in Italy and into the sixteenth century north of the Alps. C. H. Moore defines Gothic architecture as 'a system of vaults, supports, and buttresses, the supports strong enough to bear the crushing weight only, and the stability maintained by a perfect equilibrium of thrusts.' This definition is as valuable for what it omits as for what it contains. Most surprising is its lack of any reference to the pointed arch. Yet while that feature is prominent in the Gothic style, it is found in other styles, and round arches occur in Gothic buildings. Throughout the Romanesque period, wherever Saracenic influence exists, one may encounter the pointed arch; Monreale Cathedral uses it consistently, though the building is Romanesque not Gothic. The Spanish Romanesque, and even that of Provence, use pointed arches. On the other hand, in so Gothic a building as Chartres Cathedral, the nave clearstory windows, though not their smaller divisions, are round-arched, and so too are the diagonal ribs of Notre Dame in Paris. This shape is a less certain touchstone of the Gothic than is popularly supposed.

Moore's definition mentions no wall, but merely the three great structural elements. In the developed French Gothic the wall ceases to exist as a structural member. The building becomes a cage of glass and stone, with windows the full width from pier to pier. If some wall remains, for example below the aisle windows, it plays no other role than to exclude the weather. It is as though the Romanesque wall had been cut into sections, and each section turned outward at right angles to the mass of the building to become a buttress. The early French Gothic is a structural system composed of the elements mentioned by Moore. Adequate as is this definition in many respects, it has one serious defect. It applies only to early French Gothic; not to Gothic architecture in other countries, or even to later phases of the style in France.

The emphasis on structure implies the desirability of examining the several parts of the Gothic cathedral individually before we attempt to discuss any one monument in its entirety. First in importance is the vault. While logical, the vaulting of Sant' Ambrogio in Milan (fig. 119) has several shortcomings. The vaults tend to be heavy; the crown or apex of the vault, because of the use of the semicircle for all the ribs, remains domical. This produces some outward pressure along the length of the wall rib, and in addition tends to break up the interior into separate units; but above all in Sant' Ambrogio, the lack of a clearstory results in a very dark church. As we have seen, the Normans in St. Etienne at Caen (fig. 123) reverted to the clearstory, and to a vault with level crowns, but at the expense of heavy walls and of less than semicircular ribs. To meet these objections, the Gothic builders made two fundamental innovations in vaulting. First,

to raise the crown of the transverse and wall ribs to the same level as the crown of the diagonal ribs, they adopted pointed arches. This step was taken only in slow and tentative fashion. At Morienval, in the ambulatory of a very

134. *Ambulatory Vault*, Morienval (*c.* 1120).

small church, perhaps rebuilt about 1120, the arches were pointed (fig. 134), though in the earlier parts of the same building, they remained the simpler round arches. The pointed arches brought the apex of the ribs around the edges of each area to be covered by the vault approximately to the level reached by the diagonal ribs. Elsewhere, the builders pointed the arches, but not enough to give the desired result; consequently, they had to insert above the arch a small section of wall in order to gain the necessary height, as, for example, at Bury. In the fully developed Gothic, such makeshifts were unnecessary because of the bolder use of this device.

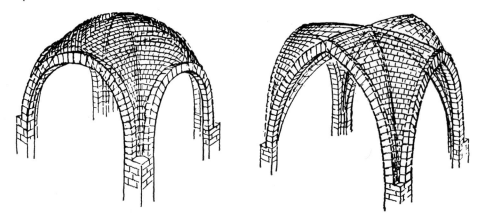

135. *Romanesque and Gothic Vaults.* Diagram.

The pointed arch could by itself produce a vault with level crowns, that is, one where all of the ribs rise to the same level. Especially in a vault over a rectangular area, if the height is to be achieved simply by pointing wall arches, they must be very sharply pointed indeed. Moreover, the Gothic builders tried to concentrate the thrusts of their vaults along a single line opposite each pier on the outside of the building. The diagram of Romanesque and Gothic vaults (fig. 135) shows that the Romanesque wall arches begin to curve at the same point as do the transverse and diagonal ribs, and therefore cover a triangle of the outer wall surface. Logically the buttress should cover that triangle, and thus become broader than the Gothic builders desired. In addition, the Romanesque scheme reduces the wall area in the clearstory, which the more open Gothic arrangement converts to window. The Gothic designers *stilt* their wall ribs; that is, instead of allowing the wall ribs to begin to curve at the same point as the diagonal ribs, they insert a colonnette to raise the springing of the wall arches above that of the others. Therefore, the under surface of the vault assumes a warped form, called the *plowshare twist*. A second result is the greater window area in the clearstory level; a third, that the wall rib does not need to be so sharply pointed to produce a vault with level crowns; and fourth, the area covered by the vault on the outer wall of the church is restricted to a line instead of a triangle. This type of vault is illustrated in the nave of Amiens Cathedral (fig. 136).

In the matured Gothic of the thirteenth century—for example, at Amiens and Chartres—the designers reverted to the quadripartite system of Lombard origin and abandoned the sexpartite arrangement. This was not true while the style was developing; on the contrary, many twelfth-century Gothic buildings converted the sexpartite system to Gothic structure, as in the nave of Notre Dame at Paris, or the Cathedral

136. *Cathedral,* Amiens (1220–79) Interior, vaults 139' high; nave width 48'; total interior length 438'.

of Laon. But one advantage of the Gothic vault is its adaptability to any area. Realizing this after the style had been perfected, the builders returned to the uniform quadripartite system and abandoned the alternate arrangement of sexpartite vaults. The domical character of Lombard vaults, prominent in a square plan, would become absurdly emphasized if the plan of the vault were oblong. The longer the rectangle, the greater the discrepancy between the crowns of round diagonal and wall ribs, if they spring from the same level. With the flexible Gothic, by pointing and stilting, any height may be reached even over a limited span.

Next to the vault, the second element in the definition of Gothic is the support, which includes the piers of the nave arcade and the shafts above them in the triforium and clearstory levels designed to carry the vault. Since the Gothic structure grows out of the Romanesque, one would expect to find a colonnette corresponding to each rib, and so one does, above the level of the capitals in the nave arcade. As the proportions of the building turn toward lightness, these shafts become more attenuated than in the Romanesque, and therefore emphasize verticality. In the piers, however, the story is different. The membered Romanesque pier, however logical, tends to large bulk; it defines and separates the space in the nave from the volumes in the aisles. Though one may pass readily from one to the other, the several parts are conceived as visual units. The first step taken by the Gothic seems retrogressive. The membered pier is replaced by the round column, whose somewhat smaller mass frees the floor area and allows the space to flow from nave to aisles, as though the two were parts of the same volume. However, to use plain columns here means that the apparent support for the vault ribs must stop at the level of the capitals, which, though not structurally objectionable, is weak in appearance. The strong verticality of the colonnettes seems contradicted or at least interrupted by the absence of a similar vertical emphasis in the piers. Therefore, the architects placed a single colonnette in front of the sixth nave pier of Notre

137. *Notre Dame*, Paris (1163–1235) Interior, vaults 110′ high, nave 46′ wide.

Dame in Paris (fig. 137), west of the crossing. Although this one member seems to support three colonnettes, it serves to continue the movement from the vaults to the pavement, or vice versa. This pier is lopsided; in the seventh pier at Paris, similar shafts were applied to the column to support the aisle vaults and under the arches of the nave arcade, as well as on the face of the pier. This symmetrical result proves effective both structurally and visually. The sturdy piers of Chartres (fig. 142) grow into the elegant shafts of Amiens (fig. 136), which suggest not only the engineering knowledge accumulated through trial and error, but also the zeal for height, which reaches its culmination in the Cathedral of Beauvais. The

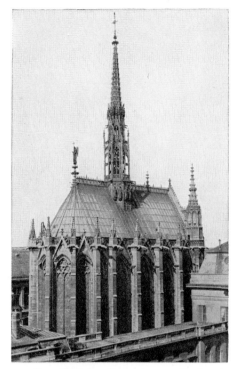

139. *Ste. Chapelle*, Paris (1245–48) Interior length 98', width 35'.

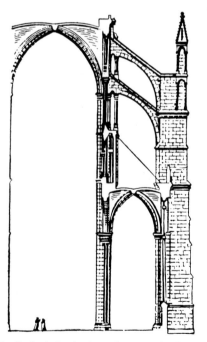

138. *Cathedral*, Amiens (1220–79) Section, vaults 139' high.

increased technical skill of the later builders in the fourteenth and fifteenth centuries permitted a partial return to the elaborately membered pier, but with its parts so small and delicate that it remained light.

The buttress is the third and last of the principal structural elements. A Romanesque pier buttress has a massiveness characteristic of the style. The problem lies in connecting the thrusts of the nave vaults with the buttress; if placed against the clearstory, its lower portion will block the aisle. The Lombards sacrificed the clearstory to galleries; the latter contain arches that transfer the thrust of the nave vaults over the aisles to the pier buttresses on the outer wall of the church. The thick walls in Norman churches appear to be heavy enough to care for the problem, but the Gothic walls are thin or non-existent. The matured Gothic buttress (fig. 138) has two parts. The first, the pier buttress, derived from the Romanesque, is built as a solid mass at right angles to the axis of the church, against the wall of the aisle, and in perfected examples rises high above it. This part through its sheer weight counteracts the outward pressure of the vaults. In such a single-aisled church as the Ste. Chapelle in Paris (fig. 139), this buttress is set against the body of the build-ing. A series of offsets on its outer edge makes the buttress heavier at the bottom than at the top. This device is effective both as structure and in appearance, since it slopes the buttress inward against the outward pressure of the vault.

The second part, the flying buttress, is peculiar to Gothic, though its germ exists in Ste. Trinité at Caen, where the Normans experimented with a half-arch under the aisle roof, as they did also in Durham Cathedral. Although too low at Caen to meet the thrusts of the nave effectively, this engineering expedient was pushed above the aisle roof as the Gothic style grew, and so was

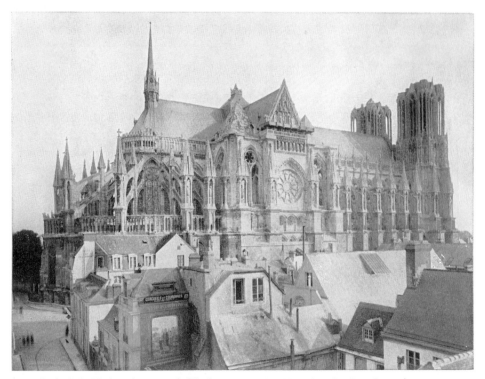

140. *Cathedral*, Rheims (1211–90) Flank, towers 267′ high; interior length 453′.

141. *Notre Dame*, Paris (1163–1235) Façade 135′ wide; towers 207′ high.

brought up to the point where it touched the lower parts of the nave vault. This exposed half-arch, which carries a diagonal course of stone, rests its lower end on the pier buttress and its upper against the clearstory of the nave. The flying buttress functions as a prop to transfer the thrusts outward over the aisle roof. This half-arch has very little inward thrust; alone it would be almost valueless to resist the powerful outward pressure of the nave vaults, but as a connective its value is enormous. Without it French Gothic could never have attained its height and openness. Flying buttresses appear on the flank of Rheims Cathedral (fig. 140), where their soaring lines express both the vertical mass and the skeletal character of Gothic structure. At first in the evolution of the flying buttress, a single half-arch sufficed, but in time the Gothic builders realized that there were two points to be resisted, the vault proper and the pressure upon the walls just above the vault produced by wind on the huge roof. Consequently, the flying buttress was doubled, one half-arch above another.

In addition to these structural components, the Gothic has many elements less fundamental, but prominent in appearance. To a greater extent than any other style, the Gothic avoids applied decoration; its richer details tend to be interwoven with the structure, which itself is made decorative. The large windows, for example, are patterned with *tracery*, bars of stone interlocked like arches. The wind pressure sustained by these windows is more than could be borne by stained glass, composed of small pieces held in place by pliable lead bars. Although iron rods divide these windows at intervals, additional support is necessary lest the rods be-

142. *Cathedral,* Chartres (1194–1260) Interior, vaults 121′ high; nave width 54′; total length 427′.

come inordinately heavy. Therefore, vertical stone members, called *mullions,* break the whole window area into smaller units, and support openwork or traceried arches.

As these changes in structure arise, a similar metamorphosis alters the façade. The west front of the Gothic cathedral, derived from such Norman façades as St. Etienne at Caen (fig. 124), reflects the interior. The buttresses of its flanking towers mark the separation of nave and side aisles, and the successive stories echo the nave arcade, triforium, and clearstory. It remained to give this division more vivid expression. The early façade of Notre Dame in Paris (fig. 141), retains these divisions, with the middle section reduced to a row of

143. *Cathedral*, Chartres (1194–1260) Façade 157′ wide; south spire 344′ high; north spire 377′ high.

sculptured figures. The doors are now larger, and the opening itself expanded by a splayed surface, that is, by a diagonal plane to either side of the doors, which emphasizes them and affords a field for sculpture. The windows, too, are splayed and larger than in the Romanesque. In later examples, such as the façades of Amiens and Rheims cathedrals, the corner buttresses of the towers project boldly from the plane of the façades. The doors become porches as deep as the projection of the buttresses. In these welcoming portals, the sculpture of the cathedral reaches its culmination.

The Gothic builders preferred to terminate the towers with spires, though in most instances local history prevented their completion. The towers of Notre Dame in Paris were intended to support spires. The powerful verticals of the buttresses demand some continuation. At Chartres Cathedral (fig. 143), the magnificent south spire to the right is approximately contemporary with the twelfth-century façade, but the north spire was not constructed until early in the sixteenth century and is consequently different in style. During the early Gothic the French felt that a spire should grow imperceptibly from the tower. Therefore, in the south spire at Chartres, two transitions were effected: that from the vertical plane of the tower walls to the sloping surfaces of the spire, and that from the square plan of the tower to the octagonal plan of the spire. The soaring dormer windows compose at once the top story of the tower and the lowest stage of the spire, making so subtle a transition from one to the other that one hardly realizes it has been made. Moldings rise above the center of each dormer and on the angles of the spire to prolong the vertical movement.

Many have observed the asymmetry of Gothic buildings, and undoubtedly that is important. However, in most cathedrals the obvious asymmetrical features were constructed at different dates. Neither the Gothic nor the Romanesque builders were hostile to symmetry; they simply did not make a fetish of it, and were willing to depart from it whenever circumstances afforded some reason to do so. The Gothic castle is usually unsymmetrical and picturesque, because the builders took advantage of the possibilities of the site. If the ground is level and the fortress built at one time, as at Aigues Mortes, erected by St. Louis in the thirteenth century, tower balances tower, gate echoes gate, and only the keep remains as an asymmetrical element. The readiness with which the Gothic builders gave up symmetry allows few Gothic buildings to be absolutely uniform around an axis. Although the façade of the Cathedral of Paris is symmetrical in its larger elements, more than twenty discrepancies can be found between the right and left halves of the design.

Important as are the elements that compose the Gothic cathedral, the whole is still more significant. Each cathedral has its personality, none more

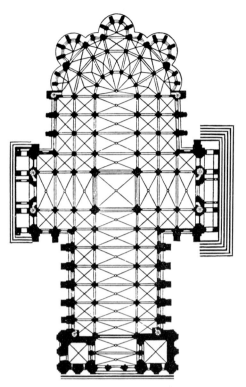

144. *Cathedral,* Chartres (1194–1260) Total length 427'.

than Chartres (figs. 142, 143), dating chiefly from 1194 to 1260. The plan (fig. 144) is different from that of all other styles. Because of the elimination of the wall, the plan comprises only a series of points, connected by lines that indicate the ribs in the vault. This lace-like pattern discloses the openness of design, as it points to the vast window area. To credit this openness wholly to a desire for light is not justifiable. The stained-glass windows of Chartres form a decorative expression of the religious exaltation of the Gothic age; but stained glass excludes a large proportion of the available light, bathing the

church in color whose beautiful tones are too dark for adequate lighting. In the detail of the Annunciation (Plate II, facing p. 269) from one of the west windows of Chartres, the figures are set on a red ground but the tone is not of uniform intensity. Blue, varying from pale to dark, dominates the costumes, with accents of golden yellow, lavender, and white. The features and details of costume are stylized; the purpose is decorative and symbolic, not realistic.

For the thirteenth century, the beauty of color compensated for the decreased quantity of illumination. As one enters Chartres Cathedral on a sunny day, shafts of kaleidoscopic color reveal the structural system. The form of the piers with four colonnettes attached to the central core is made more subtle by a slight alternation in design. Where one pier is composed of an octagonal core with four round shafts engaged on it, its neighbors reverse the scheme, having a circular core with four octagonal shafts. Most visitors to Chartres are never aware of this alternation, yet it impresses itself imperceptibly by the slight rhythm in design. These angular and curved forms add visual interest, since each catches contrasted patterns of shade, the change from a smooth transition of light to shade in the rounded surfaces to the sharper breaks afforded by the octagons.

Each pier supports five shafts, to reflect the five ribs of the quadripartite vaults. Those shafts too change from the smallest ones, which support the wall ribs, to the largest, which respond to the transverse ribs. Since the triforium occupies the vertical space cut off by the sloping roof over the aisles, no windows pierce that level; instead, in each bay a group of four arches opens on a passage. The clearstory windows spread from pier to pier, and utilize to the full the advantages for stained glass offered by the Gothic system.

Through the piers and their shafts, the builders create a dramatic expression of height, great in itself but even more accented in design. It might be hard to show a necessity for this vast space, but spiritually its worth is incalculable. As a result, the polyphony of the medieval chant reverberates from the vaults above, to fill the church with music and produce an atmosphere that can be gained in no other way. In the last analysis, though, this height is an expression of civic prestige and of the devotion of the Middle Ages. As one advances through the church, a succession of vistas meets the eye. One sees through the nave arcades to the aisles, through them to the transepts; but the culmination of the cathedral is the radiant east end, where the aisle winds around the apse and gives access to a series of chapels. The curved plan here results in great richness of effect, so that new beauties meet the eye at every step, perspectives change, and the patterns of light and shadow flow from one part of the church to another.

The same dramatic verticality governs the exterior. Soaring buttresses march along the flank of the church; each draws the attention upward until, through the crowning pinnacles, stone merges with sky. At the west end, towers crowned with spires accent the principal entrance and provide a brilliant climax for the building. Not only through its verticality does the Gothic cathedral differ from the Romanesque; its whole relation to space has altered. These buttresses and spires, unlike the wall in a Romanesque church, do not seem to enclose a volume; instead they link the building to the surrounding atmosphere. The interior space flows readily from nave to aisles, transepts, and ambulatory, with none of the divisions conceived as discrete volumes, but as ramifications of the same volume. In the same way, the large window area invites that inner space to join with the outer air. The thin sheet of glass hardly interrupts this union. As the buttresses project from the wall plane, they break up any sense of enclosure that plane might otherwise establish, and seem to soften the union with the out-of-doors. Their pinnacles and pointed spires melt into the sky.

This relation of the building to space both inside and out contradicts the method of the Greek temple, as the mystical Christianity of the Gothic age reverses the rational religion of the Greeks. The Greek temple clings to earth, the Gothic church springs heavenward. The Parthenon defines its mass; Chartres is less clear and less self-contained. It is the difference between the static and dynamic, the intellectual and the emotional. As a whole and in its parts, the Parthenon seems governed by the mind of man, and as reasonable as a proposition in Euclid; whereas the Gothic, like medieval speculation, expresses the intangible, and transcends the human in its hopeful quest for something above and beyond.

The same devotional spirit molds the sculpture, without which the French cathedral is more incomplete than the Greek temple. Like the Romanesque, Gothic sculpture is predominantly ecclesiastical, and, to be understood, it must be approached with some knowledge of medieval interpretation. It is didactic in purpose, calculated to illustrate and emphasize the teachings of the Church. Christ is glorified in all the world, and, therefore, all is worthy of representation in His temple. In his encyclopedia, Vincent of Beauvais groups the knowledge of his day under four divisions, the mirrors of nature, instruction, morals, and history. Thus the sculptor may include plants or animals; he may present symbolic figures of music, astronomy, geometry, and philosophy; or the seven virtues and seven vices; or he may deal with that part of history worthy of remembrance, namely, sacred history.

To understand Gothic sculpture, one must realize that any figure or object may be open to a threefold interpretation. Art is a script, a calculus, and a symbolic code. Iconography dictates the way an artist shall present any given figure. Thus God, the angels, and the apostles are carved with bare feet; other characters will be shod. To represent them otherwise might not be merely in-

correct; it might also be heretical. A stalk with a few leaves signifies a tree and indicates that the scene takes place on earth. A tower with door implies a town; if, however, an angel stands on the tower, it establishes the location as the heavenly Jerusalem. The nimbus, or halo, indicates sanctity; when a cross is inscribed within it, the figure is divine. Through such a pictographic script, the identification of the figures and the scene is made clear.

But the subject itself is only part of its significance. The place occupied by any figure, with relation to the center of the design where Christ usually appears, has its meaning. The higher the position in the design, the greater is the honor; the place on Christ's right hand is more distinguished than that on His left. It must always be borne in mind that, since Christ faces the observer, His right hand is on the left as one looks at the composition. The Elect are always placed on the right hand of Christ in the Last Judgment, with the Damned to the left. Some of the clearstory windows in Chartres depict prophets who carry the Evangelists on their shoulders. Medieval dogma teaches that although the Evangelists rest on the prophets, yet, because they have a direct knowledge of the Saviour, they possess a higher spiritual vantage ground and a wider outlook than their forebears. Certain numbers have precise symbolism. Because of its association with the Trinity, *three* connotes things spiritual. *Four*, the number of the elements that compose the world according to the

Middle Ages (which in this theory followed antiquity), pertains to the earth. The sum of these two numbers produces *seven*, the number of humanity and an indication of the dual nature of man, partly spiritual, partly of the earth. *Twelve*, the product of three and four, explains the selection of twelve apostles, the twelve lesser prophets, and so on.

Finally, the Middle Ages believed that profound meanings are hidden in the Scriptures, allusions yielding their significance only through analogies. Thus, types or forerunners of Christ appear frequently in the Old Testament: the brazen serpent, lifted up by Moses in the wilderness to free the Israelites from a plague of serpents, suggests Christ raised on the cross to expiate the sins of the world. Melchizedek, as priest and king, prefigures Christ, and his bread and wine given to Abraham foretells the Holy Eucharist. The parable of the Wise and Foolish Virgins recalls the account in the Gospels, and also typifies the Elect and the Lost. The lion serves as the emblem of the Resurrection; in medieval belief the lion's cubs were as though dead for three days after birth, at the expiration of which period the lion returns and breathes on them and brings them back to life. These three days of apparent death parallel Christ's descent into hell between Good Friday and Easter Sunday.

Because these interpretations are possible, it does not follow that all of them are applicable in every instance. Nor is it certain that these meanings were evident to laymen, even in the thirteenth century; doubtless the clergy understood these matters, and explained them to their flocks to illustrate some point in a sermon, but such esoteric meanings were probably hidden from the throng.

The sculpture of the Gothic period differs from that of the Romanesque, even though it grows from it. Like its predecessor, Gothic sculpture is polychromatic. The colors, until the later Gothic, are conventional; they do not imitate tones in nature, but instead are conceived as decoration. On the other hand, where Romanesque sculpture seems to have been carved after the stones were placed in the building, the Gothic statues were in most instances carved on the ground, and set in place when they were finished. Moreover, the sculptor's technique advanced. He no longer turns to ivories and manuscripts for his inspiration; he thinks more in terms of stone, and consequently develops a greater roundness in his figures. The folds of drapery are not indicated by line with little change of surface, but become more deeply modeled. The features approximate their normal human proportions and projections, and catch a richer pattern of light and shade. Rigidity of pose relaxes to allow the statues to stand easily. With the full development of Gothic sculpture, idealism dominates. The figures, like human beings but without individual traits, are generalized and perfected; conceived as types, they have a certain universality

145. *West Portals*, Cathedral, Chartres (1145–70) *c.* 50′ wide.

of expression. As a result, the Gothic figures acquire a monumentality adapted to the new style.

These new qualities did not appear suddenly. The west portals of Chartres Cathedral (fig. 145), completed in the middle of the twelfth century, are transitional between the two styles, but by common agreement they are classed as Gothic. Frequently the west front contains a series of royal figures; although these are often identified as the kings and queens of France, the Middle Ages would hardly have considered secular characters worthy of representation in so important a place; thus they must be interpreted as the ancestors of Christ,

the kings and queens of Judah listed in the first chapter of the Gospel according to St. Matthew.

The most conservative part is the tympanum over the central door, where the symbols of the Evangelists surround Christ in hieratic order. His head is backed by a halo inscribed with a cross, though such a symbol here is unnecessary for identification. His drapery is folded in linear patterns which hardly indent the mass. Indeed in some parts, such as the raised right arm, the folds swirl so as to bear only a remote resemblance to the body beneath, but a close one to the pattern-like character of Romanesque art. The Christ has a

146. *Royal Ancestors of Christ, Kings and Queens of Judah*, West Portal, Cathedral, Chartres (1145–70) 20'6" high.

greater roundness of form, more feeling for the mass of the figure. The head is more natural than the diagrammatic heads in the Romanesque, with more highly modeled features, and perhaps less use of the drill.

However, the kings and queens who line the portal (fig. 146) are remarkably elongated. They grow from the columns they rest on, and emphasize their subordination to the verticality of the architecture; not only are the proportions tall and slender, but the patterns of the clothing reinforce the direction. The long flowing sleeves of the queen, her braided hair, and the folds of her dress create an insistence on Gothic movement. Such willingness to subordinate sculpture to architecture and to distort the dimensions of the figure continues Romanesque principles. However, where the Romanesque sculpture might be applied to door jambs to enrich the architecture, but with little reference to construction, the new Gothic interest in structure compels a corresponding emphasis on it in sculpture. Also, the heads change in the degree of realism. At Chartres, these have considerable individuality, a flesh of naturalism, contradicted by the bodies, but otherwise analogous to the realism of Greek sculp-

147. *Coronation of the Virgin, Dormition of the Virgin, Prophets and Kings*, North Tympanum, Façade, Notre Dame, Paris (1163–1235) 23'3" high.

ture about the time of Myron. These heads represent an attitude opposed to the stylized, expressive heads of the Romanesque.

The west portals of Chartres Cathedral, dating from the middle of the twelfth century, are at most transitional to the Gothic. Representative of that style in the early thirteenth century in sculpture is the north tympanum on the west front of Notre Dame in Paris (fig. 147). The architectural change between the west fronts of Chartres and Paris produces here a more pointed arch, with a consequent enlargement of the tympanum area. Therefore, instead of treating the tympanum as a single composition, the sculptor breaks it up into three bands. The lowest zone contains three prophets on our left, three kings on our right. These we may interpret as the spiritual and physical ancestors of Christ, with the spiritual side given the place of honor on the right hand of Christ, whose figure appears above. The middle range depicts the Resurrection of the Virgin. When the last earthly hours of the Madonna arrived, the apostles gathered in her presence from the four corners of the world. Christ reappeared to receive the soul of His Mother and translate it to heaven. The apostles sit or stand around the bier, in meditation on the miracle before them, with St. Peter, the chief apostle in the Western church, significantly at the left, and thus to the right of Christ. Finally, in the top range appears the Coronation of the Virgin. Christ has placed the Virgin on

148. *Beau Dieu*, Cathedral, Amiens (*c.* 1225) *c.* 10′ high.

His right, and offers her the scepter in token of his intention to share His power in heaven with her.

These figures project boldly from the

background, and if the proportion of the heads is still a little large for the bodies, the discrepancy is not so great as previously. The drapery too has changed, even as compared with the carving at Chartres. Large, simple, majestic folds replace the rippling pattern, and lend to the whole concept a monumentality and breadth with a touch of idealism about it. A certain ease in pose and freedom of movement animate these figures. The artist conveys his message less through symbolism and more through human characters.

The full development of Gothic sculpture, however, is accomplished in Amiens and Rheims cathedrals. The Beau Dieu at Amiens (fig. 148), from the first half of the thirteenth century, central in the scheme of the west front, adorns the post, or *trumeau*, that divides the two halves of the middle door. He is, therefore, isolated from the saints who line the portal where stood the kings and queens at Chartres. While symbolism is still important, it is now subordinate. This is Christ triumphant; He stands on two grotesque animals, and just below two more appear in relief on the pedestal. These four animals are the adder and the basilisk, the lion and the dragon. Since the lion is a symbol of antichrist, the dragon of the devil, the basilisk of death, and the adder of sin, this figure commemorates Christ risen from the tomb and triumphant over the powers of darkness. But these symbols are no more needed to convey the message than is the crossed halo to identify the figure of Christ. This statue

is now highly idealized, its features rendered in broad planes, and all marks of individuality and all physical defects eliminated. In fact, we encounter the same careful selection of details to create idealism and impersonality that we have observed in fifth-century Greek sculpture. Indeed, the courses pursued by Greek and by medieval sculpture are curiously parallel; each started with a substitution of convention and symbolism for objective treatment, but later turned to an ideal conception, only to abandon that in the end in favor of a literal realism.

The Beau Dieu invites comparison with the sculpture of the Parthenon. Each represents the complete incarnation of the artistic ideals of its epoch. In quality, there is not much to choose between them. Different as they are, each fulfills its purpose on the building. The Gothic figure is clothed, whereas many of the Greek statues are nude. The body had become identified with evil during the earlier Middle Ages; at the very least, it was insignificant compared with the soul; the less seen of it the better. Any humiliation of the flesh might be a gain to the spirit. Fasting, flagellation, or use of the hair shirt, common during these centuries, were directed to that end. The artists avoided the nude wherever possible. When it does appear in medieval art, in scenes of the creation of the world, of Adam and Eve, or of the Resurrection and Last Judgment, the figures were rendered on a small scale, hardly bigger than puppets. Hence, in absolute contrast with antiquity, all the larger figures of medieval art are clothed.

The amount of sculpture on a medieval cathedral is too great to have been executed by a single man. Differences of hand are inevitable, but the similarity of expression, not the difference, is remarkable. However, the Annunciation and Visitation groups at Rheims Cathedral (fig. 149), in the second half of the thirteenth century, vary widely in treatment. The Annunciation figures to the left are youthful in face and figure. Their costumes fall in broad folds, analogous to the treatment of the Beau Dieu. Mary and Elizabeth in the Visitation, on the other hand, are mature; their figures are bulkier, their features particularized, though not beyond the limits of idealization. In the head of Elizabeth, a few lines in the face and even more the general treatment of the head sympathetically suggest old age. A maze of small folds complicates the drapery. Instead of reverting to the drapery type of Chartres, these folds point the way to later developments; they do not create a pattern, but suggest softer stuff with a view to representation. By comparison with the Beau Dieu, these characters in the Visitation are more animated. Their gestures are not so restrained, nor do they stand so quietly as the figures from Amiens Cathe-

149. *Annunciation and Visitation*, Cathedral, Rheims (*c.* 1280) 10′2″ high.

dral. Though it is not pronounced, these figures foretell the trend toward realism, with a partial loss of the union with architecture so clear in earlier medieval sculpture.

The larger figures by no means exhaust the sculpture of the cathedral. Its encyclopedic character is even more evident in the reliefs and the stained glass. A single example, chosen from the two rows of quatrefoils below the principal figures on the west front of Amiens Cathedral (fig. 150), shows in the upper tier the signs of the zodiac and in the

settings are reduced to a minimum; a stalk with a few leaves on it, or the tendrils of a vine identify the scene. And yet even in these tiny figures, the feeling for roundness is evident. If not masterpieces, such compositions fulfill their decorative function, and widen our knowledge of the Middle Ages.

Finally, the exuberant spirits of Gothic times find an outlet in the grotesques. Some serve as gargoyles, or water spouts, with the figures, especially the legs, contorted to adapt them to this purpose. But most of them balance

150. *Signs of the Zodiac and Activities of the Months*, West Façade, Cathedral, Amiens (*c.* 1225) 2'6" size of single quatrefoil.

lower the activities of the months. In this particular group the Ram, corresponding roughly to the month of March, is paired with a farmer spading the soil; the Bull, for April, matches a hunter with a falcon on his wrist; and the Twins, for May, parallel a man seated out-of-doors, basking in the spring sun. These reliefs exhibit the same selection of detail as the larger figures;

on the buttresses, peer over the parapet, or crouch on the cornices; an exception to the rule in Gothic, they serve no structural or liturgical purpose. If a few of them are human, the majority are pure figments of the mind, hybrids of real and imaginary animals. Doubtless God could have made such creatures, but certainly God thought better of it. Carved in the same broad planes as the sober sculpture, these monsters animate the cathedral to its top. Such carvings, and in fact all Gothic sculpture, bereft of their settings, are meaningless. They are too closely related in interpretation and in design to the sculptural ensemble, as well as to the architectural design, to bear separation. When studied in their setting and combined with the cathedral, they contribute to the most complete expression of spiritual exaltation yet produced by Christianity.

XI THE DIFFUSION AND LATER HISTORY OF GOTHIC ART

Little doubt can exist that the focus of Gothic art lies in France. The very name, *opus francigenum,* by which it was known in the Middle Ages proves that. But the influence of the French style spread in all directions, and as each country accepted the new fashion, it modified French Gothic art to meet its own local needs. Buildings with indigenous variations, moreover, are almost as early as those that adhere to the French manner. León Cathedral in Spain follows the style of the thirteenth-century cathedrals of northern France, in plan, structure, and elevation. The vast Cathedral of Seville, on the other hand, has many points that contrast with French work, some of them traceable to climatic differences. The flat roof, or at least a roof of gentle slope, produces a fundamentally different exterior. Since a triforium is caused by the sloping roof over the aisle, a flat roof there results in a contraction or even a suppression of that internal division. The brilliant southern sun makes it desirable to curtail the window area characteristic of French Gothic buildings. Thus in Spanish Gothic architecture, broad wall surfaces, pierced only here and there by windows, supplant the glazed areas of French Gothic. Such small openings protect the building from excessive heat in summer, but leave a gloomy interior. A Spanish interior is apt to be interrupted by a high *coro,* or choir screen, which separates that part of the church from the rest.

With these and many other differences in detail, Spanish Gothic architecture is no mere copy of French.

In Italy, a series of monasteries, including San Galgano near Siena, imported a French style. It, however, was the Gothic of Burgundy, more austere than the better-known architecture of northern France. Climate and the Italian love for the horizontal soon exerted their influence so that the cathedrals of Siena and Orvieto, in spite of a decorative scheme of pointed arches, tracery, and pinnacles, rejected the northern version of the Gothic style. The nearly flat roofs, the polychromy inherited from Tuscan Romanesque architecture, the indifference to Gothic structure, the small windows and broad wall surfaces, all betray an Italian feeling for the horizontal in contrast to the verticality of the northern style.

Cologne Cathedral in Germany, begun in 1248, though different in many details, is modeled on Amiens. More original are the *Hallenkirchen* or hall churches. Though a similar type may be found in southwestern France, the Germans developed their own form and showed great distinction in handling it. Such churches as St. Elizabeth at Marburg exemplify the system. The aisles are built as high, or almost as high, as the nave itself, and are covered by the same roof. The interior system of nave arcade, triforium, and clearstory is eliminated. The piers soar upward to support the vaults directly; this arrangement permits the windows in the aisles sufficient height to light the nave.

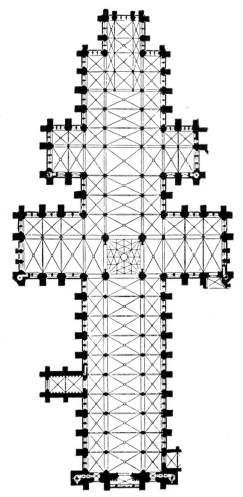

151. *Cathedral,* Salisbury (1220–58) 473′ x 230′.

The main steps in the history of the Gothic style in France are duplicated in other countries. Thus, in the late twelfth and early thirteenth centuries, much of the Romanesque spirit was retained; then the local style, under French influence or otherwise, formed itself, and as proficiency in building increased, the expression was further modified during later years. These divergent styles are too numerous to be discussed here; we must be content with one or two examples chosen arbitrarily to demonstrate national contrast in architecture and the general course taken by Gothic architecture in its later years.

The cathedrals of Amiens and Salisbury were both begun in 1220, but the latter shows the English solution of the problem. The plan (fig. 151) in the shape of an archiepiscopal cross has two pairs of transepts, a large one approximately in the center of the building from end to end, and a smaller one further to the east. Instead of the complex polygonal apse and ambulatory of Amiens, the English substitute a square east end. The nave is long in proportion, with ten bays instead of the seven

152. *Cathedral*, Salisbury (1220–58) Interior, nave 40' wide; vaults 81' high.

customary in France. The façade projects beyond the sides of the church and is treated as a screen, without emphasis on the portals; indeed an English cathedral is normally entered through a porch on the side of the nave, or sometimes through a transept portal. A cloister fits into the corner between nave and transepts.

The interior (fig. 152) retains more of a Romanesque flavor than does the French cathedral. The quadripartite vaults recall those across the Channel, but the support is not visually continued to the floor and does not correspond to each of the ribs; instead, at Salisbury clusters of shafts rest on brackets in the triforium level. The unbroken horizontal lines of the lower edge of the triforium emphasize the length of the church, not its height. The vaults, too, are relatively low. Where the French vaults rise to well over 100 feet, the English are rarely more than 80 feet high. One reason is that the ribs of the French vault do not begin to curve until well up in the clearstory; at Salisbury, the ribs spring from the upper level of the triforium, and in many English cathedrals from an even lower point. A thick wall, pierced with larger windows than those of the Romanesque period, helps to support and buttress the vaults. Therefore, the buttress system, as we see on the exterior (fig. 153), does not need to be so fully developed as in France. Some English cathedrals have flying buttresses, but they are less prominent than in France. Usually the English cathedral is beautifully set in

153. *Cathedral*, Salisbury (1220–58) North Flank, total length 473'; height of spire 404'.

lawns and foliage, with sufficient open space around it to make it possible to see the building as a whole. Since the structure can be perceived in its entirety from many points of view, the principal tower, with or without a spire, is made to rise from the crossing of the main transept and the nave. If western towers appear, as they generally do— Salisbury is exceptional in this—they are apt to be dominated by the central accent which culminates the whole design.

The English cathedral is of a type quite distinct from the French. Many of its points of divergence can be credited to its monastic origin. More than half of the English cathedrals were built by Benedictines, and even those cathedrals governed at first by a college of secular canons followed many of the practices typical of monastic buildings. The English cathedrals are often referred to as minsters (monasteries). Patently the cloister comes from this source. So too does the open setting, a reminder of the monastery grounds. Then the English orders accepted literally the need of orientation. In the French system of radiating chapels, if the altar be placed in its proper architectural position on the axis of the chapel, it cannot face east unless the chapel also faces east. But only one of the chapels around the chevet can be so directed. This consideration apparently prompted the English to abandon the apse in favor of the square east end, so that all the altars might be oriented. Processions played a large part in monastic ritual. The procession started in the choir, passed around the east end to visit the altars located there, through the transepts where still more altars were found in each bay, out through the cloister, and sometimes even through the churchyard. The need for such ceremonial goes far to explain the particular forms of the English church.

Many have compared the French and English cathedrals, and have concluded that one is a greater and better architecture than the other. Such a judgment is neither necessary nor desirable. The two styles express different qualities, which must be considered separately; to measure the English by a French yardstick is absurd. The French has a superb energy and an inspiring result, like some triumphant anthem. The English is reticent, almost private by comparison, calm and restrained. Each in its own way is supreme.

Gothic architects through the early thirteenth century, especially in France but to some extent in the rest of Europe as well, were absorbed in structural problems. Little creative energy remained to devote to an elaboration of design. Even the decoration became a revelation of and an emphasis on structure. But after the structural difficulties were solved, the designers refined the forms and imagined richer variations of solutions already discovered. Piers and

154. *Cloister*, Cathedral, Gloucester (1351–1412) 147′ long, 12′ wide, 18′6″ high.

tracery were made thinner as experimentation showed it possible to contract their mass. Decorative carving spread over more of the moldings than before. Extra ribs were added to the vaults. In England, the way to this elaboration was easier because of certain peculiarities in laying the stones of the vault. The English method of construction suggested a multiplication of ribs, especially the addition of a ridge rib running down the length of the church at the apex of the vault.

About the middle of the thirteenth century, the first phase of English Gothic architecture, represented in Salisbury Cathedral and called the Early English or Lancet style, gave way to the second phase, the Decorated style. The widely spaced piers of Exeter Cathedral permit a fusion of the volumes of nave and aisles like that of Amiens. Intermediate ribs subdivide the four triangles of quadripartite vaults. The larger windows require complex patterns of tracery whose reversed curves in the early fourteenth century were to influence later French Gothic.

The English vaulting technique led ultimately to what amounted to a new system of construction, which produced the fan vault. The cloister at Gloucester (fig. 154), begun in 1351, where the fan vault is first demonstrated on any scale, shows ribs radiating from the pier like the ribs of a fan. The ribs look like tracery applied to the under surface of the vault, though in reality cut in the thickness of the vaulting stones; they

serve to strengthen the vault much as an engaged column stiffens a wall. An emphasis on the vertical line at this time and for the following century and a half in England, particularly in the tracery, prompts the term Perpendicular style for this phase of Gothic architecture, in which, also, various kinds of pointed arches gain popularity.

Though by no means identical, the late Gothic style in France, called the Flamboyant, probably borrowed a good deal from England, especially from the Decorated style. The region where the Flamboyant flourished is also the region in closest contact with England. The course of development in France had been interrupted by the Hundred Years'

155. *St. Maclou,* Rouen (1432–1511) Façade 75' wide.

156. *Cloth Hall*, Ypres (1200–1304) 440' long.

War, fought on French soil. This calamity impoverished the country and helped to end the earlier Gothic era. It opened the way for the Flamboyant style, whose name is derived from the flame-like curves characteristic of its tracery. In St. Maclou at Rouen (fig. 155), begun in 1432, the façade is no longer planned in simple parallel planes. Instead, it bows outward, the central bay normal to the axis of the church, those to the right and left bent back at a slight angle, and finally the two side bays at a greater angle. An openwork gable, whose curved lines of tracery sweep across one another in interlacing patterns, crowns each of its five bays. The old structural emphasis has vanished in favor of a dexterous openness of design, that betrays exuber-

ance without the spiritual exaltation of the thirteenth century.

To most people, Gothic architecture is identified with the church, and undoubtedly the major expression of the period does lie in the cathedral. However, to imagine that the church alone represents the age is wrong. In reality, the style is a vernacular applicable to all sorts of problems. Where cities rose to virtual independence, as in Flanders, the town and guild halls are almost as great civic monuments as the cathedral itself. The power of the Flemish guilds is evidenced by the size of the Cloth Hall at Ypres (fig. 156), its character established by a great central tower wherein hung the bells to summon the citizens. The architectural vocabulary is that of the thirteenth century, when the structure was largely completed. Its distinction depends on the simple majesty of its proportions. Similar in purpose, the municipal buildings of Italy, such as the Palazzo Pubblico in Siena, the Palazzo Vecchio in Florence, and the Ducal Palace in Venice, follow the styles of their respective localities. So, too, does the Knochenhauerampthaus, the butchers' guild hall, at Hildesheim.

In the earlier Middle Ages, domestic architecture reflected the unsettled conditions that compelled as much fortification as the owner could afford. While the peasantry lived in cottages of wattle and daub, and green twigs matted with clay, or more rarely of permanent materials, the home characteristic of the nobility all over Europe was the castle, picturesque but forbidding, cold and uncomfortable by modern standards—though as time went on it developed a few conveniences. Bodiam Castle (fig. 157) in Sussex, built late in the four-

teenth century, is typical and quite complete, at least externally. A moat provides the first line of defense. The solid stone walls, punctuated by towers at the corners and around the entrance and crowned with battlements to protect archers defending the castle, have as few openings as possible, and those only of small size.

Since the castle is planned (fig. 158) around an open court, the living quarters are more ample and better lighted than might be supposed from the exterior. Across the court from the main entrance is the hall, flanked by the kitchen on one side, with its pantries and services, and on the other by the solar and bower, the private chambers of the master and mistress of Bodiam. In a very real sense, the hall is the center of life, where, under the paternalistic system of feudalism, the owner meets and mingles with his retainers. Here are served the meals to the entire

157. *Bodiam Castle*, Sussex (1386) 175' wide; towers 60'4" high.

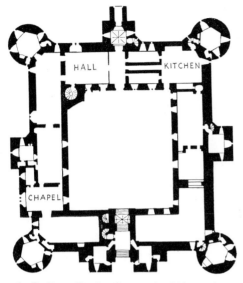

158. *Bodiam Castle*, Sussex (1386) 175' x 178'.

household, and here most of the communal activities of life are carried on. In earlier times, the hall had been used as sleeping quarters for the retainers, though that custom had generally disappeared by the fourteenth century. Bodiam reveals a remarkable progress in convenience over earlier castles. Much more living space is enclosed; larger windows on the court are adequate for the rooms they serve; sanitation improves; and more hearths or fireplaces help to take away the chill. Nonetheless, however picturesque Bodiam may be, and however much one may admire the intimacy between owner and dependents, few of us today would care to live there. Glass, though not unknown, was still very valuable; probably few, if any, of the windows were glazed. Therefore, one had a difficult option;

sufficient light at the expense of free access to wintry winds, or, by closed shutters, few drafts and little or no natural light. Since the sanitary facilities drained into the moat, that feature can hardly have been as attractive when the castle was in use as it is today. Moreover, while an open fire is cheerful, it does not provide either the amount or the diffusion of heat to which we are accustomed.

Public safety and peaceful living conditions improved with time. The late fifteenth-century town house of Jacques Cœur at Bourges (fig. 159) in France, though built around a court, is without provision for defense, since cities were walled and fortifications of separate buildings within them unnecessary. Consequently, windows of considerable size appear in the outer wall. This house is a splendid example of the Flamboyant style in domestic architecture. A Gothic directness of solution is evident throughout. The house is faithful to the principles of symmetry only where no reason can be found to abandon them. The central tower has its large window on axis, filled with Flamboyant tracery, the reversed curves forming a *fleur de lis* at the top. On the other hand, a stairway in the single turret on one side of the tower gives access to the upper stories of the tower. The entrance to the court provides for both equestrian and pedestrian traffic; it may be desirable at times to admit one kind but not the other. Two doors of different sizes pierce the wall unsymmetrically below the tower. A traceried parapet emphasizes

159. *Jacques Cœur House*, Bourges (1443) Façade *c.* 150′ long.

the junction of the steep roof and the walls. The windows vary in size in proportion to the room they are intended to light. They are composed of multiples of simple units: the openings in a single window are separated from one another by stone mullions and transoms, which form a very plain kind of tracery. All the architectural elements are characteristic of the time, and most may be found at similar dates in church architecture.

The medieval spirit persisted in the north long after it had disappeared in Italy. As late as the early sixteenth century in England, such a house as Compton Wynyates (fig. 160) is still Gothic, with nothing borrowed from the Italian Renaissance. Though Compton Wynyates is a country residence unlike the Jacques Cœur House, the settled conditions of Tudor England made it possible to dispense with fortifications even in the country. A moat once surrounded the building, but that was a heritage from less peaceful days, and was intended less for defense against military operations than to hinder marauders. Picturesque in its irregularity, the house seems to throw out gables and bay windows wherever the interior demands them. The warm color of brick walls, with a little stone around the doors and windows, contrasts with the blue

160. *Compton Wynyates*, Warwickshire (*c.* 1520) Façade *c.* 120′ long.

roof and with the brown half-timbered gables. The court is retained, as is the traditional arrangement of the suite of rooms around the hall. However, the latter has shrunk in size and importance; by this time, the family's comradeship with their retainers at meals and on other occasions was fast disappearing; a new recognition of the conveniences of privacy was growing. Comfort of the occupants increased tenfold. More ample sleeping accommodations have been provided for the dependents as well as for the family. Every important room is now warmed by a fireplace, as the grouped chimney pots attest. Glass for the windows has become general, so that light and warmth are possible at the same time. The result of these advances is a sense of domesticity, informality, and charm that has attracted the admiration of later days. While the

house lacks 'modern improvements,' it is not wholly foreign to current conceptions of a home. Though we can hardly imagine ourselves living in comfort at Bodiam, and still less so in the earlier castles, Compton Wynyates meets quite closely our ideas of domestic architecture.

By modern standards at least, houses during the Middle Ages were underfurnished, though the quantity and variety of the furniture had increased by the time of Compton Wynyates. Tables, in our sense of the term, were rare. The old phrase, 'to set the board,' meant precisely that: the table top of planks was set on trestles when a meal was in prospect, and removed after the meal was completed. Family and guests alike sat on stools or benches, though throne-like chairs might be available for the master and mistress. Paintings of the

161. *Vierge Dorée*, South Transept Portal, Cathedral, Amiens (*c.* 1280) Figure *c.* 10′ high.

bench and at times even as a bed, as well as for storage purposes, and from it the late Middle Ages developed the cupboard. The few preserved examples of Gothic furniture show the same frank solution of its structural problems, the same respect for its materials, and the same decorative tracery that are to be found in late Gothic architecture and sculpture. These examples, built in oak, look and are sturdy.

While architecture and furniture underwent these changes, sculpture did not stand still. Just as the house developed its plan and its equipment to meet human needs, so that same concern with a more human quality modified the idealization of mature Gothic statues. Even in the late thirteenth century, the new spirit began to be apparent; the Vierge Dorée at Amiens (fig. 161) betrays a maternal interest tinged with sentiment. Her hip, thrown out to support the child's weight, gives to the figure more movement than had the Beau Dieu (fig. 148). The drapery becomes complicated and more realistic, though the latter development is only suggested.

The bare hint of realism in the Vierge Dorée leads at the outset of the fifteenth century to such statues as the Moses adorning the well head at Champmol near Dijon, by Claus Sluter (fig. 162). This figure of the patriarch in its voluminous folds of drapery, with its flowing beard and the noble realism of its face, conveys the clearest statement of the dignity of man. Sculpturesque in

time testify to the existence of massive beds, but the principal object of furniture was the chest, which served as a

162. Claus Sluter (active 1375–1405) *Moses*, Well of Moses, Champmol (1395–1403) 5'8"
high.

mass, the plastic art dominates the architecture, which serves as a setting for the figure; whereas in Chartres, the figures enrich a larger architectural composition. This Burgundian work, however, is restrained in its realism when compared with German sculpture of the fifteenth century. Such artists as Veit Stoss, Adam Krafft, and, at times, Tilman Riemenschneider display the fullest possibilities of realism in stone, bronze, or wood. Consummate in technique, their work turns to pictorial effects that undermine the sculptural massiveness of Claus Sluter.

Such realism provoked a revolt in the movement known as the *détente*, which centered in the Loire valley in the late fifteenth century, and was characterized by a relaxation of extreme realism. Especially the head of the Female Saint (fig. 163) from this epoch is idealized, less spiritual than the distant creations of thirteenth-century art, and not devoid of sentiment, but far from the complete realism of late German Gothic sculpture. The poses are quiet and restrained, the draperies simple, and the heads ennobled from middle- or lower-class French types, without individual peculiarities. Nevertheless, the sculptors of the *détente* cannot forget their background. Many details of costume reflect the elaborate fashions of the day, and the accessories show that these artists could have transferred this interest in minutiae to the head had they so desired.

This later development of medieval sculpture curiously parallels the story of classic art after the generation of

163. *Female Saint* (15th–16th cent.) Museum of Historic Art, Princeton University. 3′10″ high.

Phidias. An increased sentiment, coupled with an interest in more human form, characterizes alike the fourth century before Christ and the late thirteenth and fourteenth centuries. Then, in each case, the artists turn toward realism, which after becoming extreme gives way at times to a partial return to idealism. Although one should not force cyclical patterns upon history, such similarities do appear to mark certain stages in the history of human culture.

Italy presents a different story. Even in architecture, the Italians resist the Gothic fashion as foreign to their culture. They divorce the French marriage of sculpture and architecture, and continue to regard sculpture as an independent art. The Italian preference for marble as a medium for sculpture,

regardless of the stone used for the building, changes the character from the freestone cathedral statues of the north. Also, in Italy the individual sculptors build reputations remembered through the centuries more than do any of the northern sculptors.

Nicola d'Apulia, usually called Nicola Pisano, came to Pisa from the south of Italy, where, it will be remembered, a singularly classic school of sculpture flourished under the Emperor Frederick II and at his court in Capua in the early thirteenth century. If, as seems probable, Nicola was trained in this milieu, it explains the Roman quality in the relief of the Nativity (fig. 164) from the pulpit in the Baptistry at Pisa, where his known career centered in

164. Nicola Pisano (c. 1206–80) *Nativity*, Detail, Pulpit, Baptistry, Pisa (1260).

165. Nicola Pisano (*c.* 1206–80) and Giovanni Pisano (*c.* 1250–1320) *Nativity*, Detail, Pulpit, Cathedral, Siena (1266).

the late thirteenth century. Although classed as Gothic, little trace of that style is discernible in his work, except in some architectural details of the pulpit. The Madonna, half reclining on a couch, Roman fashion, is envisaged as a Roman matron, swathed in large folds of drapery and wearing a tiara. Her features are demonstrably classic. The heavy proportions, especially of the heads, of the other figures in this relief, the undercut curly beards of the men, and a plastic approach further betray a similarity to certain phases of Roman sculpture. With no Gothic spirituality about them, Nicola d'Apulia's figures are stolid, massive, and mun-

dane. They have monumentality but do not equal in technique the best contemporary French sculpture.

In his later work, Nicola collaborated with his son, Giovanni Pisano. The younger man, who lacked the south Italian background of his father, had absorbed the Gothic feeling which flooded down from the north like a wave and, for the moment, extinguished the classic character of Nicola's sculpture. The Nativity (fig. 165) on the pulpit at Siena exhibits a remarkable increase of later Gothic qualities. The composition of the panel is more pictorial than in the Pisan pulpit. Lighter proportions, a smaller scale, greater

166. Andrea Pisano (*c.* 1270–1349) *South Doors*, Baptistry, Florence (1330–39) Bronze, 18′6″
high.

movement, and an increased naturalism characterize all these figures, perhaps most obviously the Madonna herself, who has now become a winsome young woman, with none of the dignity of Nicola's independent conception. These differences may imply the influence of the younger man. In the Visitation group, just to the left of the Madonna, the face of St. Elizabeth is old and haggard, and the whole composition has become looser and more pictorial, like the later stages of Gothic development in the north. These qualities were yet more pronounced when Giovanni Pisano worked independently of his father, as in the pulpit of Sant' Andrea at Pistoia.

Early in the fourteenth century, Andrea Pisano, who, in spite of his name, was unrelated to the two previous sculptors, modeled the first set of bronze doors for the Baptistry of Florence (fig. 166), the south doors. Twenty-eight square panels enclose quatrefoils to decorate the doors, the small size of the panels being in accord with the architectural scale of the building. The shape of these quatrefoils is Gothic, like the similar motives on the Cathedral of Amiens (fig. 150). The upper twenty panels deal with incidents from the life of St. John the Baptist, to whom the building is dedicated. The Feast of Herod (fig. 167) shows that Andrea Pisano was influenced by the paintings of Giotto, in whose circle he belonged. The story is told with directness and simplicity. A Giottesque economy of figures and of setting helps to achieve

167. Andrea Pisano (c. 1270–1349) *Feast of Herod*, Detail, South Doors, Baptistry, Florence (1330–39) Bronze Quatrefoil 15".

the architectural quality of these doors. Just enough indication of background, either through landscape elements or by very plain architecture, is included to explain the story, but is not developed in depth to an extent destructive of sculptural values.

Just as she did in architecture, France early in the thirteenth century assumed the lead in manuscript illumination. At the same time, important changes modify the output of the illuminators, who begin to become professional and known at least by name. The books are written in finer script and in a smaller format than before, perhaps for the benefit of itinerant friars. Architectural enframements of the miniatures, and architectural settings when they appear at all, follow such current details of

168. *Metz Pontifical* (1302–16) Fitzwilliam Museum, Cambridge.

the exuberant fancy of the artists finds an outlet in imaginative figures and animals, in this case a mermaid and a rabbit playing a harp. These borders become still more elaborate in the fifteenth century and combine with greater naturalism of the miniatures. Painting in northern Europe becomes more independent of books, whereas in Persia, at this time and for the next few centuries, the miniature continues to be a major art.

During the early fourteenth century, painting in Italy, as distinct from manuscript illumination and from mosaics, began to gain importance. While some painting was produced throughout the earlier Middle Ages in Italy, the stream trickled thin, and the artists almost without exception remained anonymous. When the new painting began, the artists turned for guidance to the Byzantine mosaics of Sicily. The Death of the Virgin (fig. 169), in the church of La Martorana in Palermo, is as Byzantine in style as the mosaics of St. Mark's in Venice. The formal design has an architectural balance. The horizontal movement created by the Madonna on her bier is stopped at either end by groups of apostles. Christ stands in the center behind the couch with the doll-like soul of the Madonna in His arms, while from the sky symmetrical figures of angels sweep down to receive it. The artist substitutes a gold background for any indication of deep space; he has no interest in, and no knowledge of perspective; and, since his figures are

Gothic buildings as pointed arches, tracery, and pinnacles. A close approximation to normal human proportions replaces the Byzantine and Romanesque conventions. As the century progresses, and still more in the early fourteenth century, diapered patterns in gold, bright reds, and blues serve as a background for the figures. A page from the *Metz Pontifical* (fig. 168) illustrates this and other characteristics of later Gothic illumination. The figures tend to sway in pose as did the Vierge Dorée. Initial letters begin to sprout pendants that border and enframe the script. Conventional or naturalistic foliage grows from these borders at irregular intervals, while

169. *Death of the Virgin*, La Martorana, Palermo (1143) Mosaic.

religious characters, not ordinary human beings, he is content to indicate them in an unreal manner. Figures and drapery alike are defined by flowing lines, the hands reduced to the simplest of linear patterns, the Madonna's head to a circle, while the narrow eyes and long aristocratic noses have an other-worldly tinge about them. With their sumptuous color, these mosaics complete their purpose: they indicate the story with perfect clarity through the diagrammatic rendering, and as decoration they are unsurpassed.

The mosaics of La Martorana are Byzantine, even to the inscriptions in Greek letters. Soon the Italians adapt the lessons of this style to painting. Generally these native works are inferior to the Byzantine productions in technique. The dignity of Byzantine art, with its unreality, was undermined by the influence of St. Francis of Assisi. His emphasis on the humanity of Christ, and his love of nature, called forth a premature attempt to picture this new emotionalism; premature in that the painters' means were not adequate to such an expression, and the results lost the noble Byzantine formality without compensating success.

From these mosaics and the styles they inspire spring the two principal schools of Italian fourteenth-century painting. The more conservative is the school of Siena. While it retains much of the Byzantine, it modifies the eastern austerity by a less hieratic attitude, more human figures, and a taste for sprightly narrative. Duccio di Buonin-

segna, the founder of the school, seems to have worked largely in *tempera,* one of the two common media of Italian painting for the next two centuries, and the one preferred by the Sienese, although they adopted fresco for mural decorations.

The Italian altarpiece is painted on a poplar panel, covered with plaster worked to a smooth hard surface. On this, after making his design, the artist laid sheets of gold leaf wherever that material must appear in the finished picture. Then he sketched the figures with *terra verde,* a greenish pigment that added body to the final colors. An apprentice prepared the pigments in small pots, three for each color, and mixed them with egg to bind them to the panel. Since the strongest color in each group is lightened by mixture with white, it follows that any change of tone intended to suggest roundness in the figure or in the folds of drapery will change from red, for instance, in the shadow to white in the lights. To the eye, the most intense red appears in the lights, though not in the high lights, and from there the color becomes less intense as well as deeper in value as shadow increases. The early Italian method reverses this optical effect, but, so long as it is consistent, the results are satisfactory. The lower value limits in this medium are restricted, so that tempera tends to produce panels of bright clear color, light in value, and decorative, but usually on a small scale.

However, the Rucellai Madonna, in Santa Maria Novella in Florence, proves that tempera can convey considerable scale. This seven-foot panel was ascribed by Vasari to Cimabue, the founder of Florentine painting, but today all critics agree the painting is Sienese, while many believe it a work of Duccio, dated about 1285. This more than life-size Majesty, made between 1308 and 1311 for the high altar of the Cathedral of Siena. The principal panel depicts the Madonna as the Queen of Heaven surrounded by her court of saints and angels (fig. 170). Mary is a regal figure, but compared with Byzantine concepts,

170. Duccio di Buoninsegna (c. 1255–1319) *Majestas* (1308–11) Opera del Duomo, Siena. Tempera, 6′11″ x 13′10″.

Madonna sits on a paneled throne, her feet on a footstool. The mass of her dark blue robe strikes the main accent, visible from a distance against the gold background, while to each side in adoration kneel three angels, whose forms extend the central mass laterally. This design creates a clear two dimensional pattern; neither the Madonna nor her throne has great depth; and the flanking angels in the same vertical plane kneel above one another's heads with no visible support.

The one surely dated painting by Duccio is the Majestas, or Madonna in less cold and distant, more human, more appealing, a person at whose feet mankind may come to lay its troubles and receive an understanding sympathy. The design is clear, as it has to be in order to carry from a distance in the confusing cross lights of the building. The Madonna forms a large vertical mass of strong blue; she is bigger in scale than the figures beside her, partly for emphasis and partly for design. To the right and left range the saints, each head ringed by its halo, to create horizontal bands supporting the central vertical. One can perceive the order of the

171. Duccio di Buoninsegna (c. 1255–1319) *Corruption of Judas*, Detail, Majestas (1308–11) Opera del Duomo, Siena. Tempera.

painting from a distance, long before one can distinguish the details.

Closer inspection shows much of the Byzantine tradition to be still preserved. Little attempt is made to render natural figures; on the contrary, they are predominantly linear, silhouette playing a major role both in the whole and in the parts. Some shading does occur, but it is minor in effect. Conventions define the figure: a circle outlines the head, a linear pattern indicates the hands with their long slender fingers, and an undulating line the hem of the drapery. A slender nose, narrow slanting eyes, and a small mouth, together with delicate hands give to these sacred characters

the aristocratic distinction the Sienese felt they must have had. The rich quality is further enhanced by sumptuous blues of powdered lapis lazuli, reds, bronze greens, the solid gold background, and the profusion of gold details.

The back of the Majestas is lined with small panels that depict incidents from the life of Christ. The Italian feeling for telling a story comes out here. In the Corruption of Judas (fig. 171), Duccio masses his crowd of characters, whose rolling eyes betray their consciousness of wrongdoing as they whisper to one another. But the group also forms a rectangle similar in proportions to the panel and to the shape of the architectural setting. The loggia set against a gold sky describes the general location of the incident rather than attempting to create much depth in the design. These figures, painted more as silhouettes than as solid human beings, need no great depth. Their meaning is clear without it, and a realistic illusion would neither improve the composition nor enhance the narrative force of the painting.

Duccio's composition and narrative power is further illustrated in the Temptation of Christ (Frontispiece). The Bible says the devil took Christ up on a mountain and showed him all the kingdoms of the world. Christ refused to worship Satan, who went away, and angels came and ministered to Him. The high mountain has become in Duccio's hands an outcropping of rock, and the kingdoms of the world walled cities in toy boxes. What if Christ is taller than the mountain? It is not his size but his spiritual importance that concerned Duccio, and that is immeasurable. Nor is Duccio interested in space; the gold leaf of the sky forms a solid ground to silhouette the figures and to enrich the sumptuous blue and cinnabar red of Christ's robes. These colors, the strong-

172. Simone Martini (c. 1283–1344) *Sant' Ansano Annunciation* (1333) Uffizi, Florence. Tempera, total dimensions 9'10" x 8'7"; central panel 5'4" x 4'.

173. Simone Martini (c. 1283–1344) *Guidoriccio da Fogliano*, Detail (1328) Palazzo Pubblico, Siena. Fresco, figure life-size.

est in the panel, draw attention to Christ.

Duccio established the traditions and general manner of early Sienese painting. Though often grouped with the Italian primitives, his paintings belong there only in their historical position in Italian painting. True, the Majestas is not realistic; it is not drawn in scientific perspective, nor does it suggest depth; but those are neither the aims of the artist nor implied in the true meaning of primitive. Duccio's art stems from the age-long traditions of Byzantine painting. He marks not the beginning of a new development but the culmination of an old. His is a highly sophisticated art, produced by a consummate craftsman, who knows what effect he wants to achieve and how to achieve it.

The scanty records give no indication of travel by Duccio. His pupil Simone Martini (c. 1283–1344) was anything but a stay-at-home. His journeys from Siena to Naples in southern Italy and to Avignon in the south of France gave him an opportunity to scatter the methods of Sienese painting far and wide. Especially important was his sojourn, late in his life, at the papal court in Avignon, since he must have come into contact there with artists from all over Western Europe. In most respects, Simone seems not quite the artistic equal of Duccio; his much damaged Majestas, a fresco in the Palazzo Pubblico in

Siena, complicates the arrangement of Duccio's Majestas, and thus loses its clarity; but as a draftsman he is supreme. The Sant' Ansano Annunciation (fig. 172), named for that patron saint of Siena in the left panel, carries mastery of line to the point of virtuosity. In his use of line Simone suggests the suavity of the angel whose suspended motion is conveyed by the flowing cape, while the angular lines of the Madonna bespeak her agitation. Nowhere is there a better example of line serving all three sides of the artistic triangle: decoration, representation, and expression. Moreover, the color accentuates the decorative side through the solid gold background, the customary blues and reds of the Madonna's robes, and the particolored wings of the angel. The same decorative quality was no doubt paramount in the original frame (now replaced), which was so integral a part of the picture that it was as much a responsibility of the artist as the painting itself. The same linear expressiveness dominates his portrait in fresco of Guidoriccio da Fogliano (fig. 173).

174. Giovanni Cimabue (c. 1240–1301) Madonna Enthroned (1270–85) Uffizi, Florence. Tempera, 7′4″ x 12′6″.

To this linear style the Lorenzetti brothers, Pietro and Ambrogio, brought the human emotions of ordinary men and women, less consciously regal than their predecessors. Their vivid narratives gain clarity through careful organization of space both for interior settings and for landscape. Through the fourteenth century and well into the fifteenth, this style lingered on in conservative Siena, where the new spirit of the Renaissance was accepted reluc-

tantly. Meanwhile, the second important school of Italian painting arose in Florence. Here were laid the foundations on which European painting of the next five centuries was to build. Especially in Florence, the new energy, the desire for progress, the love of reality in contrast to the mysticism of Siena, fertilized a soil where new developments flourished. In Giovanni Cimabue of the late thirteenth century, however, the old forms persist at least in externals. His Madonna Enthroned (fig.

174) displays the Byzantinesque conventions, the slender fingers, circular heads, and pointed eyes, but with an undercurrent of fresh vitality. This new energy ill accords with the old forms and can be felt as a contrast to them, which made inevitable the development of painting adequate to convey this zest for reality.

This original and basically realistic goal is outstanding in the painting of Giotto di Bondone (1266–1336), much of whose work is in the medium of fresco. The small windows of Italian Gothic architecture left large wall areas that invited the color loving Italians to mural painting. This could hardly have developed in the north, where stained glass provided both color and pictorial expression. *Fresco* is the application of pigment to wet plaster. After the design is made, it must be transferred to the dry plaster of the wall. Over that, the artist spreads enough fresh plaster for a single day's work. This obliterates part of the drawing, which must then be remade. The pigments, mixed with water, when applied to the wall become an integral part of the lime plaster. Therefore, no changes or corrections are possible without the arduous process of scraping off the plaster and starting afresh. Although the artist may paint on the wall after it is dry, such additions often flake away. Certain limitations are inherent in this medium. The chemical reactions of the lime in the drying plaster limit the artist to earth pigments, which have not the brilliance of color possible in tempera and are more restricted in both color and value than are oils. Furthermore, the difficulty of change demands a rapid direct procedure. From its very limitations, however, stems the mural character of fresco. Its directness forces broad conceptions, an emphasis on the larger elements, and a partial suppression of detail. Also, the restrained palette accords with the function of such painting as architectural decoration.

Giotto probably painted three great cycles of frescoes, the first in the church of San Francesco at Assisi, the second in the Arena Chapel at Padua, and the last in several small chapels in Santa Croce in Florence. His mature style is best studied at Padua. This building, lighted from the end wall and from small windows along one side, is lined with Giotto's designs. There are three tiers of paintings, separated by decorative patterns, and with a monochrome band at the bottom in imitation of marble, punctuated by figures of the Virtues and Vices. The subjects of the pictures are the lives of Christ and of the Virgin. The most important innovation of Giotto is his expression of mass. In the Return of Joachim to the Shepherds (fig. 175), the figures have ceased to be two-dimensional as in Sienese and Byzantine art. Instead, they appear to have weight, volume, and consequently depth. Through shading, slight though it is, Giotto portrays the roundness of a shoulder, or the mass of a head, and insists on this expression of weight as the most important single

175. Giotto di Bondone (c. 1266–1336) *Return of Joachim to the Shepherds* (1303–6) Arena Chapel, Padua. Fresco, 7'7" x 7'9".

factor in his painting. It is an enhanced emphasis on mass as a fundamental reality, which appeals through our eyes to our sense of touch. This step taken by Giotto is the first in Western painting toward an accurate rendering of the phenomena of vision, and yet he is not a complete realist. He simplifies his figures to eliminate whatever might hinder his emphasis on weight, and to reduce figure and design alike to fundamentals. As a great innovator, Giotto could hardly develop all the implications of his great discovery. He had to feel his way toward the ideal he had in mind

and, in this respect, he is properly called a primitive.

In so far as expression of mass is concerned, Giotto reaches his goal, but such three-dimensional figures call for a convincing indication of space. While the flat figures of Duccio rest comfortably on flat thrones, the solid Giottesque characters must exist in front of or behind others. Consequently, Giotto creates a limited space, a shallow box or stage where his characters can act. Their movement from side to side, rather than from front to back, parallels the plane of the wall and expresses its surface. However, Giotto never invites the spectator to enter his designs. His setting, whether architectural or landscape, is of the simplest, a statement of the locale, not a realistic background. The sky, a uniform plane of strong blue that accords with the simple colors of figures and architecture, serves as a foil for the other parts. A few leaves, twigs, and a stem, or some formalized rocks, are enough to show that the scene takes place out-of-doors. The spectator must supply the rest. Such economy of setting recalls the limited properties and scenery in the original productions of Elizabethan drama. That is all that Giotto feels is needed—and he is right. His primary concern is with the figures and their reactions; to this everything else is secondary.

Giotto's warm human sympathy grasps the essentials of character. The Synagogue had rejected Joachim's offering on the ground that, since he and his wife Anna had no children, he was not favored by the Lord and his offer-

176. Giotto di Bondone (c. 1266–1336) *The Bewailing of Christ* (1303–6) Arena Chapel, Padua. Fresco, 7′7″ x 7′9″.

177. Giotto di Bondone (c. 1266–1336) *Death of St. Francis* (after 1317) Bardi Chapel, Santa Croce, Florence. Fresco.

ing would be unwelcome. Joachim must have been depressed, and, to recover from the shock, he wandered off to his shepherds in the fields. Giotto imagines him as strolling along, lost in contemplation, perhaps in self-examination. Joachim's sorrow is revealed not only in himself but in the conduct of his shepherds and his dog. The shepherds know that something is amiss, yet hesitate to break his revery, and merely look at one another in doubt. The dog, with that strange sympathy of animals, pushes its muzzle up toward its master's hand, but its tail droops sorrowfully.

The Bewailing of Christ (fig. 176) is often cited as an illustration of Giotto's ability to render emotion. But the violence of that painting is not characteristic of Giotto. He feels emotion intensely, but expresses it, as in the Joachim, with restraint. The specific subject in the Bewailing, a lamentation over the body of Christ, permits a display of more extreme emotion than is customary with Giotto, but even here his painting is restrained in comparison with the face-clawing women of his successors.

Giotto's late work in Santa Croce in Florence has been restored, but even the cycle of six frescoes of the life of St. Francis in the Bardi Chapel shows how far ahead of his contemporaries and immediate followers Giotto is. Although the sense of form is less effective in the Death of St. Francis (fig. 177) than at Padua, that is due to restoration. The possibilities of line are not abandoned but, even in the silhouette, line is subordinated to other things. Giotto focuses his design on the head of the dying saint. Each of his kneeling figures begins a spiral movement that coils around the halo of St. Francis and so leads our eye to that point. As at Padua, the action takes place within a shallow box, with distance limited by the wall in the background.

After Giotto's death the Florentine school could not maintain his innovations. Its later members in the fourteenth century reverted toward the traditional Sienese style, as the influence of Giotto waned and the feeling for mass faded. Some of his successors realized their inability. Taddeo Gaddi, in the next generation, said that Florentine painting had been declining steadily since the death of Giotto and was still doing so in his day. Though a few artists, like Orcagna, partly stemmed the tide, no one was found to wear Giotto's mantle until the appearance of Masaccio, early in the fifteenth century.

Toward the end of the fourteenth, and lasting on into the following century, all schools of painting in Europe had so many qualities in common that the result has been called the International style. This linear style, formulated partly by the school of Siena because of Simone's trip to Avignon, and partly by the calligraphic line of Gothic manuscripts, is enriched with charming if sometimes unreal color. The exuberance of the late Middle Ages and its chivalry, reflected in the romances, call forth a fanciful, fastidious, and fairy-like painting, without seriousness. St. George

Killing the Dragon (fig. 178) by Bernat Martorel is Spanish, but its style could be matched in Italian, French, Flemish, or German art. There is an episodic naturalism of details but no concern with reality. The dragon's ferocity we perceive less in the monster himself, in spite of his rows of horrid glistening teeth, than in the spare ribs, skulls, and tibiae of his victims strewn around so liberally. These recognizable objects provide circumstantial corroborative detail for an otherwise bald and unconvincing narrative. The painting really tells a fairy story. The kneeling princess wears an ornate crown, St. George's white charger is the very steed for a hero of romance, and his armor reflects the light from each polished surface. A Gothic city in the background is equally rich and incredible. The story can have but one end—St. George must kill the dragon. If St. George should miss his stroke, so polite a dragon would give him a second chance. Such paintings as this cannot be taken seriously, but who can resist their ingenuous charm?

The International style obtains in some of the illuminated manuscripts of the time in northern Europe. For example, the Chantilly Book of the Hours, a pictorial religious calendar painted by Pol de Limbourg and his brothers for the Duc de Berry, depicts the Temptation and Expulsion of Adam and Eve from the Garden of Eden with fairy-tale unreality. However, of the illustrations for each month, that for February (fig. 179) displays a genuine

178. Bernat Martorel, *St. George Killing the Dragon* (*c.* 1430) Art Institute, Chicago. 4'8" x 3'2".

179. Pol de Limbourg (active *c.* 1400–55)
February, Chantilly Hours (early 15th cent.)
Musée Condé, Chantilly. 11½" x 8".

interest in nature, though even here the artist thinks more of the details of nature than of her larger aspects. He removes the side of the house in this snowy landscape to let us peep at two women and a man warming themselves before an open fire. He records how a flock of birds in the foreground feeds on grain dropped when the animals were being foddered. Snow clings to the twigs of a thicket hard by, where a man gathers faggots.

It is from such manuscripts that northern, especially Flemish, painting grows. Whereas in Italy mosaics provide a principal origin, and hence a tendency to paint on a monumental scale, the source of Flemish painting in manuscript illumination bequeaths to the artists a small detailed manner. Probably these details reflect an extensive merchant patronage in the Flemish cities. The good burghers asked for paintings they could examine closely, as they might inspect a piece of cloth to detect flaws in the weave. They wanted their pictures to record light and shade cast from definite light sources, often within the picture itself. The types must prove their reality by their wrinkles and other physical defects, or by the selection of ill-favored individuals. Bric-a-brac furnishes the rooms, or, if the scene is out-of-doors, towns, rivers, trees, and flowers in microscopic detail lend interest to the landscape. The breadth of fresco could have no charm for Flemish artists or their patrons, nor did the medium of tempera satisfy them for panel painting. Therefore, the Flemish evolved an oil technique that made possible panels of enamel-like smoothness. These panels are usually of oak; the pigment, mixed with oil, is applied in layers, with something of the same technique one finds in Italy of building up the design through underpainting. A wider range of color and value is available in the oil medium. Though brilliant in color, a painting in tempera is opaque and does not glisten, since the light and color are reflected to one's eye as from the surface. In the Flemish method, the light seems to penetrate into the paint before it is reflected, which gives great luminosity and polish to panels in this technique.

Though not its inventors, the Van Eyck brothers in the early fifteenth century did much to popularize the oil medium. As the founders of the Flemish school, their work on the Ghent altarpiece is basic. This polyptych, or painting of many panels, was begun by Hubert, the older brother, and completed after his death by Jan. The problem of what parts were done by one brother and what by the other remains unsettled. The principal subject, the apocalyptic Adoration of the Lamb, fills the central panel in the lower half and also the four lower panels on the wings, hinged so as to close over the center. Christ, wearing the triple crown of heaven, is enthroned in the middle of the upper tier. His heavy black beard violates our usual conception of the Saviour, based on Italian paintings. But reflection shows this version to be as legitimate as the Italian and equally expressive of the power, justice, and mercy of the Son of God. The red-haired Flemish Virgin, in the panel next on the left, is balanced by the panel of St. John the Baptist, while beyond them are groups of musical angels and finally panels with coarsely realistic representations of Adam and Eve. Portraits of the donors and other subjects in monochrome adorn the outside of the wings.

To select a single example, the group of the Singing Angels (fig. 180) shows the Flemish realism. These figures are modeled in light and shade, their brocades deeply folded. Light plays over

180. Hubert van Eyck (c. 1366–1426) and Jan van Eyck (c. 1385–1441) Singing Angels, Panel, Ghent Altarpiece (1432) St. Bavon, Ghent. Oil on panel, 5'3" x 2'3".

the music stand to illumine its traceried panels as well as the carving of St. Michael slaying the dragon in its base. The patterns of the floor tiles vary.

181. Jan van Eyck (c. 1385–1441) *Madonna of the Canon van der Paele* (1436) Town Gallery, Bruges. Oil on panel, 4' x 5'2".

Their recession in converging lines approximates perspective. Even in the individuals, the Van Eycks exploit their observations of nature: those angels who sing notes high in the register of their voices contract their brows, a reflex everybody has experienced.

This realism becomes even more apparent in the Madonna of the Canon van der Paele (fig. 181) by Jan van Eyck (c. 1385–1441). The donor kneels to the right, a great hulking man whose face is scored with wrinkles. Nothing like the Italian sense of physical beauty idealizes this figure, whose strength depends on veracity. The patterned carpet, the brocades of the bishop on the left, the armor of St. George on the right are all presented by the artist to the observer at close range. One needs a magnifying glass to discover all the detail. Moreover, though the laws of perspective are not yet formulated, the artist approximates them with sufficient closeness not to contradict the realism of detail. Finally, many tones adopted by the artist fall into the lower value range; as a whole, the painting appears darker than Italian work in tempera.

As court painters, the Van Eycks had few direct pupils, and therefore less personal influence on the Flemish school than had Rogier van der Weyden. Himself at times inspired by the Van

Eycks, Van der Weyden does much to spread the Flemish style. In his Deposition (fig. 182), he selects an emotional theme, and handles it with a poignancy that the Van Eycks rarely attempt. The weeping and swooning women convey the tragedy and its bitterness. These figures are placed within a box-like setting reminiscent of the elaborate Flemish and German late-Gothic wood carvings, which are also suggested by the solidity of the figures.

The scale of most of these Flemish paintings is small. To this generality, the Portinari Altarpiece (fig. 183) by Hugo van der Goes (c. 1435–82) is a notable exception. The central panel, the Ado-

ration of the Shepherds, ranges the figures in a circle around the kneeling Madonna and Child with consequent depth in the design. Flemish realism is everywhere in evidence; the shepherds crowding in to the right come straight from the fields; their long jaws, unshaven chins, and tousled hair testify to the artist's objectivity by an exaggerated homeliness. Or again, in the sheaf of wheat and the jar of flowers we see closely observed passages of still life. Tommaso Portinari, an Italian businessman who commissioned it, sent his painting back to his native Florence. The scale of the work forced it on everyone's attention; its realism coincided

182. Roger van der Weyden (c. 1399–1464) *Deposition* (c. 1435) Prado, Madrid. Oil on panel, 7′2″ x 9′2″.

183. Hugo van der Goes (*c.* 1435–82) *Adoration of the Shepherds,* Portinari Altarpiece (*c.* 1475) Uffizi, Florence. Oil on panel, 8′1″ x 10′.

with Italian taste in the late fifteenth century and surpassed anything the Italians had yet accomplished. Soon after, several Italian paintings plagiarized the shepherds and the jar of flowers. Not every painting from Flanders would have aroused such enthusiasm; the scale and monumentality of the Portinari Altarpiece proved that these qualities could co-exist with minuteness of detail.

The Flemish school was bound to turn to portraiture, not only as parts of religious compositions, such as the Madonna of the Canon van der Paele, but as wholly or semi-independent paint-ings. A favorite commission was a diptych, one leaf of which represented the Madonna and Child, or a patron saint, and the other a portrait of the donor. So in Hans Memling's (*c.* 1430–94) portrait of Martin van Nieuwenhoven (fig. 184), the subject on the right, with his hands clasped in prayer, looks across at the Madonna. Some realism is necessary in portraiture to facilitate recognition, and there is every reason to believe that Memling has rendered accurately this none-too-clever young man. Still, that realism affects only detail not the whole scene. The man looks stiff

184. Hans Memling (c. 1430–94) *Martin van Nieuwenhoven* (1487) St. John's Hospital, Bruges. Oil on panel, 17″ × 13″.

and hard. We see every knot on his costume and each detail of the room, such as the stained-glass window where the young man's patron, St. Martin, divides his cloak with a beggar—with a clarity impossible even if this scene were reconstructed before us. Paradoxically, the Flemish record everything, but fail to reach the effect of reality. This contradiction results from their reluctance to understate some facts in order to emphasize others; therefore, in the absence of any visual focus, the eye roams over the panel from one detail to another. Also, though the distant landscape is often bluish in color, its minutiae stand out sharply, unscreened and unenveloped in atmosphere.

This school of the Van Eycks and their followers is contemporary not with the painting of Duccio and Giotto, but with the early Renaissance painting of the fifteenth century. It has many of the characteristics of the Renaissance: for example, the love of nature and the desire to represent it with more observed detail than in the early Middle Ages.

Indeed, the turn to nature is more evident in the fifteenth century in the north than in Italy itself, not only in painting but in late Gothic sculpture and in manuscript illumination. Religious enthusiasm in Flanders declines from the earlier Gothic centuries and secular interests grow. The new concern with portraiture implies a growth of individualism absent from the thirteenth century. Nevertheless, this school remains more Gothic than Renaissance. Not only does it issue from Gothic manuscript tradition, but it is innocent of the enthusiastic classicism that heralds the new spirit in Italy, an innovation not to affect the north until the sixteenth century, and then only as a fashionable importation. Though the issue is merely one of classification, Flemish painting of the fifteenth century has not the same character as contemporary Italian painting, and its similarity proves only that some elements are common to the century but not basic in the new spirit known as the Renaissance.

The Renaissance, or rebirth, is a movement so widespread and complex that no succinct definition is possible. Various phrases have been used to describe it, and many of them suggest certain of its features. The Renaissance is called the Revival of Learning. A new energy is evident in the fifteenth century; it dominates all fields pertaining to the intellect and to the arts and sciences. The great thirteenth-century wave of energy that had produced Gothic art was spent by the end of that period, and in the fourteenth century a new surge was gathering momentum to break only in the fifteenth century. Or, to change the metaphor, during the fourteenth century, Europe was catching its breath after its Gothic paean and before delivering its Renaissance oration.

But the Renaissance is neither exclusively nor exactly a revival of learning. The Gothic age was not one of barbarism, though men of the fifteenth century thought it such. An age that produced a Roger Bacon, the vast knowledge of Vincent of Beauvais, or the philosophy of Thomas Aquinas was neither ignorant nor barbaric. The difference is that the mind, ideals, and energy of the Renaissance were directed elsewhere. Late in the fourteenth century and early in the fifteenth, Italy rediscovered her past. The Roman remains were at her door, and had always exerted some influence on Italian thought and art. Witness the classicism of the Corinthian columns in Pisa Cathedral, or in the sculpture of Nicola d'Apulia. But the previous contributions from Rome had been accepted by instinct; now there was to be a conscious revival of the past, a deliberate return to Rome as the source of civilization. This first manifested itself in the study of classic literature and in the avidity with which scholars vied to rediscover ancient manuscripts. On these, they formed their own rhetorically pure Latin styles, very different from the dog Latin of the Middle Ages. One group, the Ciceronians, carried their desire for purity and correctness in Latin diction so far that they would accept no word not used by Cicero in his known writings, even if other Latin authors, such as Horace, Virgil, or Quintilian, had employed it. The Roman Academy revived even the supposed manners and morals of Rome—unfortunately those of the Empire rather than those of the Roman Republic.

The effect of this conscious revival on the arts, especially on architecture and sculpture, was profound. Even in philosophy, an attempt was made by the Neo-Platonists to reconcile classic philosophy to Christianity. With this new spirit abroad, to expect some revival of paganism is logical, but that one field, religion, remained unaffected or nearly so. The tendency of the humanists, as the classic scholars were called from their studies of the humanities, was to avoid the issue, or, in north Italy, to champion Christianity wherever it came into conflict with paganism. However, the fervor of Christianity was not so intense as in the Gothic period. Still, the fifteenth century and even the sixteenth, which marked the culmination of the Renaissance, hardly abated a jot in their adherence to the Church.

Humanism was the goal of the Renaissance, but the motive power was individualism. During the Middle Ages man had looked at life on earth as it bore on the life eternal. In the Renaissance man became concerned with the world as it bears on the life temporal. The individual man gains importance, where earlier his individuality had been submerged. Now arises a desire for fame, a will to be known to one's fellow man while alive and to be remembered after death. The urge to individualism produced two manifestations. Portraits appeared, where they had been all but absent in the early Middle Ages, and moreover portraits of life-like accuracy. Hardly any important figure crossed the stage of Florentine life whose features do not look down at us from some sculptured bust or painting. Biographies and autobiographies emerged. A few had been written during the Middle Ages, but most of them dealt with the lives of saints. Now Cellini wrote his autobiography, and Vasari compiled his *Lives of the Most Eminent Painters, Sculptors, and Architects.* Nor are these accounts necessarily edifying, however informative they may be. Vasari gossips about his subjects, and throws a flood of light on their personalities, even when his facts are not accurate; while Cellini, with a good conceit of himself, magnifies his own prowess in art, love, and war.

The best phrase to characterize the Renaissance is the Age of Discovery. On the one hand, it was the age of discovery of the classic past—humanism; on the other, of the dignity of man—individualism. This was when the world was discovered as it affected man's life on earth, both in the larger and in the smaller sense. The explorers of the fifteenth and sixteenth centuries, Columbus, Magellan, Vasco da Gama, enlarged the physical horizon. Similarly, men looked at the world with a scientific attitude, a desire to prove for themselves rather than to accept statements on the basis of authority. Much that was believed then was incorrect, but Leonardo da Vinci conducted dissections to discover the structure of the human body. Long before him, the artists had begun to observe the exterior of the body. They studied human anatomy and zoology, botany and geology, as those subjects had never been studied before. The Gothic age had turned to nature, but more as a manifestation of God than as a field for scientific observation.

The return to nature cannot affect architecture, but humanism does. When Filippo Brunelleschi (1377–1446) lost the competition for the bronze doors of the Baptistry in Florence, he went to Rome with Donatello, who was to become the dominant sculptor of the early Renaissance, and the two young men

185. *Cathedral*, Florence (1296–1462) Total length 508'; height of dome 367'.

spent their time drawing the fragments of classic architecture and sculpture in the Forum and elsewhere, until the Roman populace thought them mad. Characteristic too was Brunelleschi's resolve to be first in one art, if not in the other. The stories Vasari tells of him present a vigorous personality with a will to be famed for his achievements.

The dome of the Cathedral of Florence had not been built. Therefore Brunelleschi studied Roman construction, especially the dome of the Pantheon, as well as Roman design. When the committee for the cathedral had considered many expedients, some of them ridiculous in their unsuitability, they entrusted to Brunelleschi the task of building the dome, but one may imagine his chagrin to find himself yoked with Ghiberti as co-architect, the very man who fifteen years before had beaten him in the competition for the Baptistry doors. He could not accept that as final. Vasari tells us how Brunelleschi, though he appeared to accept the situation at first, publicized Ghiberti's architectural incompetence until the latter was discharged and Brunelleschi left in sole charge; to him, and to him alone, remains the fame of designing and constructing the dome. In reality, the forms of the dome contain little of the Renaissance (fig. 185). Its scale suggests a new desire for monumentality. And yet that size, almost the same as the dome of the Pantheon, is established by a plan that dates from the Gothic centuries. In structure the dome is closer to the Tuscan Roman-

esque Baptistry of Florence than to the Roman Pantheon. Like the Baptistry, Brunelleschi's dome is pointed in section, not hemispherical; based on an octagonal plan, its ribs project at each angle on the exterior. Its minor ribs divide each side of the octagon into thirds. Unlike the architects of the Roman dome and of the Baptistry, Brunelleschi expected his vault to be imposing from the exterior as well as in the interior. The full curve is visible, while in the Pantheon (fig. 87) most of the curve is hidden within the mass of the building. Thus, though the dome has about it little that is specifically classic except the lantern, built some years later, its spirit and the story of its building typify the new energy and bespeak the architect's courage and imagination.

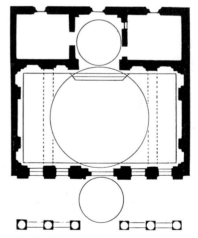

186. *Pazzi Chapel*, Florence (c. 1429) Interior 59′9″ x 35′8″.

Brunelleschi first displayed the forms of the Renaissance in the façade of the Foundlings Hospital in Florence, dated

187. Filippo Brunelleschi (1377–1446) *Pazzi Chapel*, Florence (*c*. 1429) Height, main cornice, 40'.

1419, but that design is less distinguished than his Pazzi Chapel, begun ten years later, beside Santa Croce in Florence. This little gem abandons the Gothic style save possibly in the vault. The square central area (fig. 186) is covered by a ribbed vault that looks like two Gothic apses set face to face and carried on pendentives, but at the sides barrel vaults rest on broad arches. These in turn spring from a continuous entablature supported by Corinthian pilasters whose projection hardly interrupts the wall plane. Except for the gray stone of these architectural members and of the frames of round arched panels between them, the walls are plastered.

Thus, the effect of the interior is cool and restrained, and the basis of the design has been changed from an expression of apparently revealed structure to a reliance on proportion, scale, and composition.

On the exterior (fig. 187), the pinnacles and tracery, the buttresses and soaring lines of Gothic architecture have been discarded. In their place, a portico of Corinthian columns carries an entablature. Above it paired pilasters divide the wall into panels. The polychromy of the Tuscan Gothic style yields to monochrome. Brunelleschi, for all his study and energy, had not mastered the Roman style. His design may be compared to the first exercises of a student of a new language; he has learned a few words but his accent and grammar are imperfect. His Corinthian capitals are stiff and wooden in their foliage, not plastic as in the best Roman examples. In general the design is delicate but flat, as though conceived in lines on a sheet of paper, not in the plastic forms of the past. Brunelleschi's thin walls, light columns, and surface panels have created a new style, despite the derivation of some of its details from antiquity.

The Pazzi Chapel is small; San Lorenzo in Florence, designed for the Medici, is on a larger scale. This remarkable family dominated Florence through most of the fifteenth century. Cosimo de Medici, called *pater patriae*, devoted his talents and his wealth from 1434 to his death in 1464 to the government of Florence, as did his son Piero to 1469, and his grandson, Lorenzo the Magnificent, until 1492. Although the *de facto* rulers of the city, these generations of the family remained technically private citizens, and the forms of Florentine liberty were preserved. Each of them patronized the arts.

Brunelleschi's plan for San Lorenzo turns to the Early Christian Roman basilica; he abandons the vault over the nave, and reverts to the wooden roof, thin clearstory walls, light nave arcade, and the general arrangement of the

188. Filippo Brunelleschi (1377–1446) *San Lorenzo*, Florence (1425) Nave 250′ long x 95′ wide x 69′6″ high.

early church type. However, Brunelleschi's design (fig. 188) does not look like a basilica. It lacks the color of those buildings, and its colonnade, like that in the Pazzi Chapel, is inexpert in detail when measured by classic standards. That free-hand nonchalance of the basilica is admitted nowhere. Light in construction, delicate in detail, and monochromatic, San Lorenzo charms through its simplicity, which came to Florence as a change from the colored and confused Gothic churches of the region. Thus, Brunelleschi's position in the Renaissance is that of originator and pioneer.

Michelozzo, on the other hand, was almost a private architect to the Medici family. His plan (fig. 189) for the

lights them and focuses life around itself to suggest that the street was neither attractive nor safe.

Externally (fig. 190) it is austere. Though the Riccardi Palace now has

190. Michelozzo (1396–1472) *Riccardi Palace*, Florence (1444–59) 225′ long x 80′ high.

pedimented windows in the ground floor, those are later than the rest of the building. This composition translates the medieval palace into a Renaissance vocabulary. The design of the second-floor windows, a double arch supported by a colonnette and framed within a larger arch, is inherited from the Gothic, save that the arches have ceased to be pointed. The massive rugged stonework, too, derives from tradition. And yet an emphasis upon the horizontal, created by bands of classic moldings under the windows of the second

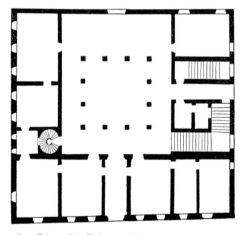

189. *Riccardi Palace*, Florence (1444–59) 225′ x 190′.

Medici, or Riccardi, Palace in Florence retains the disposition around a rectangular court typical of Florentine medieval palaces. This court serves as communication between the rooms; it

and third floors, and especially the magnificent ⟨cornice⟩ that terminates the design, shows its Renaissance character. Sensitive too are the proportions, the sequence in height of the floors from the tallest in the ground story to the lowest in the top, and the wall treatment, which varies from smooth blocks in the third floor to rustication in the ground floor.

If Brunelleschi founded the architectural Renaissance and Michelozzo applied it to the palace, Leon Battista Alberti brought the scholarship of the century to bear on building problems. Himself a humanist, Alberti wrote extensively on architecture—basing his books on those of Vitruvius, the Roman architect—and through them influenced a line of Renaissance theorists. This scholarship dictates his design of the Rucellai Palace in Florence, 1451-5 (fig. 191), which differs from the Riccardi Palace in the application of superposed orders in pilaster form. A full entablature instead of a string course separates the stories. The cornice at the top of the building must be proportioned to the uppermost order, and thus less effectively terminates the whole building than the cornice of the Riccardi. The window forms too have changed; Alberti introduces a lintel on the colonnette below the arch, which tends to create the effect of a rectangular window. Details of the Rucellai, such as the door jambs and a few moldings, betray a knowledge of Greek architecture unique in the Italian Renaissance,

191. Leon Battista Alberti (1404–72) *Rucellai Palace*, Florence (1451–55) 69′ high.

where Rome forms the almost exclusive source of inspiration. All in all, the Rucellai Palace exhibits its classicism not only in the orders and in the windows, but in a certain articulation of design, each part stated as a unit rather than submerging its individuality in the whole. Even here the linear appearance of the composition is Renaissance, not Roman.

In his remodeling of the exterior of San Francesco at Rimini, in 1447, though it was never completed, Alberti advanced further on the road to Rome. The façade (fig. 192) adapts the composition of the Roman Arch of Augustus in Rimini, an arch order repeated three times with engaged columns instead of pilasters. This gives the design a plastic character not hitherto found in Renaissance work, as do the deep

192. Leon Battista Alberti (1404–72) *San Francesco*, Rimini (1447–55) Façade 97′ wide.

arches along the sides of the building. The whole begins to mold itself in light and shade. Alberti's design of 1470 for Sant' Andrea at Mantua combines the temple front, that is, pilasters to support the entablature and pediment, with a triumphal arch. In the interior, which was decorated in the sixteenth century, the Roman barrel vault, with apparently solid supports and wide arches opening into the nave, grasps the Roman spatial sense. Alberti's style is just what one would expect of a scholar who built on the foundations Brunelleschi had laid, but who carried further an understanding of Roman principles of design. In him, not only is the Roman architectural vocabulary more complete, but the rhetoric is closely followed.

The seriousness of the Renaissance during the fifteenth century is confined to Florence, its birthplace. What attracted the north of Italy were not Roman orders and arches, volumes and mass, but the decorative detail the Romans had used and which the north Italians now created in quantity. The façade of the Certosa near Pavia (fig. 193), from the end of the fifteenth century, is appalling in its richness and confusion. Its designers considered it a field for exuberant detail, and plastered that detail, exquisite in itself, over every surface. The colonnettes within the ground floor windows undergo all sorts of ad-

193. *Certosa*, Pavia (late 15th cent.) Façade *c.* 125′ wide x 100′ high in center.

ventures between the base and the capital, with floral designs, grotesque heads, and medallions applied to their surfaces. Bands of delicate arabesques frame the windows, with colored marble panels, sculptured heads or figures, or anything else that a bubbling fancy could suggest. No Florentine sense of restraint hindered these designers, Amadeo and others, from drowning their design in a sea of detail. If this work did not promote the development of the Renaissance movement in Italy, its historical importance is immeasurable, since it was this style that the French, coming down over the Alps, first saw and admired, and which afforded the root of the early French experiments in the Renaissance manner.

The abundant Roman ruins account for the influence of antiquity on Florentine architecture. In sculpture, also, a large corpus of Roman art was extant. The change in sculpture from Gothic to Renaissance was not so sudden as in architecture. For the jambs of the doors of San Petronio at Bologna, Jacopo della Quercia (1374–1438) modeled panels of the stories in the Book of Genesis. The Temptation (fig. 194) retains traces of the Gothic style; the lounging pose of the Eve is reminiscent of late Gothic figures. Also the tree, indicated by a stem with a few leaves on it, and the serpent with a woman's head derive from the medieval background. On the other hand, the bold modeling of the figures is Renaissance; so too is

their strength and energy. The languid
Gothic pose is transformed into the
vigorous portrayal of Adam remonstrat-
ing with his wife, as he twists his body

and jerks his head around to speak to
Eve over his shoulder. That torsion of
the body's axis, coupled with a reliance
on the figure for expression, anticipates

194. Jacopo della Quercia (c. 1374–1438) *Temptation*, Detail, Portal, San Petronio, Bologna
(1425–38).

195. Jacopo della Quercia (*c*. 1374–1438)
Wisdom, Fonte Gaia (1414–19) Cathedral
Museum, Siena. 3'7" high.

Gothic drapery. Indeed, Quercia's modeling approaches the generalized statement of classic statues. One of the world's great masterpieces of sculpture, the Tomb of Ilaria del Caretto in Lucca Cathedral, whether his or not, has an exquisite idealism of features and costume, while the children with garlands of fruit along the sides is a classic motive.

The competition for the north doors of the Florence Baptistry, whose loss turned Brunelleschi from sculpture to architecture, was won by Lorenzo Ghiberti (1378–1455). In view of its date, 1401, it is only natural that the competition required the shape of the panels, a Gothic quatrefoil, to be identical with those of the earlier south doors (fig. 166). In a general view, the duplication of their larger design makes it difficult to distinguish the two. The curved figures in the panels retain much of Gothic tradition but exhibit a few pictorial elements, a trace of the new naturalism, and a touch of the antique, especially in the borders to the panels and around the jambs of the doors.

Michelangelo, who while still young was destined to work on this very portal a century later. The monumentality gained by Quercia in these small panels is extraordinary; it derives from the fine sense of selection and amplification, and from the treatment of the parts as large units of design.

That monumentality is even more evident in the allegorical Wisdom from the Fonte Gaia at Siena (fig. 195), damaged though it is. The voluminous masses of drapery fall in rounded folds, deeply modeled and distinct from the finicky linearism of fourteenth-century

The east doors, awarded to Ghiberti in 1425 without competition, show more of the Renaissance point of view. Rectangular panels supplant the quatrefoils. The number of panels is reduced from twenty-eight to ten and their size increased (fig. 196). These changes affect the relation of the doors to the building, and in this respect one must admit that the earlier sets are more architectural and in better scale with the Baptistry. The larger size of the panels and their

196. Lorenzo Ghiberti (1378–1455) *East Doors*, Baptistry, Florence (1425–52) Bronze, 18′6″ high.

smaller number made it possible and
necessary to introduce more than a single incident in many of them in order
to satisfy the demand for narrative. In
the story of Abraham (fig. 197), his tent
is at the side, he welcomes the angels

197. Lorenzo Ghiberti (1378–1455) *Story of
Abraham*, Detail, East Doors, Baptistry, Florence. Bronze, 2'5".

in the center, and the sacrifice of Isaac
takes place at the top. To separate these
incidents from one another calls for
technical dexterity. Unlike most relief
sculpture, where the background lies in
a single vertical plane, that of Ghiberti
slopes back in proportion to the distance at which the incidents are supposed to occur. The depth of relief
changes from the foreground figures,
partly in the round, to those in the sacrifice, where the relief is extremely low.
Thus an indication of depth results that
impinges on the pictorial. Ghiberti resorts to rocks, bushes, and trees which
add to the pictorial impression, as does
the architecture that occasionally re-

198. Donatello (1386–1466) *David* (1411)
Bargello, Florence. Bronze, 5'6" high.

places the landscape setting, since the
buildings are shown in correct perspective. The criticism that these doors are
paintings in bronze has much justifica-

tion. The panels are conceived as three-dimensional pictures. And yet Ghiberti's handling is so subtle, his craftsmanship so exquisite, that no less a sculptor than Michelangelo could describe these doors as worthy to be the Gates of Paradise. The subsidiary sculpture in bands beside the panels and in the border on the door jambs illustrates the Renaissance scientific naturalism. The floral border, composed of a garland of the blossoms of Tuscany interspersed with squirrels, birds, and other fauna, parallels the enthusiasm for nature felt by such contemporary painters as Pisanello.

But the sculptor whose leadership really corresponded to that of his friend Brunelleschi in architecture was Donatello (c. 1386–1466). Hardly a field developed by the later men of the century was not surveyed by him. In him, both the classicism and realism of the Renaissance bear fruit. His bronze David (fig. 198) is the first important free-standing nude in European art since Roman days. The Middle Ages had clothed the body, but under the influence of his classic studies Donatello saw no reason to continue this practice. He could not fail to notice the frequency with which male figures were carved or cast in the nude by the Greeks and Romans. His study of the figure of David is quite deliberate, and must represent his ideal; nothing in the story of David calls for such a rendering; on the contrary, every indication points the other way. The body is further emphasized by the subordination of the head; the hat, whose brim

199. Donatello (1386–1466) *Lo Zuccone* (1423–26) Campanile, Cathedral, Florence. Marble, *c.* 6′8″ high.

projects over the lad's face and shades it, drives our attention from the head to the figure. Donatello conceives a boyish form whose anatomy might have been observed from nature, possibly from the youths of Florence bathing in the Arno. However, in this statue the sculptor holds realism in check. The details of the figure are selected to emphasize the youthful nature of the subject, and simplified for clarity of expression. The smooth surfaces and the sense of volumes in the figure are well adapted to the bronze medium. The lithe proportions, plastic modeling, and breadth are reminiscent of Hellenistic developments.

Donatello can, however, be brutally realistic as, in the statue on the Campanile of Florence called Lo Zuccone (fig. 199), which means The Pumpkin Head. The insistence on the baldness that earned the figure its nickname, the modeling of the skull, the bony hands, and muscular arms are not beautiful in themselves but are powerful and indi-

200. Donatello (1386–1466) *Gattamelata* (1443–46) Padua. Bronze, 10'6" high.

201. Andrea della Robbia (1435–1525) *Annunciation* (1490–1500) Ospedale degli Innocenti, Florence. Glazed terra cotta, 5′6″ x 9′4″.

vidual. Even the drapery, whose amplitude creates a sense of volume sufficient to contain the figure completely, has caught the new spirit.

These two major strains in Donatello's work, his humanism and his realism, combine in the portrait of Gattamelata (fig. 200), the first free-standing equestrian monument since Roman days. Donatello conceives his figure in terms of a Roman Imperator, the extant equestrian statue of Marcus Aurelius, and gives him the Roman baton of command and the Roman short-skirted armor. The horse resembles the famous horses of St. Mark's in Venice, whose origin is unquestionably classic. The scientific anatomy of this charger matches the realism of the eyebrows and wrinkles

on the head. However, the small scale of the features makes it difficult to appreciate them from the ground. In one respect, Donatello's adherence to truth has betrayed him. The mass of the animal, large in comparison to the man, is so prominent that it detracts attention from his master, who has not quite the dominance that he should have. But such a criticism is carping when applied to so obvious a masterpiece.

All these monuments are in the round, but Donatello is no less original in relief sculpture. He probably invented and certainly popularized the mode called *rilievo schiacciato*, crushed relief, where objects melt into one another and barely rise from the background. A good example is the Assumption of the Virgin in Sant' Angelo a Nilo in Naples, in which the subtle projection of the figures suggests not pictorial depth but spiritual importance. Though pictorialism is possible in this technique, Donatello's instinct is too plastic to admit it. This plastic quality helps to adapt his compositions to the buildings in which they are placed. The figures in high relief of the Annunciation in Santa Croce in Florence are framed in an architecture so rich that more of it would overwhelm the eye; as it is, these decorated moldings make an opulent accent in the church.

Sometimes Donatello's vitality so animates his scenes as to open to question their dignity as ecclesiastical fittings. A band of romping children streams across the breadth of the Singing Gallery he designed for Florence Cathedral. It is now shown to the public, with its sober companion piece by Luca della Robbia, in the Opera del Duomo in Florence. Which one prefers may be a matter of temperament. Donatello feels that the joyous dance of these children will not be unwelcome to God. Luca illustrates the verses of the One hundred and fiftieth Psalm. His figures are not inert but they are less energetic, and their architectural setting is plainer than Donatello's.

The shadow of Donatello fell on the other sculptors of the fifteenth century, as though they merely exploited his attainments. Some of these men are conservatives, or perhaps more justly are described as following the middle of the road; others seem absorbed in scientific realism. The Della Robbia family, in their chosen medium of polychromed glazed terra cotta, turned a craft into sculpture through the creative effort they applied to each product. A typical example by Andrea della Robbia is the Annunciation (fig. 201) on the Foundlings Hospital in Florence. Both the figures and floral border are freely modeled, with realism in the latter, and in the former the plastic effect of simplified forms. If the medium has not the inherent monumentality of stone or bronze, it invites a simple color scheme that avoids the full polychromy of nature. The figures themselves are white, relieved against a vivid blue ground,

202. Desiderio da Settignano (1428–64) *Madonna and Child*. Museum, Turin. Marble.

with a few other colors in the border. Later members of the family sought greater realism of color, and lost the effectiveness of the works by the first two important members of the family, Luca and Andrea. Such products as these, cheap because of their medium, win popularity through their prettiness and their exploitation of refined sentiment.

Desiderio da Settignano, probably a pupil of Donatello, borrowed his master's technique, *rilievo schiacciato*, for his

203. Bernardo Rossellino (1409–64) *Tomb of Leonardo Bruni* (1444) Santa Croce, Florence. Marble.

Madonna and Child (fig. 202). The figures seem sketched in marble with exquisite subtlety, reinforced, however, by real firmness of structure. Realism, to him, might be subordinated to a gentle emotion conveyed through elegant forms and detail. Such sculpture is capable of great charm; but unless the artist has a grasp of structure it can degenerate into routine productions, meretricious in appeal, like much of the popular work of Mino da Fiesole.

A magnificent example of the early Renaissance tomb is that of Leonardo Bruni, the Florentine humanist (fig. 203), by Bernardo Rossellino. The scholar's effigy rests on his bier above his sarcophagus, within a niche terminated in a round arch supporting figures and heraldry above. Inside the arch, the lunette contains a Madonna and Child in low relief. Three red porphyry panels in the back wall of the niche accent the figure by contrast. This conception of a tomb is dignified, through its design and its architectural and sculptural decoration.

Among the ardent realists, Antonio Pollaiuolo confesses his absorption with anatomy in movement in both the sculptured (fig. 204) and the painted versions of his Hercules and Antaeus. The subject, drawn from classic mythology, recalls the humanism of the century, but Pollaiuolo makes this particular selection because of the opportunity to represent powerful figures, their muscles strained to the utmost. The desperate effort of Antaeus to free himself from the python arms of Hercules in-

204. Antonio Pollaiuolo (1432–98) *Hercules and Antaeus* (c. 1460) Bargello, Florence. Bronze, 18″ high.

in every detail, with saddle and harness elaborated like goldsmith's work. The horse, with one foot lifted clear of the pedestal, is a more literal study than even the horse of Donatello. In the rider, individualism in portraiture gains salience. This deeply scored face gives evidence of likeness to the famous captain it represents. Its detail is larger in scale, and easier to perceive from the ground, than in the case of Gattamelata. Except in so far as realism is characteristic of Roman portraits, nothing of the classic remains. The fifteenth century drew from the past only what was already part of itself; the age demanded realism, but rationalized that urge as a revival of Roman civilization. The fame of the work does not rest wholly on its realism. We perceive the individual, but were that all, our interest in the statue would be aroused in proportion to our knowledge of Bartolommeo Colleoni. Instead, Verrocchio creates a human type, the man of action, transcending time and space. The commanding pose expresses leadership and is recognizable as such in our own day and in countries far removed from Italy. This grasp of something basic in humanity gives the Colleoni its position in the history of art.

volves every tense muscle and sinew. Hercules' legs betray the fact that they support the weight of two bodies; this reveals a close observation by the artist of the appearance of nature. For such realism, bronze is the obvious material, well-fitted to convey his love of energy and violent movement.

At the end of the fifteenth century was modeled the second great equestrian monument of the early Renaissance, the Colleoni (fig. 205) by Andrea del Verrocchio (1435–88), whose very name, 'true eye,' suggests his observational powers. Verrocchio was familiar with the Gattamelata, but he rejected its classic features and stressed its realistic traits. The Colleoni wears the armor of the fifteenth century, explicit

Sculpture and architecture feel the influence of antiquity more strongly than painting owing to the preservation of classic work in those two fields. Almost nothing of ancient painting was known to the Renaissance, so that the influence of humanism must be traced in other

205. Andrea del Verrocchio (1435–88) *Colleoni*. Venice. Bronze.

ways. The painters borrow their architectural backgrounds from the classic past, or from the styles of contemporary architects themselves so affected by antiquity. The orders, the round arch, and other marks of Rome replace the Gothic arches and frames that enrich the paintings, for example, of Simone Martini. Certain classic buildings seem to have been especially popular; the Arch of Constantine in Rome (fig. 90) recurs constantly with variations, as does the Colosseum (fig. 88). Fragments of architectural carving, such as arabesques and molded cornices, add their decorative value to the paintings. Some figures may be clad as Roman legionaries. Noted examples of classic sculpture inspire the artist; the Venus de Medici forms the basis for Botticelli's Birth of Venus (fig. 216). As in sculpture, an interest in the nude reveals the new spirit. Finally, the painters draw on the past for subjects. Classic mythology, the labors of Hercules, or descriptions in classic poets may afford inspiration. However, these themes are metamorphosed when seen through the eyes of the fifteenth century. A Botticelli may turn to Horace or Lucretius for his subject, but what he paints has little in common with them.

The new interest in man prompts the development of portraiture. Through most of the century the painters select the point of view that most clearly presents the individuality of their sitters, namely, the profile. Federigo da Montefeltro, the Duke of Urbino (Plate III, facing p. 300), might have been standing on a balcony of his palace when Piero della Francesca painted him. Every feature is peculiar to this man; the strong chin, firm mouth, and especially the nose broken in a duel many years before. His brilliant red hat and robe contrast with the blue sky, which becomes paler as it nears the horizon. The river, fields, and hills, detailed where they first appear, a long distance behind the figure, fade away toward the horizon. Such a landscape adds its decorative value to the painting without distracting attention from the portrait. Later in the century such figures would be set indoors or against a plain background.

During the last quarter of the century, the profile in portraiture yielded in popularity to the three-quarter-front view, wherein the subject looks out at an angle of 45 degrees to the picture plane. In the so-called Condottiere (fig. 206), Antonello da Messina displays this new attitude, possibly imported from Flanders together with the oil technique that Antonello helped to introduce in Italy. This young man is rendered with Flemish realism, illustrated in his scarred lip and in the care devoted to each strand of hair. Strong contrasts of light and dark replace Piero's vivid color. Sometimes a window in one corner of such a portrait produces a composition similar to that of the Memling portrait (fig. 184). The realism and focused attention in the later examples involve some loss of decorative quality. Portraits also appear in religious paintings, sometimes as spec-

206. Antonello da Messina (1430–79) *Il Condottiere* (1475) Louvre, Paris. Oil on canvas, 14″ x 11″.

oil technique, either entirely or mingled with tempera. This northern influence finds its way into the peninsula by devious routes. The economic connection between Venice and Germany brought a knowledge of German art, which employed an oil medium inspired by Flanders. Though this in itself bore little fruit, it prepared the way for the Venetian acceptance of the technique when Antonello da Messina arrived in the city about 1475. Whether this Sicilian artist visited Flanders or not, his method is northern and its possibilities of realistic detail were welcomed by the Italians. In Umbria at about the same time, Justus van Ghent, a Flemish artist, was active at the intellectual and artistic center of Urbino. And finally, some Flemish paintings found their way into Italy; the Portinari Altarpiece (fig. 183) by Hugo van der Goes, aroused tremendous excitement on its public exhibition in Florence about 1476. Its influence can be traced in several Florentine paintings shortly thereafter. However, this northern technique is only a minor variation, late in the century, on the established media of Italian painting.

tators, sometimes even as models for the principal figures.

In spite of the corpus of examples illustrating individualism or humanism, the vast majority of fifteenth-century paintings remain religious in subject. Almost all commissions are given either by or for the church, to decorate its buildings or as public or private altarpieces. The devotion expressed in them weakens as the century progresses. At its outset, Fra Angelico revealed as serene a faith as any painter of the preceding epoch, but later the religious spirit was modified by other interests.

The techniques of fresco and tempera continue from the Gothic age unabated in popularity and, in the early fifteenth century, unmodified in any important respect. Some panels from the second half of the century adopt the Flemish

The diversity of distinguished painters makes the fifteenth-century history of painting particularly difficult to organize. The simplest plan is to group the artists in two categories: the experimentalists, and those who are comparatively conservative, though no labels are satisfactory because the grouping itself is artificial. By the former term, we refer to those artists whose major concern is with the technical problems of painting.

It includes those who experiment in their paintings with perspective, the anatomy of men and animals, the rendering of mass in their figures, and so on. To these artists, the subject matter of their paintings is an opportunity to expound any problem that interests them. On the other hand, those painters, whom we reluctantly call conservatives, express the character of the subject in preference to the technical sides of their craft. Some of these men are conservatives in the full meaning of the term, but many are alive to any contributions made by their contemporaries; they seize upon each step toward realism taken by the experimentalists and use it for their own ends. It is important also to bear in mind that a painter in one of these categories may have some characteristics that belong in the other.

The painter who played the same role in his art as Donatello in sculpture and Brunelleschi in architecture, and who was an intimate friend of both, was Masaccio (1401–28). His frescoes in the Brancacci Chapel in Florence reestablished the ideal of mass or solidity as a primary goal of painting, returning in that respect to the road laid out by Giotto. In the Expulsion from the Garden (fig. 207), he modeled two human beings to express their weight. Masaccio did not always attain his goal, but the substantial figure of Adam looks like a man of flesh and bone. Although the form is simplified, Masaccio observed the external masses of the body in more detail than his contemporaries. Also, he

207. Masaccio (1401–28) *Expulsion from the Garden* (*c.* 1426) Brancacci Chapel, Santa Maria del Carmine, Florence. Fresco, 6'9" x 2'11".

endowed his characters with emotions: he underscored the tragedy of the Fall of Man by a wailing Eve and by an

208. Masaccio (1401–28) *Tribute Money*, Detail (*c.* 1426) Brancacci Chapel, Santa Maria del Carmine, Florence. Fresco, 19′8″ x 8′4″.

Adam whose hands are pressed over his eyes in shame and despair.

Masaccio's monumentality is nowhere better revealed than in the Tribute Money (central group, fig. 208). The apostles grouped around Christ are conceived as patriarchs, not pretty but with an epic grandeur in them; in the tax-gatherer, with his back toward the spectator, you feel that you could touch his calf and find it round and solid. By modulating his shade, Masaccio creates an image that appeals to our sense of touch, as though designed to convince us that these shapes rendered on a flat surface are three-dimensional volumes. This impression, though to a large extent gained by shadow, did not lead

Masaccio to experiment with light and shade. The shadows are cast for the sake of the form they create, not to produce an effect of light.

So far, Masaccio attempted what Giotto had done before him, and carried it only a little further in anatomy. But he also introduced aerial perspective in his background. He noticed in the hills around Florence that not only do objects appear to become smaller as they recede from the eye, but that also they become indistinct in outline, and lighter in value. The range of hills behind the apostles is clear near them but vaguer in the distance. The architectural value of the painting is not neglected either. The group of apostles fills a rectangle

Thutmose I and Queen Sensonbe (c. 1450 B.C.) Metropolitan Museum, New York.

PLATE I

PLATE II

Annunciation, Chartres Cathedral (13th cent.).

Apse Mosaic, San Vitale, Ravenna (540–550) Diameter of apse *c.* 25'.

whose proportions are similar to those of the whole painting, and so brings it into accord with the wall area at Masaccio's disposal. In one respect, Masaccio is immature. To tell the whole parable of the Tribute Money, he has squeezed three incidents into a single frame, just as Ghiberti did in the east doors of the Baptistry. In the center, the tax-gatherer demands his money from Christ, on whose right hand stands St. Peter. At the extreme left, St. Peter takes the money from the fish's mouth. At the right he appears a third time to give the coin to the tax collector. Incidentally, Masaccio paints his own features for the apostle at the right of the central group.

Masaccio's rediscovery of mass for Florentine painting did not prevent his fellow artists from availing themselves of the possibilities of line. In his own work it plays a subordinate role, but his successors made expert use of delineation as well as shading to indicate the form. The science of linear perspective, a tool essential to any artist whose purpose is optical realism, absorbed Paolo Uccello (1397–1475) throughout his life; he exploited its laws and became so enamored of it that he even wrote sonnets to his beloved perspective. One can hardly expect that his paintings will fail to display this passion. In the Battle of San Romano (fig. 209), the horsemen ride at an angle to the picture plane in order to introduce complex problems in perspective. A casualty obtrudes his feet toward the observer. Spears and shields bearing intricate devices, each of which affords another outlet for his study, litter the battlefield. In the background, the lines of partly harvested grain roll over the horizon. Such use of linear perspective enabled

209. Paolo Uccello (1397–1475) *Battle of San Romano* (1432) National Gallery, London. Tempera, 6′ x 10′5″.

210. Piero della Francesca (1416–92) *Resurrection* (*c.* 1463) Palazzo Communale, Sansepul-
chro. Fresco, 9′6″ x 8′4″.

the painter to indicate depth and space
with great success. Therein lies Uccello's
historic importance; but as an artist,
whether because of or in spite of his
use of perspective, Uccello realized a
splendid decorative value. The constant
interruption of the surface by his little
problems creates a pattern in cool

211. Luca Signorelli (1441–1523) *The Damned*, San Brixio Chapel, Cathedral, Orvieto. Fresco.

brownish tones to which the steps toward illusionism are subordinate.

Uccello's enthusiasm was quickly accepted by his contemporaries and successors in Florence and elsewhere. In his Resurrection (fig. 210) Piero della Francesca (1416–92), an Umbrian painter under Florentine influence, places a group of soldiers asleep in the foreground, some of them in profile but others propped against the tomb with their bodies and legs coming forward to the observer. Given the standpoint from which the perspective is drawn, the recession of these forms carries conviction. Piero's design is thought out in stark monumentality. Like the figures in the Brancacci Chapel, his gaunt Christ with the banner of the Resurrection in hand rises as a solid from the tomb to provide the culmination of the design up to which the soldiers lead. Piero did not concern himself with movement, even though the postures of some of his figures imply motion. The design itself is static, and gains impressiveness through the immobility of his figures, as though they were a sculptured group.

Piero's most famous pupil, Luca Signorelli (1441–1523), frescoed the Capella di San Brixio in the Cathedral of Orvieto at the close of the century. His conception of the Damned (fig. 211) betrays his enthusiasm for the body in vigorous movement. These naked souls who suffer the tortures of hell or are being hurled into it assume violent and contorted positions. Signorelli selects these attitudes not merely to portray the pains of hell, but to display his knowledge of muscular structure. Individually, the figures seem to have been flayed; they look as though the outer layer of flesh had been removed, the better to reveal the muscles beneath. Each sinew is strained to the utmost, as one woman has her toes twisted by an energetic devil; a man nearly breaks his back as his satanic bearer hurls him down from the sky. The mass of figures interlace in a struggling knot. The Resurrection, another of the series, depicts humanity as it answers the trumpets of doom. As the dead arise from their graves and push themselves out of the ground, some skeletons in movement have not yet clothed themselves in flesh. Signorelli knew the body not only from inspection but also in its structure. If his overactive figures are too hard in surface and too angular to be convincing, his concentration on anatomy helped to lay the groundwork for Michelangelo.

All these men either belong to the school of Florence or are closely influenced by it. The same inquiring spirit characterizes the north Italian painter Andrea Mantegna (1431–1506). His master, Francesco Squarcione, stressed the drawing of mass; his pupils demonstrate it in their garlands of fruit and flowers and fragments of classic decorative sculpture and architecture. The classic columns and entablature that frame the large San Zeno altarpiece in Verona, finished in 1459, form the front of a pergola, whose other sides Mantegna paints in perspective to establish a rectangular space wherein to place his saints, and his Madonna and Child, raised on a pedestal in the center. Swags of fruit, each pineapple and grape rendered with the maximum solidity, festoon the architecture.

212. Andrea Mantegna (1431–1506) *St. James Led to Execution* (1448–52) Eremitani, Padua (now destroyed). Fresco.

The persons in his St. James Led to Execution (fig. 212), one of a series of frescoes in the Eremitani in Padua (now destroyed), are painted with a grasp of mass that Mantegna stresses by his knowledge of perspective. The painting was placed in the chapel so that its lower edge was just above the eye level. Mantegna therefore conceived his characters as actors on a stage. The soldier in the foreground projects his heel in front of the stage; the sole of the foot is visible. As the actors move up stage, first their feet, then their ankles, and finally their lower legs disappear as though blocked from view by the front of the stage. Thus perspective creates an illusion of distance. Within the space, the setting is Roman. Mantegna pushes his love of the classic to the verge of archaeology, to such an extent that Berenson says the humanist in him is always killing the artist. A Roman triumphal arch, rich with low reliefs, stands in the background. The soldiers wear the short Roman armor, carry Roman shields and weapons. Of course St. James lived during the Roman Empire, but the humanism of the Renaissance must explain this panoply of classicism.

The Gonzaga Palace in Mantua has

213. Andrea Mantegna (1431–1506) *Ceiling,* Camera degli Sposi (*c.* 1470) Gonzaga Palace, Mantua. Fresco.

several examples of secular art by Mantegna. On one wall, the Duke and Duchess are seated in the midst of their family and court. This group appears to exist in an extension of the room itself. The ceiling of the Camera degli Sposi (fig. 213) takes a long step toward illusionism. Mantegna imagines the room to have a circular opening in the ceiling surmounted by a roof garden. A parapet becomes essential for safety, but people on the roof may peep down into the room below. This parapet is drawn in perspective as though seen from the floor; cupids stand inside it on the cornice; a tub of flowers rests partly on a bar that crosses the void; and men and women crane their heads over the parapet to look within. Their faces looking down are in shade, but the sides of their heads are lighted from the sky. Thus Mantegna does everything to persuade the spectator that the room of his imagination is the room of actuality. And much about the painting is convincing. Still, a certain fifteenth-century hardness of rendering, coupled with the limitations inherent in the fresco medium, interfered with any achievement of an illusion as convincing as later painting of the sixteenth and seventeenth centuries. Perhaps this is fortunate. One may wonder whether it is desirable to contradict the existence of the surface on which one is working. Mantegna does not do this, but there seems little doubt that he tried to do so, and moreover, that his day applauded the attempt.

Mantegna and Signorelli lived in the

second half of the fifteenth century and into the sixteenth. To consider the so-called conservative painters, one must return to the beginning of the fifteenth century. Fra Angelico (1387–1455) is often described as an attractive but backward artist. His panel paintings, especially those executed early in his career, support this view of the Dominican monk of Florence. His Coronation of the Virgin (Plate III, facing p. 300) sparkles with the blues and reds of tempera on a gold background. The figures are still linear, and there is in this heavenly scene no reality of setting. Even the mature Madonna dei Linaiuoli of 1433, though by no means flat, only partly realizes that statement of form

that Masaccio expounded ten years before. The saints in the wing panels are more solid than the Madonna, to be sure, but the lesson of the Brancacci Chapel has not been learned. Within the frame of this painting, Angelico sets those musical angels that today are so often reproduced on Florentine cards. None can deny their sweetness, the grace of their almost Gothic drapery, or the charm of the clear blue, pink, and violet robes flecked with gold. But however delightful these may be, they should not form the basis for an estimate of Angelico's place in art. No great master has ever been judged by his picture frames.

His larger frescoes in San Marco in

214. Fra Angelico (1387–1455) *Annunciation* (*c.* 1438–45) San Marco, Florence. Fresco, 7'6" x 10'5".

215. Fra Filippo Lippi (1406–69) *Madonna and Child* (1452) Pitti Palace, Florence. Tempera, 4'5" diameter.

Florence prove Angelico to have been abreast of his time, and indeed a leader in painting. His Annunciation (fig. 214), at the head of the stairs in the upper corridor of San Marco, is inscribed in Latin, 'When you come into the presence of a spotless Virgin, beware lest by negligence your Aves be silent.' It might have been Angelico's motto. To him, painting was an act of worship, a vehicle for his unquestioning faith, which was of an intensity unique in the Renaissance. His Gabriel kneels in reverence before the Madonna. The Virgin, a humble handmaid of the Lord, bends forward in submission. But this beatified monk is aware of the new spirit abroad in Florence, and is in sympathy within it. His scene is enacted in a cloister drawn from the up-to-date architecture of his own San Marco, which Michelozzo had just completed. The columns and arches recede in perspective. The figures have roundness, not so powerful as that of Masaccio or Piero della Francesca, but no mere repetitions of the traditional shapes of late medieval painting. Angelico's development shows that while medieval at the outset —since he had begun to paint before Donatello, the Brancacci Chapel, and the dome of Florence had started the Renaissance movement—his style grew with his time. Like his contemporaries, Fra Angelico had a great interest in nature. The cloister garden of the Annunciation is spangled with blossoms; many are identifiable with the flora of Tuscany. He was one of the first to paint specific towns and landscapes in his backgrounds. Important as these contributions were, they did not absorb Fra Angelico's attention as completely as the study of anatomy did that of Pollaiuolo and Signorelli. These matters he subordinated to the expression of devotion, and the character of his subject.

Active around the middle of the century, Fra Filippo Lippi (*c.* 1406–69), though also a monk, had none of the devotional spirit of Angelico. He was more excited by the visible world than by the invisible. His misfortune was his entry into religious orders when hardly more than a child, since his spirit was anything but monastic. To mention the lurid details of his career is unnecessary. His *tondo*, that is, circular painting, of the Madonna and Child (fig. 215) is admirable. Its fine adjustment within this difficult shape is achieved by the architecture in the background, a typical upper-class Florentine bedroom. In view of its date, it is at least as con-

216. Sandro Botticelli (1444–1510) *Birth of Venus* (1486–87) Uffizi, Florence. Tempera, 5'7" x 9'.

servative as Angelico. There is better knowledge of perspective and the sense of form is surer. On the other hand, all religious spirit is missing; his figures are types from the streets of Florence. Filippo loved these ordinary men and women; his long-necked Madonnas have the features of his mistress, Lucrezia Buti, formerly a nun in the convent to which Filippo was chaplain. The portrait groups to either side in his frescoes at Prato link the monumentality of Masaccio with that of Ghirlandaio.

The style of Filippo Lippi is transformed to exquisite subtlety in the hands of his pupil, Sandro Botticelli (1444–1510). This rare spirit admits his enthusiasm for antiquity in his Birth of Venus (fig. 216). Not only is the subject borrowed from mythology, but the pose of the Venus is inspired by the Venus de Medici, a famous example of Hellenistic sculpture. And yet, though Botticelli may have believed that he was being Roman, no Roman would have thought so. This etherealized vision, an image Botticelli conjured up in his own mind, has little to do with the past. It is, in fact, the purest Botticelli. A master of line unsurpassed in the Western world, he disregards the Florentine interest in mass except as it is asserted in delineation; not that he could not accomplish it, but that he would not. For him, the flowing curves of the silhouette, the v-shaped convention for the waves, and the swirls of drapery combine to produce a subtle linear pattern that better meets his expressive needs. With line Botticelli weaves the fabric of his designs.

His Primavera (fig. 217), an allegory

217. Sandro Botticelli (1444–1510) *Primavera* (*c.* 1478) Uffizi, Florence. Tempera, 6'8" x 9'9".

218. Perugino (1446–1523) *Crucifixion* (*c.* 1495) Santa Maria Maddalena dei Pazzi, Florence. Fresco.

of spring, he draws from Latin authors. Horace describes how the three Graces, in loose transparent dresses, danced before Mercury, and Lucretius tells of Spring's arrival, preceded by the goddess of flowers, who strews her path with blossoms as the west wind blows her forward. A pregnant Venus, symbol of nature's fruitfulness in the spring, stands in the center. But the Graces of Horace are not the nostalgic maidens painted by Botticelli. The Roman spirit was more vigorous than this scene, with its undercurrent of melancholy. However, the artist's virtuosity in line is nowhere better revealed; through it the movement, energetic in the west wind, changes to easy rhythms in the Spring and to a sharp staccato vibrancy in the Flora. The quiet figure of Venus almost concludes this garland of action, but her outstretched hand just throws out a hint of it, to be caught up in the lilting curves of the Graces and only stopped by the masculine Mercury at the left. By means of such line, evanescent wisps of drapery or the solid structure of the male figure can be defined. The landscape is unreal, like the figures, and yet it shows that Botticelli is not indifferent to nature but makes it subservient to his purposes. The foreground is lush with daisies, iris, and other botanically accurate blossoms, and they trickle from the mouth of Spring to indicate her flowery breath. Not everyone will enjoy the highly personal art of Botticelli. It has not, with rare exceptions like the demonic St. Augustine in the Ognissanti in Florence, the vigor and masculinity of the experimentalists, but on the other hand they have not his refinement, his consummate mastery of delineation, or the nostalgia for a half-seen vision that gives a peculiar charm to Botticelli's painting.

His contemporary, Domenico Ghirlandaio (1449–94), has none of this lyricism. The frescoes by this industrious man, in the choir of Santa Maria Novella in Florence, are monumental but prosaic. Groups of Florentine socialites witness the stories or pay calls on St. Anne, who is recovering from the birth of the Virgin, and look down at the visitors to the paintings, anxious to be observed. But if all the interest in the spiritual has vanished, these worldly men and women in typical Florentine interiors are rendered with a grasp of form and an understanding of fresco painting which played its part in Michelangelo's training.

The fresh spirit of the closing fifteenth century may be symbolized by the spring-like landscape developed by Perugino (1446–1523). His Crucifixion (fig. 218), in Santa Maria Maddalena dei Pazzi in Florence, is limited to a pair of figures against an idyllic background in each panel. The point of view toward landscape has altered radically since the days of Giotto. Perugino is not content to create an emblematic setting. He has behind him the studies of a century in natural forms, the landscape and flower experiments of Angelico, Baldovinetti, and Botticelli, to mention only three. Perugino grew up in the hills of Umbria with their quiet valleys. His trees are saplings with the pale green foliage of spring. The grass is clean, and hardly a breath of air disturbs the fields that roll out into the

distance. This serenity created by the landscape pervades the figures and enhances their devotional spirit. Although the figures stand or kneel on the grass, the landscape is conceived as background; the figures seem to be in relief against it, not placed in it, because of the absence of foreground details. Strong and clear in color, the Crucifixion is one of Perugino's most satisfying paintings.

In the city of Venice, Giovanni Bellini (c. 1430–1516), though influenced by his brother-in-law Mantegna, and later by Antonello da Messina, to modify tempera by a partial introduction of an oil technique, provides a transition to the High Renaissance. This mundane city rarely produced religious painters, but Giovanni Bellini is the exception. His Frari Madonna (fig. 219), framed with pilasters, arches, and arabesques, proves that the city of the lagoons is aware of the Roman past. Bellini designed three panels, but like Mantegna before him in the San Zeno Madonna, he imagined the space within them as one, as though the frame is but a screen, prolonged into the background of the painting itself. It might be the transepts and apse of a church that Bellini had in mind, with the Madonna enthroned in the center of the apse under its gold half-dome and with musical angels below, while in the transepts stand pairs of saints who look toward the Madonna. The form of these saints and the Madonna has a monumentality of expression conveyed in rich color, the Venetian heritage and glory. That grandeur is furthered by the pyramid of the central

219. Giovanni Bellini (c. 1430–1516) Madonna (1488) Santa Maria Gloriosa dei Frari, Venice. Tempera, center panel 6'1" x 2'7"; side panels 3'10" x 1'7".

group, the very motive with which Leonardo da Vinci was experimenting during these years.

The complexity of the fifteenth century makes generalization about it hazardous. Its most engaging quality is its eagerness, that enthusiasm for the new, which may be the old as well; its exuberant plunge into the classic past, which it glorifies to its own satisfaction; and its joy in the world. Sometimes the century is misled by its enthusiasm. In its zeal for discovery and self-improvement, it occasionally overemphasizes the very qualities it brings to light. The organization of its pictures may be sacrificed to detail; its realism at times defeats a sculptural expression. In his eagerness to prove himself classic, Brunelleschi is sometimes mastered by his own Roman details. But if the century is not always balanced, the youthful spirit of the Renaissance has its naïve charm.

XIII   THE SIXTEENTH CENTURY IN ITALY

The Renaissance in art began in Florence and received its greatest impetus when the Medici controlled that city. When members of that family rose to high ecclesiastical posts in Rome, first as cardinals and later as popes, the artistic center of the Renaissance moved to Rome. Though other factors played a part in this shift of activity, the coincidence is singular. The High Renaissance, as the movement is called at the beginning of the sixteenth century, carried the tendencies of the early Renaissance to their logical conclusion. Individualism crystallized the great personalities of Leonardo, Raphael, and Michelangelo. If each contained in his style much that was common to his genera-tion, each had his own personal mode of expression.

The attitude toward humanism changed too. Less superficial, perhaps less obvious, the High Renaissance turned more to the principles than to the externals of antiquity. The figures were idealized, the forms more monumental than they had been. The girlish fifteenth-century Madonna grew to womanhood with its ample proportions. If these figures lost their youth, they gained in grandeur. The type was ideated by the artist, selected and dictated by his mind, not his feelings. It does not follow that the High Renaissance failed to convey emotion; on the contrary, it did so by means and through

forms evolved in the brain for such expression. This intellectuality was evident in the geometrical basis of the
compositions. The informal arrangements of the early Renaissance were
swept away in favor of the pyramid or
other geometrical schemes woven of
interlocking forms, related to each other
in height, width, and depth. The greater
plasticity or three-dimensionality demanded a visibly organized space.

The experiments of the fifteenth century in perspective, anatomy, and studies of natural objects also bore fruit.
The artist of the early sixteenth century
took them for granted. He used them as
his tools with no feeling that they were
exciting discoveries. His energies could
be directed elsewhere. Occasional vistas
in perspective were introduced, but their
purpose was less to display mastery of
perspective than to serve the composition or to create space.

The discoveries of Brunelleschi, Alberti, and other fifteenth-century architects prepared the ground for the classical High Renaissance style, which centered in Rome. The key figure of the
Roman school in architecture was Bramante. Though born in Urbino, his
early career centered in north Italy. His
remodeling of Santa Maria delle Grazie
in Milan, 1492–9, especially in the east
end, is marked by Lombard detail, and
by its small scale, though neither quality is so extreme as in the Certosa at
Pavia (fig. 193). When Milan fell to the
French at the end of the century, Bramante drifted down to Rome, where he

220. Bramante (1444–1514) *Tempietto* (1502)
San Pietro in Montorio, Rome. Diameter of
colonade 29'; total height 46'.

studied classic buildings and revolu-
tionized his style. The Tempietto in San
Pietro in Montorio in Rome (fig. 220)
of 1502 shows his mature academic
manner. Backed by a thorough knowledge of the Roman orders, and by an
acquaintance with such Roman round
temples as that of Vesta at Tivoli, Bramante gave the Tempietto none of the
freedom of the fifteenth century. Each
part of the Roman Doric order occupies its appointed place and fulfills the
rules of disposition and proportion that
apply to it, like a well-studied academic
exercise, correct in every detail. Nevertheless, this is no copy of a Roman
building. Circular in plan and surrounded by a ring of columns, the core

221. Antonio da San Gallo, the Elder (1455–1534) *San Biagio*, Montepulciano (*c.* 1518–37) Interior *c.* 120′ x 120′.

of the building supports a dome whose full curve, unlike the dome of the Pantheon, rises visibly to climax the mass. The austerity and grandeur of proportion give to the Tempietto a monumentality unexpected in view of its small size. The concentration of the central type, symmetrical around a vertical axis rising through the dome, is significant. Though examples of this scheme occur in the fifteenth century, its inherent monumentality brought it into favor in the High Renaissance. The outstanding example is St. Peter's itself, where Bramante and his sixteenth-century successors were to work variations on the theme. Since most parts of this building were modified and executed in the

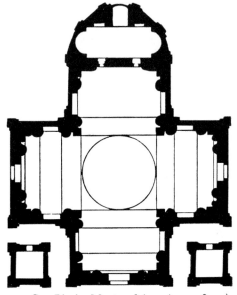

222. *San Biagio*, Montepulciano (*c.* 1518–37) *c.* 120′ x 120′.

horizontal contrasted with vertical & curving lines

223. *Cancelleria Palace*, Rome (1495–1505) Façade 295' x 80'.

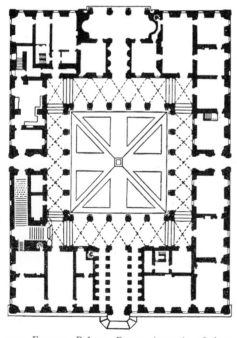

224. *Farnese Palace*, Rome (1534) 185' x 235'.

second half of the century, we shall discuss it later.

The church of San Biagio at Montepulciano (fig. 221), by Antonio da San Gallo the Elder, is another illustration of the central type, built between 1518 and 1537, this time a Greek cross plan (fig. 222). The four arms of the cross support barrel vaults on broad arches that help to buttress the dome, or, more precisely, the pendentives on which the dome rests. Although the High Renaissance borrowed much from imperial Rome, it did not forget the late Roman or Byzantine dome on pendentives. An engaged Roman Doric order breaks forward from the wall to carry the arches. Where the fifteenth century employed pilasters, the sixteenth turned to the engaged column. Consequently, a plastic

expression in the High Renaissance replaced linearism and went hand in hand
with an increased spatial sense and a
feeling for mass. These results are the
architectural analogues of the plastic
solidity and monumentality of sixteenth-century compositions in painting
and sculpture.

The new spirit was not attained overnight. The palace, exemplified in the
Cancelleria in Rome (fig. 223), retains
much from the fifteenth century.
Though ascribed to Bramante, in spite
of the fact that it was built at the end
of the fifteenth century while he was

still in the service of the Dukes of
Milan, it seems closer in style to Alberti's Rucellai Palace (fig. 191). The
rustication and the superposed pilasters recall that building, but several
changes are introduced. Instead of resting the pilasters of the upper orders on
the entablature below, the architect of
the Cancelleria inserts a pedestal between them that serves as a conclusion
of the lower story and as a base for the
upper. The origin of this transition
member is the Colosseum (fig. 88).
Thus the palace illustrates the archaeological spirit developed to maturity in

225. Antonio da San Gallo, the Younger (1485–1546) *Farnese Palace*, Rome (1534) Façade
185′ x 96′6″.

the sixteenth century. The pilasters are no longer evenly spaced, as they had been in the Rucellai Palace. Those flanking the windows are set further apart than those between which no window occurs. Such an alternation gives rhythm. The fenestration shows sequence, from the round arched windows of the ground floor, through the arched windows enframed in rectangular panels with horizontal cornices on top, to the rectangular windows of the top floor. Finally, the façade is not designed in a single plane; the corners of the building project a foot or two as pavilions, to terminate the design. Such a use of accented corners is common in France, but most unusual in Italy.

The Cancelleria is not typical of the Roman school, but the Farnese Palace is. Designed by Antonio da San Gallo the Younger, about 1534, its plan (fig. 224) surrounds an open court, entered through a colonnaded passageway. The rooms are ranged along the front and side of the building with little effort to provide communication to them save by passing from one room to another. The cliff-like façade (fig. 225), almost 100 feet high, has one principal accent and only one, its door, colossal in scale, and emphasized by rustication. Similar accented blocks of stone recur at the angles of the façade to express the strength needed on the corners of stone buildings. Though the orders on a large

226. Antonio da San Gallo, the Younger (1485–1546) and Michelangelo (1475–1564) *Farnese Palace*, Rome (1534) Court 81′ square.

scale are abandoned, the windows prove that they have not been forgotten. Columns flank each window and support entablatures with alternate triangular and segmental pediments. No frivolous detail, nothing playful, is allowed to disturb the sobriety of this design or to mitigate its scale.

The court (fig. 226) of the Farnese Palace illustrates the new plastic feeling. Light columns support the court walls in early Renaissance palaces, but they are replaced by the Roman arch order with engaged columns on rectangular piers. Such piers make possible a greater mass at the corners, visibly to express strength without loss of continuity. The rich shadows caught by the arcade and by the projecting orders convey the plastic character of High Renaissance buildings. This power could hardly have been reached without the experiments of the fifteenth century, but its severe monumentality opposes the delicate linear compositions of Brunelleschi, Michelozzo, and even Alberti.

Such palaces as the Farnese, and even fifteenth-century homes such as the Riccardi Palace in Florence, reflect the sophistication of the Renaissance in the quantity and variety of their furniture, as compared to medieval houses. The chest, or as the Italians call it the *cassone*, still leads in importance, but its shape is less structural, its surfaces enriched with arabesques or swags of fruits and flowers, or its sides painted. The greatest artists of the Renaissance produced panels for these dower chests. Chairs are plentiful and lighter in design; in the sixteenth century, cushioned seats testify to an appreciation of comfort. Ornate carved tables cannot, as in the Middle Ages, be dismantled after each meal. Though large, beds are lighter in design. The sideboard, as distinct from the cabinet, and the chest of drawers put in their appearance.

The High Renaissance manner, exemplified in architecture by the Farnese Palace, is difficult to date precisely. Though it culminates early in the sixteenth century, one of the men who did much to establish it spent most of his active life in the fifteenth century. Leonardo da Vinci (1452–1519) is the most amazing illustration in history of the universally talented man, a phenomenon common to a lesser degree in the Renaissance, when men felt that they might turn their minds in many directions. We think of Leonardo as a painter, but he runs the gamut of the arts, including architecture, city planning, sculpture, literature, and music. Leonardo himself and his own age regarded him as an engineer and a scientist. In hydraulics, aerodynamics, and military engineering, in geometry, botany, zoology, anatomy, physics, mathematics, and astronomy, he led his age and plotted lines of development that sometimes waited centuries for recognition. His is the modern point of view: to reach truth by objective experiment. Volumes have been written about Leonardo; it requires volumes to do him justice.

One effect of this versatility is the paucity of his paintings; another is that

227. Leonardo da Vinci (1452–1519) *Madonna of the Rocks* (1483) Louvre, Paris. 6′5″ x 4′.

many of them were never completed. Perhaps Leonardo's interest in any task was sustained just so long as a problem remained unsolved; when he saw the way to that solution, rather than incur the drudgery of completion, his mind sought other fields. He knew himself competent in the media of his day; as a young man he proved himself in them; why, then, spend his time doing what others could do? Leonardo's attitude is understandable, but of doubtful wisdom. He lacked the mental discipline needed to finish his works. Pope Leo X said of him in despair, 'This man thinks of completing a painting before he begins it.'

Leonardo twice defined the aims of painting, but very differently. In one place he says that the object of painting is to create an illusion of the third dimension, where none exists. This definition states a cardinal aim of the fifteenth and sixteenth centuries. The Madonna of the Rocks (fig. 227), painted in 1483, summarizes the accomplishments of the early Renaissance. The four figures are set in a landscape whose details betray the naturalism of the fifteenth century and the scientific observation of Leonardo. In the foreground the rocks are stratified, and flowers and low shrubs are meticulous. And yet it is doubtful whether the setting should be described as natural. Its effect is unusual, with a dramatic emphasis on a dark background against which the figures may be relieved in light. The strong illumination is designed to model the figures, and to enhance the projection of their parts. To that end, also, the poses are selected and drawn with masterful foreshortening, as in the Madonna's hand extended toward us, the light visible only on the finger tips. These gestures serve to tie the figures together, to knit them into a related group. Leonardo uses his light naturalistically. Where a lighted form is visualized against a dark ground, or vice versa, its outline is sharp. If, on the other hand, the figure be in shadow against a shaded background, the silhouette disappears as it would in nature. Thus the lighted features and breast of the Christ Child are prominent against the Madonna's dark robe, but the outline of His back is barely perceptible. This full chiaroscuro, or study of light and shade, in the Madonna of the Rocks fulfills Leonardo's first definition of the aims of painting. It creates forms on a flat surface which the eye interprets as three-dimensional. This effect is reached by drawing in masses, not in line, and in value instead of color. Indeed color is subordinate to the primary purpose. In the Madonna of the Rocks Leonardo employs his famous Madonna type. Her smooth modeled features, soft cheeks, and small chin have a subtle reticence, a modesty stressed by the downcast eyes and the half-smile on her lips.

But if this masterpiece is the culmination of fifteenth-century art, it lacks the monumentality and intellectuality of the High Renaissance. Those qualities are obvious in the Last Supper (fig. 228) in the refectory of Santa

228. Leonardo da Vinci (1452–1519) *Last Supper* (1495–98) Santa Maria delle Grazie, Milan. 14′5″ x 28′3″.

Maria delle Grazie in Milan, Dissatisfied with fresco because its necessary boldness of execution prevented the long study Leonardo intended to give to each detail, and with tempera because it was unfitted to the scale at which he wanted to work, Leonardo experimented here with oil paints on a prepared surface of pitch and mastic plaster. The result was not successful, and the painting is in poor condition. It must be admitted, however, that to cut a doorway, blocked up later, through the lower part of the painting, and to store hay in the same room, is not the proper treatment for a masterpiece.

As a result of its condition, one sees little more than the composition and the artist's general approach to his problem. The painting covers the upper wall at one end of the refectory. Leonardo gives the illusion that the upper room where the Last Supper took place is an extension of the space of the refectory itself. The plane of the side walls within the painting prolongs the planes of the walls in the room. In the composition, everything accents Christ. First, through perspective, the receding beams of the ceiling, the tops of the tapestries along the walls, and the floor pattern, converge on a vanishing point within the area occupied by Christ's head. Next, the architecture concentrates on the same purpose. Three windows in the back wall are rhythmically designed; the smaller ones are plain but the largest in the center enframes Christ, and through its size and richer design draws the eye to Him. The segmental pediment above it curves from a center within the figure of Christ.

In the third place, the subsidiary characters focus attention on Christ. All twelve apostles as well as Christ sit on the further side of the table. Many earlier versions of the story had placed Judas alone on the nearer side of the table, as though to emphasize his isolation among the apostles and to bring him into that physical proximity to Christ demanded by the Scriptures. To do this is to make Judas, not Christ, the most prominent character. In Leonardo's painting, the apostles are arranged in two groups of three characters each on either side of Christ. By their poses and gestures the apostles provide transitions from one triad to another without confusing the identity of any group. Thus St. Peter, his head second to the left from Christ, starts forward and carries the eye with him from the outer part toward the inner. At each side the action is subdued, but undergoes a crescendo toward the center. Finally, at that point Leonardo contrasts the quiet form of Christ with the agitation elsewhere, and isolates Him visually from the figures of the apostles overlapping one another. This equilateral triangle of Christ focuses attention on itself, and particularly on its apex, the head of Christ; His light face surrounded by dark hair is itself contrasted to the light background.

Furthermore, the Last Supper illustrates Leonardo's second definition of the purpose of painting: namely, that the greatest painting is that which through the motions of the body reveals the feelings of the soul. He advises painters to study deaf-mutes to learn the expressive possibilities of gesture. Leonardo has characterized each individual as much by his action as by his face. To facilitate this, he chooses the dramatic moment at the Last Supper, the instant after Christ said, 'One of you shall betray me!' To Christ, this truth was sad, but no occasion for surprise. Its effect on the apostles, however, was startling; so sudden an announcement of a traitor in their loyal group was perfectly calculated to expose their several natures. To the right of Christ, St. James Major draws back with outstretched arms to deprecate the possibility of such dastardy. Next to him, St. Philip leans forward, his hands pressed to his bosom to assure Christ of his devotion. Behind them both, starting forward from the outer group but by his action brought nearer the center than St. James, is St. Thomas. He has been called 'doubting Thomas'; his instinct would be to question Christ's accuracy, to ask for proof as though to argue the point, against the Master Himself if need be.

To the left of Christ, St. John, the beloved disciple, thinks only of the tragedy and slumps away from Christ as though about to swoon. The action of St. John and St. James, by isolating Christ, symbolizes that within a few hours His closest followers will desert Him. Then St. Peter starts forward toward Christ, his head appearing next to St. John's. A man of action, St. Peter is angered at this disclosure; with never a thought that it might be himself, he proposes to discover the villain and to avert the disaster by direct action. One alone, besides Christ, knows the meaning. Judas, having a guilty conscience, feels himself exposed. His figure is tense; aware of danger, his emotions find their way through his fingers to strangle the money bag in his hand. Symbolically, too, Judas draws away from Christ, his elbow upsets the salt, and, as he turns away from the light, his face alone of all the apostles is in shadow. Finally, the other apostles, less vivid in the Gospels, are grouped toward the ends of the table; their gestures reveal agitation, doubt of Christ's meaning, or whether they have heard Him aright. Its dramatic intensity and its pictorial unity explain why this painting has been from the moment of its execution the most famous version of the Last Supper. It has become the measure by which we gauge the success of other treatments, the last word on this theme.

A third pillar of Leonardo's fame is the Madonna and St. Anne (fig. 229), probably executed early in the sixteenth century. If the Madonna of the Rocks be a summary of the fifteenth century, the St. Anne is a prediction of the High Renaissance. Indeed, the St. Anne *is* the High Renaissance. The figures abandon the slenderness Leonardo had preferred earlier in favor of mass and monumentality. St. Anne's feet point to the left, her hips are frontal; but her head faces to the right; the axis of the body has turned through 90 degrees. That torsion of the body, called *contrapposto*, produces tension within the figure and gives to it balanced movement. Since the Madonna sits in her mother's lap and reaches downward to Christ and the

lamb, the figures create a pyramid. The outlines of this geometric shape are constantly repeated. The outstretched arms of the Madonna and of Christ, the lamb's body, and the line of St. Anne's shoulders and her glance, parallel one side of the pyramid; they are balanced by the lamb's feet, the torso of the Madonna and of Christ, and the legs of St. Anne. Carried through with the completeness and intellectuality of a mathematical proposition, this type of composition reappears in many Raphael Madonnas, and the reliance on geometry remains constant through the first generation of the sixteenth century.

The most celebrated example of Leonardo's type is the Mona Lisa, a portrait of the Neapolitan wife of Francesco del Giocondo. She had been saddened by the loss of children, and it is said that Leonardo employed musicians to charm a wan smile to her lips. Many have praised the beauty and mystery of Mona Lisa; others have found her repellent; but one proof of her power lies in the strength of people's reactions to her. No common portrait could provoke so much comment. Whether one likes Mona Lisa as a person is unimportant. In this painting, Leonardo demonstrates his power of draftsmanship, his ability to create form, his analytical grasp of character, his accuracy in natural objects, and his fertility in composition. These matters establish his position in the history of art.

If Michelangelo's range of interests hardly compared with Leonardo's versatility, his output in sculpture, painting,

229. Leonardo da Vinci (1452–1519) *Madonna and St. Anne* (1506) Louvre, Paris. 5′7″ x 4′3″.

230. Michelangelo (1475–1564) *Pietà* (1498–1500) St. Peter's, Rome. Marble, 5'9" high.

architecture, and literature was greater. During his long life (1475–1564), he accomplished colossal tasks in each of the major arts. A giant in spirit, Michelangelo Buonarroti was physically small, and his misfortunes darkened his already somber disposition. In him a deep Christianity worked in opposition to his pagan love of beauty in the body. He saw his beloved Italy become a battleground of nations barbarous to him, and his native Florence, nominally a republic in his youth, converted into a duchy. Moreover, he had to work for the very men who subverted Florentine liberty, the later Medici, and for ecclesiastics who were to blame for the religious lethargy of the Church in the early sixteenth century. His personal misfortunes must be added to these—the unworthiness of his brothers and sisters and their children, to whom Michelangelo was, nevertheless, generous; and his inability to complete his project for the Tomb of Julius II, which proved a thorn in his side for decades.

Though he learned to paint under Ghirlandaio, Michelangelo studied antique sculpture in the Medici collections and considered himself primarily a sculptor. The subject of the Pietá in St. Peter's (fig. 230) is tragic; nowhere have the lassitude of death and its pathos found more sympathy than in this restrained group. The Madonna's sorrow is idealized in her face, and echoed in the sobriety of the broad folds of her costume. These polished surfaces retain something of the fifteenth-century spirit, but the High Renaissance mass of the

pyramid forms the basis of the composition and compels compactness in the group. Michelangelo alters normal proportions to suit his needs; through his

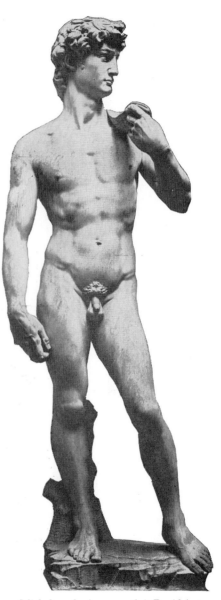

231. Michelangelo (1475–1564) *David* (1501–4) Academy, Florence. Marble, 13'5" high.

whole career, he is the master of the figure, which in his hands becomes a ve-

232. Michelangelo (1475–1564) *Bound Slave* (1513) Louvre, Paris. Marble, 7′5″ high.

hicle for expression. In this case, Christ, though an adult male, is made smaller in mass than the Madonna on whose lap He lies, in order not to appear to crush her, or to destroy the pyramid of the group.

His colossal David (fig. 231) was carved a few years later from a block of stone that had been abandoned by earlier sculptors. Michelangelo again shows his preference for marble; his glyptic instinct contrasts with the plastic quality of most fifteenth-century work. His love of sheer size opposes the smaller scale of the early Renaissance. The body attests Michelangelo's thorough knowledge of anatomy. Its powerful structure, its features, and the veins and sinews of arms and hands are realistic in detail only. These forms are selected and, under the influence of the antique, given breadth so that they may be infused with his titanic personal energy. Michelangelo does not copy a human body; the head and the right hand are enlarged for expression. The pose, particularly that of the right arm, is similar to that carved by Donatello on Lo Zuccone (fig. 199). Like the Renaissance itself, Michelangelo's David has grown to maturity; he is presented as older than the best-known fifteenth-century versions of the hero by Donatello (fig. 198) and Verrocchio. Where they had imagined David triumphant after the fight, Michelangelo presents him grim with determination before the battle, as though such intensity were inherent in the sculptor himself.

233. Michelangelo (1475–1564) *Tomb of Giuliano de' Medici* (1521–34) New Sacristy, San Lorenzo, Florence. Marble, Giuliano 5'8" high.

These examples belong to the beginning of Michelangelo's career. The figures designed for the Tomb of Julius II come from his maturity. Because of the curtailment of that project, the so-called Bound Slave (fig. 232), which with its unfinished companion pieces symbolized the realm of nature as conceived

in Neoplatonic philosophy, was disso-
ciated from the final design. Here
X Michelangelo applies contrapposto to
sculpture; this powerful figure struggles
not against an outward adversary but
within himself, muscle against muscle,
the torture of a spirit. The completed
tomb in San Pietro in Vincoli is the
merest fragment of Michelangelo's conception. The Moses, its most important
statue, is terrific; possibly he had just
returned with the tables of the law under his arm to find that the Israelites
had forsaken Jehovah; he rose, and in
anger threw down and broke the tablets.
Michelangelo's figure has the full Old
Testament energy, that expression of

unmeasured will, Michelangelesque
power and anger, called *terribiltà*.

The Medici Tombs, for which Michelangelo designed the new sacristy of
San Lorenzo in Florence, commemorate
Giuliano, the Duke of Nemours, and
Lorenzo, the Duke of Urbino. Each
contains three figures, a seated man in
a niche above, and a pair of nudes reclining on the sarcophagus below. The
seated figures may be portraits, but if so
they are generalized; they symbolize in
the Tomb of Giuliano (fig. 233) the
active life, and in the Tomb of Lorenzo,
the contemplative life. The nudes below, perhaps suggested by a hymn of
St. Ambrose to St. Lawrence, represent

234. Michelangelo (1475–1564) *Night*, Tomb of Giuliano de' Medici (1521–34) New Sacristy,
San Lorenzo, Florence. Marble, 6'4" long.

235. Michelangelo (1475–1564) *Creation of Man*, Sistine Chapel, Vatican, Rome (1508–12) Fresco, *c.* 8' x 17'.

four times of day: in the Tomb of Lorenzo, Dawn and Twilight, and in that of Giuliano, Night (fig. 234) and Day. This epic conception is matched by the design and execution. The architectural setting is arranged to afford a pattern of light and shade rather than to follow any laws of architecture. Michelangelo makes up his own laws and thus becomes the founder of the Baroque style.

In the Night, Michelangelo releases his energy and sense of movement in sculpture. This tortured body, writhing in her dream, reflects Michelangelo's dismay and disgust at the condition of the world, and particularly of Florence,

bereft of liberty. Nevertheless, sculptural compactness persists. The original prismatic shape of the block is recalled by one arm thrown across the figure and by the crossed legs; these force the eye to travel from front to back or from bottom to top. Parts of these figures are unfinished, the chisel marks still visible in the stone. The pressure of other commissions compelled Michelangelo to abandon the project before it was completed. In the early Pietà all the surfaces are finished, and in the Night also, which suggests that had he had time he would have provided the same polish on all the other figures.

His most famous production in painting is the barrel vault of the Sistine Chapel in the Vatican, executed under protest between 1508 and 1512. Thanks to his training with Ghirlandaio, Michelangelo was proficient in the techniques of painting, especially in fresco, but he affected to despise the art as fit only for women. He believed that his enemies had forced this commission on him to discredit him. The project was colossal, and needed a gigantic imagination to solve it. The nine main panels, four large ones alternating with five smaller scenes, recount the story of the Creation and Fall of Man down to the Flood and the Drunkenness of Noah. They are framed in painted architecture. Twelve immense figures, five sibyls and seven prophets, flank the five smaller scenes or find space at either end of the vault. In the remaining areas, Michelangelo painted other Bible characters, and unified the whole with decorative nudes, perched on the painted architecture to soften its lines and to afford transitions.

Michelangelo adopts a lighter color scheme in the center to call attention to the principal panels, since the eye seeks an area in higher values. A characteristic scene, the Creation of Man (fig. 235), displays Michelangelo's complete reliance on the figure. Landscape is reduced to a minimum; Adam lies on the earth, which is important only as a support and background for the man. Jehovah with his angels floats through the heavens, to inspire life in the new-formed man by the bare approach of his finger. Adam looks back toward his Maker reluctantly, as though he realizes that life involves tribulation. Two centuries before Giotto had established the ideal of form as the goal of the Florentine school. Michelangelo reaches that goal. His figures are massive; they speak to the mind through the sense of touch; their weight might be estimated accurately. And yet Jehovah can drift through the sky without seeming impossible. The superb Adam demonstrates Michelangelo's ideal of the body. He turns easily, his muscles rippling, with each mass selected and amplified to enhance the effect. The artist is so familiar with anatomy that the body becomes a language to him; he does not copy figures, he creates them.

The Jeremiah (fig. 236) illustrates Michelangelo's love of power. Such a patriarch seems worthy of a great religion. It has been well said that these prophets must be immense because of the weight of thought they carry. The tragic character of Jeremiah must have been congenial to this artist; into it he has poured his own distress at the condition of the world, and his own lamentation over the state of the Church.

The decorative nudes (fig. 237) bind these larger elements together. Many attempts have been made to discover some allegory in these figures. These athletic youths are powerful. Michelangelo thinks instinctively in terms of the male figure. Even when the subject demands the female form, as in the sibyls, or in the sculpture on the Medici Tombs, he tends to endow it with the physique we associate with manhood.

PLATE III

Fra Angelico (1387–1445) *Coronation of the Virgin.* Uffizi, Florence. Tempera on wood.

Piero della Francesca (1416–92) *Federigo da Montefeltro.* Uffizi, Florence. Tempera on wood.

Titian (1477–1576) *Madonna of the Cherries* (c. 1515) Kunsthistorisches Museum, Vienna. 2' 8" x 3' 3".

PLATE IV

The variety of these nudes is amazing. Michelangelo boasted that in sculpture, painting, and drawing he had created ten thousand figures and had never repeated himself. One can believe it, since the figure is limitless in its possibilities

236. Michelangelo (1475–1564) *Jeremiah*, Sistine Chapel, Vatican, Rome (1508–12) Fresco, *c.* 9′ high.

and can be used to express the epic nature of his imagination.

Thirty years later, Michelangelo re- turned to the Sistine Chapel to paint the Last Judgment on the end wall. This Mannerist (p. 322) composition,

237. Michelangelo (1475–1564) *Decorative Figure*, Sistine Chapel, Vatican, Rome (1508–12) Fresco, c. 5′6″.

Christ enclosed in a parenthesis of figures, is confusing. Massive as the characters are, they are small in comparison to the total area. Even though combined in groups, so large a design cannot succeed with only small elements. By that time, Michelangelo had become embittered at his, and Italy's, misfortunes. He has lost none of his power, but the exaggerated might of these figures defeats itself, and the result loses the grandeur of the ceiling. His vision of the end of the world is hardly Christian. Michelangelo conceives the Saviour as He returns on the day of wrath to hurl humanity to perdition, urged on by naked saints around him. Sober as is the ceiling, its view of man retains a youthful hope of redemption, but the Last Judgment is hopeless, sinister, vengeful. The power of the ceiling has turned to vehemence, the movement to strain, the sorrow to bitterness. The Last Judgment has not the clarity or the universality of the ceiling.

The times had changed too. No protest was raised in 1512 against the nudes on the ceiling of this papal chapel, but in 1541 Michelangelo was absurdly accused of immorality in so representing the sacred characters, and was asked to clothe these figures. Michelangelo refused. His follower, Daniele da Volterra, was engaged to drape Michelangelo's characters, and was promptly nicknamed the 'breeches' maker.'

Michelangelo's influence could not but be immense. So titanic a figure was bound to start a fashion. His power aroused a taste for similar figures, but the secret of Michelangelo's greatness does not reside in his heavily muscled men and women. Such externals might be copied, but these forms become effective only when they are imbued with a titanic spirit, and with the epic poetry of Michelangelo's nature—something that could not be imitated. A Bandinelli in sculpture becomes ludicrous in his ineptitude. The bombast of the Michelangelesque painters is tiresome, but the inadequacy of his successors highlights the genius of Michelangelo.

A more complete contrast of temperament than that between Michelangelo and Raphael would be hard to imagine. Raphael (1483–1520) was the soul and definition of geniality. His urbanity was bound to make him popular among his contemporaries. Where Michelangelo was venerated, Raphael was loved. If Leonardo foretold the modern spirit, and if Michelangelo's fervent Christianity recalled the Middle Ages, Raphael was wholly of his own day. He borrowed from many, from Perugino, Pinturricchio, Leonardo, and Fra Bartolommeo; but he so fused their contributions with his own manner that they became his own, sublimated, personalized, and perfected to his purposes. The only artist from whom Raphael could not borrow with impunity was Michelangelo. Their spirits were too divergent; the power and tragedy of Michelangelo were impossible for the sunny nature of Raphael to absorb, and his worst failures were caused by his attempts to imitate Michelangelo's power.

238. Raphael (1483–1520) *Madonna del Cardellino* (1505–6) Uffizi, Florence. 3'6" x 2'6".

Born in Urbino, his early work shows the influence of Perugino in the quiet figures, as well as in the idyllic landscape of Umbria. Had Raphael died in 1504, he would have been an attractive minor master. In that year, he moved to Florence, where he met the progressive atmosphere of the metropolis. This gave him a feeling for structure and a monumentality absent from his earlier manner, but Raphael welded them to his own modesty of expression. During the next four years a series of Madonnas came from his brush that have made his name remembered. The Madonna del Cardellino (fig. 238) is named from the finch brought to Christ by St. John. The color is strong, fresh, and clear; the dark blue and red of the Madonna's costume contrast with the light blue sky and green grass. The landscape retains the peace of Umbria; young trees break into leaf under a fair sky; accurate in its details, the scene has the serenity of a morning in spring. Some trace of Perugino lingers in both landscape and figures. But the type is Raphael's own, lovable and human. The figure is more ample, the face a perfect oval with a broad forehead, widely set eyes, and a Cupid's bow mouth. These Raphael Madonnas are noble idealizations of womanhood. Under the influence of the Florentine concern with reality, he paints no figures that might not be of the earth, none of the winged cherubs that occur in his production both before and after this period. Nevertheless, these paintings reveal their devotion. They gain monumentality through

the pyramidal arrangement, borrowed from Leonardo's Madonna and St. Anne (fig. 229), but the Raphael is less elaborate and less intellectual as a study in design; here is the same contrapposto, but not so insistent. Raphael subordinates scientific interests, movement, and power to admit more fully his sweet but never cloying spirit.

Later, after he moved to Rome, Raphael painted the Sistine Madonna. The intimacy of this painting is consequent on the motive, which allows the Madonna to approach the spectator down a path of clouds composed of the heads of cherubim. The composition is again geometrical, a rhomboid with the head of the Madonna at its apex, the figures of St. Sixtus, from whom the painting is named, and St. Barbara at its sides, and two cherubs resting on their arms at its base. The open-eyed Madonna has not the modesty of his best Florentine examples, and its intimacy involves theatricality, as though this tableau had been posed before the curtains were drawn.

Generally, when we imagine the Madonna, we do so in terms of Raphael. He establishes the standard. Raphael's portraits of Pope Julius II and of Pope Leo X with his nephews betray his power of characterization. In the latter, Raphael introduced the chased bell, the magnifying glass, and the illuminated manuscript to reveal the cultivated tastes of this member of the Medici family. The fleshy cheeks imply that Leo loved the pleasures of a not too frugal table, but do not conceal his in-

239. Raphael (1483–1520) *Baldassare Castiglione* (1516) Louvre, Paris. 2'8" x 2'2".

tellectual power. Simpler is the portrait of Baldassare Castiglione (fig. 239), author of the *Book of the Courtier*, a book of etiquette of his day. Castiglione was a gentleman and a friend of the artist, and never did Raphael compose a more sympathetic portrait. The color scheme in black and gray contradicts the brilliant color of many fifteenth-century portraits. Male fashions sobered down at this time; the costume is rich without ostentation—'Costly thy habit as thy purse may buy, but not expressed in fancy, rich not gaudy,' Castiglione, like Polonius, might have said. That quiet restraint suited Raphael.

The greatest of Raphael's undertakings are the decorations of the Vatican

Stanze, four rooms of moderate size. The first to be executed is the Stanza della Segnatura, whose paintings are almost entirely from Raphael's own hand. Next come in order the Stanza d'Eliodoro, the Stanza del Incendio del Borgo, and finally the Sala di Costantino. These show more and more of his pupils' work, until in the last the execution at least is wholly by his students. Raphael conceives the Stanza or Camera della Segnatura as a chamber of the faculties, with subjects that reflect theology, philosophy, poetry, and jurisprudence on the four walls. A rich ceiling includes allegorical figures corresponding to the paintings below. The School of Athens (fig. 240) is a symposium of classic philosophy. In the center stand the figures of Plato, carrying the *Timaeus*, and Aristotle with his *Ethics*, as the fountainheads of ancient thought. To the left of Plato, Socrates argues some proposition with a group of followers. Diogenes sprawls on the steps, while among the characters in the foreground can be identified Pythagoras with his mathematical table, Euclid drawing a geometric figure, Ptolemy and Zoroaster as astronomers. Not only does the inclusion of these figures testify to an extensive knowledge of the past, but the way that they are conceived has the breadth and idealism of classic times. These patriarchal characters, clad in large draperies and massive in form, achieve monumentality. The spirit of humanism more than its externals flows through this conception, even in its architecture, which reflects Bramante's

240. Raphael (1483–1520) *School of Athens* (1508–13) Camera della Segnatura, Vatican, Rome. Fresco, 18′ x 26′.

scheme for St. Peter's, itself strongly classic.

In this composition Raphael reaches his clearest expression of space as an element in design. With perfect assurance he organizes his arrangement in three dimensions: the figures create a ring or horseshoe, open in the foreground, to guide the eye around the group. The architecture defines the space so that it becomes almost tangible. In spite of the movement within this volume, the symmetry of the whole design establishes a feeling of repose. Individual figures have possibilities of action, but the design is quiet, its monumental equilibrium created by each part located in its

appointed place. This clarity, completeness, and assurance are the essence of the High Renaissance in Rome.

While Leonardo, Michelangelo, and Raphael fulfilled the destiny of the High Renaissance in Florence and Rome, an analogous but modified development took place in Venice. This city, wealthy through its trade with the East, had acquired a semi-Oriental richness, an exotic flavor unique in Italy. Although its painting during the fifteenth century, like Florentine, had been predominantly religious, the Venetian attitude toward the subject in the sixteenth century became more secular. In spite of some masterpieces of reli-

241. Giorgione (*c.* 1478–1510) *The Tempest* Palazzo Giovanelli, Venice. 2′6″ x 2′4″.

gious painting, such as Titian's Assumption of the Virgin, it is hard to imagine a Fra Angelico or a Raphael in Venice. The Venetians were attracted to splendor of costume, to elaborate architecture, to luxuriant physical types, and above all to color.

They adopt the Flemish oil medium, but modify it in the direction of modern practices, and thus develop a technique appropriate to their painterly approach. While they still underpaint their canvases, building them up layer by layer with semi-transparent glazes, they think in terms of the brush. The Florentines never understood this point of view. The Tuscan artists design their paintings in terms of drawing in black and white; during the fifteenth and earlier centuries in terms of delineation; and later in terms of form drawing in light and shade; but color is subordinate in a composition worked out with the pencil. With such a history, the looser Venetian drawing with a brush is bound to seem to the Florentines an indication of incompetence, whereas in reality it is a different method and one much closer to later painting. Venetian paintings rely on their color, which bears the same basic relation to the school of Venice that form does to the Florentine school.

The painter who introduced the later style is Giorgione da Castelfranco (c. 1478–1510). His short career produced only a small number of canvases. The basis for a discussion of Giorgione's paintings is the Tempest (fig. 241). The painting has also been named the Soldier and the Gypsy, and Adrastus and Hypsiphile. All these titles are modern. Some definite subject always existed for earlier paintings; an incident from the life of some minor saint may not be recognized, but it is clearly a specific incident that the artist had in mind. In the Tempest, the illustrative purpose of the painting is minimized. The subject as such becomes of less importance because the painting deals with mood. The soldier and the woman nursing her child have no obvious connection. They do not even look at one another; their appearance suggests day-dreaming in a moment of idleness.

The landscape, too, and its relation to the figures have changed. Throughout the fifteenth century, painters experimented with landscape as a background. The figures had been dominant, and were painted at a large scale in the foreground, where they were prominent in the composition. Here they occupy but a fraction of the painting. They are not in the foreground; the landscape surrounds them, and a bush sends up its shoots in front of the nursing mother. Where previous artists had placed their figures on the landscape, Giorgione puts his in the landscape. The scene itself has altered. In place of the quiet, sunny, and panoramic landscapes of a Perugino, the Venetian prefers a thunderstorm with its dark clouds ripped by lightning. He introduces ruins not for their archaeological interest, but for their pictorial qualities. His trees grow in the foreground as well as in the background, and therefore only the trunks of some of them find space within the frame. In short, this landscape paints a mood appropriate to the figures. All these considerations indicate that the point of view toward painting has changed; a visual and emotional approach has replaced the intellectualism of the Florentine tradition.

This alternate emphasis is neither better nor worse than the Florentine; it is different, and calls for a new type of appreciation.

The Madonna of Castelfranco, the principal altarpiece in the principal church of Giorgione's native village, is called by Ruskin the most beautiful painting in existence. Though the composition is symmetrical, like the fifteenth-century designs, the Madonna and Child, elevated on a pedestal, form the apex of a triangle completed by the full-length figures of Saints Liberale and Francis. As in the Tempest, these figures are introspective, a peculiarity of Giorgione's. St. Francis gazes at the ground, and if St. Liberale looks out of the picture, his eyes seem to see nothing.

Historically, Giorgione's Venus (fig. 242) is significant as the first example of the reclining nude female figure in Western painting, a motive exploited since then by almost every important painter. The landscape, as in the Tempest, creeps out to the picture plane to enclose the figure. The leaves, sod, and rocks are clear, but are not scientific or microscopic. The painter sweeps them in boldly; his brush leaves a band where one color merges with another. The outlines of the figure in the landscape show this penumbra. The idealized Venus is sensuous but not sensual; the surfaces of her body melt into one another until the form looks as though it had been poured out on the landscape. This conception marks the acme of lyrical visions of the human figure, asleep in an idyllic setting.

Giorgione and Titian were fellow

242. Giorgione (c. 1478–1510) *Sleeping Venus* (c. 1508–10) Museum. Dresden. 3′7″ x 5′9″.

pupils of Giovanni Bellini, but Titian (1477–1576), although a year older than Giorgione, was influenced by him. During almost a century of production, this grand old man of Venetian painting passed through several modifications of style. With an eye to his personal comfort, but with a miserly eagerness, Titian begged for sinecures and pensions from the state and from princes who patronized him. These positions freed him of financial worries, though no painter of his ability in the sixteenth century would have gone unrecognized. Few artists have ever subjected their own work to more stringent criticism. On completing a canvas, Titian might set it aside till the first ardor of creation had faded, and later re-examine it as though it had been painted by his worst enemy. Any defects might then be remedied, and possibly the criticism and revision might be repeated several times. Such reworking commonly blurs the freshness of the original, but Titian avoided this too. As a result, his greatest canvases contain a balance and serenity, classic in the broadest sense of the term.

Giovanni Bellini had popularized half-length Madonnas seated behind a parapet against a curtain. Titian amplified this type in his early Madonna of the Cherries (Plate IV, facing p. 301). The sumptuous contrast of the Madonna's orange and blue costume against the red brocaded curtain and blue sky show the Venetian colorist tradition at its best.

By 1518, the date of the Assump-

243. Titian (1477–1576) *Assumption of the Virgin* (1516–18) Santa Maria Gloriosa dei Frari, Venice. 22′6″ x 11′9″.

tion of the Virgin (fig. 243), Titian had outgrown the influence of Giovanni Bellini, and had so digested his borrowings from Giorgione that they no longer betrayed their source. Thus, at the age of forty-one, Titian reached his early maturity. The painting glows with the golden tonality associated with Venetian art. The local colors are strong, but a superposed translucent yellowish glaze draws them together, as would a golden haze. Like the High Renaissance paintings of Florence and Rome, the composition has a geometric basis, a circle supported on a horizontal base. The head of the Madonna marks the center of a circle composed of the frame and the flight of child angels. The Madonna's followers look upward or raise their arms; by glance and gesture they visually join with the upper part, while their compact mass serves as a pedestal for the circle.

This dramatic conception reveals the temperamental difference between Giorgione and Titian. To Titian, the Assumption is the moment of the Madonna's triumph; naturally her friends are exuberant. Had Giorgione attempted this problem, he might have supposed that the followers of the Madonna would feel some pangs at their personal loss. Such a possibility could never occur to Titian. It would be involved; it could not but confuse the main theme, and should not be considered. Like the

244. Titian (1477–1576) *Bacchus and Ariadne* (1523) National Gallery, London. 5′9″ x 6′3″.

245. Titian (1477–1576) *Young Englishman* (1540–45) Pitti, Florence. 3′8″ x 3′.

Raphael Madonnas, Titian's Assumption has become the standard for that subject.

Titian imagines Bacchus and Ariadne (fig. 244) as none of the various fifteenth-century painters of mythology could. His interpretation is vigorous, and the figures robust and physical. They need no archaeological attributes, because their lusty spirit is that of

Mount Olympus. Titian catches the fundamental quality of classic myths, a sensuous ideal of physical perfection. Therefore, he discards his predecessor's display of humanism. The composition abandons symmetry; if Bacchus is nearly on the axis of the design, the lonely figure of Ariadne on the left is enough to balance the boisterous Bacchic band who stumble out of the woods to the right. Such a design gives a deceptive appearance of the accidental. Throughout the canvas Titian repeats forms and shapes for harmony; thus, though the unity of the composition is evident at a glance, the means of its accomplishment are not.

In addition to his mastery of mythological and religious paintings, Titian is one of the great portraitists of all time. The Young Englishman (fig. 245), sometimes identified as the Duke of Norfolk, is dressed in sober black, relieved only by the golden chain around his neck. The design is reduced to three spots of light against a dark background,

246. Titian (1477–1576) *Rape of Europa* (1559) Fenway Court, Boston. 5′10″ x 6′9″.

the head and the two hands. Through an adjustment of size, shape, and emphasis, these accents establish equilibrium. So economical a composition eliminates every nonessential, and concentrates all on the man. Moreover, Titian so discusses the character of his sitter that one feels him to be an individual. Titian draws on his canvas not only a face but also a personality.

These paintings are High Renaissance in spirit; though contemporary, the Pesaro Madonna foretells a change in the point of view. The plane of the columns recedes into the design, as do the planes of the figures. Serenity and repose give way to the dynamic and incomplete, a foretaste of the future; but its promises were not to be fulfilled for some decades.

By about 1545, another change modified Titian's style. He was then sixty-eight, an age when most men have either died or retired. The Rape of Europa (fig. 246) is looser in handling than Titian's earlier work; it testifies to a decline of interest in detail coupled with an increased concern with the whole. Details are suggested rather than defined. The pigment is spread broadly over the canvas. The design is now wholly dynamic; Europa riding on the bull duplicates in ideation a cupid sprawled over a dolphin; the movement of these figures slashes diagonally, with smaller diagonals in the flying cupids of the upper left corner. As in the Pesaro Madonna, these tendencies anticipate Baroque painting, as do some of the

247. Correggio (1489–1534) *Madonna of St. Jerome* (1527–8) Gallery, Parma. 6'8" x 4'7".

later works of Michelangelo. Titian's conception of color has changed radically. He deserts color for tone; in place of the sonorous blues, reds, yellows, and greens of his early maturity, Titian's late palette is subdued, with silvery gray, blue, and old rose predominant.

Titian's place in painting is like that of Beethoven in music. His art is controlled and organized, with a grandeur of spirit, classic in its balanced perfection. He combines visual structure with vigorous emotion. His works are not exercises in organization, though they are complete in that respect; nor are they spasms in paint, though they give a stimulus to mood. They fuse the best of the intellectual and the emotional, placing Titian on the mountain top of pictorial achievement.

Having reached such a pinnacle, Venetian painting might have continued on that path, even if not at the same level. But art no more than life ever stands still. It is constantly changing, and a change from even a Titian is not necessarily deterioration. Any alteration of standards, or any adjustment of values in life, calls for a new interpretation. The geometric repose and the intellectual assurance of the High Renaissance began to crumble as soon as they were attained. Even in the hands of its most characteristic figures, we see premonitions, at times, of the impending change.

More than any other man, the painter who underlined this change, long before Titian's death, was Antonio Allegri (1489–1534), a north Italian artist, called Il Correggio from his native village. Active chiefly in Parma, Correggio must have been influenced by Leonardo, who had devoted followers in Milan not far away. In the Madonna of St. Jerome (fig. 247), the disappearance of shaded contours against a dark background, which Leonardo had demonstrated in his Madonna of the Rocks (fig. 227), is carried further. The forms melt into one another, while the sweet types cloy the taste of the present day. Sentiment abounds, but whether this is objectionable depends on the observer. One thing is certain: in spite of its subject, this painting is not primarily religious in spirit. Correggio exulted in the beauty of flesh, particularly feminine flesh. The

248. Correggio (1489–1534) *Io* (c. 1530) Museum, Vienna. 5'4" x 2'5".

Madonna, the Child, the angel, and St. Catherine are dangerous in their loveliness; the gaunt St. Jerome on the left seems out of place.

With this secular love of feminine beauty, Correggio should be at his best where the subject and his instinct work in harmony: for example, in mythology. Fortunately, Correggio was commissioned to paint the amours of Jupiter. One of these is the Io (fig. 248), whom the god visited enveloped in a cloud. This voluptuous canvas is the very ecstasy of love. The cloud, within whose mist the features of the god are barely visible, serves as a foil for the luscious pearly body of the nymph, a glorification of the feminine figure, appealing to the senses. These are passionate Olympians, classic in spirit. Such a vision is worlds removed from the young athletes Michelangelo spread over the Sistine ceiling.

That same sensuous physical exuberance pervades the Assumption of the Virgin, frescoed on the dome of Parma Cathedral. Correggio imagines the hemisphere of the dome as a void where a rush of angels on beating wings transport the Virgin to heaven, while in the center Christ Himself descends tumultuously to greet her. Around the sides, within the painted balustrade, stand the apostles, and behind them a crowd of nude boys, like classic genii, hurry to and fro. These figures are all conceived as though they existed in space and were seen from the floor of the cathedral. While Mantegna on the ceiling of the Camera degli Sposi had tried to create an illusion of space, Correggio carries the idea further than ever before. The turbulence of the apostles, and the optical approach make Correggio the prophet of Baroque decorations a century later. And yet Correggio was only a few years younger than Raphael, and

died almost half a century before Titian.

Venice itself shows the changing times and the trend toward Mannerism (p. 322), partly in Titian's later paintings, and partly in the younger men, all of whom are influenced by him. Jacopo Robusti, known by his nickname, Il Tintoretto (1518–94), chose the motto, 'the color of Titian and the drawing of Michelangelo.' He achieved neither, though influenced by both. In spirit more violent than Titian, he has not the titanic character or the *terribiltà* of Michelangelo. His Presentation of the Virgin (fig. 249) is rich in golden browns; the palette has not the color of the early Titian, or the subtle tonality of his last manner; it is Tintoretto's own vigorous combination. Light, too, has become prominent to enhance drama. The line of beggars on the steps of the temple is half concealed in shadow, while other rich passages of shade play over the pattern. The figures swing from shadow into light with greater agitation than before. These muscular characters, influenced by Michelangelo, are often distorted, with small heads on elongated bodies. Depth plays a prominent part in the composition. The little Virgin stands well back in the design at the top of the temple steps. An irregular ring of figures, including the beggars and several Venetian mothers with their children, reaches a climax in the Virgin and the High Priest silhouetted against the sky. The simple lines of a pyramid in front of the Virgin help to lead the eye to her. Both light and perspective are means of dramatizing

249. Tintoretto (1518–94) *Presentation of the Virgin* (1551–6) Santa Maria dell' Orto, Venice. 14′1″ x 15′9″.

this point of interest, placed well back from the foreground; in Titian's paintings the center of interest is at the front or near it.

The figures in Tintoretto's foreground bear the same relation to the subject that we do; they are spectators over whose shoulders, or between whom, we glimpse the incident. Thus the spectator is brought into intimacy with the subject. The scene is not presented to him; he becomes a part of it. This is true too in the Miracle of St. Mark. A naked Christian slave lies bound in the foreground, saved from execution by his patron saint. An eager crowd surges around him; its members jostle each other, or climb on columns to see better, but nothing impedes a clear view of the slave. Therefore, Tintoretto expected that the observers of his painting would imagine themselves as continuing the circle of curious spectators. The color in this canvas has greater range than in the Presentation of the Virgin, and to that extent is closer to Titian. Also the foreshortening of St. Mark, poised in the air above his follower, suggests the inspiration of Michelangelo. That influence is further illustrated by the figures from the Medici Tombs, on either side of the pediment in the garden wall behind.

In these paintings Tintoretto retains the geometrical basis of earlier compositions, but enriches it. The decorations in the Scuola di San Rocco display his ability to handle complex schemes, notably in the Crucifixion. Everything focuses on the head of Christ, though one hardly realizes it, so apparently casual is the disposition. The glances and gestures of the characters who form a ring of figures on the ground, a ladder lying near by but unused for the moment, the cross of one of the thieves, which is just being raised into position with ropes, and many other details, establish lines that fan outward from the head of Christ. The effect of the scene is one of reality. Tintoretto makes no attempt to treat his subject with archaeological precision, but he imagines a heterogeneous crowd, including a small

250. Tintoretto (1518–94) *Marriage of Bacchus and Ariadne* (1578) Sala del Anticollegio, Ducal Palace, Venice. 4′9″ x 5′2″.

group of loyal disciples, executioners engaged in their tasks, members of the Synagogue come to gloat over their success in suppressing this man, and the idly curious, pausing to view a public execution. In other words, Tintoretto conceives the Crucifixion as history, not as a symbol of Christianity.

His Marriage of Bacchus and Ariadne (fig. 250), in the Sala del Anticollegio in the Ducal Palace in Venice, is arranged like the spokes and rim of a wheel. The curved arms of the three figures converge on the wedding ring proffered by Bacchus. The three bodies form similar curves; each starts inside one adjacent curve and ends outside the other. The elegant forms are idealized. They have a full-blooded healthiness and vigor that make it easy to imagine them as denizens of Olympus. Notable in the Venus is the influence of Michelangelo. Tintoretto made models and suspended them from wires to assist him in learning to draw human beings in any position, including those which could not be held by a model. He displays a mastery of the human figure second only to that of Michelangelo himself.

In his paintings for the Ducal Palace, Tintoretto draws upon Venetian ceremonies for inspiration. The Marriage of Bacchus and Ariadne by analogy symbolizes the marriage of Venice and the Adriatic. Annually, the Doge and his corps on the state barge *Bucentaur* were drawn into the sea, on which the prosperity of Venice depended, and there deposited a gold wedding ring. In these superb decorations—there are three others by Tintoretto in the same room—the artist abandoned drama in favor of a Titianesque serenity. Different as they are, to love Titian does not prevent enjoyment of Tintoretto. One may relish the drama of the latter, finely organized though less perfected and serene in form, just as one may savour the exuberance of Tschaikovsky without losing one's taste for Beethoven or Bach.

Finally, the fourth of the leading painters of sixteenth-century Venice is Paolo Veronese (1528–88). The Marriage at Cana (fig. 251) is religious in subject only. To Veronese, the magnificence of Venice sufficed; the scriptural subject becomes an excuse to record the pomp of Venetian life. This scriptural feast looks like a state banquet. The guests are decked out in brocades of fashion; the setting is elaborate architecture, rich in light and shade, with the gorgeousness of such Venetian buildings as the Library by Sansovino (fig. 252); waiters and pets circulate through the crowd, and a private orchestra provides incidental music. The players are portraits of artists; Titian with the double bass, Tintoretto playing the cello, Jacopo Bassano blowing the flute, and Veronese himself at the viola. The last, as his name suggests, is a native of Verona; his silvery tonality, like that of the north Italian schools, modified the golden tonality of Venice. The architecture is designed either parallel or at right angles to the picture plane, to give the stateliness that so

251. Veronese (1528–88) *Marriage at Cana* (1562–63) Louvre, Paris. 21'10" x 32'6".

formal a composition demands. When seen in perspective, that architecture focuses attention on Christ, seated in the center of the table at the principal vanishing point. This composition is magnificent as decoration; on the other hand, one may look in vain for any deeper meaning in it; Veronese is uninterested in other matters. He displays the social glories of his adopted city as enthusiastically as any society journalist, but his characters have neither intellectual nor spiritual depth. The women in particular are stolid. A St. Catherine in another of his pictures has been described as having 'a heavy placable nonchalance, like a performing cow.' Everything is present that can be achieved by technique, perspective, color, compo-

sition, and external splendor. His are magnificent paintings, nothing more; but perhaps it is enough.

These Venetian artists play a pivotal role in European painting. Their painterly point of view links the earlier Italian schools to later European art. For centuries to come, almost all the major artists of Europe turned to Venice for inspiration. El Greco was trained here. Rubens and Van Dyck studied the work of these Venetians. The whole English portrait school was affected by them, and painter after painter of the nineteenth century owes some debt to these masters. In view of their accomplishment in composition, color, and decorative quality, there could have been no better school.

After the death of Raphael, Leonardo, and Giorgione, and even before that of Titian, Michelangelo, Tintoretto, and Veronese, the development known as Mannerism showed itself in Rome, Florence, and elsewhere. The traditions of the High Renaissance masters could not continue unaltered, partly because the ideals of that generation could no longer be maintained under the new conditions. The outbreak of the Protestant Reformation in the north undermined the assurance of the High Renaissance, and though its impact on Italy at first was distant, it brought with it in 1527 the sack of Rome by German mercenary troops. After that orgy of rape, loot, and desecration, though

Rome regained some of her power, she could not recapture the carefree exuberance of her halcyon days; insecurity, restlessness, and change were inevitable.

The successors of the High Renaissance artists in the second third of the sixteenth century are influenced by them, but their pictorial aim is not identical. Giulio Romano does not paint like his master, Raphael, nor do Daniele da Volterra and Pontormo preserve the earlier Michelangelesque point of view. Some of these men are powerful draftsmen of amazing, restless energy. This is obvious in Angelo Bronzino's painting of Venus, Cupid, Folly, and Time (fig. 253). Figures fill the foreground of this composition to choke the

252. Jacopo Sansovino (1486–1570) *Library*, Venice (1536) 275′ long x 58′ high.

253. Angelo Bronzino (1502–72) *Venus, Cupid, Folly, and Time* (c. 1546) National Gallery, London. 4'9" x 3'9".

whole rectangle and eliminate the depth and the three-dimensional sense of Leonardo's and Raphael's pyramids. These figures seem too large for the space and interlock in complex patterns. Though cleverly tied together, the composition sacrifices the clarity of an earlier generation. The figures themselves are conceived decoratively, with a sensuous feeling for the nude; their mincing grace has neither the spiritual import of the Michelangelo nudes, nor the Olympian robustness of Titian's mythologies. Perhaps the impulse to decoration is one reason for the elongated mannered proportions. Preternaturally tall, the figures sway to and fro, bend over backward, or turn in spirals as though searching elegance in pose, even at the price of affectation. So pronounced is this attenuation that a painting by Parmigianino is called the Madonna of the Long Neck. Such mannered proportions and poses appear in some of the men already considered. Certain late paintings of Titian, and many of the works of Tintoretto—for example, the mother standing halfway up the temple steps in the Presentation of the Virgin (fig. 249)—testify to this development. But the late Titian and much of the work of Tintoretto is contemporary with Mannerism and characteristic of it. In color, also, the Mannerists tend to forgo the

254. Annibale Carracci (1560–1609) *Ceiling Detail*, Gallery, Farnese Palace, Rome (1595). Gallery 30'10" long x 15'10" wide.

sonorous primary chords of the High Renaissance, and turn instead to off shades, like lemon yellows, lavenders, steely blues, metallic colors, in place of the more straightforward tones.

Opposed to Mannerism in theory were the eclectic painters of the Bolognese Academy, founded in 1583 by the Carracci brothers, who thought to outdo their predecessors by borrowing from each painter those qualities in which he had excelled: the strength of Michelangelo, the color of Titian, the repose and balance of Raphael, and the sweetness of Correggio. It was a laudable ideal, but the difficulty lay in combining these divergent traits. Raphael and Correggio exerted the strongest influence, save in murals, where the Sistine Chapel inspired emulation. The Carracci altarpieces continue the types and color of the men they admire, but modify these contributions; the effects are strained, the sentiment obvious and cloying, and the composition too involved for clarity.

Their most prophetic work lies in the field of decoration. Annibale Carracci and his assistants fuse the effects of architecture, sculpture, and painting in the gallery of the Farnese Palace in Rome (fig. 254). Since the artist takes account of light sources within the room itself, and since his technical ability in perspective and modeling is supreme, one is often at a loss to know what is real and what painted. In fact, the whole ceiling above the cornice is painted, but the corners seem to open to the sky beyond, colossi in mono-

chrome suggest sculpture, dark medallions like bronze reliefs contrast with the simulated marble, while pictures are introduced in molded frames. The illusion carries added conviction, since sculptured figures overlap the painted moldings of the frame or cast painted shadows around them. The mantle of Michelangelo falls on the muscled figures as well as on the conception of the ceiling. But the Sistine ceiling is illusionistic only to a mild degree, while the Farnese gallery partakes of the character of a trick, and so forms a halfway stage leading to the fullest development of illusionism and to the complete denial

255. Caravaggio (1569–1609) *Death of the Virgin* (1607) Louvre, Paris. 12'1" x 8'.

256. Jacopo Sansovino (1486–1570) *Bacchus*, Bargello, Florence.

streets, and others drawn from the tavern, the brothel, and the gutter. No longer are the apostles richly clad, and the Madonna conceived as the Queen of Heaven. Their clothing is poor, their features old, wrinkled, and grimy. Such types do not belong in a palace; they are at home in a cellar, with a shaft of light streaming down from some open areaway and falling in stark brilliance on forms set against an inky background. The dramatic shadows of this *Tenebroso* style almost reduce the scene to two planes, one of light and one of shadow.

Though Caravaggio and his followers are called the Realists, we may take exception to the term. Cellar lighting is just as artificial as the diffused lighting of the High Renaissance masters. Also, there is room for doubt as to whether types from low life, though more accurate in the narrow historical sense, are artistically preferable to noble types that indicate the importance of the scriptural characters as the founders of Christianity. Powerful as these paintings are, they lose something. Bald statements supplant the serenity of earlier works, and, while helping to destroy the older conceptions, this substitute does not satisfy everyone. Still, the influence of Caravaggio is extensive. His lighting opens the way to the Baroque in that field, and ultimately to the personal treatment of light by Rembrandt, while several of the Spanish masters, notably Ribera, are affected by it.

Sculpture also displays the new spirit. Jacopo Sansovino in Florence, in the

of the surface in the later Baroque of the seventeenth century.

In protest against eclecticism the Realists led by Caravaggio (1573–1610) arose. He rejected the ideal types inherited from Raphael. In their place, Caravaggio peoples his Death of the Virgin (fig. 255) with characters drawn from the slums, plain folk from the

first half of the sixteenth century, carves his classic Bacchus (fig. 256). The rounded forms of the figure and the generalized treatment produce as finished an academic expression in sculpture as Bramante's Tempietto is in architecture. One of the few sculptors not influenced by Michelangelo, Sansovino stands almost alone. He settled in Venice while still young, became intimate with Titian, and is the sculptor who best expresses the classic ideals of that generation.

The voluble Benvenuto Cellini, on the other hand, is Mannerist to the core. His Nymph of Fontainebleau exhibits the elongated proportions and the affected grace of contemporary painting. Often brilliant in detail, thanks to his goldsmith training, most of Cellini's sculpture lacks largeness of conception. His Perseus, of whose casting we read so exciting an account in his *Autobiography*, acquires a scale that the filigree ornament of the base and the complicated gore dripping from Medusa's neck cannot quite destroy. However, the artificial pose and modeling hardly justify Cellini's encomium on his own work.

The principal Mannerist sculptor, Giovanni da Bologna (*c.* 1524–1608), also displays slender proportions in his bronze Mercury (fig. 257), an incarnation of movement and a proof of technical skill. His academic Rape of the Sabines (fig. 258) shows sensuous naturalism in the modeling. The stone has become flesh, soft and yielding in the woman to the pressure of the man's

257. Giovanni da Bologna (*c.* 1524–1608) *Flying Mercury* (before 1574) Bargello, Florence. Bronze, 5′9″ high.

fingers, but firmer in the masculine flesh. The problem itself is complex, as these three figures of different sexes and ages spiral upward. Where sculpture hitherto had been designed to be seen primarily from a single point of view, this group is interesting from all sides. The forms draw the eye from the front, around the sides, to the back; they de-

258. Giovanni da Bologna (*c.* 1524–1608) *Rape of the Sabines*, Loggia dei Lanzi, Florence.

mand a peripatetic spectator; one must see this group from all angles to realize the purpose of the sculptor.

Architecture, too, gradually modifies its design. The Library in Venice (fig. 252) by Sansovino the sculptor, with its Venetian love of richness already had abandoned in 1536 the austerity of the Bramantesque manner. This well-proportioned two-story building has enriched the arch and column by modeling these elements in light and shade. The open gallery of the ground floor has a severe Doric arch order. On the other hand, the second floor, with its deep window reveals and its combination of arches and Ionic columns, is exuberant. Carving almost buries the architecture with statues on the skyline, garlands in the frieze, medallions within the spandrels, and yet this façade is controlled as the fifteenth-century designs, such as the Certosa at Pavia, are not.

The Library in Venice has much in common with the High Renaissance, as does the earlier painting of Titian. However, the latter half of the sixteenth century prepares the way for the Baroque architecture of the seventeenth century, as Mannerism prepares the way in painting and sculpture. The man who fathered the Baroque style was Michelangelo. Thinking in terms of sculpture even when working in architecture, Michelangelo saw no reason to adhere to the rules of classic design. He said he intended to 'free architecture from the bonds and chains which she had laid upon herself.' He developed his forms with an eye to creating patterns of light and shade, regardless of their previous use. If a column embedded in an embrasure of a wall seemed to him effective, however illogical it might be, he did not hesitate to use it,

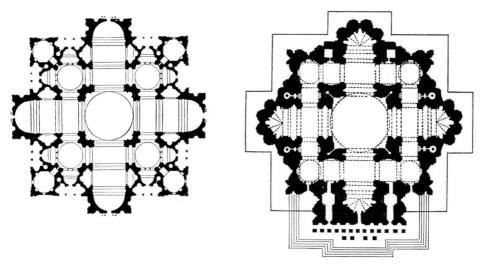

259. *Bramante's Plan* (left—1506) and *Michelangelo's Plan* (right—1547) St. Peter's, Rome.

as in the stairway to the Laurentian Library in Florence. Appointed chief architect of St. Peter's in 1547, he announced his intention of returning to the ideas of Bramante, though in practice he altered his predecessor's conception.

The idea of rebuilding the venerable Early Christian basilica of St. Peter's had occurred as early as the fifteenth century, but not until the pontificate of Julius II (1503–13) was any serious work done. He appointed Bramante in 1506 to begin construction of the new edifice. In the spirit of his day, with respect to classicism and scale, Bramante dreamed of piling the Pantheon on the Basilica of Constantine, choosing two of the largest Roman monuments to produce an even grander scheme. He planned a building of the central type (fig. 259), a Greek cross whose equal arms joined in the space covered by the great dome, almost the same in diameter as the dome of the Pantheon. The whole was to be inscribed in a square. Bramante retained enough smaller features in his design to convey its scale. These elements, whose size could be measured against man's stature, were juxtaposed against the major portions, too large in themselves to permit such measurement. His dome modified the Roman type, more prominent than that of the Pantheon, but still buttressed on all sides by rings of masonry around its base, and by a continuous colonnade. Bramante did not live to see much of his project executed; the foundations had been laid, and the building had begun to rise when he died in 1514. After his death, a succession of architects were appointed, each of whom drew his own plans, many of the central type that modified without rejecting the original project. Others, supported by cogent

260. Michelangelo (1475–1564) *St. Peter's*, Rome. West End (begun 1546) Total height 470'.

arguments, attempted to convert the scheme into a Latin cross form.

When Michelangelo became chief architect, he admired the monumentality of the central type. His conception of the dome required more concentrated supports than had Bramante's. Therefore, Michelangelo's plan (fig. 259) made the solids more solid, the voids more open. The four central piers, like magnets, drew to themselves the smaller supports that Bramante had left isolated. That change destroyed the sense of scale and made it impossible to appreciate at a glance the immensity of this building, particularly in the interior. Michelangelo's love of the colossal had betrayed itself.

One may still perceive Michelangelo's conception of St. Peter's around the apse or west end (fig. 260). An attic story crowns a colossal order of pilasters, almost 100 feet high, as tall as many eight-story buildings. Windows and niches give scale to the exterior. The dome rises from a drum whose perimeter is punctuated by paired columns engaged to solid masses of masonry. Each mass seems to buttress one of the visible ribs of the dome, whose full curve rises in soaring lines. To achieve this effect, so expressive of the unity and power of the Catholic Church in the Counter Reformation, Michelangelo thinks as a sculptor, searching for visual effectiveness with a disdain for structure.

To him, the engineering side of architecture is the handmaid of design, to execute what his eye demands. The pairs of columns below are illogical and inadequate to buttress the vast dome: illogical, because a dome, in spite of the ribbed system, has a continuous thrust that calls for continuous buttressing; and inadequate, because their mass is too small to resist any considerable thrust. The stability of this dome depends on chains embedded in the masonry, and even then there has been trouble. Giacomo della Porta constructed the dome in 1585–8, twenty years after Michelangelo's death. He altered the silhouette by raising the apex of the dome about 20 feet, while retaining the same diameter. This change produces an impressive effect that Michelangelo's model does not attain. Whether the dome is great architecture may be debatable; it depends on the relative emphasis placed on design and on structure; but few will deny the visual power of this culminating feature on the largest church in Christendom.

Early in the seventeenth century, Carlo Maderna was commissioned to complete the church proper by the addition of the nave, which found no place in the plans of Michelangelo or Bramante. There were several reasons for this change. The Latin cross form adapts itself to the needs of Christian ritual better than does the Greek cross. The congregation cannot take part in the service from behind the altar, or even from the sides. The altar must be placed at the architectural focus under the center of the dome, lest it seem pushed into a corner. Three quarters of the area in a Greek cross plan are behind or to the side of this point. Moreover, immense as St. Peter's was to be, the early designs did not occupy all the ground covered by the nave of the Early Christian basilica. Centuries of use had hallowed that ground, and many were reluctant to see any part of it deconse-

261. Carlo Maderna (1556–1639) *St. Peter's*, Rome (1606–26) Façade 390′ wide x 167′ high.

crated. In any case, the papacy, not the architect, decided on a nave.

The architectural effect of this addition is unfortunate. The façade (fig. 261) is no higher than is necessary to cover the vaults of the nave, whose height was determined by Michelangelo's building. Nevertheless, the façade conceals the drum and even some of the dome, except from a distance, and ap-

262. Carlo Maderna (1556–1639) *St. Peter's*, Rome (1606–26) Nave, total interior length, 710′.

PLATE V

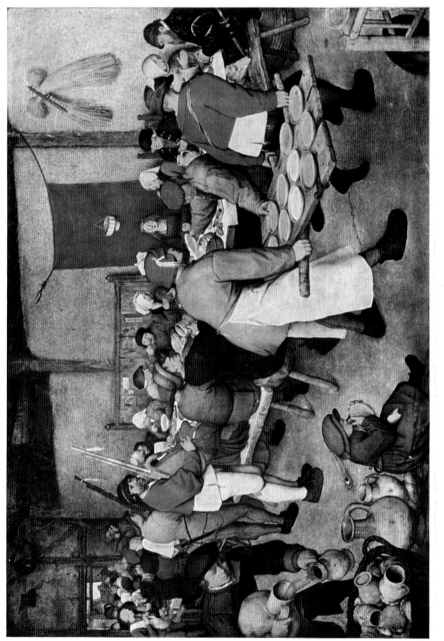

Pieter Bruegel the Elder (1525–69) *Peasant Wedding*. Kunsthistorisches Museum, Vienna.

PLATE VI

El Greco (1541–1614) *Niño de Guevara* (1596–1600)
Metropolitan Museum, New York. (5′ 7″ x 3′ 6″)

pears to tip the dome over backward. Therefore, from the front the dome cannot accomplish the purpose it fulfills for the west end of pulling the lower masses of the design together. Maderna could not but follow Michelangelo's executed work. The latter had planned a porch of colossal columns, but to have retained that with the new length would have accentuated the ill-effects on the dome. The height of the order and of the attic story was already determined. Maderna substituted pilasters for columns, and his detail is less personal than that of Michelangelo, but the unsuccessful result of the façade is the consequence of the work of Michelangelo modified by the demands of the papacy.

The interior of St. Peter's (fig. 262) is vast, but like much of the exterior, lacks scale. A barrel vault continues in dimensions and design the vaults with which Michelangelo surrounded his dome. Pairs of pilasters carry an entablature to support the vault. This order, almost as large as that of the exterior, has little to convey its size. Though added later, the child angels supporting the stoups of water are giants and consequently deceptive. This lack of scale can hardly be charged to Maderna, who merely continued the earlier design. From the entrance the long nave prevents the immediate perception of the space within and around the great dome that Bramante and Michelangelo had

263. Andrea Palladio (1518–80) *Villa Rotonda*, Vicenza (1552–53) 80′ wide on each side; porticoes 32′6″ high; dome 70′ high.

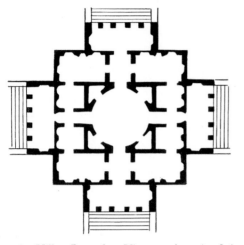

264. *Villa Rotonda*, Vicenza (1552) 80′ square.

as much through their writings as by their architecture. Andrea Palladio in his *Four Books of Architecture*, published in 1570, lays down his rules for the proportions of the orders. These books became architectural gospels to England and thence to America. His style, as seen in the Villa Rotonda at Vicenza (fig. 263), 1552, depends for its effect first on proportions, and second on restraint and formality. The Villa Rotonda is of the central type, square in plan (fig. 264), with a portico

in mind, but this again was impossible to avoid. Any nave would have had the same result. Maderna followed the scheme Michelangelo had already built in large part. He had to introduce windows in the vault, and he was able to lighten both vault and piers, since they did not need to support the dome. St. Peter's took a little over a century to build. Begun by Bramante in 1506, it was changed and carried further by Michelangelo, and the church itself was completed early in the seventeenth century by Maderna, though its approaches and some of its fittings had still to be added in the High Baroque style. St. Peter's is the central monument of its time in Italian architecture.

Michelangelo was far in advance of his own day. Not until well on in the seventeenth century did architecture catch up with him. Two architects of the latter half of the sixteenth century, however, exerted great influence later,

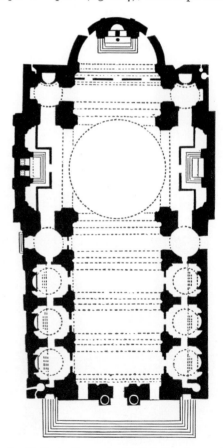

265. *Il Gesù*, Rome (1568–84) Interior 225′ x 115′.

on each face and a domed chamber in the center. All sides of the building are identical and gain monumentality from the flights of steps that approach their porticoes. Designed as a country residence, the regularity of its plan is not adapted to the asymmetrical requirements of a house. On the other hand, its stateliness is admirable as a background for a formal life, which explains Palladio's popularity in Georgian England and America. The adherence to rule and the emphasis on correctness, which produce the academic flavor, are more Renaissance than Baroque, though in some of Palladio's buildings a hint of the later style can be detected.

The second of the late-sixteenth-century architects, Giacomo Barozzi da Vignola, is more advanced. He, too, wrote of architecture, but his volumes, *Rules of the Five Orders of Architecture*, 1562, had their chief influence in France, and through their use by the Ecole des Beaux Arts, on those Americans who received their architectural education in Paris. Though his books are not much less conservative than Palladio's his executed work shows more freedom. Vignola's church of the Gesù in Rome (1568–84) establishes a milestone in the history of Baroque architecture. The plan (fig. 265) is more compact than the three-aisled type.

266. Giacomo Barozzi da Vignola (1507–73) *Il Gesù*, Rome (1568–84) Interior 225′ long x 115′ greatest width.

Short transepts hardly project beyond the rectangle of the church, and are broader than they are deep. The nave is wider in proportion than had been usual. Chapels replace side aisles and open into the nave through large arches so that the space of the chapels seems rather an extension of the space of the nave than a separate volume.

Such a design suggests a different type of religion from that for which the medieval churches were built. It argues a growth in the importance of preaching. There had been great preachers in the previous centuries, some of them so popular that they had to address their throngs out-of-doors. However, the medieval church was designed for the rich ceremonial preparatory to and connected with the Mass. That service was so familiar that it made little difference whether all within the church could hear distinctly, or whether they could all see the altar. Ease of hearing and, to a lesser extent, of sight are fundamental to preaching. Since the sermon plays a large part in the teaching of the Jesuits, their churches have to be so arranged that the whole congregation can have an unobstructed view of the pulpit. This functional requirement works toward the same result as the Baroque feeling for unity of space. The barrel vault springs from an entablature carried on paired pilasters (fig. 266). A half-dome crowns the apse, while over

267. Giacomo della Porta (1537–1604) *Il Gesù*, Rome (1568–84) Façade *c.* 115′ wide x 114′ high.

the crossing a full dome is raised on a drum to light the eastern part of the church. These unbroken volumes inaugurated a new conception of space that played a central role in the seventeenth century.

The façade of the Gesù (fig. 267) was redesigned and erected after Vignola's death by Giacomo della Porta. Vignola displayed some Baroque freedom in his scheme, but Della Porta goes further. This two-storied front is of a type that became standard for Italian church façades at this time and later. The lower story must be as wide as the nave and the lateral chapels, but the upper story screens only the vault over the nave, and is narrower. Buttress-like masses rise along the sides of

the church to support the barrel vault. Those are expressed on the façade in scrolls at the sides of the second stage, and soften the transition between the stories. Such a façade, while some of its elements reflect the building behind it, is a screen and can be treated as a problem independent of the building. One could hardly guess the existence of a barrel vault behind the upper story, and the freedom of design reflects a breakdown of architectural properties unknown in the High Renaissance and beloved by Bramante.

The detail has not the correctness of a Palladio, but begins to exhibit the florid quality of the Baroque. A single feature suffices to illustrate the indifference to logic. Over the central door,

268. *Fountain of the Organ*, Villa d'Este, Tivoli (begun 1550).

Della Porta has set a triangular pediment inside a segmental pediment. This is preposterous. If the function of the pediment is to discharge rainfall to the sides of an opening, then one or the other pediment is useless. These architects do not pretend to logic; they are designing in light and shade, and if the pattern consequent on such a use of classic features interests the eye, their use is justified. But the Gesù has little of the plasticity of the Baroque. Only a few inches separate the planes of its façade, and no strong projections interrupt it; its flat members cast thin lines of shadow without the boldness of seventeenth-century designs.

One of the most successful creations of Italy at this time is the villa. Its variety is infinite. The Villa d'Este at Tivoli has many characteristic features. Placed on the side of a hill to drain the utmost value from a stream that is diverted to feed the fountains, its paths lead the visitor down from level to level through ramps, alleys, and steps shaded with trees and cooled by fountains. The balustrades, urns, stairs, and fountains are coarse in detail. Who would want the refinement of a drawing room in features destined to be covered with moss and lichens? Playfulness and even broad humor find a place here. Jets of water once drenched any visitor who unwarily stepped on certain stones in the path, or on certain steps, though these booby traps no longer operate in our fastidious days. But fountains are the glory of the villas. One never escapes the sound of splashing water as it spouts from a thousand jets, dribbles from one basin to another, or rushes down a cascade or over some constructed waterfall. In the Villa d'Este the culmination is the Fountain of the Organ (fig. 268), where great jets, like the pipes of an organ, contrast with the plunging mass of water in the center. Such villas are pleasant indeed on summer afternoons, and are among the most lasting contributions of the Italians to the history of art.

The Gothic style was indigenous to the north; the Renaissance was not. By the sixteenth century the Gothic energy had worn itself out so that the ground was ripe for something new. In the Renaissance Italy gave birth to a civilization of greater sophistication, with a consequent emphasis on the amenities of life. The northerners slowly became aware of this refinement, though until the end of the fifteenth century its effects were hardly perceptible. Then the series of Italian wars started with the raid of Charles VIII of France into Italy in 1494, followed shortly by those of Louis XII and Francis I. Since many of the French aristocracy accompanied these excursions, the upper class was thrown into contact with the new style and culture at the source, and wanted to adopt it immediately in their own homes.

The Renaissance style in France, therefore, grafts Italian elements on the native stock. The builders had been accustomed for centuries to work in the Gothic tradition. When their patrons called upon them for something different, they were bound, at first, to take the superficial details of Italian art to adorn their works, while retaining much of the earlier tradition. To assist in the importation of the new fashion, Francis I invited to France such Italian artists as could be induced to come. Leonardo da Vinci, to whom Francis I gave the Château of Cloux near Amboise, where the great Florentine spent his declining years, is the most famous, though his productive days were already over when he went to France. Cellini, also, came to Paris and Fontainebleau for a brief time, but such men as Il Rosso, Prima-

269. *Francis I Wing*, Château, Blois (1515–19) *c.* 150' long.

ticcio, and Serlio, who made Fontaine-bleau the training ground for the dissemination of new ideas, exerted the formative influence.

The wing added by Francis I, in 1515 to 1519, to the Château at Blois (fig. 269) illustrates the peculiar combination of traditional French and imported Italian styles. It is, so to speak, the offspring of a marriage between the Jacques Cœur House at Bourges (fig. 159) and the Certosa at Pavia (fig. 193), one of the first buildings in the new manner that the French saw on their Italian journeys. The former contributes the visible roof, the vertical continuity of Gothic buttresses, the mullioned and transomed windows, and the dormers in the roof. From the latter stem the translation of the buttress-like forms into classic pilasters, misunderstood in purpose but recognizable in design; the substitution of the round for the pointed arch; the decorative motives, like arabesques, carved wherever possible; and the rich cornice that replaced the parapet. There was in France the same misunderstanding of a new architectural language which had hampered Italy at the beginning of the fifteenth century, but with this difference: the Italians at first mistranslated classic architecture to

270. *Château*, Chambord (1526–50) *c.* 525′ long.

create the Renaissance; the French mistranslated Italian architecture and were therefore one step further removed from the classic. Their detail is coarser but no less profuse than the exquisite carving on the Certosa. However lawless, this French style has an exuberant joy in life that parallels the richness and energy of Rabelais in contemporary literature.

As time went on, the French became more at home in the new fashion, and the foreign details were naturalized. The Château of Chambord (fig. 270), eight years later than Blois, is strictly symmetrical, though it preserves the courtyard of the medieval castle, and the keep at one point in its walls. Tower balances tower, themselves French although their regularity bespeaks the Renaissance influence. Thus the plan (fig. 271) is reminiscent of bygone military needs, but the absence of fortifications and the

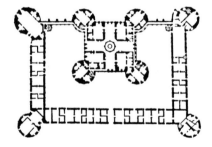

271. *Château*, Chambord (1526–50) 525′ x 370′.

many windows attest a new security. Each unit in the plan, each tower, and each building mass connecting them retains its independent roof as though the edifice were composed of associated elements—a peculiarity of French architecture at least until the middle of the seventeenth century. The effect is less vertical than in the earlier design at Blois; double bands above and below the windows in each story cross the structure, towers and connecting masses alike, and thus unite the whole. The detail has more of the Renaissance than has previously occurred—for example, the numerous but flat pilasters. The plan of Chambord and its broken silhouette thus distinguish it from any Italian design, while on the other hand its regularity and its detail separate it from the Middle Ages.

When in 1539 Charles V paid a visit of state to Francis I, the lack of any modern palace to receive his distinguished guest embarrassed the French king. He therefore commissioned Pierre Lescot to design a building to replace the medieval Château of the Louvre in Paris. Though only a few parts of the existing Louvre date back to Lescot in 1546, those parts (fig. 272) demonstrate his evolution of a co-ordinated style from the charming but lawless vagaries and richness of the châteaux. This style is still French, with its visible roofs, its conception in terms of accented vertical pavilions alternating with less emphasized horizontal blocks, and its peculiar French feeling for elegance.

The vocabulary of this style is now coherent and Renaissance. The orders are prominent both as engaged columns

272. Pierre Lescot (c. 1510–78) *Lescot Wing* (on left, 1541–48) Louvre, Paris. c. 175′ long x 95′ high.

and as pilasters. A Composite order on the principal floor is superposed on the Corinthian order of the ground floor, each with a full and correct entablature. Every fourth bay makes a pavilion with bold membering, engaged columns instead of pilasters with an entablature broken forward above them, deep window reveals, rich ornament, and a dormer roof at the top rising higher than the neighboring bays. No one of these factors would call attention to itself, but collectively they distinguish these bays from the others, and so establish a rhythm in design. For the rest, round arched niches on the ground floor contain Renaissance windows, while pediments and pilasters enframe those above. The detail is rich but elegant, much of it carved by Jean Goujon and his assistants, and yet it takes a subordinate place in the design instead of running riot over the façade. The humanism of the Renaissance, at this time better understood in architecture, also prompted the mythology of the Goujon decorations. In short, by the middle of the sixteenth century, France had absorbed the Renaissance but extracted her native version from it.

The diffusion of the Renaissance in other countries follows the same pattern. In Spain, the Plateresque, or silversmiths', style toward the end of the fifteenth century shows the same exuberant energy in half-understood Italian forms as the earlier châteaux. Here, some trace of the Moorish gives its local flavor to the style. By mid-century, the Griego Romano, as its name suggests, parades the classicism of the High Renaissance with greater austerity than the contemporary work of Lescot in France. In Germany, also, the same course is pursued, with first the influence of the north Italian style being felt, then of the Bramantesque manner, and finally of the developing Baroque. The precise steps, however, are confused, and elements from more than one phase may exist in a single building. In general, the detail in Germany is apt to be treated in a heavy-handed and ugly manner.

Owing to local conditions, the story in England is a little different. Early in the reign of Henry VIII there occurred the same importation of Italian craftsmen that had helped to established the French style, but England, further removed from Italy and with less to offer, could attract only third-rate artists, whereas the French could at least get second-rate men to serve them. The parts of Hampton Court built under Cardinal Wolsey in the first half of the sixteenth century show an application of Renaissance details to a Gothic building similar to what one sees in the earliest French examples. Doubtless the English would have moved along lines parallel to the French had it not been for the marital troubles of Henry VIII. Because of his divorce of Catherine of Aragon, a break with the Roman Church, though at first merely in church government, became inevitable. Since the papacy was virtually an Italian institution, the colonies of Italian craftsmen in London and Winchester dwindled and disappeared, and thus deprived

the English of their source of Renaissance inspiration. The subsequent religious troubles under Edward VI and
Mary engrossed the attention of the
English too completely to permit much
to be accomplished in the way of architecture. During the reign of Elizabeth
I the art revived, but turned for inspiration to other countries affected by the
Reformation—to Germany and the Low
Countries. These countries were by
then aware of the developing Baroque
style, which they interpreted in a heavy-
handed manner that became typical of
Elizabethan palaces such as Burghley
House in the second half of the sixteenth century. Much of the Perpendicular Gothic tradition is retained, for example the large multiple windows, but
is coupled with such absurdities as
Doric columns used for chimney pots.
This fashion was better mastered in the
Jacobean style under James I, early in
the seventeenth century, though it was
still apt to be heavy in detail.

The gradual assimilation of the Renaissance in the Gothic north is just as
apparent in sculpture. A relief of St.
George Slaying the Dragon by Michel
Colombe, very early in the sixteenth
century, treats the subject in much the
same episodic manner as the International style in painting, discussed before
(p. 235). Remnants of its victims surround the dragon, itself a wondrous fig-
ment of the imagination. Like a playful
puppy, it worries St. George's lance. The
princess at the left prays for her champion; her type, her simplified drapery,
and her partial idealization link her

273. Jean Goujon (c. 1510–68) Nymph
(1547–49) Paris. 6'4" x 2'4".

with the Détente. And yet Italian artists frame this late Gothic panel with Renaissance pilasters and an entablature embellished with north Italian detail, producing the same mixture of styles characteristic of the Francis I wing at Blois.

The influence of Italian Mannerism molds the Nymphs from the Fountain of the Innocents in Paris (fig. 273), by Jean Goujon, a contemporary of Lescot, who couples it with a distinctly French quality. These slender figures in low relief create appropriate decoration. The drapery clings to and reveals the bodies, as they turn languidly in studied poses; the proportions are reminiscent of such mannered figures as Cellini's Nymph of Fontainebleau, with which Goujon must have been familiar. Here the head is one ninth of the total height of the figure; she therefore appears to be a courtly lady, tall and slender. On the other hand, the linear design is more delicate, the conception exhibits a French elegance, and the type of face and figure is quite distinct from the Italian. Through such works as these Goujon shows his subtlety and refinement.

Germain Pilon (1535–90) in his Christ of the Resurrection (fig. 274) is self-conscious in his attack on the problems of realism. His zest in detail conveys his desire for a literal summary of the form, and for precise anatomy to express suffering. The statue has power, though its design, delicacy, and charm seem unequal to Goujon's fountain. In the other countries in Europe, the same sequence of style may be traced as in architecture, running from slight mod-

274. Germain Pilon (1535–90) *Christ of the Resurrection* (c. 1583) Church of St. Paul-St. Louis, Paris. 5′7″ high.

ifications of the Gothic to more complete acceptance of the Renaissance and Italian point of view.

Much the most important development of painting outside of Italy during the sixteenth century took place in Germany. The technique practiced in the north derives from the oil painting of the medieval Flemish school, not from Italian tempera or fresco methods. It offers the same opportunity for minute detail on a lacquer-like surface that existed for the Van Eycks and their followers. The earliest and greatest of these northern painters, Albrecht Dürer (1471–1528), is still a medieval or at most a transitional figure. Little of the Renaissance affected his earlier work, and yet in his career as a whole something of the Renaissance can be detected. His love of microscopic detail is purely northern. On the other hand, his concern with perspective, the zest with which he seizes any opportunity to sketch exotic animals with fidelity, and occasionally the weight of his figures and his compositions imply that he was familiar with Italian Renaissance ideals —no doubt through the constant com-

275. Albrecht Dürer (1471–1528) *Adoration of the Magi* (1504) Uffizi, Florence. 3'3" x 3'8".

276. Albrecht Dürer (1471–1528) *Four Saints* (1526) Museum, Munich. Each panel 6′8″
x 2′5″.

munication of the two countries at this time—even before his own trips across the Alps into Italy.

The commanding position occupied in Dürer's output by religious subject matter betrays his medieval origin. The Adoration of the Magi (fig. 275) is characteristic. The Flemish oil technique, but slightly modified, makes possible the polished surface and the clarity of detail. What joy he takes in the butterfly and beetle on the steps, the iris growing from a joint between the stones, the jeweled brocades of the costumes of his Magi, and the anthropological painting of the Negro! The Virgin, as always, adheres to the local physical type—in this case to the blonde complexion, light hair, and tendency to fleshiness that, rightly or wrongly, we associate with German womanhood. There is little of the Renaissance here. To be sure, the ruins in the background show round arches, but they are too elementary to be called classic or even Italian. The naturalistic detail, though typical of the early Renaissance, is equally pronounced in the northern late-Gothic painting of the fifteenth century, and in itself can hardly be accepted as evidence of the Renaissance. The form of the Madonna and the largeness of conception, however, do suggest the existence of a new spirit creeping in to the northern schools.

The painting of the Four Saints, John, Peter, Mark, and Paul (fig. 276), being later, is more affected by Italian sources, though it does not lose its Germanic character. In this case, the sense of form is increased. A genuine monumentality inspires these figures, clad in ample draperies whose very plainness adds to the grandeur of the types. Naturalistic in detail though the heads are, some of them even prosaic, the avoidance of enrichment in the massive folds of the costumes lends a noble simplicity to this design. Dürer gives us here a microcosm of mankind, since the four saints symbolize the four temperaments or complexions—sanguine, choleric, phlegmatic, and melancholic—into which current belief divided humanity. For such a purpose, the elemental grandeur of these figures is vital.

Although Dürer never deserted the Catholic Church, he was not unaffected by the religious ferment that, during his lifetime, gave birth to the Lutheran Reformation. Criticism of the Church in Germany was widespread, and was expressed not only by the spoken and printed word, but in some respects with greater effect by graphic illustration. Dürer's master, Michael Wolgemut, for example, made an engraving of the Church as the Whore of Babylon. The age called for serious thought on religious problems, though it is only the exceptional woodblock or print that is anti-clerical. Dürer was even more important in the graphic arts than in painting. Two series, the Large and the Small Passion, reveal Dürer's medieval intensity of belief in the tragic incidents of Christ's trial and death. In the Four Horsemen of the Apocalypse, a woodcut, he shows the figures riding roughshod over the burghers of his native Nuremberg, artisan, merchant, and housewife alike. The engraving of Knight, Death, and the Devil shows a knight-errant in sixteenth-century armor accompanied on his way by a skeleton armed with scythe and hourglass, and followed by a devil whose horn and piggish snout seem unlikely to tempt anyone. These works prove how sober was Dürer's view of life. They also reveal him to be a great master in the graphic arts, with a power in black and white rarely equaled and never surpassed.

The same sobriety raised to the acme of religious mysticism dominates the celebrated Isenheim altarpiece by Matthias Grünewald (c. 1485–c. 1530). It builds up to its startling effect in all possible ways. The enamel-like surface enables the literal detail to be observed with unnatural clarity. The figures are posed with outlandish angularity. The dark sky throws them into prominence as they point toward the Crucifixion. But above all, the unearthly greenish tonality makes this painting look, as it was intended to look, like a scene from another world, gaunt, powerful, and tragic.

Very different was Lucas Cranach the Elder (1472–1553), who lived in Saxony, the birthplace of the Reformation. Religious subject matter accounted for a smaller proportion of his work than of his predecessors', and what there was was somewhat affected by Protestantism. On the other hand, he was eager to keep abreast of the classic spirit of the Renaissance. His paintings of mythology, such as Venus and the Judgment of Paris, are laughable in their naïveté. These slender blonde-haired German girls, who seem coy and a little embarrassed by their nakedness, parody Olympian characters. Such conceptions are worlds removed from the sensuous idealization given to similar themes by Giorgione and Titian.

Cranach's best paintings are straightforward half-length portraits. In some, the costume of the sitters is amazing for its wealth of elaboration rendered with microscopic precision, but in many of the finest paintings the sitters are plainly dressed. The Dr. Scheuring in the Brussels Museum, clad in a fur-trimmed robe, is typical of these figures in the artist's unpretentious presentation of his subject. Though not devoid of modeling, Cranach's portraits rely more on delineation, on a clean-cut silhouette against a background of a single tone of clear color—light tan, pale green, or most often, a robin's egg blue. The decorative value of this simple combination of color and line is undeniable.

Hans Holbein the Younger (1497–1543), almost a generation later than Dürer and Grünewald, shows a quite different attitude toward religion. Born and trained in Swiss Basel, he belonged to the same cosmopolitan group as Erasmus and Melanchthon. He became a painter for the merchant class, and therefore religious subjects played an incidental role in his career. They were not wholly neglected, however, as the engraved series of the Dance of Death can testify. His most important paint-

277. Hans Holbein the Younger (1497–1543) *Georg Gisze* (1532) Museum, Berlin. 3'2" x 2'9".

ing, the Madonna of the Burgomaster Meyer, seems to prove that Holbein is indifferent to the religious characters. What interests the artist are the kneeling portraits of that substantial citizen of Basel and his wives and family. One cannot help wondering whether Meyer's living wife relished the prominence given to his deceased and shrouded wife. Even the Madonna looks middle class. This secular attitude is more Renaissance than Dürer's had been.

Further, where Dürer adopts a subjective attitude, and comments on his theme, Holbein is objective, dispassionate. No one more keenly analyzes the characters of his sitters than Holbein, but his purpose is to show exactly what they are like, rather than what they might be. Georg Gisze (fig. 277) is a shrewd merchant of the German Steelyard in London, the establishment of the Hanseatic businessmen. In his office Gisze is surrounded by the materials of his trade, a box of coins open on the table before him, ink, receipted bills, other business documents on the wall beside him, and a curiously wrought container for a ball of string over his head. The texture of each of these details Holbein treats with objective realism, and their presence assists in the characterization of the individual. One understands Gisze better than if he were present in the flesh before us, because the portrait is not only a speaking likeness, but one where the personality of the man has been underscored visually to bring out those traits of character which Holbein, the analyist, discovered in him. Without allowing his own personality to appear, Holbein concentrates on this objective presentation.

The Gisze was painted shortly after Holbein's arrival in England, partly to demonstrate his ability. It is therefore more elaborate in its setting than most of his portraits. The Jane Seymour

278. Hans Holbein the Younger (1497–1543) *Jane Seymour* (1536) Museum, Vienna. 2′2″ x 1′7″.

(fig. 278) is simpler. While hardly less literal in effect, a linear style is adopted with little shadow or modeling of the form. The result is an exquisitely finished, enamel-like panel. Each detail of costume or feature is precise from a graphic point of view. The plain background concentrates all attention on the features of the sitter. Such an analysis appears to be based on a careful drawing in line, executed at a single sitting; this might then be translated into the finished portrait at the artist's leisure in his shop. Such details as those of the costume could be taken from whatever dress the subject chose to select and have sent to Holbein's studio, but the personality must have been established

279. François Clouet (*c.* 1505–72) *Elizabeth of Austria*, Louvre, Paris. 14″ x 10″.

through a short period of observation, and especially through the artist's intellectual analysis of his subject.

The technique of Holbein, like that of Dürer, still continues the Flemish oil medium. The method proved equally applicable to the religious sobriety of Dürer, the merchant portraiture of Holbein, and the court portraiture of the Clouets in France. François Clouet, painter to Francis I and later to Henry II, in his Elizabeth of Austria (fig. 279) is quite similar to Holbein in technique and in his two-dimensional pattern-like approach. He differs from Holbein as one would expect a court portraitist to differ from an artist many of whose patrons belonged to the merchant class and whose point of view was colored by

that fact. Holbein, to be sure, also painted members of the court of Henry VIII of England, but always with unsparing honesty. Clouet is less analytical and less frank. His portraits do not convey the same impression of a human personality dissected before us; rather his figures present themselves less as they are than as they would like to be. Perhaps Elizabeth of Austria was as handsome as she is rendered, but Clouet's portrait of her does not inspire the same feeling of authenticity as do Holbein's portraits, or of power. Nevertheless, Clouet's portraits are exquisite in drawing, and have an egg-shell fragility in them fraught with infinite charm. The same elegance that characterizes Goujon's sculpture recurs here, and helps to give them their peculiarly French flavor. These portraits, like Holbein's, were based on quick sketches, but many such drawings were never intended to be used for paintings; they were collected as we collect photographs of our friends. Francis I and his successors loved to thumb through albums of these drawings, and sometimes to write remarks upon them concerning the sitters, compliments or frank and even ribald comments on the beauty, personality, or conduct of the subjects.

Meanwhile, the imported Italian artists were enriching the gallery of Francis I at Fontainebleau, or the Château of Ancy-le-Franc, with Mannerist paintings and schemes of decoration. In the former, effects of architecture, sculpture, and painting are mingled. Decorative nudes, echoes of the Sistine ceiling, combine with elongated figures in mannered poses and with cartouches bearing the royal monogram. In his panel, Geometry, at Ancy-le-Franc, Francesco Primaticcio (1504–70) accepted the muscular male figures of Michelangelo together with the complex compositions of the Mannerist painters.

As in Germany, so in Flanders the medieval school gradually became aware of the Renaissance. One man after another, such as Jan Gossaert, called Mabuse (c. 1478–1533), made the pilgrimage to Italy, to return with more or less Italianism in his baggage. Others, less affected by the prevailing wave of southern influence, showed the spirit of the times in different ways. The extraordinary fantasies of Jerome Bosch (c. 1450–1516) provided a precedent for the Surrealist painters of the twentieth century. Save for his sacred characters, he reveled in grotesque types; but even more fantastic are such details as a pair of enormous human ears pierced by an arrow and separated by a knife, or a body whose legs are gnarled trees and whose egg-shell torso is broken to admit a glimpse of human figures within it. The inexhaustible wealth of his imagination nowhere found a fuller opportunity than in the Temptation of St. Anthony and The Garden of Earthly Delights; such paintings cannot be described; they must be examined in detail.

Pieter Bruegel, the Elder (c. 1525–69) wove together the diverse threads of Flemish painting in the early sixteenth century in his epoch-making canvases. Like many of his predecessors he traveled to Italy in 1553, but unlike them he made no attempt to borrow Italian motives. When he painted the Fall of Icarus, he relegated that incident to the background despite the inclusion of all the details of the story mentioned in Ovid's *Metamorphoses*. In the foreground, he substituted a Flemish peasant plowing a field. The influence of Bosch on Bruegel is prominent in the kaleidoscopic wealth of detail in such paintings as the Flemish Proverbs, or the Children's Games, compositions that show Bruegel's encyclopedic interest in the life of his time.

The canvases commonly called Huntsmen in the Snow, The Harvesters, The Return of the Herds, and others show Bruegel's grasp of the possibilities of landscape painting at varying seasons of the year. The many small Flemish figures, engaged in activities appropriate to the month, give some genre quality to these paintings, but that is so subordinated to the larger conception of the landscape as a whole that Bruegel may be called the first great landscape painter in the European tradition.

Even more important was Bruegel's preoccupation with the vitality of Flemish life. To him, the common man offered all the opportunity he needed for his study of humanity; it was a passion that dominated his work whether the subject was mythology, a religious incident such as The Carrying of the Cross,

280. Pieter Bruegel the Elder (c. 1525–69) *Peasant Dance* (c. 1567) Museum, Vienna. 3′9″ x 5′5″.

landscape, or genre. The Parable of the Blind Men was to him a file of beggars tumbling into a ditch, while the Hireling Shepherd was a Flemish shepherd. His innate Flemish realism, with a spirited emphasis on the awkward peasant types, found full play in the Peasant Dance (fig. 280). A century before, Van der Goes had introduced Flemish peasants into his Portinari Altarpiece (fig. 183) as participants in a devotional scene. By Bruegel's time, the secularism of the Renaissance had left not a trace of religious motive in this genre subject, based on daily life. How these clodhoppers and their wives pound through the vigorous movements of the dance, clumsy in person and uncouth in cloth-

ing, but amazingly energetic withal! The lust for life was strong in the sixteenth century.

The composition both in the Peasant Dance and in the Peasant Wedding (Plate v, facing p. 332) is informal, as befits their subjects. In the former, certain shapes repeat themselves in the gables of the houses and the heads and shoulders of the figures. The table in the Peasant Wedding creates strong diagonals that serve to define the figures in space. Accurate as these figures are in essentials, the old microscopic detail has disappeared. Instead, the forms are enough simplified to yield a pattern of shapes and colors. Great patches of red and blue, large shapes and masses, create a stirring arabesque of fine visual consequence. So effective are the forms, space, and color that it makes little difference whether the subject is a Peasant Wedding or, as has been suggested, a Harvest Festival. Surely Bruegel, both as a painter and as an observer of the lusty vitality of life, still is not accorded a sufficiently high niche in the history of art.

XV   THE ITALIAN BAROQUE

To a considerable extent, the Baroque style, though it reaches its full development only in the seventeenth century, is the fruit of the Catholic Counter Reformation of the sixteenth century. Although that style made itself felt even in non-Catholic countries, such as England and Holland, the style originated in Italy and found its fullest expression in Italy, Spain, and Catholic Flanders. The sad condition of the Church, that provoked the Reformation in the north, did not pass unnoticed in Italy itself. Therefore, a small group of devout men, during the pontificate of the worldly Leo X, formed the Oratory of Divine Love to work for the purification of the Church from within. The reform movement grew with such landmarks as the establishment of the Dominican Inquisition, the Index, and the

Council of Trent (1545–63), while the Jesuit Order, founded in 1540 by St. Ignatius Loyola on military lines, proved to be a powerful weapon in the hands of the Church in its fight against the spread of heresy. One product of the purification of the Church and its consequent strength was a renewed and almost arrogant affirmation of the authority of the Church and its unity. The scale and size of St. Peter's in Rome suggest that.

Another result was an emphasis on the sufficiency of faith and its emotional nature. The religious experience of such a typical Counter Reformation saint as St. Theresa of Avila was physical in its emotionalism and violence. Moreover, the renewed faith made its appeal to the emotions through the senses more than through the mind. Hence one finds a growth in the dramatic conception of art which often produces a desire to astonish the observer by effects that seem unbelievable, or by a theatrical presentation in sculpture and painting of both miraculous and common events. Naturally, this leads to violent movement. Individual figures throw themselves around in excited gesticulation, enhanced by wind-tossed flights of drapery. Turbulence may at times help the intensity of expression; at other times, it becomes mere restlessness. This tendency is not found in the figures alone but in the composition as well. The geometric schemes of the Renaissance, the triangle, the circle, and the symmetrical shapes, which are, so to speak, complete in themselves, give way in the Baroque to asymmetrical designs that often emphasize the diagonal line, a motive in itself incomplete and dynamic.

Such a diagonal may cross the picture plane, or it may consist of movement leading the eye into the composition, accenting the depth of space the artist has at his disposal. The three-dimensional designs of the Renaissance—the ring of figures in Raphael's School of Athens (fig. 240) and the pyramid in Leonardo's Madonna and St. Anne (fig. 229)—exist in space and have more or less distant backgrounds. But the spatial depth of the Baroque is more dramatic and important to the design; the movement in depth predominates over both lateral and vertical motion. The design opens up as though to imply the existence of still greater areas beyond and ever beyond, instead of being contained and complete and final in itself.

Coupled with this depth, and at times an instrument to attain it, is a fresh concern with light and shade and an extensive exploration of its possibilities. The Renaissance had confined its interest in light and shade largely to the modeling of the figures. Indeed, in many cases, though light molds the objects, it casts little shadow. The Baroque, however, ranges from the personal treatment of light by Rembrandt, through the theatricality of Rubens' Descent from the Cross (fig. 296), to the naturalistic light of Velásquez (fig. 294). The same interest in light provokes the sculptors to undercut the drapery, and so to play with the surfaces as to induce a variegated design in shade over them. Similarly, the architects develop plastic arrangements, an opulence that creates a sense of movement through bold patterns of light and shade. In painting, this study introduces a painterly approach with an appreciable degree of optical realism. It does not follow that the results will be naturalistic, though they sometimes approach that, but simply that the appeal is visual. Hence we find illusionism in some mural paintings, and a tendency to make other canvases credible in appearance, even when they deal with the miraculous or with the supernatural.

Such purposes call for a high degree of technical skill, which becomes an end in itself—that is, virtuosity. Whether in architecture, sculpture, or painting, one is amazed at the dexterity of the performance of the Baroque artist. This may or may not be desirable; such facility may contribute to legitimate ends in the arts, or, if allowed to dominate, it may destroy the feeling for the material by playing tricks with it.

These various characteristics are not combined in every example of the Baroque, still less in all the works of the seventeenth century. Some of them are present in sixteenth-century artists, as for example the cellar lighting of Caravaggio, or the turbulence of Correggio's frescoes. The late sixteenth century, indeed, leads into and merges with the Baroque. Also, local conditions modify the completeness with which the Baroque is adopted. At its purest in Catholic Italy, Spain, and Flanders, some elements of the style affect the contemporary art of France, Holland, and England in varying proportions and in different ways, according to the spirit of those countries and the background of the artists. Even in a single country, wide latitude is possible.

Although Michelangelo's rejection of the laws of architecture reached its culmination in the High Baroque, not all monuments of that style are radical. When in 1656 Bernini was commissioned to create a setting for St. Peter's, he divided the space in front of the church into two parts. The portion nearer the façade he treats as a trapezoidal piazza, which is, in turn, entered from an elliptical area outlined on either side by colonnades four rows deep (fig.

261). The detail is conservative, though the proportions of the Doric columns are more slender than usual. Each column of the inner row is bound to be seen against parts of the columns behind it, a fact that tends optically to widen the diameter of the shafts; no doubt this suggests the lighter proportions of the columns to prevent an effect of too great heaviness.

On the whole, the design is austere. Those who consider that the Baroque is by definition florid and ornate must modify their opinion when faced with this monument, where decoration is reduced to a minimum. The Baroque character of the design is unmistakable. Over each column of the inner row rises a statue to interrupt the skyline and to produce the broken silhouette so common in Baroque designs, though the motive can also be found in the work of Palladio and Michelangelo. But above all, the plan establishes the Baroque quality. The trapezoidal shape, foretold in Michelangelo's group of buildings on the Capitoline Hill in Rome, lacks the regularity and geometric simplicity of the Renaissance. The oval of the front piazza is an unstable form; a dependent shape, it demands something else for its completion, in this case the trapezoidal area and the façade of St. Peter's itself. Not only do these forms dramatize the great space, but they bring movement into the design, and, like claws, pull the spectator forward.

Perhaps because of the quantity of Bernini's commissions, or perhaps because he is primarily a sculptor, he

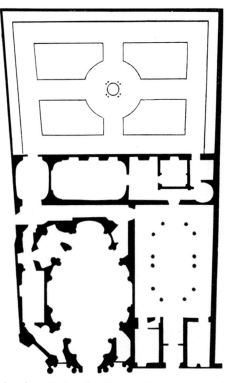

281. *San Carlo alle Quattro Fontane*, Rome (1638–67).

shows little interest in architectural detail and is content to follow precedent in this respect. Not so with Francesco Borromini; his interest is architectural, and few are the elements of that art with which his fertile mind does not experiment. The Church of San Carlo alle Quattro Fontane, begun 1638–40, often called San Carlino from its diminutive size, is built on a tiny and irregular plot. Borromini displays the greatest ingenuity in his solution. Like Bernini in the colonnades of St. Peter's, Borromini bases his design upon an oval (fig. 281), but makes the long rather than the short axis dominant. Unlike Bernini, he

does not stop with a simple shape, except in the dome, whose inner surface is paneled with crosses and irregular hexagons instead of the usual square or octagonal coffers. The oval plan is not obvious at first glance, because of semicircular protrusions at the ends and semielliptical extensions at the sides. The entablature winds in and out of these shapes.

The serpentine façade of San Carlo (fig. 282) of later date recalls this undulating movement. It is composed of three bays: the central one on the ground floor is convex in plan, and the lateral ones concave; but in the second story all three are concave with an elliptical sentry box in the center to provide a transition. Thus the whole façade is thrown into movement. At the top, flame-like curves replace the usual pediment. Engaged columns are preferred to pilasters, with a resultant enrichment of the light and shade patterns. The columns give an impression of verticality peculiar to much of Borromini's work; this impression is due partly to their exceptional height but more to the close spacing he prefers. Moreover, even the capitals are designed anew. Borromini is not content to repeat the time-honored members of the Corinthian order; he must turn the corner scrolls inward upon themselves instead of outward as usual. Or, as in his remodeling of the nave of San Giovanni in Laterano, he alternates wide and narrow flutes in his pilasters. To the conservatives such experiments are perverse license, calling forth the strictures of such critics as

282. Francesco Borromini (1599–1667) *San Carlo alle Quattro Fontane*, Rome (1638–67)
Façade.

Ruskin or Warren; but unless one assumes a sacrosanct immutability of the orders, they provide novel and exciting variants on the norm, despite the fact that not all of these experiments are successful.

In spite of his originality, Borromini was overshadowed by the tremendous popularity of Bernini, so that his opportunities were few and frequently on a small scale. The same was true of the sculptors. As the favorite of Urban VIII and of Alexander VII, Gian Lorenzo Bernini (1598–1680) could choose his own projects and skim the cream of the commissions flowing from the papacy and elsewhere. His high fortune was foretold by Urban VIII, who, on his election to the chair of St. Peter said, 'It is well for you that I, Maffeo Barberini, am become pope, but we are even more fortunate that the Cavaliere Bernini should live to decorate our pontificate.' Even when Bernini's star passed under a cloud during the pontificate of Innocent X, which separates the other two, he won his way back into partial favor before the end of that reign. His fame brought from Louis XIV an invitation to Paris and Versailles to consult on the design for the Louvre; on his journey thither in 1665, he was received with honors generally reserved for royalty. The cities through which he traveled turned out to do him honor, and built temporary triumphal arches over his route. Few artists have ever enjoyed such esteem.

As a young man, Bernini studied in the gardens of the Villa Borghese, and worked for that family. One of his commissions from them is the Apollo and Daphne (fig. 283). This prestidigitator of the seventeenth century would convince us that we do not look here at stone, but at many other substances. The texture of male and female flesh is subtly distinguished and contrasted with the textures of cloth, bark, and leaves. Each surface is so handled that it almost deceives the eye, and appeals to the physical senses.

Even more startling is the arrangement. The dynamic figures throw their arms about in actions that lead the eye on a diagonal out of the group rather than into it. Sculptural compactness is not an aim here, nor is there the slightest indication of the original limits of the block of stone. Michelangelo had said that sculpture should look as if it could be rolled down hill without injury, and his work, however capable of movement within the block, retains that sense of compactness. The Baroque desire for visualized movement induced Bernini to select the dramatic climax, the very instant Daphne is being metamorphosed into the laurel to escape capture by Apollo. Everything must be momentary and in transition.

But that same movement occurs in portrait busts, where no story exists to explain it. Francesco d'Este (fig. 284) turns his head to his right, but this movement is answered by the drapery fluttering off his left shoulder. Why drapery over armor! Why, indeed, save that the metallic surfaces of armor seem

283. Gian Lorenzo Bernini (1598–1680) *Apollo and Daphne* (1622–24) Villa
Borghese, Rome. Marble, life-size.

284. Gian Lorenzo Bernini (1598–1680) *Francesco d'Este* (1650–51) Museo Estense, Modena. Marble, over life-size.

at the sides support concave bits of entablature, which then break back to permit a convex plan for the center of the entablature and pediment. This convex portion gives Bernini the opportunity to conceal a small window, whose light runs down gilded rays to the figures like the spotlight of a theater. Even the side walls of the chapel play their part in the scheme; portrait groups in high relief of members of the Cornaro family attend the performance in boxes, some looking toward the stage, and others glancing around at the rest of the audience. This operatic setting belongs to the same century and country that gave birth to opera as a musical form.

Such a setting calls for the dramatic group of St. Theresa and the angel, an interpretation in white marble of the ecstasy of the saint. She tells how in her dreams an angel appeared to her and transfixed her body with an arrow. At that moment, she felt a combination of exquisite pleasure and of such agony as to cause her to swoon. Bernini translates this vision literally into stone. Momentary as the scene is, the story is told as though it were re-enacted for us in living characters. Every texture of flesh, cloth, and metal is suggested. The sensuous figures evoke physical responses in the spectator. A spiritual orgasm is given expression in physical shape. The sweetness of the angel and the ecstatic suffering of the saint, fainting on a bank of clouds, tax our credulity. The Baroque dramatic sense is thus coupled with the Baroque wish to astonish the spectator.

to Bernini to need a contrasting texture, a pattern of light and shade that deep folds of drapery could supply, a suggestion of movement that would convey a counter action to the head. The finely characterized face breaks into undulations of surface to induce a dynamic play of light impossible to attain in simpler forms. The undercut curls of the wig complete the effect in texture, movement, and shadow.

These qualities remain paramount in sculpture designed for the Church. The religious spirit of the Counter Reformation receives full expression in the altarpiece of St. Theresa of Avila (fig. 285), in the Cornaro Chapel of Santa Maria della Vittoria in Rome. The whole chapel is arranged as a theater. A proscenium bent forward like the front of a stage frames the altar. Paired columns

285. Gian Lorenzo Bernini (1598–1680) *Vision of St. Theresa of Avila* (1645–52) Cornaro
Chapel, Santa Maria della Vittoria, Rome. Marble.

PLATE VII

Peter Paul Rubens (1577–1640) *Emperor Maximilian I.*
Kunsthistorisches Museum, Vienna.

PLATE VIII

Jan Vermeer (1632–75) *Girl with Water Jug.*
Metropolitan Museum, New York. 1′ 6″ x 1′ 4″.

John Constable (1776–1837) *Hay Wain* (1821)
National Gallery, London. 4′ 3″ x 6′ 1″.

286. Gian Lorenzo Bernini (1598–1680) *Tomb of Alexander VII* (1671–78) St. Peter's, Rome.
Marble and gilt bronze, 24′2″ high x 19′4″ wide.

Equally dynamic and typical of the Baroque point of view is such a tomb as that of Alexander VII in St. Peter's (fig. 286). Four allegorical figures, whose gestures bear little relation to their meaning, begin the scheme, two in the foreground and two behind. A grim skeleton pushes aside the billows of fringed drapery carved in colored marble, and struggles upward to reach the kneeling pope at the top. Thus does the Baroque represent even death as a melodrama. The Renaissance feeling of repose has given way to movement, restraint to abandon. This type of tomb remains the vogue until the end of the eighteenth century.

The St. Theresa group and the Tomb of Alexander VII combine sculpture and architecture. One hardly knows whether to describe the Baldacchino of St. Peter's (fig. 262) as one or the other. This vast canopy has to accent the high altar of the church, itself a small feature, and yet must not block the vista down the nave to Bernini's own composition enclosing the Chair of St. Peter at the end of the church; it has to challenge the scale of the church without confusion with the architecture. Dark bronze serves this purpose well; its color contrasts with the lighter travertine stonework of the building, and yet its strength allows the four twisted columns to rise as high as an eight-story building. These vine-covered shafts that enframe the altar spiral upward in answering curves, the direction of turning reversed in each pair. From their architraves hang bronze draperies, embroidered and tasseled. The columns support angels and scrolls that join in the center to hold the ball and cross. Over all these architectural members crawl thousands of bees, the heraldic emblem of the Barberini family. Since the bronze for this monument

came from the beams of the Pantheon roof, the wits of the day coined the quip, 'Quod non fecit barbari, fecerunt Barberini'—'What the barbarians did not do, the Barberini have done.'

No painter arose in Italy to challenge the position occupied in sculpture by Bernini, though the art of painting was hardly less flourishing. Guercino's Burial of St. Petronilla (fig. 287) is characteristic. Here is the same Baroque dexterity, the control over perspective, the figure, and the sense of depth. The design be-

287. Guercino (1591–66) *Burial of St. Petronilla* (1621) Capitoline Museum, Rome. 23'7" x 13'10".

288. Fra Andrea Pozzo (1642–1709) *Ceiling of Nave*, Sant' Ignazio, Rome (1691–4).

comes open by contrast with the closed designs of the Renaissance. Our eye runs from the men who place the body of the saint in its grave at the bottom, through curving masses that sweep to one side and back to the other, always striving upward and inward. A succession of dynamic diagonals carries the observer through the painting; they do not permit his attention to rest at any point. The scene itself has the same sensationalism, and the figures the same physical appeal as Bernini's St. Theresa. It calls upon our faith for appreciation, and we must not expect the moment represented to last. It is the dramatic climax that absorbs Guercino's interest.

Similarly, in the ceiling of Sant' Ignazio (fig. 288), one of the huge Baroque decorative schemes, Fra Andrea Pozzo gives us a glimpse of the Apotheosis of St. Ignatius Loyola. Here is illusionism carried to its conclusion. The vault of the church is imagined away. An elaborate ensemble of columns and arches, bits of entablature and so on, rises above the walls and in their plane the center of the vault is open to the sky. Within this void, Pozzo explodes a host of figures. Saints and angels with fluttering draperies rest upon clouds, sit on the painted architecture, or rise and fall in space. The perspective is calculated from a specific point on the

289. Giovanni Battista Tiepolo (1696–1770) *Institution of the Rosary*, Gesuati, Venice.

floor of the church, and from that point the effect is astonishing. So perfectly has Pozzo taken into account the light and painted shadows, that one cannot tell where the real architecture stops and the painting begins. These figures spill over on constructed parts of the building as well as on those that are merely envisioned. We may question the validity of this *tour de force* on the ground that a surface can hardly be decorated by denying its existence, but Pozzo and his contemporaries would have rejected this theory, and if we accept his premise, the result could not be improved.

A testimonial to the force of Baroque decorative tradition lies in its continuation in the eighteenth century. The Institution of the Rosary (fig. 289) on the ceiling of the Gesuati in Venice, by Giovanni Battista Tiepolo (1696–1770), retains the movement, the fancy, and

18th Cen

the dynamic composition of the Baroque, but combines them with traditions in drawing and color inherited from Veronese. The explosive energy of the Baroque lessens as the Rococo spirit of the new century lightens the motives it has inherited, and replaces gusto with vivacity. The color also betrays its date in its lighter value and softer quality. By this time, Venice had become a tourist center, catering to a taste for gaiety and entertainment. Such painters as Antonio Canale, called Canaletto, whose work was popular in England, and Francesco Guardi recorded the pageants and spectacles of Venice as well as its buildings, canals, and lagoons, while Pietro Longhi chronicled the frivolous social life of the city. If these later Italian painters lack the stature of their forebears, at least they portray the city and its society in their day.

Though Italy was untouched by the Protestant Reformation and remained the home of the papacy and the Church, it was too weak to play an important role in European politics during the late sixteenth and early seventeenth centuries. Therefore, Spain became the prop of the Catholic Church and the real home of the Catholic Counter Reformation. It is significant that the Inquisition was associated with Spain in the popular mind, and that the founder of the Jesuit order and many of the other early Jesuit saints were Spaniards. Spain has been described as a land of contrasts, of the subtropical coastal area and the bleak and arid plains of the center, of the fabulous wealth of the hidalgos and the abysmal poverty of the peons, of gaunt austerity and sentimental emotionalism.

Domenikos Theotokopoulos (1541–1614), the first Spanish painter of international importance, was born at Candia in the island of Crete. Like the rest of the Greek world, Crete was still Byzantine in culture; therefore El Greco, as this painter was nicknamed, must have been aware from his childhood of the Eastern willingness to distort the figures for the sake of either design or emotion. However, he received his training in Venice, probably from one of the Bassani family, contemporaries of Tintoretto and of Titian's old age, the generation of Mannerism. That training left its mark on his work for years afterward.

For example, the Purification of the Temple (fig. 290), painted shortly before he settled in Toledo in 1577, is still strongly Venetian. Its architecture be-

290. El Greco (1541–1614) *Purification of the Temple* (1571–74) Institute of Arts, Minneapolis. 3'10" x 4'10".

trays that origin, and so too does the sumptuous color, not yet personal to El Greco himself. Moreover, the figures and the calculated geometry of the composition (p. 9) testify to the thoroughness of Venetian training. The subject, too, has significance. El Greco repeats it at least six times during his career, though in earlier history the motive is rare. Surely one is justified in recognizing here an allusion to the purification of the Church by the Council of Trent, one of the most important fruits of the Catholic Counter Reformation.

Indeed, El Greco more than any other artist becomes the painter of that movement; its mystic emotionalism, its fervid faith, find in him an interpreter. For example, the Burial of Gonzalo Ruiz, Count of Orgaz (fig. 291), records a local legend of Toledo. St. Stephen, whose martyrdom is embroidered on the hem of his robe, and St. Augustine reappear on earth to lower the body into the grave. Dressed in the sumptuous vestments of the Spanish church, their identity has not yet become apparent to the noble friends of Orgaz or to most of the clergy. Mean-

291. El Greco (1541–1614) *Burial of the Count of Orgaz* (1586) S. Tomé, Toledo, 15′9″ x 11′9″.

while, the heavens have opened to receive the soul of this just man, an ecstatic vision witnessed by the priest in
the right foreground. El Greco paints

Christ in the center; below Him to
either side, the Madonna and St. John
the Baptist intercede for the soul of
Orgaz, a vague form wrapped in swad-

dling clothes and borne aloft in the arms of an angel. El Greco does not hesitate to distort these heavenly figures; their proportions are elongated, in part through Mannerist tradition, and perhaps through some dimly remembered Byzantine conventions, but more as a personal and expressive element of El Greco's style. Here, too, his individual color scheme, characterized by a luminous white, is displayed. El Greco is attempting to express the supernatural by means of the unnatural.

The lower half of the painting forms a deliberate contrast. A portrait group of the Spanish nobility have gathered to attend the last rites of their friend. They stand in sober grief behind the group of priests and saints in the foreground. Neither the palette nor the proportions are unnatural in this scene, but then these figures are of the earth. Contrasted as are the upper and lower halves of this design, they are visually co-ordinated with magnificent success. Curved lines rise from the backs of St. Augustine and St. Stephen through the angel into the rhythms of the upper part, and bind the two sections together. One may examine details of El Greco's painting in photographs, but such details never look complete. They always appear to need something else, so completely has El Greco subordinated each part to the whole. This cannot always be said even of great painters; one can sometimes find a part of a painting that is an entity in itself; but with El Greco, the building of a picture is so integrated

292. El Greco (1541–1614) *Resurrection* (1595–1600) Prado, Madrid. 9′ x 4′2″.

that nothing can be added or taken away.

The Orgaz was painted within ten years of the time that El Greco had arrived in Spain. His later work, such as the Resurrection (fig. 292), is further removed from nature. By this time his dynamic sense, foretelling the Baroque, has grown apace, and the forms themselves partake of the action. Especially is this conveyed through El Greco's peculiar light, a whitish light, which flickers over the forms where it is needed, not so much for its own sake as to increase the upward movement. That light helps to give El Greco's palette its unique flavor; his reds and blues, yellows and greens mold the forms they enrich, but each of them models toward this living whiteness found in the work of no other painter. One reason for the mysticism of El Greco's paintings and for their religious poignancy is the upward movement of the light. Not only are the forms elongated and accented by light, but they are piled one above another. The risen Christ with the banner of the resurrection ascends above a sprawling devil, whose arms and legs conduct our eyes up to the Saviour.

Though most of El Greco's work is religious, he does not confine himself to that field. The View of Toledo in the Metropolitan Museum is said to be the first pure landscape in the European tradition—that is, the first with no figures to provide an excuse for the scenery. A more dynamic landscape would be hard to find, as El Greco resolves the hill where Toledo is built into a succession of swirling curves, answered in the stormy sky. The strong greens of the land create a base for the steely blues and whites above. Even in this field, his personality transforms the subject; landscape, religious themes, and portraits alike are filtered through El Greco's mystical nature.

In portraiture, too, he ranks with the best. The Niño de Guevara (Plate VI, facing p. 333) is a solid painting of that leader of the Spanish Inquisition. His puritanical conviction of the justness of his cause and austere determination to prosecute it to the limit do not conceal the intellectuality of this head. Was the piece of paper on the floor that might have slipped from his fingers an anonymous accusation of heresy that has caused the cardinal thus to deliberate? Perhaps so; in fact it bears El Greco's signature. The gorgeous crimson robes of the cardinal are set off against a background of yellowish tones, subdued in intensity. Significantly, El Greco places the sitter in an armchair neither facing the observer, nor in profile; rather the chair is at an angle that introduces diagonal planes for the front and sides of the figure, and thus enhances the space by which the figure is surrounded. This is combined, however, with a linear pattern of curves in sequence, each leading to the head, a succession of drop-shaped loops which establish harmony of line. The patterned leather of the wall completes the design, so that even the setting becomes an integral part of the scheme.

Very different from El Greco, and a generation later, is José de Ribera (1588–1656), who spent most of his active life in Naples, at that time under Spanish domination. His violent spirit vibrates between themes of sentimental piety, such as in the St. Agnes, and ferocity,

as in the Martyrdom of St. Bartholomew. The vigorous types and deep
shadows attest the influence of Caravaggio and the Tenebroso style, and at
best give his paintings strength akin to
his own swashbuckling nature; but the
shadows are apt to produce an unpleasant griminess of tone.

With but one important exception,
El Greco received no patronage from
Philip II. That cold and bigoted monarch could not appreciate El Greco's
fiery intensity. On the other hand, Don
Diego Rodríguez de Silva y Velásquez
(1599–1660) became court painter to
Philip IV. Though he made two trips
to Italy, he seems not to have been affected by the work of any particular
artists he saw there. This is not surprising in view of his instinct for optical
realism. Few painters have observed the
facts of vision so clearly or recorded
them so easily. The subtlest changes in
light or atmosphere flow from his brush.
Velásquez could paint anything that he
could see; therein lies his strength and
his weakness, for he lacked the ability
to envision what he could not see.
Whenever his subject deals with an unreal world his imagination collapses, so
that in his few Madonnas and mythological characters he is not at his best.
In the painting called the Topers, Los
Borrachos, an initiation of a follower of
Bacchus, the god is the least effective
figure of the group. On the other hand,
the older devotees, as human figures,
are magnificent. His Mars has been described as an undressed policeman. A
Spanish smithy serves for the Forge of

293. Velásquez   (1599–1660)   *Innocent   X*
(1650) Palazzo Doria, Rome. 4'7" x 3'11".

Vulcan, with the sturdy blacksmiths at
home but the god in his aureole of light
distinctly out of place.

With this ability to catch the essence
of visual reality, one would expect
Velásquez to be successful in portraiture, and so he was. The portrait of Innocent X (fig. 293) in tones of red and
white, a product of his second trip to
Italy, shows an intensity of characterization rarely equaled. The intellectual
force and strong personality of the pope
are portrayed with a vividness at once
faithful to externals and analytical. In
pose, Velásquez seems here to be influenced by the Greco portrait of Niño
de Guevara: Innocent X sits in an armchair placed at an angle to the picture
plane, as though to involve the sense of
depth. But Velásquez does not com-

294. Velásquez (1599–1660) *Las Meninas* (1656) Prado, Madrid. 10′5″ x 9′.

pose his figure or its background with the richness of El Greco. He is content to leave the painting as a plain statement of the looks and character of his sitter, the fruit of his vision and his keen analysis. El Greco went on to synthesize his observations with the pictorial interest of composition.

Velásquez zeal for optical realism has full scope in such canvases as the Maids of Honor, Las Meninas (fig. 294). This is a genre scene, a painting of everyday life. It happened one day that Velásquez was busy painting the portraits of the king and queen, as he must frequently have been. The little Infanta, surrounded by her ladies-in-waiting, wandered in to observe the progress of the picture, and while there sent one of her attendants for a glass of water, which has just been brought. The princess stands in the center with her maids, nuns, dwarfs, and pets. To the left, the artist works at his canvas, while a courtier looks back from the open door on the scene he has just left, and finally the king and queen themselves are reflected in a mirror on the studio wall.

This incident has no particular significance, and yet Luca Giordano once referred to the Maids of Honor as a theology of painting. The handling is broad; details are summarized to record their visual effect. A few touches suffice to establish the flowered headdress of the kneeling lady-in-waiting, and the pleats and ribbons of the Infanta's gown. In such breadth, as well as in the optical realism, Velásquez anticipates the nineteenth-century Impressionists. Space envelops the figures. One senses the volumes of air within the room, and even the visual effect of the atmosphere on distant as compared with nearer objects. In distinguishing no less than four planes of light within a small interior by subtle gradations of values and intensities, Velásquez accomplishes a *tour de force* of painting. These planes define the spatial relationships of the composition. Light from the window whose jamb is visible to the right bathes the principal group. Being close at hand, these persons are most sharply seen. Farther back a second plane, marked by a second window, includes canvases of Velásquez and a mirror on the wall. Not much of pictorial interest occurs here, lest this zone compete with the main subject, though its recession is clear. Outside the door is a courtier, not merely smaller than the foreground figures, but with a thicker veil of atmosphere between him and our eyes. Finally, the king and queen reflected in the mirror, though they stand in the position of spectators to this canvas, are visually the furthest away. The light from their persons must travel to the further wall and back to our eye. Not only are they small through perspective but, though still recognizable, they are the least precisely painted characters in the whole canvas. To render four planes in the limitless spaces of out-of-doors involves great depth, but there the contrast between the several planes is large. Velásquez finds that contrast within the limited dimensions of an interior, and renders it with so sure a touch that the space has become real.

His feeling for space and his interest in light link Velásquez to the Baroque, but the religious side of that movement touched him not at all. Bartolomé Esteban Murillo (1617–82), however, exemplifies the sentimental side of Baroque faith in his Immaculate Conception (fig. 295), one of his many versions

295. Bartolomé Esteban Murillo (1617–82) *Immaculate Conception* (1678) Louvre, **Paris.**
9′ x 6′3″.

of a theme popular in his day. Once a general favorite, Murillo is now less admired. His compositions are satisfactory, with a predilection for the diagonal, here created by the attributes, and the angels who flutter around the Virgin. On the other hand, the drawing is weak, and the color, chiefly pinks and blues, suggests the tones of the nursery. These qualities go hand in hand with the pietistic sentiment revealed through the hands clasped on the bosom, the head thrown back, and the eyes rolling upward. Such sentiment comes close to the saccharine banalities of religious calendar art, which has not infrequently been inspired by it. On the other hand, Murillo could be realistic in his genre paintings of the gamins of his native Seville. These brats, though not devoid of a sentimental appeal, are lively; their clothes are ragged, they are dirty and tanned, but they have a vitality lacking in his sacred characters.

XVII

FLANDERS

During the early seventeenth century, the southern Netherlands was still under Spanish domination. Among the richest and most industrious of the Spanish possessions, Flanders remained within the fold of the Catholic Church, though it required the bloody persecutions of the Duke of Alva to stem the tide of the Reformation in those provinces. Also, an aristocracy continued to play an important role there; like the Church, it patronized the arts and so helped to form the character of Flemish painting. That character was embodied in the work of Peter Paul Rubens (1577–1640), the greatest Baroque painter of the north, if not indeed of Europe. As a child, Rubens served as page in the court of Margaret de Ligne-Aremberg,

and received a schooling in court etiquette of great value to him in later life. That he knew how to behave in the presence of royalty was proved by his reception at the court of France, where Marie de Medici, then the Queen Mother, loved to watch him at work and to talk with him; and again in England, where Charles I did him the singular honor of commanding from him a self-portrait.

Rubens received his training as a painter from several minor Flemish masters. Going to Italy after he was trained, he spent eight additional years copying and studying the works of the Italian 'old masters.' This extraordinary length of what one might call a post-graduate course is worth observing by those who think they can learn to paint in a few years. On his return from Italy Rubens opened a studio that soon grew to the proportions of a picture factory. By 1611, two years after his return, 200 painters and students were active there. Apparently, there was a division of labor in this shop; there were independent painters such as Snyders, who specialized in animals, and Jan Bruegel, called Bruegel de Velours from his interest in textiles. Rubens recognized this method in his scale of prices; so much for a canvas painted entirely by himself; somewhat less for one where his students had carried out some of the work; and still less for products of the studio, untouched by the master. Such a system was financially successful. Rubens made two large fortunes during the course of a career of about thirty years in Flanders. The method was adapted to decorative work, and indeed that point of view dominated Rubens' style, which perhaps reaches its culmination in the Marie de Medici series in the Louvre. Rich in color, which is inherited from Venice, his paintings, regardless of the subject, have vigor and a robust, sensuous, physical character.

The Descent from the Cross (fig. 296), painted not long after his return from Italy, is dramatic. Rubens slashes a spotlight across his scene; it follows the arms of Christ, the diagonal sweep of the sheet on which he is being lowered, and the Magdalen kneeling at the foot. The man leaning over the cross, the body of Christ, and the red-robed figure below restore the equilibrium. The figures sway backward and forward,

296. Peter Paul Rubens (1577–1640) *Descent from the Cross* (1611–14) Cathedral, Antwerp. 13'10" x 10'1".

partly because of their roles in the incident, but more because of the Baroque love of movement. These men and women are strong and healthy, as yet without that exaggerated fleshiness that today in Rubens' paintings has repelled so many. They have a material reality that enhances their vigor.

The Rape of the Daughters of Leucippus by Castor and Pollux (fig. 297) shows this animal exuberance at its best. There is a robust grandeur in these characters who glory in their energy; such rousing love of being needs physical expression. The composition seems to be based on that of a lost painting by Leonardo da Vinci, the Battle of Anghiari, which is known through a sketch

297. Peter Paul Rubens (1577–1640) *Rape of the Daughters of Leucippus* (*c.* 1618) Museum, Munich. 7′3″ x 6′10″.

made of it by Rubens himself. But the diamond shapes have become dynamic. One point throws itself across the canvas to catch another, one movement sweeps into the next. The actors toss themselves around, even more violently than the subject demands, especially since the two women do not seem to

fight their captors. Moreover, the forms are rendered in short quick curves; the abundant flesh of human beings and horses, the clouds above and the features of the ground below, all repeat this curving motive with variations. Such a design becomes decorative; it appeals less to the mind than to the eye. It is not so much concerned with telling a story, though it does that too, as with the sheer exuberance of these lush forms.

That sense of the decorative dominates even his portraits. Helena Fourment, Rubens' second wife (fig. 298), is sufficiently analyzed, but the painter

298. Peter Paul Rubens (1577–1640) *Helena Fourment* (c. 1631) Hermitage, Leningrad.

is less eager to create a personality on canvas than to establish a decorative pattern of color and form. The full-length figure, with its rich costume, feather fan, and flowing hat, forms its own justification. Even half-length portraits, such as his Self-Portrait, Rubens paints in the same way, again with the broad-brimmed hat cocked at a rakish angle above his bearded face. These are brushed in with boldness in full color, a masculine technique, dashing and supremely confident of itself. Just how sumptuous the color can be is apparent in the portrait of the Emperor Maximilian I (Plate vii, facing p. 364). His glittering armor with its gold decorations has for a foil the red curtain and blue sky. With such color, the character of the sitter must play a secondary role.

One measure of Rubens' greatness lies in his diversity. Religious paintings, mythologies, landscape, and hunting scenes spring from his brush with equal readiness. His two principal followers each took up one or two fields of Rubens' activity, but could not match his scope. Jakob Jordaens (1593–1678) had much of his predecessor's vigor in his genre composition, The King Drinks. In this Flemish feast, the king of the banquet, usually the heaviest drinker, regulates the pace his subjects must follow. The table groans, as well it may under such bounty, and if not all the men live up to standards approved by Emily Post, nevertheless good spirits overflow the picture. The gusto with which these vulgar people are recorded forms a seventeenth-century version of the zest for life seen earlier in this region in the peasant scenes of Pieter Bruegel. A sober piety of the middle and lower classes finds its way into Jordaens' religious compositions. In color, too, the warmth of Rubens' palette is continued. It has been said that Rubens dipped his brush in blood, Jordaens in fire.

But where Jordaens accentuates his predecessor's animal spirits, Anthony van Dyck (1599–1641) concentrates on the courtly side of Rubens' nature. Van Dyck's religious canvases and his mythologies have a restraint that deprives them of the exuberance of Rubens' paintings. He is, of course, best known for his portraiture, especially that of the court of Charles I of England. His Maria Louisa van Tassis (fig. 299) displays Van Dyck's exquisite drawing. The costumes and accessories retain something of Rubens' decorative quality, but without that passionate energy that lends power to Rubens' smallest work. Van Dyck's are society portraits at their best; as such they have neither the vitality of Rubens, nor the dispassionate accuracy of Holbein. His court ladies are always seen to their best advantage. Surely not all these beauties were so attractive as they appear to be in Van Dyck's canvases. At its worst, this idealization may produce the vacuity of a routine society portrait, as it does in some of the beauties of the court of Charles I, even at the hands of Van Dyck himself. At its best, however, such an approach can create a sense of innate distinction that sheds its social prestige over any room where the por-

traits are displayed. Very often these finely dressed men and women stand against a generalized landscape, or perhaps against the pedestal and lower drums of a classic column, while a decorative sweep of drapery may fill in the canvas without distracting too much from the sitter. The color, influenced by the Venetians, is fresh, but not so intense as to violate the elegant and restrained technique that matches his characterizations. Through his creation of the society portrait, Van Dyck goes far to establish English portraiture, which reaches its finest native expression toward the close of the eighteenth century in the paintings of Reynolds and Gainsborough.

HOLLAND

Holland, the northern half of the Low Countries, during earlier times had been the poor sister of the Flemish school of painting. In the seventeenth century, local history molded conditions there, different from those in Flanders, which helped to give rise to an independent school of equal or greater eminence than the Flemish. For one thing, Holland had become predominantly Protestant. Therefore, religious painting was almost eliminated. When we reflect how large a proportion of the work of all previous painters had been religious in motive, we must realize how profound was the change when painting ceased to serve the Church. Rembrandt, to be sure, dealt with scriptural subjects, but both his choice and his treatment were in-

299. Anthony van Dyck (1599–1641) *Maria Louisa van Tassis* (*c.* 1629) Liechtenstein Gallery, Vienna. 4'2" x 3'.

spired by a Protestant intimacy with the Bible, not by Catholic faith or dogma.

The spread of Protestantism in Holland drove the Dutch on to win their independence from Catholic Spain in the long wars that ended with the Peace of Westphalia in 1648. One might expect a school of historical painting to commemorate with legitimate pride the heroic incidents of that struggle. In reality, the Dutch were indifferent to historical painting. The burghers who had fought that war displayed their patriotism in their satisfaction with their own civilization. They admired painting that looked as much as possible like what it purported to represent. They were not interested in painting as a vehicle for the expression of abstract ideas or stories of mythological personages. What they wanted was portraiture, if

one may use the term, not only of themselves, but of their lives and all matters that bore on them. They lived not in palaces but in comfortable houses, more or less the size of our homes today, and their paintings were domestic in scale and in subject. The canvases could not be too large to hang in a room of normal size, and they dealt with themes appropriate to being hung in a home.

Moreover, the Dutch burghers had the means to command such painting. Through her proverbial industry, her dairying, her printing, and above all her trade, Holland won prosperity for several generations. The Dutch captains sailed their craft far and wide. For a brief moment they snatched control of the seas from England. Holland had a monopoly of the spice trade, more important then than today, since before

300. Frans Hals (c. 1580–1666) *Officers of St. Andrew's Company* (1633) Frans Hals Museum, Haarlem. 6'9" x 11'.

the days of electric refrigerators spices were not merely condiments but essential preservatives.

Thus portraiture of individuals and of all the ramifications of their lives became the dominant production of the school. Most artists sought reputations for their handling of a given type of subject, and, willingly or otherwise, specialized in that field. That jolly soul Frans Hals (c. 1580–1666) was a portraitist both of individuals and of groups. During the wars of liberation many of the merchants joined the civic guard to maintain order, and the officers of these pseudo-military companies naturally formed clubs. These lived on after the emergency had passed as businessmen's clubs, analogous to the Lions, the Kiwanis, and the Rotary Clubs of America today. Such groups wanted records of themselves. Today, photographs of classes in school or college, of fraternity memberships, even of banquets, testify to the same urge.

The Officers of St. Andrew's Company (fig. 300) is such a portrait group by Hals. Aside from the usual requirements of portraiture, this type of subject raises two special problems: first, at least reasonable prominence must be allotted to each member of the group, without producing the monotony of seried rows of figures; and second, the artist must avoid the posed artificiality that makes many group photographs today look stilted. In this painting Hals masters these difficulties. He depicts the club around a table in the yard of their clubhouse. A natural light, free of theat-ricality, molds each member, but the trees and foliage in the background are kept dark and too vague in detail to obtrude themselves. Someone, perhaps the painter himself, must have entered suddenly to utter a remark that has caused many members to break off their conversations and turn toward him. Some do not. Many are seated, others stand and look back over their shoulders, while still others bend over the table; thus no rigid line of heads appears. Everyone's face has adequate space in the picture, and all are at ease, with one notable exception. One pompous individual has turned around and is posed stiffly with his hands resting on his cane. Surely Hals paints him this way to enhance the characterization.

He is equally sure of himself in sin-

301. Frans Hals (c. 1580–1666) *The Jolly Toper* (c. 1627) Rijks Museum, Amsterdam. 2'9" x 2'3".

gle portraits. The Jolly Toper (fig. 301) leans back in his chair, glass in hand, perfectly relaxed. As in most of the Hals portraits, the man seems in a right good humor. The joviality of the painter himself must be reflected in these merry individuals. From their expressions one might illustrate an encyclopedia of the laugh and smile. Such men would be out of place at court, but very much at home in a tavern or at a drinking bout. The technique is suited to the subject. Hals indicates the necessary details without drawing them. The pleats of the toper's jerkin Hals sweeps in with a flowing stroke of his brush, loaded with pigment. Such a stroke may be a quarter of an inch wide but neither needs nor receives further definition. Therein it anticipates nineteenth-century paintings by Manet and others. Like some of the later works of Velásquez, notably Las Meninas (fig. 294), such boldness of indication foretells the Impressionists of 1870.

Hals spent his life in Haarlem; Rembrandt van Rijn (1606–69), the miller's son of Leyden, made the Dutch metropolis of Amsterdam the site of his career. To him, light was the vehicle through which to reveal his love of mankind. Where others had studied the effects of this or that kind of illumination for its own sake, light was to Rembrandt only

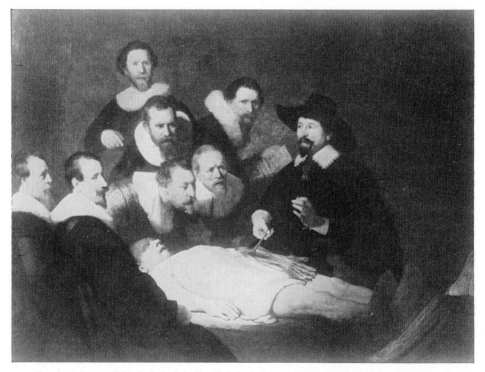

302. Rembrandt van Rijn (1606–69) *Dr. Tulp's Anatomy Lesson* (1632) Museum, The Hague. 5′5″ x 7′2″.

the means to an end. He was its master. During the ten years of his first Amsterdam period, 1632 to 1642, he was fashionable and prosperous. At this time, his style in painting coincided with the tastes of his clientele. Although he produced only four group portraits, it so happened that three of these were milestones in his career.

Dr. Tulp's Anatomy Lesson (fig. 302), famous though it is, succeeds only in part. The dramatic concentration of interest on the corpse which forms the subject of this demonstration yields a lively group of portraits. And yet this concentration is won at a price. Strong light intensifies the center of interest, but to achieve this intensification Rembrandt sacrificed the outer members of the group. While the men close to the corpse are painted in full light and color, those on the outskirts are depicted in shade and in subdued tones—an obvious suppression of the corners to stress the pictorial possibilities of climax. Moreover, Rembrandt was not yet sure of himself in the matter of space. Those doctors leaning over the cadaver for a better view are solid down to the waist, but there seems hardly room for them to stand. Rembrandt appears to have forgotten the lower half of their persons. The artist himself attended the lectures upon which this painting is based; it is therefore curious that he should have represented the fingers of the corpse extended almost flat on the leg when the tendons were raised by the doctor's spatula. Rembrandt must have known that under these conditions

the fingers would flex more than in this painting. The explanation must be that Rembrandt wanted to carry the diagonal toward the corner of his design, there to stop the movement with the open book that cuts across the angle. To permit the fingers to curve upward and inward would have interrupted this movement. Rembrandt sacrificed what he must have known to be true to his desire for pictorial rightness.

On the whole, however, the Anatomy Lesson was sufficiently like the scene to satisfy his patrons. The portrait of his first wife, Saskia in a Red Hat, reveals Rembrandt's aims at this time and the reasons for his popularity. The artist painted his subject's profile carefully and freshly. The bright carnations of Saskia's face, the richness of red velvet, feather, and embroidery, of necklaces and dress, are precise and descriptive. Each part invites inspection. Beautiful as the portrait is, it can be described as a painting of the surface, rich in color, and silhouetted against the dark background. Its objectivity, its gay tones, its accuracy, and its finish are enough to ensure its reputation.

For ten years Rembrandt was content to exploit this style, but the year 1642 marked a turning point in his career. Up till then he had been financially successful and happy. He owned a large house, had accumulated a collection of works of art, and was a favorite portraitist of the wealthy Amsterdam merchants. In that year his wife Saskia died, and he painted the so-called Night Watch (fig. 303), properly entitled

303. Rembrandt van Rijn (1606–69) *The Night Watch* (1642) Rijks Museum, Amsterdam. 11'11" x 14'4".

Frans Banning Cocq's Company of the Civic Guard. The nickname can be explained by the personal treatment of light. Where Caravaggio had explored the possibilities of strong light contrasted with black shadows, Rembrandt makes the shadows glow with reflected light. Instead of representing night illumination in this painting, Rembrandt shows the members of the club as they issue from the city gate in the morning to welcome to Amsterdam Marie de Medici, the Queen Mother of France. Contrary to the common opinion, the painting was recognized from the first

as remarkable, and was given a prominent position in the club house of the group.

Unlike most group portraitists Rembrandt did not give nearly equal importance to each of the sixteen members of the company. To be sure, the captain in a red scarf and his lieutenant clad in a white-satin suit dominate the center, and other figures to the right and left are prominent, but the light and their positions to the rear subordinate a number of the members. That these matters improve the picture is undeniable. The composition assumes the form of an E arranged in perspective. A bar of four figures at the back forms the upright, from which three groups come forward, to the right, in the center, and on the left, with an opening between each of these groups.

The death of Saskia and the growth of his own pictorial sense opened the way to the introverted style of Rembrandt's later years. After 1642 he painted more and more for himself, to meet his own ideals rather than those of possible patrons. Like many another more recent artist, he separated himself from the public. A few trusted friends, such as the burgomaster Jan Six, still appreciated and helped him, but his fortunes declined.

Twenty years later, Rembrandt had a last opportunity to handle group portraiture in the Syndics of the Cloth Guild. Then he solved the problem, not only as a picture, but also as representation. Light falls evenly on the group. Each of the five men around the table is an individual, and even their servant who stands behind them can be seen as a subordinate. Their poses are natural, and yet Rembrandt produced a painting of great variety. Some of the syndics have their natural hair, others wear wigs; some are seated, others stand; and some look out of the picture, while others gaze at their companions. The painting was realistic enough to satisfy his patrons without any loss of artistic integrity.

It was in these later years that Rembrandt's sympathy for humanity reached its climax. He turned to old age in The

304. Rembrandt van Rijn (1606–69) *The Rabbi* (1657) National Gallery, London. 2'6" x 2'2".

Rabbi (fig. 304) to develop psychological portraiture, which then absorbed his attention. This old man seems to have endured most of the experiences of life, and they have inscribed their record on his face. His haunting eyes look beyond the grave to everlasting peace. But this was not what the Dutch wanted; the successful merchants had no interest in these old men, who were of no importance as the world measures importance. Nor are such portraits decorative as paintings. There are no vivid colors and no picturesque costumes to lend a superficial attraction. A strong light plays over the faces as though to extract their personality and to suppress all else in the dark brown background. If one loves mankind for its own sake, in all its joys and sorrows, then these men and women become significant, for Rembrandt here explores the human soul through his own sympathy deepened by grief. Others may have dealt as well with objective appearance, but Rembrandt stands alone in his warm love of mankind.

He liked nothing better than to paint himself. A long series of these canvases that reveal his instinct for self-dramatization stud his whole career. He had a passion for dressing up and acting another character, Rembrandt in a Plumed Hat, Rembrandt in a Steel Gorget, Rembrandt with Haggard Eyes, and here at the end, Rembrandt Laughing before the Bust of a Roman Emperor (fig. 305). His late method differs from his early style of the Saskia. The *im-*

305. Rembrandt van Rijn (1606–69) *Rembrandt Laughing before the Bust of a Roman Emperor* (c. 1668) Museum, Cologne. 2'8" x 2'1".

pasto, or layer of pigment on the canvas, is heavier and its surface broken. No longer does it create the glitter of a smooth finish. Spread unevenly, it picks out the pictorially significant elements, the heavily pigmented head emerging from the shadows. One likes to think that the self-dramatization, in this example, may be symbolic. By this time Rembrandt had undergone heavier personal misfortunes than fall to the lot of most men. His fine house had long since been sold; his art collection and his studio equipment were sacrificed to his creditors; he had passed through bankruptcy; his son Titus had died; his devoted housekeeper and second wife, Hendrickje Stoffels, had died; he stood alone. But nothing could subdue that spirit. So long as he had brush and paints, or burin and copper plate, he could record the life he loved and let the rest go by.

Rembrandt was not typical of the Dutch school; he transcended it, though his style had many elements in common with his time. His interest in portraiture, his concern with light, though of a more personal quality, and the scale of most of his canvases fitted into the pattern of Dutch painting. But he was exceptional in the subjective analysis he substituted for the prevailing objectivity of vision, and in the range of his undertakings. Though the Dutch tended to specialize, Rembrandt did not. A Protestant simplicity characterizes his paintings of religious subjects. Portraits occupied a larger place in his output than any other kind of subject, but he also handled still life, genre, and landscape themes with equal aplomb, both in painting and in etching. He even experimented with the style of Mughal painting, examples of which had come to Holland through the Dutch East India Company. The same diversity of subject marked his extensive production in the graphic arts. His mastery of light and his intrinsic perception of values endowed his work in this field with such distinction that Rembrandt has seldom been equaled and never surpassed.

Rembrandt alone would suffice to transfigure the art of any country, but for so small a land in so short a time Holland produced an extraordinary number of other painters. These artists had to be competent to meet the Dutch demands. Those who specialized in genre and who recorded the life of Holland have come to be known as the Little Masters. Each had his chosen field of subject matter. For example, Adriaen van Ostade deals with the lower classes, drinking or brawling in a tavern, lounging outside the door of an inn, or simply passing the time of day. Nicholas Maes, a pupil of Rembrandt, steals something of his master's light to show his servant girls peeling apples or active in other culinary and domestic pursuits. Gerhardt Terborch caters to the merchant class. His paintings show the wives and daughters of the well-to-do burghers at their music lessons, playing an informal concert, or washing their hands. The rooms where these everyday scenes take place are not pretentious. Small, and furnished with chairs and tables, beds, stools, and clavichords, with pictures or maps on the wall, they create a familiar volume of space wherein the figures may live. The ladies dress in silks, satins, or velvets, exact in their appearance of texture. One can almost hear the satin rustle as the figures move; one can almost feel the softness of the velvet, or play with the long silky hair of the family spaniel. The paintings of Pieter de Hooch record Dutch interiors. The diffused light of indoors plays over them from some definite light source, such as a door or window. Strongest near the opening, the light fades away in imperceptible transitions as the depth of the room is reached.

Jan Vermeer of Delft (1632–75) belongs with this group because of his subject matter, the small size of most of his paintings, and his realism. The Girl with a Water Jug (Plate VIII, facing p. 365) reaches the climax of the mode of total visual effect. Every fact of vision is observed. The graded lighting models the forms with full appreciation of the existence of reflected light and reflected color. The blue dress prints a blue reflection on the pewter jug and modifies the other colors near it. The change of values and colors is accurate; a blue or yellow passage in light remains that same blue or yellow as it darkens into shade. And yet Vermeer is not photographic. He has an instinct for selection. The forms are simplified to retain only those elements pertinent to his purpose, that is, the visually significant parts. Though informal, the composition is nevertheless calculated. It has neither the geometry of the Renaissance nor the Baroque diagonals. Based on a series of rectangles created by the bits of wall, the picture or maps hanging on it, and the shape of the table, Vermeer arranges these shapes to produce a design perfectly balanced and adjusted. Just enough curves vary this system to avert any touch of rigidity; the curves of the figure, or of the water pitcher, serve as a foil for the straight lines of the rectangles.

Moreover, Vermeer's interpretation of his subject differs from that of the other Little Masters. None of them has the same intimacy of vision. He confines himself as a rule to only one or two figures, and they are so absorbed in what they are doing that they seem oblivious of any spectator. The ladies painted by Terborch are on their best behavior; they conduct themselves with full consciousness that others are watching them. The girls of Vermeer are too engrossed for that. Through that very absorption they seem to be accorded more respect; their privacy is unviolated. They are no mere decorative adjuncts around the house, attractive enough, but a useless luxury; Vermeer's women are the household, and through their occupations lend domesticity to the hearth.

If the Dutch are well enough satisfied with their society to want it painted, they are also proud of their country— its gardens and meadows, its canals and harbors. Therefore, a group of landscape painters is inevitable. Jakob van Ruysdael (1628–82) in The Mill (fig. 306) depicts an intimate bit of Holland. The scene with its water and its windmill serves as a symbol of his country. In this alluvial land, the sky is bound to bulk large in any normal view, and in Dutch landscapes it may occupy two thirds or more of the canvas. Billowing clouds roll in from the North Sea and cast fleeting shadows on the ground. Certain devices are so regular that they may be called conventions. A shadow darkens the foreground, while the middle distance and the background are sunny. In this example, jetties and marsh grass lower the foreground values, but light focuses on the mill and the water. Possibly several planes of light and shade may succeed one another. The result is to accent depth and space, and thereby to draw the eye from the foreground into the distance. Even in the paintings of the sea, one can often find this device of the dark foreground where it is difficult to explain on rational grounds. In color, though the range is considerable, the prevailing tone is apt to be brownish. The love of warm color, so common in the Baroque, impels these painters to record the shadows as brownish, the trunks of the trees in brown, and even the foliage as affected by the same tone. There is every reason why the artist should do this. He is painting a picture, not creating a landscape or even recording one, and if the adoption of a specific tonality aids in pictorial creation, then it belongs in his painting despite any conventional character it may have. In spite of these conven-

306. Jakob van Ruysdael (1628–82) *The Mill*, Rijks Museum, Amsterdam. 2′9″ x 3′4″.

tions, however, Ruysdael's picture looks like a particular scene. Though doubtless painted in the studio, not in the open, The Mill is not an abstract conception of landscape. The Dutch prefer the specific and therefore identifiable scene, and though the painting may symbolize the country, it still remains a view of a particular mill in the surroundings that building probably had.

Ruysdael painted landscape for its own sake, largely devoid of people and animals; Aelbert Cuyp, on the other hand, dealt with landscape and cattle. The lush meadows of Holland pastured the sleek cattle which contributed to its prosperity and which were shown with the same objectivity and with the same grasp of pictorial possibilities that one finds in the pure landscape painters or in the Little Masters. Others painted the sea and shipping, or buildings. Nowhere does the technical virtuosity of the seventeenth century find more vivid illustration than in the flower compositions of Jan van Huysum and others. These bouquets, convincing in themselves, are filled with naturalistic detail. Points of light glitter in crystal drops of water on the leaves or petals, while bees and butterflies sip honey among the blossoms. Still other artists specialized in piles of vegetables on kitchen tables, combined with culinary utensils, with game, or poultry. Indeed, no facet of Dutch life escaped the attention of these painters. The school as a whole gives a picture of a civilization in all its aspects, a record as complete as that found in the reliefs and paintings of the Egyptian tombs, but even more vivid in that it is more realistic.

XVIII The Seventeenth Century in France and England

While Dutch painting stemmed from its merchant patronage and Holland's democratic way of life, the aristocracy and the growth of absolutism dictated the art of France. However, the concentration of power did not arise overnight. After the death of Henry II in 1559, his three young sons, who succeeded each other on the throne, were not strong enough to unite the country when Protestantism, at that time a disruptive force, was injected into the situation. The dismal story of the Wars of Religion and the massacre of St. Bartholomew's Day in 1572 need not be told here. Suffice it to say that these troubles exhausted France and ended its Renaissance. The civil wars were finally healed by Henry IV, Henry of Navarre, who began to recoup the resources of France and thereby laid the foundations on which Louis XIV in the last half of the seventeenth century could build.

The architecture of Henry IV in its combination of brick and stone suggests the poverty of the country. The houses lining the Place des Vosges in Paris show that the style can be restrained, though it is affected by the early Baroque of Italy. The successive French styles of the sixteenth, seventeenth, and eighteenth centuries are named for the kings, but do not coincide with them in date. Thus the Luxembourg Palace in Paris, built in 1615–20 for Marie de Medici after the assassination of her husband Henry IV in 1610, is one of the largest buildings of his style. The queen directed her architect, Salomon de Brosse, to model the building on the newer parts of the Pitti Palace in Florence, which she had known in her childhood and drawings of which she had had sent up from Italy. The rusticated columns, composed of alternate large and small blocks, come from that source. But De Brosse was a Frenchman, conscious of French tradition. Consequently, the Luxembourg retains the rhythmical pavilion and link scheme, with a central motive and wings that protrude from the plane of the façade and have their own semi-independent roofs. In plan, though the enclosed court remains, one side has been lowered to a single story, and thus the palace is more open than the Château of Chambord.

Under Louis XIII, the architectural pendulum swung in the direction of sophistication, restraint, and even, to a minor extent, of classicism. The Pavillon de l'Horloge (fig. 272) in the Louvre, next to Lescot's wing, was designed by Jacques LeMercier, 1624–30. Quieter than the work of De Brosse, it lacks the elegance of the very French buildings of François Mansart, the uncle of Jules Hardouin Mansart. The Château of Maisons-Laffitte of 1642–51 testifies to Mansart's exquisite sense of proportion and composition. His style leads on into that of Louis XIV. At the same time, from the brush of Philippe de Champaigne flowed a stream of stately and somewhat Flemish portraits, well suited to His Eminence Cardinal Richelieu.

But the spirit of the century flowered under the personal rule of Louis XIV. This monarch ascended the throne as an infant in 1643, assumed personal command of the state in 1660, and fashioned French civilization in his own image until his death in 1715. His life covers the classic period of French art. The word *classic* is ambiguous; it may refer to productions that have stood the test of time as in the phrase *the classics of literature*; it may indicate the influence of antiquity; or it may describe a quality of restraint, an emphasis on the intellectual as contrasted to the emotional, and a control or reserve. As applied to the age of Louis XIV, it has all these meanings. This is the time of the classic drama of Racine. That drama is, to some extent, modeled on the ancients, though the latter might not recognize the fact. Much of the subject matter of the painters and sculptors is borrowed from Rome. In art, the academic point of view with its respect for codified rules dominates. At best, these productions are superb; their effects, and the means whereby these effects are realized, calculated and formal. Personal emotion yields to order and system— to regularization. In 1648 the Academy of Painters and Sculptors was founded under royal protection, paralleling the Academy of Letters established earlier. But the arts do not readily submit to such standardization; it tends to stifle originality and vitality, and if it adds concentration and organization, it is questionable whether the gain compen-

307. Nicolas Poussin (1594–1665) *Kingdom of Flora* (c. 1635) Museum, Dresden. 4'4" x 5'11".

sates for the loss. However, to the people of that time, formality and order outweighed all other considerations.

The two greatest painters of France in the seventeenth century, Poussin and Claude Lorrain, spent most of their lives in Italy. They matured before the Academy had gained the power it was to enjoy under Le Brun. Nevertheless, the spirit of the age was strong upon them. Nicolas Poussin (1594–1665) borrowed from Raphael, Titian, and the Carracci and their school, but a French logic and clarity of mind illuminated all he did. The Kingdom of Flora (fig. 307) draws its subject from mythology, but its prevailing quality is that of organization, thought out in terms of drawing. These are no lusty Olympian figures comparable to Titian's Bacchus and Ariadne (fig. 244); they are too sober to survive the hearty existence of Olympus. Instead, the spirit is restrained and ordered until a perfect adjustment of the parts is achieved.

Classic, too, in subject is Et in Arcadia Ego (fig. 308), wherein four figures ponder the cryptic inscription on the tomb that gives its title to the painting. Some of the actors hark back to antiquity, such as the woman on the right with her Greek profile, or the kneeling shepherd with his heavy curly beard. They are types, not individuals; they have the same abstraction as the characters of Racine's dramas. Their actions, unimportant as movement, form part of the larger organization of the painting,

308. Nicolas Poussin (1594–1665) *Et in Arcadia Ego* (1638–39) Louvre, Paris. 2'9" x 3'11".

or tie in with the generalized landscape. No Baroque abandon disturbs the equilibrium of this composition in three-dimensional space. The arm of the kneeling shepherd tracing out the inscription carries the eye across to the younger man opposite, whose staff, in turn, parallels the leg of the first figure. The tree trunk behind continues the axis of the woman's figure, as the tree in the left background prolongs the movement begun by the leg of the man standing on that side. It is possible to discover some compositional and pictorial purpose in every part of this design. A shape, so to speak, is presented on the canvas. From that, everything follows inevitably, just as in the French classic drama a situation is stated and its consequences rigorously pursued to a conclusion. So organized a structure has something analytical in its intellectuality. It does not appeal to the emotions but to the mind. It offers no charm to the eye, no seduction of color, however much the latter may abet the design. Nothing unexpected can take place in this painting, which pursues its goal with the infallibility of a mathematical proposition. Whether or not such adherence to the demands of picture construction can command popular love, it has an abundance to offer to the professional. Hence Poussin has been exceptionally influential. Artists have recognized his demonstrations of their own problems, and among the French he has found wide appreciation because of the

309. Claude Lorrain (1600–1682) *Marriage of Isaac and Rebecca* (1647) National Gallery, London. 4′11″ x 6′7″.

lucidity of his mind and his feeling for logic and for abstract types.

Claude Gellée (1600–82), called Claude Lorrain, had a wider vogue in England. As compared with Poussin, his mind is less dominant over his emotions. The structure of the picture, therefore, is not so fully developed. On the other hand, his drawings testify to a poetic love of nature, which affected even his paintings. The Marriage of Isaac and Rebecca (fig. 309) does not attempt to be natural, although it is based on a profound study of tree forms. In it, two seventeenth-century conventions of landscape painting, the dark foreground leading out to the lighted middle distance, and the brownish tonality, are present, as they were in Holland. But unlike the Dutch landscape, this does not represent any particular scene. Claude paints landscape in the abstract, with a formal conception of nature analogous to the formality of Versailles. These wooded scenes leave an impression of tidiness, as though the ground keepers had just been through them to gather any dead branches and sweep up all the fallen leaves. Nature has had its face lifted to give it the order demanded by the times. Figures are incidental to such designs and were often added by another hand. The stateliness of these landscapes derives much of its impressiveness from the feeling for space. Frequently, as here, the largest and nearest trees in one corner, commence a spiral which then sweeps across the dark foreground to include the more distant trees on the other side. These, well behind the picture plane, lead us out to the background. All is suffused with a glow of light, golden and warm, playing over trees, grass, and water from a sun that in many paintings may be seen in the sky just above the horizon. These serene creations, formal and ordered as they are, yet have a fine poetic quality.

The reign of Louis XIV found at least as full an expression of its love of order in architecture as it did in landscape painting, and a still greater opportunity to display its magnificence. Bernini's trip to Paris to consult on the design of the Louvre in 1665 proved abortive. His scheme called for a Roman Baroque palace that was foreign to the French spirit, and would have required the destruction of the already existing parts of the Louvre. Therefore, when he had returned to Italy, his design was shelved in favor of Claude Perrault's (fig. 310). The new scheme suited the taste of the day. Magnificent in scale, it had just the pomp and brilliance expected by the young monarch. Perrault's design combines French, Italian Baroque, and Roman classic elements, a mixture typical of its time. These three strains interweave with now one and now another predominant. A plain ground floor, whose solid walls are pierced by windows crowned with segmental arches, provides the strong base needed by the richer treatment above. The colonnade in the Corinthian order is proportioned with classic cor-

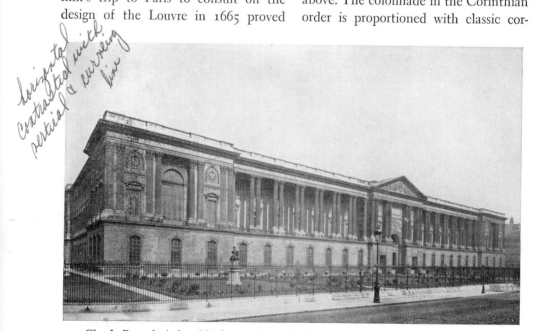

310. Claude Perrault (1613–88) *Louvre*, Paris (1667–74) East Façade *c.* 600′ long.

rectness. A majestic file of paired columns in front of a gallery create a robust pattern of light and shade, and have something of the Baroque about them, as do the cartouches with the reversed initials of the monarch surrounded by floral bands. Some break in the French tradition occurs in the abandonment of the visible roof, which the earlier part of the century had maintained. The roof is now constructed with such a low pitch that it is hidden behind the balustrade. And yet though the elements are borrowed, the colonnade of the Louvre is conceivable nowhere but in France. Its fundamental scheme adheres to French tradition; accented features at the center and at either end advance forward of the mass of the colonnade as pavilions, and while they resemble the colonnade in design enough to compose with it, at the same time they differ from it enough to be distinct and articulate. The end pavilions, for instance, retain the order but not the gallery behind, and the central accent is crowned by a pediment. The rhythmic disposition descends from French châteaux in the style of Francis I, such as Chambord (fig. 270), which also has corner accents and a central motive, and beyond that stems from the medieval castle.

The largest project of the reign was the Palace at Versailles. Louis XIV selected a site where a small hunting lodge already existed, in barren countryside, so that when his new work was completed it might be said that its splendor was his own creation, with a minimum of help from nature. To appreciate Versailles one must try to understand the point of view of the seventeenth century, and of Louis XIV in particular. His phrase, L'état, c'est moi, succinctly stated his conception of France. His country might be compared to a pyramid, the base provided by the numerous lower classes, and each successive stratum of society, smaller in number, built up to the king at the summit. Never had such concentration of power been known in Western Europe. If the monarch could not make all the decisions of state himself, he could review them, and cancel or alter enough of them to keep control in his own hands. Granted his identification of himself with France, it followed that anything done to display his own magnificence shed glory on the country.

Unless we understand this, Versailles must seem a monument to egotism. This vast design focuses on the bedchamber of His Majesty. In front, an avenue from Paris marks the axis of the palace, while other roads converge at equal angles on the Place d'Armes. Between these arrow-like avenues are the stables. A succession of axial courts, each smaller than its predecessor, forces the attention inward to the three windows of the royal bedchamber (fig. 311). The axis continues behind the palace between patterns of topiary work and pairs of lagoons, along a canal, through formal gardens and woods designed by Le Nôtre. Sculpture, fountains, and straight

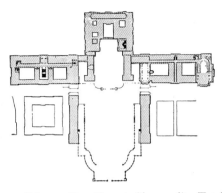

311. *Palace*, Versailles (1661–1756) Total length 1903'.

Its state apartments in the central block provide an appropriate background for the grandeur of the Sun King, as his courtiers called Louis XIV. The principal access leads up a stairhall, monumental in its proportions and resplendent in polished marble, through chamber after chamber, each more magnificent than the last, to the garden front. There only three rooms exist, the small Salon de la Guerre and the Salon de la Paix at the ends, and the huge Galerie des Glaces (fig. 312) or Hall of Mirrors between them. This last chamber is the setting for state functions. Designed by Jules Hardouin Mansart, who built or remodeled much of the

paths lead to statues, more fountains, or garden pavilions, which close each vista through the woods.

The palace itself is also symmetrical.

312. Jules Hardouin Mansart (1645–1708) designer; Charles le Brun (1619–90) decorator; *Hall of Mirrors*, Palace of Versailles (1678–84) 240' long x 34' wide x 43' high.

palace, and decorated in part by Le Brun, the director of the Academy, it epitomizes the reign. Its mirrors reflect arched windows. A pilaster order, where a Gallic cock modifies the normal Corinthian capital, punctuates walls enriched with marbles, gilding, and Baroque decorations, and supports a barrel vault whose surface is covered with gilded stucco and paintings of a warm brownish tonality. Individually, the paintings and the sculpture are not masterpieces, but as a whole they complete the sumptuousness of the hall.

Nor is the furniture less ornate. Baroque scrolls form the arms and legs of upholstered chairs. The shell motive, masks of human or animal heads, and acanthus leaves encrust beds, chairs, tables, cabinets, and chests of drawers. Inlaid designs of veined wood had developed in the Italian Renaissance; under Louis XIV, Boulle gives his name to a type of inlay or marquetry wherein tortoise shell and ormolu are employed.

The latter is a composition of gold, mercury, and copper. Such opulent materials are climaxed by the solid silver furniture the Sun King provided for his halls of state.

To see Versailles properly requires an effort of the imagination. One generally visits it in company with a motley group of tourists in the charge of some pensioner, who is eager to complete his patter as quickly as possible. But one should envision Versailles as the setting for a court. The costumes, gorgeous in lace, silk, and velvet, the powdered wigs and red-heeled shoes, the lights from thousands of candles redoubled in the mirrors, the hundreds of lackeys bustling about and the incidental music from Lully's orchestra, the buzz of conversation suddenly hushed at the announcement that His Majesty is about to make his state entrance—these circumstances made Versailles and its king impressive indeed to the ministers of foreign states. What tales they took

313. Jules Hardouin Mansart (1645–1708) *Garden Front*, Palace of Versailles. Total length 1903'.

home of the power and glory of France! Such a life is the cause of Versailles.

To make his court splendid, Louis XIV drew the upper nobility into dependence upon himself, and forced it to attend his every act from the *lever du roi* to the *coucher du roi*. The extent of Versailles as seen from the gardens (fig. 313) is inexplicable unless one bears in mind that it is not a residence, even of a king, but the seat of the government of France. At its prime, Versailles housed ten thousand people in the palace. Men preferred to leave their own estates to live in an attic bedroom in Versailles, because only by attendance in person could they obtain the royal favors. The garden façade of the building is, if anything, richer than the entrance front. Rustication marks each course of stone in the plain ground floor. The principal floor gains prominence by its orders in pilaster form, with three groups of free-standing columns in the center and near the ends. A decorative attic story tops the design. The roof is not visible, but Baroque accents enrich the skyline. The smaller of these accents are urns placed over each single pilaster below; the larger, repeating the corners of the colonnades and the paired pilasters, are trophies: piles of armor, cannon, shields, and other weapons heaped together and carved in stone; together, the urns and trophies recall in the silhouette of the building the rhythm of its design. This rhythm is fainter than at the Louvre, and thus implies the fading of the tradition of rhythm in French design.

The triple strain of classic, Baroque, and French occur also in the sculpture and painting of the reign. Pierre Puget's (1620–94) Milo of Croton (fig. 314) was a commission from the state. With

314. Pierre Puget (1620–94) *Milo of Croton* (1672–82) Louvre, Paris. 8'10" high x 4'7" wide.

academic formality, Puget creates a parallelogram whose sides are the torso and the tree trunk, the arms with its fingers caught in the cleft stump, and the legs, echoed in the lion and the drapery that falls between the legs of Milo to the ground. A Baroque openness may be detected in the void in the center, in the movement of the figure turning its head around, and in the pictorial details that complete the group. And yet the effect is neither more nor less Baroque than is the effect of the Louvre. It is more controlled than the Baroque; it has the academic regard for rule; and in its anatomical treatment, its proportions, and its muscularity, it may recall the Hellenistic statue, the Farnese Hercules.

Puget preferred to work in Genoa or Toulon rather than in Paris. Antoine Coysevox (1640–1720), on the other hand, spent most of his career in Paris and Versailles. His portrait of Le Brun

315. Antoine Coysevox (1640–1720) *Le Brun* (1679) Louvre, Paris. 2′2″ high.

(fig. 315) betrays the influence of Bernini. The drapery, Baroque in its movement and in its undercut pattern of light and shade, contrasts in texture with the curls of the flowing wig. How-

ever, the movement is not as pronounced, the features not as animated as in the works of Bernini. Details are realistic, but the total effect is academic. More so, however, are Coysevox's decorative works at Versailles, such as the oval relief of Louis XIV in Triumph in the Salon de la Guerre. So powerful an organization as the Academy, under royal control, could dictate the kind of design in sculpture.

Charles Le Brun (1619–90), as the leader of the Academy and dictator of design, reflects the reign in his canvases. They are not appreciated today, because of the lack of sympathy with the life they were painted to adorn. Gigantic in size, they need a palace as a setting. The subject of his Alexander Entering Babylon is superficially classic, but compliments Louis XIV, who impersonates Alexander in triumph. Great columns, elephants, and burly men carrying loot compose a design no classic artist would have recognized. The lavishness of this design is artificial; the effect has a heavy-handed grandiosity which the rich browns do little to relieve.

The state portraiture of Hyacinthe Rigaud, late in the reign, is as formal as the official art of Coysevox. Less staid than paintings by Philippe de Champaigne, his rendering of Louis XIV is a record of an official position, not of an individual. The king appears in robes of state; behind him is a sweep of curtain, the base of a column, and all the accoutrements common in official portraiture. These decorative accessories, the drapery and the column, originate in Venetian paintings of the time of Titian, and become stereotyped later. Vitality and individualism are subordinate to pomp and circumstance.

ENGLAND

While these developments were taking place in France, England produced but little sculpture and painting. During the first half of the seventeenth century Van Dyck painted portraits for the court of Charles I. Under the Protectorate and after the Restoration, Sir Peter Lely and later Sir Godfrey Kneller, both German by birth and both trained in the Low Countries, continued the externals of Van Dyck's style, but without his strength. Some little-known native

painters, such as Michael Wright, were more vigorous.

In architecture, however, the century produced two of the greatest figures in the history of that art in England. The first of them, Inigo Jones, was equally eminent in stage design; he is credited with the development of the proscenium arch and of movable scenery, and his sets for Ben Jonson's masques were so ingenious as to steal attention from the masques themselves. He developed an enthusiasm for Palladio that induced him to take at least one and perhaps two trips to Italy, chiefly to Vicenza, Venice, and Verona, where might be seen the works of his idol. When, in 1619, he designed the Banqueting House in Whitehall in London (fig. 316), he composed it in an academic

316. Inigo Jones (1573–1652) *Banqueting House*, Whitehall, London (1619–21) 120' long, 75' high.

and Palladian vein. It has no element that is not duplicated in one of Palladio's palaces. The plain basement supports two floors, treated with superposed orders of pilasters at the sides and of engaged columns in the center. The entablature breaks forward above every pilaster and column. Garlands of fruit and flowers enrich the second floor at the level of the Corinthian capitals. Triangular and segmental pediments alternate over the windows. A balustrade crowns the rusticated wall. These features reinforce the distinguished proportions that really account for the success of the building. To say that this design is Italianate in origin is not to deny that it is also English, just as to recognize the Italianism of the Luxembourg Palace need not blind us to its French character.

To exaggerate the historical importance of the Banqueting House is impossible. Few Englishmen had ever had an opportunity to see what Italian architecture was really like. Its sense of order was diametrically opposite to the lawlessness of the Jacobean, and its Palladian purity to the florid ornament of its predecessor. Thus the Banqueting House was a revolution in English architecture that brought the island in step with continental developments. Though its style would have been current in the last part of the sixteenth century in Italy instead of in the early seventeenth century, it provided a closer approximation to the developments on the Continent than anything England had produced since the reign of Henry VIII.

The academic style of Inigo Jones was hardly launched when England found herself in the whirlpool of the Great Rebellion. Its disturbances particularly affected the cavalier classes who employed Jones, and so minimized the opportunities for the spread of his style. When architecture revived with the Restoration in 1660, it assumed a Baroque quality in the work of Sir Christopher Wren. This astronomer, mathematician, and charter member of the Royal Society had much of the universality that appeared in Leonardo da Vinci; his discoveries and interests ranged from new methods of sailing and better types of street pavements to improved forms of embroidery and a device for writing double. Wren always had an amateur interest in architecture, but after the Restoration his appointment to the committee in charge of rebuilding old St. Paul's Cathedral in London led him to a closer study of building problems.

The great fire of London in 1666 burned for a week and destroyed much of the medieval city. This offered Wren an unparalleled opportunity. First, he drew up a plan for rebuilding the city, one of several that were submitted. His plan displayed an insight into the problems of civic design in advance of his day. Instead of imposing a geometrical pattern of streets, Wren attacked the problem of traffic, and planned residential streets 30 feet in width, business streets of 60 feet, and thoroughfares 90 feet wide, so disposed that passage through the city and to its principal centers would be facilitated to the utmost. At the intersection of avenues and wherever else a vista might be created, Wren reserved sites for public buildings, usually parish churches, while the two foci of the city, St. Paul's and the Royal Exchange, had splendid approaches to them. Modern city planners would not design as Wren did, but had his plan been carried out, it would have prevented many of the traffic jams that hamper London today. But although his scheme would have given to every landowner as much ground as he had before, and a site at least as desirable because of its accessibility, the lots could not in all cases be identical with the pre-fire holdings. The conservatism of the English was not to be overcome, and the city was rebuilt on its old lines.

Among the losses caused by the fire were many parish churches of London. As Surveyor General to the King, it was Wren's task to redesign them. Many of the old sites had been irregular, but that merely challenged Wren's ingenuity. The spirit of his time called for axial designs, and these Wren provided; in each instance he adapted a regular plan to the limitations of the site with little sacrifice of available space. The variety in plan and elevation is amazing. Some churches are domed, others barrel vaulted, while still others are arranged with flat ceilings, or any conceivable combination of these forms, and with an equal variety in the type and arrangement of the supports. Pews had come into general use, but since their seating capacity was small in proportion to the space they occupied, they prompted the addition of galleries to supplement the accommodation. Although the altar remains in the center of the chancel and the pulpit to one side, the decline in emphasis on the service of Holy Communion allows a shallow chancel to replace the deep sanctuary of medieval times.

The towers and steeples of these buildings are often the only parts of the exterior visible from the street; the rest is hidden behind other buildings. The same fertility of imagination that distinguishes these features in the Wren churches also marks his interiors. The steeple of St. Mary-le-Bow (fig. 317) in

317. Christopher Wren (1632–1723) *Steeple of St. Mary-le-Bow*, London (1671–83) Tower and steeple 223' high; steeple 104' high.

1680 shows Wren's appreciation of the value of silhouette. A tower must be seen against the sky, therefore the outline is its most telling feature. The tower is usually square in plan and severe in masonry; its upper story, where the bells hang, is enriched by arches, columns, or pilasters. The lowest stage of the steeple in St. Mary-le-Bow is circular, with a ring of free-standing columns. Baroque scrolls and urns soften the transition from the square to the circular form above. Above that, more scrolls lead to a smaller colonnaded story that supports a pyramid, a frequent conclusion of these steeples. St. Mary-le-Bow is exceptionally rich, but the steeple is only one of many Wren designs.

St. Paul's Cathedral, begun in 1675, is his masterpiece. Wren preferred a church of the central type, his model for which still exists, but the English tradition called for length. The final arrangement (fig. 318) combines the length, the western transepts, and the choir of the English medieval plan with a system at the crossing that was in part suggested by the Sorbonne in Paris. Shallow transepts separate the nave and choir and create a crossing covered by the great dome. The external dome of wood and lead expresses the existence of a lower dome of masonry embedded within the drum. The visible dome dominates the exterior (fig. 319), its curve exposed and supported on a continuous colonnade. This unbroken entablature encircles the drum like a band, as

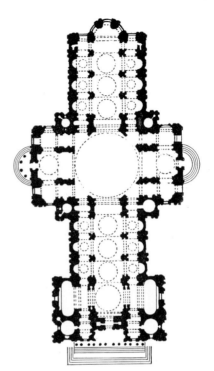

318. *St. Paul's*, London (1675–1710) 514′ x 250′.

though to buttress it. The façade, influenced by the east front of the Louvre, has two stories of paired columns, the lower story somewhat wider, to indicate the presence of aisles as well as nave, whereas the upper colonnade corresponds to the span of the nave alone. Flanking towers enframe the dome as one looks up Ludgate Hill; like the steeples of Wren's parish churches, their design is fraught with Baroque license in the treatment of the orders, providing interest in silhouette. His towers and steeples are influenced by Italian towers of the High Baroque, familiar to him through publications, but the fre-

319. Christopher Wren (1632–1723) *St. Paul's Cathedral*, London (1675–1710) Total height 366'.

quency with which they occur must be traced to the English tradition of tower building.

St. Paul's is more structural than St. Peter's in the disposition of the dome and drum. In scale, St. Paul's, though smaller, is infinitely superior. Wren incorporates small features on both interior and exterior to emphasize the size of his building, while the lack of these elements, human in scale, renders ineffectual the vastness of the papal monument. St. Paul's is the only one of the major cathedrals in Western Eu-

rope to be completed by the man who had designed it. The final stone in the lantern was set in place in Wren's presence by his son in 1710. All the other great churches took centuries to build, and involved the designs of several architects. What could be more appropriate, then, that when Wren died in 1723 his bones should be laid within the church that he had conceived? Above them is a simple inscription ending with the words *Si monumentum requiris, circumspice*, 'If you seek a monument, look around you.'

XIX The Eighteenth Century—Rococo and Georgian Art

When Louis XIV assumed personal control of France, his spirit was in accord with that of his day, but the old monarch had lived too long. By 1715, the ideals of France were changing beneath the surface. The repression of this new spirit by Louis XIV, who was under the influence of Madame de Maintenon during the closing years of his reign, made the reaction the more violent when he was succeeded by his grandson, Louis XV. The new century revolted against formality and heaviness. Whenever possible, society escaped from Versailles to seek diversion in elegant private mansions in Paris.

If the Hall of Mirrors symbolized the seventeenth century, the salon and the boudoir were emblems of the early eighteenth century. In these smaller rooms, groups became intimate, and their types of entertainment less pretentious. No age has ever been so shaped by woman as the age of Louis XV. She expected delicacy and politeness; the arts of the drawing room, conversation, and the *mot juste* met with her approval; etiquette prescribed every word and action. She was the supreme arbiter of conduct, the dictator of society. Such a life was artificial. Indeed, pretense lay at the core of the times, and yet the simplicity of nature, as then conceived, had infinite charm. Later in the century the affectation of society evoked a nostalgia for the natural man, who, free from the evils of society, pursued a noble and simple existence. But no group that had grown up in Versailles could possibly become natural, as we understand the term.

The age of Louis XV rebelled against the rules and order of the seventeenth century. People craved pleasure, frivolity; they wanted to be gay. They demanded freedom and license in art as well as in life, and achieved them. The Italian comedy, which because of its salacious character had been banished during the closing years of the reign of Louis XIV, came trooping back. Amateur theatricals, pageants, and tableaux afforded an outlet to the craving for amusement. And yet, however licentious the age might be, it was never coarse; its very immorality had an elegance about it.

Toward the end of the century the freedom of the reign of Louis XV provoked its own reaction. Pleasure had sated society and immorality in itself had ceased to satisfy. Skepticism and rationalism ridiculed certain aspects of French life. The pendulum swung from liberty to sobriety. The style of Louis XVI began before his accession to the throne in 1775; it preserved the elegance of the earlier period, but the expression was controlled, the effect quieter, as

320. Germain Boffrand (1667–1754) *Salon de la Princesse*, Hôtel de Soubise, Paris (*c.* 1740) *c.* 33′ x 26′.

though the serious times of the French Revolution were casting their shadows before them.

In architecture, the classic strain of Louis XIV faded away. The boldness of the Baroque melted into the playfulness of the Rococo. The full effect of this new manner was felt only on the interiors in France. To be sure, in their enthusiasm for all things French the Germans tortured the exteriors of their buildings, like the Zwinger at Dresden, with Rococo details that had been devised for the salon and the boudoir; but in its native country the style is less marked externally. The orders lose their prominence, windows are apt to have segmental tops, and the whole project

is smaller in scale. The Salon de la Princesse in the Hôtel de Soubise in Paris (fig. 320), designed by Boffrand about 1740, is typical. A small room supplants the immense halls of Louis XIV. Such a chamber provides a setting for and an expression of sophisticated life and witty conversation. The orders have vanished; in their stead delicate panels, whose upper and lower edges bend in free reversed curves, line the walls. The panels may be left in the natural surface of the wood, but more often they are painted white and the moldings gilded. The language of classic architecture is avoided, so that in extreme cases the panels become asymmetrical. In such instances, a panel in one part of a

321. Jacques-Ange Gabriel (1698–1782) *Petit Trianon*, Versailles (1762–68).

322. Jacques Germain Soufflot (1709–80) *The Panthéon* (*Ste. Geneviève*), Paris (1764–90) 265′ high.

room may balance one in another part. Even the walls and ceilings of the rooms are no longer separate; the upper moldings of the panels so interweave with the decoration of the ceiling that one cannot say where the wall ends and the ceiling begins. This is especially true when the plane of the wall curves into that of the ceiling, as it does in this example. Such designs do not pretend to monumentality, or often to more than interior decoration, but they do have charm and delicacy.

Asymmetry, lightness, and a rejection of classic motives characterize Rococo furniture under Louis XV. The straight line almost vanishes as the legs of tables and chairs bend in sinuous curves which are playful at the expense of sound construction, while the fronts of writing tables, commodes, and cabinets bulge, echoing in their shapes the slender flowing scrolls of the wall and ceiling decorations. Tapestried upholstery, lacquer, marquetry, ormolu, and even porcelain inserts add their beauties to designs that illustrate the virtuosity achieved by the master craftsmen of this time.

Just after the middle of the century, 1762–8, the Petit Trianon at Versailles (fig. 321) rejected that freedom and turned toward classicism. A cornice crowns rectangular windows. The orders regain popularity, but without the pomp of the preceding century. The Petit Trianon, by Jacques-Ange Gabriel, has such beauty of proportion that it deserves a place among the greatest masterpieces of architecture, small as it is. The relation of height to width, of sides to center, of solids to voids comes close to perfection. These beauties are reinforced by the exquisite delicacy of detail. Without sacrificing the lightness of the Rococo, Gabriel introduced a control that gives to each smallest part its due place. It is no accident that in the days when architecture was taught, in part, by making measured drawings of the great monuments of the past, the Petit Trianon was almost invariably one of those selected for instruction.

Still later, and still more sober, is the church of Ste. Geneviève in Paris. Called the Panthéon (fig. 322), it was executed by Soufflot between 1764 and 1790. Its Greek cross plan (fig. 323) is remarkable for its spaciousness. Just before the French Revolution, society turned its attention to England with enthusiasm; its political forms, its organization of society, its gardens, and its art all received the approval of an influential part of the French public. Hence St. Paul's inspired the dome of the Panthéon. The ring of columns that forms its drum is based on Wren's masterpiece.

Even more important is the increase of classic influence. Remarkable activity

in archaeology characterizes the second half of the eighteenth century, such as the excavation of Pompeii and Herculaneum, and the publication of scientific drawings of Roman and even of Greek monuments, though the latter do not bear fruit until the next century. Under this influence, Soufflot designed the portico of the Panthéon in the Corinthian order, with a full entablature

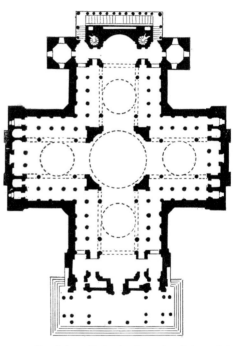

323. *Panthéon*, Paris (1764–90) 360' x 262'.

and pediment like the front of a classic temple. The archaeology of this colonnade is not only purer than that of the Baroque—one might expect that—but it is also more classic than that of the Renaissance. When Roman art was first revived, such artists as Brunelleschi permitted themselves great freedom. Even the buildings of the High Renaissance are not copies of any Roman, still less Greek, edifice. The portico of the Panthéon, however, leads on to the still more archaeological adaptations of the early nineteenth century. Its unbroken walls contribute to this increased classicism. As it was originally designed, Soufflot had intended to have tall windows in those walls, but the amateur archaeologist Quatremère de Quincy forced his hand and made the building measure up to a standard of correctness more exact than it might otherwise have been.

The increased sobriety of the age of Louis XVI makes itself felt in furniture design too. Straight lines reappear in the legs of tables and chairs, in the paneling of the walls, and in the sides of commodes and desks. The lightness of the Rococo remains without its asymmetry and its extravagance. The decorative vocabulary in furniture is simpler and acquires a restraint to which fluting and other classic motives contribute.

The painting of the Fêtes Galantes corresponds to the Rococo in architecture. Antoine Watteau (1684–1721) is the most perfect, if not the most characteristic, painter of his age. The Embarkation for Cythera (fig. 324) is the antithesis of the vast canvases of Le Brun. Painted on a small scale, it is intended for a small and intimate room. The exquisite figures are hardly a foot high, and in many of his other paintings

324. Antoine Watteau (1684–1721) *Embarkation for Cythera* (1717) Louvre, Paris. 4'3" x 6'4".

are still smaller. Their gay costumes sparkle like jewels, with flashes of green, blue, yellow, and lavender in place of the somber browns of the previous reign. In spirit too the painting reveals the aristocratic society of its day. Here is

325. Antoine Watteau (1684–1721) *Gilles*. Louvre, Paris. 6′ x 4′11″.

no attempt to glorify the state, or to compliment its ruler. These ladies and gentlemen of the court stroll through a world of Watteau's imagination to Cythera, the enchanted isle of love. A delicate eroticism colors the motive, but is always refined. Moreover, this scene has no classic background. The characters go out of doors, but find themselves in a park. Their silks and satins bespeak their sophistication; these dainty courtiers transfer themselves for the moment from the salon to a well-groomed wilderness, or perhaps a stage set. The life they lead is artificial, and though they, or their successors like Jean Jacques Rousseau, may talk of their love for nature and the natural man, it is at

326. François Boucher (1703–70) *Vulcan Presenting to Venus the Arms of Aeneas* (1757) 10′6″ x 10′6″.

most a lip loyalty, a mannerism and a pose.

There is a tinge of melancholy beneath the frivolity, but that is Watteau's personal contribution, not present in other painters of his day. Gilles (fig. 325) is a character from the Italian comedy, whose other players are behind him. He is dressed as a clown, but Watteau's painting belies the comic costume. This clown, like *He Who Got Slapped*, is pathetic. Perhaps the painter had a premonition of his early death. In any case, the Gilles is exceptional in his scale, almost life size, and demonstrates Watteau's ability to develop plastic forms at that size, and to conceive a figure who might serve as a monument to his own nostalgic spirit.

François Boucher (1703–70), the favorite painter of Madame de Pompadour, is more typical of the Rococo in that he is less serious. The Vulcan Presenting to Venus the Arms of Aeneas (fig. 326) has none of Watteau's sparkle, but then Watteau is a master draftsman. Boucher's drawing is adequate but undistinguished. His palette has the softness of the boudoir in its pinks and blues. This scene, though based upon mythology, might be one of the tableaux enacted by society in some of its select parties. This Venus and her attendants could never survive the lusty life of Mt. Olympus. One cannot imagine her taking an active part on the battlefields of Troy and being wounded while defending her favorite, Paris. She represents aristocratic beauty of her day, small of head and delicate in body, with powdered whites and pinks, fresh from the hands of the hairdresser. The swirling movement of the composition shows the Rococo to be a development of the Baroque, but in a lighter vein. These designs, with their eighteenth-century cupids, set the type for tapestries and even porcelain.

The aristocracy molded the character of the age, but the middle class was increasing in numbers and influence. Jean Baptiste Simeon Chardin (1699–1779), in addition to doing a series of powerful still lifes, became the painter of this group. The Blessing (fig. 327) has none of the frivolity of the upper class but rather the sober virtues of the bourgeoisie. The pause while the younger daughter says grace before the noonday meal is restrained and dignified, ennobled into a type scene. This genre subject does not have the descriptive character of the Dutch; however much it reflects its day, it also transcends time and place. The figures have a monumentality absent in the paintings of Boucher. All details are conceived with accuracy and freedom. Less meticulous than in Dutch painting, the objects may be realistic but are not naturalistic: that is, the essential character of each is enhanced and its accidentals of appearance suppressed. A superb control over his medium, a feeling for the brush in rich scumblings of pigment, a grasp of solidity, and a distinguished sense of composition in space mark Chardin as one of the soundest painters of his or any other time.

During the second half of the century, Jean Honoré Fragonard (1732–1806) prolonged the spirit of the first half even though that spirit was chang-

ing. He represents the frenzied quest for pleasure maintained by a dwindling group of the upper class. The Swing

327. Jean Baptiste Simeon Chardin (1699–1779) *The Blessing* (1740) Louvre, Paris. 1'7" x 1'3".

328. Jean Honoré Fragonard (1732–1806) *The Swing* (*c.* 1766–69) Wallace Collection, London. 2′8″ x 2′1″.

329. Jean Baptiste Greuze (1725–1805) *The Return of the Prodigal Son*, Louvre, Paris. 4′3″ x 5′4″.

(fig. 328) was ordered and its subject dictated by a young nobleman. Watteau's delicate eroticism develops into ribaldry. The fresh color, the drawing, and the technique raise a trivial theme into a painting of distinction. Elsewhere Fragonard exploits the possibilities of light and shade; he paints with strong color and impressionistic breadth such canvases as the Bathers.

Fragonard's willingness to cater to the amorous whims of his clients brought down upon him the condemnation of Jean Baptiste Greuze (1725–1805), who pretended to be more serious and perhaps more moral. The lat-

ter's narrative compositions, of which The Return of the Prodigal Son (fig. 329) is typical, are banalities. It would be hard to imagine a more stilted gesture than that of the mother calling her son's attention to his dead father, the extravagant sorrow of these gesticulating daughters, or the trite remorse of the son. The characters overact their parts. Greuze tops this type of work by a series of young women who masquerade under such titles as Innocence, Girl with a Lamb, or The Broken Pitcher. They have little to recommend them beyond their youth. Often badly drawn, they assume a modesty that is belied by their costumes, disarrayed to reveal their charms. Greuze, not Fragonard, exemplifies the spirit that provoked the French Revolution.

The type popularized by Boucher recurs in The Bather (fig. 330) by his contemporary, the sculptor Étienne Maurice Falconet (1716–91). Its slender figure, lithe and graceful, supports a small head with a fashionable coiffure, expressing in marble the courtly ideal of feminine beauty. Though The Bather turns slightly, the movement is less violent than in the Baroque, while the modeling shows the naturalism of the eighteenth century. In Falconet's equestrian statue of Peter the Great at Leningrad that naturalism is extended even to the pedestal, in which an irregular, pseudo-naturalistic outcropping of rock supplants an architectural base. The horse, rearing on his hind legs, is balanced by a flowing tail weighted with lead. Nevertheless, active as the group is, it does not lack characterization. Falconet also designed for bric-a-brac. A frivolous interpretation of classic material, his Venus Spanking Cupid, for example, does not pretend to be serious; it is a light and amusing piece of genre intended for a casual glance, not for analysis.

A generation later, Claude Michel, called Clodion, formed one of a group that met the demand of society for this sort of thing. He modeled terra-cotta figures and groups, like the Nymph and Satyr (fig. 331). Conceived on a small scale, it mocks mythology by the trivi-

330. Etienne Maurice Falconet (1716–91) *The Bather* (1757) Louvre, Paris. Marble, 2'8" high.

331. Clodion (1738–1814) *Nymph and Satyr*. Metropolitan Museum, New York. Terra cotta, 1'11" high.

ality of the motive and by the amorous quality, which is more outspoken in these *objets d'art* than in most paintings and monumental sculpture. These nudes, overflowing with animal spirits and fleshy in physique, he conceives with dainty naturalism. Notable, too, is the momentary quality, a transitoriness appropriate to such a theme and such a scale.

Many of these characteristics find their way even into the tombs of the

332. Jean Baptiste Pigalle (1714–84) *Tomb of Marshal Saxe* (1756–76) Church of St. Thomas, Strasbourg. *c.* 16′ high.

century. That of Marshal Saxe (fig. 332) by Jean Baptiste Pigalle, dated 1756–76, developed from the Baroque but carried its movement and its pictorialism even further. The drama of death

is yet more extravagant than in Bernini's tombs, and finds its climax here. Such elaboration is ill adapted to our conception of the purpose of a tomb. Its sentiment, its drama, its naturalism of detail would be more appropriate on a small scale in the salon or the boudoir. Nevertheless, Pigalle is the incarnation of his century; its growing confidence in science finds expression in anatomical accuracy. His animated figures convey the feminine ideals of the Rococo as fully as do the paintings of Boucher.

At the very end of the century, France produced in Jean Antoine Houdon (1741–1828) a figure who ranks with her greatest sculptors. The increasing sobriety of the age spared Houdon the necessity of catering to the less sculpturesque aspects of the Rococo, and the reviving classicism had not progressed so far as to insist on archaeology as basic to success, although Houdon did return to the Roman portrait bust as a form. The Voltaire (fig. 333) is clad in simple drapery with none of the furbelows of the Rococo to disturb its sculpturesque lines. In fact, it is too general to suggest historic costume of any period. Its ample folds avoid the naturalism of the mid-century, lest by superfluous detail they distract attention from the head and the hands where lies the characterization. With consummate taste Houdon selects those details best calculated to reveal the personality of Voltaire: the vivacious eyes, the cynical twist of his lips, the intellectual animation of his features. Voltaire leans

333. Jean Antoine Houdon (1741–1828) *Voltaire* (1781) Théâtre-Français, Paris. Life-size.

forward, gripping the arms of his chair as though absorbed in conversation and as though he had just uttered one of his provocative sallies.

The Rococo does not constitute a major style comparable to the Gothic, the Renaissance, and the Baroque. It is slight and affected, and as such has been bitterly attacked by more sober times. Nevertheless, this boudoir style has many admirable qualities. If it does not inculcate any moral and intellectual precepts, at best its proponents are exquisite draftsmen and delicate colorists, who display a sympathetic understanding of their media in sculpture and painting that may well be the envy of other generations.

ENGLAND

Meanwhile in England a different history was being shaped. The Georgian period was not exciting, and did not want to be. Its ideal was stateliness, serious and academic, but it was without the pomposity of the reign of Louis XIV, as it was also without the political absolutism of that age. A desire for rule and order affected everything, and compelled a sophisticated propriety. This sounds stuffy, but no century that produces a Hogarth or a Dr. Johnson can be dull. In fact, the Doctor and his circle are typical of the time. Moreover, the very order of the century provokes eddies of protest—a shadow of the Rococo, or the vagaries of the 'Chinese taste' or of the 'Gothick taste.' These are not serious studies of Chinese or Gothic art or architecture; they are variants, mostly of a flippant character, on the sober norm of Georgian architecture.

The Baroque style of Sir Christopher Wren and his successors did not permit the academic rule demanded by the new age. Under the leadership of Richard Boyle, the Earl of Burlington, architecture in the first half of the eighteenth century turned instead to Inigo Jones and Palladio. Burlington himself was an amateur, though his circle included many trained architects. Such amateurs, like Quatremère de Quincy in France at the end of the century, needed a formula wherewith to measure architectural success, as with a yardstick. In the case of Quatremère de Quincy, the standard was archaeological; for Burlington, it was academic. The proportions and members of the classic orders were all important; symmetry was to be achieved at any cost; imagination was subordinate to regularity. Jones himself had been less narrow than this, while Wren was great enough to be a law unto himself.

No outstanding architect appeared in this group, but many of its members were competent. Colin Campbell compiled the *Vitruvius Brittanicus*, a collection of the best examples of English architecture as measured by the standards of the Burlington clique. Significantly, many of Jones's buildings were illustrated, but few by Wren. The best

Georgian designers were more independent. James Gibbs was less academic and was, therefore, disapproved of by the Burlington group. More than any other mid-eighteenth-century architect, he carried on Wren's Baroque manner, confirmed in this tendency by his own trip to Italy and by the Italian stucco workers whom he brought back with him. His portico on St. Martin's in the Fields in London, 1721–6, is Georgian in spirit, but the steeple would do Wren himself credit in its beauty of silhouette. Gibbs has importance for Americans as the immediate source of inspiration for many colonial designs.

The best site for the study of Georgian domestic architecture is the city of

334. John Wood (*c.* 1704–54) *Prior Park* (1735–43) Bath. 147' long; columns 32' high.

Bath, which became fashionable at this time. Its regular lines and its blocks of uniformly designed houses make whole streets and squares units of design. The best architectural expression of the quiet culture of Bath is found in the work of the John Woods, father and son. Prior Park (fig. 334) near Bath, built from 1735 to 1743, shows the Georgian at its best. It was the estate of Ralph Allen, the prototype of Squire Allworthy in Fielding's *Tom Jones*, who promoted much of the new work in the city. The main block of the house is rectangular in plan and strictly axial; quadrant wings curve forward from each corner of the façade to connect with smaller blocks that often functioned as kitchens and stables, their masses serving as a foil to the central building. This triple scheme can be traced back through designs of Inigo Jones to the villas of Palladio. Its effect is stately, but presupposes a corps of servants and some sacrifice of convenience in the separation of the kitchen from the dining room. The spacious apartments are designed more for display than for domestic use as understood today. However, this impression that the house is designed for show is partly due to its monumentality. On the façade, window balances window in number, size, and design. A free-standing portico, complete with entablature and pediment, accents the center, but notice that this feature is in the middle of the long side of the house, and the pediment does not, therefore, terminate the principal roof, as it did in classic art. Such a portico adds the final touch

to the dignity and formality of the life within.

The smaller Georgian interiors, with their paneled walls sometimes painted in quiet colors and elsewhere left in the natural color of the wood, were very satisfactory. In the larger houses the de-

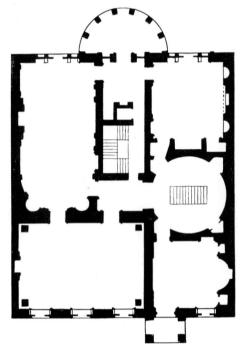

335. *Home House*, London (1775–77).

sire for display led to the introduction of polished marbles and columns, pediments, and other features too large in scale and too public in character to be appropriate. Hence toward the end of the century the Georgian style, especially on the interior, gave way to the style created by the Adam brothers, who were partly under the influence of the increasing classicism. Robert Adam returned in 1760 from his travels in

336. Robert Adam (1728–92) James Adam (1730–94) *Lord Derby's House*, London (1773).

Italy, where he had shared in an archaeological investigation, which he later published, of the Palace of Diocletian at Spalato.

The new classic vogue betrays itself, on the façade of Kedleston, in the choice of such Roman motives as the triumphal arch and the saucer-like dome, but the Adam exteriors differ from the Georgian manner less than do other parts of their designs. In plan (fig. 335) the Adam style varies the volumes of several rooms in a suite, from the square to the rectangle or circle, with large or small niches and exedrae to enrich the impression of each changing area; Home House, London, is an excellent example. Lord Derby's House

(fig. 336) in London shows the result of such a plan and also its substitution of elegance for grandeur. The forms become lighter and better adapted to an interior than to an exterior. A rich vocabulary of small decorative features enlivens walls and ceilings alike. Rosettes, festoons of corn husks, urns, and floral motives modeled in plaster create an interior of sophistication and refinement suited to the polished life of this generation. A few touches of bright color, or perhaps decorative paintings by Angelica Kaufmann, enhance these details. The whole room is homogeneous in design, thanks to the application of like motives in the furniture, and even in the locks, keys, and hinges. These were the fashionable interiors which housed the social celebrities painted by Reynolds and Gainsborough.

The eighteenth century is recognized as the great age of English furniture. Walnut began to supersede oak as the favorite material as early as 1660, giving way in turn to mahogany about 1725. However, these dates are approximations only, and walnut pieces were made long after 1725. Many familiar motives, such as the cabriole leg and the ball-and-claw foot, prevail in the first half of the century in both walnut and mahogany designs, which were characterized by vigor and restraint and executed with such skill that the unknown craftsmen need not bow to the celebrated cabinet-makers who succeeded them.

The first of these craftsmen to give his name to a style of furniture was Thomas Chippendale. Several types of design are associated with him on the basis of the illustrations to *The Gentleman and Cabinet Maker's Director*, first published in 1754. He continued the cabriole leg and the ball-and-claw foot; he popularized the tripod support for screens and small tables; fretwork in either the Chinese or the Gothic tastes create playful variants; and at other times, the influence of the French Rococo style is paramount. Chippendale also worked for the Adam brothers after 1766, but then the design is more theirs than his. The same motives—corn husks, slender urns, and fluting—that characterize the Adam style in architecture also adorn the furniture that bears their name.

George Hepplewhite lived a few years later than Chippendale. His book, *The Cabinet-Makers' and Upholsterers' Guide*, was published in 1788 after his death. He preferred tapered legs; curved fronts for sideboards and commodes, perhaps with shutters; oval, shield, heart, or hoop-shaped backs of chairs; and sometimes light woods in fine veneers. However, these characteristics also occur in furniture not connected with him. The designers of the eighteenth century drew on the same traditions and also borrowed motives from one another.

Finally, Thomas Sheraton published *The Cabinet Makers' and Upholsterers' Drawing Book* about 1791. Though he was scornful of the designs of his predecessors, his own manner draws on the same sources. In general his models are simpler, less influenced by the Rococo and more by the developing classic fashion. Legs are usually straight, chair backs square or with quadrant corners, and although curved fronts are not eliminated, they become less common. Greater reliance is placed on the beauty of workmanship and veneers. The level of craftsmanship faded during the nineteenth century when the rise of industrialism, mass production, and materialism led to a striving for effect without taste. In protest, the arts-and-crafts movement of the late nineteenth century, led by William Morris, attempted to revive craftsmanship in printing, wall paper, textiles, and furniture. The Morris chair, with its adjustable back, was the most functional piece of furniture

337. William Hogarth (1697–1764) *Marriage à la Mode I* (finished 1744) Tate Gallery, London. 2'3" x 2'11".

developed during the nineteenth century.

Before the eighteenth century not much painting had been produced in England by native artists. Foreigners like Van Dyck established a tradition of aristocratic portraiture. Some Georgian houses contained Baroque decorative paintings, perhaps in the stair hall by the Italian Verrio, or the Frenchman Laguerre. The dome of St. Paul's was decorated by Sir James Thornhill, a native artist, but on the whole English decorative art is not important.

Aside from portraiture, however, the English spirit demanded narrative of its pictorial arts. William Hogarth (1697–1764), the first great English painter, presents vivid narratives in sets of pictures, each canvas comparable to a chapter in a novel. Such a work is the Marriage à la Mode series. The first design (fig. 337) introduces the characters. The social position of a nobleman is to be bartered for the money of a wealthy tradesman. A gouty earl on the right points with pride to his position in a family tree that traces his ancestry back to a knight in medieval armor. In exchange for this social eminence, he receives back the mortgage on his estate, and a cash settlement as well. The father of the bride-to-be inspects the marriage settlement with the same care and the same absence of emotion he might feel in reviewing a business contract. The engaged couple sit beside each other to the left, but Hogarth allows them to turn their backs upon one another. The young woman twirls her ring on her handkerchief and listens to the charming conversation of the lawyer in charge of this job. With such a beginning, one can hardly expect a happy issue from this marriage, and the remaining five pictures show the progress of the tragedy—the boredom of the couple in each other's company after marriage, the empty gaiety of the household, the infidelity of the bride leading to a duel in which the young nobleman is killed, and the subsequent death of his wife.

This and Hogarth's other series of paintings were made to be engraved and the reproductions sold broadcast. Financially, they were very successful. The lucid story would ensure that. These satires on social customs of Hogarth's day are historical documents of the first importance. They are often mistakenly described as moralistic. A moral teaches that the consequences of wrongdoing fall upon the transgressors, but Hogarth allows the guilty to escape untouched. The young couple have their union arranged for them, but they, and not their parents, bear the brunt of the tragedy. Rather than describe Hogarth as a moralist, one should recognize in him a realist, who takes a custom of his day and demonstrates its probable consequences without a trace of sentiment.

These compositions may well, like the novels of Dickens in the next century, have borne their share in ameliorating the conditions they attacked.

But however biting the satire, and however vivid the narrative, these qualities alone could not make Hogarth's canvases great paintings, nor should the effectiveness of these satires overshadow Hogarth's power as a draftsman. Detailed as these are, he is capable of extraordinary breadth, as in the Shrimp Girl, or of keen character study, as in his portrait of Captain Coram. His composition appears to be accidental, or, more precisely, defined by the narrative demands of his subject. In reality, Hogarth shows a remarkable feeling for space, and for the co-ordination of the figures with the rooms they occupy. The pictorial strength of these designs rests on an organization that is none the less present for not being obvious.

But after all, it is the portrait school in the second half of the century that is most characteristic of the age. Its leader Sir Joshua Reynolds (1723–92), destined to be the first president of the Royal Academy, studied for years in Italy. His color and even his lighting are affected by the Venetians, through his own study, and through the Venetian influence upon Van Dyck and Rubens, who laid the foundations of English portraiture. Reynolds is often said to be at his finest in his paintings of women, for example, Mrs. Siddons as the Tragic Muse, inspired by Michelangelo's Isaiah from the Sistine ceiling. He infuses that portrait with a histrionic character through the pose and background lighting, appropriate since Mrs. Siddons was a great Shakespearian actress.

But Reynolds' best male portraits are more powerful than his female portraits. Dr. Johnson (fig. 338) could hardly be better characterized. The painter and his sitter were friends, as intimate as the

338. Joshua Reynolds (1723–92) *Dr. Johnson* (1772–1780) National Gallery, London. 2'6" x 2'1".

spirit of the eighteenth century and the reserve of Reynolds himself would permit. The painter catches the ponderous intellectually of Dr. Johnson perfectly. The Doctor might be formulating a definition of some word for his Dictionary, or characterizing one of the English poets. He looks the part of a dictator of English letters. Reynolds is at his best in these intimate portraits, concentrated against a plain background. In the more pretentious canvases, custom dictates such accessories as the lower part of a column, a sweep of drapery, or a bit of landscape. Lord Heathfield, the defender of Gibraltar, is reinforced by a cannon and other objects that allude to his profession. The lighting is generalized and no attempt to be natural is made. Sufficient to bring out the modeling, it comes closer to the diffused light of an interior than to sunlight. Technically, the middle range of values in nature is recorded with nearly its actual contrasts, and therefore a crowding together of the high and low values comes inevitable.

This English school is one of society portraiture. Thomas Gainsborough (1727–88) has a flair for infusing his characters with all the social graces. In his portrait of the Honorable Mrs. Graham (fig. 339), she looks as though she might just have come from a reception at St. James's Palace. She looks to the manner born, with that self-confident distinction caricatured in the March of the Peers in *Iolanthe*. The color, stronger and fresher than that of Rey-

339. Thomas Gainsborough (1727–88) *The Honorable Mrs. Graham* (1775) National Gallery of Scotland, Edinburgh. 7′9″ x 5′.

nolds, and the pictorial accessories of landscape and column create a sumptuous effect. The portrait sheds its richness and its social eminence wherever it may be displayed. Gainsborough is not so intellectual in his analysis of character as Reynolds. He never, like Reynolds, traveled to Italy, nor was he so influential in his day. On the other hand, Gainsborough is more brilliant as a painter; he has sheer genius. His dash and verve, his freedom, his pictorial instinct, and his virtuosity with the brush are pronounced.

The danger of such brilliance of technique lies in its charm. Many painters in the late eighteenth and early nineteenth centuries follow the lines laid down by Reynolds and Gainsborough, men like Henry Raeburn, George Romney, and John Hoppner, to name only three. But these portrait manufacturers, as a more critical age has called them, lack the intellect of Reynolds and the pictorial structure of Gainsborough. Sir Thomas Lawrence carries the school to its glittering extreme in sparkling color and virtuosity, but the means have become an end in themselves, and only the shell of the school of Reynolds and Gainsborough is preserved. At its worst this school indulges in all the superficialities of society portraiture, and adheres to a monotonous pattern. In this formula, established by Van Dyck, a fashionably dressed figure is placed against a generalized background or one filled with vague accessories that hint at some achievement or interest of the sitter. However, even the weaker members of the group retain the decorative color and the social poise that typified the school at its best.

Over a long period of time and in relatively small groups, the American Indian migrated across the Bering Straits into this hemisphere from northeast Asia. Evidences of human occupancy of the Americas have been traced back to about twenty-five thousand years ago, while habitation sites in caves in Oregon and elsewhere are over seven thousand years old. The immigrant peoples were nomadic hunters who roamed over the extensive reaches of both North and South America, as far as the southernmost point. They were of Mongoloid stock; but differences in physical type and languages suggest that they came from different areas or groups in their northeast Asian homeland. At some point long after their arrival, the Indians domesticated such plants as maize, beans, squash, and tobacco, and became either sedentary small village dwellers near their fields, or semi-nomadic groups dependent for their subsistence diet on agriculture as well as on hunting and fishing.

With the domestication of plants, numerous structural and conceptual changes occurred in the various Indian cultures. Agriculture was diffused all over the Americas and was fundamental to the formation of high cultures in Mexico, Middle America, and Peru. It was also basic in the survival pattern of the majority of tribal groups elsewhere.

It is necessary in the study of Indian art to make certain temporal and cultural distinctions. Chronological differences must be observed between the undocumented archaeological arts of Pre-Columbian times and the tribal arts recorded by Europeans at about the time of contact with the Indians. Differences must also be noted between the high and tribal cultures. The high cultures are distinguished by such elements as a consolidated government, a unifying institutionalized religion, specialization in the arts and vocations, uniformity of institutions and customs, and a planned and organized use of manpower for the prosecution of such extensive plans as large architectural projects and warfare. Tribal cultures, on the other hand, have a simpler pattern of life in which many of the elements above are either lacking or are modestly developed within a small isolated group.

The high cultures developed in the Peruvian (Central Andean) area of South America and in Middle America (Central America and Mexico), but there are suggestions of a near-high culture in the archaeological material from the Ohio-Mississippi area. Knowledge of these high cultures has accumulated from archaeological investigations of the past hundred-odd years. The dating of them, however, is still somewhat hypothetical, although a relative time sequence is now generally agreed upon. Hence, the dates used here will be broad and general.

The ancient Peruvian region extended along the western part of South America from Ecuador in the north to northern Chile in the south. Topographically and culturally it can be divided into a lowland coastal strip and a highland zone, often over 10,000 feet in elevation within the Andean escarpment. Our knowledge of these peoples derives to some extent from the written records of the Spanish following their conquest of the Inca Empire in 1532, but is scientifically based on archaeological work of the past seventy-five years. Although these Indians evolved a culture with a well-organized religious, political, and social structure, they lacked knowledge of the wheel, the arch, and any method of writing and dating.

Ancient Peruvian art encompasses many of the so-called minor arts, such as pottery and textiles, and the major arts of architecture and sculpture. The greater number of surviving examples from all eras, however, are of pottery and textiles. Throughout the long timespan of this art emphasis was placed, regardless of medium, upon technical excellence.

Three broad chronological periods, early, middle, and late, may be characterized in Peruvian art. The early period, roughly 1000–400 B.C., is best represented by the stone sculpture of the Chavin culture of the northern highlands; the middle period, A.D. 400–1000, by Mochica pottery of the northern coastal region and by Nazca pottery and textiles of the southern coast; and the late period, 1000–1532, by the stone sculpture of the Tiahuanaco culture in the southern highlands and by the architecture and decorative arts of the Inca Empire. But pottery, art forms in metal, usually gold or silver, and evidences of textiles appear in all periods and areas, while wood sculpture has survived in some regions.

In the highlands throughout the length of Peru an abundance of stone led to the development of stone sculpture and architecture; good clay furnished material for pottery and adobe; and the llama, alpaca, and vicuna provided food and wool for textiles. Chavin, the earliest highland culture, derives its name from the site of Chavin de Huántar, where the most extensive remains of it have been found. The art is dominated by a single all-pervading motive—a heavy, fanged feline head. It appears on stone sculpture, ceramics, and gold work, in profile, top and front views, often moderately or considerably stylized. The head is attached in some examples to a feline body; in others it is appended to a bird, or fish form; while in all three it is often used to indicate joints or body details. Often the fanged mouth alone is used. This motive is rendered in a two-dimensional incised style composed of curving, somewhat angular lines, frequently used as parallel pairs to produce a strap-like effect.

Characteristic Chavin relief sculpture appears on the cornice soffits of extensive architectural ruins discovered at Chavin de Huántar (fig. 340). These ruins include sunken plazas, platforms, terraces, and structures of several floors, together with subterranean drains, galleries, ventilation shafts, ramps and stairways. Carefully dressed stones were set without mortar or dowels in alternating wide and narrow courses to face the interior and exterior walls. Within the buildings two large stone sculptures were found: one, a 6-foot-high flat relief

340. *Relief, detail of Cornice Soffit,* Chavin de Huántar (1200–400 B.C.).

carving of an anthropomorphized feline form with an enormous headdress of superposed feline faces and serpentine forms; the other, a 15-foot-high lance-like shape carved with a large feline head. Examples of both architecture and sculpture reveal an accomplished technique of stone cutting; while the ever-present feline motive, certainly a pervading symbol, has contributed to the belief that Chavin de Huántar was a religious center of a theocratically dominated culture. The large architectural complex also hypothecates a religious or political organization strong enough to utilize and control mass labor.

The ubiquitous feline head or face motive has been found at early cultural levels over much of Peru, an indication that Chavin culture may have been pan-Peruvian in its distribution. It is certainly one of the most interesting of early American Indian art styles.

Mochica art of the middle period is best represented by a distinctive pottery shape, modeled, well polished, and painted red, white, and black in a unique and characteristic manner (fig. 341). The pottery was used as an adjunct to burials, possibly indicating the

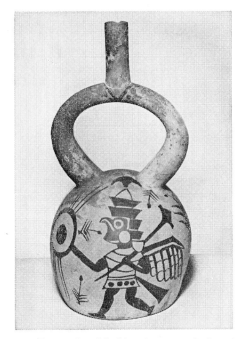

341. *Pottery Jar*, Mochica (400–1000) American Museum of Natural History, New York. 11½" high.

social, political, or religious importance of the deceased. Mochica decorated pottery was mold-made in two identical vertical halves, which were joined together and topped by a so-called 'stirrup-spout' consisting of an open tubular loop surmounted in the center or to the side by a tubular spout. These vessels were decorated either by modeled and painted forms, or by linear designs painted on the surface. The subject matter was often a genre-like description of various mundane activities or a lively representation or symbolic depiction of religious, mythological, and military scenes. The forms were human, bird, animal, or hybrid, arranged as groups or as single figures. A fanged

anthropomorphic feline, presumed a deity, is fundamental to this art; while other human and anthropomorphic animal figures, such as the lizard and dog, are considered as menials in the religious hierarchy. Because of the pottery decoration, more is therefore known or may justifiably be surmised about Mochica culture than about any other early culture of Peru.

In the dry desert coastal region to the south, textiles as well as ceramics have survived from the Nazca middle period culture. Here the decorated pottery was coil-made and molded by hand. Distinctive of this art, both in pottery and textiles, are the range and variations of colors: on a white, cream, gray, or buff slip as many as eleven different colors may be distinguished in the painted ceramics, and a similar color range is found in the textiles. The designs, often outlined in black, are rather descriptive or stylized, and are usually less pictorial than in Mochica art. A wide variety of shapes, including the bowl and open cup, are typical of the pottery (fig. 342). The decorative subjects include birds, plants, fish, cat-demons, centipedes, trophy heads, and a number of geometric designs.

Nazca textiles consist of both cotton and wool fibers, while embroidery and tapestry were the preferred techniques (Plate IX, facing p. 556). Textile designs, like those of ceramics, are usually composed of small units and often represent highly conventionalized anthropomorphic figures. Outstanding in the textile designs are the numerous varia-

342. *Pottery Jar*, Nazca (400–1000) American Museum of Natural History, New York. 7½″ high.

tions, alternations, and inversions used, together with changes in color, in the composition of a single design unit, or several, in the same cloth.

The later period culture of Tiahuanaco, found at the site of that name, south of the shore of Lake Titicaca in Bolivia, is typified by an art style most clearly defined by stone sculpture and painted ceramics. A particular motive also dominates this style—a conventionalized human figure with a short, heavy body and a large rectangular head. Facial features of these figures consist of low-relief rectangular eye, nose, and mouth elements, with a vertical rectangular band of three 'tear-drop' forms below the eyes. A conspicuous variant of the human head is that of a bird, a condor; while other constantly recurring elements include stars, puma, fish, winged-eye, and a geometric stepped design.

A number of monolithic stone sculptures have been found at the site of Tiahuanaco in an enormous architectural ruin measuring almost 4000 feet by 2000 feet. The most famous of these sculptures is the so-called Gate-way of the Sun, a monolithic structure approximately 7 feet high, 13 wide, and 18 inches thick. On the front surface the basic motives of Tiahuanaco art appear in a very low relief and an incised technique: a frontally posed stylized human figure, flanked by running condor-headed figures. Several colossal stone sculptures, ranging from 6 to 24 feet high and representing humanoid figures, have been uncovered at this site (fig. 343). The over-all proportions serve to emphasize the large rectangular head, while the body below has a similar rectangularity of shapes. All of the forms are blocky and four-sided, with descriptive details of costume and facial features incised or carved in low relief on the surface. The motives of Tiahuanaco style spread all over Peru and became dominant influences in the formation of later art styles.

The year 1438 is the date accepted for the establishment of the Inca Empire. In many respects this Empire, conquered by the Spanish in 1532, was a cultural synthesis of what had been developed by earlier Peruvian cultures; but the Inca were more deeply concerned with the formation of a tightly knit social and political organization and less with the creation of a distinctive art

343. *Stone Figure, Stela Bennett,* Tiahuanaco (1000–1300) American Museum of Natural History, New York. *c.* 24' high.

achieved, however, through the medium of architecture. Numerous fortresses, cities, and ceremonial structures were built in various types of heavy stone masonry. Some of them were constructed of huge megalithic blocks of irregular sizes and shapes, carefully cut so that they would fit perfectly together; other structures were built in a similar type of masonry but of smaller stones; and still others were built of large blocks with the surfaces cut as a convex or expanding plane, producing a rusticated effect (fig. 344). The Inca also used a dressed stone and coursed masonry, and rough or split stones laid in courses of clay cement, as well as a common type of adobe brick construction. Although the aesthetic character of Inca architecture largely derives from the excellence of technique in the cutting, shaping, and fitting together of the stones, it is also important to note a sculptural quality in space—the way the bulky, voluminous forms are arranged in relation to each other.

Ancient Peruvian art consists predominantly of two-dimensional designs, as on ceramics and in textiles, although three-dimensional forms are also well represented in stone sculpture, ceramics, metal work, and in the massive architectural shapes. There are very few style elements common to the entire area; but there was a continuing and universal emphasis on technical dexterity, and a close adherence to local or regional art styles.

style. Their art, although technologically accomplished, produced relatively few typical shapes and patterns in ceramics, textiles, and metal-work; a significant, and awe-inspiring art was

Middle America, comprising parts of Honduras, Guatemala, and all of Mex-

344. *Detail, Stone Architecture,* Tampumachay, near Cuzco, Inca (1438–1532).

ico, may have had, as present archaeological knowledge suggests, a cultural depth comparable to that of Peru. In this extensive region there evolved a considerable number of cultures and art styles for which a chronological sequence has been established by both archaeological and historical evidence. Middle-American art may also be divided into early, middle, and late periods, the three periods covering a time span extending from about 300 B.C. to A.D. 1521, when the Spanish conquered the Aztec state.

Within each of the three periods there developed a number of different, and in most cases distinctive cultures and their attendant art styles. The major arts of architecture, sculpture, and painting were more highly developed here than in Peru, although ceramics and elaborate metal-work were also given important artistic expressions. Several pre-writing systems or notations were evolved: one consisting of glyphs composed of natural forms and symbols arranged to record a date or a period of time; and the other a pictorial account of ceremonies or events painted on deerskin or a type of parchment.

In Middle America, the so-called pyramid is a conspicuous feature of civic-religious sites. The pyramid was, with few exceptions, truncated, and it served as a massive, lofty base for the temple built on its flattened top. The temple was reached by steep steps arranged on the outer slope of the base. This was essentially an architecture of mass and bulk, constructed of rubble, cut stone blocks or slabs, and adobe brick, the exterior and interior walls frequently being decorated with sculpture or fresco painting. The true arch was not known, but the corbelled arch was used extensively, particularly as a covering for the narrow interior rooms and galleries. In Middle America the civic-religious urban centers were often enormous in size and complex in plan.

Sculpture in stone, pottery, or jade was an outstanding art, carved or modeled in high and low relief, or in the round. Color was sometimes used to clarify a design and inlays of various materials were employed. Bulk and volume of component shapes were stressed, although descriptive or symbolic details were often elaborately rendered by small-scale, multiple-design elements.

The early-period Middle-American arts developed in four main centers: at Monte Alban in the Oaxaca Valley of western Mexico, tentatively dated 100 B.C. to A.D. 550; the east Mexican Vera Cruz area, known as La Venta, 100 B.C. to A.D. 600; the Mexican Valley site of Teotihuacan near Mexico City, 300 B.C. to A.D. 900; and the early Maya cities of Guatemala, Honduras, and Mexico, A.D. 325–900. These four art styles have a considerable geographical spread and a marked distinctiveness of character. The middle-period arts are those of the east Mexican Totonac area, dated A.D. 800–1200; from the Toltec sites in the Valley of Mexico, not far from Mexico City, 900–1200; of the Mitla-Mixtec center in Oaxaca, 900–1300; and in the Yucatán Maya cities, 900–1204. Knowledge of the art of the early and middle periods is derived from archaeological investigations; and, since these are still continuing, this knowledge is being added to and modified with each year of research. The late-period art is that of the Aztec state, which may be dated 1325–1521; and possibly that of the northwestern Mexican area of Tarascan, where a strongly developed local art evolved and for which at the moment no dates can be given. Only the late period may be considered historical, owing to the recording by the Spaniards of the culture of their conquered peoples.

Associated with the Zapotec tribes or peoples, the ceremonial center of Monte Alban consists of a number of fairly stubby truncated pyramids, plazas, temples, ball courts, and shallow subterranean tombs, and was used for a long time apparently as a combined religious and mortuary center. Among the earliest arts from Monte Alban are a series of 3- to 4-foot-high vertical stone slabs set up to line the entranceway to the tombs, and carved in an incised or island-relief technique, depicting dramatic, energetic 'dancing' figures. In style, irregular curving lines boldly and simply delineate the forms and the sparse details.

The best-known examples of art from this site are clay-modeled, well-fired anthropomorphic urns, ranging from 1 foot to over 2 feet high and from a gray-tan through a red-tan in color (fig. 345). They were found in the tombs and represented a seated or kneeling figure in a ceremonial dress consisting of an often very elaborate headdress and a cloak-like costume believed to be that of a priest. The earliest of these figures wear a simpler costume. In early and

represented by a few colossal stone heads, measuring as much as 7 feet high, found in association with architectural ruins. The significance of these massive and strongly sculptural heads is not as yet known. In the La Venta area carved calendar stones and complex glyphs, at present undecipherable, have also been discovered. The influence of this culture may have extended south to Guatemala and west to Monte Alban; and it may have been basic in the formation of other Middle-American cultures.

At Teotihuacan there was located a vast early-period ceremonial center comprising two large, stepped, truncated pyramids, the so-called Pyramid of the Sun, 216 feet high, and the Pyramid of the Moon, 140 feet high. They served as lofty foundations for temples, which have now disappeared, and were built of sun-dried brick covered with a thick

345. *Anthropomorphic Urn,* Monte Alban-Zapotec (500–1000) Museum of the American Indian, New York. 26⅜" high.

late examples there is a naturalistic interpretation of form, rendered by a sensitive modeling of shapes and structure. Carved jades and highly stylized fresco paintings are also typical of Monte Alban art.

The most important evidences of La Venta art, formerly known as Olmec, are finely sculptured jade and stone objects, including mask-like forms, statuettes, votive axes with human features, and colossal heads (fig. 346). Body shapes are consistently squat and fat, while the facial features have heavy Mongoloid eyes and a composite feline and infantile mouth. The style is well

346. *Face Type from Stone Head,* La Venta-Olmec (100 B.C.–A.D. 600) c. 7' high.

layer of adobe mixed with broken stone and surfaced with stucco. Nearby are ruins of houses built of the same materials, with developed ground plans and elaborately stylized fresco paintings on the plastered walls of some of the rooms.

The largest building complex at this site, known as The Citadel, was a ceremonial structure. It measures over 1300 feet long by 250 feet wide and consists of high embankments reached by stairways and surrounded by a courtyard. The Temple of Quetzalcoatl is located within the citadel and is one of the most famous buildings in Middle America. It is a stepped truncated pyramid, which was covered over by one built at a later date; hence its front face or façade was protected and has suffered only slight deterioration. This structure is 55 feet high, built up in 6 terraces or steps faced with stone. Each terrace is richly decorated with sculptures representing alternately the mask of the rain-god, Tlaloc, and the feathered serpent, a symbol of the deity-culture hero, Quetzalcoatl. These symbolic sculptures, large in both size and scale, were carved in stone in low and high relief, the head of the serpent projecting in the round, the teeth painted white, and the eyes inlaid with round obsidian disks. It has been calculated that there were originally 366 carvings on the pyramid.

Teotihuacan art also includes carved stone masks and a quantity of small hand-molded pottery figurines with mold-made faces and headdresses, probably used as temple votive offerings. This art is in general architecturally rigid, formal, and highly symbolic, particularly in the painted frescoes, but also in the sculptures. The symbolism at times seems a forerunner of the glyph notation and writing developed by the Maya and other Middle-American peoples.

The original homeland of the early-period Maya tribes is not known, although it is believed that it may have been to the northeast. They apparently migrated south and southwest, one group continuing into Guatemala, and the other breaking off and moving northeast into Yucatán, where a Mayan culture was evolved just a little later than that to the south. In both the north and south early Maya art is characterized by large, well-planned civic centers, where architecture and sculpture combined to produce an awesome, spectacular effect.

Despite the agrarian character of the economy, Maya culture centered around a unique type of city plan. Each city with a population estimated as ranging from a few thousand to over a hundred thousand had a large, often enormous religious-civic center. These centers consisted of numerous courts and sunken plazas, surrounded by temples raised on very high pyramid bases and palaces or civic buildings built on lower platforms. From this hub the small farms and the simple mud-and-stick homes of the commoners or peasants spread out in all directions, forming a heavily populated area dependent upon the civic-religious center. Labor, food, and other services were exacted of the population of a city by the numerous priests and officials, thus making possible the often astounding architectural achievements.

The Maya, like all Pre-Columbian Indians of Middle America, had no metal tools until after European contact; they quarried, cut, and carved stone with stone or wooden tools and abrasives. Surviving Mayan monuments well attest to an amazing proficiency in the use of these tools, but a great deal of time and manpower must have been involved. Their architecture consisted essentially of monolithic lime-concrete walls or core, covered with cut stone, usually limestone, and surfaced with a lime plaster. The cut-stone work was therefore nonfunctional. In the south, the temple bases are lofty, truncated, stepped pyramids, frequently over 100 feet high, the highest at Tikal in Guatemala measuring 240 feet. Steep stone steps lead up one side of the base to a platform on top where the temple was constructed. The temple was rectangular in plan, with a single or three-doorway entrance, and an interior of only a few rooms covered with a corbelled vault, a trait unique in America to the Maya Indians. The exterior façade was usually divided into two almost equal parts by a medial cornice, with a capping cornice at the top; while the flat lime-concrete roof was surmounted in the center by a very high wall parallel to the front façade, a purely decorative form known as a *roof-comb*. Above the medial cornice the exterior façade was frequently decorated with relief sculptures, and the roof-comb was always given a decorative treatment.

Characteristic of the southern Maya area were the carving and erecting of large, vertical, slab-like stone stelae, 10

347. *Stela 14*, Piedras Negras, Maya (436–534) The University Museum, University of Pennsylvania, Philadelphia (on loan from the Government of Guatemala). *c.* 9′ high.

to over 20 feet high (fig. 347). Stelae were set up to mark the conclusion of five-, ten-, or twenty-year calendrical cycles, when important ceremonials took place. They were usually carved on the back and sides with a series of square-shaped glyphs which recorded the date and other matters. Large priest figures, replete with an elaborate headdress and costume, were sculptured in very high and low relief on the front surface of stelae, figures usually frontally posed and often so lavishly costumed that the human form is almost completely hidden. Highly stylized hybrid human, animal, and serpentine forms and detailed costume and iconography are characteristic of this essentially descriptive and didactic art. Other carvings, made for the inner sanctuaries of the temple and depicting priests and ritual scenes in low relief on stone panels, have a less profuse costume and iconography. Here the human form is rendered in a strongly articulated, modeled style. Examples of these sculptures were found at Palenque and Yaxchilan in western Guatemala.

Southern Maya style defines forms and details with sharply rendered single or often double strap-like outlines. The forms are frequently broken up into multiple parts by small rectangular units, while contrasting short or angular curves give contrast and variety to the design. In relief sculptures a half dozen or more parallel planes may recede into depth, although some details may be carved in the round in very high relief. Early northern Maya art appears in unique architectural forms and decoration. Supporting bases or platforms are moderately low and decorative roofcombs are replaced by 'flying façades,' a continuation upward of the front façade as a decorative wall. Large stone mosaics of considerable elaboration were frequently set into the walls above the medial cornice as symbolic decorations, and a thin, finely cut stone veneer was used to cover the wall below this cornice. The stone mosaics, which constitute the important sculpture in this area where stelae time-markers are exceedingly rare, are often projecting forms carved in the round before being embedded in the surface of the wall. The ubiquitous Mayan serpent-deity figure, together with human heads and figures and geometric forms, is typical of this sculptured stone work. The best examples of northern Maya art are found at the Yucatán city of Uxmal (fig. 348), while other excellent examples appear to the northeast at the famous site of Chichén Itzá, although this city was to reach its greatest development during the following period.

Maya art, both in its uses and subject matter, was the product of a theocractically dominated culture in which both spiritual and secular matters were largely in the hands of priests. Religious rites centered around a large pantheon of nature deities, particularly those favorable to agriculture, such as the rain god. Complex and accurate calendrical systems were worked out by the Maya, who had observatories and various techniques for determining sea-

348. *Detail, Stone Architecture, The Nunnery,* Uxmal, Maya (700–1000) 189' x 33½'.

sonal changes. The development of the arts, together with the organizational character of this culture, indicates an advanced degree of specialization. Technical excellence in architecture and sculpture and the abundance of finely decorated pottery supports this assumption.

In the ninth century the many large southern Maya cities were abandoned. It seems most likely that this was a result of the collapse of their method of agriculture in the face of an increasing population. The Maya thereafter wandered or migrated in various directions, some to the northwest and north and others to the northeast, eventually arriving in Yucatán, where a revival of

their culture, modified by peoples and elements from the west, took place in the following period.

Totonac art of the middle period is best represented by that found at the city-ceremonial site of Tajin. The most important ruin at Tajin is a six stepped pyramid temple base, with each step containing a continuous row of deep niches. In association with this pyramid, many carved stone panels and rectangular blocks suggest that the temple had sculptured stone wall panels and cornices. The sculptures, carved in a low relief, represent gods and humans often engaged in sacrificial ceremonial scenes. A relatively open spatial setting for the figures distinguishes this style, in which the forms and details are described by strongly marked double outlines of angular curves. Glyphs are sometimes carved on the heads of the figures. Other unique Totonac forms include three enigmatical types of stone sculpture: heavy, horseshoe-shaped stone 'yokes,' sometimes of polished diorite, carved in a relief style similar to that of the architectural stones; axe-shaped forms sculptured with a human or animal head; and vertical ovoid shapes, called 'palmas' (fig. 349), sometimes 24 inches high and covered with low-relief representations of single figures or animals, or compositional groups. Totonac relief sculptures are frequently heavily stylized and sometimes difficult to read visually. Characteristic of this art, too, are three-dimensional terra-cotta figurines and heads, and stone figures and mask-like faces interpreted in a sensitive naturalistic manner, often carved with somewhat infantile faces and pleasant smiling features.

In the middle period at Mitla, near Monte Alban, the Mixtec tribe of northern invaders established an art of new forms and greatly modified earlier-Monte-Alban elements. The outstanding achievement at Mitla is the ceremonial building with its attendant stone shaft tombs. This structure, raised on a relatively low platform, is dominated by long, low horizontal lines. Built around a central court, it comprises a number of narrow rectangular rooms and a large wider room in which the wooden ceiling beams are supported by round monolithic stone columns. On the exterior

349. *Stone Palma, Totonac* (800–1200) American Museum of Natural History, New York. 18″ high.

façades and interior walls are geometric mosaic designs composed of small white stones, fitted together without mortar and set in a hard red stucco background. The geometric designs, supposedly stylizations or symbols of a feather-serpent deity, consist of frets, stepped frets, and angular spiral motives, often arranged in a diagonal direction. Various kinds of polychromed pottery and richly worked gold ornaments have been found in the Mitla tombs.

The Toltecs, another invading northern tribe, in the Tula area developed unique cultural elements, including new architectural and sculptural forms. They were an aggressive people who had as important culture traits warrior societies and extensive human sacrifice. Although human sacrifice was common to other Middle-American groups, sacrificial altars and structures for the display of victims dominated the ceremonial center at Tula.

Toltec art appears in a pure form at Tula and in a slightly modified style at the Yucatán-Maya city of Chichén Itzá. Temples were raised on a low or high truncated pyramidal base. A wide molding marked off the sloping or battered lower wall area from the upper part of the flat-roofed structures. Frequently the wall above the sloping base and the space between the upper capping cornice and a parallel molding slightly below it were decorated with elaborate low-relief carvings. These, painted descriptively red, white, and black, represented the military societies symbolized by jaguars and eagles. Ceremonial scenes involving combat or human sacrifice are often graphically depicted in these low reliefs by a distinct, didactic linear style.

Other Toltec architectural innovations included the colonnaded court and the use of great feathered-serpent columns as structural and decorative forms flanking the entrance to temples. These columns consisted of three parts: a large, sculptured serpent head lying horizontally along the ground; the columnar body rising vertically above it; and the tail and rattles placed at right angles to the body and projecting forward in an L-shaped manner to function as supports for the stone entrance lintel. Three-dimensional sculptures in this style represent a recumbent figure, known as Chacmool, and various small caryatid or atalantid supporting-figures for low bench altars or table-like altars. All of the characteristic Toltecan architectural and sculptural forms appear at Chichén Itzá, where the building activity during this middle period was extensive. A quantity of finely wrought gold work from this period has been recovered from the deep cenotes or natural wells in the Yucatán area, objects which had been thrown, together with living human sacrifices, into the wells on ceremonial occasions.

The Aztecs were still another northern tribe who came into the Valley of Mexico and established their power by 1325. They, too, were an aggressive, warlike tribe with an innate ability to assimilate and synthesize the cultural elements they encountered in their conquest of the Mexican area. Their culture was therefore largely of an eclectic nature, a summation of what had been achieved by the earlier peoples. Aztec achievements are found in the fusion and organization of conquered peoples into a consolidated militaristic state in which there was a complete and oppressive control over the masses of the pop ulation. Religious beliefs were largely derived from the Toltecs, but Aztec deities were even more fearsome and bloodthirsty, and ritual surrounding them demanded constant human sacrifices.

Architecture followed the usual Middle-American pattern of large, complex civic-ceremonial centers with lofty temple-pyramids, courts, and altars. Added, however, were trophy platforms for the exhibition of human heads and hearts. But the most important Aztec artistic achievements were in the medium of three-dimensional stone sculpture. Their figures were often gruesome in appearance and colossal in size, such as the Mother of the Gods in the National Museum in Mexico City, a Janus-figure over 8 feet high, represented with the heads as pairs of confronted serpent heads, the feet as claws, the hands as snake heads. She wears a large necklace of human hands and hearts with a death's-head pendant, and as a skirt, a writhing mass of braided rattlesnakes. Other deities are represented by equally awesome figures, or are depicted by carefully wrought skulls encrusted with a mosaic of turquoise and obsidian and skulls carved in rock-crystal. Other Aztec sculptures represent deities as simple and strongly rendered naturalistic forms (fig. 350). Their sculpture stresses full volumes and structurally heavy masses; and although the forms are emphatically three-dimensional, they are frequently somewhat four-sided, and almost always express the original square or rectangular shape of the stone block.

350. *Stone Figure, Aztec* (1325–1521) Museum of Primitive Art, New York. 14½″ high.

Aztec culture, as that of the Inca, was documented by the Spanish who conquered the Aztecs in 1521. This recorded knowledge was supplemented by a number of codices or pictorial manuscripts painted on parchment or deerskin by the Aztecs and other Middle-American peoples. These depict ceremonies, events, and histories involving particular persons and scenes in the art style characteristic of the period and area in which they were painted. A number of significant Aztec manuscripts have survived.

A distinctive art of undetermined age developed in the mountainous area of northwest Mexico among peoples known as Tarascans, and among related groups in Nayarit to the north and Colima to the south (fig. 351). These people maintained their independence from the

351. *Figure, raised arm in form of vase,* Tarasca (Colima area) (*c.* A.D. 1200?) Coll. Diego Rivera. 14′ high. Photograph from Medioni and Pinto, *Art in Ancient Mexico,* Oxford University Press.

Aztecs and created a modeled-pottery art of unique character. Large and small solid and hollow figures were modeled, fired, covered with a red slip, and often painted with black and white details, interpreting in a sensitive, often humorous, but never realistic manner men and women engaged in ordinary activities, the crippled and the deformed, and chubby dogs and birds. The forms, poses, and expression have a sturdy nat-

uralism, a remarkable vitality, and an instantaneous appeal.

North of Mexico the Indian cultures of the vast area of the United States and Canada can also be divided into archaeological and historical periods, the archaeological being a cultural reconstruction based on excavated sites and areas, and the historical or tribal derived from the facts recorded at the time of, or subsequent to, European contact. In both the archaeological and tribal phases, large regions are dominated by a basically similar culture and art style. The art is extremely varied in materials and techniques, including such materials as stone, wood, clay, fibers, bark, hides or leather, shell, and quills. Various forms and designs were evolved in the media of architecture, sculpture, pottery, and two-dimensional designs.

The basic areas of archaeological or Pre-Columbian art are the Southwest, comprising largely the region of Arizona, New Mexico, Utah, and Colorado; the east-central region, containing the Ohio-Mississippi River drainage basin and the area to the east along the Gulf of Mexico; and the far northwest, including areas around the Columbia and Fraser rivers. Chronologically the Southwest, together with the Valley of Mexico, has produced archaeological evidence of being among the oldest habitats of the American Indian, the evidence indicating an occupation going back many thousands of years before Christ to a time when mammoth and other now extinct animals were present on this hemisphere. But the more developed culture from which there is an abundance of art remains has been dated back to about the beginning of the Christian era. By that time, agriculture was established as the staple for subsistence, and the arts of architecture, polychromed pottery, weaving, and some stone sculpture were well beyond an early formative stage. Although hunting contributed to their diet, the Indians of the Northwest Coast were largely fishermen, and other early peoples were agrarian sedentary village-dwellers.

The great period of Pre-Columbian art in the Southwest dates between A.D. 1000 and 1300 and has three main centers: a northern or plateau area in the regions of the San Juan and Colorado rivers; a central one in the lowlands of eastern Arizona and western New Mexico; and a southern one in the desert region, largely near the Gila and Salt rivers in Arizona. The northern region was the home of the Pueblo peoples; the central, of the Mimbres, a sub-group of the Mogollon culture; and the southern, of the Hohokam. While all of the arts typical of the early Southwest were produced to some measure in all three of these centers, in each area certain arts reached a high level of accomplishment.

Architecture was the outstanding achievement in the Pueblo area, especially during the great period when the apartment house type structures such as the famous 'cliff houses' and 'pueblos' were built. The cliff-dwelling, built within a deep recess high above the ground level, below and underneath large overhanging cliffs, consisted of a huge multistoried structure or structures capable of housing in some instances over a thousand persons. Each floor was set back from the one below, and in the famous Mesa Verde so-called Cliff Palace in southern Colorado some of the structures were four floors high. Here the walls were of loaf-shaped stones set within a thin mortar. One of the most renowned of the architectural remains in the Southwest is that of Pueblo Bonito in Chaco Canyon in northern New Mexico. This large single-structure pueblo, built on the canyon floor, was of D-shaped ground plan. The building surrounded and faced a large central court. The curve of the D consisted of five floors; each one faced the court and was set back from the one below, while the connecting arm of the D consisted of a single story. Walls were massive, decreasing in thickness as they rose from floor to floor, and built of stone, adobe, and rubble faced on both sides with thin, dressed, perfectly-fitted stones, mostly of a tabular shape. Pueblo Bonito contained over 800 rooms and had an estimated 1200 inhabitants.

Aside from these large houses, the greater majority of Pueblo peoples lived in small-unit houses in communities scattered throughout the area. These were built in a similar way and, as all of the Pueblo buildings, had flat roofs of cross-timbers, matting, and adobe. By 1300 the great houses and the entire Pueblo region had largely been deserted or abandoned. The reason or reasons for this are still not agreed upon, but it seems likely that erosion of the soil from their method of farming, the great drought of 1276–99, and possibly an increase in population had combined to enforce this exodus.

In every area of the early Southwest many distinctive styles of painted pottery are characteristic of a region or even of a single site. Among the finest of this pottery are the shallow bowls of the Mimbres peoples. Found associated with burials, with a hole knocked or cut in the bottom, they were apparently thus 'killed' at mortuary rites in order to accompany the dead (fig. 352). Only the interior of these shallow bowls are painted, in a black or dark design on a white ground. The design usually consists of an elaborate geometric wide-rim pattern, so composed as to suggest a movement around the inner perimeter of the bowl; while in the central field

352. *Pottery Bowl*, Mimbres (950–1050) Museum of the American Indian, New York. 10½″ diameter.

geometric, fantastic, or stylized naturalistic forms were painted. Even lines, ranging from a hair in thickness to a moderate thickness and often used in parallel groups, are basic to this style. The designs are carefully composed of sharply angular, frequently combined with curvilinear, lines and shapes.

Both the Mimbres and the more southern Hohokam peoples relied on an irrigation agriculture, and much effort and time were devoted to the construction and maintenance of ditches. Houses were of a single story semi-subterranean or surface type, usually of single-unit character. The Hohokam also produced a fine painted pottery, with designs on a buff ground of large and small geometric forms, either angular or curvilinear, at times even spiral. Their pottery was usually shaped as bowls and jars, sometimes large in size. But the most significant Hohokam art is perhaps its stone sculpture. Small stone bowls and mortars were sometimes decorated with reliefs of animal forms, often the snake or toad, and sometimes shaped as an animal. Other extant Hohokam stone sculptures include small fragments of figurines representing simplified human figures, and many shallow palettes used as mortuary offerings and found in cremation pits. The edges of the palettes are decorated with sculptured birds and animals or with incised geometrical relief designs. Painted pottery and pottery figurines were also used as offerings to the dead.

The dating of the early Pre-Columbian period in the Southwest has been more certain than in other areas because of the discovery in 1929 and the subsequent perfecting of a tree-ring calendar, whereby it is possible to date the timbers in the early structures and so the year or years when they were built. Objects found at these sites may therefore be given a comparable terminal date.

The archaeological period of the east-central part of the United States, that of the Ohio-Mississippi drainage area and the eastern Gulf Coast region, is characterized by the presence of earth mounds and by the numerous art forms found in burials. Because the mound was a distinctive cultural element, these peoples have been called the 'Moundbuilders.' In the northern part of the area, centered in the Ohio Valley, the majority of these structures were conical in form and sometimes over 100 feet high, carefully and regularly shaped. Within them have been found one or more logged-in burial chambers, large enough to contain the body and the numerous and various kinds of offerings. In these graves a profusion of flaked flint and obsidian blades and points have been found, together with grizzly-bear claw necklaces, both the claws and the obsidian obtained from the Rocky Mountain area. Other grave offerings included freshwater pearls, mica from the Carolinas cut in pierced designs as ornaments, and hammered surface-copper breastplates, the copper from the Lake Michigan region.

But the most important art forms in the graves are innumerable pipes made of *pipe-stone*, a stone which is soft when quarried and hardens with exposure to air. Termed *platform pipes*, they are made with a flat, moderately wide base surmounted in the center by a hollow bowl, a hole drilled lengthwise through the base leading to the bowl. They were used without a stem. The bowl was given a variety of shapes, but those carved as animal or bird forms, such as the hawk, beaver, and squirrel are the most artistic (fig. 353). These animals, carved in the round, have a direct and

353. *Stone Pipe,* Moundbuilder, Ohio (?–A.D. 500) Museum of the American Indian, New York. 5½" high.

strongly expressive naturalism; while descriptive details, rendered in low relief or incised lines, often distinguish surface textures. Pipes of this kind are unique to the more northern Moundbuilder peoples, who had, as the variety of materials found in the graves indicates, trade or other contacts over an extensive geographical area.

In the southern Mississippi region, the most significant forms are mortuary pottery jars, some sensitively modeled to represent fully rounded human heads.

Others are modeled with large surface bosses incised with spiral or concentric circular designs; and still others are painted with geometric curvilinear patterns. The outstanding art achievements of the southeast, also used as mortuary offerings, are small, finely carved limestone heads, some only a few inches high, and carved stone bowls, delicately and carefully shaped as birds, or with bird heads, wings, and tails attached to them. These bowls often have a pierced design around the sides, and they too were 'killed' when placed in the grave. In the southeast, sculptures are not usually found in the mounds but in burial grounds nearby. Southeastern earth-mounds were truncated, stepped pyramids, and served as bases for religious or secular structures which have now disappeared. They are therefore comparable in shape and function to the pyramids of Middle America.

The date of Moundbuilder culture is at present controversial. It has been dated by archaeological methods from 900 to about 1400; but as a result of a new technique of dating known as *Carbon 14*, it now seems probable that it may date from about the beginning of the Christian era.

Numerous aesthetically significant Pre-European stone sculptures have been found in the Columbia River and Fraser River areas of the Northwest. The majority of examples of this sculpture appear on, or as, stone bowls, mortars, and palettes of various sizes. They are numerous in the Columbia River Valley, where they were carved as high

and low reliefs of stylized animal heads and forms, particularly the owl and turtle. In this area, too, fairly large stone slabs were shaped in a pecked-and-ground technique to represent conventionalized owls and mountain goats, while some carvings in the round depict the same animals with a sculptural feeling for volumes and natural forms.

In the Fraser River region, the majority of stone sculptures represent in a more sculpturally descriptive and dramatic manner a seated or squatting human figure holding tightly gripped in front of it a bowl. The bowl was often carved as an animal head or form and served as a mortar. A dramatic physical and psychological relationship between the human figure and the bowl is always evident. While in this area too the form is often achieved by grinding and pecking, cut surfaces and incised lines are also used. Here, as in the Columbia River area, there are no clearly determinable dates. It is certain, however, that, since the Indians in both regions considered the stone sculptures ancient at the time of European contact, they date considerably earlier than the tribal art of historical times.

The dating of our knowledge of tribal art is for most areas that of the period when there was continuous contact with the Indians. Since these contacts were established by the gradual extension of frontiers following the initial era of discovery and colonization, the dates vary widely for different parts of the country. In the Southwest, for example, Spanish contact dates from early in the sixteenth century, while in the Northwest it occurs in the early nineteenth century.

By the time of Spanish contact the centers of Pueblo culture had, following the migrations of the late thirteenth and fourteenth centuries, become established in the Rio Grande River region and in the older Zuni and Hopi areas to the west. Architecture was by then only slightly modified for defensive purposes to protect against the marauding sorties of their neighbors, the Navaho and, especially, the war-like Apache. As in the earlier period, the varied shapes and painted patterns of polychromed pottery were perhaps the most characteristic expression of the artists of the Southwest. As time went on, however, the traditional designs were either forgotten or became modified by European influences. Although this was common to all Pueblo groups, it is well represented by the large pottery jars of the Zuni, with floral, geometric, and animal forms painted red and black on a white background.

Meanwhile, the new art of silversmithing, introduced in the late sixteenth and early seventeenth centuries, had developed into a distinctive Southwestern art, now largely that of silver jewelry, often inlaid with turquoise. The Navaho peoples greatly modified the traditional designs of their woven blankets to produce rugs commercially. They retained unaltered their ceremonial art of 'painting' on the earth symbolic and realistic designs in fine pulverized varicolored sands and rocks, an art originally acquired by them from the Pueblo peoples. The tribal arts of the Southwest also include numerous styles of decorated baskets as well as ceremonial masks and figurines carved in a soft wood or fabricated with leather, cloth, or wooden boards.

There is relatively little knowledge of early tribal arts along the eastern coast, where contact dates back to the end of the sixteenth century and the beginning of the seventeenth century. From this early period a few clubs in European collections are the oldest examples of the art of this area. Other early examples include large incised pottery jars and numerous stone, pottery, and wooden pipes, sometimes decorated with tiny carved animal and human figures. But the best-known examples of the art from the east are the somewhat later wooden masks of the Iroquois Confederation. These masks, usually carved in a living ash tree and then detached, emphasize facial bone structure and the heavy creases or wrinkles expressive of tension and aggression. Each mask, painted red or black or both, was used in communal therapeutic rites and represented or symbolized a particular supernatural being who had the power to cure or prevent illness.

In the New England area the significant art was two-dimensional and consisted of sewing shell beads on hide or cloth to form abstract designs symbolic of the magical properties of plants. Basically curvilinear, these designs are usually arranged bilaterally and often with a symmetry of upper and lower elements. This so-called *double-curve* motive appears as far north as Labrador, where it is pressed on the edging of leather coats as a decorative and protective element; in the St. Lawrence River region it occurs as positive and negative designs on birchbark containers. These containers were made from a single sheet of bark by folding, cutting, and stitching together the edges, a technique of aesthetic importance in this area.

In the Great Lakes region a type of finger-weaving or plaiting of reed and wood fibers was employed to make shoulder bags. These bags were originally decorated with a woven design representing the beneficent, protective Thunderbird, a stylization of the eagle; but shortly after European contact, occurring here in the seventeenth century, the designs became greatly modified to include foreign floral and geometric elements.

The acquisition of the horse in the early seventeenth century converted the earlier agricultural Plains peoples into nomadic, meat-eating hunters. They also became aggressive, war-like, and egocentric; and their arts, applied to clothing and horse trappings, were largely of sociological significance, symbolically recording the position and ex-

354. *Painted Buffalo Robe,* Dakota tribes (19th cent.) American Museum of Natural History, New York. 107" x 91".

ploits of the warrior leaders and decoratively indicating their rank and position. The arts of the Plains are almost exclusively two-dimensional, highly polychromed, and include such techniques as incising and painting on buffalo hide (fig. 354), and the delineation of a design on leather by the use of porcupine quills or European beads. Fundamentally it is a geometric decorative art, the same geometric motives used individually for symbolic purposes. Simplified naturalistic forms were painted on buffalo robes or on tepees to record exploits or to represent the source of an individual's supernatural power.

The most significant tribal sculpture was produced on the Northwest Coast, an area extending from Oregon north to and including the southeastern-most part of Alaska. The crucial environmental elements in the culture of this region were the seasonal run of salmon and the abundance of the cedar tree. As a consequence of the availability of salmon at certain seasons of the year considerable time was freed for leisure, particularly during the winter months, when elaborate religious and social ceremonies were performed; while the vast stands of cedar provided material for an extensive wood sculpture, for the building of plank houses and canoes, and for the making of clothing and utensils. Many masks, varied in size, color, and expression, were used in the complex ceremonials of Northwest Coast peoples (Plate IX, facing p. 556). In design, some masks are realistically

355. *Totem Pole*, Haida, Northwest Coast (mid 19th cent.) *c.* 35′ high.

human, but the majority of them are of hybrid, often fantastic human-animal forms.

A most spectacular form of American Indian tribal art is the often lofty so-called totem-pole, unique to the Northwest Coast (fig. 355). These poles were made as memorials, burial-poles, and as decorative or partially functional architectural adjuncts, and always represented the crests and legends owned by and denoting the rank of the person who had them set up. Human, animal, and composite beings provide the motives for the low- and deep-relief carving on the poles; the figures are arranged in superposed and overlapping manner, with forms and details further clarified by a light wash painting in various colors, largely red, white, blue-green, and black.

Numerous other art expressions of the Northwest Coast included the incising and painting of wooden boxes, made by steaming and bending cedar planks; painting of crest designs on wooden house fronts; weaving; basketry; and the sculptural decoration of clubs and cere-

monial rattles. In style, the carved shapes are large in scale and strongly sculptural; while the forms range from a descriptive realism to a conventionalized, almost abstract expression, such as on the Chilkat blankets of southeastern Alaska. After European contact the art flourished and remained largely unmodified for many years, the only marked difference appearing in the use of brighter and more varied commercial colors.

The most significant single feature of American Indian tribal art was the numerous techniques developed in the use of a wide variety of materials, the aesthetic effect often being the result of the technical manipulation of the material. Although much of this art was of decorative or sociological importance, a sizable proportion of it was also charged with religious-philosophical meaning.

XXI   THE BIRTH OF AMERICAN ART

The early settlements along the Atlantic seaboard varied in origin; the largest colonies in Massachusetts, Pennsylvania, and Virginia were English, but the Dutch settled in New York, the Swedes in Delaware, and the Germans in and around Philadelphia. Before the end of the seventeenth century, however, the English absorbed all of these settlements, and their origins began to be eclipsed by the prevailing English culture. The colonists in this new land might have laid the groundwork of an indigenous art appropriate to the country and the climate, based on the available materials and the conditions of life under which they found themselves; actually they did not attempt to be original. The fact that settlers had sailed across the ocean from England did not in itself alter their traditions or their habits of thought. They built in the wilderness the same type of house they had known at home, modified as little as might be by the circumstances they encountered in the new land. Consequently the formative force in colonial art was its European background, generally English, but with some Dutch influence in New York and the Hudson Valley, and traces of other Continental origins elsewhere on the Atlantic seaboard; and of course in Florida and the Southwest the background was Spanish.

In 1620, the date of the settlement of Plymouth, English building traditions were still medieval. Inigo Jones, to be sure, had just begun the Banqueting House, but its influence was still in the future. The Renaissance had appeared in England a century before this, but, as we have seen, the classic side of that movement was misunderstood and its application was confined to the estates of the wealthy. It was not from such families that the colonists came. The houses of the lower and middle classes in 1620 were Gothic and continued to be so, even into the eighteenth century. Though smaller and simpler than Compton Wynyates, the style is fundamentally the same. Many of them were built of timber, or of half-timber; the house was made half of timber and half of something else, the spaces between the timbers filled in with brick, or with clay matted on twigs. One does not expect vaults, flying buttresses, and membered piers in wood construction, but a directness of solution and a frank exposure of structure are essentials of Gothic architecture, and these qualities characterized the cottage architecture of England at the time of the settlement of America.

Thus the afterglow of the Gothic day, whose high noon had produced Canterbury Cathedral and Westminster Abbey, can be seen in the seventeenth-century colonial house. The best preserved examples of this type are found in the North, though the form was common in Virginia. The Parson Capen House in Topsfield, Massachusetts, built in 1683, shows that the type remains unchanged through the seventeenth century. In plan (fig. 356) the house huddles around the great central chimney, as though for warmth. It usually consists of two rooms only on each floor, one to either side of the chimney, with narrow stairs to the second story be-

356. *Parson Capen House*, Topsfield (1683) 42' x 21'.

tween the chimney and the door. These two rooms differ in size; therefore the house, like most medieval designs, is asymmetrical.

The forest, which had to be cleared anyway, provided material. Rough-hewn logs compose the frame of the building, the half-timber of English tradition, but experience showed the colonists that the colder climate of New England demanded additional protection. Hence the exteriors of these houses (fig. 357) are clapboarded—thin boards overlapping one another to make a blanket of wood around the house. Clapboards were more common in seventeenth-century England than they are today, but in New England they are almost universal. Consequently the sturdy framework becomes visible only at the corners, and not always there, but is often expressed by pendants that project below the overhanging second story. These pendants, the only enrichment of the house, recall the Gothic style since they are structural members made decorative rather than decoration applied as something distinct. A good deal of variety exists between the colonies and also between different houses in the matter of the overhang; sometimes it is found

[handwritten margin notes:] influence in Gothic evolution in Colonial American.

[handwritten footer note:] pendants: decorative piece suspended from roof, esp. in Gothic arch.

357. *Parson Capen House*, Topsfield, Mass. (1683) 42' long x 21' wide.

only on the front, sometimes only on the ends of the house, and at other times in both places. The idea comes from the Middle Ages, not only in England but in the timbered houses of France and Germany, where it increased the room within the house by encroaching over the street in the crowded medieval towns. That reason carried no weight in colonial America, but tradition was strong enough to ensure its retention. A steep gable roof covers the mass. As the family expands, more space may be gained by adding other gables, as in the famous House of the Seven Gables in Salem, Massachusetts, or by adding a lean-to. Small casement windows are placed wherever light is needed; no preconceived principle of symmetry dictates their arrangement. They are composed of multiples of small units; a single opening for small chambers, but two, three, or even more units, to light the larger rooms—though none of the rooms were large by present-day standards. Leaded glass in rectangular or diamond-shaped panes is known from the earliest days of the colonies, but cannot have been general, since letters advise prospective colonists to bring paper and linseed oil for the windows.

No porch mitigates the severity of these designs. The door of sturdy planks opens on the stair hall. The stairs are too narrow to permit more than one person to ascend at a time, and are dangerously steep. Each room centers on its fireplace, which warms it, and where the cooking is done. Into such fireplaces one could roll a tree if necessary; like everything else in these modest houses, they are designed for a specific purpose, and their beauty is consequent on the directness with which they meet that purpose. The ceilings are so low for additional warmth that tall men cannot walk under the exposed beams and joists of the second floor without stooping. So, too, are the posts of the walls visible on the interior. But rarely do these builders permit themselves the luxury of sheathing the walls on the inside, and then usually only on the fireplace wall. In fact, when Winthrop sheathed the interior of his house with plain boards the governor of the colony called him to task for such ostentation, so that Winthrop had to explain that this sheathing was inexpensive and added to the warmth of his house.

Houses in masonry were rare indeed because of the difficulty of procuring lime. Bricks were imported, but they were also made in the colonies from the time of settlement, and all the evidence points to the prevalence of the local product. Bacon's Castle, Surry County, Virginia, built before 1676, is a remarkable example of the Jacobean style. A projecting chimney at either end breaks the simple rectangular plan of the Parson Capen House, as do the three-storied vestibule in front and the stair turret behind. The grouped chimney-pots and especially the gable ends with their quadrants and right angles are earmarks of that style.

Simple as they are, nothing more functional has ever been built, or ever will be built, than these seventeenth-century colonial houses. In whole and in part they follow the needs of the day; they take no thought for their appearance, and perhaps in consequence achieve their homespun beauty, as sturdy as the men who built them.

The need for shelter made it inevitable that the house first should absorb the energy of the builders. And yet worship was so vital to them that it had formed a major reason for their migration. Few churches have been preserved from these days, but those few are instructive. St. Luke's, Smithfield, Virginia, in an Anglican settlement, was built in 1632 of brick and retained the plan and even the buttresses, pointed arches, and tracery of Gothic parish churches in simplified form. In New England, the Old Ship Meeting House, in Hingham, Massachusetts, dated 1681, had the open frame construction of the houses on a larger scale. The great curved timbers of the roof resemble the beams of a wooden ship. Its square plan, the pulpit centered on one wall, and a general openness reflect the democratic form of Congregational worship in contrast to Anglicanism.

By the eighteenth century conditions had changed along the seaboard, prompting an architectural revolution. The thrifty and enterprising merchants of the North and the Southern plantation owners alike had accumulated sufficient wealth to tempt them from the Spartan rigors of the days of settlement. The modest houses of their forebears could not accommodate the genteel and formal life that now became possible. Luxuries and amenities, far from being suspect, were now sought.

With their greater wealth the colonists turned to the mother country, not for traditions but for the latest fashions in building. Consequently America jumped from the fifteenth century to the eighteenth, from the medieval to the Georgian. Floods of architectural textbooks, simple carpenters' handbooks, submerged the traditional style. Many of these were imported from England, but a considerable number as the century progressed were local products. These inexpensive volumes began with descriptions of the orders, went on to explain the intricacies of carpentry, and concluded with designs for windows and doors, staircases and fireplaces in the latest fashion. When some well-to-do merchant determined to build a house, he called in the builder, his neighbor, and together they thumbed through these handbooks to decide on the approximate model for the living-room fireplace or the balusters for the stairs.

These manuals establish the Georgian style as the model followed in Massachusetts and New York, in Philadelphia and Charleston. Such differences as had existed in the seventeenth century because of divergent national origins no longer obtain. The differences in the several colonies are traceable to climate and available materials. The warm climate and plantation life of the South allow a more open design than that found in the compact New England houses. Also, brick walls are more popular in Virginia than in Massachusetts, while the available ledge stone near Philadelphia colors the architecture of that region. Nevertheless, these differences are negligible in comparison to the unity of style in the colonies. The same fundamental plan and the same principles of design govern the style from north to south, and one may find identical details, inspired by the same handbooks, in Virginia, Pennsylvania, or New Hampshire.

The sophisticated Georgian spirit not only demanded larger houses; it also required symmetry. Therefore the typical house—such as Westover, Virginia, the Chew Mansion in Germantown, Pennsylvania, or the Royall House, Medford, Massachusetts (fig. 358)—is a rectangle in plan and has four rooms, each larger

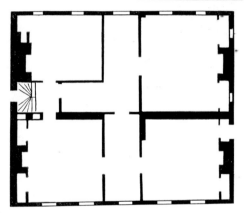

358. *Isaac Royall House*, Medford (1747) 45' x 38'.

than those of the preceding century, two on either side of an ample central hall. The hall contains the stairs and provides access to the rooms. Nothing, in plan, suggests the use to which these chambers were to be put. Since each room needs its own fireplace, a single chimney no longer suffices; two are possible, but more often four chimneys, two in each

359. *Isaac Royall House*, Medford, Mass. (1747) 45′ long x 38′ wide x 36′ high.

side wall of the house, indicate the rooms within.

This symmetrical plan dictates the exterior of the Isaac Royall House at Medford, Massachusetts (fig. 359), cited in mid-century as one of the grandest in the colonies. The roof is lower in pitch than in the seventeenth century, and occasionally is flattened at the top; perhaps it has a balustrade to finish the design. Pilaster orders accent the corners of the house, or in other instances the place occupied by the hall. Perhaps the Ionic order is the favorite, but the Doric is almost as popular; though the Corinthian is known, its complexity forbids its common use. These builders, though influenced by an academic style, will not sacrifice much to it. Thus the pilasters carry blocks of entablature, but almost never do the builders allow more than the cornice to support the eaves of the house: to adopt a full entablature would interfere with the second-story windows.

Five windows of the second floor repeat four windows and a door on the ground floor. These symmetrical openings are larger than those of the seventeenth century, and the sash slides up and down in the plane of the wall. Leaded glass has given way to larger panes set in wood bars. In wooden houses only a cornice may finish the second-story windows, but pediments, either triangular or segmental, enrich those of the ground floor. The door focuses the design and gives character to the house. Here again the orders with entablature and pediment express the dignity of the owners, though even now no porch offers shelter to the visitor.

A complete change remodels the interior also. The plastered ceilings, higher than in the seventeenth century, no longer expose the floor beams of the second story. At least the principal rooms are paneled, and may even admit the orders in pilaster form, especially around the fireplaces. Occasionally native or imported wallpaper takes the place of the panels. We are apt to think of these Georgian interiors as white, when in reality wide latitude in color prevails: dull blue, oyster gray, green, red, and even marbleized interiors are not uncommon, though often the original color has been changed. The fireplaces are large enough to be serviceable, but since most of them are no longer intended for cooking, they are less ample than before. Early in the century, a molding frames the fireplace, but in the decades just before the American Revolution, elaborate mantels and overmantels establish the hearth as the focus of the room. The stairway is commodious and its slope gentler than hitherto; a balustrade offers an opportunity for the carpenters to demonstrate their ability, and all manner of spiral turnings and complicated designs in the newel posts attest their skill. Such an interior suits the sedate existence of its day. Its rooms with their plastered ceilings and paneled walls match the change from the austerity of the seventeenth-century costume to the colorful garb of the colonial worthies portrayed by Copley.

As the colonies grew, they needed public buildings, though these remained simple until after the Revolution. The Old State House in Boston and Independence Hall in Philadelphia are in essence enlarged private houses, bigger in scale but with no fundamental change in conception. Time after time, local tradition points to a colonial church as designed by Sir Christopher Wren. Except for the College of William and Mary at Williamsburg, Virginia, no foundation exists for these attributions. Like the houses, the churches of the eighteenth century are Georgian, some of them, such as the First Church in Providence, Rhode Island, inspired by the designs of James Gibbs. These white churches are distinguished by a tower, perhaps with a steeple built up in the manner of the Wren steeples, but simpler and conceived in terms of wood. The interior of these meeting houses centers on the pulpit, which is raised above the floor in the position occupied by the altar in a Catholic church. Even Anglican churches, such as Christ Church, Alexandria, or Christ Church, Philadelphia, subordinate the altar to the pulpit, and minimize the chancel. The exquisite craftsmanship, as demonstrated in the box pews and the pulpit, turns to the same basic motives and moldings as in the houses.

Sculpture in colonial America was negligible save for tombstones and figureheads in wood on the ships. Civic life had not grown enough to command monuments, and the cost of sculpture militated against its spread if it depended on private patronage. Perhaps the Puritan hostility to luxury acted more in sculpture than in painting; perhaps the unimportance of sculpture in England was responsible. Whatever the reason, the demand for the representative arts was satisfied by painting, and even this only got under way by the middle of the eighteenth century.

Some of the limners, as they often styled themselves, were English trained, like John Smibert; others, such as Robert Feke of Newport, Rhode Island, were native products. In either case, their subject was portraiture. The colonial gentlemen had sufficient pride in themselves and their families to demand likenesses from their painters. Smibert's most important canvas, Bishop Berkeley and His Entourage, reveals his European training, among other ways in its sophisticated arrangement.

That this canvas influenced Feke's painting of 1741 of Isaac Royall and His Family is obvious; the Feke portrait shows the same man for whom the Royall House at Medford in its present form was built, and is unusually elaborate. The rich costumes and the carpet table cover tell of the social position of the family, but the artist's desire has outrun his performance. Though his aim was realistic, his draftsmanship was inadequate; some of the characters are little dolls, though others are more at ease. The design leaves something to be desired, as though Feke was attempting a

360. John Singleton Copley (1737–1815) *Jeremiah Lee* (1769) Museum of Fine Arts, Boston. 8' x 5'.

composition that was too difficult for him. Nevertheless, he had great native ability, and his painting shows an instinct for formal design.

The greatest of the colonial painters was John Singleton Copley (1737–1815) of Boston. He painted Jeremiah Lee of Marblehead and Boston (fig. 360), matching his colors to those of his sitter and his costume. There is little of the fluency or the sophistication of a Gainsborough. Painting did not come easily to Copley; the form was painstakingly rendered, but to achieve this absorbed Copley's energy too much to permit him to fall into superficialities. The portrait has an unpretentious honesty about it. We have every reason to suppose that the sitter looked like this, and that Copley did not tamper with reality in order to give social graces to his models. Probably the independence of these portraits, their unwillingness to seem what they are not, may be due to the clients also. One is tempted to see in this sober honesty and this hatred of affectation qualities outstanding in those men who laid the foundations of our country.

In 1774, just before the Revolution, Copley went abroad, and in the following year settled in London, where he was admitted to the Royal Academy, and where he lived for the rest of his life. Despite considerable success in his profession, at least down to 1800, the cosmopolitan atmosphere of the metropolis was not an unmixed blessing; what his style gained in facility, it lost in vigor. His later portraits lose the sturdiness of his earlier work without achieving the brilliance of a Gainsborough.

It is natural to suppose that the American Revolution broke our cultural relations with the mother country, but it did not. Many revolutionary heroes maintained that they were defending their rights as Englishmen, and with them a large party in the mother country agreed. In any case, no abrupt break in tradition occurred. The period after the Revolution and down to about 1820 has been called the Post-Colonial or the Early Republican, but the best name for the era is Federal. Culturally, the generation was dominated by the group that formed the backbone of the Federalist party in American politics, and the duration of the style almost coincided with the life of that party. Though some members of what we might call the colonial aristocracy belonged to the Democratic party, on the whole (particularly in the North) the wealthier individuals of the community tended to be Federalist, and it was for them that the art of the time was produced. That class did not change its traditions with its allegiance.

When at the outbreak of the Revolution Copley went to England, he found Benjamin West (1738–1820), a Pennsylvanian, established in London. West, despite his backwoods origin, or perhaps partly because that background made his modest achievement seem remarkable, won notable success in England. He became the historical painter to George III, and succeeded Reynolds as president of the Royal Academy. His painting is not inspired; one can almost agree with Byron's strictures about 'that dotard West, Europe's worst daub, poor England's best.' West was personally both genial and generous, and his home and studio became a center for American artists who had come to London to study.

Among them was Charles Willson Peale (1741–1827), who filled the gap between Copley and Stuart; if not inspired, he was so enthusiastic about his art that he named several sons after old masters, such as Rembrandt and Raphael. It would be fortunate if our image of Washington were based upon his portraits by Peale, made when the first President was in the prime of life, instead of on those by Stuart, which were painted just a few years before Washington's death. In one of his finest paintings, a self-portrait, Peale lifts a rich red curtain so that the spectator may peep at the exhibits lining the walls of his museum in Philadelphia, devoted

361. Gilbert Stuart (1755–1828) *Thomas Jefferson* (1799) Bowdoin College, Brunswick, Maine. 3'11" x 3'3".

partly to painting and partly to natural history.

Although Gilbert Stuart (1755–1828) studied with West in London, he was little influenced by him and became a better painter. When Stuart returned to America in 1792, he was the best-trained painter in the country. His portrait of Thomas Jefferson (fig. 361) shows the cosmopolitan technique of his English experience, as compared with the more provincial style of Copley before the Revolution. Painting came easily to Stuart; his brush flowed with a readiness that yields something of the decorative value of the English portrait school. His characters seem a little more aristocratic than Copley's, and their social poise is greater. They sit easily, and the likeness is gracious, but to reach this cosmopolitan style in place of the provincialism of the earlier men, Stuart has lost something. His portraits have not the self-evident honesty of Copley's. His sense of structure is less powerful, and his figures a little flatter.

Stuart's famous portraits of Washington are too well known to need much comment. One regrets this, because the portraits of Washington are not the best of Stuart's work. Stuart had a faculty for putting his sitters at their ease by his conversation, but Washington's innate dignity appears so to have awed Stuart that he could not himself be comfortable in the presence of the man he so admired. Also, Stuart only had the opportunity to paint Washington a few years before Washington's death, when physical vigor was beginning to fail and

the founder of his country was suffering from a badly fitted set of false teeth which gave a prognathous appearance to his jaw and lips.

Very different from Stuart is John Trumbull (1756–1843), son of the Revolutionary governor of Connecticut. An intellectual haughtiness revealed in the clear-cut features, with none of Stuart's geniality, characterizes both Trumbull and his portraits. Congress commissioned him to paint a series of Revolutionary battles and scenes of the formation of the Federal Government for the rotunda of the United States Capitol. The artist studied each subject in detail; every character is a portrait, and therefore these paintings have great historic value. Moreover, they are well drawn and fresh in color, at least in the sketches preserved in New Haven, Connecticut. The few large paintings completed by him for the Capitol fail to preserve that spontaneity, nor are they well adapted as murals.

This portrait school survived until well on into the nineteenth century, when American artists turned their allegiance from their English origin to Düsseldorf, Munich, and ultimately Paris.

The same English origin persists in the Federal style in architecture. This is woven of three strains: a continuation of Georgian tradition, a strong influence from the Adam style, and a new archaeology that reflects the incipient Roman revival. To these we may add at times some influence from the style of Louis XVI. The Georgian elements are more apparent early in the period, and the Roman features later, though many exceptions to this generality can be cited. Books continued in use, but the books themselves reflect the new ideals. More complex architectural needs arose, caused by the growth and independence of the country, and called into existence architects as well as builders. The style is consequently more architectonic than the American Georgian, as evidenced in Latrobe's work on the Capitol in Washington.

Even the houses catch the new spirit, though the absence of any single type makes generalization difficult. Protruding bays, or a salon bulging on axis, complicate the simple rectangular plans. The rooms also cease to be always rectangular; the varied volumes of Adam interiors won popularity on this side of the Atlantic. Furthermore, a niche to contain a sideboard or an alcove for a four-poster bed shows that some architects now had specific purposes in mind for such rooms. A balustrade or parapet at the eaves of the house often conceals the roof. Especially in the South, a two-storied portico dignifies the design, but, like those of the English Georgian, it is placed in the center of the long side of the house, not on one end. Since these colonnades reduce light in the second story, the North preferred a smaller porch, only large enough to shelter the door, whose composition is complicated by semicircular or elliptical fanlights above, in addition to rectangular sidelights.

The interiors of these houses have higher ceilings than before. Wallpaper, silk, or plain plaster replace paneling, though the latter is not unknown. Much of the detail, especially in the work of Samuel McIntire of Salem, is influenced by the Adam manner. No less exquisite in craftsmanship, often even more dexterous, the sturdiness of the Georgian yields to a refinement that approaches virtuosity.

The two leading architects were Charles Bulfinch and Thomas Jefferson. Bulfinch belonged to the Boston aristocracy; he had traveled abroad, especially in England, and as a young man had cultivated a gentleman's interest in architecture without the need to turn his taste to financial profit. Unfortunate investments in real estate compelled him to become a professional architect to supplement his civic career as the Great Selectman of Boston.

The Boston State House, begun in 1795, the second of his three state capitols (the others being in Hartford, Connecticut, and Augusta, Maine), reflects his European travels. Traces of English and French influence suggest the architectonic Federal approach, but his sense of proportion gives the State House its distinction. The white trim in wood and stone contrasts with the warm brick of the walls. A noble colonnade above a high arcaded basement marks the original lower house of the state legislature. To the right was the chamber of the upper house, and to the left the administrative offices of the state government, though these uses have now been altered in part, owing to the growth of the legislature. The dome, though visually insecure above the pediment, serves to tie the design together and to provide stateliness to the whole. One might almost say that the dome introduced here became standard for state capitols throughout the country. Bulfinch's design shows the conservative side of the Federal style. The proportions of the order are a little more slender than usual, and much of the interior detail shows the influence of the Adam style, which was still fashionable at the time of Bulfinch's sojourn in London. As yet there is little to suggest archaeology.

With Thomas Jefferson the case was different. Like Bulfinch, Jefferson repre- sented the cultured upper class, but his career left him with no need to become a professional architect. When he became enthusiastic about Roman archi- tecture he threw himself into a study of that style. His design for the Richmond State Capitol, sent back from Paris in 1785, was modified in execution (fig. 362), but its classic elements and pro- portions were retained. Jefferson studied the Maison Carrée in Nîmes (fig. 83) with Clérisseau, a French archaeologist. To Jefferson, the little Roman temple was the 'model of cubical architecture'; he could find no more fitting source for the Virginia capitol. The exigencies of use compelled him to admit windows

362. Thomas Jefferson (1743–1826) *State Capitol*, Richmond, Va. (1785–98) 146' long x 84' wide x 53' high.

along the sides; the difficulties of execution presented by the Corinthian capital prompted the substitution of the Ionic order; but on the whole Jefferson followed his model closely.

Though not a copy of the Maison Carrée, the Richmond capitol demonstrates the new interest in the classic in its revival of not only the Roman vocabulary but also the Roman type of building. This is the first application anywhere in the world of the complete Roman temple form to a building intended for practical use. Before this, some temples had been copied on a small scale as garden ornaments; after this, the temple form would be widely revived in Europe and America, and for such buildings Jefferson's design was pioneer. Whether such a borrowing from the past of complete types of building is desirable, and whether it does not entail a great sacrifice of its functions to cram a state legislature into the box of a Roman temple are debatable points, but to Jefferson the beauty of the form justified its use, and the extent of the sacrifice can be exaggerated.

With his interest in architecture, Jefferson naturally used his own house, Monticello, near Charlottesville, Virginia, as a proving ground for his ideas.

The plan is complex but ingenious and workable, and the building has been called the 'finest piece of proportion in America.' His last great design is the academical village for the University of Virginia at Charlottesville, dated 1817–26. Long colonnades flank the lawn on the each and west, and screen the student's quarters. These are punctuated at intervals by larger pavilions that served at first as the homes of the faculty and the classrooms of the university. The colonnades approach the climax of the scheme, the library, whose source is the Pantheon in Rome, believed by Jefferson to be the 'model of spherical architecture.' Although, as in the Richmond capitol, windows had to be introduced and some other changes made, the library is almost a replica of the Pantheon at one quarter the size. The pavilions also are modeled on specific Roman temples, each different, in part as demonstrations of correct design for the gentlemen students. To Jefferson, a knowledge of architecture was essential to the education of every gentleman, and to him the proper guide for young America was Roman architecture. That style he did his utmost to foster in this country.

XXII

NEOCLASSICISM IN EUROPE

The years in Europe corresponding to the Federal style in America, 1785–1820 or somewhat later, witness the flowering of that branch of Romanticism known as the Neoclassic, with which indeed the Federal style itself may in part be classed. This new revival of antiquity differs from the revival of Roman art under the Italian Renaissance in the degree of its accuracy. The Renaissance had great enthusiasm for Roman times; it did recapture the vocabulary and something of the spirit of the past, but modified both form and expression to suit its own needs. Later ages ascribed even less importance to archaeology. Under Neoclassicism, success is judged by archaeological accuracy. Moreover, at least in later Neoclassicism, a Greek inspiration, unknown to the Renaissance, challenges and often supplants the Roman.

This new scholarship was rooted partly in the excavations carried out through the second half of eighteenth century at Pompeii and Herculaneum, cities that had been buried by an eruption of Mt. Vesuvius in A.D. 79. The discoveries there showed types of Roman domestic architecture which were quite different from the better-known monuments of the Roman forum. Moreover, scientific archaeology, based on measurement, was pursued in the later eighteenth century, and a series of important volumes were published that familiarized the European world as never before with the exact nature of Roman architecture. Robert Adam's work at Spalato, already mentioned, was paralleled by Wood's studies at Palmyra, by Clérisseau's *Monumens de Nismes*, and, most important of all for later history, by Stuart and Revett's *The Antiquities of Athens*, which first opened the eyes of Europe to the difference between Greek and Roman architecture.

The revival of the classic was not confined to the arts, by any means. It was part of the spirit of the times. The growing republican sentiment, rife in France even before the outbreak of the Revolution, sought a precedent in the republics of Greece and Rome, however different they were in actuality from the civilization and background of Europe in the late eighteenth century. That enthusiasm for the past was sufficient to induce men to call one another after the names of classic characters, and at times to modify their costumes in the direction of classic garb. In literature, Mme de Staël's *Corinne* was a pastiche of classic fragments, Walter Savage Landor became an enthusiastic proponent of Rome, and Keats was inspired to write an *Ode on a Grecian Urn*.

In architecture, Neoclassicism has two sources, Roman and Greek. In general, the Roman Revival is earlier than the Greek, and the latter receives its fullest development in those countries that had not formed part of the Roman Empire. But little of the Greek Revival occurs in Italy, and almost none in France or Spain, whereas it flourished in the second quarter of the century in Germany, England, and America. One obvious reason why the Roman Revival appears first is that, since the Renaissance, European architecture has derived from Roman architecture. The late eighteenth century produced the forerunners of

Neoclassicism; the Adam style in England, the portico of the Panthéon in Paris by Soufflot, and Jefferson's Richmond State Capitol herald the movement in their attention to archaeology or their increasing seriousness. The full character of the Roman Revival appears in the Madeleine, 1806–42 (fig. 363), by Barthélemy Vignon, originally intended to celebrate Napoleon's victories. If we cannot visit a real Roman temple, we can still get an accurate idea of its external form from this building. Like a Roman temple, it is raised on a base and approached by a flight of steps across the front. A colonnade surrounds the building, and supports an unbroken entablature and pediments, which terminate the low pitched roof. The Corinthian order is correct, like an academic study. And yet, like such a study, the Madeleine is cold and precise; it is a mummy from the past, without the life that the best Roman buildings display.

Furthermore, aesthetic unity in a building demands consistency. At least the major units of the interior should be visually expressed on the exterior. The Parthenon, the Pantheon in Rome, the Romanesque and Gothic Cathedrals all predict through their external forms the major divisions within them. The visitor is therefore prepared before he enters to find a single room, the cella of the Parthenon, the vast dome of the Pantheon, the nave, aisles, transepts, apse, and radial chapels of the medieval cathedrals. What these buildings say on the outside, they confirm on the inside. This is not true of the Madeleine.

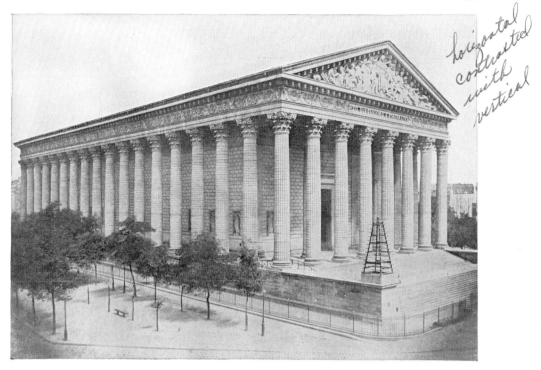

horizontal contrasted with vertical

363. Barthélemy Vignon (1762–1829) *La Madeleine,* Paris (1806–42) 350' long x 147' wide.

No one would guess from the exterior that the building is roofed by three consecutive domes; on entering, the visitor sustains a sense of shock. The design of the interior and the exterior are not co-ordinated.

At best, the Madeleine has an icy dignity. But the Roman revival is not always so rigid in its archaeology. The Arc de Triomphe in Paris, built by Chalgrin from 1806 to 1836, though inspired by a Roman triumphal arch, is like no known example of Roman work. Its heroic scale, its bold proportions, and its reliance on sculptured groups for enrichment instead of on columns, give Chalgrin's arch a vitality not approx-

imated in the Madeleine. The latter relies on archaeology, but the Arc de Triomphe has an architectural basis. As a matter of fact, Chalgin's masterpiece touches a higher peak of architectural distinction than any similar Roman edifice.

By the 1820's the Greek temple form begins to be the motive for houses, churches, and public buildings. The Walhalla at Regensburg, built 1830–42 by Leo von Klenze, is based on the Parthenon, save for its picturesque setting. The absurdity of a Greek temple dedicated to Norse heroes bothered nobody. Langhans's Brandenburg Gate in Berlin, an exceptionally early example,

dated 1788–91, derives from the Propylaea. These two sources, with the addition of the Erechtheum, the Choragic
Monument of Lysicrates in Athens, and
the Temple of Hera at Paestum provide
the direct inspiration of almost all the
Greek revival works, and can be recognized over and over again. However,
some features of the Brandenburg Gate,
such as the arrangement of the triglyphs and the separate bases for the columns, betray a modification of the
Hellenic style by Roman models. The
details of the Walhalla, on the other
hand, or of Thomas Hamilton's Edinburgh High School of 1825–9, adhere
rigidly to Athenian precedent.

As with the Roman revival, not all the
Greek revival monuments are so strict.
In the Bank of England, 1788–1835, Sir
John Soane borrows at will from the Roman Temple of Vesta at Tivoli and the
Erechtheum in Athens, but conceives
parts of his design in geometric volumes,
almost stripped of detail, and thought
out, like the works of some modern
architects, as designs in abstract shapes.
The simplified detail of his own house,
now the Soane Museum in London,
hardly interrupts the surface; therefore,
the block-like masses dominate any
traces of archaeology. In fact, the end
of the Greek revival so purifies its designs that they have style without
styles; they are conceived as architecture, not as Greek architecture, and
through this elimination of historic
precedent they parallel certain developments of modern architecture.

364. Antonio Canova (1757–1822) *Perseus.*
Vatican, Rome.

Similarly strict and free phases, Roman and Greek precedents, influence
Neoclassic sculpture. The Italian Antonio Canova (1757–1822), at the outset of his career, retained much of the
very late Baroque spirit. His Hercules
Hurling Lichias into the Sea incorporates
turbulent energy. The open design has
a violence and an interest in pictorial
detail, handled with some realism, that
testify to the influence of Bernini. The
heavy beared type of Hercules and its
muscularity and proportions may be inspired by the Farnese Hercules, a famous
Graeco-Roman statue, but these early
works of Canova are no more than transitional to Neoclassicism.

His later work, after the beginning of
the nineteenth century, is purely Neoclassic. The Perseus (fig. 364), ordered

by the Vatican to replace the Apollo Belvedere, which had been stolen and transported to Paris by Napoleon, is inspired by that statue. The movement of his earlier manner has gone. In its place, we have a quiet Neoclassic work, its surface generalized to such a point that all interest has been lost, in spite of a trace of eighteenth-century softness of modeling. The affected grace of pose, derived from its model, has a deliberately 'artistic' character; but Canova's statue is no worse than its dull Hellenistic prototype, once so extravagantly admired.

If Canova represents the Roman revival, Bertel Thorvaldsen (1770–1844), the Dane, prefers an emasculated Hellenism. For all his study of the monuments of Athens, and despite his borrowing of motives and details from them, he misses the Greek breadth and freedom of spirit. His Jason again restudies the Apollo Belvedere, but with even less vitality than Canova. In him is nothing of the majesty of Hellenic idealism, none of the largeness of conception or the feeling for the material Greek art had demonstrated in its earlier and more vital periods; only the hard and empty shell remains.

For both sculpture and architecture, artists had a wealth of precedents to which they could and did refer. Painters were more fortunate in this respect. With the exception of Greek vase paintings, really drawings, and a few second-rate mural compositions mostly on the walls of Pompeii, nothing of ancient painting has been preserved. Conse-quently, the painters were not hampered by direct comparison, nor could the dead hand of the past stifle originality. None the less, Jacques Louis David (1748–1825) had the evangelist spirit, and the will to impose the tenets of his creed on a world that was ready to receive them as an antidote to the frivolity of the Rococo. An ardent Jacobin, high in the councils of the Revolution, he reorganized the old Academy as the *Institut de France* and promulgated a code on the basis of the seventeenth-century academic formula, which became the accepted doctrine for a generation.

First, art must be noble and public. Anything that smacked of triviality fell under the ban. Dutch genre paintings and the frivolity of the Fêtes Galantes could not meet this goal. But nobility of subject matter to David meant subject matter drawn from Roman or Greek history or mythology, invested with the stern virtues of the Roman republic. Nature as a whole was an undesirable source of inspiration; only the most beautiful aspects of nature were worthy of the artist's attention. Painting was like poetry, and the painters allowed the poets to select and interpret their subjects. This view unfortunately ignored the difference between verbal and visual modes of expression, and prompted the desire for clarity of statement that could best be achieved by drawing. Color, therefore, must be subordinated. It became merely a means to elucidate the drawing that told the story or described the scene; it was an afterthought instead of being the principal medium of the painter.

The Oath of the Horatii, first exhibited in 1785, is the ultimatum of this new style. The figures, modeled in cold light, are firmly drawn. Only in the group of women to the right is there a trace of eighteenth-century grace. The severe architecture has already assumed the guise of the Roman revival. The men seem inspired by grim determination; they might well become Jacobins, pledging themselves to the cause, so austere is their zeal and so high are their principles. Such a painting is too anxious to preach its lesson ever to relax its severity. Its cold intellectual approach forbids any emotional treatment of form.

This is the type known as a historical canvas, on which David expected his reputation to rest in later ages. Another example is the Death of Socrates (fig. 365). It is hard thus to visualize the scene after reading the Platonic dialogue of Phaedo, on which it is based. However, the histrionic attitudes, the jailer who covers his eyes as he hands Socrates the fatal cup of hemlock, the philosopher who blandly accepts the cup and points upward to indicate the immortality of his soul, which he has been discussing, and the mourning of his friends may all find their excuse if not their feeling in Plato. These characters do not ring true; their sentiment is obvious and fails to carry conviction to the spectator. However clear its didactic les-

365. Jacques Louis David (1748–1825) Death of Socrates (1787) Metropolitan Museum, New York. 4′11″ x 6′6″.

366. Jacques Louis David (1748–1825) *Madame Sériziat* (1795) Louvre, Paris. 4′4″ x 3′2″.

son, the whole scene is badly conceived. Each form is modeled as though cast in plaster. The drawing is accurate but academic. In spite of the reds and blues, the impression persists that these tones have been applied to a design in black and white by some later process; they are not integral to the conception, so that the painting hardly suffers in a monochrome reproduction.

Occasionally, David is shocked out of his academic ivory tower. The assassination of his friend Marat inspired a realistic design, stark in its contrast of light and shade, and hard in modeling, which in this instance enforces the expression of gaunt tragedy. To some degree, portraits evoke this power of realism, since the necessity of adhering to the sitter's appearance helps to blast David loose from his formulae. Madame Sériziat (fig. 366) is dressed in the fashion of her day, a plain high-waisted gown simplified through classic influence. Details of figure and costume are precise and firmly modeled in cold light. And yet David can observe and present with loving care such details from nature as the spray of flowers in her hand. To many, the portraits and the handful

of David's other works in a realistic vein are more stirring than those official canvases he himself believed to be his masterpieces.

Whatever be the final judgment of David's painting, its historical importance is enormous. Not only does it reflect the civilization of his day, its aims and ideals, but it lays the tracks on which the Academy and official art are to run through the nineteenth century. To be sure, not even the Academy preserved indefinitely David's kind of historical painting. The pressure of later developments and new tastes drew the Academy further and further away from its origins. But the pseudo-intellectualism and the insistence upon drawing as basic to success in painting have characterized official art for the whole century. They helped to turn this influential group, the Academy, into a reactionary force which opposed each new movement of the nineteenth century. By investing official patronage in this conservative body, which popular opinion was apt to follow, David made difficult the path of progressive painters for many generations.

In its underlying aspects, Romanticism may have been an escape mechanism prompted by the sordid living conditions of the nineteenth century. The Industrial Revolution, that substitution of machine power for handicrafts, accompanied by the rise of the factory system and therefore of large cities, had been manifest through the eighteenth century, especially in England. It is significant that Romanticism took deep root in England and that it first appeared there. Whatever advantages may have accrued to humanity in the long run from the Industrial Revolution, it brought in its train chaotic, overcrowded, and unsanitary cities, grimy with smoke and filth.

Three possible ways lay open for escape. First, past centuries, when life was different, beckoned the imagination to vicarious adventure and romance. Second, exotic lands enchanted and allured through distance. Finally, the mind might turn to the subjective, and to flights of fancy having no connection with reality. To these three possibilities, and in certain ways connected with them, must be added a renewed interest in nature, its freshness in contrast to the dingy cities, its beauty as opposed to sordid urban reality. Probably all periods would claim to love nature in some measure, even the age of Louis XIV, but under the impulse of Romanticism nature was accepted more nearly as she is, in her intimate details as well as her larger effects. This interest accompanied the scientific explanations of natural phenomena reached in the eighteenth century and marked by Réau-mur's invention of the thermometer or Lavoisier's discovery of oxygen.

On the surface, no two movements seem more opposite than Neoclassicism and Romanticism in the visual arts. In architecture, it is the gulf between the Roman and the Greek revivals on the one hand and the Gothic revival on the other. In painting and sculpture, the Romantic movement assaults the subject matter, the style, and the very purpose of painting as laid down by David. And yet, these two movements are not discrete; they are the obverse and reverse of the medal, or two leaves growing from a single stem. The roots of Neoclassicism reach back into the eighteenth century; so also the origins of the Gothic revival occur at least as early as 1750. An archaeological note is common to both, though the archaeology of the Middle Ages was slower to mature. Often the same persons contributed to both aspects of the movement. Keats not only admired the classic in the *Ode on a Grecian Urn*; he also loved the Gothic as in *The Eve of St. Agnes*. Most significant, in so far as Romanticism is an escape in time or place, the reversion to Rome or Greece is as much of an escape as the return to the Gothic.

The Gothic revival started as a variation on the Georgian, as playful as the *Chinoiseries*, those wallpapers, bits of china, and decorative carvings that the eighteenth century loved to call Chinese. The fad of working in Gothic, at first sponsored by the *nouveau riche*, became socially respectable when Horace

Walpole played with the style at Strawberry Hill about 1752. His interest lay in the details of Gothic, in its picturesqueness, but not at all in its principles or in its construction. The Gothic details were a stage setting, and often frankly a sham. The eighteenth century considered Gothic buildings as a setting for a mood, a background for self-dramatization. Some fortunate individuals owned estates where the crumbling walls of medieval abbeys remained, but for those whose property was not so well equipped there was always the possibility of beautifying the place by building a ruin. William Mason perfectly describes this curious point of view in his poem, *The English Garden*.

Fonthill Abbey (fig. 367), designed by Wyatt at the turn of the century for the eccentric millionaire, William Beckford, was not built as a ruin, though it shortly became one. It is simply the most extravagant manifestation of this urge for the picturesque. This must have been the most inconvenient house ever built. Its four great wings consist chiefly of corridors that lead to nothing. The entrance hall, with a broad flight of thoroughly un-Gothic stairs, is big enough to accommodate larger crowds than the house itself could hold. This hall exaggerates the proportions of a Gothic church, its doors and windows tall and narrow. Externally, the picturesque asymmetry of the Middle Ages becomes a goal instead of the result of the building's purpose or its site. Such an edifice denies the principles of Gothic construction and its unself-conscious

367. James Wyatt (1748–1813) *Fonthill Abbey* (1796–1813) Interior *c.* 245′ long x 35′ wide.

spirit. Wyatt gave thought to his effect; indeed he thought of little else. It is fortunate that Fonthill Abbey should have vanished. We can revisit the building only in imagination, where its inconvenience and its flimsy construction can be forgotten. Built as a fantasy, Fonthill Abbey should be veiled in a haze of unreality.

Neither Wyatt nor Beckford, nor for that matter Walpole, were hampered by much knowledge of medieval styles. Indeed, their day had not realized that the Middle Ages produced more than a single style. Still archaeology, stimulated by antiquarian interest, gradually collected the information essential to any serious adaptation of the style. Thomas Rickman devised the first intelligible classification of the medieval styles; he demonstrated their sequence and made impossible an unwitting combination of Early English, Decorated, and Perpen-

dicular elements. Then John Britton spread a popular knowledge of the style through volumes of fine engravings, sold extensively because of the growing interest in and enthusiasm for Gothic architecture. Finally, the elder Pugin published measured drawings of details that gave the architect who had to design a Gothic building the information he needed. A new church or castle cannot be planned on the basis of general views, however picturesque, but Pugin, himself an architect, knew just what sort of information was requisite.

These men laid the archaeological foundation for the sober maturity of the Gothic revival. The identification of Gothic as a national architecture, when nationalism was beginning to be powerful in England, fostered the style. The English believed that Gothic was local in origin, whereas the Roman and the Greek were foreign. It had not yet been

368. Charles Barry (1795–1860) *Houses of Parliament,* London (1840–60) 940' long.

369. François Rude (1784–1855) *Departure of the Volunteers*, Arc de Triomphe, Paris (1836)
41′8″ x 26′.

realized or admitted that however native the Gothic became, it was first imported from France to England.

Even more influential was the identification of Gothic as Christian architecture. The revival within the Anglican Church known as the Oxford Movement provided a stimulus to faith and worship that turned to the ritual of the Middle Ages for expression. That ritual needed a setting. Therefore, religion converted the spirit of the Gothic revival from superficiality and picturesqueness to sobriety and a seriousness comparable to a Quest of the Holy Grail.

The most famous building of the Gothic revival in England, where the movement was strongest, is the Houses of Parliament (fig. 368) designed by Sir Charles Barry in the middle of the century, but with its Perpendicular Gothic detail supplied by the younger Pugin. Barry was by training and preference a classicist. If his plan and mass are not classic, neither are they Gothic. The plan has a coherence no Gothic revivalist could have attained. The silhouette is so picturesque that the Houses of Parliament has long been a theme for painters, but its style, the Perpendicular, was identified at the time with the decay of Gothic architecture, and went out of fashion before the building was completed. For his own work, such as St. Augustine's at Ramsgate in 1842, A. N. Welby Pugin preferred the Decorated or sometimes the Early English style. His profound knowledge of medieval architecture and his

religious spirit enabled him to withstand the contemporary tendency to display. At their best, his buildings are correct in detail, sound in construction, and devotional in character.

If Romanticism in architecture is perfected in England, its sculpture and painting, save in the field of landscape,

370. François Rude (1784–1855) *Marshal Ney,* Luxembourg Gardens, Paris.

can better be illustrated on the Continent. The Departure of the Volunteers (fig. 369) by François Rude (1784–1855) on the Arc de Triomphe in Paris is transitional. Though the youthful nude carries over from Neoclassicism, the proportions and the modeling to bring out the tenseness of the forms are not academic or classic. The armor is Romantic, based upon French armor of the sixteenth century. The group has a surging movement that Neoclassic sculpture abhorred. Under the patriotic stimulus of the *Marseillaise*, this band of volunteers leaving for the front inspires emotion as the cold intellectuality of Neoclassicism never does. Rude becomes completely Romantic in the portrait of Marshal Ney (fig. 370). Neoclassic portraits had been generalized; their subjects were arrayed in some garb that would identify them with well-known examples of classic sculpture, such as Canova's portrait of Pauline Bonaparte Borghese as a semi-nude Venus Victrix. Rude dresses Marshal Ney in his Napoleonic uniform. He is rendered not as a type but as an individual. His upraised arm, with sword aloft, and mouth open as though commanding a charge create a dramatic moment of action to characterize the figure.

In the actuality of Marshal Ney, the Romantic return to nature is manifest. So too, but more pungently, does it appear in the animal sculpture of Antoine Louis Barye (1796–1875). His Jaguar Devouring a Hare (fig. 371) testifies to his study in the Paris Zoological Gardens and his measurements of its exotic animals. Though Barye never saw them in their native habitats, no one has so

371. Antoine Louis Barye (1796–1875) *Jaguar Devouring a Hare* (1851) Louvre, Paris. Bronze, 3′5″ long x 1′5″ high.

grasped their Romantic wildness and ferocity. The style is at once realistic and broad. No detail is present that might not be found in reality, but many details that exist in nature are suppressed to stress the essential and the expressive. Through such a treatment, Barye creates a succession of dynamic and sculpturesque animal groups. His understanding of character in animals is unsurpassed. The action of the big cat with ears laid back, its tail flicking to and fro, and its tense crouch while feeding can be observed in the domestic cat, but they are, naturally, increased in scale. The exotic nature of these creatures and the selection of a moment of feeding or combat to emphasize their wildness are fundamentally Romantic traits. No animal sculptor has ever reached the height scaled by Barye, partly through his combination of realism and the sculpturesque, and partly through his use of animals to parallel human emotions. We, as humans, respond to the qualities Barye discovers in his subjects.

The painters of Romanticism, like the sculptors, reject Neoclassic doctrine. They ignore the formulas laid down by the Academy, and turn to subject matter of greater range. Not only do they exploit the Middle Ages—in fact, they do that only to a limited extent—but they also turn to their own day for material that touches their lives and arouses their emotions. Thrills, excitement, horror, not born of the mind but of the emotions, replace the aridity of Neoclassicism. Such a purpose demands a change of technique. Therefore the insistence on drawing and especially on delineation must be reduced. In its place, the emotional possibilities of color once more come into their own. Although the color and vitality of Rubens had been anathema to David,

372. Goya (1746–1828) *Maja Desnuda* (1799) Prado, Madrid. 3'3" x 6'3".

373. Goya (1746–1828) *Execution of Madrilenos* (1808) Prado, Madrid. 8'9" x 11'4".

the Flemish painter helped to mold the foremost Romanticist, Delacroix.

One forerunner of the full-blown Romantic movement calls for comment. Francisco Goya y Lucientes (1746–1828) was as turbulent as were the days of the Napoleonic occupation of Spain through which he lived. Strongly erotic —he almost lost his life in consequence of one ill-starred escapade—Goya was never happier than when embroiled. The best Spanish painter since Velásquez, he became portraitist to the decadent court of Charles IV. It is astonishing that Goya retained this post unchallenged. His realism enabled him to characterize to the point of caricature.

Goya painted the queen as a sensual vixen, and the king as a moron—accurate characterizations, but only the inability of the court to recognize their truth prevented these paintings from being suppressed and Goya with them. In many of his early works, Goya is not above criticism. His figures are often stiff and wooden; they do not stand firmly, nor have they much atmosphere around them.

The Maja Desnuda (fig. 372), the same motive as Giorgione's Venus (fig. 242), is entirely representative of Goya. No more sensual or naturalistic portrait of the female figure can be discovered in the annals of great painting. Every-

374. Goya (1746–1828) *Hasta la Muerte* (*Los Caprichos*) Etching, 7½" x 5¼".

thing is done in drawing, in color, and in pose to make this figure as seductive as possible. Nevertheless, Goya does not neglect composition. The figure ranges the diagonal of the canvas, and the arms, folded behind her head, provide a counter movement to stop the action. Goya once said, 'Lines, always lines, and never body. But where do we see these lines in nature? I see only forms which advance, forms which recede, masses in light or in shadow.' Clearly, Goya was not in sympathy with the delineation stressed by the Academy, and intended to turn from it to the observed appearances of nature.

The incidents of the Napoleonic occupation of Spain gave him a perfect opportunity to dramatize the horrible. The Execution of Madrileños (fig. 373) depicts a military execution of those who resisted the French occupation. They say that Goya came upon the scene the morning after, when the bodies were still lying in the gutter, and dipped his handkerchief in blood to make his first sketch of this composition on a nearby wall. Whether this be true or not, it is just the sort of thing that Goya would do. A dramatic light brings into prominence the victims filled with horror at impending death, and silhouettes the soldiers with their leveled rifles in the foreground. Here Goya expresses his interest in 'masses in light or in shadow.' None of these figures is delineated; that would have destroyed the turbulence, and therefore the emotion of the scene.

This macabre strain in Goya finds expression in the series of etchings called Los Desastres de la Guerra, and to a lesser extent in the series, La Tauromaquía, a sort of history of the bull ring. His wild fancy and his sarcasm prompt the other two series, Los Caprichos and Los Proverbios. A single plate, Hasta la Muerte (Till Death) (fig. 374), shows his grim humor. The age-old desire to retain the habiliments of youth after they have ceased to be appropriate receives here a sarcastic commentary. If these etchings are humorous, there is also present much that is less pleasant to contemplate, as Goya dissects the foibles of humanity with pitiless accuracy.

The French Academy naturally never had the power in Spain that it wielded in Paris. Hence, an independent spirit like Goya could arise in Spain at the height of the Neoclassic movement. The rise of Romanticism in France comes a little later. It is foretold in Baron Antoine Jean Gros, who in 1815 succeeded David as leader of the Academy when David on the restoration of the Bourbons was exiled as a regicide to Brussels. Baron Gros concurred in the ideals of historical painting set down by David, but Gros had served with Napoleon during the Egyptian campaign, and the military life of his own day interested him, not the wars of Hannibal or the battles of Marathon and Thermopylae. Napoleon in the Pest House at Jaffa (fig. 375) has first of all the interest of an historical event known to Gros. The members of Napoleon's staff wear their full military regalia. Nothing of the

375. Antoine Jean Gros (1771–1835) *Napoleon in the Pest House at Jaffa* (1804) Louvre, Paris. 17′5″ x 23′7″.

classic in subject matter belongs in such a scene. Perhaps the nude man in the foreground may recall the academic concentration on the figure, but a strong natural light falls on the central group and defines the planes of the distant buildings, quite different, for example, from the cold lighting of the Death of Socrates (fig. 365).

Also transitional, but further along on the road to Romanticism, is Théodore Géricault (1791–1824). Because of its military glory, the Academy might condone the Napoleon at Jaffa, but the Raft of the Medusa (fig. 376) came as a grenade to the Salon of 1819. It happened that the ship *Medusa* had been allowed to leave port in an unseaworthy condition and had foundered. After days of suffering on a raft in mid-ocean, a few survivors were rescued and brought to port. Many had died of exposure and starvation; others had gone insane. Their gruesome tales invoked a wave of sympathy, and of criticism of the Government, which seemed partly responsible for the disaster. Géricault was among those who were stirred. He was accused of criticizing the Government; that such was his intention is not certain, but there can be no two opinions about the dramatic horror of his painting. The moment is that when a rescuing ship has just been sighted, and the strongest

376. Théodore Géricault (1791–1824) *Raft of the Medusa* (1819) Louvre, Paris. 16′1″ x 23′5″.

survivors struggle upward in hysterical joy at the prospect of rescue. The old man at the left has lost all hope of deliverance, and perhaps all desire, as he drops his hand in a protecting gesture over the corpse of his son. The survivors have not strength enough to clear the raft of their comrades who have died, such as the body dragging through the waves to the right. No one in 1819, with the tragedy still fresh in his mind, could look at this painting unmoved. Its gruesome tale inspired pity in all who saw it. No one feels emotionally stirred by David's historical designs. This is why the conservatives of the Academy condemned the Medusa. It is not foreign to their traditions in color; the prevailing tonality is brown. The large size of the painting is not different from academic standards. The emphasis on drawing and the academic love of the figure are still present, as Géricault uses the opportunities afforded by his theme for a study of the nude. The contrasts of light and dark, however, are more dramatic than in Neoclassic paintings. With that exception, the technique remains conservative, but the spirit of Romanticism is already rampant.

Had Géricault lived, he might have led the Romantic rebels. His premature death allowed the torch to fall into the hands of Ferdinand Eugène Delacroix (1798–1863). A well-informed and intelligent man, Delacroix was anything but revolutionary by nature. He had no desire to head a movement with whose excesses he had little sympathy, no matter how fully he might adhere to its less

radical sides. Already in his Bark of
Dante in 1822, Delacroix had proclaimed his willingness to paint a theme
of the Middle Ages drawn from the

Inferno, and with its horror paramount
in the result. Nevertheless, the browns
and the academic interest in the nude
still remained, though with heavier

377. Ferdinand Eugène Delacroix (1798–1863) *Massacre of Scio* (1824) Louvre, Paris. 13'10"
x 11'6".

modeling of the figures. As in Géricault, the spirit, not the forms, had altered.

A few years later, partly under the influence of Rubens, Delacroix's color and forms began to change. The Massacre of Scio (fig. 377), like the Raft of the Medusa, came from a contemporary event. In this case, the source was the Greek war of liberation from Turkey. The prosperous island of Chios had not joined that revolt, but a raid by the rebels caused the Turkish governor to lose his head and permit the Janissaries to massacre thousands of civilians. Liberal sentiment in Western Europe was appalled. Sympathy for the Greeks already existed there, where it stimulated the Greek revival; Delacroix's epic vision of the Greek war illustrated that sympathy. The painting is restrained; in the foreground, men and women wait their turn for slaughter, helpless and hopeless. They do not even struggle against the inevitable. The scenes of tumult are relegated to the background. Nor are the Janissaries more violent; their mission, foreordained by Allah, is to slay the Christian pigs; they complete their task with contempt but with little more emotion than a butcher plying his trade. Horrible as is the subject, the expression seems controlled merely to heighten its grimness through contrast. No longer does delineation dominate; the brownish tonality has been modified in favor of richer color. The use of complementary tones, such as violet shadows on a yellow passage, or green to serve as a foil to red, probably came to Delacroix through observation, though it did exist in paintings by the Venetians, Rubens, and Watteau with whose works Delacroix was conversant, and in Constable's contemporary English landscape paintings.

More riotous in color, with a strong dash of Rubens, is the Death of Sardanapalus. The subject of this sensational canvas is drawn from Byron, that is, from English Romanticism. What an opportunity it affords Delacroix to study the female figure, as the eunuchs put to death the women of the harem lest they fall into the hands of the king's enemies! The theme gives Delacroix a chance for action, rich contrasts of light and shade, and sumptuousness of color.

Delacroix returns to French life for inspiration in Liberty Leading the People, a portrayal of an event that occurred 28 July 1830 (fig. 378). In it he creates an apotheosis of the July revolution, which ejected Charles X, of the older branch of the Bourbon dynasty, from the throne of France and installed the younger branch in its place in the person of Louis Philippe, who promised to be favorable to the business classes. In the center, the allegorical figure of France bears the banner of the revolution. On the right is an irrepressible youth who, like a western cowboy, strides over the barricades with both guns swinging, a splendid interpretation of a type, to whom the ends of the revolution appear to be subordinate to its excitement. The lower-class support of this revolution inspires the man at the extreme left, but that figure is shadowed, while next to him is an eminently respectable businessman. One expects sideburns, a frock coat, and a top hat on 'change; they look anachronous in the melee of street fighting. And yet the class he represents controls this political upset; they want a government favorable to them, but they do not want a social upheaval like the French Revolution; that would be bad for trade. This solid businessman seems to have picked down from his mantel an old fowling piece, as antiquated as he himself is unexpected in these surroundings. The dramatic lighting, the color, the contemporary scene, and the excitement in the painting make it a landmark of Romanticism.

During the 1830's, France began to expand into North Africa. The Moorish civilization there and the exotic wild life of the region attracted Delacroix. As a member of a mission to the Sultan of Morocco, he had first-hand knowledge of this part of the world. Lion hunts with turbaned and burnoosed Bedouins provide Delacroix with an opportunity to achieve the movement and color that he finds in Rubens. Here, too, he begins to exploit the qualities of paint, and therefore his draftsmanship becomes looser or, more precisely, free. The old linearism is deserted. Nor does he restrict his themes to animals and

378. Ferdinand Eugène Delacroix (1798–1863) *Liberty Leading the People* (1830) Louvre, Paris. 8'6" x 10'8".

379. Ferdinand Eugène Delacroix (1798–1863) *Algerian Women* (1834) Louvre, Paris. 5′11″ x 7′6″.

the hunt. The Algerian Women (fig. 379) is as exotic as his paintings of lions. The hot stillness of this inner room, its Oriental color in the pink, orange, black, and white tiled wall echoed in the costumes, and the life represented in this scene is foreign to life in France. Such a scene is alluring, when seen through the medium of painting. It provides those elements of romance that were fast disappearing from European civilization. Moreover, such paintings attest the European interest in colonial expansion under economic and imperialistic stimuli.

Delacroix's fight for recognition of the Romantic point of view met the opposition of Jean Auguste Dominique Ingres (1780–1867). Older than Delacroix, Ingres had been a pupil of David; later he spent years in Florence and Rome, supporting himself in part by exquisite pencil portraits. These tight drawings are sharp in detail around the face, but sketchy in their indication of costume. Essentially linear, Ingres suppresses shadow. Small areas under the chin or below the nose suffice to establish the form of the head. The passages fade so subtly into white that the pencil strokes are imperceptible and suggest a waxy smoothness of surface. Such elegance and refinement recur from time to time in French art, in the paintings of the Clouets, and the drawings and paintings of Watteau, as though they were sympathetic to the French temperament. These drawings testify to Ingres' consummate skill as a draftsman, and are often fresher than his paintings.

They suggest that draftsmanship lies at the basis of his style. When Ingres became the leader of the Academy, he modified its ideals and, even more than David, determined its character for the rest of the nineteenth century. By his time, the spirit of the day had so changed that the historical subjects of David could no longer maintain their dominance. Instead, Ingres substituted the figure, sometimes male but more often female, as the prime requisite. His Odalisque (fig. 380) represents the type. The figure is not individualized; on the contrary, the form is generalized, the principal divisions of the body accurate enough, but with all sensuous details eliminated. His control of line emphasizes delineation; we are first aware of the outline of the figure developed with lyrical beauty and clarity. The figure as such means nothing. It is an excuse for Ingres to display his draftsmanship. Such a nude may be posed in many ways, though in fact the poses are normally quiet; it may be called Truth or Venus, a Fountain or an Odalisque. The title changes but the essential figure does not. Through such works as this, Ingres established the academic nude as the subject of official art for the rest of the century, and, by reason of his insistence upon delineation, draftsmanship became the prerequisite for academic recognition. 'Any-

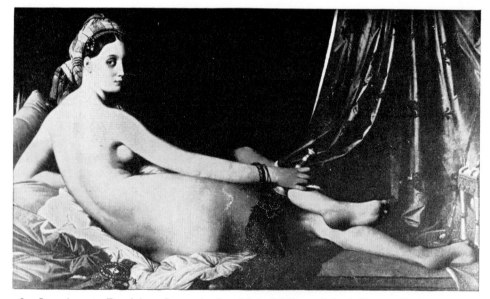

380. Jean Auguste Dominique Ingres (1780–1867) *Odalisque* (1814) Louvre, Paris. 3' x 5'4".

thing that is well drawn is well enough painted,' he said. Therefore, color is an afterthought, and from then on the Academy produced a series of coldly academic studies which, however adequate in draftsmanship, look like tinted drawings. A man of less breadth of mind than Delacroix, Ingres' spirit restricted official art for generations.

The Romantic interest in nature, as a palliative for urban conditions, was bound to have results in landscape painting. The new point of view went back into the eighteenth century to the work of the English watercolorists. More important is Richard Wilson (1714–82) who, though he retained the conventional dark foreground and brownish tonality of the French classic school of Claude Lorrain, turned to specific scenes like the Dutch landscape painters, to the rugged aspects of nature, to Cader Idris and the Welsh mountains. He substitutes the beauty of the picturesque and the unexpected for the well-groomed, carefully constructed landscapes, traditional in his day. Somewhat later, Thomas Gainsborough, who preferred landscape to portraiture, gave vent to his lyrical spirit and his pictorial power in designs like the Market Wagon, not appreciated in his own time.

It remained for John Constable (1776–1837) to effect the revolution in landscape painting. He stated his aims, which may be taken as the creed of Romantic landscape painting, in saying, 'There is room for a natural painter.' His sketches were made directly from nature, and though his finished compositions, such as the Hay Wain (Plate VIII, facing p. 365), may have been executed within his studio, they rejected the traditional scheme of landscape painting. The dark foreground and lighted distance and the brownish tonality are tossed into the limbo of antiquated notions. Instead of areas of solid color, Constable breaks up the masses of foliage into sparkling green passages, broad and free in handling, and closer to the vibrancy of nature than are the traditional solutions.

Like the Dutch, he turns to the specific, not the general, in landscape; the Hay Wain represents a bit of his native Suffolk. In consequence, we are at first unaware of a deliberate scheme. The painting appears to be well adjusted, but the house and the group of trees near the left foreground seem to be there because in this particular scene that is where they happened to occur. Though this casualness of arrangement may be, and in this instance is, more apparent than real, such informality underscores Constable's acceptance of the actual scene. He so loves nature that he clings to her not only in the structure of his trees, his clouds, and all the other elements of landscape, but even in their disposition. Therein lies his strength and his weakness. Few better grasp and render the scenes before them, but at times his passion for actuality leads him to forget that he is painting a picture, not creating a landscape. His scope is limited, through his very naturalism, to those scenes he had himself observed, and since he seldom traveled, the range of his material is narrow. Nevertheless, Constable does select his subject and modify it to construct pictures without loss of naturalism, while his study of the structure of natural forms gives his work a solidity seldom rivaled and never surpassed.

Joseph Mallord William Turner (1775–1851) was a more fluent draftsman than Constable, but did not always perceive the solid structure that empowers all of Constable's paintings. Turner admired Claude Lorrain, and in his earlier work especially, for example, Crossing the Brook, he retained the composition and something of the restricted palette of his great forebear,

but combined them with a Romantic view of nature. He bequeathed to the British nation several paintings by Claude, on the condition that they be displayed in conjunction with some of his own, to acknowledge his debt. Admirable though they are, Turner's paintings rarely achieve the pictorial ability so marked in the French artist, and want that lyric love of nature evident even through the conventions of Claude's paintings.

As his style developed, Turner became more and more absorbed in color, and, toward the end of his life, in atmosphere, which he approached emotionally with swirling masses of color and pigment. The Fighting Téméraire

381. J. M. W. Turner (1775–1851) *The Fighting Téméraire* (1839) National Gallery, London. 3' x 4'.

(fig. 381) appeals to sentiment; who does not feel the tragedy when some fine old ship, ennobled by its associations, is towed away to destruction? That drama is heightened by the contrast of the picturesque man-of-war and a most unromantic tug. Such an appeal to sentiment is quite legitimate. The ship has become a ghostly galleon, a veritable *Flying Dutchman*, with little feeling for structure. The sun sets below a dark red cloud. Turner has begun to dump his paint pot upside down for the sheer sensuous excitement of sumptuous color.

His celebrated canvas, Rain, Steam, and Speed, shows a train crossing a viaduct in a fog. The tangible subject dwindles to a mere excuse for a study of atmosphere, in which forms dissolve in a haze of smoke and mist, unsubstan-

tial and unscientific by comparison with later atmospheric studies by Claude Monet. However, these late paintings of Turner play a historic role as an influence on Impressionism a generation later.

On the other hand, Constable's influence, injected by his paintings into the Salon of 1824, is profound on the Barbizon school, a group of landscape painters who in the 1830's sought refuge from the cost of living in Paris at Barbizon on the outskirts of the forest of Fontainebleau. Théodore Rousseau (1812–67), called the eagle of the group because of his strength, turns to the *paysage intime,* the same kind of pastoral and intimate bits of landscape that Constable loves. He discards the picturesque and the scenic. The Oaks (fig. 382) occupy and block the center

382. Théodore Rousseau (1812–67) *The Oaks.* Louvre, Paris. 2′1″ x 3′3″.

383. Jean Baptiste Camille Corot (1796–1875) *La Matinée* (1850) Luxembourg Museum, Paris.
3'2" x 4'3".

of the composition and so confine our attention to the foreground. Such distance as may be necessary to establish this grove in space is relegated to the sides. The tufts of grass in the foreground are more important to Rousseau than great distance, and the structure of the trees more significant than either. There is nothing epic in the scene, save its power of observation. This delight in the smaller aspects of nature and this confidence in their pictorial sufficiency did not meet the approval of the Academy; so consistently were Rousseau's paintings rejected by the Salons that he was nicknamed '*le Grand Refusé.*'

Strictly speaking, Jean Baptiste Camille Corot (1796–1875) does not be-

long to the Barbizon school, though he sympathized with its members and helped them to the best of his ability. His own characteristic manner is easily recognized in La Matinée (fig. 383), sometimes called the Dance of the Nymphs. These idyllic figures might be the dream children of the landscape itself, with its unreal appearance. In actuality, Corot has an understanding of nature and its structure, a lyric love of the country, pervading these songs in paint which are like odes in honor of his goddess. His strict limitation of color and values avoids extreme lights and darks, and vivid colors. Instead he preferred silvery grays or gray greens. An occasional touch of stronger color serves

384. Jean Baptiste Camille Corot (1796–1875) *Honfleur, Houses on the Quay* (*c.* 1830) Mme E. Staub-Terlinden, Männedorf. 1′3″ x 1′11″.

to accent the quietness of the scene. These canvases, so characteristic of Corot, contrast with his early work, such as the Honfleurs (fig. 384), more architectural scenes with planes of strong light and shade, blocked in with a structural sense of pictorial possibilities. This same sensitive construction marks his few but powerful figure paintings. After we have become sated with the repetition of his better-known works, such designs as these come as a surprise and a relief.

The Barbizon group is primarily one of landscape painters. With them, Jean François Millet (1814–75) allies himself, but applies their directness and their unpretentious modesty to the figure. By birth a Norman peasant, Millet fully understood the types that were to make his reputation. The Sower (fig. 385) pursues his vocation in the time-honored way, strewing the grain over the fields by hand. The setting is reduced to a plane of brown to indicate the plowed earth, and a line for the horizon. Against this background, Millet creates a Michelangelesque type, a symbol of the farmer of all times and places, in his constant struggle to wrest a livelihood from the soil. This is no musical-comedy peasant with a picturesque costume; he is dressed in rough but serviceable garments. The technique of painting is as rough as the costume and the figure, as though to insist on the bulk of this monumental character.

In these types, Millet created an

apotheosis of the class he knew and loved. In his lifetime, he was accused of social propaganda; later ages discovered in him their own attitude that the underprivileged were oppressed by the exploitation of the upper classes. Such

385. Jean François Millet (1814–75) *The Sower* (1850) Museum of Fine Arts, Boston. 3'4" x 2'9".

interpretations were foreign to Millet. He was amused that his own day could find propaganda in his paintings; he would be astonished that anyone should think of his peasants as 'stolid and stunned, a brother to the ox,' as Edwin Markham wrote. On the contrary, if the peasant's lot was hard, he had, Millet believed, the strength to bear it. His characters exult in the importance of their calling; they are, in fact, the men and women upon whom the strength of France is based, and their elemental power lends them majesty. Theirs is no message of despair; it is a glowing tribute to the people Millet knew so well.

XXIV   The Later Nineteenth Century in Europe

As the nineteenth century progressed, Paris became more and more the center of the art world. There new ideas were born. Its atmosphere stimulated discussion and the existence of a large group of artists in Paris drew still more artists from all over the European world. Consequently, each new step in French art was reflected in that of other countries. Of course, academic art continued in Paris and elsewhere to supply an accompaniment and a foil to the new ideas, each of which had to battle for recognition against the persistent conservatism of official bodies.

The Academies in painting paralleled the Ecole des Beaux Arts in architecture. This school laid stress on drawing and on the effectiveness of a design on paper. Such an emphasis inevitably focused on pictorial possibilities in design, and although structural training existed in the curriculum, if one may call it that, and was expected to appear in the drawings, the position accorded it was apt to be insignificant. New materials, however great their possibilities, had to overcome academic prejudice based on the supposition that they were ill-adapted to monumental architecture.

This is a difficult era to discuss, because all manner of styles co-exist. Eclecticism is the guiding thread. The word means freedom of choice; as applied to the arts, specifically freedom to select from among the styles of the past. Either the architect or his client or both may decide in what historic style the building shall be dressed. Eclecticism did not really obtain during the earlier

Greek and Gothic revivals, though its germs were present then. Many factors may influence the choice, some of them intelligent, others minor. The association of a type of building with a given style, as for example, the identification of church architecture with the Gothic, may determine the selection. The supposed existence of a national historic style is sometimes a governing factor. The training of the architect selected, or his or his client's whims or tastes are frequently the only reasons for adopting one style rather than another. All the styles tend to be crass, whether they be some modification of the classic or the Victorian Gothic, which often turns from English and French sources to Italian or German Gothic. The architects feel free to borrow details from where they will, and to mix elements from one style with elements from another. Still underneath this veneer of style can sometimes be found a fundamental exploration of space problems for their own sake and in their relation to function, together with experiments in new materials.

From this unpromising ground sprang a few distinguished architectural monuments. The Bibliothèque Ste. Geneviève (1843–50) by Henri Labrouste derives from the early Italian Renaissance, and owes some debt to Alberti's design

386. Henri Labrouste (1801–75) *Bibliothèque Ste. Geneviève*, Paris (1843–50) Reading Room.

of the flank of San Francesco at Rimini. Severe arcades enclose the windows of the second-floor reading room, and only small arched windows and a band of garlands break the plain stone wall of the ground floor. These fifteenth-century motives lead to nothing; more prophetic is the reading room (fig. 386). The nineteenth century fostered science, a corollary to its materialism; this is reflected in the development of concrete, the availability of glass in ever-larger sheets, and especially in the increased use of metal as a structural material. Iron and bronze had been employed from time immemorial for decorative details, but the cost of metal had hitherto prevented its structural use. During the eighteenth century, it began to appear in bridges, for example the Severn Bridge, constructed in 1775–9, and from there it spread to utilitarian buildings. In 1801 it appeared in a cotton mill in Manchester, and in 1824 in the market hall of the Madeleine in Paris.

Up to the middle of the century, however, tradition hampered its adoption for monumental buildings, as did the Beaux Arts' emphasis on historic styles. Labrouste wanted his reading room to be free of heavy interior supports. He might have vaulted it in stone, but to do so would have necessitated heavy walls, which would have curtailed the light. To cover this span with wooden beams, even if it were possible, would result in a lack of monumentality. Therefore Labrouste chose iron in the form of arches and columns whose slender proportions were possible only in metal. As always when a new material is adopted, the design is conceived partly in terms of other materials. The iron columns retain the details of the Corinthian order. Moreover, the utilitarian arches are disguised with waving foliate designs, as though Labrouste had not yet found a solution in design for them as acceptable to the public as the solutions so readily at hand with the older building materials. However, in the utilitarian stacks, the architect takes full advantage of iron. The open grilled floors allow penetration of light and a frank expression of intersecting planes.

Architects are often unjustly condemned for their conservatism, and disparaging comparisons are drawn between them and engineers. In that connection, it is fair to remember that adequate designs for the automobile were not immediately discovered by the engineers, who at the outset shaped their cars in terms of wagons; it took more than a generation to reach the beauty of contemporary automobiles. Much the same can be said of the locomotive, the steamship, and the airplane. Moreover, the architect experiments with his client's money, and the latter will usually prevent any solution of a new problem that departs too radically from buildings known to him. One cannot test buildings on a proving ground, since their cost forbids their immediate destruction and redesign, even when lines of improvement become obvious. Such a scheme as Labrouste's, then, though it has some precedent in utilitarian build-

387. Charles Garnier (1825–98) *Opera House*, Paris (1861–74) Façade *c.* 200′ wide x 95′ high.

ings and parallels contemporary exposition architecture, such as the Crystal Palace in London in 1851, represents a bold experiment with a material not yet respectable in academic circles, whose perfected expressions, such as the Eiffel Tower in Paris or the skyscrapers in America, could arise only later.

If the Bibliothèque Ste. Geneviève derives from the Renaissance, the Paris Opera House of 1861–74 (fig. 387) by Charles Garnier stems from the Baroque. The well-organized plan testifies to the thoroughness of the Beaux Arts training, as does the controlled richness of the Baroque façade. Such opulence of arches and columns, cartouches and sculpture creates a festive character. The Baroque sumptuousness of opera, quite

understandable since opera is a Baroque form, seemed to call for display. Garnier's success is tragically evident when contrasted with many an American theater, whose designers were tempted to walk in the paths of the mighty without training for such an exercise. It requires a thorough understanding of composition to master so rich a style. The stairway of the Paris Opera (fig. 388), with its Baroque curves and bulging balconies, not only communicates with the boxes and seats; even more it affords a setting for the social display opera inspires.

The church of the Sacré Coeur in Paris, begun in 1873, is Romanesque in style and the quintessence of Romanticism in feeling. Its architect, Abadie, remodeled the church of St. Front at Périgueux, an example of the half-Byzantine Romanesque of Aquitaine, crowned with five domes. No doubt this suggested the new design of Sacré Coeur, but Abadie has piled up turrets

388. Charles Garnier (1825–98) *Stairway*, Opera House, Paris (1861–74).

and dome in a picturesque manner, more extravagant in effect than the medieval building. Crowning the heights of Montmartre, this church has a fairy-tale unreality about it, something un-believable, like an illustration for the *Arabian Nights.*

The same eclecticism is prevalent in sculpture—at times, even the same styles that inspire the architects are used. Jean Baptiste Carpeaux's (1827–75) group of the Dance (fig. 389) on the Paris Opera House is as Baroque as the building. The subject involves a mo-ment of violent action. The movement

389. Jean Baptiste Carpeaux (1827–75) *Dance* (1869) Opera, Façade, Paris. 15'2" x 8'6".

of these figures, even though they form a ring, often leads the eye out of the cen-tral mass. Thus the composition has the complexity of the Baroque, its openness, and its turbulence. Much pictorial de-tail finds room here. The whole design, though executed in marble, is in fact conceived for the plasticity of clay.

Just as the painters of Romanticism turn to Rubens for inspiration, so do Carpeaux and, even more, Jules Dalou. In the latter's Silenus of the Luxem-bourg Gardens, the fleshy figure, the movement and abandon, the naturalism of the modeling, and the pictorial ac-cessories justify its description as a modeler's version of a Rubens mythol-ogy. Like all sculptors of their day, Car-peaux and Dalou build up their compo-sitions in clay, which may be molded under their fingers into naturalistic de-tails. The model can then be transcribed into bronze or stone, and each modula-tion of the surface preserved. To achieve monumentality under these circum-stances is all but impossible; effects ap-propriate in clay are too readily at hand to be avoided, even if the sculptor tries to retain the qualities of the final ma-terial.

These considerations go far to ex-plain the style of Auguste Rodin (1840–1917), the outstanding sculptor of the later nineteenth century. He concludes the development from the break-down of Neoclassicism at the hands of Rude and Barye through the pictorial model-ing of Carpeaux and Dalou. That Rodin is capable of amazing naturalism is ap-parent in the Age of Bronze. This fig-

390. Auguste Rodin (1840–1917) *The Kiss* (1898) Luxembourg, Paris. 6′ high.

this been carried out, the effect when one encountered the group in a city square would have been startling.

These works were cast in bronze, but Rodin commonly chose marble, as in The Kiss (fig. 390). The surfaces of these intertwined figures undulate to induce a play of light and shade over them. These light effects parallel contemporary Impressionist painting, and hence permit a description of Rodin as the foremost Impressionist sculptor. The fluid surface modulation is not so broken as to violate naturalism; on the contrary, it gives the stone the animation of living flesh. Rodin's love of the body is sensuous, and often frankly erotic, as these figures interlock in their passionate embrace. The soft texture of flesh contrasts with the rough stone on which they sit, the marks of the chisel apparent on its surface. Often Rodin resorts to the device of allowing part of his figures to emerge from an unfinished block, as Michelangelo did. In the case of the Florentine, the lack of finish is probably due to pressure of other work; in Rodin's hand, it becomes a meretricious trick. It does not even express a feeling for the material. The sensuous naturalism and his modeler's conception and methods make Rodin typical of nineteenth-century sculptors.

ure of a young Belgian soldier caused Rodin to be attacked by his fellow sculptors, who accused him of trying to palm off a life cast as an independent work. Rodin was able to free himself from this charge, but the accusation would never have been made had not his statue been so like the human figure in every detail. The group called the Burghers of Calais is almost as naturalistic. These five figures, who commemorate an incident of local history, are each individualized, their faces stern if not haggard, their arms gaunt and sinewy, and their sackcloth pictorial. Rodin wanted to place them on a plinth only a few inches high instead of a pedestal. Had

When he was commissioned to do a portrait of Balzac (fig. 391), Rodin's patrons were outraged at the result and rejected it, though by then he had won recognition. Rodin conceives Balzac wrapped in his dressing gown and striding about the room in the throes of

391. Auguste Rodin (1840–1917) *Balzac* (1892–97) Rodin Museum, Paris. 9′10″ high.

comes amorphous. The interpretive portrait, with its beetling eyebrows and heavy features, is intended to be lighted from above to accentuate its sensationalism.

Whatever importance the architecture and sculpture of the time may have, the dominant art of the late nineteenth century is painting. So pronounced is this fact that many people today think of art and painting as synonyms, and thus fail to realize that art comprises many other media. However, there is something of the painter's attitude in Rodin's pictorial interest in light and shade, and many sculptors of his day started as painters or practiced that art in addition to their own. Perhaps even in architecture, the eclectic tendency to design for effect and to deny, conceal, or at least minimize the importance of structure may be traced to the same attitude. Possibly the methods of education in all the arts by means of the Academies produced this result. However that may be, the fact remains that painting is pre-eminent in the arts during the nineteenth century as sculpture had been in Periclean Greece and architecture in medieval Europe.

Moreover, the Industrial Revolution, against whose effects Romanticism had protested, called into being a crass materialism. Progress became identified with bigger and better production, and success was measured in terms of money. Whether or not such a scale of values is desirable, it is impertinent to painting and sculpture, and hardly relevant in architecture. Thus the values that the

literary composition. A powerful head tops a chaotic mass. The bulk of the great body, though simple in its larger outlines, like some outcropping of nature, fritters away its form in meaningless bosses and hollows, rough and broken clay-like surfaces, until it be-artist recognized, the public rejected. The success of a painting cannot be measured by its dimensions or by the quantity and cost of its pigment. Therefore, the artist became separated from the rest of the public in aims and ideals. If the notion that the artist is a queer and impractical fellow did not originate at this time, it did gain currency.

This separation of the artist, and his consequent rebellious attitude, could not but affect his work. The fact that without a market for his paintings the artist might starve is in some respects a minor matter, however vital to him. His enemies could retort that inability to earn a livelihood in painting did not close the door to gainful occupations, and if the artist chose to suffer in a garret rather than work in a factory, that was his affair. During earlier centuries, the upper class, either the aristocracy or the church, had cultivated an interest in the arts, and passed it on as a tradition from generation to generation. Their ideals could be expressed in paint or stone with no loss of artistic integrity; moreover, the artist's public sympathized with and understood his products. With the materialism of the nineteenth century, the artist could not compromise without losing his integrity. Furthermore, economic developments brought a new wealthy group to the fore. These men had no inherited appreciation of the arts. They lacked the background and traditions that had sustained painting in earlier days. At the same time, they realized, or some of them did, that patronage of art was one of the per-

quisites, if not a social requisite, of their position. To whom should they turn for guidance if not to official art and the Academies?

By reason of their control of the annual salons, the Academies wielded tremendous power. Their juries rejected not only the incompetent but also the new and original, and indeed anything that failed to meet their conservative standards. By refusing to exhibit the works of a painter, the Academy could deprive him of the opportunity to become known to that part of the public interested in art; in other words, it controlled his most legitimate form of publicity. Through its awards, it set the stamp of mastership where it chose, and by so doing increased the market for certain artists' work. The artists were aware of this and therefore tried to make sure that their canvases displayed on the walls of the annual salons would catch the public eye. This they might accomplish by sensationalism in subject or color, but sheer size of canvas was the most direct means. No matter how irrelevant is size to quality, if a large picture and others of medium or small size are hung on a single wall, it is human nature to examine the large one first. Also, the largest painting is inevitably placed in the center; it can hardly be pushed into a corner. Irreverent artists nicknamed these great compositions 'machines.' Aside from any other consideration, their size made it certain that no private patron would buy them, since they required a palace for their display. They were painted to be sold to the Government as 'great art' after winning their medals and acclaim in the salons. One example will suffice, the Romans of the Decadence, painted by Thomas Couture in 1847, master of the 'well-painted bit.' The canvas measures 15 feet 3 inches by 25 feet 5 inches. The subject itself is sensational—an orgy, whereon the statues of worthy ancestors look down as with disgust. The work is facile and competent, but though influenced by Veronese in its architectural setting, its interest lies in its subject.

Through its ability to make reputations, the Academy could open the door to portraiture, the one really lucrative field in the arts. Those who could afford to have their portraits painted turned to known artists; the wealthier the individual, the more certainly would he patronize recognized masters. Although their portraits are tight, such men as Léon Bonnat are well trained. The draftsmanship is precise, the pigment applied as though figure and drapery were waxen, and the personality and likeness caught.

However much they might covet the security of academic success, a few painters, and among them the most serious of their generations, insisted that the goals of the Academy and of the public were insufficient, and that the expressive possibilities of painting as an interpretation of life were more significant. Honoré Daumier (1808–79) stands alone in his day in his human

392. Honoré Daumier (1808–79) *Gargantua* (1831) Lithograph, 8½″ x 12″.

393. Honoré Daumier (1808–79) *Washwoman* (*c.* 1863) Louvre, Paris. 1'6" x 1'.

sympathies. His professional activity lay in the graphic arts, where his caricatures got him into trouble with the state. In such a cartoon as Gargantua (fig. 392), Daumier invited the hostility of the Government. The ministers of Louis Philippe collect taxes from the people in panniers, which they convey to the insatiable maw of Gargantua, personified as the monarch. From under his chair issue privileges and monopolies for the business classes in whose interests, under the *laissez-faire* theory of economics, his government was conducted. The taunts of this satire were too sharp to be forgiven. In lithographs and paintings based upon his observations in the courts, Daumier dissects for all to see the conduct of the legal profession, the lawyer's impassioned pleas for unworthy clients, or their hobnobbing around the halls of justice. His representation is not flattering to them either as individuals or as a group, but his grasp of the essentials of characterization is superb.

Perhaps his training as a caricaturist gave him a feeling for the economy of essentials and the elimination of the accidental, and also a realization of the power inherent in values. The Washwoman (fig. 393) is a monumental figure. The action and mass of the figure are fundamentals to which detail can be sacrificed. Little is visible within the outlines of this dark figure silhouetted against the buildings opposite, as the mother stoops over to help her child up the steps. Here is nothing of narrative; no story is conveyed by these figures. No individualism mars Daumier's preoccu-

pation with the general. His effort is concentrated in simplified forms that transcend time and space to become types of humanity always recognizable and understandable.

In his day, Daumier was hardly known as a painter. Gustave Courbet (1819–77) took pains to reach notoriety. When in the Exposition of 1855 his works were refused, he arranged his personal exhibition opposite the Exposition grounds. He coined the term 'Realism' to describe his style. Once he shouted at a friend, who had urged him to paint from his imagination, 'If you show me an angel, I'll paint one!' In brief, Courbet's interest lay in the visible world, and he considered it his function to record it as it was. His style is not photographic; it shows a keen sense of selection of what to paint among the details of nature to give the essentials of his subject.

Sentiment and idealism find no place in him. The Burial at Ornans (fig. 394) is matter of fact, too much so for the taste of his day, which was appalled at this unvarnished statement of reality. In this painting, Courbet said what everyone knew to be true, that the priest was performing his routine duties in a routine way, that the acolytes might pay no heed to the funeral, and that the presence of friends and relatives was more socially expected than prompted by real and lasting grief. These matters were familiar, but no one liked to have the veils that society had hung around such events torn down. Mankind preferred a sentimental view; Courbet gave

394. Gustave Courbet (1819–77) *Burial at Ornans* (1849) Louvre, Paris. 10′3″ x 21′9″.

his observations bald objectivity. He neither condemned nor satirized, but painted what he saw.

In reality the Burial at Ornans is a great portrait group, its members individualized and characterized. The forms on close examination turn out to be simplified in order to bring out what Courbet believed to be essential; the incidental or accidental is suppressed despite an informality of pose. Such a procedure prevents loss of monumentality. The color creates a chord of gray, red, and violet against the gray blue of the sky. The monumental composition consists of verticals created by the group around the open grave, tied together by the long horizontals of the cliffs and horizon. For emphasis, the one break in the cliffs occurs above the center of action, where the priest performs his office, and at the only point at which the verticals carry upward in the crucifix outlined against the sky.

If Courbet could be so matter of fact in figure composition, he could have no reason to be less so in the field of landscape. Sometimes his paintings represent deep woods, for he was an out-of-doors man. Other landscapes record the shore around Ornans. The Wave (fig. 395) glances along the coast at an angle, with a dory drawn up on the beach, and a great comber about to break. The diagonal planes pursue each other with fine consistency, to build up an asymmetrical composition whose accidental appearance is belied by its underlying structure. In addition, a perception of the forces of nature gives vitality to this design. What Courbet does is to take the modest accuracy of the Barbizon painters, their delight in the intimate aspects of nature, and then to intensify those aims. He gave to them monumentality, and stormed his way into public recognition. The Barbizon school was winning its position slowly, but Courbet's temperament was forceful and impatient.

395. Gustave Courbet (1819–77) *The Wave* (1870) Louvre, Paris. 3'10" x 5'3".

Courbet's influence on Edouard Manet (1832–83) is profound. Especially at the beginning of the latter's career, his studies of form in light and shade show the same absorption in reality. Manet went to Spain in 1865, but even before this he had come into contact with a group of Spanish dancers, some of whom posed for him. Moreover, he was enthusiastic about Goya and even more so about Velásquez. The 'men of 1870,' as they were called, admired the Spaniards and also Frans Hals because they found in them the qualities toward which they were themselves working. To say that the course of French painting was changed by the new familiarity with Velásquez is incorrect; that is the result, not the cause. From this interest in visual reality, it was an inevitable next step to Impressionism, which became more pronounced in Manet's later work.

The term Impressionism was coined by a journalist to deride the unconventional work of a group of younger artists. The manner of painting this described has several related characteristics. It is important to observe that these qualities occur in varying degrees in different artists, and that not all need be found in the painting of any one man for him to belong in this group. Many of them are landscape painters, but the techniques and approach can be applied to other fields as well. Beauty exists for these painters not in any particular subject, but in light as perceived by the beholder. The subject in terms of form, space, and content ceases to be important; a railroad station, coal barges, or the boulevards of Paris may be as worthy of the artist's attention as a noble panorama or a bucolic scene. Furthermore, older renderings of landscape, even those of Constable, do not pretend to paint the equivalent of sunlight. Their canvases tend to be dark when hung on a light wall. The Impressionists, for the first time, take their easels out-of-doors. Other men had sketched from nature, but the finished paintings had always been studio products; now the artists complete their works before the scene itself. This in turn stimulates a close observation of light and atmosphere. These aspects of nature are anything but constant; they change every hour. Therefore, if the artist is to catch these fleeting impressions, some method of quick notation has to be adopted, a sort of shorthand brush stroke that will transcribe light and atmosphere quickly and accurately. Finally, the range of color in nature prompts experiments in the application of pigments, called broken color.

Most of these characteristics result from the Impressionist desire to deal objectively with the facts of vision. Consequently, Impressionism has been defined as the cult of the eye. Much was said of the innocent eye, that is, of vision as nearly as possible divorced from memory. We have become accustomed by experience since our cradle days to translate what we see into what we

know. A ball with some shadow on it we say looks spherical to us. What we mean is that we know it to be spherical, though we see it as a circle with a pattern of light and shade upon it. What the Impressionists try to do is to record what they see, where other painters alter the visual appearance by what they know about the objects. Their unbiased observation of fact parallels the impersonal objectivity of the scientist.

Moreover, they represent in their paintings just as much as the eye can take in at a glance and no more. If we look at a painting by David, the artist expects us to let our eyes wander over the canvas, to examine each part of a figure separately; we may see the painting as a whole, but we may also inspect its details, and to do this the focus of our vision must change. When we look at a figure, while our gaze is focused on the head, we are conscious of the costume and of certain details, but we do not perceive those details sharply until we turn our eyes from the head to them. The Impressionist summarizes the scene for us with shorthand brush strokes and a broad indication of detail. When Velásquez painted Las Meninas (fig. 294), he suggested the flowers in the hair of his lady-in-waiting, and expected the observer to be satisfied with their general appearance in form and color but did not ask him to examine them. Seen at close range, those flowers are blurs of pigment. Were this point of view carried to its conclusion, one should expect a center of interest where the detail is sharp, surrounded by less precise zones, but in an Impressionist canvas the painting is considered as a whole, and the whole may therefore be painted with equal breadth. Taking all these factors into consideration, Impressionism may be described as optical realism carried to its logical conclusion.

Only one of these matters is clear in Manet's Olympia (fig. 396), namely the respect for appearance under specific conditions of light. This painting represents a nude woman lying on a couch, her black cat at its foot, and her Negro servant behind, flowers in hand. The diffused light of the interior falls evenly on the forms, and visually flattens them out. Slight shadows under the breast and along the edges of the figure hardly change it from a two-dimensional image to a three-dimensional form. Manet observes that under these conditions of light, the solid form appears to be almost flat, and paints it that way. Through the influence of Courbet, Velásquez, and Hals, he became engrossed in the possibilities of the brush and pigments. His flowing brush delights in the warm white tones of the flesh, the ivory of the scarf beneath the figure, and the bluish white of the linen sheet. The textures of each part are suggested for their general appearance, not to render each thread in the material. Such clear, fresh, and direct painting outraged the Academy, partly because it was so close to a sketch.

Ostensibly, this masterpiece dealt with a theme common in the Salons, the nude female figure. Manet was surprised and a little hurt that so few peo-

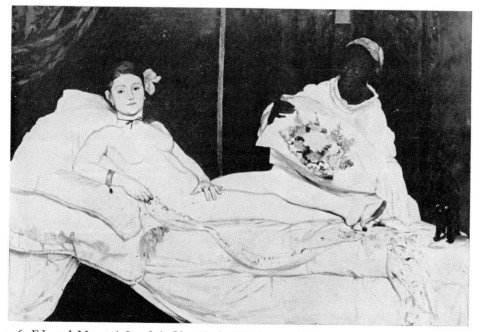

396. Edouard Manet (1832–83) *Olympia* (1863) Louvre, Paris. 4'3" x 6'3".

397. Edouard Manet (1832–83) *Bar of the Folies Bergère* (1882) Courtauld Collection, London. 3′1″ x 4′3″.

ple appreciated the brilliance of the painting. The conservative strictures were perhaps prompted by jealousy. However, the similarity to the academic nude is more superficial than real. In spirit, Olympia contrasts at every point with the vacuity of official art. Where their figures are soft and idealized, Manet's is hard and realistic; his study of flesh is firm, while theirs look like skins stuffed with cotton. Where the academic nude is no one in particular, Manet's figure is individualized and recognizable, a portrait of a well-known model. While the academic nude is surrounded by objects or by a setting purporting to give the

figure some ideal explanation such as Truth or Spring or September Morn, Olympia's household connotes her profession as an artist's model—the servant with a bouquet from some admirer, or the black cat associated with the sinister in womanhood. But the cat creates a series of short verticals necessary to stop the compositional movement of the figure from escaping at the right. There is no comparison in strength between the Manet and the academic nudes; the former has an assurance and a visual integrity which they lack.

Twenty years later, in the Bar of the Folies Bergère (fig. 397), Manet carries further his concern with the summary indication of form. The bottles on the bar are swept in with bold strokes of the brush; Manet deals only with essentials. One might suppose that such optical realism would approach the photographic. Actually, the selectivity of this technique, its very indication rather than definition of detail, leaves a gulf between this and what we understand as the photographic. However much Manet may dwell upon the facts of vision, he does not forget for one moment that he is painting a picture, and is willing to sacrifice even the visually possible to better his design. Behind the barmaid, a mirror reflects a throng in the distance, and near at hand the barmaid and her customer of the moment. But no possible arrangement of the mirror could produce these reflections seen from a position in front of the girl. Manet arbitrarily moves his reflections to one side for pictorial interest.

The subjects of Impressionism may be unimportant in themselves, but collectively they suggest the influence of the upper middle class in Paris. Manet himself was well-to-do, and, to judge by his paintings, one would say that urban entertainment and a holiday spirit had affected his selection of material. That point of view was common to the Impressionists. They sought in the country what delighted a city dweller on vacation, a stream on whose banks one might while away an afternoon, a boating party, yachting, or fields that promised repose. In the city, the theater, the boulevard, the dance hall, and the race-course, the favorite entertainments of the upper middle class, recurred in the paintings of these men.

In his later years, Manet was influenced by Claude Monet (1840–1926). Though he painted figures at times, Monet's primary concern was landscape. The scientific research of the nineteenth century here impinged upon problems of painting. Such physicists as Chevreul and Helmholtz and Professor Rood of Columbia University were experimenting at this time with the natural laws of color. They observed that disks, painted alternately in red and yellow, when revolved appeared to be orange. The original colors reflected to the eye in rapid succession could no longer be distinguished, but instead the two colors were added together to produce a third quite different tone. A painter cannot use a series of moving disks; but he can obtain a similar result from small touches of different colors placed side by side on the canvas, since, from a short distance, the eye fails to perceive the individual colors and blends them for itself. There is reason to believe that such artists as Claude Monet discovered the technique of broken color independently of the investigations of the physicists. Broken color permits more vibrancy of tone and a greater freshness than can be obtained by a mechanical mixture of the same pigments upon the palette. However, this technique entails some sacrifice. The beauties of brushwork must be abandoned, and the surface becomes rough in appearance. Thick strokes of pigment may project so far

398. Auguste Renoir (1841–1919) *Moulin de la Galette* (1876) Louvre, Paris. 4′4″ x 5′10″.

from the surface as to cast their own shadows on the painting, and thus make it necessary to regulate the direction of light relative to the canvas.

Coupled with this new technique, which is partly anticipated in the work of Constable and Delacroix, is a more or less scientific approach toward the phenomena of light and atmosphere. Where Turner had painted atmosphere from the emotional Romantic point of view, Monet was absorbed in rendering the subtlest changes in weather conditions with scientific realism. To that end, he took to the site half a dozen or more canvases. Then he begins to paint Etretat (Plate x, facing p. 557), or more exactly the light, color, and atmosphere within which the sea and rocks are seen. The subject remains important to the artist only in so far as it provides a background for his main purpose. As those conditions of light change, Monet changes his canvas, painting many versions of the same scene, each with all his remarkable accuracy of observation. A contemporary painter said that Monet was only an eye, and added, but what an eye! Degas, on looking at an exhibition of Monet's paintings, turned up his coat collar in mute tribute to the artist's success in rendering the weather.

And yet for all their accuracy, Monet's landscapes are full of lyrical beauty. A profound love of nature permeates his work and transcends its scientific aspect.

The composition is so informal as to seem accidental; coupled with the brushwork, it gives these canvases the casual quality of sketches. His color scheme becomes lighter in tonality than that of any previous school. In many museums, the visitor may look from a room where older paintings are exhibited into one devoted to the Impressionists and mark this contrast, that where the older landscapes make dark spots against the light background of the wall, Impressionist paintings bring light into their surroundings. Though not necessarily brilliant in color, their effect is that of cheerfulness.

Not many Impressionists carry their study of light as far as does Monet. Pierre Auguste Renoir (1841–1919) paints landscapes in broken color, but he seems less absorbed in the problems of atmosphere and light. His primary concern is with the figure, more specifically with Parisian womanhood, the forms well rounded and feminine. The Moulin de la Gallette (fig. 398), a gay scene in an open-air dance hall, shows a moderate use of broken color for its own sake. The Impressionist study of light is prominent as sunlight filters through leafy trees and flecks the blue dresses of the ladies, or their features. These very French men and women tend to be flattened out by scattered and diffused light as it sifts through the foliage.

As Renoir developed, he studied light less and buxom form more zealously, as in the Seated Bather (fig. 399), one of his many versions of that subject. To the end of his long life, Renoir preserved the broken color of the Impressionists but used that technique for its brilliance of tone, in touches of vivid reds, yellows, violets, and blues. Instead of a two-dimensional image, he stressed volume more and more as time went on. Though simplified and well clothed in flesh, the structure and movement of his figures remain basic. Something of Rubens reappears, but bathed in the deep well of Renoir's imagination to emerge more delicate and unmistakably French. Though Renoir must be classed with the Impressionists, more than most of them he retains elements of the French tradition that link him in spirit to the great painters of the past, to Delacroix, to Fragonard, and to Boucher.

Nor is Edgar Hilaire Germain Degas (1834–1917) fully in accord with the new movement. The exquisite draftsmanship of Ingres, even in its linearism, lies at the basis of Degas' work. A man of independent means, Degas painted to satisfy his own taste, which disdained anything pictorially vulgar, and instead sought the unusual and the dissonant in color and composition. The tones of some of his ballet scenes, or his bathing women, startle the observer if they do not shock him. He may select a vivid arsenic green and combine it with touches of brick red and of lavender, colors that ought to clash but that in fact add zest to his paintings. These dissonant colors seemed perverse discords to his day, but now our eyes have become accustomed to such effects, as our ears have become attuned to the music of Wagner, which sounded discordant to Degas' day.

399. Auguste Renoir (1841–1919) *Seated Bather* (1914) Durand-Ruel Collection. 2'8" x 2'2".

That zest for the unusual marks both his compositions and his choice of models. In feature and in pose, he avoids the pretty and prefers the awkward. The

Ballet Dancer on the Stage (fig. 400) embodies the fleeting beauty of such entertainment too well to be typical. When one examines this composition,

400. Edgar Hilaire Germain Degas (1834–1917) *Ballet Dancer on the Stage* (*c.* 1876) Louvre, Paris. 1′11″ x 1′5″.

one realizes that the dancer is far off to the right of the picture, and yet the painting is balanced. We are at first perplexed at this, until we notice that Degas has introduced the dark blur of the ballet master in the wings, just important enough to re-establish the balance. Such a design builds up from a number of spots or areas, carefully chosen in size and shape and precisely placed in relation to each other. Almost all Western painting has relied upon leading lines or movements to carry the eye from one point to another, and to tie the forms together in compositional unity. Whether the basis of the design was geometrical as in the High Renaissance paintings of Italy, or informal as among the works of the Dutch masters, some visual connection of the parts had been established. In the art of the Far East, on the other hand, a tendency to build the design of well-chosen, perfectly adjusted accents is traditional. The Orientals recognize the positive value of open space and take advantage of it; they are content to arrange a few flowers within a rectangle, and rely on their placement to complete the design (fig. 597).

The generation of the Impressionists discovered the Japanese print as they had discovered Velásquez, because they were ready for it, and more directly because of an exhibition of Japanese prints in Paris in the 'sixties. Degas borrows none of the superficial motives of Oriental art, but his own compositions betray its influence, so absorbed as to become part of his own style. To that end,

he may omit part of an object, even what might be considered the most important part, if the remainder provides the shape he needs. The ballet master, as we have observed, produces the dark accent needed for asymmetrical balance, but his head would add nothing; therefore, Degas allows the scenery to conceal it. His painting seizes upon the unexpected, and is, consequently, refreshing to the eye.

Instead of arranging his subject in normal perspective, he prefers to see it from an abnormal point of view. At times, he seems to look down upon his subject; elsewhere, the figures act upon a stage and are rendered as though perceived from below. This selection of the unusual angle of vision admits a new range of pictorial effects, such as are exploited in modern photography. Degas has not the popular appeal that has made Renoir beloved. He would have avoided such popularity, had it seemed imminent, as unworthy of his aristocratic and esoteric nature. Our taste grows up to his paintings; we learn to expect the unexpected, and to love the spicy dissonances of his color.

Neither Renoir with his interest in form nor, still less, Degas' exquisite draftsmanship and subtle compositions fit neatly into the pattern of Impressionism. It was not long before progressive painters toward the end of the century began to contradict the very premises of Impressionism. Was the sole purpose of painting to record the fleeting aspect of the moment, an ever-changing atmosphere, or transient, if not accidental,

401. Georges Seurat (1859–91) *Sunday on the Grande Jatte* (1884–86) Art Institute, Chicago. 6'9" x 10'.

conditions of light and shade? Should not the painter attempt greater permanence? Above all, should he not concentrate on structure and form rather than on appearance? Some Post-Impressionist painters, at least, began to think so, and among them was Georges Seurat (1859–91). His painting of Sunday on the Grande Jatte (fig. 401) corresponds to Impressionism in subject matter. This Parisian resort on a sunny afternoon is visited by respectable people with their pets, and its waters are alive with pleasure craft. In technique, also, broken color persists, but with a basic change. Seurat's technique, called *pointillisme*, reduces broken color to a formula, and gives it an almost mathematical regularity as each dot, like a piece of confetti, is placed in position, and graded in intensity to create space organization in depth. Monet's method had none of this calculated quality, but Seurat carries the technique even into his picture frames.

Still more significant is the insistence on form, so highly simplified as to approach abstraction. All accidentals of shape and costume are swept into the discard. In their place is an austere preoccupation with simplified outline and with the geometrical mass it contains. These forms are not chosen as a setting for light and shade; in so far as the latter play a part at all, it is to mold those forms into solids and to establish successive planes in space. Movement is abandoned in favor of nearly static shapes, like the monumental figures of Piero della Francesca (fig. 210), as though permanence and solidity were of the greatest artistic value. Their function as forms is dual: to state the essential and timeless elements in the objects themselves, conceived with sculpturesque simplicity, and to assist in constructing the picture. The apparently accidental arrangements of the Impressionists give way to a design wherein each shape is calculated with regard to every other shape in size, in location within the frame, and in color. The design is as carefully constructed as a Poussin, and as formal.

In spite of Seurat's premature death, his work formed one of the pillars of modern art. Another was Paul Gauguin (1848–1903), who turned to painting comparatively late in life after some success as a banker in Paris. This son of a French father and a Peruvian mother rebelled against the mores of his day, both in life and in painting. Though influenced by the heightened color of the Impressionists, his instinct sought those primitive cultures as yet but little affected by contact with Western sophistication. In Brittany, the childlike faith of the peasant women prompted such a composition as the Yellow Christ, where the form of the Crucified is as distorted as the twelfth- and thirteenth-century crucifixes of the early Italian painters. Gauguin makes no attempt to render Christ realistically; his version in line and areas of flat color,

like stained glass, may be called expressionistic or symbolic. The white-linen headdresses of the women provide an arabesque of flat shapes, each outline filled with a single tone.

But Brittany proved to be only a stepping stone in Gauguin's return to the primitive. A trip to Martinique in the West Indies confirmed his bent, and led to longer sojourns in Polynesia. His escape from civilization becomes complete in Manao Tupapau (fig. 402). In subject matter he rebels against Impressionism, to exploit the exotic because of its strangeness and mystery. Realism ceases to be an end. In place of plastic solids, Gauguin returns to a two-dimensional scheme. Each shape and area is outlined and painted with a flat tone of strong color, without modeling. For expression or for decorative effect, Gauguin is willing to distort the proportions of his figures, to modify perspective, or to sacrifice representation for local color. His sonorous tones have often been likened to medieval stained glass; a better analogy would be late-medieval tapestry. Intense as his tones are, their prevailing value is not high; their richness is increased by their depth. Through his personal arrangement of these shapes, as in Mahana No Atua (Plate xi, facing p. 588), Gauguin achieves the fullest decorative expression.

One debatable question concerning Gauguin arises in regard to the extent and honesty of his return to the primitive as an escape from the oversophistication of modern life. The linearism of native arts and their lack of perspective

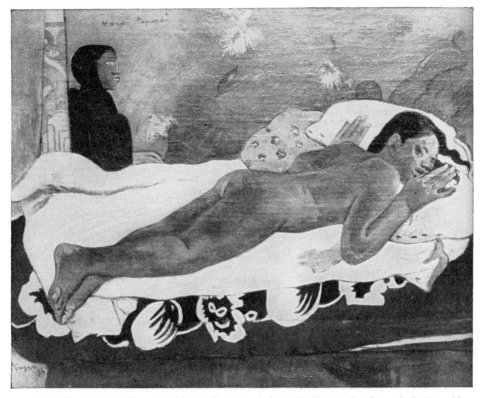

402. Paul Gauguin (1848–1903) *Manao Tupapau* (1892) A. Conger Goodyear Collection, New York. 2′4″ x 3′.

are due partly to their indifference to realism, and partly to their identification of forms and shapes with religious purposes. For a Parisian of the 'nineties, is there not an element of affectation in Gauguin's return to the primitive? Is not Gauguin deliberately sensational? In his life the answer must be in the affirmative. He craved adulation and would sacrifice anything, do anything, to become the lion of the hour. Nevertheless, so far as his painting goes, the affectation is less apparent, if it exists at all. Gauguin accepts from the primitive whatever suits his pictorial purpose,

but he cannot be said to imitate primitive art. For all their unreality, his are not the forms of Polynesian art. Even the subjects are often Occidental, and merely expressed in terms of native models. In spite of the apparent simplification, Gauguin's paintings betray a sophisticated amalgam of the decorative and non-representational attitude of semi-civilized peoples with the spirit of the Paris of his own day.

The inspired zealot, Vincent van Gogh (1853–90), threw himself with uncontrolled energy into every field that caught his attention. Like Gauguin,

Van Gogh did not at once begin to paint. As a clerk in the shop of an art dealer, Goupil, he proved unsatisfactory because of his attempts to force his tastes upon prospective purchasers. He turned thence to religion, and served with missionary zeal, first in the degrading slums of Whitechapel in London,

403. Vincent van Gogh (1853–90) *La Berceuse* (1889) Art Institute, Chicago. 3′ x 2′4″.

and then among the miners of Le Borinage in Belgium. It was typical of Van Gogh that he should feel it necessary to live under worse conditions than those to whom he would minister. When in the last five years of his life he turned his full attention to painting, he threw himself into that pursuit with the same unnatural energy; he painted furiously, as though he had to get these records on canvas before death or insanity interfered.

At one time, he came into contact with Gauguin, who claimed to have influenced him. The method of line and flat tone that Gauguin uses is approximated in La Berceuse (fig. 403), though there is more feeling for mass than in most Gauguins. The color is somewhat lighter in value, and much more intense. Above all, Van Gogh, creates a fiery and passionate portrait, expressive of the subject filtered through the screen of his own personality. He is not concerned with abstract beauty, but with emphasizing what, to him, is significant about his subject. The primary importance of woman is her role as mother of the race; hence, the deliberate enlargement of the breasts and hips. The neck offers few possibilities of expression, and therefore Van Gogh allows the large head to rest directly on the shoulders, with a heavy and rather coarse indication of the features. The eyes and mouth are magnified as centers of expression, but other parts of the face are comparatively neglected.

Van Gogh does not always paint in such an arabesque of tones, however

vivid they may be. His incandescent energy activates his Landscape at Auvers (fig. 404) to such an extent that even inanimate objects acquire vitality. The pigment was slapped on and around these things in streaks, perhaps applied with a brush, but often smeared on with a palette knife, and, to judge from the intensity of color, he used paints as they came from their tubes with no mixing of tones on his palette. The landscape itself has become emotionally excited; the trees flicker in green flames, the ground undulates, and the sky and sun are tormented in swirls of line and color. No normal mind could have imagined such an ensemble, but neither could such a mind have achieved the visual excitement or the frenzied brilliance of his paintings.

If Gauguin's foremost quality is decorative, and Van Gogh's expressive, Paul Cézanne's is structural. At the outset, Cézanne (1839–1906), who was older than the other two but developed slowly to his maturity, exhibited with the Impressionists, though he had none of the fluency, the virtuosity of brushwork, that Manet commanded. In fact, Manet described Cézanne's early work as 'foul painting.' At that time, he loaded his pigment on the canvas in patches. But Cézanne, though he admitted the value of some of the Impressionist contributions, such as their feeling for color, rejected the transient nature of their conceptions. His goal, unappreciated in his lifetime, was to combine their ideas with the firm picture construction he

404. Vincent van Gogh (1853–90) *Landscape at Auvers* (1890) Museum, Munich. 3′ x 2′4″.

noticed in the 'old masters' in the museums.

A Still Life (Plate XII, facing p. 589)

offers the opportunity for prolonged analysis. Cézanne, like Chardin, constructs the composition in an architectonic vein. The front of the table parallels the picture plane, the drawer of the table is pulled out to repeat that plane, the objects on the table recall it again, and in the background a chest of drawers finally stops the series. Horizontal planes separate these vertical planes one from another and create the necessary recession. Such a system requires the implied permanence of geometric forms. The apples are in essence spheres; to insist upon that shape, several concentric strokes of the brush may repeat its circular silhouette. Conservatives accuse Cézanne of bad drawing, and point to the top of the vase in proof. That aperture is, of course, a circle, and everyone knows that a circle seen in perspective is an ellipse. But Cézanne does not draw it so; he squares the circle. The oval shape in itself lacks the architectonic character of the rest of his design. Therefore, Cézanne modifies that ellipse, flattens its upper and lower edges, and even straightens out its sides until it becomes a rectangle with rounded corners. It is absurd to suppose that this can be owing to inability; the veriest tyro can sketch a better oval than Cézanne has painted. We must conclude, then, that the artist has done this deliberately, for the sake of his composition. Whether the result justifies that modification may be another question; whether the composition is improved by it can, dialectically at least, be challenged. To most people of his day, the shock was too great to be condoned on these or any other grounds; to most people today, no doubt remains that Cézanne was right to make such modifications.

Mere visual appearance seemed to Cézanne negligible. However pretty may be the texture of an apple, or the temporary play of light and shade over it, such matters are insignificant in comparison with the fundamental nature of the fruit and its pictorial possibilities. Apples in general approach a spherical shape, though in any individual apple accidents may have injured the perfection of the form. Cézanne disregarded these accidents; he sought its permanent and universal aspects. The creation of solid form on a two-dimensional surface of panel or canvas had been a common aim of Western art from the time of Giotto. But Cézanne wanted to encompass this form, not so much by modeling in light and shade as by means of color. He realized that some colors seem to cause surfaces to project, others by comparison to recede; through this visual phenomenon, he could model his forms solidly by color and establish successive planes by tone. In this attempt, Cézanne surveyed a new path. He has often been compared to Giotto, and in this respect with justice; Cézanne is a 'primitive' in the sense that he has a conception, an aim, a *petite sensation* as he himself says, to which the road has not yet been explored. That Cézanne sometimes failed to reach his goal is to be expected. He fumbled his way forward, and often sacrificed to his main purpose other matters of less consequence to him; but in the best of his still lifes, Cézanne succeeded, as Giotto

405. Paul Cézanne (1839–1906) *Mt. Ste. Victoire* (1885–87) Phillips Memorial Gallery, Washington. 2′ x 2′5″.

had succeeded in the Arena Chapel in Padua.

This concentration on structure and modeling in pure color lies at the basis of Cézanne's painting and of his importance in the history of art. The same approach dominates his landscape painting. Mt. Ste. Victoire (fig. 405) is typical. The landscape is analyzed into planes, each with its appointed role in the picture. At first, the observer is inclined to feel that these landscapes cannot have much contact with reality. But photographs have been made of the sites in and around Aix en Provence found in Cézanne's paintings. These are more detailed than his canvases, but the important point is that every form in these landscapes existed in the scene before him. His method is the same as in his still lifes; he analyzes the scene before him with the utmost care to extract from it those elements susceptible to pictorial and architectonic composition, and omits the rest. The branch of the pine in the foreground, which repeats the profile of the mountain and the horizon, is a case in point. We have every reason to believe that such a parallelism existed, and that Cézanne seized upon it to help unify the design by tying together the foreground and the background. As in his still lifes, Cézanne prefers the general to the particular; he emphasizes the cylindrical mass of the tree trunk and the characteristic silhouette of the mountain as essentials of the objects before him.

If Cézanne applies these principles in still life and landscape, it would be strange for him to depart from them in figure composition. His problem in dealing with figures is complicated by their animate nature. An apple will pose motionless, and will remain so for any length of time, until he is satisfied with his painting. So will a landscape. But human beings cannot be static indefinitely. Even a quietly posed model must be permitted to relax and can seldom return to the identical position. If this complicates the artist's problem, the distortion of the figure is even more difficult for the public to accept than a corresponding departure from appearance in landscape or still life. This distortion in Cézanne sometimes results from selection and simplification, in

406. Paul Cézanne (1839–1906) *Bathers* (1898–1905) Museum of Art, Philadelphia. 6'9" x 8'1".

which case, however unnatural in appearance, it is not strictly distortion; but elsewhere he alters the size and proportions of the parts of the human body. An extreme example of this is the Bathers (fig. 406). One of Cézanne's ideals was 'to do a Poussin before nature,' that is, to regain the pictorial structure of the old master and combine it with the color of the Impressionists. The composition here is geometric. The trees tip inward to establish an equilateral triangle with the group. Its sides are repeated in the forms of the nude women. Anatomical accuracy is insignificant in comparison to the requirements of the pictorial scheme. Moreover, these figures begin to be analyzed into geometric forms, just as in landscape the tree trunk becomes cylindrical, or in still life the apple becomes spherical. But the geometry of the human figure is complex, and to reduce the head or the breast to spheres, the arm or the thigh to cylinders, violates the usual notions of the figure.

The charge of distortion, leveled against Cézanne as though it were a crime against art, is absurd. Art always involves distortion; the range of color in pigments does not equal that in nature; forms are three dimensional and the painter must translate them on a flat surface, and present them in some pictorial medium. Even more important, the artist is not a divinity who can create nature, or even a human being who copies nature. He is first and foremost creating a picture, and, in spite of the old cliché, nature does not pre-sent perfect pictures. All artists have distorted to a greater or lesser degree, even the most naturalistic of them. Thus, such a charge leveled at Cézanne means nothing.

However, the debatable question arises as to how far the artist ought to contradict appearances. Dialectically speaking, the artist may depart just as far as he sees fit in order to increase his compositional unity, his decorative result, or his expressive power. If this be true, we may then ask whether the result in one or more of these directions justifies the means in any particular case. Of course it does, if improvement is effected thereby. In El Greco's case, or in that of many non-realistic painters, such as Duccio, the expression and the decorative brilliance is undoubtedly enhanced by their unreality. On the other hand, many of the greatest painters, such as Titian, Michelangelo, Rembrandt, and Rubens, distort only to a minor extent. Have their works less compositional integrity, less expression, or less decorative value than those of more recent artists, who carry distortion to such a point that it calls attention to itself? Have not the 'old masters' reached as fine pictorial qualities as the moderns? Indeed, have they not outstripped the moderns in these very respects by so restricting their departure from appearances that those departures, by not calling attention to themselves, leave the observer free to enjoy more important pictorial matters? To these questions no categorical answer can be given. Conservatives will reply in one way; en-

407. William Adolphe Bouguereau (1825–1905) *Birth of Venus* (1879) Luxembourg, Paris. 9′10″ x 7′1″.

thusiastic modernists in another. Probably no sweeping answer will ever be satisfactory. Each painting must be considered on its own merits.

If the choice were confined to Cézanne and to the contemporary academicians, there could be only one intelligent selection. Although Cézanne longed to be recognized by the Academy, he could not but feel contempt for its leaders. His paintings protest against the non-intellectual and non-structural approach of the Impressionists, and the vacuities of academicians such as Bouguereau. Just how static academic painting had become during the nineteenth century, and how much ground it had lost to progressive art is obvious if we compare characteristic canvases of Cézanne and Bouguereau. The latter's Birth of Venus (fig. 407) typifies what has been called the bar-room nude, the ideal of high art held by a stockbroker of the black-walnut generation. These slick, soft, and spineless figures are well drawn from the academic point of view. The linearism of Ingres persists with faint eclectic traces of Botticelli and Raphael. By its lights, the painting is competent—but its lights are a little dim. A less critical and less pictorially conscious generation, with some literary but little artistic background, accepted it because of its superficiality, its prettiness, and its high finish. The more powerful paintings of Cézanne have none of these qualities. The difference is that Cézanne's paintings are loaded with pictorial consequence, whereas Bouguereau's have nothing to say. They are pretty enough, but they are artistically dumb.

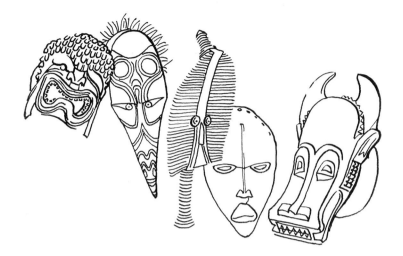

XXV   THE ART OF PRIMITIVE PEOPLES

The primitive peoples of tropical Africa and the islands of the South Seas developed an extensive art based on aesthetic principles unlike those of the high civilizations of the Western and Eastern worlds. This art should not, therefore, be considered comparatively with those of the high civilizations, but must be evaluated independently to be understood and must be placed within its own cultural setting.

There were evolved over countless centuries in these two vast areas many small, mostly tribal societies on a non-scientific, non-mechanical basis. Each tribal society was unique in the specific character of its institutions, although these were often basically similar. A compact, sometimes complex organization knit closely together the major facets of life, religious, social, political, and economic, but the degree of complexity and the facets stressed varied from place to place. Authority, vested in an elder, chief, priest, or selected council, a role sometimes hereditarily determined, controlled the temporal and spiritual aspects of life and maintained the traditional institutions, customs, and beliefs.

Life was largely sustained by the farming of community gardens, supplemented in many areas by fishing and hunting; while the domestication of food animals, usually the pig and chicken, was widespread. Ceremonies, ritual, and taboos were enacted frequently to ensure food sufficient to meet the demands of the population of a village or area, a concern often uppermost in the thoughts of these people. Cause and effect were, as a rule, unrelated on a scientific or pragmatic level and various practices were devised to explain the cause of such happenings as death. Similarly, the unknown forces of the physical and spiritual worlds were considered the concern of particular deities or spirits to whom rituals were addressed for their control.

Typical of primitive peoples were the creation of carved, painted, and fabricated art objects, such as masks and figures to be used in the religious and secular ceremonies relative to so many phases of human activity. The art forms, made by highly trained professional artists, were of traditionally prescribed designs, each with its own meaning when used in the appropriate ceremonials. To appreciate primitive art fully it is therefore necessary to know why certain forms were required for certain ceremonies. It is possible to evaluate this art, as all art, for its aesthetic character alone; but that is always only the empty shell, and to fill it in one must understand the motivation behind the forms and their content or meaning.

Many areas of primitive Africa and the South Sea Islands were not known until the age of Empire building in the nineteenth century. Initial contacts with both areas, however, began as early as the fifteenth and sixteenth centuries, and a greater knowledge was acquired during the era of exploration in the eighteenth century, when some valuable descriptions of objects and ceremonies were recorded, but few examples were brought back to substantiate these accounts. At the great World Fairs in the latter part of the nineteenth century the 'exotic' products, peoples, and 'arti-facts' from the far reaches of Empire were romantically exhibited in special pavilions. Frequently included in these exhibitions were art objects collected by explorers, missionaries, traders, and government officials, that often reveal a knowledge of the aesthetic qualities of this primitive art. These were later, toward the end of the nineteenth century, to serve as nuclei for the founding of great ethnographical museums.

The current widespread interest in this art had its beginnings in 1904–5 when young painters in Paris and Munich 'discovered' its aesthetic merits. Historically, the 'discovery' could only have been made at a time when young artists had renounced the academic or Classical-Renaissance scientific rendering of reality, a dominant Western tradition that had become stifling to artistic creativity. They recognized in Primitive art, at first particularly in Negro African sculpture, a vigorous expressive statement based on a sensitive perception of natural forms that was not a copy of nature. This form statement, rendered in purely creative sculptural terms, did not depend upon an ideal or accurate mensuration of proportions and shapes but, rather, upon a rhythmical structural interpretation of the expressive, functional interrelationships of human shapes. At the time, the painters knew little or nothing of the content or meaning of this art, nor of the setting within which it developed; but they readily and enthusiastically accepted it as a further substantiation of the aims and experiments of their own painting. African Negro sculpture was, therefore, a sustaining and contributing factor in the development of modern art.

The art-producing cultures of Negro Africa evolved during many centuries in a belt extending across West Africa south of the Sahara Desert, and across Central Africa from the Atlantic Ocean on the west to the Great Lakes on the east, and from the Egyptian Sudan in the north into Angola and the Rhodesias in the south. It was the heart of 'Darkest Africa,' an area vast in extent and almost entirely within the tropics. Here innumerable large and small Negro tribal groups established an economy based on the small-garden variety of agriculture, supplemented by some fishing and hunting. Although their cultures were varied, many elements were shared in common; and it is essential to know these elements in order to understand the art within its cultural context.

The family, the basic and smallest unit of African life, served as the model for all of the larger and more comprehensive groupings. It was structured as a pyramid, with the head of the family at the apex, his wives and children at a lower level, and the retainers or slaves serving as the base. As head of the family, a man was in absolute control of the religious, social, and economic aspects of family life. Revered ancestors and spirits or deities were worshiped within the privacy of the group, and to consummate these rites figures and other ritual carvings were often required from the sculptor. Social stability, the maintenance of traditional customs, and economic balance were all in the hands of the head of a family.

Village, tribal, and inter-tribal organizations were comparable to those of the family, with the head-man, the chief, and the king respectively functioning in the precise role of the head of a family. A considerable number of sculptures were therefore required for ritual and social purposes by all of these larger groups.

The sculptor throughout a long apprenticeship was carefully instructed in the traditionally established form patterns of his village or group, forms he could not substantially modify without incurring the unmitigated criticism or even wrath of the leader of his village or tribe. But this adherence to tradition did not impose an insuperable restriction on the artist; rather, it freed him from the necessity to invent and made it possible for him, if a perceptive and sensitive artist, to give to the traditional forms an expressive and structural interpretation that was truly creative. It is for this reason that in African Negro art, as in all art, there are genuine masterpieces, and mediocre and poor works.

Specific religious, philosophical, and social concepts served as the motivation for the greater part of this art. The belief that ancestors when ritually appealed to would intercede in behalf of their descendants was universal, and figures and masks were carved as residing places or as temporary abodes for the ancestor spirit so that it could be petitioned directly. Ancestor sculptures were generic not individualized representations; thus they largely functioned symbolically. In some areas of Negro Africa, where a pantheon of gods had control of all human activities, figures or masks sometimes denoted the deities, since it was believed that when properly requested, their spirits would enter the carvings and could thus be conveniently and satisfactorily evoked. Thus, these sculptures, too, were largely symbolic spirit containers, although in some instances iconographic details identified the god.

Throughout the greater part of Africa the secret society existed as an important and often dominant institution. The secret society may be defined as a group of men and sometimes of women who banded together to perform prescribed ceremonies more or less in secret for the purpose of achieving a desired end. The society might have religious, social, economic, or political significance; but in many areas it existed largely for the purpose of initiating adolescent youth into the traditional beliefs and customs of the tribe preparatory to acceptance as adults within the group. Secret society rites, it was believed, were celebrated under the aegis of ancestor, mythological, or deity spirits, and since their presence was essential to the performance of the ceremonies, they were usually represented or symbolized by figures or masks. These societies were therefore important patrons of the artist.

In certain regions of Africa a fundamental and basically religious concept postulates the active presence of an ambient force or power in all animate and inanimate objects. It is substantially a life essence, and is both actively and potentially dynamic. This power permeates all matter and may be construed as serving as liaison between the supernatural or spirit and the natural worlds. Some of it can, by formulas and prescribed and secret procedures, be localized in various objects, including carvings, and when certain rituals are performed can be marshaled in the cause of mankind. Sculptured figures and masks, both sometimes called 'fetishes,' amulets, and charms, are tangible agencies through which this power or force is manifested and manipulated. When evoked properly, it is believed that the power in these sculptures will cure the ill and protect against both known and unknown dangers. To a large extent this category of beliefs embraces all of those loosely designated as magical.

Ceremonial objects, needed in practically all rituals, were usually given artistic treatment; while articles of everyday utility, such as drinking cups and stools, were often enriched with decorative carvings that served no other purpose.

Sculpture is the principal art of Negro Africa. Whether figures, masks, ceremonial or utilitarian objects, the sculptures were usually carved in wood, occasionally in ivory, or cast in bronze or brass, and at times were decorated with paint, shells, beads, or fibre. This sculpture, often small, sometimes sizable, conveyed ideas and a significance of forms and designs that were largely understood by the people of a village or tribe as a whole. The art was therefore to a remarkable degree a familiar adjunct to life.

While a considerable number of styles can be characterized in this art, the basic forms are in every instance derived from nature, whether human, as is usually the case, or animal beings. Each tribe and often each village had by virtue of its cultural heritage its own style, although neighboring tribes may show in their art a shared tradition. On the basis of broad stylistic similarities, it is possible to characterize five major divisions or areas of African art: the Sudan, the Guinea Coast, Nigeria, and the Cameroons, all in West Africa; and Central Africa to the south.

The Sudan peoples, living between the Sahara and the tropical rain-forest to the south, created a sculpture marked by a formalistic, almost mathematical character, in which human and animal subjects were given an abstract and at times geometrical interpretation (fig. 408). Emphasis is upon a Gothic-like verticality and hieratic expressiveness. Both human figures and animal masks are used in Sudan religious rites associated with ancestor-protective or animal-fertility concepts. Black is in many examples the only color found in this strongly sculptural art.

The Guinea Coast, extending around the southern part of West Africa, supported numerous tribes and tribal groups. The art here is strongly interpretive of natural forms, but an element of abstraction in certain shapes suggests influence from the Sudan. The

408. *Figure,* Dogon, West Africa (19th cent.) The University Museum, University of Pennsylvania, Philadelphia. Wood, 23″ high.

ticulated; while identifying details, such as hairdresses and scarification marks, are emphasized to denote specific ancestors or deities. Among the Ashanti peoples of the Gold Coast (Ghana), small cast bronze forms used for weighing gold dust were modeled in an impressionistic manner, the subject matter often being of a purely genre origin.

In Nigeria, particularly among the Yoruba tribes, forms, often moderately

409. *Figure*, Baoulé, West Africa (19th cent.) Royal Scottish Museum, Edinburgh. Wood, 18½" high.

Baoulé tribes of the Ivory Coast carved masks and figures with a balanced and controlled reality in the creative handling of human form, achieving a style characterized by the elegant and precise rendering of surface planes and details (fig. 409). In this style component shapes are sculpturally defined and ar-

410. *Figure*, Yoruba, West Africa (19th cent.) British Museum, London. Wood, 14½" high.

small but of monumental scale, are sculptured in a vigorous naturalistic style (fig. 410), stressing volume and roundness of shapes; and although subject matter and detail interpret life prototypes, they are conveyed within the non-representational sculptural idiom traditional to the area. A heaviness of form, with a profusion of descriptive detail, characterizes the famous Benin bronzes; while the wood carvings of the Ibo and Ibibio tribes in southeastern

412. *Mask*, Cameroons, West Africa (19th cent.) Linden Museum, Stuttgart. Wood, 20" high.

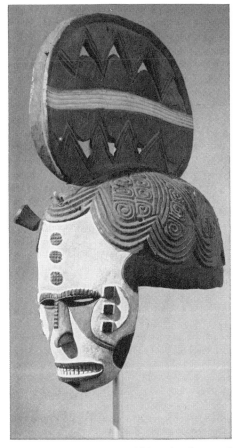

411. *Mask*, Ibo, West Africa (19th cent.) Museum of Primitive Art, New York. Wood, 17¾" high.

Nigeria (fig. 411) evidence a considerable variety of designs, notable for their intense dramatic expressiveness.

The art of the Cameroons combines the naturalistic vigor of Yoruba sculpture with the dramatic intensity of that of southeast Nigeria (figs. 412, 413). Forms, composed of expanding volumes, are often rhythmically arranged around a vertical axis to describe a dancing or moving figure. On numerous examples the sculptor's tool marks remain to give the surfaces a rough, textural finish and to contribute to the vitality in the realization of form.

Many strong and unique tribal styles developed in the extensive area of Central Africa; but certain elements may be singled out as distinctive of the sculp-

413. *Mask*, Cameroons, West Africa (19th cent.) Linden Museum, Stuttgart. Wood, *c.* 22″ high.

The varied traditional style patterns in African sculpture were maintained by a strong conservatism common to all aspects of tribal culture. On the basis of our present knowledge, it is impossible to determine why in certain areas shapes were compressed to emphasize the verticality of the human form, and why in other regions they were expanded to express the bulk and volume of various shapes; or why in some styles an angularity of outline is stressed, and in others

ture of the entire region. With the exception of the abstract brass and copper covered figures of the Bakota peoples in Gabun (fig. 414), the conspicuous expressive elements in this art are derived from a bold stylization of selective human shapes and descriptive details (fig. 415). While this often appears in the rendering of the enlarged head and facial features, it is also frequently found in the pose, proportions, and inter-relationships of body forms (fig. 416). In many of these styles, figures and especially polychromed masks are given a dramatic and sometimes fantastic appearance (Plate XIII, facing p. 620), which, although it may permeate the work as a whole, is often concentrated in the head or in certain of the facial features.

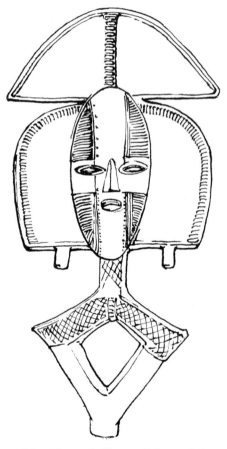

414. *Metal-Covered Figure*, Bakota, Gabun, Central Africa (19th cent.) *c.* 22″ high.

a fluidity of curving lines and surfaces. The so-called 'distortions' in African art are established by local traditional style patterns; but to view them as distortions is to deny the fundamental Negro concept of art: for the African sculptor the proportioning and shaping of figures and masks do not follow mathematically or

416. *Figure*, Western Congo, Central Africa (19th cent.) The Brooklyn Museum. Wood, 10¾" high.

415. *Figure*, Fang, Gabun, Central Africa (19th cent.) Museum of Primitive Art, New York. Wood, 22" high.

visually mensurated calculations; rather, they evolved from the intention to create sculptural forms expressive of the active force or growth of natural forms. The functional character of the human body is in almost every style stressed, such as the short, heavy legs as supports, and the enlarged head as the major center of expression. Selective details, as scarification marks and hairdresses, are emphasized as identifying village or tribal characteristics. Since the artist worked without benefit of any model or example before him, Negro sculpture may be typified as a conceptual and creative synthesis of life forms.

The primitive peoples of the South Pacific inhabit some thirty thousand islands and the sub-continent of Australia. Within this enormous area an almost limitless variety of art forms developed as a concomitant part of the many amazingly varied and rich cultures. By comparison, the art and cultures of Africa are relatively homogeneous, and those of the South Pacific islands greatly diversified.

The vast Oceanic world may be divided into five large areas: from west to east, Indonesia, Melanesia, and Polynesia, with Australia south and Micronesia north of Melanesia. Although these lie with few exceptions within the tropics, life in them differs considerably, depending upon the natural resources at hand. The people themselves represent three of the major groups of man: Caucasoid or white, Negroid or black, and Mongoloid or yellow. In many areas these groups have to some extent intermingled; but Micronesia and Indonesia are largely Mongoloid; Melanesia, Negroid; Australia, a specialized dark-skinned Caucasoid people; and Polynesia, a substantially Caucasoid stock with various admixtures. The region is therefore ethnically heterogeneous.

It is not possible to single out, as it was in Africa, the common cultural elements contributory to the motivation, character, and content of the art. But a few elements are basic to the area as a whole. Life is largely sustained by agriculture and fishing; east of Indonesia metal was unknown before European contact, and both tools and weapons were made of a variety of stone, shell, and fish or rats' teeth. In most of the islands art occupied as important a place in the lives of the people as it did among the Negroes of Africa. Although preponderantly sculpture, it also included architecture, painting, and many of the so-called minor arts and crafts.

The Oceanic artist, a trained craftsman esteemed for his skill, utilized a wide variety of materials. At times he combined these materials in various ways, to represent as preferred subject matter the human figure or aspects of it, such as the head or face. While all forms were rendered independently of a visual model, few western Pacific sculptures are expressive of physically experienced reality; instead, they usually denote the appearance, idea, or symbol of an unseen supernatural spirit. They are therefore supercharged with an emotional content. Animal forms, including birds, fish, crocodiles, snakes, and the pig, provided the artist with additional subjects, while floral motives were used largely in Indonesia. Geometric designs appear frequently as an enrichment of surfaces or with symbolic meaning.

The peopling of this vast island world and the establishing of its cultural roots were the consequence of waves of migrations from west to east extending over thousands of years. This is evident from the similarity of physical types and many cultural elements with those of the Indonesia islands of Southeast Asia, where the five basic types of design, fundamental to all Oceanic art styles, almost certainly had their origin.

Sculptured, painted, and fabricated forms from Melanesia and Polynesia best represent the art of the South Pacific peoples. In both areas the five basic types of design are interpreted in a variety of ways to convey subject matter in conformity with the style traditional to a village or tribe. These design types are: a three-dimensional sculptural statement stressing planes and volumes; a polychrome painting of surfaces or details to represent ideas and relationships other than those of the carved forms; a compositional arrangement of several figures oriented either vertically or horizontally; a two-dimensional incised or low-relief carving or painting on a flat surface; and an aerial design with forms, often pierced, having an existence and sometimes movement in light and space. Although these designs are the common denominators of Oceanic art, they are very diverse in appearance, since they are always rendered within the style traditional to a particular region.

The Melanesian ('black') islands, so named because of their Negroid inhabitants, extend for almost three thousand miles into the southwestern Pacific. The area contains both large and small islands, including New Guinea, over thirteen hundred miles long, New Britain, New Ireland, and the Solomon and New Hebrides groups. Melanesian art styles are as varied as its islands and cultures are numerous. Cultural diversity resulted from the isolation of the groups who originally migrated into these islands, an isolation sometimes imposed by physical barriers, such as expanses of open sea or lofty mountain ranges, and sometimes self-imposed for protective reasons. Such elements as inter-tribal or inter-island warfare, head-hunting, cannibalism, and language differences tended to isolate further one area or even one village from another.

In Melanesia active volcanoes, frequent hurricanes, and tidal waves give the islands a quality of violence that is often reflected in their cultures, and thus in their art. Religious beliefs in many islands center in supernatural spirits, frequently of fearsome character, in mythological beings, the power of ancestors, and in magical practices. Characteristically, spectacular dramatic ceremonies, lasting for days or months or even years, are enacted as part of the communal religious and social life. In some areas secret societies build large men's clubhouses within which sacred objects are seen and rites performed only by members. Throughout Melanesia an abundance of art is required for use in almost all religious and secular ceremonies.

Of the many varied art styles developed on the island of New Guinea that of the Sepik River area, in the north-central part, is one of the most astounding in the entire primitive world. Although the polychrome tradition domi-

417. *Mask*, Sepik River, New Guinea (19th–20th cent.) American Museum of Natural History, New York. Wood, 22" high.

expressive elements of masks and figures, producing an intense, startling, and emotionally charged effect (fig. 417). Fantastic creative shapes and proportions are freely employed, while elaborate symbolic and decorative designs are often painted on carved figures, masks, drums, sacred flutes, and many other ceremonial objects as circular patches or sinuous curvilinear surface patterns. Whether simple or complex, the rhythmic interplay or the opposition of curved surfaces and flowing lines in Sepik River art excites the eye and stimulates the imagination, an effect furthered by the use of light and evanescent colors, or stolid and heavy ones.

In many parts of the primitive world a parchment-like cloth was made by soaking and pounding the thin inner bark of certain trees. The Polynesian word for this fabric cloth is tapa. In Melanesia bark-cloth was used as clothing and in New Britain and elsewhere as a covering for palmwood frames in the fabrication of masks. Vividly painted green, red, yellow, black, and white, New Britain masks (fig. 418) represent supernatural spirits of the jungle and were often worn in brutal initiation ceremonies. They are generally based on conical, columnar, or circular geometric shapes on the surface of which are painted fantastic, quasi-human facial features in bold two-dimensional designs of concentric circles and curving lines.

The particular character of New Ireland art derives from a combination of

nates, all of the basic design types are represented in this art. The strongest of the many motivations were derived from the socio-religious ceremonies and those of the men's societies, with supernatural, legendary, and ancestor spirits providing the subject matter. Large eyes, accentuated by concentric circles, serve as focal

PLATE IX

Bella Coola, *Mask* (early 19th cent.) Statens Etnografiske
Museum, Stockholm. 1′ 9″ x 1′ 7½″.

Paracas Necropolis, Peru, *Textile* (before A.D. 1000) Neck-band of a poncho
shirt, woolen embroidery on a cotton base. Lima Museum. 7″ wide.
Photo, courtesy of Junius Bird.

PLATE X

Claude Monet (1840–1926) *Etretat*.
Metropolitan Museum, New York.

Maurice de Vlaminck (1876–   ) *Les Maisons à Chatou*.
Sidney Janis Gallery, New York.

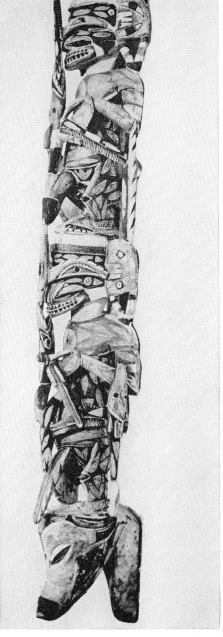

418. *Mask*, New Britain (19th cent.) The Denver Art Museum. Palmwood frame, pith covering, 42″ high.

419. *Superposed Figures*, New Ireland (19th cent.) Private Collection, New York. Wood, 66″ high.

420. *Canoe-prow Figure*, Solomon Islands (19th cent.) Museum für Völkerkunde, Hamburg. Wood, shell inlay, 8½" high.

style is the visual dissolution of sculptured forms achieved by painting their surfaces in small repeat linear designs in red, white, and black.

The strong purely sculptural style evolved in the Solomon Islands is best represented by modest-size but large-scale carvings mounted just above the water-line on the prows of head-hunting canoes (fig. 420). Heavy volumes described by contrasting rounded and flattened surfaces dramatically combine with large and intense facial features, particularly the eyes and mouth. Also characteristic of Solomon Islands art is the use of a fine and delicate mother-of-pearl shell inlay to define such details as the eyes, eyebrows, and the lines of the jaws. The iridescent shell designs stress the bold monochrome black surface planes of these aggressive heads representative of powerful protective spirits essential to success on such highly dangerous excursions as head-hunting.

Ancestor figures and masks, and various ceremonial objects, richly polychromed in brilliant earth pigments, are typical of sculpture in the New Hebrides Islands (Plate XIII, facing p. 620). They are used to represent the alert and dynamic guardianship of the ancestors in the numerous religious and secular graded societies so dominant in New Hebrides life. This was achieved symbolically in the sculptures by huge, long oval heads and enormous circular eyes, both intensified by vivid colors. In many respects, New Hebrides art is the climax of the spectacular so prominent in the art of Melanesia.

polychromed forms with pierced aerial forms (fig. 419). A variety of masks, single figures, columnar carvings of superposed forms, and other objects were made anew for use in lengthy mortuary ceremonies performed periodically to honor the recent dead and the mythological and legendary ancestors. It is a complex and spectacular art consisting of fantastic human and animal forms composed to produce an intense, fierce appearance. A unique feature of the

To the east of Melanesia the less numerous Polynesian islands are spaced over an immense area of the central and south Pacific. It is believed that the inhabitants of these islands migrated from the west into the central Pacific, possibly about the beginning of the Christian era. Later, perhaps in the 10th and 14th–15th centuries, the more remote islands of Hawaii, Marquesas, New Zealand, and Easter Island were colonized. The Polynesian groups are linguistically and culturally related to one another and to Southeast Asia. Since they are therefore a fairly homogeneous people, it is possible to characterize the basic beliefs and practices they shared in common. After the period of colonization, however, cultural variations, particularly in the art styles, developed among the widely separated groups.

Polynesian art, too, consists largely of sculpture in wood, while in some areas stone, bone, and whale ivory were used. Bark-cloth or tapa was a major art, often richly decorated with stamped or freehand painted geometric designs in various colors. On some islands a cloak, cape, or helmet was decorated with feathers attached to a net or basketry background. With the exception of its use on tapa, color was a minor element in this area.

Form in Polynesian sculpture was clearly derived from physically experienced natural form, and the motivations back of it stemmed from the importance of rank and ancestry, often traced back through long remembered genealogies to legendary times, the legendary an-

cestor being worshiped and revered as a 'deity.' Even the esteemed gods of various crafts were usually deified early craftsmen. Society was stratified according to seniority of birth, the highest rank claimed by those who could trace descent back through a line of first-born to an early ancestor. Such a system of rank had therefore religious sanction;

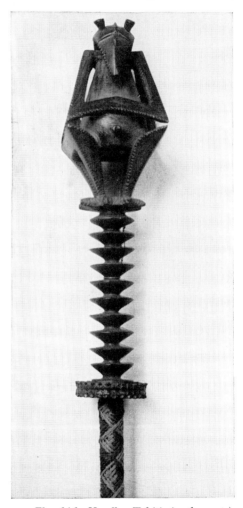

421. *Fly-whisk Handle*, Tahiti (19th cent.) Royal Scottish Museum, Edinburgh. Wood, 7½" high.

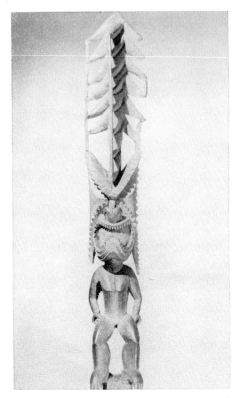

422. *Figure,* Hawaii (late 18th-early 19th cent.) Bishop Museum, Honolulu. 43½″ high.

mana; while the presence and potency of it was revealed by the skill and success of a man, weapon, or tool. Since persons and objects of great mana were dangerous to those with less, taboos were established to protect against contact; and to break a taboo was fatal, as persons with great mana could lose a bit by meeting those with less.

Specialization was as marked a feature of Polynesian culture as was rank. All activities were under the control of specialists instructed in the appropriate knowledge and skills through long apprenticeship, such as all artists, canoe makers, tattooers, priests, and so forth.

Persons of rank in Tahiti used fly-whisks as functional and prestige objects. The handles of these fly-whisks are often carved with the highly conventionalized human figure type found in central Polynesian art (fig. 421). The small seated figures are rendered in a few sharply separated geometric forms, the body parts sharp and stocky, and the heads long spherical triangles with protruding 'bug-like' eyes. No color supplements the sculptural statement of alertness and tension.

In Hawaii a strong sculpture style appears in both the very large and small carved wooden figures depicting the great public gods, who controlled such activities as war and agriculture, and the innumerable small household deities (fig. 422). Hawaiian sculpture expresses bulk, volume, aggression, and defiance. The actively posed heavy forms are completely set in space, a quality furthered by the contained and negative spaces

and the dominant and all-important feature of life may be considered a tightly ingrown ancestor worship.

Fundamental to an understanding of the culture and art of Polynesia were the concepts of mana and its corollary taboo. These were as culturally pervasive as ancestor worship with which they were closely associated and supported. Mana was the thought that a portion of an ambient universal power was contained in varying degrees in all animate and inanimate objects. A person of high birth, for example, had because of his rank a great deal of potent

423. *Relief, House Panel*, Maori, New Zealand (1842–43) Dominion Museum, Wellington, New Zealand. Wood, 6'6" high.

between the separate parts of the forms. Sharp angles and planes contrast with flowing curved surfaces and outlines to create a tension of pose and an organic unity of form; while the enlarged heads and the aggressive expression of facial features are correlated with the almost universal Polynesian concept of vigor and defiance as narcissistic qualities of both their ancestors and deities. No color appears in Hawaiian sculpture; that was reserved for the bright red, yellow, and black feather-work and the decoration of the very fine tapa produced on these islands.

The Polynesian tribes of New Zealand are known as the Maori. Their art is elaborate and complex, the primary forces behind it being closely related to the war-like proclivities of the people and to the importance of rank and ancestry. Sculptural decorations in the round and in relief for special houses and canoes and on weapons symbolize legendary and recent ancestors. Figures are large headed, heavily proportioned, and with an aggressive, almost menacing expression, the tongue often protruding from a snarling figure-eight mouth (fig. 423). In the majority of Maori sculptures, the forms are usually given a rich over-all surface design, most frequently

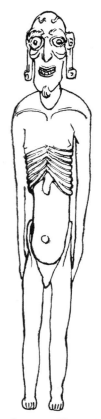

425. *Wooden Ancestor Figure,* Easter Island (late 18th-early 19th cent.) *c.* 16" high.

424. *Stone Figure,* Marquesas (early 19th cent.) The University Museum, University of Pennsylvania, Philadelphia. 8" high.

composed of geometric curvilinear elements and painted a monochrome red or black. It is a technically accomplished art and is lavish in the intricacy of its design elements.

On the Marquesas Islands the human figure was interpreted in heavy, compact, full-volumed forms carved in volcanic stone or wood and ranging from a few inches to 10 feet high. Whether large or small, the figures are massive in scale, with large heads set on a very short neck to overhang the body below. Facial features, delineated in very low relief, consist of large oval or round eyes, wide nostrils, and a wide narrow oval mouth (fig. 424). Sculptured human figures were used as symbols in ancestor rites, as implements in the practice of sorcery, and as decorations—when the body shapes are covered with wide parallel grooves arranged vertically, diagonally, or horizontally. Although Marquesan art has a static, conventionalized quality, a significant tension is conveyed through the interaction of tightly compressed large and various shaped forms.

Easter Island art also included forms sculptured in volcanic stone and wood. The stone carvings represent large half-figures and brooding heads, some of them 20 feet high, apparently made to commemorate an ancestor, the forms defined by a few simple shapes and planes arranged to emphasize depth. The smaller wood carvings depict emaciated and skeletalized male and female figures (fig. 425), and grotesque combinations of human, bird, and lizard forms. A careful and precise technique is employed to give descriptive detail and smooth and polished surfaces to these ancestor and fantastic hybrid fig-

ures, while a further descriptive note is often added by inlaying the eyes with obsidian set in a ring of fish bone.

Oceanic and African art consisted predominantly of wood sculpture, although in Oceania painting and impressive decorated architecture were produced. In Polynesia and in Africa sculpture was usually given a monochrome coloration and depended largely for its aesthetic effects upon the inter-relationships of plastic forms and details; but in Melanesia prescribed color and an array of various materials, such as shells, feathers, seeds, and grasses, had to be added to the carving to achieve full content-meaning and artistic expression.

To be more fully appreciated, this art must not only be understood within its cultural context, but must also be visualized in bright tropical sunshine or in the flickering firelight at nocturnal ceremonies, when changing patterns of strong light and deep shadows gave it an aliveness and a further dramatic intensity. Although the aesthetic impact of primitive art is direct and immediate, it must be seen again and again for a comprehension of its stature as one of the significant arts of man.

XXVI   THE GROWTH OF AMERICAN ART

If American art through the Federal period was provincial English art, its subsequent growth also has often been influenced by European civilization. Each major movement on the other side of the Atlantic has found its echo on this side, though the source is no longer predominantly English. However, the inspiration is not always foreign. At times, a local spirit wells up to hide the imported factors. These local developments can be called American in the fullest sense of the word, but it does not follow that the derivative art is un-American. The art of our civilization has been neither more nor less indigenous than our culture as a whole.

Neoclassicism, and especially the Greek revival, took firm root in this country. The latter movement, extending in America from 1825 to 1850, accompanied our sympathy for the Greek revolt against Turkey, a sentiment also felt by liberal thinkers of Western Europe, but the keener in this country because the United States was a young republic and to some degree considered the ancient Greek republics as its prototypes. One can trace the settlement of the country from 1800 to 1850 by the classical place names. Athens, Ithaca, Sparta, Ypsilanti, and hundreds of other frontier or near frontier towns thus signified their admiration for the Greeks. The contrast between such settlements and Periclean Athens might be startling, but who could tell how these rude villages might grow? Classical allusions and quotations stud the political orations of the time, and the almost exclusively classical curricula of the colleges point in the same direction. Both in date and in spirit, the development links with the rise and power of Jacksonian

426. Thomas U. Walter (1804–88) *Andalusia, Pa.* (1836).

democracy. The older styles of architecture and painting of English origin were tinged with aristocracy; the Greek was believed to be democratic in background.

Andalusia (fig. 426), on the banks of the Delaware in Bucks County, Pennsylvania, was the estate of Nicholas Biddle, the first American to travel in Greece. Under his instructions, Thomas U. Walter, later to become famous for his completion of the United States Capitol in Washington, in 1836 dressed one wing projecting toward the river in a Greek Doric portico, with a full entablature and pediment, derived in proportions from the Parthenon. Tall windows testify to the increased story heights. The walls become simple planes with plaster or smooth boarding; such un-Greek devices as shingles or clapboards are avoided in the purest examples. The portico is designed for effect. Some sacrifice must be made to force the requirements of a house into the form of a Greek temple. The very perfection of that form for its original purpose implies its imperfection for other purposes. The windows, especially those on the second floor, lose much of their effectiveness when thus hidden under the portico. Through the influence of carpenters' handbooks, detail was simplified. Greek architecture had been adapted to stone; its members were, therefore, bold. In order to translate these forms into wood, the exquisite Federal detail yielded to simplification. During the early part of the Greek revival, craftsmanship remained at a high level. Nevertheless, the demands for simplicity made upon the woodworkers, and the pressure upon them to give to their work not the forms appropriate to wood, but those suited to stone, helped to undermine the native traditions in the former material.

But even if these charges are just,

much may be said in praise of the Greek revival. Great mansions like Andalusia undoubtedly do what they set out to do; they are imposing, even magnificent in their way. We sing of our 'templed hills,' and the phrase is no empty figure of speech, as witness the Lee Mansion in Arlington, across the river from Washington. Andalusia is stately with lawns that slope down to the river bank; the Lee Mansion crowns the hill it is built on. Nor do most of these houses slavishly follow the temple form. Both these examples have wings that break the usual lines of the temple. These extensions are not emphasized from the front; they may even be concealed, but they add to the commodity and flexibility of the house.

Still more important, the bulk of the work in this period is less archaeological than these famous houses. The best architects and the builders throughout the country adapted the style to local conditions and problems, except when forced to do otherwise by the client. They retained its simplicity, its repose, its dignity, but they so far modified its vocabulary as to make it American Greek. In time, this simplified version came very close indeed to becoming a vernacular. A Phidias or an Ictinus might no longer recognize it; it might be naïve, even provincial, but these manifestations of the Greek manner, still extant in every village from Maine to Florida and west to the Mississippi, have a better claim to being American than much that we have built since that time. Generally speaking, the less elaborate it attempts to be, the more indigenous the style becomes.

The same can be said of sculpture. Ships' figureheads and local crafts are purely native, but formal sculptors imitated their European colleagues and went to Italy, where the techniques of sculpture still lived. Horatio Greenough (1805–52) of Boston was commissioned to create a monumental statue of Washington, intended to be displayed under the dome of the Capitol. When the statue arrived in Washington, it proved to be too large to pass through the Capitol doors; they had to be enlarged to admit the figure. Then it became clear that its weight endangered the floor, and it was moved outside the building, where it sat for many years facing the east front of the Capitol. Finally, in 1908, it was transferred to the Smithsonian Institution to protect it from further weathering. So large a figure needs room around it. In its present cramped quarters, it looks as out of scale as a giant in a baby carriage. The statue (fig. 427) is pompous to the point of absurdity. The idea of Washington, that Virginia gentleman, tricked out as an Olympian Zeus seems incongruous to the present-day generation, and did to some men even in Greenough's time. The trite gesture accords with the fulsome orations of the time. Nevertheless, it is only fair to remember that the dry execution and the dull over-generalization of the form are defects of the day and are not peculiar to Greenough. He is no rival of Canova, but he is no worse than

427. Horatio Greenough (1805–52) *Washington* (1832–42) Smithsonian Institution, Washington. 11′4″ high.

most sculptors of European Neoclassicism.

Nor was the academic admiration for the figure without its exponent among American sculptors. Hiram Powers won notoriety by his statue of the Greek Slave. It says much about America in the 1830's that before the statue was exhibited, a committee of clergymen in Cincinnati visited it to pass on its possible effect on public morals. (Purity Leagues and Watch and Ward Societies are not twentieth-century inventions in America.) The gentlemen concluded that since her hands were chained, her undraped condition was beyond her control, and she would not endanger public virtue. In another case, men and women were admitted separately to an exhibition of casts of Greek sculpture, as to a *Sala Pornographica*. The Greek Slave is a better than average version of the figure sculpture of its generation, graceful in pose and slick in surface, but lifeless. It owes its fame more to its subject than to its quality.

During this period, painting concentrated on portraits by late followers of the school of Benjamin West. These continued to respect the Federal traditions, which faded away as the influence of the cultivated class waned. Little true Neoclassic painting was done, save perhaps for the heavy pomposities of Washington Allston. This worthy gentleman had unbounded enthusiasm for Michelangelo, whence came the grandiose scale of his canvases and the bulk of his characters; but most of his paintings were as drab in color and as dull in execution as the mediocre work of David's followers in France.

The foundation of the National Academy of the Arts of Design in 1826, with the first important attempt to write the annals of American art, namely the *History of the Rise and Progress of the Arts of Design in the United States*, by William Dunlap, published in 1834, and countless articles in magazines testify to the enthusiasm for the arts in eastern centers. Nevertheless, the spirit of the country, thanks to the influence of the frontier, was hostile to painting. Art was a useless occupation in a frontier community, and therefore pressure developed during the expansion of the country to divert men from it to practical activities, such as mechanical invention. Robert Fulton is known to every school child in America, however wrongly, as the inventor of the steamboat; Samuel F. B. Morse as the inventor of the telegraph; but few realize that both men had been successful painters before their energy was diverted to channels congenial to the tastes, and perhaps to the needs, of their day.

At least by the 'forties, the universality of the Greek revival was challenged by the Gothic revival, which had left some examples even of its earlier phase in America. Bulfinch, in the Federal Street Church in Boston in 1809, tried his hand at Gothic with results marked by as complete a misunderstanding of the style as the faddish stage of the movement in England. The real change in spirit to the mature Gothic revival, with its archaeology and its revival of a liturgical style, occurs in the Episcopal churches of Richard Upjohn. Trinity Church, New York, 1839–46 (fig. 428), marks the turning point. Though not copied from any known building, it is sympathetic to the spirit of an English parish church. Its deep chancel, the first in America, proves the influence in the Episcopal Church of the Oxford Movement, which compelled a form closer to the medieval and better adapted to the ritual of the high-church party. Richard Upjohn, English-born and English-trained, knew well the architectural character appropriate to an Episcopal church. The nave and aisles, the piers and Gothic arches, the traceried windows, the tower and soaring spire are all admirable. At only one point does the church contradict the spirit of its style: the vaulted roof is not built in the stone its forms postulate. Evidence exists, however, to show that the architect would have preferred a structural wooden trussed roof; this was supplanted by the sham vaults because of pressure from the building committee. Elsewhere the church respects its material.

Not many other buildings of the Gothic revival in America reach the point of monumentality achieved in Trinity Church. Many of Richard Upjohn's other churches reveal less of archaeology but more sympathy with the demands of construction in either wood or stone; these are usually parish churches, smaller and simpler than Trinity. The Perpendicular style of Trinity Church, like the same style in the Houses of Parliament, was abandoned as improper after the completion of Trinity; instead, the Early English or the Decorated styles served as inspiration. As in the Greek revival, the country builder simplified the Gothic so far as to approach a vernacular. Even Richard Upjohn's design for a country church in wood bears only a remote resemblance to his larger work, though in fact its straightforward carpentry and adherence to the needs of a church have a Gothic directness. His design for a wooden Gothic church, published in 1852, can be recognized with local modifications in hundreds of towns scattered through every state admitted to the Union before 1870.

On the whole, houses and other types

428. Richard Upjohn (1802–78) *Trinity Church*, New York (1839–46) 136' x 72'; 264' high.

of buildings are less affected by the Gothic revival than churches, partly because the prototypes are less well known, and partly because the leader of the new style, Richard Upjohn, identified it with the new movement in the Episcopal Church and refused to profane it by turning it to secular use. Nevertheless, the Gothic Villa, of which Alexander J. Davis designed many notable examples, is an application of pseudo-Gothic detail to plans of great complexity. The motive in such designs is less archaeological than imaginative, a decorative exploitation of a style that once was structural. Fifty years ago, at least one example might be found in every village up and down the Hudson Valley; today, so many of them have been destroyed that this type is approaching extinction. A pilgrimage to Sunnyside, Washington Irving's home near Tarrytown, will reward anyone who wants to see how picturesque this type can be.

As the architects turned away from the Greek revival, so also the sculptors rejected Neoclassic formulas in favor of a fresh naturalism. The statue of Washington (fig. 429) by Henry Kirke Brown (1814–86) is not the first equestrian portrait in American sculpture. That distinction goes to Clark Mills's portrait of Jackson in front of the White House in Washington, finished in 1853, a month before Brown's monument. In this laughable rendering, the great democrat raises his hat to a cheering throng, while the horse rears on its hind legs. One can hardly admit Mills's monument as serious sculpture, but the enthusiasm

429. Henry Kirke Brown (1814–86) *Washington*, Union Square, New York (1853).

that greeted it—Congress more than doubled the amount of the sculptor's commission—testifies to the uneducated taste of the country, and perhaps to its new-found self-confidence. Brown's Washington is more monumental. Though indebted to Verrocchio and Donatello, it is not a copy of either the Gattamelata or the Colleoni. Clad as a general of the colonial army, Washington commands his troops. The selection of historical costume, instead of the Greek garb that Greenough chose, recalls a similar decision by Benjamin West in painting, and by François Rude for the Marshal Ney (fig. 370). The strongly modeled horse remains subor-

430. John Rogers (1829–1904) *Coming to the Parson* (1870) 1'5" wide, 1'10" high.

dinate to its rider. In technique, Brown is competent but not facile; his surfaces lack the vitality of cosmopolitan sculptors, but they have not the dullness of Neoclassic productions. Brown turns to nature for his model, but by no means sacrifices the sculpturesque to it. Sober, unpretentious, and dignified, his statue has in it much of which to be proud and nothing that is unworthy. Somewhat later, John Quincy Adams Ward (1830–1910) continued in this vein, with greater precision in his statue of Washington on the steps of the Subtreasury Building in New York. The emphasis here rests on Washington's civilian achievements, but as in the equestrian portrait, no affectation mars the effort to convey the grandeur of his personality.

These sculptors reject the European;

they reflect the growth of a national spirit in this country, a supreme faith in its destiny, a new pride in themselves and, at times, an unwarranted confidence in their ability to solve any problem. They form a counterpart to the literary development that flowered in New England in the days of clipper ships, when the American merchant marine reached its height. The spirit continued in the decades after the Civil War, until other conditions compelled a change. In minor works, and even in important productions, sentiment plays a role. John Rogers (1829–1904) became famous for his groups, reproduced in plaster or bronze and sold everywhere. Some of the subjects commemorated the Civil War; others are sentimental genre scenes, like Checkers Down at the Farm, or Coming to the Parson (fig. 430), which might be an illustration for Lowell's poem, *The Courtin'*. The use of dialect in verse and of episodic detail in these figures reveals an appreciation, not unmixed with humor, of the country for itself.

Painting, meanwhile, though it did not neglect the possibilities of genre, for example, the canvases of William S. Mount (1807–68), more often turned to landscape, just as did Romanticism in France and England. However, the cult of the wilderness finds no parallel in Europe; it must be traced to the proximity of the frontier and its effect on American life. Virgin land had long since vanished in Europe, but it lay at the back door of America. Its influence on the poetry of Bryant and on Cooper's

431. Asher Brown Durand (1796–1886) *In the Woods* (1885) Metropolitan Museum, New York. 4'10" x 3'11".

Leatherstocking Tales is obvious. So, too, in William Doughty, at times even in Thomas Cole, and especially in Asher Brown Durand (1796–1886) can be found the lure of the wild. In the Woods (fig. 431) is a glimpse into the depth of a primeval forest. Man has not left his mark anywhere. Each tree and

432. George Inness (1825–94) *Autumn Oaks*, Metropolitan Museum, New York. 1'8" x 2'6".

branch, each rotting log half damming the brook, is naturalistic, studied with crystal clarity, but with little regard for pictorial structure. The scene details the deep woods. Elsewhere, these painters select panoramic views up and down the Hudson Valley, allied to the cult of the wilderness in a topographical attitude but based upon settled regions.

The early landscape school culminated in George Inness (1825–94), whose youthful work retained much naturalism and topographic quality, but who developed toward greater breadth. *Autumn Oaks* (fig. 432), rich in color, shows him aware of the need of picture construction. These sturdy trees produce a sweeping curve in silhouette to draw the eye into the distance over the spacious country. His concern with atmosphere increased as his style matured; thus his first paintings correspond to the Barbizon school, while his later work parallels the Impressionists, but is less scientific in approach.

Somewhat different and a little younger is Winslow Homer (1836–1910), who served as a correspondent illustrator for *Harper's Weekly* during the Civil War, but settled at Prout's Neck on the Maine coast. A native product, he was not affected by European art. From this fact came both his strength and his weakness. He had little feeling for texture; in *All's Well*, a lookout aboard ship, the sou'wester is as metallic as the ship's bell. On the other hand, those qualities that spring from a study of nature, his realism and his frank observation, empower such canvases as Northeaster (fig. 433). The strong color, the sense of the surging sea, and the broken rocks of the coast attest his love of the shore. Though informal, the composition is well organized, with an effective use of repeated diagonals.

Homer's contemporary and counterpart in figure painting was Thomas Eakins (1844–1916) of Philadelphia, who took the regular medical courses in anatomy at the Jefferson Medical College to perfect his knowledge of the body. Such a painting as the Gross Clinic, an actual operation, is a documentary record of medical practice, strange to modern surgeons but accurate to the last detail. Several of his paintings, such as Between Rounds, are based on prize fights in the old arena in Philadelphia; the pugilists offered Eakins an opportunity to exploit his knowledge of the figure, and yet they are more than anatomical studies. The forms throughout are solid and structural. His serious nature leads Eakins to the heart of his subject, nowhere more so than in The Thinker, a portrait of his brother-in-law, so absorbed that his awkward pose with hands thrust deep in his pockets is indifferent to superficial grace.

The native qualities of this era were soon submerged by a new wave of foreign influence. In fact, Homer and Eakins, both of whom lived on through

433. Winslow Homer (1836–1910) *Northeaster* (1895) Metropolitan Museum, New York. 2'10" x 4'2".

this later period, gained in stature by their independence from it. The climax of the Gothic revival in America, as in England, was short-lived. After the Civil War, the full blast of later nineteenth-century eclecticism shattered any consistency of style. The Gothic revival turned into Victorian Gothic, sometimes restrained, sometimes extravagant, as in the Hartford Capitol, by Richard M. Upjohn, son of the architect of Trinity Church, New York. The uninspired Baroque descendant of the Paris Opera rears its ugly head in the old State, War, and Navy Department Building in Washington by the Government architect Mullet, who had his foot in many another government design, such as the old Post Office in New York. Tallmadge describes this time as the Parvenu period, when ignorance was bliss. The vulgarity of many buildings in the Philadelphia Centennial Exposition of 1876 suggests the unschooled desires of men whose fortunes piled up in the unbridled expansion of the country after the war. Many of these men rose from the ranks, with no tradition behind them to help them distinguish richness from glitter and sham. They confused size with scale, novelty with originality, and demanded a crass ostentation in their surroundings. The flashy landscapes of Albert Bierstadt and Frederick Church won acclaim, not through their quality as paintings but because of their subjects, such as Niagara Falls, Cotopaxi, or the Yosemite Valley. Cast-iron Indians began to hunt the stag through the shrubbery on lawns, while within the

houses mechanical advances like central heating and bathrooms helped to compensate for the lush opulence of overstuffed rooms. During this heyday of the pressed flower, the stuffed bird under a glass canopy, the gas chandelier, and the whatnot, high-ceilinged rooms were disorderly with excessive furniture. With luck, one might escape the obtrusive points of the central marble-topped table, only to trip over the bear-skin hearth rug, and fall into a Morris chair, the one comfortable piece of furniture in the house.

From this chaos, Henry Hobson Richardson took steps to free us. One of the first Americans to study in the École des Beaux Arts in Paris, Richardson returned to this country shortly after the Civil War. His won the architectural competition for Trinity Church, Boston (fig. 434), in 1872 and thereby gained a national reputation. To Richardson, the rough strength of the Romanesque styles expressed a young and growing America better than any other style. He fuses in Trinity Church elements borrowed from the Romanesque of Auvergne, of Provence, especially in the porch, and of Spain. In particular, the source of his tower or lantern is that of the old cathedral of Salamanca. These imply that Richardson is merely distinguished by the style he selects and by the genius with which he handles it. But Trinity is more than another monument of eclecticism. Its rusticated masonry is not characteristic of the Romanesque; it is personal, and reveals Richardson's feeling for the rugged

434. Henry Hobson Richardson (1838–86) *Trinity Church*, Boston (1872–77). Length 160′ x width across transepts 121′ x height 150′.

power of stone. But rarely in the nineteenth century has material played so important a part in design, or its qualities received such sympathy. The superficial style of the Beaux Arts is sloughed off, but its valuable contribution, namely training in composition, remains. This design is conceived in mass and developed in three dimensions, not the two dimensions of the drafting board. One great bulk leads to another, to pile up with monumental concentration.

The success of Trinity Church, Boston, took the country by storm. It gave birth to the Richardsonian Romanesque with its progeny in every city of the country. But the followers could grasp only the externals of the master's manner, the contrast of granite and sandstone, without his ability in composition. While they became Romanesque-minded, Richardson himself grew away from that style. His eclecticism, even in Trinity Church, is minor; the Marshall Field Warehouse in Chicago (fig. 435), of 1885–7, rejected it. This design was thought out in architectural terms, a frank use of materials as a skeleton of masonry piers and arches, an effective search for the character of the building, and a composition that relied on mass and on a vertical sequence in the fenestration. The number of windows in each bay increases from bottom to top, but the size decreases. Such designs as this earn Richardson the proud title of pioneer of modern architecture. Nor is his contribution restricted to stone. The day of metal construction began just after his death, but in wood he worked wonders. His shingled houses have the same basic qualities, the same grasp of the fundamentals of architecture that distinguish the Field Warehouse. The Stoughton House in Cambridge, Massachusetts, creates a vernacular in shingles, founded upon volume and proportion, with no historic precedent or mere-tricious ornament in a time when both were rife.

The World's Columbian Exposition in Chicago in 1893 put an end to the Richardsonian Romanesque. Although Daniel H. Burnham of Chicago, an able administrator, was a perfect selection for architect in charge, he was awed, in matters of design by Charles Follen McKim from New York, who, like many other architects of his generation on the East Coast, had been trained in Paris. McKim's silver tongue and his taste, his sense of proportion, organiza-

435. Henry Hobson Richardson (1838–86) *Marshall Field Warehouse*, Chicago (1885–87) 325′ x 190′ x 125′ high.

*horizontal
Contrasted with
curving line*

436. McKim, Mead, and White, *Agricultural Building*, World's Columbian Exposition, Chicago (1893) 800′ long.

tion, and style dictated first that a uniformity of style be mandatory for all buildings on the Court of Honor; second, that that style should be 'Modernized Classic'; and third, that external color should be expunged. The result was the 'White City,' that so impressed America and so depressed foreign visitors, who looked to the new country for something original. There was reason for both reactions. Few Americans had ever seen so large a group co-ordinated in design and dominated by a sense of order. A uniform cornice line, sixty feet high for buildings on the central court, helped to tie them together as parts of a larger whole, and the total effect must have been imposing. Its virginal purity was timid, but at least it had not the blatancy of bad Victorian color. The Agricultural Building (fig. 436) by McKim, Mead, and White illustrates the style. It differs from Neo-

classicism in that it rejects the fetish of archaeology; correct and academic though its elements are, they are adapted with sympathy and freedom. The design is admirably proportioned and marked throughout by good taste.

The Modernized Classic, derived from the architecture of imperial Rome, reflects the imperialism of business enterprise. The same wide extent, the same power, the same ramifications, and the same colossal wealth typified the business empires of the end of the century that marked the centralized government of the Roman Empire. The success of the style in expressing the ideals of one of the largest contemporary forces is the real reason for the influence of the Chicago Fair. It fixed upon America for a generation the Modernized Classic as the only style for civic and commercial buildings. State capitols, court houses, memorials, banks, department stores, and even skyscrapers fell under its spell. The memory of its beauty that America carried away from the Fair and its lessons in the possibilities of planning and of consistency of style were lasting. Austere critics of the twentieth century deplore the falsity of the Fair, its monumental architecture designed for stone but built of wood and plaster, and its arctic whiteness splashed on with a squirt gun. That the Fair was designed for effect is indisputable; but at least it was effective, and, if it had something of stage scenery about it, an exposition may be theatrical. It was probably for the best that America should undergo another generation of disciplined academic study. Not so much the architects, though even they could profit, but especially the public needed this further experience of architecture, even if it was an architecture of taste, lest in a premature attempt to fly, the American Icarus should fall into a sea of undisciplined novelty. It does not follow that this influence should continue today. Now we have had our period of training, and are better prepared to stand on our own feet in architecture.

Even before 1893, a few were ready to abandon eclecticism, and to design architecture instead of styles. European visitors to the Fair recognized in the Transportation Building (fig. 437) the hand of an original genius, Louis Sullivan, of the firm of Adler and Sullivan. Its golden door contrasted to the whiteness of the main buildings. Though influenced by Richardson, the building was neither Romanesque nor Modern-

ized Classic. Sullivan announced his creed that in architecture 'form follows function,' that each problem, large or small, contained the germ of its own solution, and that the task of the architect was to uncover this solution. Like the others, his building at the Fair was constructed in wood and plaster, but, unlike the rest, it was made to look so. This did not imply something shoddy, but rather that its design should be expressive of its materials. If a projection over the entrance was desirable, the wooden rafters might extend beyond the face of the wall. In a stone architecture, bed moldings must be present to support the overhanging blocks that make the cornice; these were unnecessary in wood and were therefore omitted. Plaster, decorative and not structural in appearance, encased the rafters. The entrance needed dramatization; concentric arches rich with sumptuous surface ornament forced the eye down to the portals. These must be wide to allow circulation, but they did not need to be high. They were proportioned to the human scale, but brought into relation to the scale of the building by the arches above. The originality of Sullivan's design and its lessons in the principles of architecture were lost on America in 1893, but not on Europe. The path he helped to cut has been the path of architectural development, and justifies his title as prophet of modern architecture.

For a generation, his was to be a voice crying in the wilderness. Apparently eclecticism won the day. Modern eclecticism differs from that of the nine-

437. Louis Sullivan (1856–1924) *Transportation Building*, Golden Door, World's Columbian Exposition, Chicago (1893). Total building 960′ long.

teenth century not in point of view, but in results. The scholarship in historic styles is sounder, the possibilities of adaptation better understood. The best of our twentieth-century eclectics do not copy any specific building. They write their architectural essays in the language of the past with a facile understanding of its grammar and rhetoric. The best buildings replace with vitality the dullness of much nineteenth-century work; in the better examples, fine craftsmanship supplants mechanical detail. Perhaps the spread of photography is responsible for this. The nineteenth-century designers had to depend on en-

gravings, accurate but metallic and linear in effect; these qualities reappear in nineteenth-century eclecticism. Only a few photographs brighten the pages of architectural periodicals before 1900, but later they flood in, less to supplant the information that engravings and measured drawings must provide than to supplement it by complete and plastic illustrations of historic buildings. Today hardly a cottage exists in the countries of Western Europe that has not been photographed from all angles.

A consequence of this fund of information is great diversity of style. Even before the Chicago Fair, McKim, Mead, and White designed the Public Library in Boston in the Italian Renaissance manner, with a strong influence from the Bibliothèque Ste. Geneviève in Paris. They adapted the composition of Labrouste's exterior, but refined it and perfected its proportions. More recently, in 1923, the Lincoln Memorial in Washington (fig. 438) by Henry Bacon turned to the Greek, but the design does not copy a Greek temple. Bacon was the master of the style, not its servant, and he modified it, for example, in the entablature. He made the short axis of the building primary, and substituted an attic story for the sloping roof and pediments of the Parthenon. Adaptation likewise transformed the modern version of medieval styles at the hands of such men as Henry Vaughan and Cram,

Goodhue, and Ferguson at almost exactly the time of the World's Columbian Exposition. Bertram Grosvenor Goodhue especially, in the Chapel of the Intercession and in St. Bartholomew's, both in New York, showed a freedom based upon profound understanding of the past, whose suggestions he so modified as to approach a modern style. That tendency to simplification he carried further in the Nebraska State Capitol at Lincoln, begun in 1920, one of his latest works, which has thrown overboard the baggage of eclecticism.

For better or worse, eclectic design dominated the 'nineties and the early twentieth century in America. A generation whose cultural leaders turned to London and Paris for guidance would borrow in the other arts as well. That

438. Henry Bacon (1866–1924) *Lincoln Memorial*, Washington (1923) 189' x 119' x 80' high.

generation was still going to school in the old world. Today, to attack eclecticism is fashionable. It can be done easily and sometimes with justice. In fairness to the past we should examine the charges leveled at any eclectic building, and test them narrowly to be certain they apply. The Orientals have a proverb to the effect that when you stand on a man's shoulders, you should try not to spit on his head. To say that eclecticism sacrifices convenience and practicality to historic style is easy and often correct. Perhaps it is always true to some extent, but in the better examples any sacrifice of convenience to style is negligible. Nor does the statement that eclectic buildings cost more than comparable structures in a modern style always hold true, even if expense were pertinent in aesthetic criticism. In truth, up to the present time, the advantage here has rested more with the conservatives than with the progressives. One may urge that the traditional activities of our lives may as reasonably claim expression as those parts of life where we differ from our ancestors. Nevertheless, the trend of architecture is away from eclecticism. That is well, since there is reason to hope that the change is based on principles of architecture, not on style. The substitution of a 'modernistic style' would bring little or no improvement. Let us avoid that by concentrating on architecture that bears directly on our lives, and not on 'style,' ancient or modern, which touches us not at all.

Most of this could be said with equal pertinence about sculpture. While the architects were going to the Beaux Arts, the sculptors also turned to the Paris ateliers. Augustus Saint-Gaudens (1848–1907) dominated his generation in America. He was a modeler, like his European contemporaries, but he was an expert with fine taste and, at best, a sculpturesque power of conception. The monument to Admiral Farragut in New York (fig. 439) he designed in collaboration with Stanford White, of the firm of McKim, Mead, and White. The pedestal is flanked by curved benches in stone, with allegorical figures in low relief. These young women who look so frank and healthy represent the ideal of his generation. Irregular slashes in the stone suggest water and seaweed, appropriate enough to the subject, who stands with legs apart, as though on the deck of his flagship. Though the figure is not remarkable for its mass, it is not devoid of sculptural plasticity. Farragut looks capable of movement, but his action stays within the composition. More sophisticated and less direct than portraits by Brown or Ward, the surfaces are marked by greater vitality. Saint-Gaudens does not attempt the undulations of surface that we find in Rodin, but he introduces enough variety to give interest to his modeling. The kind of sculpture for which he stands is wholly that of his generation. Daniel Chester French, Frederick MacMonnies, Lorado Taft, and many others worked along the same lines without Saint-Gaudens' taste or his sculptural quality.

The painters, too, went to school in

439. Augustus Saint Gaudens (1848–1907) *Admiral Farragut Monument* (1880) Madison Square, New York

Paris. James McNeill Whistler (1834–1903), though American-born, spent most of his professional life in London. The Japanese influence, found in Impressionism, is strong in him. Many externals of costume and still life in his paintings are Oriental, but more important is the delicacy and the sense of selection that strips each canvas down to a few perfectly arranged accents. The pier and roadway of Old Battersea Bridge (fig. 440) at twilight create within the frame a pattern relieved by twinkling lights reflected in the river. Such extreme simplification outraged the public in England and embroiled

Whistler in his famous lawsuit with Ruskin. The critic referred to the artist as an impudent coxcomb who flung a paint pot in the face of the public, and Whistler sued for heavy damages. He won his case, but the damages awarded to him—one farthing—exactly expressed the injury to his reputation. At his best, his paintings are fantasies, so balanced that each accent, even to his butterfly signature, must remain as he placed it. Nevertheless, this conscious aesthete, like his friend Oscar Wilde, sometimes allowed cleverness to beguile him into mistaking shadow for substance.

The most popular painter of his day

440. James McNeill Whistler (1834–1903) *Old Battersea Bridge* (*c.* 1872) Tate Gallery, London. 2'2" x 1'8".

441. John Singer Sargent (1856–1925) *Daughters of Asher Wertheimer* (1901) Tate Gallery, London. 6'1" x 4'3".

was John Singer Sargent (1856–1925), a society portraitist. The techniques of painting came easily to him; he relied upon dash and verve for facile effects. The temptation to snap out flashy likenesses, flattering to his sitters, must have been great, since they accepted them so eagerly, and not all sitters would stimulate him enough to compel a study of structure and character. Some of his earlier portraits, like those of the Wertheimer family, are among his best. The Daughters of Asher Wertheimer (fig. 441) are characterized with satirical bitterness. Sargent's fame during his lifetime was inflated, but modern critics have gone to the opposite extreme. He is not a great painter, but his best canvases, whereon the future will base its estimate of him, have some structure and decorative value as well as the fluency of their technique to recommend them.

The most unique American contribution to the history of art in the World's Fair generation is the skyscraper. This problem originates in the desire of American businessmen engaged in the same field of enterprise to be as near one another as possible. It is not due to scarcity of land, nor to high land values, of which it is the cause rather than the result. The skyscraper was born in the Middle West, not in New York. Two developments had to take place to make skyscrapers possible. First of all, some means of vertical transportation was essential, before the economic limits even of stone construction could be reached. By the middle of the century, passenger elevators began to be introduced in hotels, and later in office buildings. The early elevators were slow, but when they were sufficiently improved to make access to the tenth floor, for example, as easy as to the second floor, the tall building could and did appear. Each increase in height of skyscrapers coincides with an improvement in elevator design.

But if the elevator made the skyscraper practical, metal construction made it possible. As already noted, the nineteenth century explored the structural possibilities of metal. It remained for Leroy S. Buffington of Minneapolis to design a multi-story building with a masonry wall supported on iron. He thereby transformed the building from one in which the walls held at least their own weight, if not also the floors within, to one in which a framework of metal beams and columns carried the entire load of floors and outer walls as well. Buffington claimed that he devised a braced metal frame with iron shelves to hold the masonry as early as 1882. His claim is supported by drawings, but the dates on them have been questioned. In any case, some buildings, both in Europe and America, had already grasped this principle in part, notably the Menier Chocolate Works at Noisiel-sur-Marne in France in 1871–2, but none realized the possibility of great height inherent in this method. On the basis of this idea, Buffington designed a twenty-eight story building (fig. 442) to elucidate his principle and its possibilities. His design is remarkable for its

442. Leroy S. Buffington (1847–1931) *Cloud-scraper Project* (1887–88).

grasp of the aesthetic opportunities of the form. Though details bear the imprint of the Richardsonian Romanesque, such as the round arched entrances and the heavy rustication, and though the pointed roof seems archaic today, Buffington's design is far ahead of his time. He places the piers slightly in front of the plane of the windows and makes them continuous to bind the whole design into a vertical unity.

Buffington never had an opportunity to build a skyscraper, since his project remained unexecuted. The honor of first doing so belongs to William L. B. Jen-

ney of the firm of Jenney and Mundie of Chicago. His Home Life Insurance Building was designed in 1883 and occupied in 1885. Granite walls in the two lower floors carry the external weight, but iron beams bolted to cast-iron columns support the walls at the fourth, sixth, ninth, and tenth floors. However, the brick wall has still to be substantial, since no other provision is made for lateral bracing. Jenney hardly realized at the time the advantages of light, speedy, and flexible construction implicit in the new method, nor did he grasp its possibilities in design. Not for nothing were the early skyscrapers ridiculed as packing boxes on end. Jenney piled his ten stories, with two more added later, on top of one another, some of them grouped in pairs or threes, but each unit as distinct as a part in a sectional bookcase. He nodded to the architectural amenities with an occasional pilaster, molding, or cornice, eclectic features that could have been omitted without damage to the design.

Perhaps Jenney was more engineer than architect, but even those who claimed to be designers failed. In an eclectic age, a proper solution for a new problem was not obvious. Burnham and Root designed the Masonic Temple in Chicago in 1892, a twenty-two-story edifice, the half-dozen upper floors conceived as a German medieval town hall with steep roof and small windows. These stories, considered by themselves and placed on the ground, would make a decent if not distinguished eclectic design. They seem preposterous perched atop this mass as though a gigantic flower stalk had germinated under them. After 1893, the Modernized Classic prevailed. A skyscraper might confess its architectural allegiance by columns or pilasters, arches, and entablatures draped around the upper floors, and a similar scheme around the ground stories, with a plain shaft in between, the only successful part in such a building.

One man alone perceived the possibilities of the new problem, and accepted its challenge. In the Wainwright Building in St. Louis (fig. 443), dated 1890, Louis Sullivan vindicates his belief that the skyscraper needs no apology, that it may be a 'proud and soaring thing.' The mass of the skyscraper can be dramatized, and its height stressed to create a composition. The piers, uninterrupted from basement to roof, should be so devised as to look continuous. The wall, whose only function is to exclude the weather, must not counterfeit a supporting member; between the windows in each vertical band, the wall is treated decoratively to deny any structural significance in it. The cornice projects abruptly to reveal the flat roof, but with no trace of historic precedent to interfere with a demonstration of the new material and the new method of construction. Floors that serve a similar purpose are identical in design, but contrast with floors that have different functions. Therefore the bulk of this building, devoted to office space, is uniform; but the ground floors allotted to shops, and the top floor to services common to the whole, are distinct. Sullivan is too much of an artist to idolize consistency; in the Wainwright Building, the supporting steel rises only in every other pier. That is clear at the bottom, since the intermediate supports do not descend through the windows of the ground floor, but in the mass of the building nothing distinguishes one pier from another. This inconsistency is insignificant in view of the fact that the Wainwright Building, unlike most skyscrapers for the next twenty-five years, is a co-ordinated and expressive design.

That the verticality of the skyscraper should not have turned more eclectics to the one historic style that had stressed

443. Louis Sullivan (1856–1924) *Wainwright Building*, St. Louis (1890–91) 127' x 114' x 135' high.

Paul Gauguin (1848–1903) *Mahana No Atua (The Day of the God)* (1894) Chicago Art Institute. 2′ 2½″ x 2′ 11½″.

PLATE XI

PLATE XII

Paul Cézanne (1839–1906) *Still Life*. Wertheim Collection.

Pablo Picasso (1881–   ) *Pitcher and Bowl of Fruit*. Private Collection.

444. Cass Gilbert (1859–1934) *Woolworth Building*, New York (1913) 800' high.

the vertical, the Gothic, is curious. It must be attributed partly to the hypnotism of the Chicago Fair, and partly to the opinion that Gothic was not appropriate for business buildings. A few examples do exist, and among them the most distinguished eclectic skyscraper prior to 1916. The Woolworth Building in New York (fig. 444), completed by Cass Gilbert in 1913, was for years the tallest building in the world. To call it

Gothic is misleading; its effectiveness comes not from its Gothic tracery, its canopies, and its pointed arches in terra cotta, but in spite of them. The one Gothic feature that helps the design is the verticality. Large and small piers rise in rhythms, as they could hardly do in the classic styles, and reveal the location of the principal supports. The tower with its successive stages creates an effective silhouette against the sky. But the over-all result comes more from the mass than from the Gothic details.

By this time, it had become evident to the public that the skyscraper had brought with it many civic problems, especially a chaotic effect on land values. Moreover, the difficulty of the traffic problem, attributed to it somewhat unjustly, the building's obstruction of light and air, and its conversion of the streets into canyons made regulation inevitable. The New York Zoning Law of 1916 provided a model that spread throughout the country, its principles sometimes accepted with little change, though at other times different methods of control were preferred. In addition to restricting certain activities to specified parts of the city, the zoning law prescribed partial height limitations. The city was divided into districts, each with a number to describe it, ranging from one half to three and one half. This figure signified that on any piece of property in a '1½-times' district, for example, the owner might build a wall to a height 1½ times the width of the street. A building could rise beyond that height, but only if its upper part were

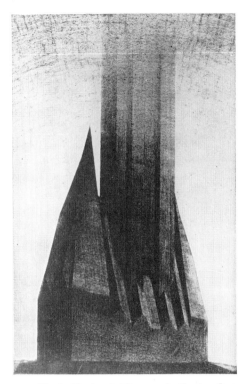

445. Hugh Ferriss (1889–   ) *Zoning Law Diagram*, New York (1916).

contained within a line drawn from the center of the street through the top of the wall. These factors operated to produce what the law described as the mass envelop, the legal maximum of building on any given site. A number of exceptions in detail complicated the law, but none of them need be mentioned except that a tower of unlimited height might be added, its area not to exceed one fourth of the area of the plot. Hugh Ferriss illustrated the provisions of the law on a theoretical city block in four drawings; the first showed the mass envelop (fig. 445), the second the excision of light courts in that mass, next the

446. Eliel Saarinen (1873–   ) *Chicago Tribune Tower*, Competition, Second Prize (1922).

walls of each story within the crowning pyramid made vertical, and finally these set-back stories grouped for simplification of construction. In spite of its restrictions on property rights, the law was accepted with little criticism, a proof of its soundness, though it was later simplified in some respects. The architectural world soon realized that the law contained and in large part compelled a satisfactory solution of the aesthetic problem of the skyscraper.

Consequently, its principles were incorporated in almost all skyscrapers, even in cities where they were not yet compulsory. However, our entry into the First World War, and the minor depression after it, prevented much building prior to 1922. That year saw the next milestone in the story of the skyscraper, an open competition for the Chicago Tribune Building. Many of the foremost architects of the country, and indeed of the world, entered. From the date the competition was announced, the *Tribune* illustrated the masterpieces of world architecture, each with the caption, 'Will the new Tribune Building look like this?' Had the publishers been able to foresee the results of the competition, they might well have asked that question. The most amazing range of designs were submitted, borrowed blatantly from all styles of the European tradition. The winning design by Howells and Hood was a sensitive piece of eclecticism, influenced by the Tour de Beurre of Rouen Cathedral, but well composed and in no sense a copy. It was obsolete before the building was finished. The second prize design (fig. 446) by the Finnish architect, Eliel

447. Holabird and Root, *Chicago Daily News Building* (1928).

Saarinen, overshadowed it. Developed in terms of mass and verticality, with no correspondence to any historic style, Saarinen's design soared aloft, while its rhythmic piers and corner accents flowered into admirably proportioned setbacks at the top.

The solution exemplified here set the type for the skyscrapers of the 'twenties, for example, the Chicago Daily News Building (fig. 447) by Holabird and Root, or the Barclay-Vesey Telephone Building in New York (fig. 448) by McKenzie, Voorhees, and Gmelin. By then, architects had realized that their buildings were so enormous that the older architectural elements, like doors and windows, no longer counted in the result. Instead, they must rely

448. McKenzie, Voorhees, and Gmelin, *Barclay-Vesey Telephone Building* New York (1924–26) 29 stories high.

upon masses, each as large as entire buildings of the past. The blocks, projected above the main mass to form the buttresses and foundations of the tower, would each, if placed on the ground, be a structure of considerable dimensions. As it is, they form mere units of the whole. Detail, as it had been conceived through the centuries, could no longer tell. The decorative conclusion of the building at the top must be designed on bolder lines. Moreover, the increasing cost of skilled labor made the traditional types of decoration prohibitive. Ornament was forced to become repetitive, and thus capable of being produced in part at least by machine. The result is magnificent in mass, overwhelming in scale, and strongly vertical in consequence of the projection of each pier in front of the windows. Skyscrapers of this type adorn all the large cities of the country, and testify to the popularity of the skyscraper idea and to the success of this solution.

A few buildings under the influence of European modernism and of what has been called the International style have rejected this solution. One is the Philadelphia Savings Fund Society Building by Howe and Lescaze. Where the designers of the standard skyscraper have not availed themselves of the cantilever principle, these architects exploit it. On the main front, the wall projects beyond the last supporting piers, and each floor overhangs the columns it rests on. Therefore, since the supports are withdrawn from the face of the building, the wall plane can be converted to windows stretched from corner to corner, and even around the corners. The result is that this face of the building becomes a series of bands, alternately light and dark. The elimination of the wall as a structural feature produces this change in the conception; the wall and windows together become a skin drawn over a frame with only the slightest projections and recessions. The thin wall is made to look so by the absence of any shadows that might create an impression of its thickness and so of its weight. Such a design expresses the structure of the building, betrays the existence of each separate floor through its bands of windows, and utilizes the possibilities of steel construction on the cantilever principle. On the Twelfth Street side, however, the vertical columns are visible.

Rockefeller Center in New York, built between 1931 and 1939, is less radical in style. So large a project called for collaboration in design; its architects included Corbett, Harrison, and MacMurray, Hood and Fouilhoux, and Reinhard and Hofmeister. They developed a group of tall buildings related to one another. Generally, it is difficult to see a skyscraper in its entirety, because it is surrounded by other buildings that partly conceal many of the lower floors and tend to minimize its height. In Rockefeller Center, low and high blocks are so disposed that each shall admit to the group as much light, air, and visibility as possible. The open space in front of the seventy-story RCA Building allows dramatic expression of

449. Skidmore, Owings, and Merrill, *Lever House*, New York (1952) 306′6″ high.

the height of this climax of the ensemble. Its thin book-like mass is based on the satisfactory depth of an office and the access to it; as each bank of elevators rises to its limit, the space it occupied is no longer valuable and a setback occurs; thus, Rockefeller Center represents as nearly scientific an approach as is possible in the art of building.

Since the end of the Second World War, the International style has dominated skyscraper design. Where some of the walls in the Philadelphia Savings Fund Society Building had been cantilevered, they are all so treated in Lever House, New York (fig. 449). Skidmore, Owings, and Merrill have here carried, perhaps to its ultimate conclusion, the Internationalist concept of volume, with its emphasis on the space contained within the curtain walls. Not only have those walls become a skin of glass and colored plastics, but most of the ground floor is open to the sidewalk, its lobby sheathed in plate glass. Hence one looks through the building under its tower, as though it floated in space. The undercutting of the shape of the tower increases its appearance of lightness. The clean precision of all surfaces, their polished textures reflecting light, suggest the impact of the machine on the aesthetics of building.

But while eclecticism was continuing even in a few skyscrapers, and commonly in other buildings, some architects were pursuing their personal ideals. Frank Lloyd Wright, who calls Sullivan his *lieber meister*, is the greatest architect of the twentieth century. While the rest of the country was building its

450. Frank Lloyd Wright (1869–   ) *Unity Church*, Oak Park, Ill. (1903) 66' x 66' x 45' high.

Gothic churches and Modernized Classic banks, Wright designed the Unity Church in Oak Park, Illinois (fig. 450), just after 1900. Considering the problem on its own merits, Wright backed the auditorium against the main street and raised its windows high in the wall to avoid noise and interruption from heavy traffic. The chief source of light is a skylight, invisible from the ground, that bathes the interior with adequate illumination. Partly under pressure of economy, Wright chose concrete, and evolved a design in that material proper to it. Up to this time, concrete had not been admitted to the Social Register of architecture as a monumental building material. Wright won it that standing. The rectangular forms, not only of the chief masses but of the smaller members as well, grasp the true nature of concrete. The medium is often called plastic, because of its fluid state while being mixed. However, since it must be poured into rigid forms to hold it in place until it sets, rectilinear shapes express the substance better than curved surfaces. Of course, concrete can be poured into a form of any shape, such as the weird curves of the Einstein Tower in Potsdam, by Erich Mendelssohn, but the prohibitive expense of such plastic forms compelled a substitution of plaster for concrete. The solution hit upon in the Unity Church is earlier, simpler, and more direct.

The so-called Prairie House, like the Coonley House of 1908 in Riverside, Illinois (fig. 451), comes as a relief from the usual residence of its day. Its

451. Frank Lloyd Wright (1869–   ) *Coonley House*, Riverside, Ill. (1908).

horizontal with contrasting vertical

452. Frank Lloyd Wright (1869–   ) *Kaufmann House*, Bear Run, Pa. (1937–39) *c.* 64′ deep x 62′ wide.

horizontality conveys repose instead of the restlessness of its contemporaries. The complex plan is difficult to read, even for those who have had wide experience in architecture. This rambling house throws forward a room here into the lawns and gardens, or draws one back there, as though to pull the exterior within the house. The inside and outside fuse so that it is difficult to say where one begins and the other stops. To this union of the house and its setting must be credited the charm of Wright's buildings. He abandoned the idea that the house must consist of cubical volumes called rooms; instead, by eliminating partitions wherever privacy was unnecessary, he allowed his enclosed space to flow from one area to another, and from inside the house to the outside and back.

The low-pitched roof overhangs the wall so that it shades the windows. Its long horizontals echo those of the projecting balconies, or of window boxes shaggy with growth. His multiple windows give an openness to the house, and yet the roofs curtail much of the light that might come through them, even when the undersides of these projections are treated in some light-toned material. The picturesqueness of these houses is romantic in spirit, as is their emphasis on individualism, Wright's outstanding personal characteristic. Many of Wright's admirers praise the logic of his work, and try to adduce practical explanations for every peculiarity. Such an attempt is not only hopeless, since his designs are not always logical, but is quite unnecessary. Wright is too much of an artist not to be ready to depart from, or to contradict, logic for architectural effect, or even for some jolly architectonic joke.

Since the early years of the century, he has continued to work in his own individual vein. The Millard Residence in Pasadena, California, built in the 'twenties, gives a decorative expression to precast concrete blocks, an ordinarily drab material. In each block, he casts a pattern, one for the wall units and another for the narrow supporting members. He adapts his solutions to the spirit and traditions of a particular region, without resorting to historic styles.

The Barnsdall Residence in Hollywood, California, is no modern version of adobe architecture in poured concrete, but its blocky masses and bold scale seem sympathetic to the older architecture of southern California. It is closer to the past in spirit than the twentieth-century versions of Spanish mission architecture. Or again, Wright injected an Oriental tinge into the Imperial Hotel in Tokyo without contradiction of his own Occidental background.

Wright is not a 'modern' architect, as that nebulous term is used today. He does not subscribe to the International style, but expresses his opinion of it in caustic terms. Indeed, his underlying romanticism compels hostility to that style. But some of his work appears to have developed along similar lines. The Kaufmann House at Bear Run, Pennsylvania (fig. 452), built 1937–9, exploits concrete and the cantilever, but combines them in a design appropriate to its romantic site overhanging a roaring brook.

More recently, in 1945, Wright de-

453. Frank Lloyd Wright (1869–   ) *Solomon R. Guggenheim Museum*, New York (1957 design, work begun 1956).

signed the Solomon R. Guggenheim Museum (fig. 453). The exhibition space consists of a spiral ramp lighted from a court covered by a dome of glass tubing supported on stainless steel. No such museum has ever been built—but neither was there precedent for the Unity Church, the Millard Residence, or the Imperial Hotel. However extravagant Wright's projects may seem, his completed buildings have always fulfilled his expectations and confounded his critics; we must learn to expect originality from genius. Until recently, America has ignored Wright; he has had but little influence here. But in Europe, especially in Holland, his genius has long been acclaimed. The openness of his plans, the originality of his houses, his sense of materials, and his avoidance of eclecticism helped to formulate the architecture of the past five decades in Europe. If its course has turned away from him in certain matters, he has not been forgotten or left without honor.

Eclecticism, so dominant in architecture during the early decades of the century but declining in recent years, pursues a similar course in sculpture. Conservatives, like Paul Manship, born in 1885, continue to design with exquisite craftsmanship in the older, more or less archaeological styles. His small bronze Centaur and Dryad in the Metropolitan Museum has borrowed the decorative patterns of archaic Greece. The Dancer and Gazelles of the Corcoran Gallery in Washington has something of the East Indian in its stylization. On the other hand, his portrait of his infant daughter, marble enframed in wood, reverts to the Italian Renaissance. We must admire the delicacy of these works, slight in dimensions and small in scale, like table ornaments, or fail to recognize the linear design on which they rely.

More progressive sculptors deny the

454. Gaston Lachaise (1882–1936) *Statue of a Woman* (1912–27) John A. Dunbar Coll., New York. Bronze, 5'8" high.

legitimacy of eclecticism as a goal. Like contemporary Europeans, they turn to a direct study of their materials, and re-examine the basic elements of sculpture. Gaston Lachaise (1882–1935) was born in Paris, worked for René Lalique, a designer of exquisite decorative pieces in glass, and after his migration to America in 1906, became Manship's assistant from 1913. Perhaps it was from Lalique that Lachaise got the admirable feeling for movement and for design in simplified curving volumes in his Dolphins. He felt that such decorative work was secondary in importance. The expressive sculptural volumes of his Standing Woman (fig. 454) create a glorification and amplification of the human body utterly in contrast to the facile grace of academic nudes. Large as its mass is, this figure standing on tiptoe and with its arms poised is peculiarly light in appearance, and yet with a masculine strength and musculature like Michelangelo's Night (fig. 234). The sex characteristics of the woman are emphasized for expression, as in Van Gogh's La Berceuse (fig. 403), only much more so, carried to an almost psychopathic extreme. Lincoln Kirstein describes his conception of woman as 'a calmly savage figure, an idea of the feminine that has a serenity more dominating than tender.'

Part of the twentieth-century re-examination of the basis of sculpture lay in the field of technique. The sculptors of the World's Fair generation and their European counterparts thought in terms of clay, of models to be turned over to

455. William Zorach (1887–   ) *Mother and Child* (1927–30) Spanish marble, 5'6" high.

professional bronze casters or stone cutters for execution in the final material. While they might add the finishing touches themselves to the bronze or marble, their concepts were not shaped by direct handling of the final material.

Some modern sculptors prefer *taille directe*; that is, they choose to do their own stone cutting. Thus, the Lithuanian-born William Zorach (b. 1887) carved his Mother and Child (fig. 455) directly in pink marble with only a small model to guide him. Even then, he departed from his sketch as the conception grew in stone under his hand.

The design of such a statue as this is calculated from all points of view, though in this instance some views of the back are less interesting than others. On the whole, each part in the mass is sculpturally related to every other part. The compact enclosed design marks and echoes the limits of the block whence these figures have been released. It dramatizes the weight and massiveness of stone in volumes sufficiently similar to the human body to be self-explanatory, and yet simplified and abstract enough to yield a sculpturesque treatment. Zorach is neither eclectic nor academic, nor does he move far in the direction of abstraction. He appears to walk in the middle of the road in his search for the possibilities of his material and of sculpturesque monumentality through working directly in stone, without a complete sacrifice of recognizable forms. John B. Flannagan (1895–1942) carried *taille directe* even farther. He said, 'I would like my sculpture to appear as rocks, left quite untouched and natural.' His Triumph of the Egg in its extreme reduction to elementary forms shows how nearly he reached this goal.

Though the work of these sculptors is hardly realistic, it certainly is not abstract or non-representational. One of the first Americans to experiment with abstraction was Alexander Calder (b. 1898), who studied with George Luks and John Sloan. Late in the 'twenties, Calder produced a number of amusing caricatures in wire. Through the influence of Piet Mondrian, he turned to

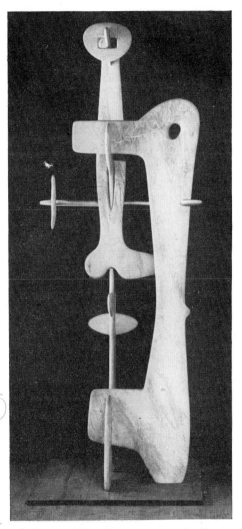

456. Isamu Noguchi (1904–   ) *Kouros* (1945) Coll. Artist. Georgia Pink marble, 9'9" high.

complete abstraction. His mobiles consist of metal rods with shapes suspended from them on swivel joints, delicately balanced and capable of revolving. A motor, a touch of a finger, or even a breeze may set these shapes in motion so that the forms describe patterns in

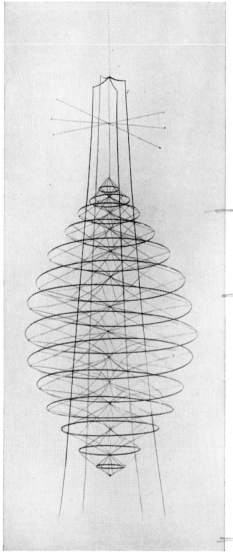

457. Richard Lippold (1915–   ) *New Moonlight* (1947).

space. These open compositions and Calder's use of unorthodox materials link him with the Russian constructivists.

The relation of forms in space is a problem that absorbs the attention of many contemporary sculptors. For example, Isamu Noguchi (b. 1904) says, 'The essence of sculpture is for me the perception of space, the continuum of our existence.' His Kouros (fig. 456) in Georgia pink marble is monumental in scale, its biomorphic forms of vaguely organic origin interpenetrating one another like the planes in cubist paintings or the masses in the Kaufman House. Like the latter in particular, the voids here seem as important as the solids. Even more recently, Richard Lippold (b. 1915) claims that space is his material. His New Moonlight (fig. 457) through its geometric spirals captures a segment of space and retains its open form. Other sculptors turn to irregular-shaped forms in dynamic and emotionally suggestive relationships, or like Theodore J. Roszak (b. 1907), to organic forms shaped in metal at white heat. One can hardly imagine a more complete revolution within the short span of half a century than that between the ideals of a Manship and those of the current generation. Perhaps a Roszak would deny the name of sculpture to Manship's work, as Manship would probably refuse to admit as sculpture the wire constructions of Lippold.

A similar revolution has obtained in American painting. At the turn of the century, a few artists like Arthur B. Davies (1862–1928) withdrew into a world of dreams as though in protest against the materialism of their times. The rhythmic spotting of the lonely figures in his Unicorns (1906) stands out against the clear blue of the glassy

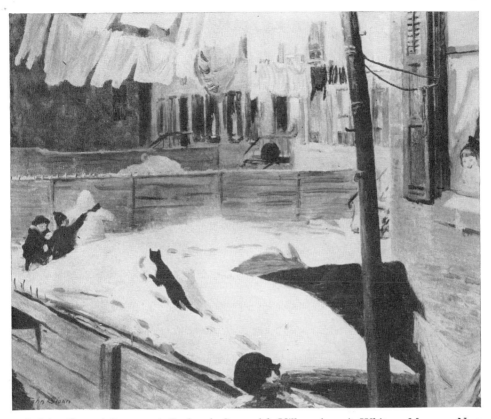

458. John Sloan (1871–1951) *Backyard, Greenwich Village* (1914) Whitney Museum, New York. 2'2" x 2'8".

sea and the brown of distant mountains. It is a fusion of the tangible and the intangible, an imaginative vision of lyric beauty. More important historically as the spearhead of the revolt in subject matter was the group known as The Eight including, among others, Davies, William Glackens, Robert Henri, George Luks, and John Sloan. In 1908, they exhibited together at the MacBeth Gallery, New York. Though by no means homogeneous in style, as a group they presented a common front against the traditional and academic standards of the beautiful in subject matter. Living in New York, they turned to the commonplace, often to the seamier, aspects of the city and its people. They were in consequence ridiculed by conservatives as the Revolutionary Gang, the Black School, or the Ashcan School, and at the same time they were applauded by progressives for creating a natural art.

Of them, Robert Henri (1865–1929) preached direct painting in a dark Impressionist manner without preliminary drawing. His best portraits have a warm-blooded realism that testifies to his keen interest in life. A product of the Pennsylvania Academy of Fine Arts, he became enthusiastic over the paintings of Courbet and Manet that he discovered in Paris, and as an inspiring teacher left his mark on many younger men. His close friend, John Sloan (1871–1951), also studied at the Pennsylvania Academy, under Thomas Anschutz, a colleague of Eakins. Perhaps he was the most complete exemplar of the Ashcan School. His Backyards, Greenwich Village (fig. 458), is reminiscent of the view from his own back windows, with wash hanging on the line, children building a snow man, and a lean and mangy cat. Not decorative, perhaps not beautiful, it is powerful through its truth; nothing shows better his intense interest in the life around him and his hatred of affectation.

Though not strictly one of The Eight, George Bellows (1882–1925) was similar to them in his early work. The Cross Eyed Boy in its dark Impressionist type, its bold modeling, and its dashing direct drawing with the brush betray his artistic lineage in Henri. As he matured, Bellows simplified his realistic forms.

459. George Bellows (1882–1925) *Dempsey and Firpo* (1924) Whitney Museum, New York. 4'3" x 5'4".

His large canvas of Dempsey and Firpo (fig. 459) selects the dramatic moment when the 'wild bull of the pampas,' as the sports writers called Firpo, knocked Dempsey out of the ring. The exciting action of the figures builds up to Firpo, whose wide-spread legs complete a pyramidal composition. The individual forms are highly simplified. Bellows does not stress details of anatomy; rather he prefers the semi-abstract geometric shapes into which the body and the parts thereof can be reduced. The heads of the spectators and officials in the foreground are almost ovoid, and firmly modeled as such. Both color and value are strong and fresh, but handled with the same stringent selection and the same simplification as the forms themselves. Such painting as this is certainly not conservative or academic, nor is it representative of the more extreme movements toward abstraction that play so obtrusive a part in any panorama of twentieth-century painting.

But America has not been unaware of those movements. Even in Bellows, the tendency to simplification testifies to their influence. Prior to 1913, a number of progressive American artists had kept abreast of Fauvism, early Cubism, and Futurism through study in Paris. Moreover, the distinguished photographer, Alfred Stieglitz, in his Photo-Secession Gallery at 291 Fifth Avenue, New York, presented an exhibition of Matisse in 1908, and followed it with exhibits of African sculpture and children's drawings, as well as the work of a number of younger American artists.

These helped to acquaint some painters and a few New Yorkers of the *avant-garde* with the new ferment of ideas emanating from Paris. It remained, however, for the Armory Show of 1913 to introduce these movements to the public at large. This historic exhibition organized by Arthur B. Davies and Walt Kuhn, with the active support in Paris of Walter Pach, won notoriety through its cubist and other near-abstract works, particularly Marcel Duchamp's painting, the Nude Descending the Stairs. The public flocked in to admire or to ridicule, but at least they came—100,000 in New York and even larger numbers in Chicago when the exhibition moved there. Celebrated as the foreign works were, the bulk of the painting and sculpture was American; almost every key figure in American art for the first quarter of the present century was represented there.

Among them, Stanton MacDonald-Wright (b. 1890) and Morgan Russell (b. 1886), while in Paris, had developed Synchromism (1912–14), a minor offshoot of cubism and a rival to Delaunay's Orphism of the same date. More completely abstract than cubism, it emphasized advancing or recessive color. Arthur G. Dove (1880–1946), who began his abstractions at least as early as 1911, may have been the first American to turn to cubism. Marsden Hartley (1877–1943) and Max Weber (b. 1881) passed through cubist phases during the years of the First World War. The former's Portrait of a German

460. Marsden Hartley (1877–1943) *Portrait of a German Officer* (1914) Stieglitz
Coll., Metropolitan Museum, New York. 5′8″ x 3′5″.

Officer (fig. 460) combines such recognizable symbols as the flag and the iron cross into a rhythmical pattern in strong colors with little depth. Joseph Stella (1877–1946), under the influence of Italian Futurism, was thrilled by the dynamic confusion of city life, its pace and rhythm. Allied to these movements but not of them is John Marin (1870–1953), perhaps the foremost American

461. John Marin (1870–1953) *Woolworth Building, No. 31* (1912) Private Coll., Mt. Kisco, New York. Watercolor, 1'8" x 1'4".

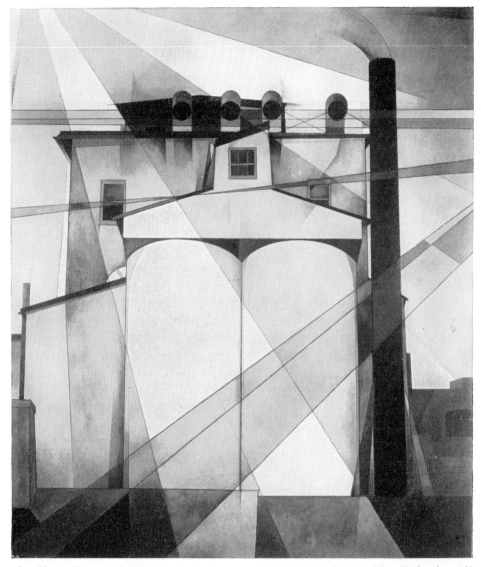

462. Charles Demuth (1883–1935) *My Egypt* (1927) Whitney Museum, New York. 3′ x 2′6″.

painter of his day. His explosive compositions like the Woolworth Building,
No. 31 (fig. 461) owe something to
cubism and futurism. In 1911, he said
he wanted 'to pile these great houses
one upon another with paint as they

do pile themselves up there so beautiful,
so fantastic.' Marin really belongs to
no school; he is so individual, so personal, as to defy classification. Neither
a romanticist nor a naturalist, his apparently unstudied watercolors have an as-

surance highly expressive of natural forces.

Some of these artists, like Dove and Russell, continued to avoid the representational in painting after 1918. With the return of peace and during the prosperity of the 'twenties, others reverted to objective painting, modified in certain ways by the lessons of abstraction. Among them are MacDonald-Wright, Hartley, and Weber. The group of painters known as the Immaculates apply the sharp lines and smooth precise surfaces of engineering to their paintings whether or not their subjects are based on industry. Thus Charles Demuth (1883–1935) chose the austere cylinders of the cement mills in Egypt, Pennsylvania, as the theme for My Egypt (fig. 462). These clear, clean forms are overlaid with a cubist pattern of diagonal shafts of light. Like Demuth, Charles Sheeler (b. 1883) was trained at the Pennsylvania Academy, that breeding ground for a generation or more of outstanding artists. His painting Pertaining to Yachts and Yachting discovers a rhythmic linear pattern in the sails and masts, a pattern that is an abstraction drawn from actuality. His Upper Deck (1929) offered him the chance to weld the machined shapes of motors, ventilators, and rigging into a design reminiscent of modern photography of which Sheeler is a distinguished exponent. With these men we may group Georgia O'Keeffe (b. 1887), who during the years of the First World War produced such complete abstractions as Blue and Green Music, but later turned toward representation. The Museum of Modern Art describes her work as 'naturalistic geometric' in that her flower studies are based on natural forms, but the geometric shapes inherent in those forms and in their relation to other objects are made dominant.

The prosperous decade of the 'twenties ended with the stock market crash of 1929, followed by years of economic dislocation. No longer was it so easy to trot off for a summer or a year in Paris or London. Perhaps that tended to force American painters to find their inspiration at home, as the rise of totalitarian states in Russia, Italy, and Germany with their avowed hatred of the democratic way of life tended to confirm American isolationism. In any case, a large group of painters turned to the American scene in all its aspects, sometimes simplifying the forms they observed, but often portraying them with forthright realism. Like the Dutch Little Masters, they are often identifiable by the type of subject they choose, as well as by the way they handle it. Thus Kenneth Hayes Miller (1876–1952) has painted the ample forms of women on the street, carrying umbrellas, in the fitting room of a dress shop, somewhat vulgar of face and figure but full of vitality and reinforced by resonant garish color. He approached these subjects with impersonal detachment, content to paint the lower-middle-class women of Fourteenth Street, New York. Their forms he deliberately simplified with a disdain for naturalistic light and a Ren-

463. Edward Hopper (1882–   ) *Lighthouse at Two Lights* (1929) Private Coll., New York.
2'5" x 3'7".

aissance admiration for sculpturesque mass that gives his designs a classic balance and repose. His pupil Reginald Marsh (1898–1954), who had studied earlier under John Sloan, was fascinated by the people of the city as they flowed before him on the Bowery, at Coney Island, in the burlesque or the subway, or walking the streets of Harlem. His *High Yaller*, a garishly fashionable Negress, is characteristic of Harlem in subject and in spirit.

While human beings attracted Miller and Marsh, Edward Hopper (b. 1882) and Charles Burchfield prefer landscape. The former, a pupil of Henri, commonly presents the character of the city not in terms of its dynamic life or

its famous monuments but through its quite commonplace buildings. His approach to these subjects is analogous to the literary realism of Theodore Dreiser and Sinclair Lewis. These scenes are not satirical, nor are they made vehicles of social protest; they are simply there. His Lighthouse at Two Lights (fig. 463) shows his love of clear-cut shapes in strong color powerfully modeled in the sun. Similar to Hopper in his choice of architecture as a vehicle is Charles Burchfield (b. 1893). Even more than Hopper does Burchfield prefer the shabbiness of neglected Victorian houses. In contrast to Hopper's objectivity, Burchfield seems to work emotionally. His buildings fit perfectly with the somber color scheme and dull weather that envelop and express them.

These painters have dealt with those limited parts of this country that they happened to know best, with New York, or in the case of Burchfield, with Buffalo. In so far as they are concerned only with the people or landscape of a limited area, they could probably be called regionalists, but that term is usually attached to painters who, perhaps consciously, try to express the peculiar flavor of certain larger parts of the country such as the Middle West. Thus, Thomas H. Benton (b. 1899), in his Arts of the West, combines figures and scenes whose associations create a sort of composite picture of that region. Cowboys, sharpshooters, horseshoe pitching, gamblers, oil wells, and Indians succeed one another in rapid and bewildering succession. The forms are not simplified into geometric vol-

umes; they are stylized in undulating shapes animated with restless energy. Mention should be made of Grant Wood (1892–1942), whose American Gothic and Daughters of Revolution attained their notoriety perhaps more through their satire than their pictorial qualities.

Though less sensational, John Steuart Curry (1897–1946) may prove to be more important in the long run than either Benton or Wood. His incidents of life in his native state, like Baptism in Kansas, or The Tornado, grow out of the specific into the general, and are sympathetic to the sturdy character of the people, or to man's impotence when faced with the fearful manifestations of nature. The epic figure of John Brown, fanatic, martyr, or traitor, dominates his mural The Tragic Prelude (fig. 464) for the State Capitol, Topeka, Kansas. This figure of fiery intensity car-

464. John Steuart Curry (1897–1946) *The Tragic Prelude* (1938–40) State Capitol, Topeka, Kansas. 11′6″ x 31′.

465. José Clemente Orozco (1883–1949) *Christ and His Cross* (1932–34) Baker Library, Dartmouth College, Hanover, N. H. Fresco.

ries the scriptures in his left hand and in his right 'Beecher's Bible,' a rifle, emblematic of those turbulent days. The soldiers, flags, and dead of the North and South surround him, while behind this compact group plods a stream of emigrants to the great plains, despite tornado and prairie fire, symbols of the destruction of the Civil War. This painting has much of the sweep and grandeur of Stephen Vincent Benét's *John Brown's Body*.

Curry's murals are painted in oil on canvas. A return to true fresco painting by certain Mexican artists, notably Diego Rivera (b. 1886) and José Clemente Orozco (1883–1949), lends their work a mural quality, not more perhaps than Curry's, but certainly greater than most nineteenth-century wall paintings. Much of Rivera's wide notoriety is due to his leftist political views, and their prominence in his paintings, which led to the destruction of his murals in Rockefeller Center, New York. Regardless of the merits or defects of his cause, such propaganda is not pertinent to the success of his works as paintings. In all aesthetic matters, Orozco seems superior to Rivera. His cycle of frescoes in the Baker Library of Dartmouth College shows, among other things, The Coming of Quetzalcoatl, a devastating satire on higher education in America, and a blistering attack on American Imperialism. The cycle culminates in Christ and His Cross (fig. 465), a terrific conception of the Prince of Peace returned to earth to destroy His cross because of mankind's reliance on warfare, symbolized by the mountain of military equipment behind Him. Through its simplification, and especially through its composition, the design fits the wall without any sacrifice of the modern brilliance of color.

The Immaculates during the 'twenties, and the painters of the American scene in the early 'thirties, supplanted our first experiments with abstraction, but increasingly from 1935 on have we turned to non-objective painting. Perhaps this is attributable to the arrival in America of such painters as Leger and Mondrian. Perhaps the emotional tensions arising from the international situation just before, during, and since the Second World War may be behind it. In any case, most of the younger artists have accepted a more or less abstract point of view since 1935, and many older artists have turned or returned in that direction too. So many have come into prominence that it is possible to mention only a few as illustrations of tendencies. Some have relied on purely geometric forms, stemming from cubism, de Stijl, and the Bauhaus group. I. Rice Pereira (b. 1907) has made some striking compositions through her varied and original use of such materials as resin, varnish, lacquer, mica, and gold leaf. Her Transversion (fig. 466) in oil and ceramic fluid has superimposed three layers of cubist designs on successive sheets of glass so that you literally see one system of lines behind another. Texture, vibrancy, transparency result without the slightest concession to representation. Stuart Davis (b. 1894), a pupil of Henri, who was represented in the Armory Show, is one of the few who have rather consistently maintained an interest in abstraction since that time. In his work, the influence of cubism and expressionism mingle with the precision of the Immaculates to produce a highly personal style. His forms, often in brilliant color, unlike Pereira's rectilinear lines, are curvilinear in dynamic relationships and sometimes identifiable with familiar shapes. The Museum of Modern Art classifies Jackson Pollack (1912–56) as 'expressionist biomorphic,' related to expressionism and dadaism. The calligraphic lines and irregular dribbles of pigment that compose his canvases sug-

466. I. Rice Pereira (1907–   ) *Transverse Parallels* (1946) Durlacher Bros., New York. 2′ x 1′10″.

gest an origin in doodling. The birds of Morris Graves (b. 1910) seem to be the romantic visions of his subconscious mind. Part of the canvas in his Blind Bird (fig. 467) is overlaid with an ectoplasmic scribble, related to the white writing of Mark Tobey, whom he admired. Graves has said, 'I paint to evolve a changing language of symbols, a language with which to remark upon the qualities of our mysterious capacities which direct us toward ultimate reality.' These and many other painters testify to the range and the extraordinary vitality of American art in the middle of the twentieth century.

The question is bound to arise how justly we may call our arts 'American.' Even a cursory survey makes it clear that each European movement from 1700 to the present day finds its faithful reflection in America. Much of it is distinguished by a provincial flavor, as one would expect. Our civilization is bound to be European; we are not descended from the American Indian, but from the stocks of all European countries, and particularly of Great Britain. As each has left its strain in our cultural life, so each is bound to be represented

467. Morris Graves (1910–   ) *Blind Bird* (1940) Museum of Modern Art, New York. Gouache, 2'6" x 2'3".

in the arts. But in so far as we have created a civilization that is distinguishable from the European, exactly so far have we expressed that difference in our architecture, sculpture, and painting. We tend to be a sentimental people, and hence produce a John Rogers and our painters and sculptors of the World's Fair generation, as well as the Longfellows, Whittiers, and Lowells. We have not been much attracted to theory or, until recently, to the abstract, preferring in all lines some more concrete outlet for our energies. We like to think of ourselves, deservedly or not, as a practical people. The formative influence of the frontier in American life, where practical results were vital, has colored our whole outlook. Affectation may have some place in a cosmopolitan society, but it has none in a pioneering community. The result is that the most purely American artists have been characterized by sober honesty, an utter freedom from pretense, which one finds in Copley and Bellows, in Hopper and Inness, Brown and Zorach, Homer and Eakins. So recurrent a quality we have every right to call American. That does not mean that it cannot be found elsewhere, or that other elements may not be present in American art; but this seems to be the central thread around which is twisted the pattern of our painting and sculpture.

What if the American past has been provincial? We have no more reason to be ashamed of or to apologize for this background than for the traditional career of the farmer's boy or backwoodsman risen to wealth and power. On the contrary, we may look on what we have accomplished with satisfaction, and feel no need to measure it with a European yardstick. If we can preserve this straightforward attitude and the openness of mind that goes with it, we may expect our art to grow more and more distinct from the European. Let us not disregard what others have done and are doing; they may offer us valuable help in solving our own problems. However, a weak strain in our art has appeared whenever and wherever we have consciously tried to be European. For all his brilliance, Stuart lacks the homespun strength of Copley; the American Homer is more powerful than the cosmopolitan Sargent. In short, we have been at our best when we have been most native, most completely ourselves. So long as we continue to adhere to these traditional American traits—not to external forms, for that would in itself be false to this spirit—we need not fear for the future of American art.

XXVII   Twentieth-Century Art

It is unfortunate that many writers on the art of the present century still find it necessary, although the century is now past its halfway mark, to 'defend' and 'explain' in pompous, confusing, if not omniscient terms, the character of this art. Such authors or critics fall into two main groups: one, the prejudiced traditionalists who try to ally modern art with some aspect of the Graeco-Renaissance; and the enthusiasts who attempt to find in it the full range of modern psychological and metaphysical concepts. In either case the approach is an emotional one and the results all too often forced, confusing, and ambivalent. To understand the historical as well as the artistic significance of twentieth-century art it is essential to turn directly to the art itself and to discover how the artist has solved the artistic problems with which he was concerned. All art, but particularly that of painting, consists of a dual set of visual experiences, that of the artist as the work takes shape under his hand, and that of the spectator who views it. But visual experiences are the sum total of one's life experiences; and in front of a painting all of these contribute to a personal understanding and an artistic evaluation of the work. It may be said that to each person a painting has a unique and highly personal significance.

In every era art is expressive of the culture of which it is one of the major components. The twentieth century can be characterized as a highly diversified period dominated by industrial and scientific achievements. In most parts of the world the tempo has been quick; while aggression and competition have led us into two disastrous world wars and have produced a restlessness, uncertainty, and tension that have increasingly permeated our lives. Decade by decade inventions and discoveries, such as the automobile, aviation, radio, television, and finally atomic energy, have further accelerated the pace of life and reduced the barriers of time and space. With the ever-increasing shrinkage of spatial barriers, new problems and anxieties have arisen. It has often been said that this is a chaotic period, but it seems more accurate to say that it is a period fragmented by highly competitive specialization within even a limited field of endeavor.

Within the complexity of this materialistic age, the art of painting has nevertheless maintained its position as an integral cultural element. Twentieth-century painters may be classified, as in all eras of world art, in two groups: those who adhere to the accepted traditional styles of their time; and those who strive to create new artistic forms from the essential fabric of contemporary life and thought. Whether these two groups be called conservative and progressive, or by any other antithetical terms, it is in the latter group that the historically and aesthetically important achievements are to be found.

The background for creative painting in the present century was postulated in the re-evaluations of the nature, possibilities, and potentialities of the art by a group of painters in the last decade of the nineteenth century, notably by Cézanne, Gauguin, Van Gogh, Ensor,

and Munch. By returning to basic problems of form, design, color, and technique, they began a 'reformation' within the art of painting. The innovations and point of view introduced by them led to the formation of new styles by several groups of young artists shortly after the beginning of the century.

In 1905 in the Salon d'Automne in Paris, the young painters Vlaminck (Plate x, facing p. 557), Rouault, Derain, Dufy, and the somewhat older Henri Matisse, exhibited together for the first time. The critic Louis Vaucelles in reviewing this exhibition derisively called them Les Fauves or The Wild Beasts, a characterization provoked by the non-representational rendering of nature, the use of foreshortening instead of perspective to describe depth, and, especially, the emotional shock induced by violent color. Vaucelles did not recognize that the vigorous, almost frenzied Fauve style was largely an uninhibited overstatement, overemphasis of a number of styles and ideas of the preceding twenty years, with the deliberate use of bright, raw color to visually and psychologically shock the viewer.

The major elements of Fauvist painting, however emphasized, may in part be traced back to the reformation group of the late nineteenth century. The large canvas by Matisse (b. 1869), The Dance (fig. 468), of late Fauve date, 1910, reveals the basic elements of the style. Bright red figures are delineated against a bright green ground and a saturated blue sky as vivid primary contrasts; forms are segmented into their various

468. Henri Matisse (1869–   ) *The Dance* (1910) Museum of Modern Western Art, Moscow. 8'6" x 12'10".

anatomical parts, with the points of articulation stressed, a style element indicating a familiarity with African Negro sculpture 'discovered' by artists a few years earlier; while rhythmic lines dynamically reassemble these marked-off parts and establish important tensions between them. In Fauve painting, the raw, pure color advocated by Gauguin was literally fulfilled; compositionally the depiction of only a portion of a larger scene, with parts of figures and details cut off by the frame, recalls various late nineteenth-century styles, particularly the Impressionism of Monet and Degas; and the enigmatical and provocative nature of the subject matter is in a way comparable to that of Gauguin and the Symbolists. Although

Fauve style persisted for only a few years, through its use of line, color, and pattern as dynamic pictorially expressive elements, not as means of describing reality, it marked a further departure of painting from the imitation of nature.

Contemporary with Les Fauves, the German Expressionist painters Kirchner, Heckel, and Schmidt-Rottluff, joined a bit later by Nolde, Pechstein, and Müller, formally organized in Dresden in 1904 as Die Brücke or The Bridge Group. The sources of this style were the paintings of Van Gogh and of the Norwegian Edvard Munch, who portrayed in emotive colors and strongly knit designs such basic human emotions as jealousy, fear, and loneliness. The

Bridge painters stressed, as did Munch, the oneness of emotion between human forms and nature, and hence their entire canvases, figure and setting, are permeated by a single strongly unified emotion. This is conveyed through the use of pure raw colors; freely expressive, non-realistic shapes and outlines; and a dynamic rhythmic design. Perspective is replaced in the spatial organization of elements by the relationships of brilliant color shapes which pictorially suggest depth and roundness. In this style, bright color is an agent used to convey a personal and emotional expression and to elicit a like response from the spectator. The Bridge painting, like Fauve, received considerable adverse publicity, and both styles were of relatively short duration, the Bridge Group being formally dissolved in 1913, after, as with the Fauve painters, the various artists began to develop in different ways.

It is important to note that about 1904–5 Vlaminck of Les Fauves and Kirchner of Die Brücke independently 'discovered' African Negro sculpture. In both styles some influences from Negro art may be detected, although they are less clearly marked or important than in other styles which were developing in France and Germany at this time.

The career of Pablo Picasso (b. 1881), one of the most important modern artists, began in Paris during the formative years of Fauve painting. Born in Malaga, Spain, in 1881, Picasso proved a prodigy who at seventeen had achieved an amazing technical facility as a painter. During the early years of this century, 1901–6, he became established in Paris as an artist of considerable stature. The work of this early period, which coincides with the beginnings of Les Fauves and Die Brücke experiments, is largely a romantic, emotional rendering in a sensitive, even tender manner of the lives of beggars, mountebanks, and circus performers, subject matter handled with a comparable degree of tenderness and pathos by Daumier half a century earlier. Two periods are evident in this early work of Picasso, an earlier Blue Period, from 1901 to 1904, during which he restricted his palette to one color; followed by a Rose, or Pink, Period, when he again used a single color, although his pink palette gave to like subject matter a more delicate and sensitive and less tragic interpretation. The forms he painted during his Blue and Pink periods are not realistic representations, but generic symbols of human emotion although the visual reality of natural shapes is not abandoned. By 1906 Picasso had become dissatisfied with the expression of sentiment and emotion and a personal rendering of subject matter; but he was opposed to the intuitive freedom of design and color advanced as major aesthetic elements by the Fauve and Bridge groups.

Between 1906 and 1908, a series of experiments led Picasso and the French artist Georges Braque (b. 1882) to a new concept of painting from which ultimately developed Cubism, one of the most important and influential styles of modern art. The influences and ideas provocative of these experiments

PLATE XIII

Modeled Figure on Conch-shell, New Hebrides (19th cent.) Museum für Volkerkunde, Basel. 1′ 9″ high.

Central Congo, *Mask* (19th cent.) Museum für Volkerkunde Universität, Zurich. 1′ 4″ high.

PLATE XIV

Marc Chagall (1887–) *Accordionist.* M. Knoedler and Co., New York.

Wassily Kandinsky (1886–1944) *Landscape with Red Spots.* Sidney Janis Gallery, New York.

came from many sources, some very distant in time and space. From the 1890's photography had increasingly provided the artist with a greater familiarity with the art of all countries and eras; and of particular interest to these young painters were illustrations of styles not intent on Graeco-Renaissance representation of nature. In 1907 a large comprehensive show of the paintings of Cézanne was held in Paris; and in the same year a letter from Cézanne to the painter Emile Bernard was published, a letter containing the now famous dictum, 'You must see in nature the cylinder, the sphere, and the cone.' Earlier, possibly in 1905–6, Picasso had been introduced, probably by Matisse, to African Negro sculpture. Many other influences were operative on the artist at this period, such as the very early Medieval sculpture of Spain; but the most important sources of influence were the paintings and the published letter by Cézanne, and the sculpture of the African Negro.

During the years 1906–8 Picasso became increasingly absorbed in the problem of forms set in space without benefit of perspective. The interest in form first appears in his portrait of Gertrude Stein of 1906 and reaches a climax during this period in the famous Young Ladies of Avignon of 1906–7 now in the New York Museum of Modern Art. In this painting much of the coloration of the Pink Period still survives; but the figures are described by semi-geometric overlapping shapes that project and express volumes set in an abstract space. The angular rhythmic shapes and heads

of several of the figures recall like elements in African sculpture and are usually considered distortions; but, since they are, as in Negro sculpture, geometric shapes created and arranged to interpret not imitate the human form, there is not any distortion involved. The forms are, in fact, new and personal pictorial interpretations of reality, created entirely within the medium of painting.

By 1908 the experiments of Picasso and those of Braque had produced a kind of painting which was to be named Cubism. This style persisted from about 1908 to 1925, and its influence continued for many years longer. Cubism was consistently concerned with the structuring of form in space on a two-dimensional surface. The name given to this style was entirely reasonable, since shortly after the earliest experiments spheres, cylinders, and cones gave way to cubical shapes and faceted planes, as in Fernande, a portrait of Picasso's model and mistress, dating from 1908 (fig. 469). In this painting, form is represented by monochrome planes, derived from cubes and spheres, that tilt and round out from the background to produce three-dimensional volumes. The hatched painting of these planes is analogous to the rendering of color planes by Cézanne; while the rhythmic relationships between them and the isolation of a few expressive elements indicate a knowledge of African sculpture. The earlier phase of this style has been called 'Analytical Cubism,' since it was a breaking down or analysis of form into such geometric shapes as

469. Pablo Picasso (1881–   ) *Fernande* (1909) Museum of Modern Art, New York. 2' x 1'5".

cubes, spheres, and planes, or usually fragments of them. Subject matter consisted of landscapes, figures, and still-lifes composed of objects of everyday use, such as bottles, glasses, musical instruments. In the earliest phase of facet Cubism, a visual approach to the object obtained, but very shortly thereafter, as in the Still-life, the visual image gave way to the mental or conceptual image, and some of the most important contributions of Cubism resulted.

In Analytical Cubism, simple outlines and thin planes, often transparent, tilted, juxtaposed or overlapping, were used to give every remembered aspect of an object. Since the mind remembers these not as isolated facts but kaleidoscopically as a series of fragmentary views of such distinctive essentials as shape, details, exterior and interior forms seen from all angles, Picasso and Braque represented these various aspects simultaneously on canvas as an organization of broken-up geometric shapes. This concept introduced into painting a fourth-dimension, that of time. Not only was the three-dimensional volume presented, but also the time intervals necessary to comprehend the object from various views were conveyed by simultaneously rendering such an analysis of form. The success of this intention depended to a large extent upon the discarding of depth and perspective and the creation of a pictorial space, as Cézanne had done, by connecting the front and background planes by angled, curving broken planes, a space in which

the objects existed as geometrical shapes in a time-capsule.

By 1911, Braque and Picasso began to introduce into their paintings letters of the alphabet and numerals as cryptic documentation of the object and where they had often encountered it (fig. 470). This was followed by pasting on their paintings pieces of textured colored paper, and shortly afterwards by the use of fragments of such actual materials as bits of newspaper, a calling card, a cigarette, labels from bottles, and playing cards pasted in a compositional arrangement on a background. Experiments of this sort are known as 'collage,' a term derived from the French word for paste. They are among the earliest examples of the use of new materials, an important feature of modern art. The materials employed have no intrinsic aesthetic quality but through their arrangement produce an artistic effect. The artists felt, moreover, that since these materials were fragments of common objects closely and constantly associated with life, the collage was composed of fragmentary elements symbolic of life—in fact, the entire iconography rendered in Cubist art was looked upon largely in this light.

Before the First World War, Cubism developed, partly out of the collage experiments, in another direction. This phase, commonly called Synthetic Cubism, differed in many respects from that of the earlier period. Geometric shapes were now not derived from remembered objects, but were invented or created to build up a design with elements recognizably related to the world of reality, although they are unlike those of natural appearances.

In Synthetic Cubist style, volumed shapes were abandoned for flat planes, often arranged vertically with varying

470. Pablo Picasso (1881–   ) *Still Life* (1911) Coll. Henry Clifford, Radnor, Pa. 2′ x 1′8″.

degrees of projection into space; the planes are frequently segmented into bright color areas and given a textured surface (Plate xII, facing p. 589); and a single point of view, rather than the multiple aspects of the object, brought painting back to a three-dimensional from a four-dimensional realm. Paintings were now decorative, often with a rich variety of shapes and objects, and in some examples, as Picasso's Three Musicians in the New York Museum of Modern Art, the expression and the activity of the human figure became the subject matter of the painting. Although there was no reversion to representationalism, this style does mark a return to content and meaning and to the importance of the sensuous element in art.

At various times throughout his career, Picasso has turned from an experimental, exploratory type of painting to a more traditional rendering of the structural character of the human figure. During his so-called Classical Period of the 1920's, while engaged in the form construction of later Cubism, he painted a number of sculpturesque figures, such as The Spring (fig. 471). In paintings of this kind emphasis is given to a simplified interpretation of mass and to an impersonality of characterization comparable to that of classical sculpture.

In Italy before the First World War,

471. Pablo Picasso (1881–   ) *The Spring* (1921) Private Coll. 2′1″ x 3″.

a group of artists, known as the Futurists, worked for a few years with the problem of the expression of the dynamics of movement in space. The development of the cinema played no small role in the experiments of these artists, to which the Analytical Cubist concepts also contributed considerably. The painter Balla, for example, painted a Dog on a Leash, with movement being represented by a sequence of multiple positions of the moving forms; while others, like Russolo, expressed the force, and the direction of the force, of the rapid movement of a train or an automobile by a more abstract fragmentation of the speeding forms. Although the time-space experiments of the Futurists also employed the device of simultaneity, unlike those of the Analytical Cubists, they recorded simultaneously the various aspects of a moving object, not those of a static object seen by various shifts of the artist.

Although in the various styles of modern painting so far considered there has been an approach toward abstraction, in no case has the object been completely abandoned, but rather it has assumed a new significance. During the nineteenth century, with the decrease of commissioned subject pictures, painters began to select subjects they believed would appeal to the public, or those which would allow them to concentrate on some particular problem. As already mentioned, the latter became the preferred choice toward the end of the century and in much of the painting of the present century. It was inevitable and logical that the twentieth-century experiments and concepts of the *avant-garde* of young artists would lead to a purely abstract painting, an art with no elements based on or derived from the world of natural appearances.

Between 1912 and 1914, the Blue Rider group in Munich carried the expressionism of the German Die Brücke group toward abstraction. The group included Franz Marc, Paul Klee, and Wassily Kandinsky, a Russian painter who was living at that time in Germany. The published intention of these artists was to create an abstract expressionism in which the inner spiritual essence of expression would be spontaneously and intuitionally conveyed in emotionally stirring colors and designs. The fulfillment of the aims of this group were to appear in the painting of Kandinsky before, and that of Paul Klee after, the group had been dispersed by the war in 1914.

Kandinsky (1866–1944) developed the concepts of the Blue Rider pronouncements beyond the realm of visible nature into that of an abstract expressionism in which color, lines, and form have no connotation of natural shapes (Plate xiv, facing p. 621). Through his writings he has made clear his ideas on painting. He considered that art lives as a 'spiritual activity' that transcends the objective material world as does music; and that the artist will create 'within himself, out of his emotion and his spiritual perception and his inner imagining power . . . the form that is externalized in color, line, and mass on canvas.' Although this was a highly personal, intuitional, and mystical attitude, many of his abstract canvases induce a vivid visual and emotional response, independent of any remembered visual image.

Paul Klee (1879–1940), a Swiss artist while living in Munich, shared many of the ideas of Kandinsky, but evolved a highly individual art in which line and fantasy combine with a sensitive color palette to effect a lyrical, original style. For Klee, the painting 'grew' under his brush in a somewhat automatic, subconscious manner until the lines, colors, and shapes were arranged in striking, often delicate harmonies. His paintings frequently relate fantastic with abstract forms, or are composed of completely abstract elements, his invented subjective forms often suggesting a spontaneous growth or creation.

In Moscow in 1913, Kasimir Malevich (1878–1935) founded a completely abstract movement which he termed 'Suprematism,' explaining it as 'the supremacy of pure feeling or perception in the pictorial arts.' The Suprematists were not concerned with the emotional, spiritual expression of Kandinsky and Klee, but rather with the formal, perceptual relationships of visual geometric shapes. At first, simple squares were used, such as by Malevich in Black and Red, a painting in which a black and a smaller red square are juxtaposed within the vertical of the canvas. Later, circles and lines were added, the composition frequently arranged along a diagonal axis.

A movement somewhat comparable to Suprematism developed in Holland in 1917. Known as Neo-Plasticism or as De Stijl, from the name of the publication in which its ideas and theories were presented, the basic elements in this painting were the rectangular plane of pure color, red, blue, or yellow, with some black and white. These color planes were distributed and juxtaposed to give a plastic organization and meaning as 'pure art.' A typical De Stijl painting by Piet Mondrian (1872–1944) (fig. 472) is divided into white rectangles by narrow red and black

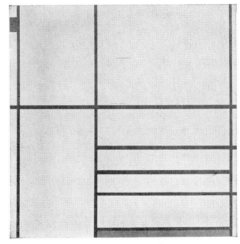

472. Piet Mondrian (1872–1944) *Composition in White, Black, and Red* (1936) Museum of Modern Art, New York. 3'4" x 3'5".

lines, so as to establish a number of formal relationships through the careful proportioning and distribution of the lines and rectangles. Mondrian and other artists of this movement were later allied to the Bauhaus group in Germany, where an association of painters, architects, creative designers and craftsmen were working in close collaboration. The De Stijl concepts, as those of the earlier Cubists, have contributed considerably to architectural forms and details and to the higher standards of design in the applied arts today.

During the early Cubist period in Paris, two young artists developed highly original styles, subsequently influential in the formation of later styles. Both artists, Marc Chagall (b. 1887) from Russia and Giorgio de Chirico (b. 1888) from Italy, combined real and unreal elements to produce pictorially arresting and emotionally provocative canvases. De Chirico composed deep city landscapes stretching back toward infinity, with arcaded buildings, statuary, a figure or two representationally rendered but given a distorted scale and set within deep airless space described by an accentuated perspective. Weird shadows cast by clearly delineated mundane objects create disturbing effects in a spatial vacuum, suggesting the unreality of dreams. This is, moreover, intensified by the clarity of design and the soft colors in these aesthetically appealing paintings.

In contrast, Chagall painted nostalgic memories of his early years in a small Russian village. These are rendered as a kaleidoscopic succession of disconnected and incoherent memories by images freed of all constraint of reason and appear as visions of forms without the density, opacity, and gravity of objects of the physical world. The color is startling, both for its brilliance and for its unrealistic depiction of life forms. These paintings have, in fact, the character of dreams of familar phantoms of life, and it was for this reason that a contemporary critic described them as 'surnaturel.' The fantasy of content, the rich lyrical color, and the unsophisticated rendering of his forms reveal the influence and inspiration derived from Russian folk art (Plate xiv, facing p. 621). In his later paintings, the pictorial equivalents of dream experiences become richer in color and are more often symbols from the deep subconscious realm of repressions and frustrations.

An international nihilist movement, known as 'Dadaism,' was founded in 1916 in Zurich, Switzerland, a movement of sociological significance and of importance as an influence on later modern art styles. The Dadaist movement grew up partly out of the bitter disillusionment of war, at a time when it had been believed that civilized man had 'progressed' too far for war, and partly out of a satirical negation of all recognized values in art and literature, which the Dadaists considered products of a decadent culture. To a large extent, their aesthetic ideas and expressions were borrowed from contemporary art and exploited by banter or satire to negate the validity of this art. The Dadaists included the Roumanian Tristan Tzara and the German Hugo Ball, both poets and critics, and the artists Hans (Jean) Arp, an Alsatian, Max Ernst, a German, and Man Ray, American-born. Important forerunners and later members of the group were the French painter Marcel Duchamp (b. 1883) and the Spanish-born French artist Francis Picabia (b. 1878), both of whom were originally Cubists.

As early as 1912, Duchamp had painted his famous series of pictures entitled Nude Descending the Staircase. These are basically Cubist paintings of a moving figure represented by a series of many juxtaposed and broken aspects, rendered in a manner comparable to the contemporary Futurist style. In these pictures, the forms have a somewhat mechanical appearance but are given a naturalistic animation. A few years later, in his so-called 'ready-mades' period, Duchamp composed his paintings of prefabricated industrial objects and gave them such titles as The Bachelors. In these satirical paintings he appears as a precursor of Dadaism. At the same time, Picabia was progressing along similar lines; while in Italy, de Chirico, who had returned from Paris in 1915, modified his style to represent human figures in mechanical forms. The French Cubist painter Fernand Leger was also using mechanical shapes to build up his forms; but neither de Chirico nor Leger had the satirical negativism of approach of Duchamp and Picabia, both of whom contributed to the formation of Dadaist painting.

The many Dadaist manifestoes proclaimed the absolute spontaneity, freedom, and license of the artist and considered free invention, the laws of chance, and the interchange of anthropomorphic and inanimate forms as important approaches of the artist. They set out deliberately to shock in a blatant, extravagant manner. A representative example of Dada painting is Max Ernst's (b. 1891) The Little Tear Gland that says Tic-Tac, now in the New York Museum of Modern Art, a ready-made consisting of stamped strips of metal painted in space as a solid wall, while below a stream flows out from a narrow tunnel, the stream and the tunnel giving monstrous scale to the canvas. At first, Dadaist pronouncements were of interest to Picasso and the Cubists, but they were later strongly opposed to them; and by 1920, the movement had largely disintegrated as the various artists began to move in other more positive directions. Meanwhile, Dada exhibitions had been held in New York, Barcelona, Paris, Cologne, and Berlin. The name of the movement is of some interest and significance: Dada was selected by opening a French dictionary at random and pointing to a word—it means a 'cock-horse' or a 'hobby-horse.'

In the final analysis, Dada must be considered a negative propaganda movement which sought by ridicule and satire to effect drastic changes in the art and aesthetics of that time. Immediately after the First World War, a more positive propaganda movement appeared in German painting, which was sometime later given the name Neue Sachlichkeit or the New Objectivity. This movement demanded, through powerful and bitter satirical paintings, a reformation in the chaotic, degenerate, and oppressive social and political life of postwar Germany. In style, the art ranged from an exaggerated, caricature-like statement to a searching, meticulous, and hard realism; but, regardless of presentation, the subjects were explicit documents of the objective material world. Important members of this group included George Grosz and Otto Dix.

It should be noted that propaganda in art, often of a nationalist-historical character, has existed almost throughout the history of art. In the twentieth century, other important manifestations of it appear after the revolutions in Russia in 1917, and in Mexico in 1925. Although substantially of documentary, historical importance, propaganda painting often has strong artistic merits and aesthetic value, as in the German and Mexican painting of this century.

In 1924, Surrealism was founded in Paris by the first manifesto by André Breton. It began as a literary movement, but shortly afterward included the visual arts. Breton, a trained psychiatrist, introduced to, or crystallized for, many artists a new source of creativity, the realm of the subconscious; although Kandinsky had explained his aesthetic concept of 'timelessness' in somewhat comparable terms. Two aspects of Surrealism developed historically: the first, one of automatic creative experiments; and the second, the turning to a dream-like subject matter or to the actual contents of dreams or dream states. In the earlier phase, the emphasis was on a free creativity; and in the later, on a new romantic, emotional vein.

The early experiments in automatic creation were attempts to block out the control of reason or thought and to release the creative impulses residing in the subconscious. Both Freud in his psychoanalysis and Bergson in his philosophy stressed the relative insignificance of the sentient, practical, conscious mind as compared to the depth of and hidden riches in the subconscious mind. The initial concerns of the Surrealists were, therefore, to release the subconscious, where they felt that the 'marvelous' experiences resided—that is, anything experienced outside the realm of controlled reason. Various methods, including that of hypnotism, were used to 'free' the subconscious.

A little later the Surrealists strove to merge the conscious with the subconscious and the real with the unreal into a super-reality. The art of this phase is perhaps best seen in the painting of the Spanish-born artist Salvador Dali (b. 1904). Among others, he realized that for Surrealism to be an intelligible art, the images 'experienced' would have to be explicitly communicated to have subject appeal. Dali, therefore, developed a descriptive, representational technique comparable to that of the Dutch Little Masters of the seventeenth century, who gave a complete reality to each texture and every detail, to the objects in a painting. The subject matter was at first based on the dream-like or nightmarish-like images and symbols recorded in psychiatric case studies, and then on a creation or invention of comparable images. In either case, the emphasis was

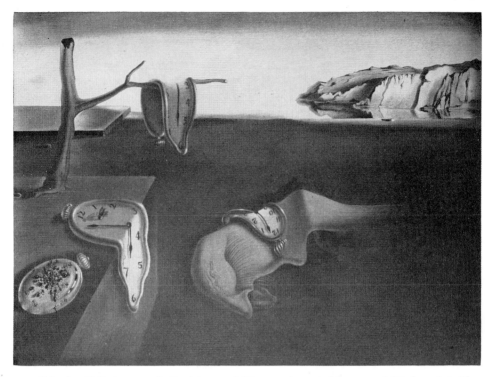

473. Salvador Dali (1904–   ) *Persistence of Memory* (1931) Museum of Modern Art, New York. 10″ x 14″.

upon a realistic rendering of subject matter.

The Persistence of Memory (fig. 473) well represents the style and subject matter of Dali. The theme of the painting is the relativity, flexibility, and destructibility of time. The painting describes meticulously a variety of forms and textures; at the left, a platform supporting a dead tree trunk; diagonally back of this a flat table-like plane; in the center of the canvas a monstrous, amorphous, nightmare-like shape; and a background of nebulous vagueness, limited at the right by seemingly suspended floating headlands of corroded rocks.

The main motives, the four watches, are represented as eroded by rust and as limp pliable forms over the platform, a branch of the tree, and the back of the nightmare-form in the middle foreground. They have a psychological and disturbing relationship with the limitless depth of space and the eroding rocky cliffs at the right background. The entire painting is given a descriptive luminous color and a clear definition of all objects and details; but an abstraction of space and an isolation and starkness of each object differentiates this painting from a realistic imitation of observed reality. Real objects have strange, enigmatical associations and are presented with a dream-like unreality.

A somewhat later and perhaps more characteristic example of Surrealism is Dali's Apparition of Face and Fruit-dish on a Beach (Plate xv, facing p. 652). Two dream-like almost amorphous double images fuse in part to represent the main theme. Ostensibly a fruit-dish, this is also the head of a girl, with deep shell-like eyes and with unpleasant hairy, semi-amorphous gourd or pear-shaped forms (the fruit in the dish) on the top of her head. The image is set deep within the side of the body of a dog, whose broken form extends, with its head at the right middle distance, diagonally toward the left foreground. The head of the dog is at the same time the headlands of a bay, and its collar a viaduct around these headlands. Below the head of the dog, vague, eroded and decayed or fragmentary forms are painted, such as decaying vegetation and a broken brick wall with grass growing from its top. In front of the wall there is a small replica of the monumental fruit-dish. A crumpled cloth and a meticulously rendered length of rope hang over a table-like plane in the right middle distance; while at the left an amorphous shell-like form marks a grooved disturbance in the sand created by the movement of the hind legs of the dog. Limitless space stretches back of these apparitions, interrupted in the left center by floating rocky hills; while a moon or sun nebulously appears in the sky above.

This painting or any like it cannot be construed as a Freudian 'dream picture'; rather it is composed of tangibly clear forms which represent simultaneously two images in a quite weird manner. This is emphasized by the disturbing unreality of the realistically devised spatial setting and by the equally disturbing strange combination of carefully delineated details. The canvas has a clarity and descriptive richness of color essential to the realistic painting of forms and details. Such a painting is not a rendering of anything seen or physically experienced, but rather it stems from a vivid imagination which fuses dream images with carefully observed objects into a pictorially rich and highly arousing picture.

In many respects Surrealism can be considered a synthesis of the elements of modern painting. Practically all of the problems of major concern to artists from the latter part of the nineteenth century on were handled in one way or another by the Surrealists. The conception of subject matter and the essential elements of their style have exerted considerable influence on recent art. A new group, the Neo-Romantics, for example, developed in Paris almost contemporaneously with the Surrealists, from whom they largely derive. They too stressed subject matter and the significance of forms in their paintings, the forms very often combining the real with the fantastic and apparently unreal; but the difference between this art and that of the Surrealists is that every object depicted by the Neo-Romantics is real or a fragment of reality, which assumes a strange appearance due to its deep spatial setting and its relationships with other objects. The Normandy seascapes by Leonid are good examples of this style. Expansive beaches, dotted with human figures and nets, marked with weird shadows, and set in a deep perspective of shoreline and sea, give these paintings a stirring and romantic, if sometimes a strange and enigmatical appearance.

Throughout the twentieth century painters have been concerned with various problems of the medium, such as form, design, delineation, and subject matter. In every case the inventive, creative artist accepted, often unconsciously, one or other of these problems as his own and worked out an unique, personal solution. From the earliest years of the century, the non-academic painter had little interest in representational or anecdotal elements; in fact, the young artist often based his paintings on a personal or enigmatical theme. The enrichment of and the balance given to our culture by these artists is at the present incalculable, but has clearly been very great.

Sculpture of the present century has followed a line of development comparable to that of painting. In the nineteenth century sculptors, even more than painters, suffered from the dictates of the academicians, with their insistence on verisimilitude and on the use of classical figures to convey an effete, allegorical subject matter. If the artist did not subscribe to these requirements, he usually received no commissions. It is no wonder, therefore, that by the beginning of the century sculpture had to a large extent lost its way and that the fundamental elements of the art had been forgotten. The exception was Rodin, who must be considered both as a product of nineteenth-century preoccupation with the technique of modeling and with literary content, and as a contributor in his expressionistic experiments in these two categories to the development of twentieth-century sculpture.

The sculptor, as the painter, is concerned with the organization of forms or shapes in space, but with this difference: the painter must create both his forms and his space, while the sculptor creates his forms in an actual, tangible space. The painter works with volatile shapeless substances, such as pigments, which he applies to a fixed ground, canvas, board, or plaster; whereas the sculptor works with materials, such as wood, stone, clay, or metal, which have inherent properties, as heaviness, bulk, density, volume, pliability, or fluidity. A basic problem of the sculptor, therefore, is the rendering of his subject matter spatially in forms meaningful both of it and of the innate nature of the material he is working with. During the twentieth century, the non-academic sculptors have, in their determination to return to the bases of the art, concentrated on one or more of three aspects of their medium: (1) the rendering of the essential or simplified structure of the human form in an impersonalized manner, so arranged and shaped as to bring out the nature of the material; (2) the use of forms either derived from human shapes or invented to stress a plastic architectural-like construction; and (3) the experimentation with a variety of materials to determine the shapes and techniques proper to them. In every case there has been a direct working in and with the material.

The Seated Woman (fig. 474) by Aristide Maillol (1861–1944) is an excellent example of the first of these three aspects of twentieth-century sculpture. Simplified massive forms, defined by smooth planes and continuous outlines, translate the essential volumes and structure of the human figure in terms of the hardness and heaviness of stone. Each shape, given a full and distinct plastic statement, approaches a geometric solid: the breasts as heavy low cones and the arms and legs as cylinders of varying and changing diameters; all of the shapes arranged in a static harmony and equilibrium to express the stolid and inert nature of stone. No mood or emotional element appears in the sculpture of Maillol, which has the impersonality of Greek sculpture. Subject matter has, in fact, been abandoned in favor of a basic sculptural organization of shapes in stone in space.

A younger contemporary of Maillol, the German Wilhelm Lehmbruck (1881–1919), also departed from a personalized representation of a model and returned to the statement of essential simplified structure of form, but with a difference in intent: Lehmbruck sought to express through his forms, in a sensitive Gothic-like manner, the fundamental spirituality or inner meaning of life, that is, the generic expression of the soul of man. His figures, composed of slender attenuated shapes, stress verticality by a rhythmic nervous upward movement of profiles; while sensitive relationships between forms, such as the space between the hand and the thigh and the long narrow openings between the arms and the body, contribute to an emotional expression.

Cubism in sculpture best exemplifies the second aspect of twentieth-century sculpture—the plastic architecture of forms. Unlike Maillol and Lehmbruck, the shapes created by the Cubist sculptors had less and less the appearance of natural forms, although in many cases they were clearly derived from nature. Those artists were familiar with Cubist painting, and their sculpture shows within the medium similar interest and aims. In 1912, The Dance by Alexander Archipenko (b. 1887), Russian-born, but then living in Paris and now an American citizen, reveals an early phase of his style when the forms were the consequence of an analysis of two figures to determine the fundamental geometric shapes, their defining planes, and inherent mass and volume. Of particular interest to modern sculptors have been the problems of statics and dynamics and the interrelationships of shapes in space. In The Dance a continuous, curvilinear plastic rhythm moving freely in space relates the two figures and contributes, together with the broken angu-

474. Aristide Maillol (1861–1944) *Seated Woman* (*c.* 1901) Tuileries, Paris. Marble, over life-size.

lar poses of the separate parts, to convey sculpturally the dynamics of the
dance. The heads of both figures are
unimportant bosses of conical form, and
serve to completely depersonalize the
group.

A few years later in the work of Archipenko and other Cubist sculptors the

analysis of form became more complete and the resulting figures somewhat more abstract in appearance. The interior, as well as the exterior, character of forms were often expressed, even in the same shape, such as the thigh, by presenting one side of the shape as a rounded convex surface and the other as a concave plane that exposes the volume and density of the shape. The French sculptor, Jacques Lipchitz (b. 1891), now an American citizen, and the Russian artist Ossip Zadkine (b. 1890), both experimented in comparable manner in the analysis of solids, and combined geometric semi-abstract elements with shapes of more complete naturalistic implications. This phase, as in painting, was soon replaced by a Synthetic Cubism, in which abstract sculptural shapes were invented or created and were composed to express a human figure, as in Lipchitz's figure The Bather. While the shapes are not derived from natural forms, they present an unmistakable image of a human figure.

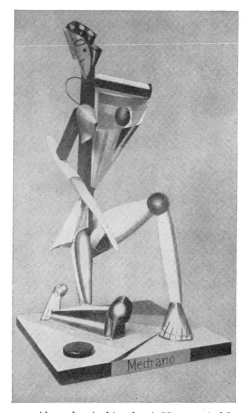

475. Alexander Archipenko (1887–   ) Medrano (1912) Wood, glass, and metal, 2'8" high.

The Cubist sculptors' interest in movement and dynamics appears in the works of a number of artists during the period just before World War I. A good example is The Horse by Raymond Duchamp-Villon (1876–1918), the brother of the painter Marcel Duchamp, a work termed by some contemporary critics 'horsepower.' The movement and power of the horse are interpreted by a disintegration of the natural forms of the horse into semi-organic and mechanical elements, so arranged as to suggest a synthesis of successive movements thrusting upward in a diagonal direction. A marked feature of twentieth-century sculpture, evident in The Horse, was the interpretation of life forms by shapes analogous to mechanical or machine-like parts, a new vocabulary of forms compatible with modern industrial elements.

About the time Cubist painters were experimenting with collage, the sculptors began to construct their figures of nontraditional materials, such as glass, celluloid, tin and other metals, materials of an industrial nature. From about the beginning of the First World War until the present time, the sculptors' interest in the possibilities of such materials and the technologies proper to them have been of major importance, and constitute the third aspect of modern sculpture. The circus figure, Medrano (fig. 475) by Archipenko, in wood, glass, and metal, is an early example; and it also represents the use of polychromy, an element often used in modern sculpture.

As in painting, Cubist sculpture approaches the abstract, sometimes closely, but it does not mark a complete break with anthropomorphism. Even the abstract, often mechanical shapes of the Synthetic phase were combined to create the image of a human figure. A nearer approach to the abstract, however, was achieved by the Roumanian-born artist Constantin Brancusi (b. 1876), one of the most widely known and influential of contemporary sculptors. Brancusi has lived in Paris since 1904, where he assisted in Rodin's studio for a short time and began to develop his own style about 1908. Almost from the beginning his sculpture has had as its starting point the nature of the material itself and not forms derived from or used to create the human

476. Constantin Brancusi (1876–   ) *Leda* (1920) Coll. Miss Katherine S. Dreier, New York. Marble, 2' high.

figure. He has said that 'sculpture is a human expression of nature's actions' and that its intent should be 'to give the sensation of reality, as nature gives it to us, without reproducing or imitation.' The true character of stone, for example, can best be found in the shape of pebbles and boulders as they have been formed by the movement of water, glacial ice, or earth over them. Whether he was working in stone, wood, or brass, Brancusi has always sought after the shapes natural to the material. He felt that the material should itself suggest the subject and forms, and that these should not be forced upon it from without.

Leda, or Bird at Rest (fig. 476) well exemplifies Brancusi's sculpture. It is composed of two carefully balanced geometric shapes, an irregular ovoid as a base, and, rising diagonally above it, an expanding ovoid-rectangular shape. Brancusi considered the ovoid the essential shape most natural to stone and to other hard materials, that is, the 'inevitable character' which he had found in these inorganic substances. In Leda he has created a work in keeping with his aim to purify sculpture of all 'associative distractions' so that it may exist as an art of forms true and natural to the material. He believed that sculptural shapes should express organic growth and should suggest or combine to suggest human or other naturalistic forms. In Leda the surfaces are meticulously finished to achieve a smoothness and high polish 'natural' to the character of stone, and the refinement of the shapes

is worked out with great mastery. The ideas and works of Brancusi have exerted a world-wide influence on sculptors for almost fifty years.

During the early Cubist period, when Brancusi was formulating his ideas and his style, Anton Pevsner (b. 1886), a young Russian artist, worked in Paris for a time with Archipenko. Later, between 1917 and 1921, in Moscow, together with his brother Gabo, Pevsner formulated the principles of the Constructivist movement in sculpture, a movement of far-reaching influence even to the present time. The ideas behind it seem certainly to have been suggested to Pevsner during his years in Paris by the Cubist experiments in new materials. He considered the essence of contemporary civilization to be its industrial content, an outgrowth of the sciences of physics and mechanics, and the development of new industrial materials and the technologies devised for their use. It is a civilization of dynamic content, one in which the space-time factors are of paramount importance in contemporary life. Sculpture, he promulgated, should be a part, as well as an expression of present-day culture, and this may be achieved through the use of new industrial materials and techniques, and by basing sculpture on new motives derived from this culture. At first a semi-abstract movement, it later became as completely abstract, as the then contemporary Suprematist painting of Malevich.

In Pevsner's Abstract Portrait of Marcel Duchamp of about 1926 (fig. 477),

477. Anton Pevsner (1886–   ) *Abstract Portrait of Marcel Duchamp* (1926) Collection Société Anonyme, Yale University Art Gallery, New Haven. Celluloid and zinc, 3′1½″ x 2′1½″.

a number of Constructivist sculptural ideas are apparent. Volume and mass as plastic elements are abandoned and are replaced by depth and space. The head is built out from a background with a number of metal plates or planes of various sizes and shapes placed at such angles to each other as not to enclose space but to present in mechanistic terms both the outer structure and inner volume of the portrait-head at the same time. Thus, the shapes exist dynamically in space through the interaction of plane with plane in the construction of the subject, and through the simultaneous presentation of the exterior and interior aspects of the forms. To a large extent this is comparable to the Cubist concept of simultaneity, in a like rendering of the concave and convex character of a form at the same time. But the important difference here is the complete abandonment of the sculptural elements of volume and mass. In later work of Pevsner and the Constructivists, and that of many other sculptors under their influence, the constructions are completely abstract in content, and a wide variety of materials, such as plastics, welded steel, soldered wire, have been used in their creation.

The Constructivists, therefore, set up as their special sculptural problem not that of form, but rather that of the organization of shapes and planes in space; and to this they added the techniques for working the new materials, and principles derived from the sciences of physics and mechanics. The fundamental aim of both Pevsner and Gabo was to create a plastic art of 'pure reality,' dependent upon no object as subject matter, an art of space and kinetics, of engineering and mechanics, which was both a 'pure' plastic creation and a symbol of the mechanical image of present-day life.

In the work of Brancusi and Pevsner, the human element in art has all but disappeared, so far as any relationship to human form is concerned. With a Brancusi-like attitude toward form as determined by the nature of the material, the English sculptor Henry Moore (b. 1898) has developed an art that expresses the forms and even the emotions

478. Henry Moore (1898–   ) *Recumbent Figure* (1938) Tate Gallery, London. Stone *c.* 4′6″ long.

of life through the 'free' creative handling of materials. In the Recumbent Figure (fig. 478), Moore has not 'freed' a figure from the stone, but has created a stone shape *as* a figure. The simple, heavy rounded shapes are those of stone formed by natural forces; the solidity and heaviness is clearly expressed; while the open spaces within the forms reveal both the density and the tensile strength of the stone, the massive arms and shoulders being analogous to 'bridges' of living rock formed in the geological past; thus, all of the shapes in this figure are those 'natural' to stone. One could say that this is the primary subject matter of this work; but these shapes are used to create a recumbent female figure which has the impersonal timelessness of both humanity and of the material, since in such a work the two are inseparable. Moore has created comparable figures in wood, concrete, and lead, but the forms always grow out of the nature of the properties peculiar to the material.

A somewhat similar attitude toward materials was basic in the sculpture of the Italian Giacometti and of the German-born artist Hans (Jean) Arp, now an American citizen; but in such examples as Human Concretion (fig. 479), Arp has merely suggested the human or organic element, and the work remains a semi-abstract rendering of balanced similar 'stony' shapes.

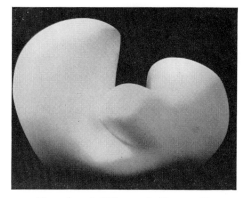

479. Hans Arp (1888–   ) *Human Concretion* (1935) Museum of Modern Art, New York. 1'8″ high.

In sculpture and in painting, the twentieth-century artists have sought as have artists of all ages to solve anew the problems of their medium in order to create an original and freshly perceptive work. The new approach to the problem he set for himself is not fundamentally one of personal choice but is the consequence of the complex of the culture within which the artist is nurtured. That there have been so many special problems set for themselves by the more progressive and creative artists of our times is to a very large extent a direct result of their lack of commissions and patronage. The pressure to invent or to develop a new 'style' in order to attract public attention has led many artists into abortive ways; but the artists of stature have withstood this and have enriched the twentieth century by their creative efforts.

The rejection of eclecticism in architecture corresponds to the rejection of realism in painting and sculpture. Though this prepared the way for some-

thing new, it alone would not have been enough. No great style in architecture has ever been born of a deliberate search for novelty. Architectural styles result from one or more of three factors: first, the emergence of new problems, which includes not only railway stations, airports, and power plants, different from any problems hitherto faced by architecture, but also an altered spirit demanding a fresh form of expression. Second, new materials, if basic and widely enough used in architecture, can create a new style as appropriate solutions are discovered for them. Today steel and reinforced concrete, sheet metal, plywood, and plastics, not to mention glass in large sheets or in the form of translucent bricks, offer countless opportunities for new effects. Finally, new methods of construction play their part. The cantilever principle has been known and used for centuries, but its application in stone and wood is limited. On the other hand, its possibilities in steel or reinforced concrete can be astonishing. Moreover, the substitution of machinery for handwork in the production of building materials and, to a lesser extent as yet, in the prefabrication of the building as a whole or in parts has led to the adoption of repetitive designs of clean-cut units, dependent for their effect upon precision instead of upon the subtleties of craftsmanship. Therefore, the proportion of manual labor in building has declined, a change accelerated by the constantly rising cost of skilled labor. The emergence of all three of these conditions since the late nineteenth century was bound to give birth to a new style.

A gradual desertion of eclecticism by progressive architects in all countries opened the way. The steps taken by Richardson, Sullivan, and Wright in America are the same as those taken by their leading contemporaries in Europe. Some of the houses by Sir Edwin Lutyens in England show the same frank acceptance of materials, the same informality, and the same direct solution, for example in the size and location of windows, that characterized late Gothic architecture such as Compton Wynyates, and yet without the architectural vocabulary of that style. In such a house as Deanery Gardens at Sonning, at the very start of the century, Lutyens' first thought was about the needs of the house, practically and as they pertain to expression, but not at all in terms of historic style. If the small building has a traditional relation of solids and voids, it comes more from the use of traditional materials than from subservience to the past. The northern European countries in particular were active in stripping away eclecticism. The City Hall in Stockholm, begun in 1912 by Ragnar Ostberg, and the Gruntvig Church in 1927, in Copenhagen, by Jensen-Klint, borrow freely from the architecture of the Baltic region but with a fresh interpretation. The widespread ignorance in America of Scandinavian architectural history makes these and other similar buildings seem less eclectic than they really are.

More advanced in style is the Postal Savings Bank in Vienna by Otto Wagner, built in 1905. Not only has it discarded eclecticism but, equally significant, the façade no longer looks like a heavy wall. Its decorative diaper patterns bespeak a light substance enclosing space, as the silk of a balloon confines its gas. Moreover, the windows are almost flush with the wall surface. The band of shadow at the top and side of the window, which in masonry expressed the thickness and therefore the firmness of the wall, no longer exists, and its absence furthers the impression of lightness. On the other hand, these windows are still vertical rectangles, taller than they are wide, a shape inherent in stone architecture. Thus the full implications of the new conditions are not yet apparent.

None of these buildings, most of which were designed before the emergence of cubism in 1909, is more than transitional. Just as pure abstraction was reached slowly in sculpture and painting, the full change to the modern point of view gradually became apparent in architecture. The Bauhaus at Dessau (fig. 480), designed by Walter Gropius in 1925, demonstrates the new style in all its scientific rationalism. Glass encases the workshop above the ground floor, and the whole exterior surface of the building on this side is cantilevered, overhanging the ground story by several feet. We can see some of the concrete columns and floors through this screen of glass. The maximum of light thereby admitted is less important than the demonstration of the new principles of

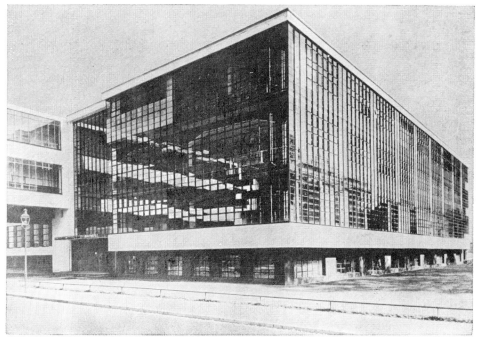

480. Walter Gropius (1883–) *Bauhaus*, Dessau (1925–26) Main block 167' x 49'.

structure and the dramatization of lightness in construction. The wall looks like a skin drawn over a frame, as thin as possible both in appearance and in actuality. The fundamental concept of the building has changed from that of a mass to that of an enclosed volume. The elimination of the wall as a weight-bearing member in itself has lightened the building and permitted an additional lightening of its component parts. Moreover, the rectangles, as units of this design, are the horizontal shapes of steel or concrete construction. Finally, the severe cubical shape parallels and is allied to the Neo-Plasticist compositions of Mondrian (fig. 472).

The plan (fig. 481) of the Tugendhat House at Brno in Czechoslovakia, designed in 1930 by Mies van der Rohe, betrays its light construction. Compared with masonry buildings, this plan seems to have no supports at all. A very slender metal column or two, and strips of thin wall here and there are sufficient to carry the light flat roof. No partitions divide the living quarters into rooms; screens, some of them movable, indicate that a given area is intended primarily for one purpose but is not restricted to that purpose. The interior space flows from one part to another with a minimum of interruption. This sense of openness and of flowing volumes stems ultimately from the work of Frank Lloyd Wright, who exerts profound influence on European architecture.

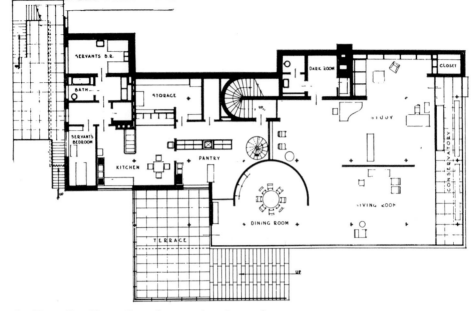

481. *Tugendhat House*, Brno (1930–31) 53' x 115'.

The house turns its back on the street. An overhanging slab shelters the entrance, with broad sheets of translucent but not transparent glass to admit light but to preserve privacy. On that side of the house are the necessary services. The owner may drive his car into the garage without that tedious process of backing and turning so often necessary in suburban homes in America where the garage is placed at the back. Here, these occupants are less concerned with the street, its noise and public character, than with the magnificent view behind, where the land falls away and where is found most of the property belonging to the house. If all is utility on the street front, the back (fig. 482) is a delight. A wall of glass hardly separates the interior from the exterior and allows the maximum advantage to be taken of the view. This window, if we may call it that, extends around the corner, and a porch and steps lead down to the lawn. The flat roof exploits the cantilever principle. Thus the house seems composed of block-like horizontal rectangles, easier to see than in the Bauhaus. These are asymmetrically disposed from the standpoint of utility and interior convenience.

This arrangement is dictated by a careful, almost scientific exploration of the purposes of the house and its several parts. In designing a modern house, the architect considers the probable routes of its occupants pursuing their daily occupations, in order to arrange the house so that these paths shall intersect as little as possible. The idea applies on a small scale the principles that govern modern highway design to minimize friction and interference. To this end, the open interior (fig. 483) greatly assists. This openness also offers communion with nature. The owner or his guests may be in the open air under partial shelter in the porch, or on cooler days may enjoy from within the beauty of the outdoors. So large a glass area admits the maximum amount of natural light when that is wanted; when it is not, movable draperies control its quantity. Modern materials, modern methods of construction, and a rational determination of as many factors in the problem as possible have produced here a charming house of great flexibility in its adaptation to its purposes.

Since 1946 extensive reconstruction has been carried on to replace the losses resulting from the Second World War. Most of this building, however, has been so hurried and under such pressure for economy as to have only moderate importance. The poverty of many countries has compelled a preference of concrete to steel as the primary structural material, except perhaps in England and Germany. Furthermore, a growing social consciousness has prompted extensive housing projects for low income families in all countries of Western Europe. In the realm of monumental architecture, the strip windows and glass wall of the Termini Station in Rome, designed in 1947 by Montuori and Callini, and others, are qualities of the International style that combine effectively with an old Roman wall. The Royal Festival Hall in London, completed in 1951 by Matthew and Martin,

482. Miës van der Rohe (1886–   ) *Tugendhat House*, Brno (1930–31).

483. Miës van der Rohe (1886–   ) *Tugendhat House,* Brno (1930–31) Interior.

demonstrates the connection of functionalism and appearance. Foyers, lounges, and restaurants, afford fine views of the city across the Thames, and completely encase the large auditorium to preserve its admirable acoustics from disturbance by noises from without.

The arts from the days of Egypt on down have always written a faithful and tangible record of their civilizations. They still do so in the twentieth century. The adoption of modern materials in sculpture and architecture in itself has created forms of expression open to no previous generation. The searching and turmoil of modern life, the impact of the machine and of science, and the willingness to experiment in every direction have left their imprint on the arts of our own times, as these same forces have been modifying our lives. No one can predict the future in the arts any more than in other fields. Indeed, dependent as the arts are upon civilization, we would have to know what the future will demand from life in order to imagine what its art may be. We can be sure of only one thing: since humanity demands the arts for enjoyment and expression, if not for existence, they will continue to live and to change as long as man continues to exist and to change. As man alters his needs, real or imagined, so too will the arts develop, and continue to reflect in the future as they have in the past whatever manner of culture man may shape for himself.

THE ANCIENT NEAR EAST

In the land lying between the Tigris and Euphrates rivers, and to the east of it, in the plateaus and sandy valleys of Iran, or Persia, archaeologists have unearthed pottery that dates back into the prehistoric period, about 4000 to 3000 B.C. From Samarra, Susa, and other sites they have taken vessels fashioned by the hands of early inhabitants which are so homogeneous that they indicate a civilization opposed to that of nearby Babylonia. Swastika and lozenge patterns, the ibex (fig. 484), and the serpent are popular, as are life-giving water (indicated by waving lines) and hills of patterned triangles. Trees in that arid land are already an important motif, as are birds, bulls, and sheep. Man plays a somewhat minor role, often reduced to geometric forms portrayed by simple angular or curving lines. Cult figures of

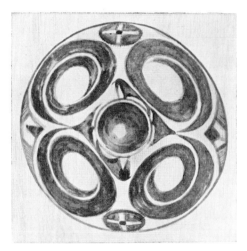

484. *Painted Jar with Conventionalized Ibex* (*c.* 3500 B.C.) Oriental Institute, Chicago. Pottery.

gods and goddesses, especially those latter who might grant children, were modeled in the round, and were found with the usual weapons and instruments of flint, stone, and clay. Fine craftsman-

647

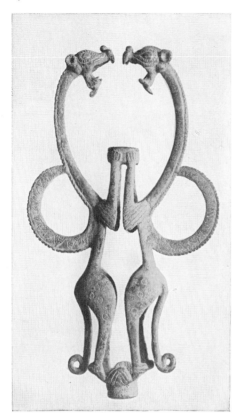

485. *Finial* (*c.* 2700 B.C.) Museum of Fine Arts, Boston. Bronze, 6¼″ high.

and Susa, showing a technical skill and artistic talent unsurpassed in the ancient Near East.

Gilgamesh, hero of the epic poem, is a frequent subject, a symbol of man the powerful hunter, the ideal of these and later generations; composite animals, winged or horned, confront each other (fig. 485), or pursue each other in the eternal combat that seemed as inevitable as day following night, and, indeed, became the symbol of day devouring darkness. Even Luristan weapons were ornamented with these vigorous and expressive animals, and their bowls and cups, dating as late as the ninth century, have similar designs in repoussé. Lithe, elegant, and spirited, filled with life though simplified to pattern, they give a hint of the particular genius that will always illumine Persian art.

THE ART OF THE MIGRATORY PEOPLES: STEPPE ART

ship and artistry of a high order are evident, marked by clarity of design and a wonderful sensitiveness in stylizing forms derived from the world around them.

By the bronze age, about 2700 B.C., many of the same motifs were adapted by metalworkers for cheek plaques, bridle ornaments, weapons, and jewelry made in Luristan. Using a technique that may have had its origin in Armenia as early as 3000 B.C., they fashioned all kinds of trappings and gear for the Lur horsebreeders who lived east of Samarra

Iranian metalwork, with its emphasis on balance and stylization, differs from the art of the migratory peoples who ranged from the eastern part of Siberia to the steppes of the Black Sea area in Russia. Nomads and hunters, shifting from place to place with their tents, carts, and possessions, swooping down on their more settled neighbors, left no records other than the metal objects placed in their tombs or dropped in combat. Weapons, tools, and bits of ornament must serve instead of books to give us some idea of their culture. In the proto-historic period, an Indo-

European group of Iranian race, called *Scyths* by Greek historians and *Śaka* by the Indian, occupied the lands north of the Black Sea; while other nomadic groups penetrated Central Asia. From about the beginning of the Christian era the movement was reversed, changing from east to west, as the *Hsiung-nu* (Huns) pushed from the borders of China into south Russia and Hungary, followed in the sixth century of the Christian era by the Mongol Avars, and successive waves of Turks and Mongols through the thirteenth century.

Between 750 and 700 B.C. the Scyths had dispossessed the Cimmerians north of the Black Sea, retaining mastery until the fourth century B.C., when the Sarmatians in turn conquered them. Though classed as Indo-Europeans in race, their customs resembled those of East Asiatic tribes in their predatory existence, their killing of sacrificial victims, their burying alive of serving people and horses around the body of the chieftain. According to Herodotus, who wrote in the fifth century B.C., to express grief they slashed their own arms, foreheads, and noses and they drank the blood of their victims; they were understandably classed by the Greeks as complete barbarians.

Near Maikop on the southern steppe in the Kuban area, and in the Ukraine, graves of chieftains have yielded up magnificent jewelry, weapons, ornaments, and plaques in gold and bronze. The most striking designs were of birds and animals common to that part of the world—creatures of the herd and hunt.

Locked in combat or intent on pursuit, they were ever alert to danger. Even on awakening a stag glances backward, feet drawn up under him, ready to spring to safety (fig. 486).

486. *Pectoral of Lioness from Kelermes* (c. 500 B.C.) Hermitage, Moscow. Gold, inlaid with amber.

Modeled with skill, vigor, and simplicity, this art is often referred to as Animal-Style Art to distinguish its dynamic and imaginative character from realistic Greek objects found in the same tombs. Its influence has been widespread; in the Far East, it was copied by less expert craftsmen in bronze and wood in the Ordos on the borders of China and in Siberian settlements, while in Central Europe and Scandinavia it was to enrich the repertory of artists for generations to come. Textiles from graves of Hsiung-nu of the Altai region and Mongolia, dating from about 200 B.C., and Persian carpets of the sixteenth century have similar patterns of combat. Twisting, interlacing forms—sometimes of the whole animal, sometimes of a part of an animal—detached and woven into compact designs, drawn directly from nature or exaggerated into the grotesque, they are to be found alike in the jades and bronzes of China and on the manuscript pages and church façades of medieval Europe, a legacy from the folklore of the moving hordes.

The Scythians wore peaked caps with ear flaps, and leather tunics and trousers, appropriate clothing for a horse-riding people who lived on the windy steppes. We see them thus as they are represented in the bas-reliefs of Persepolis, among tribute bearers to the Achaemenid kings of the fifth century B.C.

THE ARYAN INVASION AND
HISTORIC PERSIA

By 900 B.C. an invasion had taken place on the Iranian plateau by Aryan people who came from the vast plains of the Oxus and Iaxartes, westward to the area south of the Caspian Sea. Their language was one branch of the Indo-European family, and developed into Old Iranian and Sanskrit. They came with new gods and new ideas of a society divided into caste groups, which left their mark on Persian culture as on that of north India, where some of them settled. The first Iranians to be of importance historically were the Medes; in 612 their king Cyaxares took Nineveh and destroyed the Assyrian Empire, as his in turn was conquered in 550 by Cyrus, the Achaemenid. From that time until the conquest of Alexander the Great (334–327 B.C.), the Achaemenids ruled over an empire unrivaled in size and importance in the ancient world, from Lydia south of the Black Sea to the Oxus on the east, the Indus bordering India, and the Nile of Egypt, including the Chaldean or Babylonian Empire with its Syrian dependencies on the Mediterranean. They organized and welded together peoples of divergent tongues and religious practices, holding them under a humane despotism.

Cyrus, Cambyses, Darius, and Xerxes were the conquerors and builders of that empire, failing only in the conquest of Greece in the fifth century. Their tombs, palaces, rich robes, and jewels were the wonders of their time and set a standard of splendor that still colors our imagination when we think of the Oriental potentate. Out of the cliffs rising above the sandy Iranian plains they had tomb chambers cut, as the Egyptians had, so that the body of the emperor would lie inviolate. The tomb of Xerxes at Naqsh-i-Rustam near Persepolis (fig. 487) consists of a façade ornamented with relief sculpture of the ruler standing before a fire altar, supported by men from thirty nations of the empire, representing but not portraying their real appearance, for they look like a string of identical paper dolls pasted upon the face of the rock. Inside the rectangular chamber the body of the king was laid in state, clad in magnificent garments, protected by his weapons, but without the food, utensils, and favorite furniture that would have been buried with an Egyptian king, for he did not expect to return to the tomb. He was a monotheist, a follower of the god Ahura Mazda who, as the 'wise lord,' was recognized by the ruling house as the greatest of the gods, and was worshiped to

487. *Tomb of Xerxes*, Naqsh-i-Rustam, Near Persepolis (*c.* 465 B.C.). Stone.

the exclusion of all others. The deity is shown in sculpture as a human figure emerging from a disk that forms the center of a bird's body, similar to the winged sun-disk of Egypt, and he holds a circlet, symbol of power, in his hand. As the principle of Light, or Goodness, he was also represented by fire, so the fire altar is another important element of Achaemenid culture in architecture and sculpture. It takes the place of spacious temples necessary in the more

elaborate rituals of their contemporaries the Egyptians; for these makers of the Persian empire, their altars, palaces, and tombs sufficed.

Differing from the rock-cut tomb, the free-standing sarcophagus of Cyrus (fig. 488), ancestor of Darius, is built of stone blocks. Like a small, compact gabled house set upon a platform of six steps, the rectangular chamber is, therefore, at the seventh level. It was a treasure house as well as a mausoleum, for Cyrus had been buried with pomp and magnificence.

More sumptuous than the tombs were the palaces, especially those of Persepolis and Susa, built by the hands of the conquered people, using materials brought from all corners of the Empire. Until they were burned by Alexander the Great, the palaces of Persepolis were among the most stately ever erected by man, with tall, slim columns (fig. 489) that are even today fitting monuments to the 'King of Kings' who ordered them built. Under Darius about 520 B.C. work was started, destined to continue for 150 years. Judging by the elaborate sys-

tem of conduits and drains hewn in the rock platform, the initial plan of halls and dwelling quarters must have been made in the sixth century and followed by later architects.

A stairway of 106 steps, low enough for horses to walk up, led to the Gateway of the World (fig. 490) of Xerxes, through which passed the bearers of gifts at the New Year festival. On the gate were outer and inner doors, faced with bronze, about 30 feet high. These were flanked by winged guardians, bulls with human faces like the Assyrian monsters, but carved with a grace and purity missing in the Assyrian proto-

488. *Tomb of Cyrus*, Pasargadae (*c.* 530 B.C.) Stone, interior 10′ long x 7′ wide.

PLATE XV

Salvador Dali (1904–   ) *Apparition of a Face and Fruit Dish on a Beach.*
Wadsworth Athenaeum, Hartford, Connecticut.

PLATE XVI

Bihzad, *Sultan Hussein Mirza in a Garden*. Jahangir's Album,
Gulistan Library, Teheran.

489. *Apadana of Xerxes with Palace of Darius in the Distance*, Persepolis (c. 465 B.C.) Stone.

types, and without the fifth leg favored by the older artists.

Beyond were the royal buildings based on the old Iranian hypostyle house. The principal façade consisted of an open portico, the side walls were of brick, and the interior supports were limestone or wooden columns. These halls follow the same orientation, with spacious courtyards between them, formerly planted with trees and shrubs. The effect of space and height was increased by the clever use of open stairways outside of most of the halls, which added to the impressiveness of processions at audience time. The Apadana (audience hall) of Xerxes (fig. 489) must have been the scene of many such pageants; it was a square hall, with walls of sun-dried brick 15 feet thick, a ceiling 60 feet high supported by slim columns, and a great throne room which could hold ten thousand people. There were flights of steps on the north and east sides, and both stairs were adorned with sculpture of tribute bearers, the figures done in three registers, each measuring about 270 feet in length. The

490. *Gate of Xerxes*, Persepolis (486–465 B.C.) Stone.

Medes in conical caps and the Persians wearing crowns brought lotus blossoms; the Syrians brought gold vessels and a chariot drawn by Arabian horses; the Bactrians (fig. 491), coming in from the eastern deserts, led a two-humped camel. These and the others of the twenty-five nations are shown facing the stair, each group separated from the next by a cedar tree, the ancient Tree of Life, here shown as though split through the middle, with trunk and branches visible from the top to the bottom and as symmetrical and elegant as an ancient bronze. All faces, hands, and feet are directed toward the focal doorway, suggesting the procession, but the figures are as rigid as those of Egypt, without any indication of bodily motion. In contrast to Egyptian sculpture, however, the arms and torsos are seen from the side, so that there is an increasing realism; the sculptors were careful, too, in observing individual racial types and costumes of the gift bearers, but they are types, not individuals. The details of headdresses, hair, weapons, and garments are done as meticulously as in Assyrian art, and they are as patterned, but there is no emphasis here on brutality, on bulging muscles, or on constant combat; the sculptors achieved an ordered purity and clarity, a stability that may reflect the stability of the Empire. The figures project at the same level from a background that is kept

491. *Bactrian Leading Camel*, Stairway, Palace of Xerxes, Persepolis (486–465 B.C.) Stone, 3′ high.

492. *Lion Attacking Bull*, Stairway, Palace of Xerxes, Persepolis (486–465 B.C.) Stone.

bare. There is no attempt to indicate locale or to suggest space; the carvers respected the wall as a limiting member, primarily architectural. In the brilliant sunlight of Persepolis, every clearly cut line and every shadow form effective parts of the dignified, majestic pattern.

In contrast to the men, who stand expressionless in their frozen world, the animals are endowed with emotion and personality. In the angle of the stairs, flanking the spear-holders, are two scenes of a lion attacking a bull (fig. 492). Though the effect from a distance is one of heraldic grandeur, on close inspection one sees the fury in the lion's face and claws, made more dramatic by linear patterns cut sharply in the stone, which by contrast bring out the subtle and simple planes in the head of the bull. Though the same theme of attack was used so often by the creators of the Animal Art of the steppe country, the stylization of hair and muscle as seen here at Persepolis marks a difference in concept. The registers are separated by bands of rosettes repeated horizontally, each one a perfect copy of the other, clear and pure in contour, and interesting because of repetition rather than because of variety, such as one would find in the medieval carving of Europe. Another decorative motif is the ziggurat, the stepped pyramid, here used as a crowning member on stairs and platforms.

493. *Double Bull Capital*, Palace of Artaxerxes II, Susa (404–358 B.C.) Louvre, Paris. Stone, 10' high.

Within the halls, columns of wood or stone broke the space into small units. Some of the capitals and imposts, consisting of young bulls placed back to back, carried the beams that upheld the flat ceilings. These bicephalic impost blocks (fig. 493) are carved with the same precision, love of pattern, and symmetry that marked the relief sculpture. The shafts of the stone columns are relatively taller than those of Greece, some 60 feet high, and are cut by more flutes; the shaft is separated from the capital by an intervening member ornamented with volutes and rosettes. These elements, combining with a high base (fig. 494), are so characteristic that they are referred to as the Persepolitan Column, a unique development in Achaemenid art.

The living quarters, like the audience halls, emphasized spaciousness and beauty of detail. The Tachara (winter house) of Darius, which was also raised on a platform, had doors, windows, and niches of stone which survived the burning of Alexander, though the walls of brick have disappeared. The Egyptian influence is so strong here as to suggest that the architects were Egyptian. The Hadish (men's quarters) of Xerxes was placed on the highest level of the terrace, from which stairs led down into the nearby dark rooms of the Harem (women's quarters). In all of the buildings the dark limestone was polished with great care, giving it a uniform smoothness, clarity, and grace.

Within the walls of brilliantly colored brick there must have been splen-

494. *Column Base*, Palace of Artaxerxes II, Susa (404–358 B.C.) Louvre, Paris. Stone. Base, 2' high.

did feasts and gatherings. The metal bowls, pitchers, drinking horns, and cups give evidence of the same love of beauty that marked the arts of building and stone carving. This was an aesthetically consistent part of the world destroyed by Alexander the Great, in the fourth century B.C., as he swept through on his conquest to India and reduced the Achaemenids and their monuments to ruins.

That conquest left an impression of Hellenism on Iran through the succeeding period, the Seleucid, 323–250 B.C., but it did not smother the flame of creative Iranian spirit. After the intervening rule by the Parthians, 250 B.C.–A.D. 226, who were the 'middlemen' in the profitable silk trade between the Romans and the Chinese, a new Persian dynasty came to power, the Sassanian, which lasted from A.D. 226 to 642. Ardashīr, Shāpūr, Bahrām, and Chosroes are among the illustrious names of the Sassanian rulers who sought to encourage a flowering-again of the arts practiced by the Achaemenids. Like their forebears, they became world famous for their sculpture, metalwork, textile weaving, and architecture.

Unlike the flat-roofed palaces at Persepolis and Susa, the Sassanian edifices were domed and vaulted, which made for a great uncluttered interior space. A typical palace built for the Sassanian kings is the one called Tāq-i-Kisra (Arch of Chosroes) at Ctesiphon (fig. 495). In the mild climate of Mesopotamia, on a site chosen by the first of the line, Ardashīr, this winter resi-

495. *Tāq-i-Kisrā*, Ctesiphon (A.D. 242–72) Brick, 312' wide x 112' high.

dence was erected by Shāpūr (A.D. 242–72) after his defeat of the Roman emperor Valerian. A barrel vault with a span of 84 feet runs through the center of the building; smaller rooms and chambers are placed on either side, with thick outer walls in which arcades are the ornamental feature. Among them are pointed arches, an innovation at this early date. We have to imagine the brick and rubble walls as they once looked, covered with smooth stucco and relief sculpture painted in gay colors. Since the native mortar contained a large quantity of gypsum, which sets quickly, the huge central vault was made entirely without centering; it was classed as one of the wonders of the world. Beneath its majestic curve the kings held audience with a splendor rivaling that of Darius and Xerxes; even the carpet on the floor, called the Springtime of Chosroes, was famous.

Another of the palaces, at Fīrūzābād, demonstrates the ingenious use of squinches, which were built out in radiating arches from the angles of the square central chamber to meet the circle of the dome that topped it. They were used here for the first time and were to become an integral part of Moslem architecture later on, as well as an important contribution to the art of building in Europe. In the same audience hall the traditional Egyptian cornice was placed over the doorways, showing the Sassanians' pride in their past and their skill in working out new solutions.

In their sculpture they showed the same respect for the past and eagerness for the novel. Like the Achaemenids, the Sassanian rulers had huge images carved in the cliffs. These serve as monuments to the glory of the kings, but not as part of tomb ornament, rather as independent works of art commemorating investiture, victory, or the king supreme in combat and the hunt. The investiture of Ardashīr I (fig. 496) emphasizes the relation between god and emperor as Ardashīr receives the diadem from Hormuzd (Ahura Mazda). The two face each other in a composition as symmetrical in plan as that of an ancient bronze from Luristan. The heads, shoulders, waists, knees, and feet of the men are at the same level, as are the heads, bodies, and feet of the horses. That love of symmetry inherited from the past and the profile head and full-front torso technique are in contrast to the new elements—a soft modeling in surface modulation in which there is great variety in projection from the background, the use of flying ribbons, the hanging foot, and the mobility of facial expression.

Even more vigorous is the carving of Bahrām II, A.D. 276–93, in combat. Riding full tilt at his opponent, in the flying gallop, he unseats his adversary as easily as a great monarch should, showing a third-century version of a technique that will sweep over Europe a thousand years later in the Age of Chivalry. Antedating the use of chain mail in Europe, this flexible, protective armor made of rings of metal joined together was worn by the kings of the

496. *Investiture of Ardashīr I*, Naqsh-i-Rustam, near Persepolis (A.D. 224–41) Stone.

Sassanian period. It is to be seen in the large portrait of Chosroes II at Tāq-i-Bustan. There, deep in the Garden Arch carved in a cliff that rises above an artificial lake on the royal hunting preserve, he is shown in high relief in full armor, with helmet, lance, and shield, seated upon his richly caparisoned horse. On either side of this equestrian, on the inner surface of the arch, some hunting scenes were carved, showing him in action and giving us a good idea of the royal sport as practiced in the seventh century. These scenes, smaller in scale than the Persepolis carvings, are considerably broader in scope. Men, women, animals, and vegetation are suggested in an atmospheric setting, in which light and shade play an important part, though perspective and focus in the Western sense are lacking. They are charged with emotion, full of tumult and excitement. The animal forms, especially, are done with sensitiveness and understanding: the heavy elephants moving through the underbrush, which they trample with their big feet; wild boar racing across the compound; deer in the flying gallop, heads held high, or crumpling as the arrows of the king find their mark; all are remarkable studies of individual animal forms and all are a part, too, of dramatic narrative.

Roman influence had left its mark in the same site. The large arch of the

497. *Peroz I Hunting* (457-63) Metropolitan Museum, New York. Silver, 8½″ high.

Grotto is not unlike a triumphal arch in size, though it is carved in living rock, not free-standing. In the spandrels were angels of victory, the winged Nikes inherited from Greece, Western-looking goddesses with curly hair and flowing classical robes, who hold a cup of pearls and a circlet of sovereignty. As in much of the other Sassanian sculpture, the change from Achaemenid times is evident in the more careful modeling of the body beneath the drapery, a more realistic anatomical study. Flanking the arch are panels of foliate ornament, the leaves resembling prickly acanthus but adapted to a symmetrical tree-of-life pattern, which shows the ancient Iranian love of the motif.

Many of these designs cut into the cliffs as monumental sculpture were adapted by metalworkers in the gold and silver bowls and the cups and pitchers designed for Sassanian feasts. The figures are raised from the background in various levels of projection, as in the sculpture, and show the same interest in surface modulation. The contrast of human and animal forms; the excitement of the hunt (fig. 497); the calm majesty of the ruler enthroned, 'assailing the onlooker by his glance' and surrounded by his nobles; moon symbols and sun symbols; natural animals and composite creatures; all were pictured by the craftsmen, often in conjunction with leaf and flower patterns, and pearls. One of their favorite motifs was the *senmurv*, or *si-murgh*, a fabulous animal who sometimes had the head of a dog, a fox, or even a camel, the claws of a beast of prey, the tail of a peacock or rooster, and the wings of a barnyard fowl, the whole generally framed by a circlet of pearls or leaves.

These designs were used also as architectural ornaments, judging by the stucco reliefs once placed over the bricks and rubble of palace walls. They invaded the field of textiles, too. We can imagine how dearly these fabrics were prized when we find that some were preserved in the sands of the desert along the Trade Routes, that others served as inspiration for Chinese textiles, and that still others are now in the museums and churches of Europe—all monuments to the Sassanids as much as were the great domes and arches and rock carvings. The fragments now in European collections are bits from fine silken wrappings made for the bodies of early Christian martyrs, which were placed in the church treasuries and until recent times were shown as wonders from the Holy Land. Among the patterns of these ancient textiles are the senmurv and cocks, horses, hunting scenes, the tree of life, the rose, the pearl, all done in heraldic splendor. Having revived the glory of the Achaemenids in an art that touched all of the civilized world, the Sassanian princes weakened, then crumbled, before the onslaught of Islam in the seventh century.

ISLAMIC PERSIA

Mohammed was born in Mecca, Arabia, about A.D. 570, and began his teaching in his early manhood, urging his fellow Arabians to follow his leadership toward an inspired monotheism. This offended the pagan aristocracy, who sensed a threat in his desire for change, and he was forced to flee to Medīna in 622, which marks the beginning of the Moslem calendar—the year of the Hegira. He built a house that was also used as a mosque in Medīna, and set about the political reform of the rest of Arabia, coupling it with his religious fervor in winning converts to his belief in Allah, the One God; in ten years of struggle and warfare he accomplished his task. Arabia was unified politically, and the majority of the population were followers of the Prophet, fired with enthusiasm to bring the rich neighboring countries under the domination of the Arabs and Islam.

498. *Detail of Frieze*, Mschatta (743-44) Staatliche Museum, Berlin. Stone.

sisted of four porticoes (*liwan*), each covered with a flat roof supported by columns and arches, which enclosed a courtyard in which there was a fountain for purification. On the side toward Mecca the liwan was more impressive than the others, for it contained the *mihrab*, the prayer niche marking the direction of Mecca, and the preacher's pulpit, the *mimbar*. Towers, called minarets, or *mināra*, were erected beside the large rectangle so that the muezzin could call the faithful to prayer (fig.

The first caliphs lived simply as Bedouins, but, as the northern countries were brought under their sway, the Byzantine ideas that permeated Syria began to influence the internal organization of the Mohammedans and there was an increasing splendor surrounding the leader, who was established at Damascus. Finally, in the eighth century, the capital was moved to Baghdad, and a rich material civilization came into being.

Even when the court was in Damascus, the caliphs had wished to rival Byzantium, and had instructed the architects, who were brought in to build their mosques, to make them on a scale comparable to Christian churches, in richness if not in size. The mosque (*Masjid* or *Jami'*) was their first concern; it con-

499. *Interior of North Dome*, Congregational Mosque, Isfahan (1088) Brick.

507). As in Byzantine and Syrian churches, the ornament usually consisted of intricate surface decoration in mosaic, colored marbles, metalwork, and carved wood (fig. 498).

As Sassanian power was overthrown in the seventh century, Islam spread throughout the land and Iran became a stronghold of Mohammedanism. By 747 a princely Arab family, the 'Abbāsids, revolted against the caliphs of Damascus (the Ommayads or Umayyads) and set up the 'Abbāsid Dynasty, which marked a triumph of the Persian element, for they considered themselves 'Moslem Sassanids.' Like the line of kings before them, these caliphs became enthusiastic patrons of the arts.

501. *King Hunting and Holding Audience,* Detail of Silver Ewer (1232) British Museum, London. Inlaid, medallions 1½″ high.

Under the caliphs and their Turkish sultans the mosques (figs. 499, 500) developed into splendid monuments which combined some of the features of old Sassanian architecture, adapted to the needs of the Mohammedan congregation, with new motifs. Structurally, the builders used the pointed arch, the dome, and the squinch. Over these were placed stucco ornaments, glazed tile, and brick. Honeycomb elements of increasing complexity were developed in the squinches, breaking the vaulted surfaces with pockets of light and dark. The use of columns and arches in the interior gave an impression of shadowy coolness, kept from seeming overpowering and aloof by ornamental patterns and inscriptions. In both Persia and Turkestan the ceramic artist and the architect worked together to create magnificent structures, arched and domed, gleaming in various shades of blue, yellow, and rose under the clear blue skies.

Ceramic arts flourished. Some pottery was made to imitate metalwork in a less costly medium. Lusterware gave the effect of gold or silver, while other potteries made full use of blue, green, yel-

500. *Northwest Iwān,* Congregational Mosque, Isfahan (12th cent.) Brick.

502. *Bowl with Polychrome Painting* (1242) Victoria and Albert Museum, London. Pottery, 8″ diam.

low, and other strong colors. In both pottery and metalwork old Sassanian motifs persisted (figs. 501, 502), notably of the king hunting and holding audience, though in later examples he began to have a very Turkish cast of face, with slanting eyes and long black hair. Writing done by master calligraphers was considered a handsome ornament on plates, and on the mihrab and walls of the mosque. Thus old Persian elements were combined with Arabic and Turkish ideas under the influence of Islam to form a rich and decorative art.

Literature, too, flowered under this patronage. In the eleventh century, in Afghanistan, Firdausī wrote the *Shāh-namah*, the Book of Kings, which he dedicated to his patron, the Sultan Mahmud, in A.D. 1010. He had gathered together fragments of truth and legend about the ancient rulers and heroes of Persia, and fused them into one of the world's great epics. It marks the beginning of a rich literature and serves as a favorite text for calligraphers and painters in succeeding centuries.

The practice of making fine books went well back into the past. One of the most renowned artists of the book was Mani, leader of the religious sect of the Manichaeans, who lived in the third century of the Christian era in Persia. Influenced by both Christianity and Mazdaism, filled with religious fervor, and inspired by a vision of a heavenly messenger who bade him proclaim his teaching, he tried to win converts at Ctesiphon but met with little success. He was regarded by both Christians and orthodox Zoroastrians as a heretic, and was forced to go east into the desert and oasis settlements to spread his gospel. There he met with great success. Being a gifted painter, he illuminated his scriptures with brilliantly colored figures of the men and women of the congregations, of the heaven they would reach by right living, of the demons of the world of darkness, and of flowers, fruits, and other lovely things on this earth. This attractive way of recording and spreading his teaching infuriated his opponents as much as did his doctine, so the Manichaean books were burned whenever they were found. Modern scholarship knew of them only by reputation and hearsay until the German expedition of Grünwedel and Von Le Coq to Chinese Turkestan in the early twentieth century. There, in the dry sands of the desert, they found a number of fragments of the precious texts, written in flowing script and still glowing with color. They had probably been made for the Uighur Turks, ardent followers of Mani who had established houses of worship not only in the oasis cities but also in China, when they were staunch allies of the Chinese in the eighth and ninth centuries. These texts date from before the tenth century, and bespeak the long tradition of miniature illumination encouraged by the followers of the first teacher.

Turkish in type, with slanting eyes and straight black hair, the figures are very much like those painted on pottery in the twelfth and thirteenth centuries in Persia, especially at Raiy (Rhages) (fig. 502). The heads are big and the hands very expressive, costumes are painted in great detail; but the setting is often ignored. These two creative streams—of painting on pottery and of illustrating religious texts—seem to have nourished the ground from which grew the superb art of book illumination in Persia.

Under the 'Abbāsids many treatises were translated on natural history and mechanical wonders. They were illustrated in a style similar to Syrian work derived from Greek and Byzantine art, as well as to the pottery and manuscript painting of Central Asia and Persia. The early thirteenth-century Dioscorides manuscript (fig. 503) shows two physicians cutting a plant. The men face each other, separated by a large plant as symmetrical in form as the ancient tree of life portrayed at Persepolis or

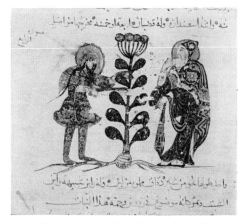

503. *Physicians Cutting Plant*, from *Materia Medica of Dioscorides* (1224) Freer Gallery, Washington. Opaque color and gold on paper, 5″ x 7″.

on a Sassanian textile. The balanced arrangement of men and plant reminds us, too, of the Luristan bronzes, almost as old as art itself in Persia. The faces, hands, and feet of the men are shown in profile, as they were at Persepolis, and their garments are as rich in pattern as those of Chosroes at Tāq-i-Bustan; they even have floating scarves like the Sassanian kings, and they exist in space untouched by cloud or shadow. Only the eyes and hands give some indication of Near Eastern vivaciousness, and bring life to a composition that might otherwise be too static for illustration. Primary colors were favored, as direct as folk embroidery. Not all of the Dioscorides illuminations are as simple as this one, but it is quite typical of the figures scattered through the text; the miniature does not occupy a page by itself—it is incidental to the writing, and fitted into whatever place was left for it by the calligrapher. It differs from

Greek manuscript illumination in that much of it seems to have been painted for the sheer pleasure of having it there, since the illustrations are not very explicit as diagrams to be used by doctors.

Another text illustrated several times in the thirteenth century was the *Maqāmāt* written by al-Harīrī, a kind of *Canterbury Tales* of the Arabs, done in rhyming prose. In his illuminations, which are gaily colored and lively, the painter al-Wasiti brings a freshness and boldness to the tale that is quite appropriate to the adventurous hero. Even when he is painting camels, and not some fabulous creature, he lets his imagination play and sets down colors that are delightful and quite unrelated to nature—pink and mauve as well as tan, vibrant tones that give as much life to the camels as the lines of their bodies. He states already one of the purposes of the Persian illustrator: though not bound by the appearance of things as he sees them, to give them such beauty of form and color that they seem more vivid to the beholder than do the natural objects from which they were derived.

In the thirteenth century a political change came, with the Mongol invasion of Jenghis Khan and his followers, which was bound to affect the arts profoundly. Baghdad escaped until 1258, but eastern Iran was overrun in 1220 in an appalling destruction, and welded into the Mongol Empire, which stretched from the seacoast of China through most of Asia (except India) into Russia and eastern Europe. With

a genius for organization that rivaled the ancient Persians, these nomads held their wide territory together and opened trade routes that allowed much freer traveling between eastern and western Asia. Culturally it brought together the two important civilizations of the East and West, the Chinese and the Arabo-Persian. Men from each section were sent to the other by the ruling khans whenever they were needed to assist in warfare and administration or to bring pleasure to the palaces. The Mongol khans soon learned to live as patrons of the arts, and began to have books illuminated as had the caliphs and their courtiers.

The Manāfi' al-Hayawān (a natural history describing the characteristics of animals and their properties useful to mankind) was painted under the Mongols in the last decade of the thirteenth century, and shows the mingling of Chinese and Persian methods. The stag

504. *Stag and Doe*, from *Manāfi' al-Hayawān* (1297) Morgan Library, New York. Painting on paper.

and doe (fig. 504) are not placed symmetrically within the border of the miniature, but diagonally; the tree, instead of being in the exact center, with an even number of leaves and flowers or fruit growing to the right and to the left, is also diagonal and to one side, like a Chinese plum in a Sung painting. Above and to the left is a Chinese cloud scroll—one of the first cloud and shadow effects to be used in a thirteenth-century painting—which does not, to the Western eye, suggest much space, but it is an attempt on the part of the artist to deal with atmospheric effects. The ground plane is more of a suggestion than a real description of locale, but, thanks to the graded tone and shading and to the Chinese hills on the right, it gives an impression of a foreground on which the deer stand. The love of surface decoration on the bodies of the animals, the patterned treatment of legs and heads, and the careful delineation of little plants are typically Persian. Another illustration is of the senmurv, which looks much more like the pheasant of Chinese art than the composite creature on Sassanian silks and metalwork. A critic was prompted to write on the margin, 'Thou fool, since thou hast never seen the senmurv, how canst thou portray it?'

In the early fourteenth century, painters were still trying to combine Chinese and Persian ideas in their illustrations. In Rashīd-al-Dīn's *History of the World*, written for the Mongols, the illuminators had a wonderful opportunity to let their fancy rove, for the history dealt with India, China, the Near East (including Bible stories), and the other countries brought under Mongol suzerainty. As David is summoned to be king (fig. 505), we note the Arabian costumes, the checkered carpet that extends vertically up the page, the detailed painting of fruit and leaves on the trees, and the use of the architectural arch with its floral ornamentation,

505. *David Summoned To Be King,* from MS. of Rashīd-al-Dīn (1307) University Library, Edinburgh. Painting on paper.

506. Bihzād, *Sultan Hussein Mirza Revelling*, from a Būstān MS. (1488) Royal Egyptian Library, Cairo. Painting on paper, 12″ x 8½″.

placed next to two trees that are quite Chinese in their irregular form. All are done by a painter trained in the Chinese method of handling a brush, making lines thick or thin to suggest vol-

507. *The Old Court* (15th cent.) and *Minaret* (*c.* 1730) Shrine of Imām Rida, Meshed.

ume or shadow. Here, line rather than color is dominant in most of the illustrations.

Gradually, as the conquerors took on more and more Iranian characteristics, the painters allowed Persian elements to overshadow Chinese, and by the fifteenth century the most accomplished and splendid miniatures came into being. The word miniature describes them properly, for the ideal was one of infinite care, painstaking detail, compositions planned with exactitude to give

the most dynamic effect, and color of the most precious and exquisite tones. The subjects illustrated lent themselves to this kind of interpretation: the *Shāh-nāmah*, the great epic based on Persian history, was still popular, and the poems of Sa'di, Nizāmī, and others, dealing with rose gardens, nightingales, mournful lovers, the wine cup, the excitement of victory, and speculation upon life and death, could be illuminated by the painters in an art intoxicating to the senses.

508. *Tahmīna Visiting Rustam*, from a Shāh-nāmah MS. (15th cent) Fogg Museum, Cambridge, Mass. Painting on paper, 8¼" x 4½".

509. Bihzād, *King Darius and Herdsman*, from a Būstān MS. (1488) Royal Egyptian Library, Cairo. Painting on paper, 12″ x 8½″.

Though political change and destruction had come with the second great conquest by a Turkic horde (that of Tīmūr or Tamerlane in 1369), one of Iran's most renowned artists flourished in the fifteenth and sixteenth centuries: Bihzād. This master of the miniature lived first in the eastern center of Herāt, and later moved to Tabriz. Both there and in Samarkand beyond the Oxus there was a ferment of artistic production under royal patronage.

Bihzād and his contemporaries painted the courtly, poetic, or mystic scenes suggested by legends of the past, or revels (fig. 506) of their time. Faithfully portraying the costumes, carpets, flowers, wine bottles, and intricate architectural ornaments, they may serve as records of that society, but they exist in a world of the imagination more vivid than what the mortal eye sees. An entrance door, encased in enamel tiles as brilliant in design and color as the architecture of the mosques (fig. 507), allows one to step into a scene of feasting and drinking inside a garden wall. Surrounded by a flaming plane tree and a poplar, and with the sound of music in the distance, the sultan and his friends are partaking of food and wine so freely that one member has to be assisted out. When we see Tahmīna entering the chamber of Rustam at night (fig. 508), we are so intrigued by patterns, colors, and the appointments of the room, by the shy tilt of her head, the dramatic gesture of the attendant as he lifts the curtain and holds the candle for her (the only indication that it is night, for the painter would not be so foolish as to darken his singing colors by making the room black), and by the interested expression of Rustam as he turns in bed to see who his unexpected caller may be, that we are trans-

510. *Queen of Sheba,* School of Bokhara (16th cent.) Anet Collection, Paris. Ink on paper.

ported into the realm of poetry. Even when out-of-doors is painted fantasy enters in. Darius, when out hunting, almost injures one of his herdsmen (fig. 509), who walks up to the King of Kings, and reproves him for not being better acquainted with a faithful servitor. Bihzād, like the makers of neolithic pottery and Luristan bronzes, uses trees, mountains, running water, and animals as his motifs, but he paints trees more exquisite than those one would see on a day's outing, and flowers scattered through the grass as though they were on a carpet, each one displayed so that the beholder gets the full impact of form and color. Rocks (still a bit Chinese) are like the inside of a shell, all opalescent hues of mother-of-pearl; horses are pink, lavender, maroon, and even sky-blue; the stream was once silver, but is now black owing to oxidation, the only pigment that has suffered with the passage of time; the men, dressed in garments of many colors, are not entirely natural in pose, but their expressions are drawn from life; the horses are done by a man of acute observation. The flowers and trees are based on things Bihzād had seen, but he has chosen to arrange and color them to suit his needs in the picture. He and his fellow painters had elevated the art of illustration to such a degree

that they were on a level with the calligrapher, and were allowed a whole page for the miniature, not just a random corner unoccupied by the writing. Line and color were used to create compositions so vibrant and clear that sheer realism was unwanted (Plate xvi, facing p. 653).

As conditions changed in the Safawid period, the patrons could not always afford such luxuries, and the tendency in the late sixteenth and seventeenth centuries was to concentrate on single figures (fig. 510) or on brush sketches left uncolored. Again Persian art came close to Chinese, but the idiom was quite strongly Iranian by that time. Much of the old power was gone; the taste seemed to be for languid men or women delicately posed. It was not illustration of epic or the glorification of kings: the lyric, poetic character and the effete refinement of a civilization nearly stagnant were reflected by the painters. The makers of textiles and carpets, however, were more faithful to the old themes, borrowed from the earlier, brilliant miniatures. They had not lost the glory, nor was it dead in painting and architecture; it was transplanted into India by the descendants of Tamerlane, the Moghuls (*Mughals*), after their conquest in the sixteenth century.

XXIX

EARLY INDIA

In the Neolithic period, 3000 B.C., people in India were busy making pottery and weapons. Excavations at the sites of Mohenjo-Daro and Harappa in the Indus Valley have thrown much light on the way men lived in the region some five thousand years ago, and show that there was actual contact between them and their neighbors in Mesopotamia. Seals discovered at Tel Asmar, near Baghdad, show elephants and humpbacked bulls of India like those from Mohenjo-Daro. The dating of the Tel Asmar finds at about 2800 B.C. is the key to the chronology of the Indus Valley cultures.

The thirty acres of ruins at Mohenjo-Daro have yielded rich materials from those early days. It proved to be a planned city with streets laid out north and south, east and west, to catch the prevailing winds which swept and ventilated it. Houses were made of burnt brick of a quality superior to that used in Mesopotamia and Egypt. Some of the buildings on the streets were designed with rounded corners so that pack animals could pass without dislodging their loads. The dwelling places and shops seem to have been spacious but of a moderate size, and uniform to the extent that no palaces or homes of nobles are indicated. Within were pleasant rooms, open courts, and separate bathrooms which were connected with sewers—as tall as a man—in the side streets. We may deduce from this their emphasis on cleanliness, and picture a society so well organized that community plans could be carried out.

The largest edifice in the center of the city is a bathing pool, 39 feet by 25 feet, with an outer wall 8 feet thick,

circular *yoni*, which in Neolithic years mark a phallus-worshiping people. The power of male and female, of generative force, already is evident in the art of India.

Among the human figures carved and modeled by the early people are some very striking examples of men and women that have a particularly Hindu

511. *Torso from Harappa* (*c.* 3000 B.C.) Archaeological Museum, Mohenjo-Daro. Sandstone.

and a row of chambers on the east side. Since other temples and sanctuaries are lacking, it is probable that this pool, fed by a well, was the gathering place for purification and healing, even as the Ganges is today.

Water, which cleanses and makes growth possible, is still associated with the conoid vertical *linga stones* and the

512. *Dancing Girl*, from Mohenjo-Daro (*c.* 3000 B.C.) Archaeological Museum, Mohenjo-Daro. Bronze.

character: a sandstone torso from Harappa (fig. 511) which has an inflated look and stresses plumpness as a mark of beauty; a slim dancing girl (fig. 512), nonchalant, angular, and bejeweled, from Mohenjo-Daro; and the countless mother goddesses, begirdled and coiffed. There is already in Indian sculpture a sensitive awareness of plastic form and a gift for endowing form with life.

Typical of India, too, is the love of animals displayed in the clay toys and in the seals. In contrast to the Near East, where combat and pursuit were so often shown, the feeling here is of affection. There are no evidences that these people admired war-like traits; instead, their energies went into the domestication of animals, for ponderous elephants are shown before mangers for the first time in either history or iconography. Men subdued animals by an inner spiritual force, it would seem, as the beasts bow down before man, their lord, or serve as vehicles for gods and goddesses. Rhinoceros, tiger, elephant, and humped bull are carved with unequaled beauty on the steatite seals, and done with a skill quite lacking in the human figures and trees, though the men bow before the tree and the tree spirit. Here, as in the Near East, there is tree and serpent worship, and here, too, composite animals are symbols of power. So compelling were these ideas that they survived the Aryan invasion and flowered again in popular Hindu imagination much later, in the medieval period. The Aryans had come down to the Indo-Gangetic plain from Iran,

probably early in the second millennium B.C. They brought their own religious ideas with them, but also gained much from their predecessors, the Dravidians, who had a highly developed culture. It was the fusion of these two elements that was to produce the basic Indian culture. Society had been divided in pre-Aryan days into three castes, the Brahmans who served as priests, the warriors, and the husbandmen. To these the Indo-Aryans added a fourth, the serfs. The priests officiated at the ceremonies to their many gods by chanting and singing hymns, the Vedas. These probably came into being about 1500 B.C., and were followed, about 1000 B.C., by the Brāhmanas, which set forth rules for ritual and sacrifice, and later by the Upanishads, which were speculative philosophical treatises. In these works, and in the later mythological texts, the Purānas, are the roots of all Indian religion, Hindu, Jain, and Buddhist. We have little to guide us in imagining any of their visual arts, but the poetry of the Vedas is magnificent. Their hymns to the Dawn, to Sūrya (the sun), to storm and wind and cosmic order, even to the fire of sacrifice, are among the most moving that the mind and heart of man have ever conceived.

In the sixth century B.C., India produced some great thinkers and masters. The two most important were Mahāvīra, founder of the Jain sect, and Gautama, who was to become the Buddha. The latter was born Prince Siddhārtha, heir to a noble family of Kapilavastu, Nepal. His mother had a dream in which a white elephant descended and entered her body, and this was interpreted as meaning that she would have a child who would be either a world ruler or a Buddha. At the time of his birth she went into a garden and when she touched a tree with her right hand the child issued from her side. All the world rejoiced: other young things were born, flowers appeared miraculously, the air was scented with fragrance, and all the birds sang. Siddhārtha was received by the ancient Vedic gods, Indra and Brahmā, and was given his first bath. He took steps in the four directions, symbolizing his universal sovereignty, and lotus flowers sprang up beneath his feet.

From this auspicious birth, his life was protected and fortunate. He married a beautiful girl when he was sixteen, winning her hand by proving his prowess in many contests. His life in the palace was one of ease and pleasure. Though his father deliberately screened him from a knowledge of human suffering, he did finally become aware of it through three sights: when driving out through the streets he saw an aged man; then, later, a diseased man; and, still later, a corpse. The realization that old age, sickness, and death existed made him impatient of the life of pleasure. He resolved, when he saw a mendicant friar, to renounce the world.

He stole out of his palace at night assisted by his grooms and by dwarf earth-spirits (*Yakshas*), who upheld the hoofs of his horse so that no one would waken to stop him. Safely outside, he took off his princely robes, cut his long hair, and began his life of asceticism. Six years of it convinced him that he was still far from illumination, that he must find it by meditation. Later, when he felt that the moment was near, he sat down beneath a fig tree, where he was tempted by the demon Māra, whose evil cohorts and beautiful daughters could not shake him from his contemplation. Māra offered him temporal power, but he remained

513. *Aśokan Capital* (322–185 B.C.) Archaeological Museum, Sārnāth. Sandstone, 7′ x 2′ 10″.

unmoved; falsely accused, Siddhārtha touched the earth, calling it to witness in his behalf. Then, having resisted temptation, the moment of enlightenment, *Bodhi*, came, and thenceforth he was a Buddha.

At Benares, in a deer park, he preached his first sermon, expounding the Four Noble Truths: that suffering must come to all living things; that its cause is desire; to eliminate suffering, one must eliminate desire; to achieve that, one must have good thoughts, good words, good deeds. That was the beginning of a long life of preaching over most of northern India, where he urged compassion and performed many miracles. He established monastic foundations for men and women, insisting that they take the vows of poverty, chastity, and obedience, and go, like him, out into the world with only a begging bowl.

In the year 483 B.C., when he was eighty, he felt that death was near, and called his favorite disciples around him. After giving them final instructions, he passed into Nirvāna. His body was cremated as the nations of the earth mourned, and the relics were distributed, some to be placed beneath earth mounds, or *stūpas*, as he had directed.

As the years passed, there were more and more adherents to the doctrine he had preached. Aśoka (264–*c.* 227 B.C.), one of the kings of the Maurya Dynasty, urged all his subjects to become followers of the Compassionate One. His edicts recommending the teachings of the Buddha were inscribed on tall pillars similar to those of Persepolis. The pillar at Sārnāth (fig. 513) was topped by four lions, symbol of the Buddha as leader of the Śakya clan, and on the abacus below were carved wheels, symbols of his teaching when he set the

514. *Stūpa No. 1*, Sānchī (70–25 B.C.) Stone, 54′ high, 120′ diam.

515. *Yakshī*, East Gate, Stūpa No. 1, Sānchī (70–25 B.C.) Stone.

Wheels of the Law in motion, and the lion, elephant, horse, and humped bull, symbols of the great rivers of India, the whole representing the Law as spreading in all directions in time and space.

To the faithful these edict pillars had a holy significance, for merit was to be gained by walking around them. As in the Indus Valley sculpture, the animal figures display unusual technical skill and a profound understanding of the forms.

Aśoka sent missionaries to Ceylon, Burma, and the East Indies, and often they carried with them the first civilizing forces known to those countries. Symbolic art, in that it could teach unlettered tribesmen about the Buddha, was one of the powerful agents in conversion and worship, and so from Mother India spread ideas and formulas for building monuments and making images that gave rise to some of the most beautiful and the most significant art in all the Eastern world.

In the Ganges Valley, stūpa no. 1 at Sānchī is well preserved (fig. 514). It consists of an outer stone railing pierced by four gateways at the cardinal points of the compass. Within is a terrace, then the hemisphere of earth and stone, and the crowning member, a platform and parasol stand, which was both axis and symbol of kingship. The gateways, done in the first century B.C., are crowded with narratives and symbols related to the Buddha in relief that reminds us of ivory carving, as well it might, for a guild of the workers in ivory probably had a hand in it. In all the richness and profusion Buddha is never shown in human form, though he is symbolized by the wheel, lotus, lion, empty throne, Bodhi tree, and by his footprint. His followers are there, as well as animals, and the spirits of air, earth, and water who had come into Buddhism from Vedic days. Swinging out from the East Gate is a Yakshī (tree spirit) (fig. 515), who embodies the

ancient tradition of the ideal feminine form, the dancing girl adorned with bracelets, lithe, sinuous, full-blown. In contrast the male Yaksha is ponderous and earthy, conforming to the male ideal of the Harappa torso, having the same 'inflated' look. Persian art glorified kingship, but these slabs show commoner and king, man and animal, for all were beloved by the Buddha.

At Sānchī, and earlier at Bhārhut, there are stories in stone of previous existences of Gautama, the *jātakas*, which tell wonderful tales of the Buddha when he was king of the monkeys, or a six-tusked elephant, rescuing his friends and repaying evil with good, done with a narrative gift that seems particularly

516. *Sūrya*, Buddhist Railing, Bodhgayā (185–80 B.C.) Stone.

517. *Chaitya Hall*, Kārlī (185–80 B.C.) Interior. Stone, 124' long x 45' high.

Indian. At Bodhgayā, there are spirits, symbols, and the ancient gods, including Sūrya, god of the sun, driving his chariot across the sky (fig. 516). The railing marked the path of the walk taken by the Buddha when he rose from beneath the sacred fig tree after the Illumination.

The believers worshiped in temples carved into the living rock, the Chaitya Halls, found in western India at Kārlī (fig. 517), and elsewhere near Bombay. Though no structural support was needed, beams were chiseled out of stone like wooden ribs, and columns spaced along the sides. Light was admitted through a clearstory window in the façade, set under a double-curved arch, one of the most characteristic features of early Indian architecture. Inside, the focal point for the worshiper was the stūpa carved in stone at the far end of the sanctuary—a smaller version in sculpture of the great mounds of Sānchī and Bhārhut. Here, too, merit was gained by walking around it in a sunwise direction.

Out in the border province of Gandhāra, beyond the Indus, the Good Law spread. Monasteries had been established, stone carvers were busy. The ruling house, the Kushāns, an Indo-Scythian or Śaka people who dwelt there from c. A.D. 50–320, were ardent Buddhists. On the coin of King Kanishka (died A.D. 160) the Buddha is shown as a standing figure wearing a flowing robe, more like a Roman orator than an Indian mystic. Graeco-Roman influence here went back to the conquest of Alexander the Great and was strengthened by the Bactrian heirs of Alexander, who, in turn, left a Hellenistic legacy to the Kushāns. Up in the foothills of the Pamirs, in the Punjab, and down the Indus Valley, these men of Greek heritage brought new forms and ideas to the service of Buddhism. Tritons, Atlantids, Herculean men with bulging muscles, women as wise as Athena and as ample as Demeter, cupbearers—even the Trojan horse—appear now associated with the Buddhist hierarchy.

It is a hybrid art, a late flowering of the Hellenistic seed, infused with a spiritual power born of India, giving

rise in time to strange and wonderful creations in Central Asia, China, and Japan. Here, and at Mathurā in the Ganges Valley, Buddha and Bodhisattva were carved in stone as majestic men, no longer simply suggested by symbol.

518. *Casket of Kanishka* (A.D. 2nd cent.) Provincial Museum, Peshāwar. Gilded metal, 8" high.

On the Casket of Kanishka (fig. 518), as well as on his coin, and on votive stele (stone memorials dedicated by the faithful) and among the figures in the round found in ruins of monasteries, the Buddha is a sturdy figure, clad in a flowing robe (fig. 519). His features resemble Apollo of the Praxitelean type,

519. *Buddha* (1st-5th cent.) Guides' Mess, Hoti-Mardan. Stone.

when he, like other princes, wore heavy earrings.

Even more Indian in form are the Bodhisattvas (fig. 520), those beings who had attained the essence of wisdom but not full Buddhahood; Gautama had been one before he sat beneath the sacred tree and received enlightenment. Instead of the robe covering the whole body, they wear the dhotī cloth wrapped around the waist, leaving the torso bare, as was natural in a hot country. Jeweled turbans, bracelets, earrings, and beads are among the 'thirteen precious objects' that distinguish them. Heavy lids droop over languid eyes, a

his hair curls back in waves from his forehead and the body under the drapery is carved in the Graeco-Roman tradition. But the mark between the eyes, the *ūrnā*, is Indian, as is the protuberance on the top of his head, the *ushnīsha*, for both are marks peculiar to the Buddha indicating especial virtue. The long ear lobes remind us of his days in the palace before the Renunciation,

520. *Bodhisattva*, from Sahri Bahlol. Stone.

small mustache often shadows the full lips, and a fold of flesh rolls above the dhotī. These are princely beings, not monastic followers of rule and discipline.

The hands of Buddha and Bodhisattvas are often shown in particular gestures, *mudrā*, which have an especial significance. These mudrā were used by the sculptors to indicate various attitudes, and were recognized by the beholders at once; they go with Buddhism into Greater India, Central Asia, China, and Japan. The hand up, palm out, meant 'Do not fear'; the hand pendant, palm out, was extended in charity; one hand laid upon the other, palms up, was the mudrā of contemplation; in discussion one hand was raised, thumb touching second finger; and when the Buddha was seated yoga fashion, legs crossed and soles of his feet turned up as he sat under the Bodhi tree, he touched the earth with his hand extended, palm in, calling the earth to witness when he resisted Māra the demon and thus symbolizing resistance of all temptation.

Some of the most beautiful Buddhist figures were made in stucco, in molds, discovered by members of the French Delegation to Afghanistan when they dug in the ruins of Hadda. Dating probably from before the fifth century of the Christian era, when the invasion of the Epthalite Huns left destruction in its wake, they show an expressive power and a love of individuality quite rare in an art that tended to become stylized in Gandhāra. All the minor deities and

521. *Mara*, from Hadda (5th cent.) Musée Guimet, Paris. Stucco, 1' high.

characters are done as portrait studies. There are Apollonian youths, angelic beings who might have come from a French Gothic cathedral, and diabolic ones who might be ancestors of gargoyles. There is a tribesman in a long coat (fig. 521), a Mongoloid person sometimes called Māra, and there are languid, graceful people who are purely Hindu; it was a meeting place of many types, all brought to the service of the Buddha, fashioned by the hands of

On such a huge scale, the work is impressive rather than beautiful, and bears witness to the enthusiasm of the devotees who came there. In the photograph, we can see the damage done by

522. *Colossal Buddha*, Bāmiyān, Afghanistan (5th cent.) Stone, 175′ high.

sculptors known to us only by fragments that remain.

The French Delegation unearthed Syrian glass, metalwork from Rome, ivory from India, and Sassanian works from Persia. Throughout the countryside there are abundant proofs of the international quality of the art of the area, which was largely due to caravan trade and to pilgrimages made by the Buddhists. In Bāmiyān, the faithful had carved two colossal Buddhas (fig. 522) in stone cliffs overlooking the valley, one 175 feet high, the other 120 feet high.

523. *Bodhisattva*, dedicated by Friar Bala (A.D. 131–32) Archaeological Museum, Sārnāth. Sandstone, 8′2″ high.

the Moslems who were offended by these images and destroyed their faces in target practice from across the valley. We should suppose that carving the enormous figures in the living rock, and attaching folds of drapery to wooden pegs set in holes drilled in the rock, would be task enough for the makers, but Chinese pilgrims of the fourth and seventh centuries speak of the great statues gleaming in the sun, so metal must have been used as well. The niches were covered by layers of plaster and frescoes were painted there, Buddhist in inspiration but international in style, Sassanian, Hindu, and Hellenistic motifs predominating.

Down in the Ganges Valley parallel developments were taking place. At Mathurā (Muttra) another great center of religious sculpture had been flourishing, probably from pre-Buddhist times, in a place now holy to Hindus, Buddhists, and Jains. The stūpa art must have been contemporary with that of Sānchī, while the practice of making Buddhas and Bodhisattvas in monumental forms was as common there under the Kushāns as it was in Gandhāra. One of the most important of these is a standing Bodhisattva dedicated by Friar Bala (fig. 523) in the third year of Kanishka, or A.D. 131-2, a figure 8 feet high, which was the ideal according to the Indian canon of proportion. In every respect the Indian ideal is followed; it has the torso of a lion, the arms of a hunter, the long supple legs of a deer. The drapery, too, is of the native type, consisting of the

dhotī, low girdle, and scarf thrown over one arm, leaving one shoulder bare, all of a light transparent material, rather than of the heavier cloth that made

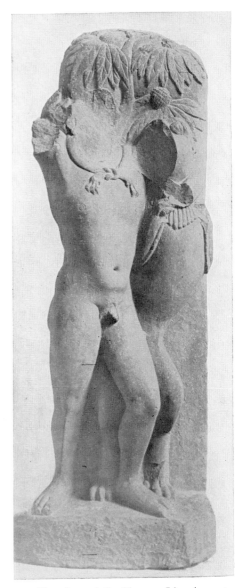

524. *Heracles and the Nemean Lion* (A.D. 50–320) Indian Museum, Calcutta. Stone, 2'6" high.

such prominent folds in the Hotī-Mardan Buddha. The relatively small head, with its round, wide-open eyes, and its smooth hair brushed back from a sloping forehead, has none of the Greek-god softness noted in the Gandhāran type. There was Graeco-Roman influence in Mathurā, to be sure, in Olympian heroes (fig. 524), but they are expressed in an Indian idiom, in the local red sandstone.

Far to the south, on the east coast, another fine group of Buddhist sculptures were found at Amarāvatī, on the Kistna River. Perhaps because the greenish marble was better adapted to the carver's needs, perhaps because it was farther away from foreign invasion, it is in many respects the most beautiful of all. Slabs once used on stūpas, since burned and looted, suggest that the southern sculptor portrayed with an effortless ease the whole panorama of life: crowded streets, palace interiors, even the realms of the Tushita heavens whence came the white elephant to Māyā, the mother of Buddha. Bodily tensions and movement, utter relaxation, drama and calmness are there (fig. 526). Compositions are sometimes unbearably crowded, sometimes done with an almost mathematical precision.

525. *Representation of a Stūpa*, from Amarāvatī (A.D. 150–300) Government Museum, Madras. Marble, 6'3″ high.

526. *Buddha and the Elephant, Nalagiri,* Stūpa No. 1, Amarāvatī (A.D. 150–300) Government Museum, Madras. Stone, 3'8" high.

Lithe and energetic, the men and women seem to pulsate with life, a splendid expression of an Indian ideal, which was able to show in sculpture the difference between a dead man and a sleeping one. The relief is generally high and well-rounded, designed by artists who had an excellent understanding of light and dark values in expressive sculpture. Gradations are more subtle than at Sānchī, indicating a more mature approach on the part of the carvers.

In architecture, too, there is a marked originality. The stūpa, as we see it in the small slabs of relief sculpture (fig. 525), was surrounded by a railing, but there were no gateways as at Sānchī. A moonstone was placed at the entrance, and five slender columns were set inside at the terrace level, both features we shall see in Ceylon. Sculpture was used lavishly, at first symbolizing the Buddha,

and later showing him in his monk's robe. The evolution at Amarāvatī from the Age of Symbol to the Age of Representation is so gradual that we are hardly aware of it, just as we feel no shock of transition from this art of the Āndhra period (220 B.C.–c. A.D. 300) to the classical art of the Gupta (A.D. 320–600).

The Gupta kings, natives of Bihār who extended their rule throughout the Aryan north, though not Buddhists, encouraged arts of all sects. Gupta images

527. *Buddha Preaching in the Deer Park* (320–600) Archaeological Museum, Sārnāth. Sandstone, 5'3" high.

528. *Cave XIX*, Ajantā (320–600) Façade. Stone, 38' high x 32' wide.

became models for later generations in India and in faraway lands. The Preaching Buddha of Sārnāth (fig. 527) is a superb example of the ideal as it had become crystallized. The seated figure is finished with a smooth perfection, and the spiritual expression reveals the attitude of the Indian sculptor toward his art, that of making God manifest in stone, present in all things, as the number *one* is present in all numbers. The crisply carved features have a grace and tenderness of form that seem almost paradoxical. The whole figure is majestic, aloof, but not haughty or arrogant; compassion is there, and serene wisdom. Just as there is the Indian emphasis on the spirit, so the very proportions are Indian, based on other natural forms; the head is oval as an egg, the shoulders strong as a lion's, the waist slim as a wasp's, and the lotus pose is one taken by followers of yoga as they seek to free the mind for contemplation. The hair is a series of tight snail-shell motifs, the ear lobes are extended, and the drapery is so light that we have to look closely to become aware of it at all. Behind the subtle curves of head and shoulders a great halo is placed, ornamented with floral and leaf patterns, beads, and, at the edge, a minute scallop design that had been used at Mathurā. The smaller attendants, flying above, or kneeling below at the turning wheel, are similar to the lithe Amarāvatī men and women. Whatever had come to India from other lands has been absorbed and changed so that the result

is now the perfect vehicle for her aesthetic ideal.

Out in the western regions, inland from Bombay at Ajantā, some mendicants had taken shelter in caves above the Waghora River. A religious community had been established gradually in the jungle country. In the solid rock above the bend of the river twenty-nine halls of worship (*chaitya*) and monastic quarters had been hollowed out and adorned with painting and sculpture from *c.* 200 B.C. to *c.* A.D. 500, some of the best work having been done in the Gupta period. The façade of cave XIX (fig. 528) shows the rough stone in which so many intricate figures were carved, and also that the chaitya window still dominates the architectural design. Beautiful as the architecture and sculpture are, it is the paintings that cause unbounded admiration. In caves I and II, especially, the walls are covered with such a variety of forms, so vibrant with life, that the earliest Europeans who saw them could not believe that they were religious. In glowing browns set off by lapis blue, pearly white, crimson, and green, men, spirits, and animals crowd about the walls in great rhythmic patterns. In cave I the central chamber is 64 feet square, a huge space to hollow out of solid rock, and contains countless figures, the most famous being the Beautiful Bodhisattva (fig. 529), which is 5 feet 9½ inches from the crown of the head to the knees. He is the lotus holder, who dwells now on earth, performing the functions of Gautama until the Buddha of the Future had come. He is a prince of noble birth and breeding, wearing jewels, aloof but not detached from the beings who crowd around him seeking salvation. As in the Sārnāth sculpture, the ideal of manly beauty has been followed, strong,

529. *The Beautiful Bodhisattva*, Cave I, Ajantā (320–600) Fresco, 5'10" high.

graceful, and supple. Highlights are brought out in skillful gradations of tone, giving volume by shading from dark to light within the limited color range.

In the narratives that relate to the life of the Buddha or his previous existence there are rich panoramas and incidents of many kinds, separated by cleft rocks and architectural motifs into horizontal units. Rocks and architecture seem to come forth from the walls toward the beholder in a perspective that is quite startling to the Western eye, accustomed to a convention that pretends to penetrate the wall. Up on the ceiling are lovely patterns fitted into carefully regulated spaces, all showing the vitality, grace, and imagination that characterize the art of the anonymous painters who worked on the plaster of these walls. Perhaps they followed the scheme of a master, for transfers were used, the outlines pricked to allow red or black chalk rubbed over them to cling to the rough plaster beneath the finely burnished surface in which the pigment was incorporated. Working in the large, dark chamber by torchlight or light reflected from the doorway by holding a white sheet there, these men expressed the ideas and methods, handed down from generation to generation in their guilds, with such success that Ajantā became the mother school for Central Asia, Ceylon, China, and Japan. It is almost the last great moment before a rising tide of popular Hinduism will engulf most of India in forms more violent than those approved by the followers of the Compassionate One.

MEDIEVAL INDIA

As we have noted, the Gupta kings were not Buddhists but Brahmanists, in whose reigns there was a revival of the old Vedic worship, bringing a need for new temples, and new tasks for the artists who must give form to a new pantheon. No longer were the forces of nature thought of as impersonal phenomena to be addressed by priests in ritual; they now became gods who dwelt in their temples, who had to be anointed with oil and cared for, who delighted in gifts, and who had to be propitiated, so that they would not bring evil into the lives of their followers. Brahmā, soul and creator of the universe, was rarely represented, but in traditional iconography has four heads and four arms (which hold the four books of the Vedas), and is accompanied by his consort, Sarasvatī, goddess of eloquence and music.

More popular with the masses were the two other members of the Trimūrti, Vishnu and Śiva. Vishnu, known also as Hari, was the great hero who appeared in ten incarnations (avatārs) to save the day for fellow gods and humans. He had been an ancient deity of the sun, and his color, blue, still suggests his heavenly association, as does his vehicle, the Garuda bird. He is generally represented with four arms, the hands holding a mace, conch shell, lotus, and disk. In his heroic avatārs his form

varies according to iconography based
on legends; as Rama and Krishna he is
the central figure in poetry, dance,
drama, music, and representational art.
Laksmi, goddess of beauty and fortune,
and Bhūmi-devi, goddess of earth, are
his consorts.

Śiva, developed from the ancient
storm-god Rudra, had to be placated
by sacrifice, for he was a destroyer; at
the same time, he was god of generative
force, represented by the linga stone,
and was shown associated with the bull.
In making this complete cycle he was
the ideal of many Hindus. He was also
lord of beasts, and dwelt upon Mt.
Kailāsa, sometimes as an ascetic, his
emaciated body covered with ashes, or,
at other times, as a consort of Pārvatī,
protecting her tenderly. His power is
shown, too, as the dancer, Natarāja, per-

530. *Dancing Śiva* (13th cent.) Government
Museum, Madras. Bronze, 3′11″ high.

531. *Pārvatī* (11th–12th cent.) Freer Gallery,
Washington. Bronze, 3′4″ high.

532. *Kālī*, Nelson Gallery, Kansas City. Bronze.

in himself, bringing release and freedom.

Śiva's consort is as full of contradic-
tions as he is. As Parvatī, she is the
daughter of the mountain, wild and
gracious (fig. 531). She is the mother of
the god of war, and of Ganeśa, the ele-
phant-headed god of mischief and good
luck, familiar to all travelers in the
Orient. As Kālī (fig. 532), she is bloodthirsty and insatiable, wearing a necklace of skulls, devouring men. She is attended by seven goddesses who spread
disease. But with her powers as a destroyer, she can also destroy demons,
and rescue her followers from care and
want, and so she is hailed as a savior.

Among the early medieval monuments inspired by these gods of popular
Hinduism are the monolithic 'raths' at
Māmallapuram down on the southeastern coast near Madras, and the famous
relief of the Descent of the Ganges
carved on a cliff near by (fig. 533). This
is 30 feet long and 23 feet high, filled
with figures of gods and men and animals. It is a seventh-century rendering
of a legend that explains how the river
goddess Ganga came to water the dry
plains of north India in response to the
prayers of a pious king who had subjected himself to austerities for a thousand years. Śiva, realizing that the shock
of the descending torrent might destroy
the earth, stood to receive it on his
head, allowing the water to trickle
through his locks, and so to come gently
to the parched earth. Magnificent elephants stand below divinities of the sky
who fly above; all manner of birds and

forming his divine dance of creation
and destruction (fig. 530). His wild
locks swing out in the dance, and on his
head are a skull, a crescent moon, and
the goddess Ganga. In one of his four
hands he holds a drum (the first sound
in the universe), in another the flame
of destruction. One hand is raised in
the mudrā 'Do not fear,' with a serpent
wrapped like a bracelet on the arm; the
other hand points down to the dwarf on
whom he dances, one of the many enemies overcome by this lord of death.
Energy is represented by a third vertical
eye in the middle of his forehead. To
the devotee, the dance took place with-

533. *Descent of the Ganges*, Māmallapuram (600–850) Stone, 23' high.

beasts are gathered there, even an ascetic cat, aping the good king who stood for so long with his arms raised above his head! Mystics and genii cluster around the stream (which is an outlet for a reservoir above), while the Naga sovereigns of the water accept their homage with calm majesty. In scale, in breadth of conception, as well as in beauty of detail, it is one of the most impressive of early medieval monuments.

At Elūrā in the Ajantā area, in the seventh and eighth centuries, a series of rock-cut cave temples and monolithic carvings were made for the three sects, Buddhist, Jain, and Brahman. The re-

markable Kailāsa Temple (fig. 534) is a representation in solid rock of the great peak atop the Himalayas which the demon Rāvana tried to take from Śiva. Note the small figure mounting steps near the center of the picture for a true idea of the scale of this tremendous shrine, cut 150 feet deep into natural rock. Tons of stone were quarried and carted away in creating the whole complex of sanctuaries, leaving vast shafts to be shaped into halls and porticos.

Sculpture and architecture form a harmonious unit. Rāvana, shaking the mountain, trying to dislodge Śiva and

534. *Kailāsa Temple*, Elūrā (600–850) Stone, 200′ deep x 100′ wide x 100′ high.

Pārvatī (fig. 535), is seen in the half-gloom of a subterranean grotto, a many-headed demon brandishing his arms in a powerful representation of an energetic figure in motion impelled by envy and fury. Sure of his eminence, Śiva sits above, languid and graceful, while Pārvatī leans upon him, frightened, clinging to her lord. All the forms are rounded, cut out in high relief, and show a singular understanding of the dramatic possibilities of light and shade.

Mystery and power are suggested in another early medieval temple, eighth-century Elephantā. In subterranean caverns on an island in Bombay harbor the worshipers of Śiva could approach the inner sanctum by torchlight. Deep in a niche the three-headed one looms (fig. 536), becrowned and bejeweled, symbol of manifold powers. Nearby, in its own chapel, the linga stone (generative force) is venerated by those praying for children, while wall surfaces everywhere are adorned with sculpture in high relief of narrative sequences.

For the evolution of the structural temple, we return to the Ganges Valley,

535. *Rāvana under Mt. Kailāsa*, Kailāsa Temple, Elūrā (600–850) Stone.

to the Mahābodhi Temple at Bodhgayā, which may have been built first as early as the fourth century of the Christian era, though in its present state of restoration (fig. 537) it looks much later. It consists of a foursided tower set upon a high base, flanked by smaller towers at the angles of the platform, all carefully oriented, and symbolic of the word of the Buddha spreading in all directions. Sculpture gives a fine surface decoration to the pyramidal mass of the tower, which is topped by a curving finial. Early Hindu temples show a tendency to combine the tower with a rectangular hall of the type found at no. xvii at Sānchī (fig. 538), as may be seen in the Durgā Temple at Aihole (fig. 539), which has an outer porch where the faithful may circumambulate

before they go within the flat-roofed cella to the sanctuary where the god lived. By the eighth century the tower becomes increasingly important (fig. 540), and begins to curve near the top in a melon shape, while its mushroom-shaped finial is a flat support for the bronze symbol of the god to whom the temple is dedicated. The emphasis is still on mass, but the surface is cut horizontally by countless sculptured reliefs. The cella seems almost an afterthought attached to the tower. By the tenth century, as the Lingarāja Temple at Bhuvaneśvara demonstrates (fig. 541), the melon-shaped tower becomes the dominant feature, adorned with myriads of small sculptured ornaments; the cella beneath is 19 feet square. Together they represent the cosmos in miniature, as does the contemporary Jaganātha at Purī, a pligrimage center. There, for the annual festival, a model of the tower is made of bamboo (suggesting a possible origin of the shape, as the poles were bent in long ellipses), placed on a heavy wooden cart, and drawn through the streets by devotees. Excitement runs so high that some have thrown themselves beneath the huge wheels of this Juggernaut, which is a symbol, even in Western thought, of crushing fate.

The temple as a cart was translated into stone in the thirteenth-century Black Pagoda of Konārak (fig. 542). Only the cella remains of the group of buildings dedicated to the sun god, Sūrya, who drove his chariot across the sky. The giant wheels of the platform

536. *Śaiva Trinity*, Hindu Temple, Elephantā (8th cent.) Stone, 12' high.

are ornamented with delicate surface carving that suggests the ivory technique (fig. 543). Other noteworthy temples are to be found at Khajuraho, where both sculpture and architecture reflect the peak of genius of Hindu medieval art in the north. In southwest India, at Belur and Halebid, the twelfth-century Hoysala kings developed a different type, star-shaped in plan, compact, with strong horizontal moldings and friezes of elephants and horses, and portals richly carved in intricate patterns of foliage and figures. At Tanjore, the eleventh-century tower to Śiva rises 216 feet, built without mortar, crowned by a stone weighing 80 tons that was pushed up a ramp 4 miles long by elephants and men.

By the seventeenth century, at Madura and other pilgrimage shrines, the South Indian Hindu temple attained its greatest size and complexity, consisting of sanctuaries, pavilions, private quarters, pools, and bazaars joined together by corridors and courtyards. They are dominated by high towers over the gates called *gopura* (fig. 544), four-

537. *Mahābodhi Temple*, (restored) Bodhgayā (4th cent.) Brick, 180′ high.

538. *Temple No. 17*, Sānchī (320–600) Stone.

539. *Durgā Temple*, Aihole (320–600) Stone, 84′ long x 36′ wide x 30′ high.

540. *Paraśurāmeśvara Temple*, Bhuvaneśvara (8th cent.) Stone, 48′ long 44′ high.

541. *Lingarāja Temple*, Bhuvaneśvara (10th cent.) Stone, c. 150′ high.

sided pyramids so covered with sculpture that no single form stands out. Power is expressed by multiplicity rather than by individual dynamism; lacking the majestic serenity of the Gupta period and the lithe grace of medieval bronzes, they are impressive in number rather than in quality, and were intended to overwhelm the beholder by sheer complexity.

Metal images, for processional use or worship in home or temple, such as the Dancing Śiva, are noted for grace and energy. Perfection of form, unblemished by accidental defect, was essential; if marred in the slightest way the figure was discarded or recast.

542. *Black Pagoda*, Sūrya Temple, Konārak (13th cent.) Stone, 100' long x 100' wide x 100' high.

MUGHAL AND RĀJPUT INDIA

The south, where Hindu art retained its classic form, had been spared the frequent invasions that penetrated north India from the eleventh century on. Fortresses, built on every strategic hill, were veritable walled cities; though they seemed impregnable, they fell one by one before the Moslems, who established themselves in Delhi. In the sixteenth century the descendants of Timur took over north Pakistan; by the seventeenth century, as the Mughals, they controlled most of India.

In the capital cities of Lahore, Delhi, and Agra they constructed palaces, gardens, mosques, and tombs, adapting marble and sandstone to Persian designs originally expressed in brick and colorful faïence. In scale and magnificence they outshone contemporary European structures, such as the palace of Versailles. The arch and dome were used extensively, particularly the bulbous, onion-shaped domes, which differed in profile and construction from the spherical Byzantine type. Columns and piers used as supporting members broke up the interior space into small units; they were sometimes joined by curving brackets like those used in Jain temples on Mt. Ābu (fig. 545), where white marble had been used in the eleventh- and twelfth-century temples—a soft marble when first quarried, which allowed intricate and delicate carving.

543. *Wheel*, Black Pagoda, Sūrya Temple, Konārak (13th cent.) Stone, 10' high.

544. *Gopuram*, Great Temple, Madura (17th cent.) Brick, stucco, *c.* 200' high.

The tomb of Humāyūn in Old Delhi, built in the sixteenth century, stood on an arched platform made of red sandstone inlaid with marble, and was topped by a dome of marble. It was the first to be enclosed in a park or garden, combining old Persian features with native Indian workmanship and materials.

545. *Jain Temple*, Mt. Ābu (11th–12th cent.) Marble.

546. *Tāj Mahall*, Agra (17th cent.) Marble, 186′ long x 186′ wide x 187′ high.

Akbar's tomb was equally splendid, and the huge palaces built in Lahore, Agra, and Delhi stagger the imagination, so vast and elegant are the halls, court-yards, baths, gardens, and mosques.

Fine as they were, it is the seventeenth-century mausoleum erected by Shāh Jahān in memory of his wife that still charms everyone by its matchless beauty, the Tāj Mahall (fig. 546). Placed between two red sandstone mosques, it gleams white and pure, reflected in the Jumna River, which flows beside it. Set on a platform 18 feet high, with tall minarets flanking each angle, a great dome crowns the central square, rising 187 feet above the platform. The entrance in each face is of the usual recessed type, consisting of pointed arches set in square frames, and inside them pierced marble screens allow a dim and subdued light to reach the interior. The proportions of platform, entrances, and dome are in perfect harmony, as are the light and dark areas of surface penetration. Equally lovely is the contrast of white marble against the green of the formal gardens that surround it; the slim dark spears of cypress reaching toward the minarets; and the low masses of the planting along the shallow pool, reminding us of the old

Persian concept of the garden as a place for cool refreshment, wherein the sound of running water and welcome shade were more important than brightly colored flowers. Only after we become fully aware of the skillful design of the building and the excellence of its setting do we begin to notice the exquisite detail of the inlaid work. Inside and out there are graceful patterns of flowers and calligraphy, consisting of thousands of pieces of semi-precious stones fitted into the marble. Moslems, Hindus, and Europeans joined together in designing and building this monument to Mumtāz Mahall, the 'Elect of the Palace,' who was given immortality by her husband in this marvel of Mughal taste and skill.

Of the mosques, The Pearl, in Agra (fig. 547) is the most notable. Built in the period from 1646 to 1653, it too is made of white marble. It is topped by three domes of equal importance, which rise above the entrance pierced by five openings framed in cusped arches. The emphasis is on beauty of proportion, fine spacing of light and dark areas, and detail work showing great restraint and finesse. Though the first impression is one of delicacy, the mosque is not small, for the court is 150 feet square, and the corridors inside are long and spacious.

For their libraries, Mughal emperors maintained hundreds of calligraphers and painters; Hindus and Persians worked together as they copied scientific treatises, religious texts, court records, and poetry, or illumined them

547. *Pearl Mosque*, Agra (1646–53) Marble, court 150' square.

548. *Rājput-Rājasthānī*, Todī Rāginī (17th cent.) Museum of Fine Arts, Boston, Painting on paper, 8″ x 6″.

with illustrations. Much of the inspiration for this was due to Humāyūn, who had spent a year in Persia with Shāh Tahmasp, visiting art centers and watching painters in the royal ateliers; he even visited the ruins of Persepolis. When he returned from exile in 1555 he brought some artists with him, and installed them in the palace. The role of royal patron was continued by his son, Akbar, though most of Akbar's life was devoted to military and administrative problems. Nonetheless he collected an enormous library and kept readers in constant attendance. He loved to discuss doctrine with Christians, Hindus, Moslems, and the Zoroastrian Parsees; he worked out a monotheism of his own and tried to establish it among his subjects. But he did not force it upon them, and they, being content with their many gods, did not accept it. One of his wives was a Rājput princess, from northwest India, and their union brought together two traditions, the native and that of the conqueror.

Rājput country had seen the continuance of a vital development in building and painting, dating from the time of the glory of Ajantā. With some of the fresco technique still in their memories, as well as the narrative style used by Jains, local craftsmen had evolved a unique method of illustration—the Rāgmālā form, which united a musical mode, a poem, and a painting, all conveying the same mood. These were male and female, Raga and Ragini, composed to express the most delicate shadings of emotion and sentiment. They were appropriate to certain seasons and times of day or night; at the top of the page there was a strip of 'weather'—blue and gray for a melancholy dark day, drops of rain for the rainy season, clear yellow for a bright day. A man or a woman was often shown playing upon a musical instrument (fig. 548). Sometimes the mood is of utter despair, at other times of rejoicing, or even of the serene peace of yoga contemplation. Like the Jain manuscript figures of the fifteenth century, the Rājputs are usually shown in profile, with prominent noses, large eyes, and receding chins; their expressive hands are extended in significant gestures. They are symbols rather than flesh-and-blood men and women. The designs are splendid, stemming from the mural tradition of Ajantā, though these paintings are page-size. The colors, too, remind us of wall painting, confined to a palette of dark blue, olive green, lemon yellow, tomato red, and chalk white. It is a folk art, handed down from generation to generation in Rajasthan. In the seventeenth and eighteenth centuries there are, besides the Rāgmālā, a great many Rājput paintings dealing with Hindu gods, myths, and legends.

At court, however, the Persian arts of calligraphy, illumination, leather tooling, and bookmaking were the fashion, as was Persian literature. When native painters joined them a mingling of styles resulted. There was still the delicacy of Persian line, the love of decorative detail, the use of Chinese rock and cloud motifs—which had been used in Persia since the Mongol invasion of the thirteenth century—the careful delineation of flowers and trees, and the radiant color of the Safawid masters, all of which were tempered finally by their contact with the vigorous native style.

549. *Illumination*, from Hamza-nāmah (17th cent.) Metropolitan Museum, New York. Painting on cotton.

The Hamza-nāmah (fig. 549), started under Humāyūn and continued in Akbar's reign, is more remarkable for power than subtlety, and two new elements are evident—interest in shading, and perspective. Akbar not only encouraged the native painters in a special effort to honor the Rājputs; he also was interested in books and gifts brought from Europe. He had received a Jesuit mission, and was delighted by the pictures of the Virgin Mary, as well as by Plantyn's Royal Polyglot Bible, brought to him in 1580, in which there were engravings by Flemish artists of the sixteenth century.

This European element in Mughal painting continued to be imporant under Jahāngīr. He received Sir Thomas Roe as envoy from James I, and like his father, welcomed the religious teachers from Europe. Traders, especially Portuguese and Dutch, played their part in bringing Western methods and motifs to India, just as they carried tales of India back to Europe. We know that Rembrandt saw and sketched from album pages owned by the president of the Dutch East India Company as well as from those in his own collection; and that Archbishop Laud had put his name and the date 1640 in a book of Indian drawings now in the Bodleian Library. Now, for the first time in India, there is an interest in the appearance of things, a searching for reality for its own sake, a desire to show shadow and cloud, and objects diminishing in size and clarity in the distance.

In the albums of Akbar, Jahāngīr (fig.

550. *Jahāngīr* (*c.* 1615) Museum of Fine Arts, Boston. Painting on paper, 1½" square.

550), and Shāh Jahān are such subjects as Durbars (daily audiences of the rulers), single portraits, equestrians, sages and poets, even abnormal people like Inayat Khan the opium-taker, who was sketched by order of the emperor just before he died (fig. 551). Rustic retreats and formal gardens were painted in full color or in dim evening light; studies of birds, flowers, and animals were portrayed so precisely that every detail could be studied. Al Mansur was noted for this type of work, as were Bishendas and Govardhan for their scenes of Indian life. Objectivity and purity of form were their goal rather than fantasy or poetry, clarity rather than emotional impact. Not until Aurangzīb took the throne in 1658 was there a falling off in power in this Mughal school, and then it was because he was a strict Moslem who thought that painting a portrait was a sin and therefore withdrew

551. *Ināyat Khān* (17th cent.) Museum of Fine Arts, Boston. Ink on paper, 3¾″ x 5¼″.

royal patronage. Artists then dispersed to the provinces to serve local princes in the foothills of the Himalayas (where the Kangra work of the eighteenth century reached a high point of excellence), or to the courts of the rajahs of Rajasthan and the Deccan. A strong tradition was maintained from which the modern revival of painting drew much inspiration.

Weaving and metalwork, already highly developed in India before the Mughals came, were encouraged by the Moslems. Cottons, stamped or printed with Hindu and Persian motifs, were exported in quantity; weapons and jewelry are still sought for museum collections.

A high level of taste and beauty of workmanship serve as a hallmark of distinction for succeeding generations in Asia and Europe.

India today is a land of renewed energy where the arts reflect an awakened nationalism. In painting, especially, she stands with other leaders of the twentieth century.

GREATER INDIA

Ceylon: Close to the Indian subcontinent, Ceylon received direct influence from the mainland. It became a stronghold of Buddhism in the third century B.C. when Mahinda, son of the King Aśoka, was sent as a missionary bearing the Relic of the Tooth and other gifts, and it is still a predominantly Buddhist island. Fortunately Sinhalese monuments and texts have been well preserved, and the course of history and art is clear. It is the Hinayana (Lesser Vehicle), rather than the rich hierarchy of northern Buddhism, that has been popular; emphasis has been centered on the Buddha's precepts, his community of monks, and symbols of his doctrine.

As in the time of Aśoka, the stūpa (*dagoba*) was an object of veneration, but the form and construction differ from the north Indian type. Heeding the instructions of Gautama when he placed his begging bowl upside down on his cloak and laid his staff beside them, the Sinhalese used a platform as base for a great mound of earth, sometimes covered with brick and plaster, crowned by a smaller platform and topped by the parasol element condensed into a solid cone. The stūpa was a reliquary with all the qualities of divinity, a combination of a thing both royal and divine. To worship it was to gain merit; to build it was even more virtuous. The location was determined by magic formulas related to directions used by builders on the mainland, for it was most important to place it propitiously. The Sinhalese dagobas lack the sculptured railings and gateways like those of Sānchī and Bhārhut; narrative episodes were rarely used, but there were many slim colonnettes of the Amarāvatī type placed near each entrance, and curving balustrades enclosed the steps. One of the largest dagobas, built about 100 B.C., the Ruwanveli, is a mound 254 feet in diameter at the base and 270 feet high, set upon 3 circular terraces about 7 feet wide which are raised on a platform extending 500 feet on each side. The surface is plaster-smooth, uninterrupted by moldings or niches; it seems like a giant bubble floating on a rim of the outer wall on which life-sized elephants face outward.

The city of Anurādhapura, in which it was erected, was colossal, extending at least eight miles in diameter, comparable in its day to New York or London. It was filled with imposing buildings, lovely pools, and the homes of all those who thronged the streets of the capital. Recent excavations give evidence of a flourishing trade with Greece and Rome; perhaps the grandeur of Rome was challenged here, for architecture and sculpture were conceived on a large scale.

The most notable early painting is to be found at Sígirya, some twenty miles west of Polonnāruva, in a natural stone fortress rising about 600 feet above the tilled fields, which was used as a refuge in the late fifth century, or early sixth, by the parricide king Kasyapa I. There are murals in two irregularly shaped 'pockets' in the west cliff; one a little over 40 feet long, the other nearly 27 feet long. In them there are processions of ladies and their serving maids, carrying lotus flowers in their hands, who are painted as if moving toward a Buddhist temple to the north of the hill. They are sometimes compared to the frescoes of Ajantā, though they differ in color and composition, red, yellow, and green being the dominant colors in Ceylon, where little blue or brown are used. There is none of the tension of forms, no narrative, no contrast of figure and background, which marked the great wall decorations of the mainland. The women have the long oval faces and long noses of the south, and each stance and each gesture suggests the languid tempo of the tropics. The gay colors in the striped gauze jackets and skirts lack the tonal intensity of the Indian mother school, though both are equally graceful and appealing. Sketching freehand, the artists changed contours at will.

The capital was moved south to Polonnāruva to escape a Tamil invasion in the eighth century; again on a vast scale, palaces, council halls, temples, and monasteries rose as, for five centuries, the jungle was pushed back. Trade with the Arabs, Chinese, and the people of Southeast Asia enriched her culture and spread the influence of Ceylon beyond her island shores. The unique dagoba form was used in Burma and Tibet, and finally introduced into China by the Mongols and Manchus. A forest of stone still gives mute evidence of the former grandeur of shrines, both circular and rectangular. Moonstones, balustrades, and stairs lead into columned halls, and records tell us of

552. *Buddha Nirvāna,* Gal Vihāra, Polonnāruva (13th cent.) Stone, 46' long.

553. *Buddha Nirvāna with Ānanda,* Gal Vihāra, Polonnāruva (13th cent.) Granite, 23' high.

buildings twelve stories high, and of the gardens and palace pools. Sculpture was massive, usually of stone covered with a plaster coating, such as the Buddha reclining at the moment of Nirvana, guarded by his disciple (figs. 552, 553). Some notable figures were cast in copper and bronze in this medieval period, usually of Śiva (fig. 554) and Vishnu, for Hinduism had penetrated into 'Lanka.' A small, precious-jeweled Buddha, containing the Relic of the Tooth and housed in the famous temple of that name in Kandy, was taken there when the last royal capital was established by the Sinhalese kings in the mountain city that is still the cultural and artistic center of Ceylon.

Java: Further out in the East Indies the island of Java had its own great art based on that of India. Early records, including the fifth-century diary of the Chinese pilgrim Fa-hsien, indicate that the people at first worshiped Brahmanical gods, then turned to Buddhism. By the late seventh century the kingdom of Śrīvijaya had been established in Sumatra, Java, and the Malay Peninsula by the Śailendras, 'Kings of the Mountains,' who seem to be descendants of the Pallavas of south India; they were Buddhists and encouraged the worship of Buddha among their subjects. In the late eighth century, in 778, the Chandi Kalasan temple was dedicated to Tārā, female embodiment of the ideal of compassion.

Under these same kings a wonderful and unique monument was made on the Dieng Plateau, the Barabudur (fig. 555). Among the palm groves and volcanic mountains it rises over 100 feet, covered with sculpture—the most elaborate expression of Buddhist doctrine made by the followers of the Compassionate One. It is perfectly orientated to the cardinal points of the compass, the east gate being the main entrance for the worshiper, who could begin a circumambulation more extensive than any other in the Buddhist world. There are six square terraces topped by three circular ones, making nine in all. The lower levels consist of galleries lined with panels of relief sculpture, illustrating narratives inspired by Buddhist texts. The first, once hidden, contains scenes

554. *Dancing Śiva,* from Polonnāruva (13th cent.) Museum, Colombo. Copper.

555. *Great Stūpa*, Barabudur (8th cent.) Stone, 100' high.

of violence and suffering, the hell of torment, the earthly desires that must be buried as the sculpture was buried; then comes the life of Gautama, and higher up, miracles of the Bodhisattvas. As the pilgrim ascends the sculpture becomes less narrative. When he reaches the three circular terraces where there are figures of the Dhyāni Buddhas carved in the round he has left the world of action behind and has reached the world of the spirit. The Buddhas were placed in small shrines perforated so that they could be seen inside. The last of the Buddhas was left unfinished by the carver—purposely, no doubt, for the pilgrim who reached the highest stage needed no more than a suggestion to spur his imagination.

It has been estimated that if all the sculpture, nearly 1000 panels of reliefs, were placed end to end it would reach three miles, and this does not include some 432 niches containing images of the Buddha a little more than life-size (fig. 556). The dark gray, pitted volcanic rock of that area was a most unsympathetic material for the sculptor's chisel. We do not know the name of the designer of this great symbol of the Law—which has all the clarity of a holy chart, or Mandala—nor do we know the names of the countless carvers who filled their panels (fig. 557) with gracious figures, tropical trees, flowers, birds, and animals. They are done with a tenderness and sweetness that surpasses anything in India itself. Based

556. *Dhyāni Buddha*, Barabudur (8th cent.) Stone.

upon the Gupta ideal and canon of proportion, but less remote, they mark the culmination of the Indian ability to produce spiritual qualities in sculptural forms.

From the eleventh century through the thirteenth both Buddhist and Hindu gods were worshiped. Temple art reflects the same violence that had marked medieval sculpture on the mainland. Even in Buddhist shrines there is a tendency toward profusion: jewels are intricate; many deities have several arms, and are surrounded by flowers and attributes, though the faces have a serenity reminiscent of Barabudur. The architectural mass serves as a compact core, whether as rectangle or stepped pyramid,

from which fanciful cornices and moldings emerge.

Cambodia: In the ninth century a Śailendra prince went from Java into the country of the Khmers, which we call Cambodia, and established himself as 'god-king,' Jayavarman II. The cult he instituted to make himself stronger was based on the principle that the king is to his kingdom as God is to the world, and he, by ceremony, allied himself with Śiva. He left Java for a country that already had a splendid art tradition based on that of Gupta India, brought in by Buddhist missionaries and traders over sea routes, or by land through Burma. He found the Khmer people divided into two kingdoms, which he united and welded into a strong state.

From the pre-Khmer art, which followed the Indian rules so closely, there developed new forms in architecture and sculpture which still make the world marvel, the best known being the Angkor Vat and the Angkor Thom. In sculpture we can see the change taking place as we look at the majestic Hari-Hara (fig. 558). It is a combination of Vishnu and Śiva in one body, the Śiva side distinguished by the 'wild locks' (reduced to waving lines on the tiara) and a trace of the third vertical eye in the middle of the forehead. It might well be a portrait of a local chieftain, tall, poised, with head held high. He looks out with a steady gaze, eyes wide open, and with his mouth set in a straight line under a light mustache. The several arms are unfortunately broken, and we notice

557. *Bath of the Bodhisattva, Hīru Lands in Hīruka,* Reliefs, First Gallery, Barabudur (8th cent.) Stone.

the stumps with surprise, for the rest of the man looks so normal that the extra growths from the shoulder are almost shocking. His drapery is noteworthy, a very light loin cloth folded over to form a flap of crisply cut, flat pleats.

The evolution from the ninth century on is toward a heavier, more massive form. In the tenth century the hair was reduced to a pattern of snail-shell motifs that fitted the head almost like a skull-cap, and met the forehead in a sharp horizontal line. There was an equally horizontal emphasis on brows and mouth. The cutting around the eyes, and on the mouth with its strangely compelling smile, was sharply and cleanly done. The lips, brows, and mustache were often outlined in two thin lines. The Indian ideal of the oval head and delicate nose has been influenced by the racial characteristics of the local people, who had wide, flat foreheads, flat noses, and thick lips. In the eleventh (fig. 559), twelfth, and thirteenth centuries the massiveness gives way to suppleness and grace, and in the Buddhist images, to a more profound spirituality, particularly in the Buddhas in meditation. One of the favorite themes is that of the Buddha raised above a flood by the Nāga king in the period following the Illumination; the body of the snake is coiled beneath the Blessed One, who is completely oblivious of the world, and protected by the many cobra heads forming a halo behind him. The smooth volumes of the central figure and the minute scales of the serpents' heads form an interesting contrast of textures.

Worship of the Nāgas dates far back into the pasts of this country and of Burma. Small wonder then that so many snakes are used as sculptural and architectural motifs. In both the Ang-

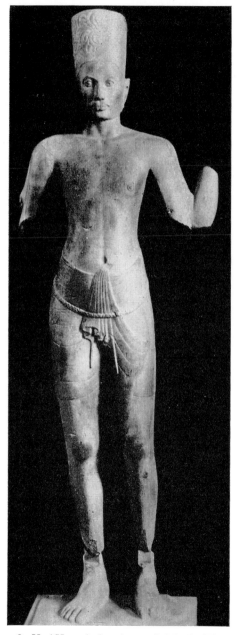

558. *Hari-Hara* (5th–7th cent.) Musée Albert Sarraut, Phnom-Penh. Stone, 6′3″ high.

559. *Head of Divinity* (11th cent.) Sandstone, 11″ high.

560. *The Bayon*, Angkor Thom (1112–52)
Stone, face 9′ high.

kor Vat and the Angkor Thom they are
to be found as balustrades, fountain
heads, and decorative finials. It is appropriate that these monuments rising out
of the jungle, reflected in countless
pools, should have so many reminders of
the kings of the waters, who were the
legendary founders of the race.

The capital of Jayavarman's line was
the Angkor Thom, the 'Great City,'
started in the ninth century and used
until the wars with Annam and Siam
brought ruin in the fourteenth. It was
planned as a huge square, surrounded
by a moat and walls 192 yards long on
each side. In the exact center, in the
late twelfth and thirteenth centuries,
the great mass of the Bayon rose, a
world-mountain in stone, tower piled

upon tower. Each of the 51 square
spires is ornamented with masklike
faces, many of them 9 feet high, facing
the four directions (fig. 560). They
were Buddhist under Jayavarman VII
(*c.* 1182–1201), who had identified himself with the Bodhisattva of Mercy; under the later kings they were dedicated
to Śiva. They are completely Cambodian, broad, flat, and smiling, with their
expressions of composure surviving the
damage of time and the cleavage of the
individual stones on which they were
carved.

A mile and a half south of the present city a temple was started in the middle of the twelfth century—the Angkor
Vat, the last of the tremendous undertakings of the Khmers and renowned
all over the world (fig. 561). It is part
of a gradual growth in the art and science of building, preceded by numerous
smaller and less ambitious temples based
on Indian prototypes and thus not
sprung miraculously in the jungle. An
outer gate on the west side allowed entrance to the worshipers of Vishnu, for
this is Brahmanical, not Buddhist—it
was the home of the god and the tomb
of the king. Down a spacious roadway,
220 yards long and over 25 feet wide,
bordered by a Nāga balustrade, the visitor walks toward the finely proportioned mass of the temple. Directly
ahead is the stately central tower, which
rises 200 feet above the top step, with
smaller towers at each angle of the rectangular central shrine, consisting of
terraces and covered galleries and steps

561. *Angkor Vat* (12th cent.) General View. Stone, central tower 200' high.

rising toward the tower, each level being twice as high as the one below it.

There is genius in the building, and genius in the sculpture that lines the corridors and graces the towers. The reliefs, miles of them, are cut so delicately into the stone that the effect is like an embroidery or tapestry, but there is much energy in the figures. One of the most impressive is the Churning of the Sea, the battle between the demons and gods, who wrapped the world serpent around Mt. Mandala and had a tug of war, each side hoping to gain possession of the *amrita*, sacred beverage, which they intended to churn up. At one time a terrible poison came up which would have destroyed them, but Śiva saved the day by drinking it. Finally the amrita appeared and was snatched by the gods, thus giving them ascendancy forever. Vishnu is present in his tortoise avatār supporting the mountain, and in heroic form above. His arms, brandishing his attributes, seem almost to move; his

knees wide apart and his ankles bent at an unbelievable angle give the impression of an elastic springiness characteristic of many of the lesser figures. Whether they fly or tug they are possessed of enormous tension, suggested largely by the use of curving lines in all parts of the bodies and costumes, and by poses of extreme angularity, which were related to the dance.

In contrast to these beings of the spirit world, some slaves are shown in another section: thin, drooping, hardly able to stand under the weight of the yokes around their necks, they are driven mercilessly by guards, who hold their whips high with an energy as terrible as the gods'. Perhaps the stones used in building the temple were brought through the steaming jungle by just such pitiful captives. Then there are the kings riding on elephants, surrounded by men and women of the court in magnificent processions, which, seen here, can also be read about in the account of the Chinese traveler Chou Ta-Kuan, who was there in 1296 and saw such pageantry as he had not dreamed of.

Among the narrative reliefs the story of Rāma is recorded in a peculiarly Cambodian way: though the Rāmāyama is faithfully followed, the idiom used in telling it is so different from that of the mother country that we hardly recognize it as the theme so popular among the Rājput painters. Rāma, going out to shoot the golden hind, stands with his knees wide apart and pulls his bow with a magnificent gesture worthy of a dramatic dancer; the trees show a finesse and grace reminiscent of Persian miniatures, each leaf meticulously done. Even in their dramatic episodes a very low relief is used, and the modeling is flattened within that slight projection. The effect is more like the Achaemenid reliefs of Persepolis than any of the medieval Indian sculpture, which is closer in time and space to Cambodia, but this has a sophistication and grace reminiscent of late Persian art.

Facing one of the pools a frieze of dancing girls (fig. 562) was carved in a somewhat higher relief than the narrative sculptures. Their supple bodies are lightly covered with transparent dhotīs, folded over flat girdles in the crisp Cambodian fashion. Their headdresses look like miniature versions of the Angkor Vat, amazingly intricate towers rising above their elaborate coiffures, which lend a vertical touch to their flat, horizontal faces, and are quite unrelated to their earth-bound feet. Again we are reminded of the time, eight hundred years ago, when harem and court existed in the present wilderness in a splendor and color that can only be

562. *Dancing Girls,* Angkor Vat (12th cent.) Stone.

hinted at in the red sandstone. This great temple, and the Bayon, and some lovely bronze figures were the last expressions of Khmer power in art, which faded away, as did their political power, before their conquerors, the Siamese.

Siam and Burma: Siam, like these other neighboring nations, received its early art impulse from India when Buddhism was introduced. The first images were of the Gupta type, having come directly from Amarāvatī, and show the power of the Gupta ideal in sculpture. Then gradually local racial characteristics alter the canon in Siam, and we witness another variation from the Indian classic norm. The sculpture reflects cultural and political changes to a remarkable degree.

To the trained eye the changes may be noted after the fifth century, when Burmese characteristics appear; the faces become rounder than the Indian oval, the eyebrows are arched over a long aquiline nose, and a smile, almost of disdain, is given to the Buddha figures. From the seventh century through the twelfth the Hindu-Javanese influence made itself felt, as the Śailendras extended their power from Sumatra and Java and finally became leaders of the Khmers; from the tenth through the thirteenth centuries, in the peak of Khmer power, the broad, flat faces of these Cambodians, the double line used to define the mouth with its strange smile, become a part of Siamese art; some of these developments took place in art centers quite close together, dif-

563. *Buddha* (15th–16th cent.) Museum of Fine Arts, Boston. Bronze.

fering because of local religious tradition and trade affiliation. Finally, from the eleventh through the fourteenth centuries at Chiengsen and Suk'ot'ai, a new group from southwest China, the Tai people, established themselves; then the true Siamese style emerges. Again the long nose is considered beautiful, as it was in Ceylon, and, as in Ceylon, a flame is added to the ushnisha mound, making the face vertical in emphasis; all that remains of the Khmer ideal of beauty is the double line around the mouth. Bronze figures of the period (fig. 563) are slim and burnished and have an aristocratic aloofness bordering on hauteur. Drapery is shown clinging to the body, defining curving volumes and

smooth surfaces that catch the light, for the metal is highly polished, and all textures—hair, skin, and cloth—gleam with equal brilliance.

In both Siam and Burma, architecture at first shows dependence upon India, and in both countries the Buddhist stūpas resemble the dāgobas of Ceylon; in the temples (fig. 564), however, they develop an exuberant style, using richly ornamented wooden cornices, glass or ceramic mosaics, and curving roof lines more fantastic even than those of China. There is a fancifulness and a gift of ornament, which have rightly made Bangkok and Mandalay synonymous with the color and romance of the East. Though the temple is still essentially

564. *Palace Courtyard*, Bangkok (19th cent.).

a reconstruction of the cosmos in miniature, as it was in India, the airy grace of
pinnacles and roofs show the mark of a
genius that is non-Indian and local. In
Pagan, the eleventh-century capital of
Burma, ruins extend for 25 miles into
the desert, crumbling brick remains of
palaces and 5000 temples. Of the un-
damaged shrines, the Ananda is most
venerated, as it rises white and gold to
dominate the plain. Frescoes, dating
from the eleventh century through the
eighteenth, reflect the life of court, village, and monastery.

Tibet: In the highest country in the
world, Tibet, art and Buddhism come
together. The early native religion had
been one of nature worship, with emphasis on sacrifice to demons, both human and animal sacrifice, made by sor-
cerer-priests. Two young princesses were
sent to Tibet in the seventh century of
the Christian era to be consorts of the
king—one from Nepal, and one from
China. Both were Buddhists. Together
they converted the king and persuaded
him to accept the Eight Fold Path.
Thanks to their success in that conversion they were regarded as earthly incarnations of Buddhist deities.

Even in northern India there had
been a certain emphasis on spells and
charms in Buddhism; by means of a
repetition of formulas and the achievement of a meditative state through yoga,
the devotee sought union with deities
of the Mahāyāna pantheon. There had
also been a belief, influenced by Hinduism, that male gods had female consorts,

565. *Jeweled Buddha* (10th–11th cent.) Museum of Fine Arts, Boston. Stone.

sisters, even dual aspects. Tārā was such
a female manifestation of the merciful
Bodhisattva Avalokiteśvara, and was
much beloved by followers of this Tantric worship. In the Pāla empire, which
controlled northeast India from A.D.
750 to 1197, and in Nepal in the medieval period, Buddhist sculpture and
painting of singular beauty had come
into being (fig. 565). The figures were
slim and elegant with the heads almost

heart-shaped and gracefully tilted; like Hindu images, they frequently had four or more arms. This was the type carried into nearby Tibet by the missionaries, who went in to convert the mountain people in the eleventh and twelfth centuries.

In the eighth century a Nepalese monk Padma Sambhava, familiar with Tantric formulas, was summoned to the court. He proceeded to subdue local demons, perform miracles, and establish the system of Lamaism, the Lama being a superior man, the leader in a monastery. He became so adept at charms that, instead of dying, he disappeared into the air. In the temple banners he is painted wearing a flowing red robe and a peaked red cap.

Though he came to Tibet to drive out magic practices, he had adopted quite a few himself, and the Buddhist church there had begun to sponsor devil dancing, exorcising, and rituals undreamed of by Gautama Buddha and his orthodox followers. By the eleventh century much needed reforms were instituted by Atiśa from Sumatra. Contact with the Mongols came in the twelfth century, and through them, closer contact with China. When the Mongols conquered China, Lamaism became popular under Kubilai Khan, resulting in an interchange of art motifs between the two countries, as well as a popular acceptance of demons and spirits that still colors Chinese folklore and practice. Even when the Ming rulers came to power and had driven the Mongols out in the fourteenth century, the emperor

of the Yung-lo period summoned the most noted Tibetan teacher, Tsong-kha-pa, to discuss doctrine with him.

Tsong-kha-pa, too, was a reformer. He instituted celibacy for the monks, and founded the Church of the Yellow Caps in Lhasa, which had been the home of the king of Tibet. The head of the church became chief of state, combining temporal and spiritual power. He introduced the two-Lama system. The Dalai Lama (Great Lama), who was believed to be a reincarnation of Avalokiteśvara, had a fortress palace in Lhasa. The present one was built in the seventeenth century. The second Lama, the Panchan Lama, had headquarters in Tashilhunpo.

Since there was little carving on a grand scale in the palaces, walls were covered with frescoes and painted banners, brilliant in color, rigidly conventional in composition. It is difficult to date Tibetan paintings, because the rules for making them were handed down unchanged from generation to generation; a nineteenth-century work may look very much like a fifteenth-century one. Pounces (pricked patterns) were used over and over again to transfer the designs to the silk or other cloth, on which flat colors were then filled in —strong blues, reds, greens, yellow, and gold. Texts had to be carefully followed in narrative detail, and canons of proportion set the figure types. Here, as we might suppose, ideas from India and China met. The form of the banners is Chinese—vertical wall hangings which can be rolled up—and they are often mounted on Chinese brocades and silk. Details (which could be done with some freedom) were often Chinese, especially flowers, cloud scrolls, and architectural motifs. The most usual subjects were: the life of Gautama; deities of the Mahāyāna pantheon (showing the tutelary god in the center, from whom rainbow-hued lines radiated to demi-gods in medallions); the eighty-four sorcerers, or church fathers, ranged in a tree-of-life design; and the Wheel of Life, a circular chart of man's existence divided into segments, each zone a world of reward or punishment.

Ritual objects include the prayer wheel (a cylinder containing rolls of prayer sheets; at each revolution of the wheel the worshiper gained merit), the thunderbolt, bell, dagger, horn conch shell, and a drum made of a human skull with skin stretched over it. Human bones are used also for rosaries and ornaments of a religious nature, thus insuring merit for the deceased.

In sculpture the Nepalese style was largely followed, especially in the casting of small gilt-bronze figurines, which were made in great numbers. They are notable for grace of form and contour, for the heart-shaped faces of north India, and for their elaborate jewels. Avalokiteśvara was often done in his eleven-headed aspect; having promised to heed all the cries of the distressed in the world, his head split into many pieces, which were gathered together by Amitābha and assembled into ten heads, topped by Amitābha's own image. The Bodhisattva usually has many arms, which reach out to carry souls to the Western Paradise, or hold symbols of mercy or chastisement.

Since even this gentlest of beings is portrayed in an awe-inspiring way, we are not surprised to find demons and demon-quellers endowed with a fierceness born of mountain winds and snows. Yamāntaka (queller of Yama, king of hell) has many heads, the principal one being of a bull or boar. He has 34 hands, grasping various attributes, and holds his female essence in a close embrace, being incomplete without her; like Śiva, he tramples upon a dwarf. Indeed there are so many Hindu elements in this art it seems much more Śaivite than Buddhist, a weird step-cousin of the serene figures from Sārnāth and Barabudur, tempered by storms and fury, and the ever-present threat of death. Out of the compassionate teachings of the Buddha this Lamaistic, Tantric form has grown and still flourishes in Tibet, while in the Ganges Valley Gautama is almost forgotten.

XXX

ANCIENT CHINA

The early Neolithic culture of China is much like that of the same age in America and Eurasia—men hunted and fished, raised grain, made tools and weapons of stone, used the bow and arrow, made baskets and cloth and pottery, and domesticated the pig and dog. Pottery of those early days has been discovered in sites widely distributed over northern China. A great variety of clays were used in the different localities to produce wares that were either plain or decorated with incised or painted designs.

Among the most striking examples are the large, thin, well-potted jars from Kansu (fig. 566), painted with broad swirling lines of black, red, and purplish-chocolate brown on the reddish-buff clay. The powerful sweeping curves and geometric patterns of this ware

show a number of similarities with early pottery from the Near East, though actual contact between the two regions is still a matter of conjecture. Of the many shapes used, the hollow-legged tripod is peculiar to China and unknown in any other culture area that flourished at the

566. *Painted Pot*, from Kansu, Museum of Far Eastern Antiquities, Stockholm. Pottery, 1'5" high.

728

same time. The earliest examples of these Chinese potteries probably date from before 3000 B.C., and the Neolithic cultures continued to flourish in the outlying regions until about 500 B.C., long after the bronze age had come, and Chinese civilization had been developing for many centuries in the Yellow River plain.

In the historic period called Shang-Yin (c. 1766–1122 B.C.), a white clay was used to make handsome pieces with designs carved on the surface. The patterns were linear, geometric versions of insect and animal forms, of which the locust (symbol of immortality), birds, and dragons were often used on the body of the vessel, while masks suggesting the heads of water buffalo, tigers, and deer were raised in relief. The background was filled with abstract fret meanders called cloud-and-thunder. Bone, ivory, jade, and marble (fig. 567) were carved with the same intricate incised lines, and bronze ritual vessels were cast from molds.

The Shang people had the highest standards of craftsmanship, great imaginative power, and a rich and complex symbolism. Their material culture has been gradually revealed to us since 1929, when systematic archaeological excavations were started on the site of the last Shang capital (c. 1350–1122 B.C.), at Anyang in Honan. The palace of the king, houses for the nobility, and workmen's quarters were discovered. The walls of these buildings were made of pounded earth; in the finer structures, painted wooden beams were used, and

567. Owl, from Anyang (1400–1100 B.C.) Academica Sinica, Nanking. Stone.

bronze fittings. The royal tombs had been carefully prepared down under the earth, and yielded every evidence of elaborate funeral ceremony and burial, including the sacrifice of human and animal victims. In these tombs, the excavators found bronze vessels, pottery fragments, shell, gold, jade, and silk. These were products of a feudal society, in which the king and his nobles hunted, engaged in battle, held court, and performed sacrifices.

From inscriptions on bones, which are the only historical records of the time, and from the Book of Poetry, written down a little later, as well as from a study of the tomb relics, we can re-create a picture of the Shang people. They could already express ideas in a

568. *Beaker, Type Ku* (12th cent. B.C.) Nelson Gallery, Kansas City. Bronze, 11" x 6¼".

of silk robes of state, the fragrance of sacrifice on the altars, formed an important part of the basis of early Chinese life.

On the altars were vessels made by the bronze casters, who were the greatest masters of the craft the world has ever known. Chariot fittings, weapons, personal ornaments, and household objects were made by them, as were also the vessels of ceremonial usage. The evolution of the different types of vessels is a rewarding but intricate study, which we can only touch upon here. In nearly all of the graves were found the *ku* (fig. 568) as a libation cup, and the *chüeh* (fig. 569), for heating liquid over the fire. A sturdier container for meat or cereal was the *ting* (fig. 570) with its three legs joining the body at abrupt angles, and with a decoration called the *t'ao-t'ieh*

pictograph writing, so developed that it gives evidence of having been started long before, in the legendary times of the Hsia. They asked advice of the spirits of ancestors, who could bring success, or could plague them with sickness and misfortune. Therefore the living served these spirits with food and sacrifice, and consulted the diviners, who wrote questions on the oracle bones and interpreted the answers from the spirit world. Ritual and ceremony, the music of drums and 'sonorous jade,' the rustle

569. *Ceremonial Wine Vessel, Type Chüeh* (1400–900 B.C.) Freer Gallery, Washington. Bronze, 10" x 9".

570. *Ceremonial Tripod Vessel, Type Ting* (1400–1100 B.C.) Art Institute, Chicago. Bronze.

on the body; this ornament consisted usually of arched eyebrows or horns, wide-open eyes, a nose and upper lip but with the lower lip omitted. The *t'ao-t'ieh* was used on many objects, sometimes in high relief, sometimes in low, and it seems almost to change expression as one looks at it. It was infused with the dynamic power that inspired all Shang design.

Having reached a high degree of culture, devoted more to the cultivation of the arts than to warfare, the Shang people were set upon by the Chou, who occupied the western borders. Anyang was destroyed. The conquered people fled, though some stayed to keep alive their traditions and to tutor the barbarians, who established a dynasty that lasted from *c.* 1122 B.C. to 256 B.C. Early Chou

art follows Shang models carefully, and the Chou conquerors soon adopted the laws, ceremonies, and precepts of the more civilized inhabitants of the Yellow River country. Chou bronzes are marked with long inscriptions, which tell the ancestors of their marriages, of honors come to the family, and of all kinds of events appropriate to these memorials that were to last forever.

In the latter part of the Chou period, texts were gathered together and written down which, for more than two thousand years, constituted the very life blood of Chinese culture. The Book of Changes was a record of divination practices, telling about the use of milfoil in long and short pieces. The long pieces represented the male (Yang, the active principle), and short ones the female (Yin, the passive principle). The long, or Yang lines coupled with two short, or Yin, lines, could be arranged in eight sets of three. Another way of representing Yang and Yin is by a circle divided into two parts by a waving line, the Yang part colored red, the Yin all black. As in India, the Chinese thought the male incomplete without the female, and vice versa, but they chose abstract linear symbols, not human beings embracing, to suggest these dual modalities.

The other classics of history, poetry, etiquette, and ceremony were recited and sung, learned by priests, politicians, and tutors. The king had to be well versed in rites and ceremonies, for by acceptable sacrifice he could bring to all his subjects good crops and favorable seasons. High-ranking nobles made sacrifices to mountains and rivers, and heads of clans and families had their ritual duties to perform. A large class of men who assisted in these rites, perhaps descendants of the Shang diviners, went from place to place, but keeping tradition pure.

Probably about the fourth century B.C., one of China's greatest philosophers, Lao-tzu, taught that men should be humble, simple, close to nature, and should avoid the distractions of public office. His teaching of the Tao, or the Way, was based on a retreat from life to solitary places, where the individual might discover himself akin to other living beings, in harmony with the laws of the universe. A somewhat earlier philosopher, Confucius, believed the good life would come only to those who fulfilled all their moral obligations, i.e., to the state, the community, and the family. Confucius and his followers and opponents lived in a time of great literary activity, the period of the Spring and Autumn Annals (722–481 B.C.), after the Chou capital had been moved from Ch'ang-an to Lo-yang, a time that profoundly influenced Chinese life for centuries to come.

In the ritual bronzes there had been a decline in technical ability and imaginative power. Toward the end of the Chou period, as smaller states broke away, there was a renaissance, a new cycle of creative activity among the bronze casters. New shapes became popular (fig. 571), as well as new versions of the old; new patterns appeared

571. *Bell, Type Chung* (600–250 B.C.) A. Stoclet Coll., Brussels. Bronze.

on the surfaces—intertwining dragons, serpents, and birds, twisting and turning with so much energy that parts of their bodies became detached and appeared in unexpected places. The *t'ao-t'ieh* still is used, with eyes popping out like a Pekinese dog's. Much of this dynamic design is contained within bands or registers, done in delicate surface patterns of knobs and dots. Bronze bells and gongs of various sizes, often richly ornamented, were cast in great numbers for ritual use. Circular mirrors (fig. 572) were polished on one side and adorned with designs in relief on the other; some were carried by priests as part of their regalia; others were used in everyday life. Jade was carved in designs similar to the bronzes and often

572. *Mirror* (600–250 B.C.) Art Institute, Chicago. Bronze.

done in a circle, symbol of heaven and of the king, the holder of heaven's mandate on earth. Many small ornaments were given to barbarian chieftains as marks of esteem, and by them were taken all over north Asia, and even into Europe when pressure drove them to the West. Certainly the animal forms, the interlacing patterns, the delicate fancifulness of design, all of which resulted from the fusion of Asiatic cultures, seem to have inspired some of the medieval art of Europe.

IMPERIAL CHINA

One of the warring states, the Ch'in, absorbed weaker states and overthrew the last Chou king in 249 B.C. Again the sturdier westerner conquered, and began a period of consolidation and reform (221–207 B.C.) that laid the foundation for the Chinese economy and administrative organization for centuries to come. The head of the ruling house

for the first time assumed the title of emperor, Shih Huang-ti, and he used every means possible to bring unity to China. He joined together and built up isolated local fortifications into the Great Wall. He had canals built, roads widened, better communication systems established, and, for himself, a fabulous palace erected. Though what he did was for the power and unification of China, he was not loved by the people. He taxed them unmercifully for his great projects; he offended them by burning the books, which were their treasured links with the past, and by throwing their ritual tripods into the river. Later, when he wanted to consider himself one of the long line of hereditary rulers rather than an innovator, he tried to recover the bronze vessels so that he could perform the kingly sacrificial ceremonies, but, according to legend, a dragon cut the cord being used to haul out the *ting*, and it dropped back into the river, safe from the hands of the usurper.

Shih Huang-ti's vision of glory for China was passed on to the next dynasty, the Han (207 B.C.–A.D. 220), especially under the emperor Wu Ti (140–87 B.C.), who extended the limits of China west and south, sent his soldiers to subdue the Turkic and other nomads of the Tarim basin, colonized Korea, and attached Tongking near Cambodia.

The tomb of one of his generals, Ho Ch'ü-ping, is near Wu Ti's tomb in Shensi, and is an interesting combination of Chinese and barbarian forms. It consists of an earth mound 50 feet high with great boulders at its base, some carved, some water-worn and smooth, the largest weighing fifteen tons, all of them brought from quite a distance. Originally they must have been placed in pairs to line a spirit path and guard the approach to the tomb, much as sphinxes were in Egypt and Assyria; but the forms are barbarian rather than Near Eastern. The most striking is that of a horse trampling a warrior beneath him (fig. 573), massive, heavy, quite unlike the fanciful and graceful figures in other parts of China. Both man and animal are of a Central Asiatic type. The idea of a conquered person being trampled upon is more extensively used in Western Asiatic art than in Central

or Eastern Asia—for example, by the Sassanian Persians in their investiture scenes (fig. 496). The other carved stones, suggestive of Turkic and Scythian ideas of combat and struggle, show animals with their feet drawn up under them and animals of totemic significance. Since a bull and a rat are among them, they may have been related to the Duodenary cycle of the Huns, who divided their days and nights into the hours of the horse, bull, rat, and so forth, as the Chinese learned to do from them.

In western China, too, in Szechwan province, a number of tombs and memorials still survive from this period. The pillars of Shên are quite Chinese in

573. *Horse Trampling Barbarian Warrior*, Tomb of Ho Ch'ü-ping, Shensi (117 B.C.) Stone.

574. *Red Bird*, Funerary Pillar of Shên, Ch'ü-hsien, Szechwan (2nd cent.) Stone.

form and decoration. The stone shafts are carved to imitate the tile roof and wooden brackets normally used in the Han house; three sides are marked with symbolic creatures of the directions— the Red Bird (fig. 574) on the south, the Dragon on the east, and the Tiger on the west. The *t'ao-t'ieh* appears, and

575. *Visit of Mu Wang to Hsi Wang Mu*, Tomb of Wu Liang Tzŭ, Shantung (2nd cent.) Stone.

all manner of strange pixy people, fantastic birds, and animals. The inscriptions (done in beautiful Han calligraphy, 'powerful as brandished lances, or waves of the sea blown by the wind') indicate that Shên was a prefect and military governor of Tongking.

In the eastern peninsular province, Shantung, there are other famous monuments of this period. One, of Wu Liang Tzŭ (fig. 575), is especially well known because of the many rubbings that have been taken from it. In registers that remind one of the late Chou bronzes, stories of all kinds are told with a wonderful animation and skill. Both Confucianism and Taoism are represented by historical scenes, by pictures of virtuous persons of the past, and by imaginative worlds of sky and water inhabited by deities who personify forces of nature. In a very low relief that projects less than half an inch from the background, the men and women in long robes bow ceremoniously to each other, or attend banquets; one is such a loyal son that, though he is in his sixties, he plays about on the floor like a child to make his eighty-year-old parents feel young again. Hsi Wang Mu, Queen Mother of the West, receives the King of the East in her pavilion, or watches her heavenly guardians, who protect the peach tree of Immortality. Mortal men ride in chariots, pulled by the famous horses of Han, heavy of body, with delicate feet and arching necks, while the immortals in their own realms ride fantastic sky and sea creatures. Though the figures are as flat as

silhouettes, and the carvers are not interested in spacious backgrounds, there is throughout a feeling of life, vitality, and the tension of carefully related forms.

The other famous Shantung slabs are from the Mount of the Hall of Filial Piety. They are also from an offering chamber, and are as flat in projection as the Wu group, with figures incised into the background. There, too, long-robed men bow to each other, or engage in very realistic warfare, hanging up the severed heads of their enemies by the hair; or they go out to hunt with hounds at their heels. Again we have an excellent record of dress, weapons, and practices.

By this time burial customs called for clay figurines, which were put into the

576. *House Model* (2nd cent.) Nelson Gallery, Kansas City. Unbaked clay, 4'4" high.

tombs to represent the people and things beloved by the departed spirits. Thus, in miniature, we see the essentials of Han life. The Chinese house (fig. 576) was a tiled-roof structure, consisting of several pavilions or wings that formed a compound and courtyards, set off from the street by a wall. The central building, in which the head of the family lived, faced south. It was approached by a ramp or steps, recalling the ancient practice of building above flood level in the Yellow River region. The sloping roof was upheld by posts and brackets, which became the essential feature of Chinese domestic and religious architecture. Inside the home of a well-to-do Chinese, the rooms were spacious. Furniture consisted of chests, small tables, or arm rests, and movable bedding rolls that were put away in the daytime. The kitchen was below the first floor or in a separate wing; the second floor seems to have been the women's quarters. We know that the exposed wooden beams were gaily painted and lacquered, and that pictures were painted or hung on the walls, though no large Han paintings have survived to the present day. Bronze fittings were carefully designed and made; even the smallest fragments are treasured still for their beauty or humor.

Out in the courtyard pigs, dogs, chickens, and children added to the color of the household. The clay figurines of the period and the stamped tiles give such a lively picture of Chinese life two thousand years ago that they are sought today as great works of art.

That civilization was carried by Han public servants into distant lands. In Korea, in the tomb of a Chinese governor and his wife, the excavators found beautiful lacquer boxes, toilet articles, and ornaments, the lacquer work painted red, yellow, green, and black in patterns full of energy and fantasy. Out on the trade routes of central Asia, other fragments of Han life have come to light, including some woven tapestries of complex colors and designs, as fanciful as Han sculpture and painting and showing a fusion of forms derived from the Near East with the purely Chinese dragons and spirits.

The Han men felt very close to the world of spirits. Taoism, which had originated as a movement to simplify the life of the individual, had now developed into an elaborate cult involving magic of all kinds and peopled with a variety of immortal beings with miraculous qualities. The Taoist priesthood sought immortality by compounding drugs, and engaged in alchemy, as popular then in China as it would be a thousand years later in Europe in the Middle Ages. Magic writing and charts were in vogue, and had their influence on the patterns of bronze mirrors, especially those carried by the priests and used in burial ceremonies. Even ritual vessels were ornamented with fairy forms, clouds, and heavenly beings. Among the smaller bronze objects, contact with the 'barbarians' is reflected in animal combat scenes similar to those found in south Russia, Siberia, and the Ordos area just north of the bend in the Yellow River. Animals common to those places were woven into the intricate patterns of belt hooks, incense burners, and weapons.

It was a time of political and creative power, drawing from the past, enriched by many contacts outside the Middle Kingdom. Silk was carried halfway across the world to Rome, Chinese palaces were filled with beautiful objects brought from far away, hands were busy making jade, bronzes, lacquers, silks, potteries, pavilions, and gardens unrivaled elsewhere—small wonder that a modern Chinese still calls himself a Son of Han.

The Han emperors had heard of the teachings of the Buddha, and texts had been translated from Sanskrit into Chi-

nese soon after A.D. 150, but Buddhism had not deeply touched the lives of the average Chinese until the troubled times of the Six Dynasties period (A.D. 317–589), when all of northern China was overrun by Tatar tribes. As the conquerors established themselves in this new territory, they brought in their own beliefs. Wanderers though they were, they had been converted to Buddhism by central Asiatic missionaries, who taught them that they would gain merit by making images and fashioning sanctuaries in the name of the Buddha. One group, the Wei, were particularly active in western and northern China.

Up in the Shansi province, just south of the Great Wall, the Wei began, in A.D. 414, to hollow out a sandstone cliff

577. *Prince Meets a Sick Man*, Shih Fo Ssu, Yün-kang (A.D. 5th cent.) Stone.

578. *Colossal Buddha*, Yün-kang, Shansi (A.D. 5th cent.) Sandstone, 32' high.

at Yün-kang, near Ta-t'ung, making grottoes filled with sculpture which were based on directions brought from India over the central Asian tracks. They had, as well, small bronze and clay images of Buddha, the Bodhisattva, the lesser deities, and the stūpa, all somewhat changed when made by the oasis artist who had not seen the Indian originals. As the Tatars and their Chinese subjects attempted to follow models and written rules, they produced results at first that were neither Indian nor Chinese (fig. 577). All of the essentials were there, but none of the Indian fluidity of form infused with life, nor the spirited energy of China. They are simple, massive symbols of ideas, with faces and drapery cut according to formulas. There is a great Buddha, 32 feet high, set in front of a flaming mandorla (fig. 578), and there are thousands of smaller ones in high and low relief, all originally colored. Gradually Chinese characteristics creep into this sculpture: the eyes become more slanting; in architecture the tile roof replaces the Indian arch; and Chinese dress is used instead of the dhotī cloth, thus covering more of the body in flat patterned folds.

In the middle of the fifth century, persecutions were ordered by an emperor who was influenced against Buddhism by Confucianists, but toward the end of the century there was a new burst of religious activity. The capital was moved south to Lo-Yang in Honan province, and the caves of Lung-mên were started, the dark marble-like limestone hollowed out into grottoes adorned with all the gods of the Mahāyāna Buddhist hierarchy. As it was a better material to carve in than the sandstone of Yün-kang, and the ideas were not quite so strange by that time, the results were finer in quality. Some of the most exquisite representa-

579. *Bodhisattva,* from Lung-mên (6th cent.) Metropolitan Museum, New York. Black marble.

tions of heavenly beings ever carved were made there (fig. 579), touched by a delicate, tender spirituality. It was estimated that nine out of ten families had been converted by that time. Emperors and empresses were donors to Buddhist shrines too, appearing with their courtiers to inspect the work and bring offerings (fig. 580), and they encouraged the study of the sūtras at court. The monk Fa-hsien was sent to India on a perilous journey that lasted fifteen years. He returned with Sanskrit books, which were translated into Chinese, and he told of the marvels of strange lands in his diary. He was the first of many

580. *Empress as Donor*, Pin Yang Cave, Lung-mên (6th cent.) Stone.

monks who risked their lives to go to India and to contribute to the Indianization of Chinese art, philosophy, and learning.

Even in the south, where the Chinese had established a capital at Nanking and strove to preserve their ancient culture menaced by the barbarians in the north, the worship of the Buddha spread, and great teachers were invited to discuss the doctrine. Ideas were interchanged, and, by A.D. 500, the Wei emperor issued an edict prohibiting the use of the Tatar language, culture, and customs in favor of the Chinese. By 589 the country was united again under the Sui Dynasty (A.D. 589–618) and Buddhism continued to play a dominant

part. The first Sui emperor ordered the construction of 3,792 temples, caused 1,508,904 images to be repaired, and 106,580 new ones, large and small, to be made in various materials.

A lovely altar group in the Museum of Fine Arts in Boston (fig. 581), cast in bronze in A.D. 593, shows the development in religious worship and artistic expression which took place as Buddhism became more and more Chinese. It is of Amitābha Buddha, who presides over the Western Paradise, receiving the souls of all who call upon him or his attendant Bodhisattva. It was not necessary to be learned, or wealthy, or high-born to seek salvation through him; he heard the prayers of all sincere be-

581. *Tuan Fang Shrine of Amitābha Buddha and Attendants* (593) Museum of Fine Arts, Boston. Bronze.

lievers. No longer were the common people condemned to suffer the vicissitudes of the Wheel of Existence; they could now find release from it, even as monks and scholars had, who had been able to lose themselves in contempla-tion and project their minds into the realms of the infinite; even the ignorant could have faith and reach the Blessed Land. In this shrine, Amitābha sits majestically upon a lotus throne. He is attended by monks who were mortal and therefore conceived as realistic portraits, and by his two Bodhisattva, who stand worshipfully on lotus flowers. The Indian elements are still there—the yoga pose, snail-shell hair, Hindu torso, and hand gestures of Amitābha; but the Chinese maker added pendants, a flaming halo, and a winsome slimness of figure. The Bodhisattva, Avalokiteśvara (Kuan Yin in Chinese), and Mahāsthāmaprāpta wear the high jeweled crowns, the necklaces and scarves of young rajas, but they have none of the masculine heaviness of their Gandhāran prototypes; they are sexless, with a feminine daintiness of gesture, and show the Chinese lack of interest in anatomical studies. This was now the proper shrine for the family altar, taking the place of the ritual vessels that held food for sacrifice in the ancient days. Spirits of the departed were still important, and Taoist monks tried to rival the Buddhists in influence; but most of the carving, casting, and painting was done in the service of the Buddha (fig. 582).

Again the Chinese began to expand. The Sui emperor was displaced by the Duke of T'ang, who had equally ambitious ideas. The dynasty changed, but Chinese conquest continued unabated, and a new era rivaling the Han came to the Middle Kingdom. As warriors, diplomats, and patrons of the arts, the T'ang rulers ushered in another epoch of political and creative power, which lasted from A.D. 618 to 907.

One of the outstanding rulers, T'ang T'ai-tsung (627–49), defeated the Turks who tried to take Ch'ang-an, the west-

582. *Kuan Yin* (6th–7th cent.) Museum of Fine Arts, Boston. Stone.

583. *Camel and Driver*, Palmer Coll., Chicago. Glazed pottery.

ern capital. By conquest or treaty he began to control the oasis cities of Central Asia. Gifts in great numbers were exchanged. Turkish and Uighur princes were invited to attend court and serve as officers in the Chinese army, and princesses were given in marriage to consolidate these ties. One, as we have seen, was sent to Tibet, for the Tibetans proved to be very troublesome at this time. Though silk was no longer a monopoly of China, the old silk road was kept open by Chinese garrisons for trade between the Byzantines, Arabs, Indians, and Chinese. Water routes were as important as land routes, and the seaport towns were thronged with foreigners, as were the two capital cities of the north. Travelers, monks, students, and soldiers poured into China from all directions. They brought new gods to worship, new fashions. The old Chinese were shocked by the ready acceptance of 'barbarian' ways, but their reproofs did not prevent the building of temples to the strange gods, nor did they keep the ladies of the palace from riding horseback, playing polo, or going about without hats. Chinese arts, like Chinese life, underwent considerable change.

The clay figurines which were still used in tombs give us a vivid picture of the times. They include many foreign ethnic types; camel drivers (fig. 583), grooms who were sent in with the tribute horses, dancing girls, Negroes, and holy men. Stone slabs are ornamented with Persians wearing the long tunic of the Sassanian period; textiles are woven with so many Sassanian motifs that it is something of a shock to find Chinese characters on them; pilgrim bottles have strong Near Eastern influences in de-

sign; and Buddhist art is injected with a direct impulse from Gupta India.

There are few architectural remains of the T'ang period in China. Except for a rare octagonal pagoda of brick or stone, little can be seen of the era; in Japan wooden structures based on Chinese models have survived (fig. 619). The cave temples, however, had not been severely damaged until modern times; experts have reconstructed the Buddhist places of worship well enough for us to see the gradual evolution in architecture, sculpture, and painting toward the cosmopolitan Chinese ideal from the simple beginnings of the Six Dynasties period. In northern and east-

584. *Amitābha Paradise*, Cave 139 A, Tun-huang (9th cent.) Painting.

ern China, work had gone on from the fifth century; in southwest China, archaeologists have recently discovered many more sites. The farthest output of all, Tun-huang, the place where caravans stopped on entering or leaving the country for the overland desert route, had been a center of religious activity since the fourth century. A monk had been led by a vision to that place; he had hollowed out grottoes in the mud cliffs above a dry stream, having in his heart the ideal of a concrete representation of the Thousand Buddhas. Other helpers had come, and there were many temples hollowed out, their walls covered with scenes of the life of the historical Buddha and the heavenly worlds to which the faithful might go (fig. 584). The donors who contributed toward this undertaking are pictured there, too, in their finest clothes. The Turkish donors are especially brightly colored, for the women wore embroidered robes and headdresses of flowers and elaborate hairpins, and their cheeks were painted with crimson circles. All the walls vibrated with color, and the sculptured figures placed against them were equally brilliant.

The mother school for all this was Ajantā, and Indian proportions were faithfully followed, as were the texts telling how the various scenes must be arranged, but many changes had taken place; Central Asiatic artists had worked out the themes, and their methods naturally influenced the Turks and Chinese, who must have been most active in the making of this outpost shrine. In the oasis cities of the northern and southern Trade Routes there were flourishing Buddhist communities, and many monasteries. The local kings, the lay believers, and the monks had all been patrons of art, or artists themselves, making countless images in clay (for stone was scarce), and adorning walls with frescoes in the Indian tradition. Central Asia was a meeting place for many peoples, each contributing some-

585. *Adoring Bodhisattva*, from Tun-huang (8th cent.) Fogg Museum, Cambridge. Clay.

586. *Avalokiteśvara as the Guide of Souls* (10th cent.) British Museum. Painting on silk.

thing to the art of the area. The subtle shading of tones used by Ajantā painters was translated by oasis artists into bands of primary colors; a kneecap, for instance, which had been modeled in light and dark shadows, was here reduced to a circle of blue, green, or yellow, making a pleasant pattern, if quite an unrealistic one. With the coming of so much activity to the Buddhist shrines of China, owing to the overland trade and missionaries, the desert and oasis art made a profound impression there.

Tun-huang is a rich mine for the student and explorer, not only because of its wall paintings made from the fourth through the tenth centuries, and its T'ang sculpture (fig. 585), but also because of the countless votive banners painted on cotton and silk (fig. 586), and the texts in many languages. One of the earliest printed books in the world was found in a walled-up library where other precious things had been hidden—a paper scroll of the Diamond Sūtra (Buddhist text) dated A.D. 868.

It was a time of literary and intellectual activity. Poets sang the praises of their emperors, of palace beauties, of the great festivals, and of the lonely men who were garrisoned in the far-flung outposts controlled by China. Courtiers and scholars discussed the classics, and called upon monks to expound the doctrine of the many religious foundations in the capitals. Students and learned men came and went, quite a few to India, the most famous of the travelers in the seventh century being Hsüan-tsang. His diary with its vivid description of oasis cities, of desert sands and mountain winds, of the marvels of India, is one of the most delightful travel stories in any literature, and served as a guide to modern archaeologists in their discoveries of many important sites rich in Buddhist remains. He came back to China with Sanskrit texts which had to be translated and interpreted, as did other monks who took similar journeys, so the monasteries were busy centers of learning.

Symbol of the law and doctrine and intellectual aspect of the church was Vairocana Buddha, a celestial being who had not lived upon the earth, but in a paradise eons of years away, where he sat upon a lotus throne, the power of his mind emanating spiritual rays that inspired confidence and hope in believers. At Lung-mên, near Loyang, the eastern capital, the Buddha was represented in a colossal image 85 feet high (fig. 587), carved in the solid rock. It was dedicated in an impressive ceremony in A.D. 672. Remote and awe-inspiring, he sits upon his throne, with a great halo containing the Seven Buddhas of the Past carved in relief behind him. The colossus is flanked by Bodhisattva and monks, and protected by muscular guardians of the law (fig. 588), who stand 50 feet high. The sculptors had to portray many different qualities in the various beings prescribed by the Buddhist texts—symbols of wisdom, compassion, kingly majesty, mystical rapture, austerity, brute force—all conceived on a scale that would have been impossible to less gifted men, but in art

587. *Colossal Vairocana Buddha*, Lung-mên, Honan (672–76) Stone, 85' high.

588. *Guardians*, Lung-mên, Honan (672–76) Stone, 50' high.

as in politics, nothing seemed impossible then to the Chinese. Poised, mature, and benign, even the small images are imbued with greatness (fig. 589).

In painting, too, there was a ferment of activity, and a level of accomplishment to which later generations pointed with pride. Artists were hired by the hundreds to adorn the walls of Buddhist grottoes and sanctuaries, monks and nuns became painters, and, in secular life, at court and among the scholars, painting was regarded as a fine art. Buddhist banners and murals, of course, were made according to rules developed in India, and reflect as much Indian and Central Asiatic influence as the

sculpture does, but there was, as well, a native tradition that stemmed from the Han period.

Though there are no painted scrolls in existence dating from the Han, we know from historical records that painting played an important role in the lives of the people; portraits of the virtuous and great were hung on the walls, and the beams and supports of palaces and temples were richly decorated. In fact, the Wu Liang Tzŭ motifs (fig. 575) are so nearly like palace ornamentation described in a contemporary poem that it is quite likely that the flat silhouettes in low relief were derived from painted figures. Lacquered objects and

589. *Buddha* (7th cent.) Metropolitan Museum, New York. Gilt bronze.

painted pottery that have survived are witness to the skill and dexterity of a brushwork that was well suited to fanciful subjects. Chang Hêng, who lived from A.D. 78 to 139, preferred to paint ghosts and demons, for he thought that real objects were difficult to represent and also that the realm of the unreal was infinite.

A renowned copy of a scroll by a fourth-century painter, Ku K'ai-chih, was based on a text called the *Admoni-* in a delicate brush style. There are reminders that whatever rises high must fall—as the sun rises, so shall it set, as the moon waxes, so must it wane. And again, 'No one can endlessly please,' a piece of worldly advice based on the experience of beauties who were brought from all over China to please the Emperor, but who held power for only a moment. Each episode is a unit to be enjoyed separately. The figures are irresistible in their delicate charm, floating

590. Ku K'ai-chih (*c.* 350–400) *Admonitions of the Imperial Preceptress*, British Museum, London. Painting on silk, 10″ high.

tions of the Imperial Preceptress (fig. 590). As its title suggests, it is courtly and Confucianist in theme. The young ladies of the palace were urged by their imperial tutor to learn proper deportment by imitating the famous heroines and beauties of the past. The horizontal silk scroll is designed in a series of scenes, each one carefully labeled, illustrating an incident or moral precept. Loyalty to the emperor, the folly of vanity, the desirability of a large family and of telling the truth are illustrated almost in an undefined space, fragile and exquisite as the flowers for which they were named. Quite unlike the voluptuous Indian beauties who wore much more jewelry and a few diaphanous scarves, the Chinese ladies were clothed from head to foot in long silk robes that give no hint of the body underneath; their appeal is subtle, sophisticated, as tenuous as a faint perfume. They are painted in true Chinese fashion by means of brush and ink on silk, in which forms are suggested by thickening and thinning lines. Some color was used, but line would be sufficient without color, it is so filled with life and rhythm, so carefully placed. Like the calligraphy labeling each scene, the brushwork demonstrates that the painter-writer had mastered one of the most difficult disciplines in the world of art.

The writer, or painter, by control and dexterity, could make a thin line or a thick one while using the same brush. Depending on his skill, imagination, and personality, he could, in a few strokes, suggest the power of an ocean wave or the delicacy of a butterfly's wing, even in a written character or pictograph. The shape of a character and the spacing of its parts were of as great concern to the writer as were the arrangement of mountain peaks and waterfalls to the maker of pictures. To both writer and painter, no matter what the subject might be, the quality desired above all was a rhythmic vitality, a suggestion of the form of life itself. As early as about A.D. 500, in canons written by Hsieh Ho, this came first on his list of directions for producing great paintings. The last canon is as characteristically Chinese as the first: he suggests that by copying the old masters one might reach toward a greater creative activity. The T'ang master, Wu Tao-tzu, has served as such a model.

Many of the poets were painters by the T'ang period, adding that highest accomplishment of the gentleman and the scholar to their poetic gift. They were founders of the tradition of the philosopher-poets, the scholar-painters, who were not bound by rules as were the craftsmen working on religious subjects, but were free to paint any subject, once they had mastered the discipline of 'good brush.' By it they expressed their attitude toward nature or their fellow man in true Chinese fashion, seeking to convey much by the simplest means, realizing that the unsaid is as important as the said, that a suggestion is more challenging than complete statement. It meant setting down the essence of the subject, which could come only after a devoted study of it. Therefore, as they tell us, they watched each flower as it grew, opening in the dew of the morning, advancing from bud to blossom to seed pod. They noted all kinds of trees, each with its own root system, trunk, branches, and characteristic leaves and watched them change appearance in the different seasons. Mountains and rocks, the flight of birds, the fall of snow, a fisherman, a spray of bamboo— all of nature was their guide and tutor. Remembering Hsieh Ho's first canon, they imbued their paintings with life and vitality instead of making objective, scientific studies; they had looked deeper than the surface, and had caught the rhythm as well as the appearance of things in the world about them.

Landscape was a favorite theme with the poet-painters, and consisted primarily of mountains and water. Like their poems, the paintings are made of mist and mountains, and reflect the mood of the artist. Wang Wei is one of the outstanding masters of poetry and scroll

painting in the T'ang period. Though
we know his painting only from copies
or descriptions made by contemporaries,
he could serve as the representative of
the unhampered Chinese style of delicate color, ink, and shading on silk or
paper, in contrast to the religious paintings of Buddhist caves and sanctuaries,
with their strong Indian and central
Asian influences.

In Tun-huang, especially, the wall
paintings and banners of the T'ang
period give us an idea of the splendor
of Buddhist art (fig. 584). The walls
were prepared with a fine coating of
plaster, applied over rougher layers, and
on it the designs were laid out according to Indian formulas, with a large
Buddha in the center, surrounded by
lesser deities and attendants. Beneath
the religious scene a row of portraits
represented donors in Chinese or Turkic
dress. The central scheme was worked
out by using chalk on string; the body
of the Buddha served as the starting
point, and, once his measurements were
correct, and a circle made for the halo
behind his head, as well as a larger mandorla behind the body, the craftsmen
then placed the Bodhisattva at intervals,
snapping the chalk against the plaster
to establish radial lines. The outlines of
the figures were drawn freehand or
made by using pounces; each one had
to be made in the proper proportion
and with the proper garments, hand
gestures, and attributes, according to
Indian texts. Colors, too, were assigned
to certain figures. They were more vivid
than the browns, blues, and greens of

Ajantā (fig. 529), for the Central Asian
communities and the Chinese had different pigments and different interpretations of the texts. The primary colors,
red, blue, and yellow, with some brilliant
secondaries, were popular in Tun-huang.

The hidden library there contained
countless banners as well as texts on
silk and cotton (fig. 586). Some had
already been dedicated to the Buddha
or one of the Bodhisattva, others had
been prepared but the dedication had
not yet been written in the space designed for it. They vary in workmanship
from the marvelous in color and composition to the poorest provincial copies.
Some are as magnificent as the wall
paintings in scale, others are small vertical hangings with hastily sketched
figures on them. Good and bad, they
are authentic, and they reflect T'ang
ideas in religious art; we must turn to
them, and to a few pieces preserved in
Japan, for our knowledge of the period.
It is invaluable for our study of Chinese
art, and also of Tibetan art. The Tibetans came and went at all times from
the outpost city nearest their own territory. They took some of the banners
home and brought their own to dedi-
cate to the Thousand Buddhas; a number of the banners show Tibetan influence, and in the earliest Tibetan paintings are Chinese motifs which stem
from the T'ang era.

In banners as well as murals the
painter had some opportunity to let his
imagination guide him in portraying
tales of the previous existences of the
Buddha and episodes from the life of

the historical Buddha or the Bodhisattva. These scenes were smaller in scale than the big Buddhist Heavens, and they were narratives. In them we see a blending of foreign and native styles, and the introduction of Chinese costume, architecture, landscape, even of the playful, fanciful sprites and demons stemming from old Chinese art. Though they are small and sometimes badly preserved, they are among the most important and delightful treasures of the Caves of the Thousand Buddhas.

Mural painting on a grand scale was continued in China in the succeeding periods, but the most sought-after paintings in later epochs are done on silk or paper, such as small album pieces or the horizontal and vertical scrolls.

When the next dynasty came to power, the Sung (960–1279), one of the emperors, Hui-tsung, became a poet-painter, as well as a great collector of masterpieces of the past. He was the patron of artists who were called to the capital to the Academy he directed. Members of the Academy wore special robes and insignia, and were expected to maintain a high level of excellence in their painting. The Emperor specified the subjects to be portrayed, and rewarded the best competitors. Some of these subjects seem more fitting for poets than painters and were a great challenge to the ingenuity of the artist: 'The hoofs of his steed returned heavily charged with the scent of the trampled flowers,' or 'A boat lying idle the whole

591. Hui-tsung (1082–1135) *Ladies Preparing Newly Woven Silk,* Museum of Fine Arts, Boston. Painting on silk, scroll 1′2½″ high x 4′9″ long.

592. Hui-tsung (1082–1135) *The Five-Colored Parakeet*, Museum of Fine Arts, Boston. Painting on silk.

day long as nobody wishes to cross the river,' were solved by the winners by showing a swarm of butterflies clustering around the horse's hoofs, and by a boatman daydreaming with his flute beside him.

Hui-tsung copied a T'ang design of Ladies Preparing Newly Woven Silk (fig. 591), faithfully depicting costume, textile patterns, coiffures, and beauty marks, but ignoring any specific setting. His Five-Colored Parakeet (fig. 592) is typical of album painting, the bird perched on an apricot branch, with an inscription in delicate calligraphy be-

side it, and seals of approval above. Instead of showing the whole tree or shrub, by choosing a few branches that come up dynamically from a place outside the limits of his silk, he suggests the whole growing organism. Tiny buds, some beginning to open, and some full-blown blossoms cluster together as they would on a growing fruit tree, developing in a cycle as inevitable as spring itself. A firmer brush stroke was used on the branches and twigs, for 'old branches are like dragon's horns, young ones like angling rods,' and the parakeet clings confidently to the longest. As we study

593. Fan K'uan (act. 990–1030) *A Temple Among the Snowy Hills*, Museum of Fine Arts, Boston. Painting on silk, 10" x 10".

it we become aware of the subtle repetition of curves in the body of the bird and in the branches, and of the importance of the unpainted areas. Though it looks unpremeditated, it is deliberately asymmetrical and carefully planned. Only an artist who had observed the parakeet and apricot for a long time could thus catch the inner character of each, and only a skilled painter could paint on the silk without a preliminary sketch, never erasing line or color, and seem to do it so effortlessly.

Even before Hui-tsung's time great landscapes were painted, both as album pieces (fig. 593) and horizontal scrolls (fig. 594). The latter were as carefully planned as the little circular or rectangular studies, and gave fuller scope to Chinese genius, with its longing for infinity and space. The two characters that make up their word for landscape are 'mountain and water,' both suggesting vastness, solitude. We have to look closely for man in the valleys if we are to find him at all; he is usually a traveler carrying a pack on his back, or a boatman. He is all men on their journey through life, with their burdens, their stony paths, their visions of beauty beyond as the mist clears. He is not so great as a mountain, nor does he live as long as a pine; he is beaten low by storms, but he goes on his way. He belongs in the scheme of things; he does not tame nature; he accepts his place, patiently and with humility, a being at home in his universe. Through him, and through the world about him, flows a vibrant life, movement and change and rhythm. In the Clear Weather in the Valley by Tung Yüan (fig. 594), the landscape elements are arranged in changing groups of motifs woven together horizontally, with vertical accents rising or falling behind them. If we follow from right to left, seeing only a few inches of the scroll at a time as it is unrolled, we find that we are actually in a moving picture; but our eyes are doing the moving, drawn up, over, down, and across by a constantly moving focus, by variations on the themes that are broken occasionally by moving water. After showing the majesty of mountains with evergreens crowning their summits, the sturdiness of trees in the foreground, distant land, tiny men in boats, open stretches of river, and bubbling streams, the painter closes his composition with a repetition of his opening harmonies—and yet he does not close it, for we must imagine the rest of it, as the river flows down to the sea.

While the Emperor and his masters of the brush tried to capture the fragrance of a flower and the delicate pattern of bamboo reflected on silk in the moonlight, the barbarians closed in again from the northwest. Hui-tsung fled, giving up his collection of over six

594. Tung Yüan (10th cent.) *Detail of Clear Weather in the Valley*, Museum of Fine Arts, Boston. Ink on paper, scroll 1'3" high x 5'11" wide.

thousand scrolls, but he was taken captive and killed by the Golden Tatars. Kao-tsung, his successor, went south to Nanking, but could not escape, and in 1141 signed a treaty with the invaders giving them most of the northern provinces. The Tatars made their capital in Peking, while the Chinese court was established in the south at Hangchou. Some of the finest works of art ever produced were done in the southern Sung period. It was a time of sorrow for most of China, when they could do little more than dream of the past or face the hard work and bitterness of the present. More than ever the poets found beauty in small, exquisite things, in the sound of rain, or the jade-white petal of a flower, or the melancholy music of the flute. They retired to their bamboo groves, as did former statesmen; for the time being, the teaching of Lao-tzu, with its emphasis on nature, seemed more in key with the times than the precepts of Confucius did.

The pomp and color of Mahāyāna Buddhism and its texts and rituals began to pall. A more personal approach had been introduced in the sixth century by Indian teachers who believed in the efficacy of contemplation in which each worshiper had to find the Buddha in his heart. No one could intercede for him, nor would the building of temples or memorials increase his merit; he had to rely on himself, with the guidance of a few masters who could only suggest, not prescribe, how he might find the Way. Thus Ch'an Buddhism and Taoism grew into a religion very agree-

595. Liang K'ai (act. 12th cent.) *The Poet Li T'ai-po*, Count Matsudaira Coll., Tōkyō. Ink on paper.

596. Liang K'ai (act. 12th cent.) *The Priest Hui-nêng*, Count Matsudaira Coll., Tōkyō. Ink on paper, 2'6" high.

nation often came while chopping wood, drawing water, or fishing. If it seemed slow in coming, a box on the ear or some other unexpected shock might bring it about. Teachers talked in riddles, for 'the Tao of which one can speak is not the Tao.'

Painters in these monasteries no longer decorated walls with formal pictures of the heavens of the future. Now the painter-monks cleared their minds of distracting thoughts, and set to work with brush, ink, and paper. Even light color was discarded, for the ink painting was more of a challenge, leaving much to the observer to fill in. Instead of painting each leaf, the brush swept quickly over the paper, giving an impression of the forms. Thus Liang K'ai did a masterly portrait of the famous T'ang poet, Li T'ai-po (fig. 595), with the fewest possible strokes, and in a staccato style he painted Hui-nêng Tearing up the old Buddhist scriptures (fig. 596) in the frenzy of energy of one who believed that the only way to Illumination was through contemplation, not the written word. The motion of Liang K'ai's brush must have been as abrupt as if *he* were tearing them; he put the ink on the paper in quick angular lines, and made a pine branch up above shoot like a rocket across the scroll. As in the early ink paintings, these figures exist in a very real but entirely anonymous space. A fellow monk-painter, Mu Ch'i, showed equal skill in suggesting much through simple means; his painting of Persimmons (fig. 597), daring in its simplicity of form, looks more like a

able to the Chinese temperament. Monasteries had been established near Nanking as well as in the north, and were run by abbots who, though enlightened, might be quite unlettered. Menial tasks were assigned to the novices, for Illumi-

597. Mu Ch'i (13th cent.) *Persimmons*, Ryū-kōin Temple, Kyōto. Ink on paper.

which must be about to put out the pale yellow-green buds of early spring. The timber bridge lies ahead, with water flowing under it, and, once safely across it, he may go through a bamboo grove to the house nestling in a cove. The damp mist is rising, almost obscuring the bamboo and the house, cloaking the base of the mountain that rises in the distance. There is the mood about it of the twilight hour, of a journey almost done, of the need to hurry before the fog settles. The curve of the willow branches, of the bridge, and of the mountain are in perfect harmony with the circle of the silk. The dark accents of the lower right, repeated near the bridge, in the tree tops, and on the mountain ridge, add to the impression of a vibrant radiation, which gives life to a scene composed of undramatic elements. The design of these parts, of the light and dark areas, of the empty spaces and the filled, was done by a master hand, sure and subtle.

Fan K'uan also chose the circular fan-shaped silk for his album piece of A Temple Among the Snowy Hills, and like Ma Yüan he emphasized the curving patterns of rock, shore line, tree trunk, bamboo, and mountain (fig. 593). He, too, places the heaviest elements in the lower right-hand corner, and he expands the design radially from there. But the mood of his snow scene is quite different; there is a suggestion of the soundless chill of winter, of a world blanketed in white. Contours are sharp, contrasts more striking. Man is still small, he still labors toward shelter and

work of the twentieth century than one of the thirteenth. Landscape, too, was a favorite theme for the Ch'an philosophers, and was painted with the same freedom of brush.

This is the great moment of painting in China. Future generations will look to the Sung masters and collect their works with as much love as they have lavished on the classics of literature and ancient bronzes, which were catalogued in this period. Famous names abound as they do three centuries later in the rich era of the Renaissance in Italy.

Ma Yüan, in an album piece (fig. 598), shows a tiny traveler, his possessions tied to a stick held over his shoulder, as he approaches a bridge flanked by willow trees. We identify ourselves with him as he nears the tall, graceful willows with their curving branches,

598. Ma Yüan (act. 1190–1225) *Bare Willows and Distant Mountains*, Museum of Fine Arts, Boston. Painting on paper, 9½″ x 9½″.

peace, but this time with a hat as big as an umbrella, and, as he bends into the wind, he lifts his feet to get through the heavy drifts.

More violent in mood, free and powerful in brushstroke, Hsia Kuei's Rain Storm is another Sung masterpiece (fig. 599). The vertical, hanging scroll gave the artist more scope and space, but he is careful not to fill the space. Far down in the right-hand corner, the traveler is about to leave a solid bank to cross a rickety bridge, and he, too, braces himself against the wind that tears autumn leaves off the trees. He almost crouches under his umbrella, and will have to be careful of his footing before he reaches the pavilion. A bold cliff juts out on the left side, to which the trees cling, their roots cutting into it like dragon claws. Everything is unsteady, designed in sweeping diagonals. Hsia Kuei's brushstroke is free and forceful, his ink rich and black, or shaded to thin wisps.

600. Mi Fei (1051–1107) *Misty Landscape,* Freer Gallery, Washington. Painting on silk, 4′11″ x 2′7″.

The mass of foliage on the trees is done by a few quick dabs of the brush loaded with ink, and even the leaves blown by the wind are small, bold dots. Behind the trees, the mist comes in obscuring a hill that appears high up in the picture. A small sapling growing from the mountain is mercilessly beaten by this autumn wind, a force to be endured, not tamed.

Equally original, Mi Fei became famous for his technique of placing small 'blobs' of ink in varying tones close to-

599. Hsia Kuei (act. 1195–1224) *Rain Storm,* Baron Kawasaki Coll., Kobe. Painting on paper.

gether, a twelfth-century 'pointillist' approach in monochrome (fig. 600). The effect is one of softness and subtle shading, well adapted to the portrayal of mist, mountain, and trees that have a vaporous, undulating quality. Though the method of painting was original and unorthodox, Mi Fei achieved a serene peacefulness that was the ideal of more academic painters.

One of the academicians who moved south after the collapse of Hui-tsung's regime was Li T'ang. He was inspired by the beauty of the Hangchou hills to paint bold landscapes, and he was equally inspired by rice wine. His Man on a Water Buffalo Returning Intoxicated from a Village Feast (fig. 601) might well be a self-portrait. The pitiful old man is kept astride his lowly steed by a faithful retainer walking beside him. A ragged boy pulls the unwilling beast. They are all unkempt, stooped, and dejected; the old man had tried to

601. Li T'ang (act. 1100–30) *Man on a Water Buffalo*, Museum of Fine Arts, Boston. Painting on silk, 10″ x 11″.

602. Ma Lin (act. 1215–25) *Ling Chao-nü Standing in the Snow*, Museum of Fine Arts, Boston. Painting on silk, 9½" x 10".

forget the sorrow of the Sung, the shame of the barbarians flourishing in the north. Li T'ang, the former court painter, was meticulous in his brushstroke. Every tiny willow leaf is done carefully and the hair of the buffalo is equally fine in texture. The willow trunks are covered by rough bark, and the bamboo leaves are painted with smoother contours. Hundreds of delicate lines indicate the rippling surface of the river flowing beside the slow-moving procession.

The quietness of winter and the loneliness of a gray day are expressed by Ma Lin in his painting of Ling Chao-nü Standing in the Snow (fig. 602). His subject, the daughter of a good Taoist who did not disturb his spirit by mingling in worldly affairs, had to go out to seek food and firewood. Though there are cracks in the silk, which is seven hundred years old, and it has yellowed with age, we are still touched by the mood. The slim figure of the girl, the leaves blackened by frost, branches broken and bent, the path blanketed by snow suggest stillness and solitude.

Something of the same melancholy is conveyed by an anonymous painter of the twelfth century who did a narrative scroll of Lady Wen-chi's captivity in Mongolia and her return to China (fig. 603). Illustrating a favorite story of Han times, he showed the delicate Chinese girl as she was taken out into Mongolia by her captor, who made her his wife. She had to live in a tent and grow accustomed to the uncouth ways of nomadic people. Finally money for her ransom came, but it was with sorrow that she parted from her husband and the children she had borne him. She ar-

rived back in the Chinese capital, bewildered by crowded streets and the rush of many peoples, as she mounted the steps, clad in the white robes of mourning. We look down upon the scene of her return, into a picture divided into small segments by diagonal roof lines. As in many Oriental paintings, the lines suggest space extending out from the picture plane toward the beholder, and they create a simple setting for the lively panorama of street and palace.

Dragons were regarded as particularly beneficent creatures: they served as symbols of the East, they were the bringers of rain, and of good crops. They lived in lakes or pools, or in the Eastern Sea, and they could rise like the mist, disappear into a cloud, become invisible at will, moving like lightning. Though it would seem almost impossible to portray a creature of sky and mystery on a piece of silk or paper, the painters often devoted themselves to dragon subjects.

603. *Return of Lady Wen-chi to Ying Ch'uan* (12th cent.) Museum of Fine Arts, Boston. Painting on silk, 10″ x 22″.

604. Ch'ên Jung (act. 1235–55) *Detail of Nine Dragon Scroll*, Museum of Fine Arts, Boston. Ink on paper, scroll 1'6" x 36'.

One of the greatest was Ch'ên Jung of the thirteenth century, a governor of Fukien, who painted as a hobby. Like Li T'ang, he was often inspired by wine, and was known to shout as he flung his ink on the paper, probably feeling as powerful as a dragon at the moment. Part of a 36-foot horizontal scroll (fig. 604), done in ink with light color on bamboo paper, is a detail of one of his

605. Ma Fên (act. 11th cent.) *Detail of the Hundred Geese Scroll*, Academy of Arts, Honolulu. Ink on paper, 1'2" high.

606. Hsi-chin Chü-shih (13th cent.) *One of the Ten Kings of Hell*, Metropolitan Museum, New York. Painting on silk, 3'8" x 1'7".

an ambitious project when he painted The Hundred Geese, showing them flying, settling down on the water, swimming, feeding, always varied and full of life. A copy of his scroll (fig. 605) is one of the most delightful ink paintings in the Sung style, sure in its brushwork, beautifully spaced, done with acute observation of the birds.

This freedom of expression that came with the Sung period affected even the religious painting of orthodox Buddhist subjects. One of the Ten Kings of Hell (fig. 606) sits like a Chinese magistrate at his desk, interviewing the wicked. Though the flames of Hell burn near by in this thirteenth-century painting by Hsi-chin Chü-shih, the King goes calmly about his judgments, full of ceremony and etiquette. All his attendants, even misshapen demoniac guards, are individuals. We are aware of what a change had taken place as we compare this with the T'ang painting of Buddhist worlds (fig. 584), where deities existed in a remote heaven, attended by spirits of superhuman, hieratic aspect, each placed at a prescribed distance from the Buddha.

In the series by Chou Chi-ch'ang and Lin T'ing-kuei of the twelfth century (fig. 607), there is the same interest in portraiture and individuality. The sages, or Arhats, are shown as men of supernatural power drifting down toward the earth, clad in monks' robes, but they look like prosperous Chinese citizens bestowing alms on the ragged beggars below them. There is striking contrast

greatest masterpieces, full of fury and spirit.

Some of the painters who specialized in birds and flowers preferred to do long scrolls rather than album pieces. Ma Fên of the late eleventh century undertook

607. Lin T'ing-kuei (act. 1160–80) *Arhats Giving Alms to Beggars*, Museum of Fine Arts, Boston. Painting on silk, 3'8" x 1'9".

ture, suggesting an infinity of space and movement.

Buddhist painters showed a tendency to break away from the magnificent crowded composition and to prefer as a subject the solitary monk, engaged in contemplation. Lu Hsin-chung of the thirteenth century painted Vanavāsi Gazing at a Lotus Pond (fig. 608), so intent in his concentration that he is not aware of an attendant who has approached with a tray. He is oblivious of

608. Lu Hsin-chung (13th cent.) *Vanavāsi Gazing at a Lotus Pond*, Museum of Fine Arts, Boston. Painting on silk, 3'8" x 1'4".

between the misshapen, grotesque ragamuffins who are almost caricatures of misery, and the bland, plump Immortals. The Chinese artists have thus rebelled against the strict formality of composition dictated by the Indian sutrās, and place their figures in unsymmetrical groups: clouds, trees, and rocks are cut by the border of the pic-

ducks playing among the lotus, and of the wind in the willows; he is completely lost in thought. Unlike the Ch'an paintings, which were monochrome, black and white, these Mahāyāna Buddhist paintings are colored. Vanavāsi wears a red and gold brocaded priest's robe over a green undergarment, his attendant wears a blue gown tied with red cords about his waist, the ducks are brown and blue-green, the lotus blossoms a fragile pink, and the lotus and willow leaves are green. In this—as in other paintings of the same series in Boston—the artist shows a master's skill in arranging forms, textures, and patterns, demonstrating his interest in the concrete world and the realms beyond reality.

These are a few among the great names of the Sung painters. Figure painters, landscape artists, specialists in birds, flowers, dragons, and bamboo— all were splendid. Many were innovators, experimenting in techniques and styles that have influenced Chinese painting down the ages, and still set a standard for all the world to admire.

This is the great moment in the ceramic arts, too. Based on the tradition handed down from Neolithic times, which reached a high point under the Han and T'ang, pottery-making in China now outstripped that of other lands in refinement, beauty of shape, and glaze. The imperial family took a great interest in its production, choosing the rarest and finest pieces. Shapes were modeled on the bronze ritual vessels, or were designed especially as

flower holders or tea ceremony dishes. The thickness of the body varies from heavy stoneware to delicate porcelain that rings when flicked by the finger, some of it fired at high temperatures. Glazing advanced beyond anything known before; the potters learned how to make crackle in the glaze, and how to control the size and direction of the cracks. Most of the Sung ware is monochrome, described by Chinese names in a truly poetic way, 'blue as the sky after rain,' 'ice crackle,' 'fish roe crackle,' 'onion green,' 'hares' fur,' or 'palm eyes.' Sometimes a design was cut into the body before glazing, or was painted in the glaze, done with as much skill as in calligraphy or painting on silk. A bowl

609. *Ting Ware Bowl* (10th–13th cent.) Museum of Fine Arts, Boston. Pottery.

of Ting ware (fig. 609), glazed creamy white, is as delightful as an album painting. The curve of the bowl is repeated in the curve of the grasses, the swans, and the waves that buoy them up. It is

610. Kuan Tao-shêng (14th cent.) *Bamboo* (1309) Museum of Fine Arts, Boston. Ink on silk, 11" x 4'6".

graceful, exquisite, and a miracle of restraint.

LATER CHINESE ART

The southern Sung dynasty came to an end with the Mongol invasion. Under Jenghis Khan, the nomads had harassed the north, and had established themselves there by 1234. The Chinese attacked the Yüan, as they named them, and started a conflict that lasted forty-five years, ending in the subjugation of all China, and the annexation of Chinese territory to most of Asia already under Mongol rule. Chinese were sent to Mesopotamia, and tribesmen from all parts of Asia flocked to the big eastern cities. Under Kubilai, who was the Khan of China from 1260 to 1294, Peking was proclaimed the winter capital, and was rebuilt under Moslem direction. Many halls, gardens, and even a zoo were in 'Khanbaliq,' as it was called, and Marco Polo was not the only traveler to report on its charms. Since Kubilai was interested in all kinds of things and people, we can imagine how the city's streets looked as the caravans came in from the desert, bearing gifts from Persia, Russia, and Damascus, or when traders came up from the south with spices, jewels, and rare animals. Tibet and Lamaism played important roles in the life of the north and west, for the Mongols supported that sect, as well as allowing Buddhism, Taoism, and Confucianism to continue.

Painting followed the Sung tradition as the 'non-collaborators' tried to ignore their conquerors and lived in solitude apart from the Mongol cities, but some of the most gifted artists were patronized by the newcomers. The 'barbarians' liked paintings of horses and the hunt, those which tended to emphasize vigor and strength rather than delicacy; but the most renowned names are those of artists who followed the principles of the past. Chao Mêng-fu and

611. Ni Tsan (1301–74) *Landscape* (1362) Freer Gallery, Washington. Ink on paper, 1′ x 1′8″.

his son and grandson were so famous as painters of horses and animals that nearly every Mongol period scroll that has a horse in it is ascribed to this family. Chao's wife, Kuan Tao-shêng, is one of the few women who rank high in the Chinese records; she was known as a specialist in bamboo painting (fig. 610). Wu Chên, basing his ink painting on the Sung ideals of life, rhythm, and simplicity of form, did many studies of bamboo. Another traditionalist is Ch'ien Hsüan, whose bird and flower scrolls would have pleased the Sung emperor-painter Hui-tsung.

Many landscapes were painted, often in the old styles, but there were several innovators who tried out different brush techniques, using line rather than tone for rocks, trees, water, and hills. As might be expected in a time when parts of Europe and Asia were under the same rule, the Chinese concept of space began to undergo changes; distant mountains, instead of rising majestically as they so often had in earlier painting, were reduced in scale. Ni Tsan (fig. 611) and Huang Kung-wang were among the experimenters, bringing a new power and originality to landscape painting. The former, particularly, won for himself an honored place by pioneering in the dry-brush technique. By it he achieved a solidity of form in rocks and trees that formed the basis for some of the great Ming painting to follow.

Owing perhaps to their contact with other civilizations where realism was stressed, the Mongols had portraits made. Their gay embroidery and headdresses are similar to those seen in T'ang paintings of Turkic people of

Central Asia. In style, the Ming ancestor portraits followed the same meticulousness for several centuries.

Much of the Buddhist painting of the Yüan period follows the tradition of the past. Of the scroll painters of this group, Yen Hui is one of the most interesting, reflecting in his work a popular belief in folklore, for Chinese fairy folk were joined by Tibetan demons and Persian djinns in the minds of the common people. His Immortal (fig. 612) is one of the dwellers in hills and forests who had been given the secret of immortality. His astral body issues from his mouth, soaring up into the air, while he remains sitting above the abyss as the mist closes in. He looks like an unkempt foreigner, with bushy hair, flat, knotty fingers, and a Persian pilgrim bottle hanging at his side. Largely through the artist's skillful use of tone, he is endowed with a magic quality equal to that of the Sung arhats.

In the decorative arts, as in painting, there was a considerable exchange of ideas with the outside world, particularly with the Near East. From Russia, also under Mongol domination, the art of cloisonné enamel was introduced as practiced by Byzantine craftsmen. Thus China became a great center for the making of highly colored vases and dishes.

The Mongols were unable to maintain their sovereignty long. Strong as they seemed, they were driven out by forces from the south in 1368. A Buddhist monk, leader of the Chinese army,

612. Yen Hui, An Immortal, Chion-ji, Kyōto. Painting on silk.

established a new dynasty, the Ming, which lasted until 1644. At first there was a great expansion, for the Chinese were victorious in military campaigns and had impressive fleets plying the coastal waters, and voyaging to India and Africa.

The early capital of the Ming dynasty was in Nanking, but in 1403 it was moved north to Peking, which was rebuilt on the plan we know today by the Emperor of the Yung-lo period. Except for the imperial tombs near Nanking, this northern capital affords the best examples of Ming genius in planning and building imposing edifices. The imperial palace, the 'Forbidden City' of later days, contains three courtyards around which are grouped pavilions, halls, terraces, gardens, and ornamental waterways. Like the ancient house in plan, but expanded to magnificent dimensions, it has been called the grandest palace in the world. The tile roof is supported by brackets that branch out from vertical supports, but the roofs are colored blue, green, gold, and red rather than a somber brown or clay, and the bracket system has grown increasingly complex. The courtyards are laid out symmetrically according to definite concepts of order and auspicious direction inherited from the past, but the white marble of the walls marks a break with tradition. It is in harmony, however, with the colors of tiles and ornaments. The Altar of Heaven (fig. 613) consists of three circular terraces with their balustrades joined by imposing stairs and ramps that were used by the emperor when he went there in the early dawn to perform his sacrificial rituals. Like the jade symbol of heaven, the circle of the altar suggested completeness that was both heavenly and imperial.

In Peking there was a revival of the arts and a renewed activity in the making of encyclopedias, books on crafts and agriculture, and fine editions of re-

613. *Altar of Heaven*, Peking.

ligious and philosophic works. Increased trade carried Chinese porcelains, silks, carved ivories, and jewels to other parts of the world, where 'chinoiserie' later became a great vogue, especially in the seventeenth and eight-eenth centuries, and China, in turn, became acquainted with products from the Western world. Then in the seventeenth century the Chinese were forbidden to go abroad, and trading on a large scale was not encouraged; the

614. Tai Chin (act. 1430–50) *Details of Breaking Waves and Autumn Winds*, Freer Gallery, Washington. Ink on paper, scroll 1' x 36'6".

Chinese turned their eyes on the glorious past.

While some Ming painters studied the past with reverence, others produced works notable for their originality and power. So great was their versatility, in fact, that they are difficult to classify in limited compartments. One group, the Chê, consisted of court painters. They had as their models the Sung masters, such as Ma Yüan (fig. 598) and Hsia Kuei (fig. 599). Though some of them produced copies more remarkable for precision than for boldness, their leader, Tai Chin, was imaginative and original, capable of working in several methods. His interpretation of nature shows the sensitiveness and understanding that we look for in the best of Chinese painting. In his scroll of fishermen bringing their boats to harbor in a hard blow (fig. 614), the brushwork is strong, demonstrating how expert he was in that exacting medium. The handling of tone, which he graded from light to dark to suggest volume, shows how well he knew that much could be expressed if every brush stroke counted. Like the masterpieces of former days, the painting is filled with life and rhythm; one follows the moving focus through the 36½-foot-long scroll, from scene to scene, each a part of the other, and each perfect in itself. The wind, bending trees, filling the sails, and blowing travelers before it, has rarely been painted so successfully. Hsia Kuei would have looked upon it with delight.

Of the non-professional painters, the Wu school of literary men produced versatile amateurs; Shên Chou, poet and gentleman, was a real leader among them. With delicate humor and fine brush work he gave individuality to both album pieces and large compositions. Whether he painted persimmons or majestic landscapes, he did them with a mastery of technique that set him above the hundreds of painters of the period. He followed the Yüan masters, especially Ni Tsan (fig. 611), taking the dry-brush method and adding color. Of his pupils, T'ang Yin is noteworthy for his swift brushwork, his delicacy, and his humor, and Wên Chêng-ming for his independence and versatility. In the sixteenth century Tung Chi-ch'ang was outstanding as scholar, statesman, art critic, and friend of Matteo Ricci, the Jesuit priest who took such an interest in Chinese painting. Chu Tuan, another important Ming painter, produced traditional subjects in the freer Ming style (fig. 615).

The use of color is one of the important contributions of the Ming artists to the history of Chinese painting. Many of them loved the exquisite festivals of the court, which took place behind walls that shut out the noisy city, in a setting amid rocks, dwarfed pines, willows, and curving bridges, for the courtiers and ladies who feasted there. Ch'iu Ying gives us a good picture of such entertainment. No longer do the moods of nature touch these people. They and their music live in a protected world, painted in subtle tones of mauve, vermilion, and blue-green.

While the name of Ming has long

615. Chu Tuan, *Man and Boy in a Boat under Trees* (1518) Museum of Fine Arts, Boston. Ink on paper, 4' x 2'.

been familiar to students and collectors of Chinese porcelain, it is only in the last decade or so that we have come to know the really great examples of Ming ceramic wares. At Ching-to-chên, which had been a former center of activity under imperial patronage, the factories were re-established in 1369. From that time on for almost three centuries, in unbelievable quantities, came the finest porcelain the world has ever

seen. Never was the porcelain more purely white, the glaze more flawlessly translucent. Among the greatest achievements were the vases decorated in under-glaze blue with cobalt imported from Persia, and the pieces decorated with red derived from copper.

Monochrome ware was equally fine. Shapes of unparalleled purity and beauty were enhanced by reds, yellows, greens, and other colors. It was at this time, too, that the famous 'five-color' enameled wares were made, the enamels applied over the glaze, both in combination with under-glaze designs and alone. Floral designs, good luck symbols, dragons, butterflies, and sages were some of the popular ornaments. The 'three-color' wares were usually heavy pots, big bowls, and garden seats, and the technique consisted of separating the patterns of colored glazes by means of cloisons of clay or by incisions in the paste, so that in firing there would be no intermingling of colors; some of these were carved in openwork designs. Aside from the standard wares, the beautiful creamy white called *blanc de chine* was made in Fukien province; in I-hsing, west of Shanghai, were made the teapots for the scholars' tables, of unglazed clays in chocolate brown and shades of red and yellow, sometimes intricately carved. Other regions, too, had their specialties.

Ming porcelains have been so skillfully imitated that assignment of a piece in its proper period is an extremely complex and puzzling task. The vases of at least ten of the seventeen Ming reign periods can be distinguished by a careful study of the paste, glaze, color, and type of design, but the mark of a Ming ruler on a piece of porcelain may mean nothing more than that a copy was made by a later workman emulating the honorable past.

Wood-block printing was used extensively in this period in the making of encyclopedias, in the illustration of religious texts, and in copybooks used by art students. The color print had been developed into a thing of exquisite beauty by Ming craftsmen. Textiles, which had always kept pace with the major arts of China, assumed a new importance. Robes for state ceremony and sacrificial rituals were made according to imperial edict and ornamented with symbols handed down from prehistoric times. These robes were so much admired by the conquerors of the Ming, the Manchus, that they adopted the designs for their own imperial costumes.

In 1644, the Manchus, who later conquered Turkestan and Tibet, infiltrated into northern China and took Peking for their second capital, which it remained until 1912 when the Republic was proclaimed. For forty years they waged campaigns in the south, and finally extended their power to Indo-China, bringing all of the country under their rule which they called the Ch'ing Dynasty. They readily adapted themselves to Chinese law, manners, and customs, and brought years of peace in which the arts could flourish. Since they admired so much of what had been done under the Ming, it was natural that they should encourage artists of all kinds. More than ever the past was examined and copied, and a display of skill for its own sake, rather than originality, was the goal of craftsman and painter.

Brush-stroke types were classified and made into copybooks, which were studied more earnestly by apprentices than was nature herself; as a consequence countless painters proved to be proficient, but their work was academic and lifeless. They were charmed by meticulousness and were inclined to overload their compositions, often stressing the decorative values at the expense of power and vitality. Though they turned to the Sung and Yüan periods for instruction, they failed to capture the simplicity and grandeur that had been a part of the heritage of the past. The eighteenth- and nineteenth-century painters were often frame-conscious, allowing the border of a scroll to serve as a real stopping place for the imagination, instead of suggesting more than was included in the picture; they ran their mountains up to astonishing heights to fit them into the vertical composition, and arranged other motifs to suit themselves within the pattern; they were fascinated by different textures, and by multitudinous objects that could be squeezed into the composition. Man did not occupy a humble place any longer; portraits were popular, especially if rank could be indicated by 'mandarin squares,' the embroidered insignia indicating the exact status of civil

616. Lêng Mei (18th cent.) *Lady Walking on Garden Terrace*, Museum of Fine Arts, Boston. Painting on silk, 3'6" x 1'10".

spontaneity that marks a real progress in the long development of brush techniques. Because the painters retained inherited discipline, there is still vitality, subtlety of form, and sly humor. Such men as Tao Chi, Yün Shou-ping, and the Four Wangs were interested in the variety in nature, rather than in its uniformity. Some made careful descriptive studies, trying to capture what the eye sees, but, unlike their copybook contemporaries, they drew from nature and endowed their studies with personality. A bird on a branch, by Chu Ta, for instance (fig. 617), is done with the fewest possible strokes of the brush; each stroke is essential, placed in exactly the right relation to the other strokes, and, what is more important in Chinese painting, in the right relation to the unfilled areas. This paint-

and military officials. Lovely ladies were shown swooning in delicate melancholy (fig. 616), and courtiers in their richest robes in audience with the emperor. Men gathered in pavilions for sociable meetings, and the painters delighted in depicting every detail.

In spite of the popularity of copying, and the widespread worship of the past or of the materialistic present, some Ch'ing paintings shows a freedom and

617. Chu Ta (act. 1630–50) *Kingfisher on a Lotus Stalk*, Kuwara Collection, Kyōto. Ink on paper.

ing seems to have been executed more rapidly than similar studies of the Sung and Ming periods, and is very modern in its freshness and bold simplicity. Men of this caliber were the true inheritors of the past and the guardians of the future. It is their work, rather than the mannered, decorative pieces that inspired 'chinoiserie,' which link a stirring twentieth-century China to her creative tradition of the dynasties long since gone, a heritage unrivaled by any other nation.

The wood-block print again was used extensively to illustrate treatises and literature. We can turn to them for a faithful picture of the times, now valuable to the student of genre art, porcelain, furniture, naval architecture, and even of warfare. A series of prints, the Conquests of the Emperor, were engraved on copper in France, and other prints were designed in China and printed in Europe or vice versa. Naturally there was more European influence than ever before to be found in perspective used in the Western manner, in costumes, and in racial types that appear in Ming and Ch'ing art. An Italian monk, Castiglione, combined both Western and Oriental ideas in his painting of the Ch'ien-lung period, and won great favor with the emperor, who used his services as architect in creating pavilions in the Summer Palace. The flourishing trade with the United States and Europe in the eighteenth and nineteenth centuries had a profound influence on those lands, as ivories, lacquer, fans, and Canton enamels were shipped out to grace the homes of seafaring men. Ceramic wares from China were in demand everywhere, and foreign influences were registered in that art as in so many others, but pieces made for the imperial household had to meet the rigid standards of imperial patronage just as they had in the past. The reigns of the K'ang-hsi emperor (1661–1722) and the Ch'ien-lung emperor (1736–95) are noted especially for the porcelains. Those emperors were connoisseurs, collecting the finest Sung pieces, which now bear their poems or marks of approval, and they demanded the best from their own workers in the imperial factories. Blue and white ware was popular, made with more mechanical perfection than in the Ming Dynasty. Among the enameled wares, the most sought-after in Europe were those called by the French collectors 'famille verte, jaune, rose,' if the ornamentation showed a preponderance of those colors. Monochromes came into favor again, with magnificent glazes such as *sang de boeuf* (copper red), Imperial yellow, *clair de lune*, 'mirror black,' and 'camellia-leaf green.' Shape and glaze were superbly suited to each other, so that a delicate vase the color of moonlight seemed really to capture the fleeting beauty of a summer night.

By the twentieth century, corruption, especially in the palace, marked the downfall of the Manchus. By the time the dowager empress had been laid away, pressure was brought on the boy emperor to retire to the shelter of the Forbidden City, and in 1912 the Republic came into being. For the last time an emperor of China had climbed the marble steps of the Altar of Heaven (fig. 613), and the sacrifices were discontinued. There on the white platform surrounded by its three tiers of balustrades, the ancient rituals had been performed for the last time.

Now new ways of life and new theories have come to China, with a European orientation. Wood-block prints carry a propaganda message in a style hardly distinguishable from Western prototypes, though traditional prints of flowers, birds, animals, and landscape still appear. Artists in exile and masterpieces in museum collections have inspired the Western world to a keener appreciation of the virtues of Chinese art.

XXXI

JAPAN

EARLY ART

The islands of Japan, lying off the east coast of Asia, were the last to receive the Asiatic culture that was carried there from India and China and the Near East. Hokkaidō in the north, the large island of Honshū stretching south and west, with Shikoku fitting into a curve of its southern shore, and Kyūshū almost due east from Shanghai are a beautiful group of volcanic lands that inspired the early inhabitants to a worship of mountains, streams, and trees. We know little about their culture before about 500 B.C. and have no written records until Buddhism was introduced in A.D. 552. Their myths of the creation of the islands, which were under the special protection of the sun-goddess and her earthly descendants who form the imperial house of Japan, indicate the love felt for their country

by the aborigines and the peoples who may have come up from the South Seas and the mainland to join them. According to legend, the Three Precious Things —a jewel, a sword, and a mirror—were given in 660 B.C. to Jimmu Tennō, who founded the empire.

There is some prehistoric pottery showing the use of the potter's wheel, as well as pottery figures of hollow tile. These were set around the graves, not placed inside them as in China, but set on stems that were pushed into the ground. They were of men, women, and animals, about 3½–4 feet high. Though not great works of art, they offer the student a chance to study early costume, especially the armor, and they indicate the Japanese preference for things that are 'bright and clear' in their simplicity and doll-like appeal. We are impressed at once by the difference between this

782

and Chinese art, which embodied the forces of nature and dealt with mysteries that stirred the souls of men.

Early bronze articles are less accomplished in casting than mainland pieces; Daitoku bells, very thin, have quite primitive designs in their panels of matchstick men, animals, and houses. Chinese influence came via Korea in the Han Dynasty, bringing the mirror form and ornament, to which were added jingles similar to those used in Siberia.

Judging from early clay models of houses, and from houses built in the traditional manner today, the high pitched roof with spreading gables was the most characteristic feature of archaic dwellings. No doubt the 'palace' erected by the descendant of the sun-goddess in western Japan was of this type, which is still followed in the modern Shintō shrine at Izumo (fig. 618). Like most Indonesian houses, it is set up on a platform of posts and planks, and is almost dwarfed by the great roof, which should serve to protect it even in a torrential downpour; the roof is thick, made of layers of cryptomeria bark or thatch, originally kept in place by the crossed timbers on the ridge pole which are retained now as a decorative

618. *The Great Shrine*, Izumo, Shimané Prefecture. Wood.

feature. In Japanese construction, the post and lintel are the basis of design and support, rather than the wall. Wood, the only material at hand for the early builders, was appropriate because of the emphasis on purity and simplicity in Japanese ritual. Some of the modern shrines are rebuilt on these traditional lines every twenty or thirty years, so that there is no decay; they are not adorned with color, plaster, or clay; the wood speaks for itself. Inside the shrine there was one chamber, almost divided in two parts by a partition; there were no images at first, only matting on the floor and an altar; the worshiper did not go inside.

The entrances to the early places of worship, which were generally in groves of trees or on mountains, were marked by simple gateways made by placing a horizontal log on two vertical tree trunks. This practice is continued in Shintō shrines in the erection of the torii, though the simplicity of ancient days has been discarded; the bark is stripped off of the logs, the surfaces are smoothed and frequently painted, and the topmost horizontal piece often is curved. The torii is used, for instance, at the famous shrine of the sun-goddess at Ise. Shintō, the 'Way of the Gods,' which was closely associated with creation legends and the sacred groves of nature spirits, embraces the ruling house of Japan, and those who give their lives to protect the emperor. In the nineteenth and twentieth centuries this relationship has been used to inspire patriotic fervor in the people, who were promised immortality through the sacrifice of a life in the line of duty. Whether in an isolated place like Ise, with its clear, bubbling streams and giant trees, or in modern Tōkyō, where elaborate edifices have been erected to the patriots, the Japanese recognize the torii as a symbol of the things they have revered most.

Except for the South Seas influence in architecture and in the early bronzes, the chief source of arts and crafts seems to have been Korea. In the Han period Korea became a Chinese province, and thus had received her bronzes and pottery from the Middle Kingdom, as well as Confucian ideals. These made their way into Japan. Then in the fifth century, when the Tatars swept over north China and a ferment of activity began in the service of the Buddha, Korea shared in that, too. Image makers, temple builders, and painters followed monks as the Law spread north and east.

A king of Korea sent an image of the Buddha to the emperor of Japan in A.D. 552, with sacred texts, and a letter recommending the adoption of the new religion. The emperor submitted the problem to his ministers, who were torn between the old and the new; they could not agree, and thus was caused a long cleavage at court. In spite of dissension and suspicion, Buddhism gradually took hold in Japan. Its early days were stormy; sometimes it was in favor, sometimes not, but the missionary zeal of the believers did not flag. Though scourges of illness were attributed to the foreign god, and persecutions took place, the practice of the Law became widespread toward the end of the sixth century. As the demand grew, more holy relics were brought over from Korea, priests and monks hastened to instruct the 'children' of the Land of the Rising Sun, temple carpenters came, as did skilled painters, carvers, and sculptors in bronze and clay.

In 593 the Empress Suiko came to the throne following the murder of the reigning emperor. In her time, inspired by her regent, Shōtoku Taishi, the first art period begins (Suiko, A.D. 552–646). This regent, her nephew, was one of the great men of Japan in the early historic period. In 604 he gave a Code of Laws to his people, incorporating much of Buddhism and Confucian doctrine in it. He recognized in Buddhism a civilizing agent of prime importance to his country, and therefore encouraged the building of temples and the translation of texts (in which Chinese characters were used, since up to that time the Japanese had had no written language), and made use of the knowledge of the monks in the development of agriculture and crafts. By the end of A.D. 624, there were 46 temples, 816 priests and monks, and 569 nuns.

One of the temples, the Hōryū-ji, still stands today, the oldest wooden building in the world (fig. 619), and the best example in Japan of the early seventh-

619. *Hōryū-ji Temple*, Nara Prefecture (7th cent.) Wood, plaster, tile.

620. *Lecture Hall*, Tōshōdai-ji (8th cent.) Wood, plaster, tile.

century style which followed Chinese lines. Since there is nothing so well preserved in China itself, it takes on an added significance. It served both as monastery and training school for monks. The various buildings are inclosed in a rectangle by a wall, on the south side of which is the Great South Gate. Within are the Golden Hall, the five-tiered pagoda, the lecture hall (illustrated by the one at Tōshōdaiji, fig. 620), and the Hall of Dreams which was added later in the eighth century. The roofs are of tile, not thatch, showing the change from the old Japanese system to the fashionable Chinese type. The weight of the roof is carried by wooden beams that rest on tall, mast-like posts, and on the brackets, or corbels, of the wall, which were derived from the Han Dynasty supports (fig. 576); the wall itself is of wood and plaster. It is an example of simple and honest construction, in which the materials were used to the greatest advantage for space and beauty, appropriate to the setting. The buildings and surrounding hills blend in a harmonious whole.

Early sculpture, like the architecture, is close to Chinese and Korean models, which followed Buddhist texts written in India. Akin to the images of the Wei and Sui periods of China (fig. 579, 581), the figures are rigid, faces and robes have been based upon patterns rather than living models, and in these figures the spirit shines forth serenely.

Though plagues of illness were attributed to followers of the Buddha who had broken with the nature gods, miraculous cures were credited to him by those who prayed to him in his healing aspect, called the Yakushi Buddha. Several of the most notable figures of the Suiko period are of Yakushi, or of the Bodhisattva of Mercy (Kwannon). The historical Buddha inspired many more dedications. Chinese and Korean masters, both wood carvers and bronze casters, taught their native pupils all the secrets of their arts, and the pupils proved to be so apt that the Suiko period and following eras produced some of the finest masterpieces of Nipponese sculpture. We cannot say now which were made by the teachers and which by their apprentices; the motherland, China, has so little left in wood or monumental bronze of the same time that we can only be grateful for the Japanese examples.

Of them, one of the most precious in the eyes of Buddhists and connoisseurs is the Kwannon (fig. 621), shut away from most mortals in the Hall of Dreams of the Hōryū-ji, a favorite place of retirement for the prince-regent. According to popular belief, the slim, six-foot wooden figure was based on that of the regent, who must have been taller than his countrymen. The Bodhisattva (Bosatsu) holds a flaming jewel of immortality, and looks out with a benign smile for those who call upon his mercy. He is crowned with a diadem of pierced bronze set upon the flat waves of his hair, which follows the neckline, and descends in regular curls over the shoulders. This type of diadem, the long, stylized curls, and drapery arranged in rigid folds are characteristic of most of Suiko sculpture. The Indian prototype has been followed to the extent that the ūrna between the eyes is included, as well as the long earlobes, and the dhotī, scarves, and jewelry of a prince; but they show Chinese influence in the flattening of volumes, the lack of interest in the body beneath the

621. *Kwannon*, Hōryū-ji Temple (6th–7th cent.) Wood, 6′ high.

622. Tori Busshi, *Shaka and Two Bosatsu*, Golden Hall, Hōryū-ji Temple (623) Bronze, central figure 2′10″ high, attendants 3′ high.

623. *Kudara Kwannon*, Hōryū-ji Temple (7th cent.) Wood, 6'8" high.

624. *Guardian Figure Bishamonten*, Golden Hall, Hōryū-ji Temple (7th cent.) Wood, 4'4".

drapery, and the flowing robes, which are like Six Dynasty and Sui dress. The halo, too, seems to be a combination of Indian and Chinese ideas, as it extends upward in a flame, ornamented with lotus flowers and the stūpa symbolizing the Buddha.

Within the simple, spacious interior of the Hōryū-ji, there are other splendid figures of the Suiko period. Two gilt bronze groups are attributed to the sculptor Tori of the early seventh century, one of Yakushi with attendants, and one of the historical Buddha and two Bosatsu (fig. 622). Like the Kwannon, some Indian features in iconographic details are retained, but the character of the whole is much nearer Chinese Six Dynasty work in drapery treatment. The stylized folds flow over the pedestals in sharply marked patterns of curving lines, which emphasize the smooth modeling of each face and throat as they emerge from the upper garments with architectonic simplicity. Another, called the Kudara Kwannon (fig. 623) because it was reputed to be from Kudara, Korea, was carved from a solid tree trunk, and painted. The paint has worn off in places, revealing the sure stroke and sweep of the carver's knife. Side drapery runs parallel to the body, allowing the spectator viewing it from the front to see the thin profile of the folds, which are in marked contrast to the full, long arms and the rounded volume of the vase holding the dew of immortality suspended from the left hand. Placed in the corners of the room are the guardians of the Four Quarters (fig. 624), the kings who safeguard followers of the Buddha, each of whom holds his weapons and attributes in his hands, and stands upon a miserable creature. Later versions of these guardians will be full of fury, but at this early stage the sculptors were content to make them majestic, as unyielding as the tree trunks from which they were carved, massive, yet crowned, as

625. *Bodhisattva in Meditation*, Chūgū-ji Nunnery, Hōryū-ji Temple (7th cent.) Wood, 5'2" high.

were so many other Suiko figures, by pierced bronze diadems.

In the Chūgū-ji Nunnery in Nara, a seated Bodhisattva is enshrined. The nuns have taken such excellent care of it in these thirteen hundred years that it looks as though it were made of polished bronze rather than wood (fig. 625). The bare torso of the Indian rajah has been retained, but two knobs adorn the head instead of one; the pose may be seen in countless figures taken from the caves of Yün-kang and Lungmen in China, but the true Japanese style begins to manifest itself in the marked feeling for decorative folds and sharp, linear rhythms of hairline, ears, and shoulder curls. Because the body is heavier and nearer the human form in modeling, it is sometimes attributed to the following period. The gentle smile and subtle carving have made it, for many people, the most beautiful figure in Japan.

Almost as famous as these pieces of sculpture is a small painted shrine called the Tamamushi. The panels represent scenes from the life of the Buddha, or symbols of Buddhist worship. They are framed by strips of pierced bronze under which are imprisoned iridescent beetle wings, which give the shrine its name. One of them (fig. 626) illustrates an event in the life of the Buddha in which he gave his life to save some starving tiger cubs. He is shown, in the upper section, standing on a cliff, hanging his garment on a small tree; then he plunges through space, and we see his lifeless body in the lower

626. *Base of Tamamushi Shrine*, Golden Hall, Hōryū-ji Temple (7th cent.) Painting on wood, 2′1″ high.

part as he is being devoured. Delicate bamboos mask the stark painfulness of this latter part, however, and they serve, in the composition, to balance the heavier upper areas. Colors are laid on the 'banded style' of the early T'ang painters of China. The upper part of the shrine is a fine scale model of a Chinese temple, interesting to architects for the structural details.

Direct contact with China in the T'ang Dynasty wrought a change in Japanese art, as did the maturing of native artists. The Hakuhō period (646–710) was enriched by contact with mainland cultures, as travelers of all kinds flocked to the great T'ang cities. As we have seen, the western capital,

627. *Shrine of Lady Tachibana,* Golden Hall, Hōryū-ji Temple (7th cent.) Bronze.

Ch'ang-an, was a cosmopolitan place, a revelation to the Japanese, who became acquainted there with other Asiatic people and with sumptuous wares offered for sale. Their art at home began to take on a more mature aspect, becoming richer and heavier, closer to T'ang sculpture, painting, and architecture.

In Buddhist art Amidism, with its idea of salvation for the masses, had a profound effect. In one of the best examples of Hakuhō art, the shrine of the Lady Tachibana (fig. 627), Amida oc-cupies the central position. The three figures sit or stand upon lotus, which grows from a pool in his heavenly paradise. The saviour, benign and welcoming, sits in Indian fashion upon his flower pedestal, flanked by standing Bodhisattva. Features, hair, drapery, and hand gestures are integral parts of circular and oval linear rhythms, which enhance the massiveness of their ponderous, cyclindrical bodies—an effect that is unusual in small-scale sculpture, for these figures are only a few inches high. Throughout, the shrine shows the

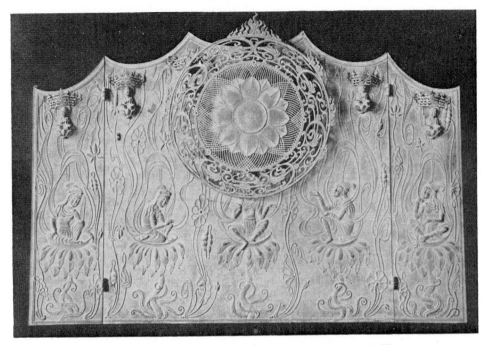

628. *Screen and Halo*, Shrine of Lady Tachibana, Golden Hall, Hōryū-ji Temple (7th cent.) Bronze, screen 1'9" high, halo 1'.

utmost care in design and execution, even in parts not visible at first to the onlooker. The pool is made of bronze, a sheet of the metal ornamented with patterned waves and lotus, which one can see only by standing above the little group; a delicately designed halo nearly hides a screen (fig. 628), which is an exquisite portrayal in low relief of the souls of the blessed. They, too, are seated on lotus, which grows up from the pool, guarded by the tentacles of an octopus, and clad in scarves that float upward in their watery world.

Amida is one of the four impressive deities painted on the walls of the Golden Hall of the Hōryū-ji (fig. 629). These murals, about 10 feet high, mark the easternmost flowering of the Buddhist fresco tradition, which had stemmed from Ajantā. In magnificence of conception, purity of line, and beauty of color, they are among the finest wall paintings in all of Asia.

Plumpness of cheeks, neck, and hands, so much admired in T'ang art, and a certain languid grace associated with India are to be found in the big black bronze Yakushi of the Yakushi-ji in Nara (fig. 630). The healing Buddha sits upon a pedestal ornamented with motifs borrowed from Sassanian Persia, India, and China. There are clusters of grapes in the upper border, jewels surrounded by pearls, and, on each of the four sides, the Dragon, Red Bird, Tiger, and

Tortoise in combat. Strange dwarf people with kinky hair and protruding
teeth look out from caves in the lower

sections, and yakshas hold ornaments
over their heads, which divide the panels
in two parts—symbols of civilization

629. *Amida Enthroned*, Golden Hall, Hōryū-ji Temple (7th cent.) Fresco, 10′ high.

630. *Yakushi*, Golden Hall, Yakushi-ji Temple, Nara Prefecture (7th–8th cent.) Bronze, 7′4″ high.

631. *Pagoda*, Yakushi-ji Temple, Nara Prefecture (8th cent.) Wood, plaster, tile.

tectural monument, for it has the subtlety of proportion and the honesty of construction found in the Hōryū-ji buildings, plus a grace and lightness that mark later Japanese design. From the central mast (fig. 632), the horizontal beams extend to support the roofs, five in number, which form an interesting and uneven pattern in silhouette. A nine-ring soren serves as a crowning member, recalling the parasols that topped the stūpas of India, the source of inspiration for the Pagodas of China and Japan.

The later Nara period, called Tempyō (710–794), was one of constant

and barbarity are brought together to serve the Buddha. He sits cross-legged, and gazes into space, ignoring his two attendants who stand on either side. All three figures have survived several fires that destroyed the temple building; and their survival has been attributed by the Japanese to magical qualities in the bronze. There is a large amount of silver in the alloy, which has turned black with time; this blackness and the smooth round volumes of faces, necks, and hands catch the light and give a richer appearance than the simple wood carvings of the earlier era.

A similar black bronze figure is housed near by in the three-storied pagoda (fig. 631), an outstanding archi-

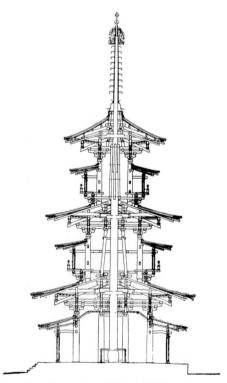

632. *Pagoda*, section. Yakushi-ji Temple, Nara Prefecture (8th cent.).

633. *The Priest Ganjin*, Kaizandō, Tōshōdai-ji Temple, Nara (8th cent.) Dry lacquer, 2'8" high.

prayers of the devout, gold was discovered miraculously in the north—just enough gold to cover the colossus. Amid great rejoicing, the Emperor called out his whole court to see him as he painted the pupil of the eye, which was the finishing touch. Like the big stone Buddha at Lung-mên (fig. 587), this was dedicated to Vairocana the Illuminator, the source of all wisdom and law.

The Tōdai-ji became a center of Buddhist learning, favored of the royal family. An illustrious Chinese monk was invited to establish a platform for ordination there, and did finally succeed, though he survived perils that would have stopped a less determined character. On his sixth attempt, in 754, he reached Nara, after having been delayed by pirates, storms, shipwreck, and the Chinese authorities. Blind and feeble, this Ganjin held his first triumphal ceremonies at the Tōdai-ji, in which he received more than four hundred persons into the church, including the Empress Dowager. A portrait of him (fig. 633) made after his death is one of the finest in Japanese sculpture.

One devout Buddhist of the royal family, the Emperor Shomu, abdicated in 746 to become a monk. His wife gave his art collection to the Tōdai-ji, where a special house, the Shōsōin, was built to receive it. He had collected things made in all parts of Asia, among them textiles, screens, lacquer, paintings (fig. 634)—a priceless treasure brought together before the mid-eighth century, which has not been augmented since,

activity. The capital was established in Nara, laid out on lines similar to Ch'ang-an. The court became entirely Buddhist, modeling itself on the Buddhist hierarchy; courtiers were referred to as Bodhisattva, and sūtras were read by every cultured person. Many new monasteries and temples were built, in which members of the royal family and nobility retired to a life of contemplation. As a climax, the dedication of the huge bronze Buddha of the Tōdai-ji in 752 was unequaled for pomp and ceremony. The building itself, later destroyed by fire, was the largest wooden building in the world, and the 53-foot-high Buddha had kept the bronze casters busy for months. In answer to many

634. *Bodhisattva*, Shōsōin, Nara (8th cent.) Painting on hemp, 5′ x 5′.

giving it unique value to the student of art and history.

In the Tōdai-ji, too, some of the outstanding contemporary sculpture is housed. Tempyō sculptors were modelers rather than carvers. Clay and lacquer were used, which allowed more variety of pose and greater freedom in surface modulation than was possible in carved wood. Building out from a wooden armature, the clay—or cloth dipped in lacquer juice—could be molded into folds of garments (fig. 635), or protruding muscles and veins, or even whirling draperies and scarves. Just as in China, where Indian ideas had come in a fresh wave in the T'ang period, Tantric formulas proved to be popular. Kwannons with eleven heads and many arms were made according to such directions, but the Tempyō sculptors failed to give them the inner fire

635. *Bonten*, Hokkedō, Tōdai-ji Temple, Nara (8th cent.) Clay, 6'7" high.

and energy notable in India; Japanese examples of thousand-armed Bodhisattva are overwhelming because of the sheer conglomeration of forms, not because of tension and power (fig. 636). The lacquer Aśura (fig. 637), enemy of the gods, looks bewildered and rather dismayed at having spidery projections coming out of his armholes, and shows no affinity to his fellow demons of Cambodia or Tibet. Like other contemporary religious images, he wears a carefully painted garment, for the Japanese love of textile patterns begins to enter all their art.

MEDIEVAL JAPANESE ART

Because members of the royal family retired to monasteries and continued to influence national policy from a distance, and much tax-exempt land had passed into the hands of religious foundations, an edict was issued removing the capital from Nara to Kyōto, 'capital of peace and tranquility,' where a new palace was made ready in 795. For the next ten years there was building on a grand scale. Kyōto, like Nara, was modeled on Ch'ang-an, symmetrically divided by broad roads into squares, and subdivided by narrow roads. By each was a moat; in fact, water from nearby Lake Biwa flowed into the gardens of all fine houses. Since there were many shrines already in Kyōto before it became capital, the Emperor Kwammu issued an edict soon after his accession (782) limiting the number of temples and restricting the admission of priests to holy orders; but soon the hillsides

636. *Thousand-Armed Kwannon*, Tōshōdai-ji Temple, Nara (8th cent.) Dry lacquer, 17′6″ high.

the art of the Jōgan period (A.D. 794–897). A more mystical Buddhism, touched by Hinduism, replaced the tender and protective teaching of the Suiko days. Instead of Yakushi the healer, Kwannon the merciful one, and Amida the saviour, there were Fudō the chastiser, and Dainichi, the remote source of unearthly power. The Red Fudō from Mt. Kōya (fig. 638) was considered too terrible a painting for average mortals to look upon; he sits in his fiery cavern, holding a thunderbolt and

637. *Aśura*, Kōfuku-ji Temple, Nara (8th cent.) Dry lacquer, 5′ high.

were covered with monasteries, and hot rivalry sprang up between the various sects. War-like monks proved to be a greater menace than anything dreamed of in Nara. Intrigue among the high-ranking clansmen in the palace kept the people in a turmoil; there were fires and ambushes, plots and counterplots that made ironic mockery of the name of the city.

This change of mood is reflected in

638. *Red Fudō*, Myōōin Temple, Mt. Kōya (9th cent.) Painting on silk, 5′1″ x 3′2″.

sword entwined in serpents, and a lasso to catch the wicked, attended by two youths who look more frightened than vengeful and have a cast of face that is decidedly Japanese, even to the prominent teeth. It belongs to one of the big monasteries founded in the ninth century by Kōbō Daishi. He had gone to China to study, and returned in 807, imbued with the doctrine of Dainichi Nyorai, the eternal Buddha from whom emanate all other Buddhas, who is to be approached by incantations, magic formulas, and ritual gestures. In sculpture (fig. 639) and painting, he is depicted as holding the forefinger of one hand in the five fingers of the other, each finger standing for an element—earth, water, fire, air, ether, and wisdom. He was the Great Sun surrounded by flames, the highest vehicle of mystic union.

A rival institution, the Enryaku-ji monastery on Mt. Hiyei near Lake Biwa, had been founded in 805 by Dengyō Daishi. He, also, had gone to China to study, and adhered to the Lotus Sūtra, which stressed meditation, self-discipline, and esoteric projections.

One of his monks, Genshin, defected and started a popular sect based on worship of Amida. He reassured his followers by emphasizing faith, not deeds, and a reliance on the Buddha of Boundless Light. If they said 'Namu Amida Butsu' often enough to reach his ear, he would assure their rebirth in his Western Paradise. This comforting philosophy appealed to laymen.

Not far from Kyōto, at Uji, a noble-

639. Unkei, *Dainichi*, Enjō-ji Temple, Nara Prefecture (*c.* 1176) Wood, 3'3" high.

man built a country house, which was later given to the church and dedicated to Amida. The courtiers of the Fujiwara period (897–1185) were very cultivated, given to a study of literature and the arts, and dedicating their lives to proper etiquette and ceremony—all in the midst of constant strife among the clans. This country house (fig. 640), true to the taste for fantasy, was designed in the shape of a phoenix (pheasant), the body and tail a corridor stretching out behind it, and the wings spread on either side. It is in the tradition of post and lintel construction, using the simple bracket inherited from the Chinese. The proportions are exquisite, and the sloping tile roofs delight the eye, twice lovely because they are reflected in the lotus pool. Affixed to the roof of the central

640. *Phoenix Hall, Hōōdō, Byōdōin Temple, Uji, Kyōto Prefecture* (1053) Wood, plaster, tile.

pavilion, the graceful bronze male and female phoenix face each other. Within the hall, now a sanctuary, the Amida Buddha presides (fig. 641), calm and majestic, a gilded wooden figure attributed to Jōchō, done in 1054. The high lotus pedestal, the stiff spareness of the Buddha, and the elaborate halo, canopy, and wall decoration are characteristic. The ceiling is inlaid with mother-of-pearl and painted in flower medallions of rose, green, and blue. On the side walls a joyous throng of Bosatsu carved in wood seem to sweep down, playing on musical instruments and sporting on clouds. The sweetness, tenderness, and elegance of this are in perfect contrast to the brooding and terrible figures of Kōyasan. The inner facing of the wooden doors was painted

with more Bosatsu and with a few bits of landscape, which begin a style uniquely Japanese, decorative, resplendent, like a textile pattern.

This Tosa style of painting was started by a Fujiwara nobleman, and it reflects the ideals of Japan so perfectly that it has been labeled Yamato-e (Yamato being the homeland of Japanese culture). It is used to illustrate the Tales of Genji, the *Genji Monogatari* (fig. 642), written by a lady-in-waiting, Murasaki Shikibu, in the early eleventh century. It is a remarkable romance, one of the world's great books, which we may read in the English translation by Arthur Waley. Genji was a courtier, a man of tender sentiment who left a trail of broken hearts behind him. Lady Murasaki was one he loved and left, but

641. Jōchō (d. 1057) *Amida of Hōōdō*, Byōdōin Temple, Uji, Kyōto Prefecture. Gilded wood, 9'8" high.

642. Takayoshi? (12th cent.) *Illustration of Genji Monogatari*, Tokugawa Collection, Tōkyō. Painting on paper, 8½″ high.

643. Toba Sōjō (12th cent.) *Hare Chasing a Monkey*, Kōzan-ji Temple, Kyōto. Ink on paper, 1′ high.

she manages to remain detached enough
to tell her tale with charm. Written on
tinted paper flecked with gold, in a
delicate, flowing script, it is a perfect
reflection of courtly refinement. The
scenes that illustrate the narrative are
painted in tones of violet, green, rose,
gold, and beige, set off by clear black
lines. The perspective angle is from
above and to one side, so that we seem
to look into palace rooms made roofless
for our inspection. As in other Asiatic
painting, the lines come toward us instead of vanishing to some point within
the picture plane. The background is
established by the use of sliding panels
and screens, and by emphasizing the
diagonal lines of the floor matting.
There are no cast shadows, the whole
things is done in clear light, space being
linear not atmospheric. Figures are cut
into segments and patterns by the
screens; it makes little difference whether
one looks at the scroll right side up or
upside down—the pattern is always
striking. The ladies sit on the floor
dressed in their court robes, with sleeves
so wide that they look like butterfly
wings, and their straight black hair is
brushed to the hem of the garment, a
mark of especial beauty. Their oval
faces are all of a type, there is no individuality. All have rosebud mouths, in-
finitesimal noses, slanting eyes, and
heavy eyebrows. They are well named—
Wisteria Blossom, Cherry, Chrysanthe-
mum—sentimental participants in poetry contests, as adapt at intrique as are
palace beauties all over the world. The
men, too, wear brocaded robes and a

characteristic tall black hat; they seem
to be accomplished eavesdroppers and
sportsmen, engaging in sallies of wit or
arms with equal aplomb. In design the
scroll reaches a high mark in Japanese
art. The intricate spatial relations and
color areas are the work of a master who
would feel perfectly at home in twentieth-century painting.

The pomp of court and religious ceremony proved too tempting to the abbot

644. *Kichijōten*, Jōruri-ji Temple, Kyōto Prefecture (12th cent.) Wood, 2'11" high.

of a monastery for him to resist mocking them. Maybe Toba Sōjō painted four scrolls caricaturing the occupations and games of his contemporaries. As we unroll these Kōzan-ji makemono and chuckle over the incidents—monkeys, frogs, and hares (fig. 643), acting like courtiers and priests, ragamuffins and bums—we can enjoy a different side of Japanese personality expressed superbly in line and satire. The whole of each scroll in the set should be seen to get full enjoyment of them, for the time element in the unrolling is important, but even a fragment is delightful. In one part, beneath a tree worthy of a Sung master, we see a monkey garbed as an officiating priest making an offering to the Buddha—and Buddha is a frog. His legs are folded in yoga fashion, his hands raised in the right mudrās, his smile benign and blank, his halo of leaves and his cushion of a lotus are as correct as a courtier's hat. In the next scene another priest-monkey is receiving gifts of tiger skins, fruits, and scrolls,

checking them in with a pious smugness all too familiar to the painter. Long before Walt Disney, a Japanese discovered the joys of poking fun at man and his foibles in the guise of animals. There is no text nor is there need—the pictures speak for themselves.

These, and the three scrolls of the Shigisan Engi, which are done in light color and with a brush as remarkable as the Kōzan-ji set, begin a secular art that developed into the wood-block prints of the eighteenth and nineteenth centuries. The Tosa courtly style became so popular that it even intruded into the religious fields; the sūtras dedicated to the Taira family are as gay as fans and as delicate as dew on a cobweb. Kichijoten, goddess of beauty and fortune, is no longer an Indian goddess but a noble lady (fig. 644) and a colorful Japanese one.

This frivolous world was shaken from its dreams when Yoritomo established himself as Shōgun in 1192 in Kamakura, the ancient seat of his clan. The real

645. *Detail of the Burning of the Sanjō Palace* (13th cent.) Museum of Fine Arts, Boston. Painting on paper, scroll 1'4" high x 22'11" wide.

government then moved north, though
the emperor was allowed to keep his
nominal power in Kyōto. Military men
took over the running of the country,
which left the court nobles with a beautiful, empty etiquette to maintain. The
glorification of war and its terror were
depicted in scrolls dealing with the
Heiji wars; one, the Burning of the Sanjō
Palace, is in the Museum of Fine Arts in
Boston (fig. 645). This last detail, which
follows a vivid continuous picture of
hurrying crowds, and smoke billowing
from the palace, as courtiers, nuns, and
attendants were trampled underfoot
and horsemen rushed through the palace, comes as a quieter moment in all
the excitement. The emperor is protected by his guard, who go forward
gingerly, expecting an ambush. After
the crowded ovals of frantic people, this
makes a final wedge-shaped pattern
pointing toward the equestrian on the
black horse and the archer who tiptoes
toward the unknown. It is one of many
splendid narrative scrolls based on the
lives of national heroes, churchmen,
and men of letters.

Religious painters were as active as
secular artists, still doing the large, magnificent vertical scrolls that were hung
in the temples or carried to the bedside
of those about to die; such paintings of
Amida, resplendent in gold, were thus
taken as a kind of extreme unction to
the faithful, a reassuring vision of the
Western Paradise where they would be
reborn. Jizō, special protector of little
children (fig. 646), was a popular figure,
portrayed as a young monk in a rich

646. *Jizō* (12th–14th cent.) Metropolitan Museum, New York. Painting on silk.

robe, carrying a staff. He was a boyish
and pleasant youth especially dear to
the Japanese. Even a Shintō god of war
is shown as a mild monk (fig. 647).

One of Japan's greatest sculptors was
active in the Kamakura period—Unkei,
son of Kōkei. He and his relatives went
to Nara to restore some of the Suiko
period figures. They, too, worked in
wood, but they preferred joining pieces
together rather than carving from a
solid trunk, a method that allowed more

647. Kōshun, *Hachiman as a Priest* (1328) Museum of Fine Arts, Boston. Wood.

freedom of action and pose than the Suiko sculptors had achieved. It is a period of realism and dynamic power. They made the two guardians that are placed inside the great gate at the entrance of the Tōdai-ji monastery in Nara, muscular, fierce, with exaggerated veins and tendons, bulging eyes, and wide-spread fingers. In a quieter vein there is the portrait of Muchaku, an interesting character study of the traveling Chinese monk, Hsüan-tsang (fig. 648). One of Unkei's followers carved a full-length figure of the Indian teacher Basu-sennin who looks as lean as a Donatello St. John the Baptist, the miserable flesh hanging on his bones, eyes sunk in their sockets, and his rags flapping on his bent body (fig. 649). Another, Jokei, did a muscular guardian with swirling drapery (fig. 650), which must have pleased the military leaders. Most of the wooden sculpture had crystal eyes (fig. 651) set in to make the faces more natural, and one figure was left nude so that it could be clothed in brocaded garments. The Japanese feeling for pattern and simplicity of form

648. Unkei, *Hossō Patriarch Muchaku*, Hoku-
endo, Kofuku-ji Temple, Nara (1208) Wood,
6'2" high.

is demonstrated in the carving of a
courtier, Uesugi Shigefusa (fig. 652),
which looks to us more like a twentieth-
century piece than one of the thirteenth
century. It is a pity that one of the inferior works of this magnificent period
is the best known, the Great Amida in

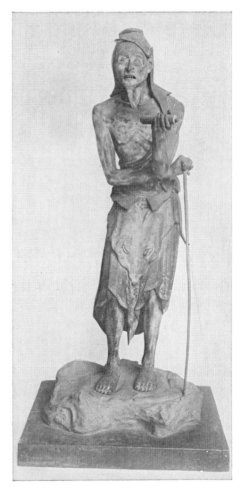

649. School of Unkei (13th cent.) *Basu-
sennin*, Sanjūsangendō Temple, Kyōto. Wood,
5'3" high.

650. Jōkei (13th cent.) *Kongōrikishi*, Kōfuku-ji Temple, Nara. Wood.

Thus the Japanese, like the Indians, escaped Mongol domination. But Kamakura power was waning, and there was a restlessness in Kyōto where intrigue reached its height when five ex-emperors, all of whom had abdicated, tried to exercise the authority belonging to a ruler. By 1330 two lines were in conflict, and Daigo II was victor; Kamakura was captured in 1333 and destroyed by fire. Kyōto again became the seat of government, though the Emperor entrusted the administration to the Ashikaga family, who were appointed Shōguns, and they were the actual rulers from 1392 to 1568.

Numbers of Chinese moved to Japan when the Mongols destroyed the Sung Dynasty, and they continued to follow

Kamakura (fig. 653). The temple housing it has been destroyed so often that there have been no more attempts to rebuild it, and Amida now sits in the midst of beautiful trees, a sanctuary in itself.

Kubilai Khan twice attempted to invade Japan, in 1274 and 1281, but each time his fleet was destroyed by storms.

651. *Red Fudō*, Hokkēdō (13th cent.) Wood.

652. *Uesugi Shigefusa*, Meigetsuin Temple, Kamakura (13th cent.) Wood, 2′3″ high.

the philosophy that emphasized meditation, the Ch'an form of Buddhism, called Zen in Japan. The simplicity, rugged individualism, and disregard for metaphysics appealed to the military minds of the Ashikago period. Zen priests were placed in key positions; they were important politically, and their teaching influenced all of the art and life of that time. They controlled trade, and they brought 'modern' spoken Chinese to Japan, where the language of China of four centuries before was still used.

Following the inspiration of the Sung Dynasty artists, many of whose masterpieces had been taken to Japan, there was an upsurge of creative activity as soon as peace and order were restored. Turning their backs on their own rapidly developing styles, Japanese painters and other artists received this Chinese influence with enthusiasm. New temples were built, gardens were constructed to look like Chinese scenery, flower arrangement became· a pastime of monks and military men alike, the tea ceremony offered a change from the battlefield or affairs at court; priests and courtiers tried brush painting with such good results that it is hard to tell some of the Japanese painting from the Chinese.

653. *The Great Buddha*, Kamakura (1252) Bronze, 33' high.

The third Shōgun, Yoshimitsu, built the Golden Pavilion in 1397, and ruled from there like a retired emperor. The Pavilion (fig. 654) is a three-story house made of fine woods in the simple manner dictated by Zen. The balustrades, supports, and walls are unadorned, and the only curving lines are to be found in the roofs and the windows on the third floor. Burned recently, it has been restored; a gilded replica and memory of it remain. It was reflected in a pool, and surrounded by austere gardens consisting largely of pines, rocks, and sand, until recently destroyed by fire.

The eighth Shōgun, Yoshimasa, was a noted patron of all of the arts during his rule from 1449 to 1474. He built the Silver Pavilion, and had its gardens laid

654. *The Golden Pavilion*, Rokuon-ji Temple, Kyōto (1397) Wood.

655. Sō-ami, *Chinese Landscape Screen* (late 15th cent.) Rockefeller Coll., New York. Ink on paper.

656. Jōsetsu (act. 1394–1408) *Catfish and Gourd*, Taizōin Temple, Kyōto. Painting on paper, 2'6" x 3'11".

out by the painter Sō-ami, who imitated Chinese waterfalls, rocks, mountains, and trees. His family, called the Šan Amī, were prominent exponents of Chinese brush techniques and connoisseurship (fig. 655).

Japanese painters, in true Zen fashion, learned to suggest more in the black and white paintings than was actually described. Jōsetsu, at the end of the fourteenth century, did the Catfish and Gourd (fig. 656), which is composed of bamboo, river grasses, misty mountains, and a ragged fisherman, who looks, in the Chinese manner, like a child of nature trying to catch his lunch; but it is actually a symbol of man's endeavors in which he reaches beyond himself. It is as hard to catch a slippery catfish in a small gourd as to be a true follower of the Tao.

Since it was a period of great artistic activity, there are many names that should be included; but one outshines all the others—that of Sesshū. Oda Tōyō, for that was his real name, lived from 1420 to 1506, most of his life a Zen priest. In training for the priesthood he had the opportunity to learn to paint, and became a pupil of the distinguished priest-painter Shūbun. As he studied the Chinese masters whose works had been taken to Japan in considerable numbers, he was fired with the ambition to go to China, a journey he made from 1467 to 1469. He traveled extensively, steeping himself in the landscapes that had had such a profound influence on the painters of the

657. Sesshū (1420–1506) *Winter Landscape*, Manjuin Temple, Kyōto. Ink on paper, 1'6" x 1'.

Sung period, especially the rugged, dramatic places that might have served as models for Hsia Kuei, whose work he particularly admired. On his return to Japan he devoted himself to perfecting a similar style (fig. 657) by which he could portray the crystalline hardness of rocks, the tortuous twisting of tree branches and roots, the rough thatch of a cottage roof, with a few vigorous brush strokes. A human being could be done in ten strokes. Among his more ambitious works is the horizontal scroll, 51 feet long, now in the possession of Count Mori. This he did in his sixty-seventh year, a masterpiece of sustained effort. If we compare it with the Chi-

658. Sesson (16th cent.) *Boat Returning in a Storm*, Nomura Tokushichi Coll., Ōsaka. Ink on paper, 9″ x 12″.

nese scrolls, we find that there is less grading of tones, less poetry, less interest in actual space, but more in the relationship of forms, which he handles in a personal and exciting way; portions of it would seem to anticipate some paintings of Van Gogh. Like other Japanese, the decorative qualities interest him. He worked in three styles, and toward the end of his life seemed to prefer a free and powerful tonal painting, done with unbelievable speed and sureness, leaving so much unsaid that the imagination is called into full play. Of his many followers, one, Sesson, learned to use his ink with freedom and power, and with a marked feeling for decorative design (fig. 658).

LATER JAPANESE ART

While priests and scholars were trying to paint in the Chinese way, courtiers continued to love the Tosa style. Thinking to combine the good qualities of both, a group of professional painters formed a school called Kāno, led by Masanobu and his son Motonobu. They were in demand as painters of screens, especially for the Kyōto monasteries. They decorated the sliding panels that separated one room from another, and large six-fold or eight-fold screens which could be placed against the wall; appropriate subjects were the changing seasons, sages and leaders of the past, and the birds and flowers. Since they

659. Kanō Sanraku (1559–1635) *Peonies, on Sliding Screen Panels*, Daikaku-ji Temple, Kyōto. Painting on paper, 3'3" x 6'1".

were to be seen from a distance, they had to be boldly designed and executed, using definite lines, brilliant colors, and gold leaf laid on in squares (fig. 659).

In the following period, the Momo-yama (1568–1615), civil wars again

660. *Castle*, Nagoya (1611).

661. Sanraku (1559–1635) *Uji Bridge,* Mizoguchi Munehiko Collection, Tōkyō. Painting on paper, 5′6″ x 11′2″.

troubled Japan. Military men had influence even in the world of art. They erected big castles in the European fashion, built of stone with strong foundations (fig. 660). To bring color to the severe walls they used magnificent screens, much as Europeans of the Middle Ages had used tapestries. The taste of the military did not run to the delicate, so the Kanō makers had a splendid opportunity to give rein to the Japanese genius for striking design. A six-fold screen attributed to Sanraku (fig. 661) of the Bridge at Uji has been much admired. The background is covered with gold leaf, willow trees with reddish brown trunks and branches droop over the bridge which sweeps across the panels in a bold and distorted pattern, dominating the whole design. The water under the bridge flows in patterned waves, bronze-colored, and seems to mingle with clouds on the right, which are equally patterned.

By this time Buddhist art was on the decline, and Tosa was almost dead; it was the great moment for the decorators and the few who still worked in the Chinese manner. Of the latter, the most interesting is Tohaku. He is renowned for his screens (fig. 662), which differ from the brilliant Kanō products, being usually black and white, or in light colors, relying on soft tone and brushwork rather than striking pattern. Sotatsu and Koetsu were as versatile and gifted as Renaissance Italians; they were the leaders of the gentleman-painters.

As the church and nobility ceased to be patrons, the way was paved for a popular, plebeian art, something gay, rich in color, and not too profound. In the next period, the Tokugawa (1615–1867), just such an art developed. Painters made designs for pottery, screens, and panels, men like the Ogata brothers Korin (fig. 663) and Kenzan.

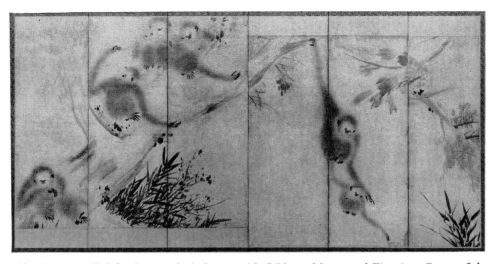

662. Hasegawa Tōhaku (1539–1610) *Screen with Gibbons*, Museum of Fine Arts, Boston. Ink on paper, 1'11" x 5'.

They and the lacquer makers, porcelain manufacturers, and wood-block print makers had an opportunity at last to make their wares completely Japanese in style. Some of them co-operated with architects to make the sumptuous buildings of the seventeenth and eighteenth centuries.

The famous shrines at Nikko (fig. 664) reflect the change from the simplicity of the past to the richness of the Japanese Baroque. In a setting of trees and streams, which would have been shrine enough for worshipers in earlier times, they erected gates, pagodas, and halls of prayer so elaborately carved and gilded that it would take days to study all the panels. A brilliant red lacquered bridge was reserved for the use of the royal family, but all pilgrims could enter the gate, with its curved roofs and its many corbels, flanked by corridors adorned with carved, painted panels of birds and fish. Among the temple buildings was the sacred stable, and there the famous monkeys of 'Hear no evil, see no evil, say no evil' were carved and colored, green, brown, white, and gold. Moving away from the dazzling colors of the temple, the patriot could go up a long flight of steps to the mausoleum of the Shōgun Ieyasu, a peaceful place guarded by giant cryptomeria trees, more like the original Shinto shrine at Ise.

One of the eras, the Genroku (1688–1704), was a time of great luxury, famous for lacquer, porcelain, and other decorative arts. The nobility became alarmed at the prosperity of plebeians, and had laws that forbade them to own things as elaborate as those of the hereditary families, but these laws were circumvented by the people who were taking the fortunes from the nobility, and wanted some of the tempting things

663. Kōrin Ogata (1658–1716) designer, and Kenzan Ogata (1663–1743) *Plate*, Museum of Fine Arts, Boston.

seen in the shops of Tōkyō, the new capital.

Travelers came to the city from other parts of Japan to see the sights, especially of the theater and the Yoshiwara district, where the ladies of the Green Houses lived in a world of their own; and they wanted souvenirs to take home. The inexpensive wood-block print proved to be the means of satis-fying the demand. The process had been perfected in China, where it was being used extensively at this same time, but the Japanese made of it an art that has not been rivaled by any other coun-try.

In the late seventeenth century, Moronobu made a series of prints of occupations in Tokyo, as well as single sheet souvenirs for visitors, pictures of

664. *Yōmeimon Gate*, Tōshōgu Shrine, Nikkō, Tochigi Prefecture (17th cent.) Wood.

a Floating World (Ukiyo-e). Usually small in scale, they resemble book illustrations that had been made for centuries, except that he recognized more than anyone else the possibilities of the woodcut. Some were colored by hand, but most of them were patterns in black and white in which there were no cast shadows, no grading of tone; space was established by diagonals set against curves, and by the placement of figures. They are animated, gay, sometimes satirical. Though we think of the Ukiyo-e masters as being primarily interested in prints, which are better known to Westerners, they did paintings as well.

Moronobu's pupil Kiyonobu was a sign painter for the theater, accustomed to bold compositions and swirling patterns, ample curves and splendid textile design in the garments of the actors. He began to do these in the wood-block technique, and became the founder of the Torii school specializing in theater work. His eldest son, Torii Kiyomasu, worked in a style so similar that it is not easy to tell their prints apart (fig. 665).

As the trade became more profitable and interesting, all kinds of refinements were thought of; the simple prints were enriched with gleaming black lacquer, water colors, and gold, and gauffrage began to be used—a kind of relief, made by raising the surface of some areas. The next step was the use of separate

665. Torii Kiyomasu (1679–1763) *Actor Mat-sumoto Shigemaki as a Woman,* Museum of Fine Arts, Boston. Wood-block print.

blocks for printing each color; at first, pink and green, or other simple two- and three-color prints were made, and finally, under Harunobu (1725–70), the art of printing many colors was brought to its highest point, using as many as eleven separate blocks to print the 'bro-cade' colors, which he started in 1764.

From that time on, he experimented, producing delicate and subtle prints. In-stead of drawing inspiration from the city streets or the theater, he concen-trated on young girlhood with all its moods and fancies, the refined daughters of the well-to-do, graceful and appealing. In their most casual occupations, ad-miring cherry blossoms, doing their hair, he found subjects worthy of his most painstaking care. He liked to emphasize their frailty by showing them buffeted by wind or rain, or standing beside a building much larger than they. One, called the Crow and the Heron (fig. 666), is of a white-robed girl and her escort, who is swathed in black, as they walk through the snow, stepping softly on their high wooden shoes and holding an umbrella on which the snow has drifted. The feeling of a chilly day is brought out by his restraint in handling this little genre scene. He purposely dis-torts his figures for effective design, and uses the traditional contrast of diagonals and curves, as well as color, to indicate space.

His success was so great that the other print makers almost stopped work in dis-couragement. Two of his pupils, how-ever, Koryusai and Shunsho, strove to develop the color print into a great art, and succeeded nearly as well. Shunsho specialized in doing actors of the popu-lar theater in their favorite roles. As in the time of Shakespeare, men were the only actors on the stage. They took women's parts, spending their lives act-ing and speaking like women, even off the stage, practicing a mincing walk that made the flowing kimono move in graceful lines, and speaking in a fal-setto. They were so proud of their art that they handed the tradition from father to son, or to an adopted child

666. Suzuki Harunobu (1725–70) *The Crow and the Heron*, Louis V. Ledoux Coll., New York. Wood-block print, 11″ x 8″.

667. Torii Kiyonaga (1742–1815) *The Debarkation*, Art Institute, Chicago. Wood-block print.

who was brought up to be a specialist in these parts.

Toward the latter part of the eighteenth century another master of the Torii line, Kiyonaga, brought out prints in still a different style (fig. 667). He liked mature women, tall, classic, and poised. Flowing kimono and the obi tied around the waist are of varied patterns and colors, which are shown to advantage on their ample figures; stylized coiffures are a special study in themselves. He preferred spacious backgrounds, with a grand sweep of riverside or garden. Sometimes he found one piece of paper too small, and made a design that was printed in three parts, a triptych of eighteenth-century Japanese life. He was inspired by breadth and grandeur rather than by the delicacy and frailty Harunobu loved.

At about the same time two other artists of unusual talent came to the public eye—Utamaro and Sharaku. Utamaro considered himself the high priest of the ladies of the Green Houses (fig. 668); he gloried in showing every pose and mood of the famous beauties, who were often cultivated women. The half-length figure appealed to him particularly, for it allowed him to concentrate on the face, throat, and shoulders, the delicate hairline or tiny ear. His outline is so tenuous that it is hard to see; at times he dispensed with the black line entirely, and had colors printed side by side. He and some of his contemporaries enriched the whole print by using powdered mica on the background, giving it a sparkling quality. This seemed to make it too precious in the opinion of the nobles, so sumptuary laws forbidding it were passed. By some he is considered one of the greatest of the Ukiyo-e masters; by others, a decadent practitioner of an art that lacks dynamic quality or nobility of theme.

Sharaku, the mystery man of the whole group, appeared like a comet and disappeared as quickly. In the year

668. Kitagawa Utamaro (1754–1806) *Three Geisha*, Art Institute, Chicago. Woodblock print.

669. Tōshūsai Sharaku (18th cent.) *Ichikawa Ebizō IV as Washizuka Kwandayū* (1794) Metropolitan Museum, New York. Wood-block print.

1794, in a few months, he designed one hundred thirty prints caricaturing actors of the popular drama (fig. 669), caricatures of such power and venom that it is hard to believe that they were done by an amateur. We know only that he was an actor in the classical Nō drama, attached to a nobleman's household, and forbidden to mingle with actors in the plebeian theater. So far, no early works have been discovered that could account for these accomplished satires; we are reminded of Toba Sōjō and his rebellion against the pompousness of the Fujiwara court and church (fig. 643), and of dramatic masks worn by Nō actors, and even of old religious sculpture—of guardians particularly (fig. 624) that might have inspired the

painter by their energy and fury. He is the master of the expressive eyebrow, the pig-like eye, the hooked nose, and the vicious mouth; and the master, too, of interesting hands and of elegant, simple robes, in which he used the actor's crest very effectively. He stopped as suddenly as he had started, and retired, perhaps to the sheltered world of an aristocratic household. Whether it was done by choice, or by order of his lord, or through pressure on him by the popular actors he lampooned, we do not know.

In the late eighteenth and early nineteenth centuries the color print was used by two outstanding landscape artists, Hokusai and Hiroshigé, to picture the whole of Japanese life and most of the beauty spots of their country. Ho-

670. Katsushika Hokusai (1760–1849) *Thirty-six Views of Fuji: The Wave,* Museum of Fine Arts, Boston. Wood-block print, 10″ x 15″.

671. Andō Hiroshigé (1797–1858) *Fifty-three Stages of the Tōkaidō: Shōno*, Museum of Fine Arts, Boston. Wood-block print.

kusai, the 'old man mad with painting,' lived to be eighty-nine years old, and at his death his only regret was that he had neglected to make more pictures of his homeland. During his long life he illustrated books, made single prints of birds and flowers, and did series of views, the best known being the Views of Fuji. He included everything he could in his landscapes—peasants working in the rice fields, going to festivals, or fishing. In his famous print, The Wave (fig. 670), he gives a vivid impression of the life of those who go out on the sea in frail boats. In a composition of sweeping curves, he shows the boatmen almost swamped by the ocean, their heads hardly larger than the fingers of foam that reach toward them. There are the surge of the sea, the mist rising from it,

and Fuji in the distance, all done in tones of blue with a suggestion of yellow in the sky. The energy with which he did this is characteristic of him and his unfailing zest for life.

Hiroshigé, too, did series of landscapes (fig. 671), and bird and flower prints. Like Hokusai he succeeded in recording the most beautiful aspects of his country—the postroad from Kyōto to Tōkyō, mountains, and rivers. Even today, wherever the traveler may look he is sure to see a bit of land that reminds him of a Hiroshigé print. Unlike Hokusai, whose prints are crowded with details, the younger man learned to leave out some of the non-essential elements, and thus gave to his work a breadth and subtlety that are a constant delight. He relied more on color and tone, less on line, for his interesting effects; the Japanese had become acquainted with European perspective techniques, and his work shows that he had studied them, though the total impression is entirely Oriental. He not only pictured specific places, he caught as well the changes of season, the insignificance of man, and the majesty of mountains; his was a poetic expression. Rain pouring down, making of bamboo and hillside a study in tones of gray, geese flying across the moon, a bridge at sunset—all are done with singular beauty.

He and the others mark the final development of a unique art, which struck nineteenth-century Europe as a fresh, lovely, and admirable thing. These prints served as ambassadors of good will to a world waiting for something new and they changed the course of Western art in a trend that has become reciprocal as the people of the world are drawn closer together. The tradition on which Ukiyo-e was based is as old as civilization itself, growing out of the infinite riches of the Orient. The poetry of Persia in all its brilliant color, the intellect and emotion of India made visible in stone and bronze, the secret harmonies of nature echoed in the rhythms of Chinese art, the youthfulness and boldness of Japan—all are ours now to enjoy and study. We can take pleasure in them without knowing more than that the design and color are appealing, but that pleasure can be increased immeasurably by learning something of the peoples and places that produced them, for there is no art for art's sake in the Orient. The disciplines of the various crafts were perfected to serve the glory of man or god; therefore we must look beyond technical facility to the inner vision that inspired it.

Glossary

Abacus   The uppermost member of a classic capital; a simple plinth in the Doric, the abacus becomes a thin slab, sometimes decorated in the Ionic, and in the Corinthian order a molded block with concave sides.

Acanthus   A Greek plant that served as the inspiration for the foliage of the Corinthian capital and other architectural motives.

Acroteria   Figures or decorations placed above the angles of a pediment.

Adobe   A method of construction using dried clay, especially associated with southwestern United States.

Aisle   A longitudinal division of a plan separated from other parts of the building by colonnades or arcades; especially the narrower lateral divisions of church plans.

Ambulatory   The semicircular or semipolygonal aisle encircling an apse.

Anta   A thickening of a wall provided with a plain capital and base, to receive the end of a beam. Somewhat similar to but not to be confused with a pilaster, the anta is simpler and its capital and base plainer than that of the order with which it is to be used.

Apanada   An audience hall.

Apsaras   Angel.

Apse   A semicircular or polygonal part of a plan, particularly one terminating the main axis of a church.

Arabesque   Originally signifying the rich surface patterns of Mohammedan art, the word has come to mean any elaborate scroll pattern in paint or low relief.

Arcade   A row of arches supported by piers or columns.

Arch   A device for spanning an opening, consisting of wedge-shaped blocks called voussoirs.

Arch Order   An arch, enframed by engaged columns or pilasters and entablature, developed in Rome, but also used in the Renaissance and in the derivatives of either style.

Architrave   A beam, particularly the lower of the three principal divisions of a classic entablature.

Archivolt   An architrave turned into an arch; a group of moldings adorning and emphasizing the curve of an arch.

Arhat or Lohan   A disciple of Buddha.

Armature   A frame of wood or metal serving as the support for the clay of a statue while the sculptor models it.

Arris   A ridge formed by the intersection of two planes; particularly the ridge that separates flutes in a Doric column.

831

Ashlar Cut stone masonry; in regular ashlar, the blocks are rectangular and uniform in size; in random ashlar the blocks vary in size.

Atrium An enclosed but unroofed forecourt such as those found in Roman houses and in Early Christian and later churches.

Attic (1) A low story placed above a cornice. (2) The uppermost story of a house, curtailed in volume by the slope of the roof. (3) Pertaining to the land of Attica; i.e. Athens.

Axis An imaginary central line around which a design or any of the parts thereof is balanced.

Baldacchino The word comes from the canopies carried in religious processions; hence, a free-standing architectural canopy over an altar.

Barrel Vault A semicylindrical vault.

Bas Relief Low reliefs; sculpture in which the roundness of the forms is expressed by planes projecting slightly from a flat background.

Basilica A hall-like structure flanked by aisles; Roman basilicas served as business buildings; the Early Christian basilicas were churches.

Batter An inward slope of the surface of a masonry wall, used to add strength.

Bay The space between the centers of adjacent supports, and thus a unit of design.

Beam A horizontal member to support a weight over an opening.

Bodhisattva Saintly Buddhist beings who deny themselves eternal blessedness to save others from misery.

Bond The interlocking of stones or bricks in a wall by laying one unit over parts of two or more other units. The commonest bonds in brickwork are (1) American Bond, one course of headers (the short ends of brick exposed) out of every six or seven courses of stretchers (the long side of the brick exposed); (2) English Bond, alternate courses of headers and stretchers; and (3) Flemish Bond, alternate headers and stretchers within each course.

Cartoon The final full-size preliminary drawing for a painting.

Cartouche An ornament in paint or low relief carving, composed of scrolls, heraldry, or foliate designs.

Caryatid A sculptured female figure used in place of a column.

Casement See *Sash*.

Cella The sanctuary of a classic temple.

Cement A material that when mixed with water will dry into a stonelike mass. Cement should be carefully distinguished from concrete, of which it is one of the ingredients; cement is also used in some mortars.

Centering The temporary mold of wood or metal used to support an arch or vault until construction is completed; the centering is then removed.

Chaitya Hall for worship, India.

Chamfer A diagonal plane cut from the corner of a rectangular member, such as a square pier, or a window or door opening.

Chancel The area of a Christian church around the high altar, reserved for the clergy; the sanctuary.

Chapel A small church; also a part of a larger church housing one of the secondary altars.

Chevet The complex of apse, ambuatory, and radiating chapels in medieval churches.

Chiaroscuro Light and shade in painting.

Choir That portion of a church between the altar and the nave or crossing reserved for the lower clergy, especially the singers. Occasionally the liturgical choir may extend down into the architectural nave.

Chryselephantine Of gold and ivory, as was the Zeus of Phidias.

Cire Perdue Lost wax; a method of bronze-casting wherein the shell of the statue is duplicated in wax which is then replaced by molten bronze.

Clapboard A thin board nailed horizontally to the frame of a house; clapboards overlap one another like shingles.

Clearstory Part of a building raised above the roof of a neighboring part to admit light.

Cloister A rectangular courtyard beside a medieval church to provide a sheltered walk for the clergy.

Coffer A decorative panel sunk in the under surface of a vault or ceiling; most coffers are rectangular or octagonal but they may be of any shape.

Collage Compositions created by glueing bits of paper, cloth, cigarettes, and other scraps on a flat surface; parts of the design may be painted.

Colonnade A row of columns supporting beams or lintels.

Colonnette A small column.

Column An architectural support, round in plan or nearly so, and composed of a base, shaft, and capital.

Compound Pier An architectural support composed of colonnettes, and rectangular members around a masonry core.

Concrete A building material similar to stone when dry but semifluid while being mixed. The ingredients are cement, sand, crushed stone or gravel, and water.

Contrapposto A torsion of the axis of the body to produce a sense of balancing movements within the figure, as when the shoulders face in a different direction from the hips.

Corbel A stone or brick whose face projects beyond that of its support to serve as a bracket. A Corbel Table consists of a series of small arches resting on corbels. A Corbel Arch is composed of stones laid in horizontal courses, each corbelled out in turn until the opening is covered.

Cornice The uppermost division of a classic entablature, projecting sharply to support the edge of the roof; any similar molded projection.

Course A horizontal layer of stone or brick in a wall.

Court An area open to the sky but enclosed on three or four sides by walls or blocks of building.

Crocket A projecting stone, usually carved with foliage, on the edge of a gable or the angles of a spire.

Crossing The space in churches occupied by the intersection of the nave and transepts.

Crown of an Arch The apex of an arch.

Crypt The basement of a church, not necessarily underground, often containing some of the relics.

Cyclopean Masonry Large, irregularly cut blocks of stone built into ponderous walls.

Dāgoba *See Stūpa.*

Dentil A small rectangular block; a molding composed of such blocks, commonly used to support a cornice.

Dhoti Draped skirt, India.

Diptych A painting composed of two balancing panels.

Dome　A hemispherical vault.

Dormer　An attic window with its roof and enframement projecting through a sloping roof.

Drum　A cylindrical block of stone to form part of the shaft of a column; also the cylindrical wall on which a dome rests.

Eaves　The portion of a roof overhanging the walls.

Echinus　The cushion-like member of the Doric capital immediately below the abacus.

Elevation　A scaled architectural drawing portraying the front, back, or side of a building.

Engaged Column　A column part of whose diameter is incorporated in a wall.

Engraving　A process in the graphic arts in which the design is scratched on a metal plate; ink wiped over the plate will remain in the scratches and thus enable the design to be printed.

Entablature　The portion above the columns and below the roof on the exterior of a classic temple, consisting of the architrave, frieze, and cornice; these same members may also be used to terminate a wall.

Entasis　The slight vertical curve or bulge in a shaft when compared with a straight line run from the top to the bottom. Most columns taper somewhat, but this is not entasis.

Etching　A graphic process wherein the design is scratched through a film of wax onto a metal plate; the plate is then bathed in acid which attacks the metal wherever the wax has been scratched off; after the acid has been washed off, and the remaining wax removed, the plate is inked and prints made from it.

Façade　The front of a building.

Fenestration　The arrangement of windows in a building.

Fêng　"Phoenix," bird of pheasant type in Chinese art.

Fillet　A narrow flat molding.

Flute　A groove, usually vertical; especially that in the shaft of a column or pilaster. Collectively these grooves are called fluting.

Flying Buttress　A half arch supporting a diagonal course of stone to transfer the thrusts of the nave vault over the aisle roofs to the pier buttress on the outer wall of the church.

Fresco　A technique of painting on wet plaster. See p. 231.

Frieze　A horizontal band, sometimes sculptured, especially the middle third of an entablature.

Frontality, Law of　Figures in which the axis of the body is not twisted or curved laterally are said to obey the law of frontality. The action of the arms or legs of such figures, however, need not be identical in pose.

Gambrel Roof　A roof with two slopes in each half; the upper slope comparatively gentle, and the lower one steeper.

Gandharva　Sky minstrel, India.

Gargoyle　A waterspout, frequently carved as a grotesque in mediaeval architecture.

Garuda　Bird enemy of Nāgas, India.

Gauffrage　Relief printing without color.

Gesso　The layers of plaster mixed with glue applied to panels to provide a smooth surface for the pigment.

Girder　A strong horizontal member supporting the beams of a floor or roof.

Groin Vault   A type of vault created by the intersection of two barrel vaults of equal span, the ridges of their intersections being called groins.

Half Timber   A form of construction in which the spaces between the heavy timbers of the frame are filled with brick or other material.

Hatching   Repeated small parallel lines frequently adopted to provide a transition from one value or color to another in early paintings. Cross Hatching refers to a crisscross of such lines.

Haunch   Roughly the middle third of the height of an arch.

Hināyāna   Lesser Vehicle of Buddhist doctrine.

Hip Roof   A roof that slopes up from three or four sides of a building, as distinguished from a gable roof which rises only from two sides.

Hypostyle   A colonnaded hall, particularly those in Egyptian temples.

Iconography   The identification of religious characters, incidents, and symbols in the arts.

Illuminated Manuscript   A hand-written book in which designs are introduced to adorn the text, such as initial letters, decorative borders, or even miniature paintings.

Impasto   The layer or layers of pigment in a painting.

Impost Block   A block placed between the capital of a column and the arches or vaults it supports.

Intercolumniation   The space between two columns.

Isocephaly   Heads of figures on the same level, as in a frieze.

Jātakas   Tales of previous existence of the Buddha, India.

Joist   A small beam to support a floor or ceiling.

Kakemono   Vertical scroll painting, Japan.

Keystone   The central stone in around or segmental arch. As a rule, there is no keystone in pointed arches.

Kōdō   Japanese, lecture hall.

Kondō   Japanese, Golden hall.

Ku   Chinese ritual vessel.

Lantern   A cupola placed at the apex of a dome or roof to admit light.

Lean-to   A roof with a single slope; a shed roof.

Li   Tripod with hollow legs; Chinese ritual vessel.

Linga   Phallic stone, India.

Lintel   A beam over a door, window, or intercolumniation.

Lithography   A graphic process in which the design is drawn on stone or metal with a greasy pencil. The stone may then be inked to permit printing of the design.

Liwan   A chamber or hall opening on a court, usually with a vaulted passage giving access to the interior, Persia.

Lokopala   Guardians of the four directions, India.

Mahāyāna   Greater Vehicle of Buddhist doctrine.

Makemono   Horizontal scroll painting, Japan.

Mandala (*Mandara,* Jap.)   Holy chart, India.

Mastaba   An Egyptian tomb form, rectangular in plan, low, flat-topped, and plain externally.

Metope   An approximately square slab in a Doric frieze between two triglyphs, sometimes enriched with sculpture.

Mihrab   Prayer niche in mosque, Persia.

Miniature   A small painting.

Modillion   A bracket-like form, often carved with an acanthus leaf, supporting the over-hanging members of Corinthian or Composite cornices.

Molding   A small band used singly or in combination with other moldings to decorate or divide architectural members.

Mortar   A mixture of cement or lime with sand and water to provide a cushion for stones or bricks in masonry.

Mosaic   A design composed of small cubes of stone or glass set in mortar to decorate floors, walls, or vaults. The designs may contain figures, or they may be floral or abstract.

Mudrā   Significant hand gestures, India.

Mullion   A vertical bar of stone or wood subdividing a window.

Nāga   Serpent kings, India.

Narthex   The vestibule of Early Christian or Byzantine churches.

Nave   Architecturally the central aisle of a church, and by extension, the entire western arm of a church. Liturgically, the portion of a church assigned to the laity.

Nave Arcade   The arches that support the triforium and clearstory, and therefore mark the separation of the nave and aisles.

Necking   The lowest portion of a capital which serves as a transition from the shaft to the upper members of the capital.

Obelisk   A tall, tapering rectangular monolith with a small pyramidal top, commonly used in front of Egyptian temples.

Obi   Sash worn by Japanese women.

Order   A formal system of base, column, and entablature in classic architecture.

Organic Architecture   An architecture in which ribbed vaults concentrate their weight and thrust at isolated points and are logically and visibly supported and abutted.

Patina   A discoloration of the surface of bronze, or by extension of stone sculpture, acquired through time or artificially induced.

Pediment   The low triangle at the end of a building corresponding to the pitched roof; a similar motive used over a door or window for accent or to discharge rainfall to the sides of the opening.

Pendant   A projection below the architectural member to which it is attached; pendants sometimes mark the junction of ribs in late Gothic vaults, or the lower ends of structural timbers under the overhanging second floor in early colonial houses.

Pendentive   A triangular section of a vault used to support a dome; four pendentives enable a dome to be supported over a square area.

Peripteral   Surrounded on all sides by free-standing columns.

Peristyle   A colonnade surrounding a building or within a court.

Perspective   The science of graphic presentation of the relative distances of objects. Linear Perspective resorts to line and relative size for this purpose; Atmospheric Perspective relies on the relatively sharper definition of nearby objects.

Pi   A circle, symbol of heaven and heaven's mandate held by the emperor of China.

Pier   An isolated architectural support, especially one whose plan is not circular. Pier is a more general term than column, but should be reserved to refer to those supports that cannot be called columns.

Pietà   A representation of the Virgin holding the dead body of Christ.

Pilaster   A columnar form flattened against a wall.

Pinnacle   A decorative turret projecting above a surface. Pinnacles appear in late Gothic buildings at the apex of gables and around the base of the spire, or above the buttresses along the parapet of a roof.

Plastics   Any of a number of fabricated precast or premolded materials available to-day for architecture and sculpture.

Plinth   A flat rectangular block; particularly the lowest unit of the base for an Ionic or Corinthian column.

Pointing   A mechanical method for reproducing in stone from a plaster model at any desired size the shape of a work of sculpture.

Polyptych   A painting of many panels.

Portico   A porch whose roof is supported by columns or piers.

Post and Lintel   A basic system of construction in which vertical supports carry horizontal beams.

Predella   In painting, the row of small panels below the principal panels of an altarpiece.

Pseudo-peripteral   Having a free-standing colonnade on one side, continued by pilasters on the remaining sides.

Pylon   A pair of solid masses of masonry flanking and forming an entrance; particularly in an Egyptian temple.

Quadripartite Vault   A four-part vault; a vault supported by ribs with the two diagonal ribs dividing the rectangle covered by the vault into four triangles.

Quoins   Alternate long and short blocks of stone at the corner of a masonry building for strength and accent.

Raking Cornice   A cornice following the sloping lines of a pediment.

Reinforced Concrete   Concrete in which steel bars have been embedded to add to the tensile strength.

Relief   Projection from a plane; particularly sculpture whose figures or objects are represented by their relative projection from a background.

Rib   An arch used to support a vault.

Rilievo Schiacciato   Crushed relief; very flat relief in which the forms seem to melt into the background; popularized by Donatello.

Rinceau   A pattern composed of a series of connected spirals of floral design.

Rustication   A treatment of stonework in which the individual blocks are accented either by leaving the exposed surface undressed, or by cutting back the edges of each block

Sanctuary   The area in a religious structure especially consecrated to the god.

Sash   The frame of a window holding the glass; the earlier type of sash was the Casement either fixed in place or hinged; late in seventeenth-century England the Double Hung Sash became popular, in which one or both halves of the window may slide up or down in grooves.

Senmurv or Si-murgh   Fabulous composite creature, Persia.

Set Back   Upper stories of smaller area than lower stories which therefore break back from the plane of the lower walls; particularly the upper stories of skyscrapers treated in this way.

Sexpartite Vault   A vault whose ribs divide the surface into six compartments, common in late Romanesque and early Gothic buildings.

Shaft   The portion of a column between the base and the capital comprising most of the height of the column.

Soffit   The exposed under surface of an arch or beam.

Soren   Crowning member of pagoda consisting of metal rings, Japan.

Spire   A tall pyramidal form placed over a tower.

Splay   A diagonal plane commonly used in mediaeval architecture to enlarge the areas of doors or windows.

Springing   The point at which an arch begins to curve.

Squinch   A device to support a dome over a square area; it may consist of an arched niche, or blocks placed diagonally across the corners of the square.

Steeple   Similar to a spire but different in that a steeple is composed of several distinct stories or stages whereas a spire is a single more or less enriched pyramid.

Stele   Memorial slab or tablet.

Stilting   The vertical portion of an arch between the impost or capital and the point at which the arch begins to curve. In Gothic architecture, stilting may be so pronounced that it requires a colonnette above the main capital. This is not true of Roman, Romanesque, or Renaissance arches, many of which, however, are slightly stilted.

String Course   A horizontal molding used to mark primary divisions in a wall.

Stūpa   Memorial mound, sometimes a reliquary, India.

Stylobate   The top step or platform of a classic temple on which the columns rest.

Sūtra   Buddhist scriptures, India.

Swag   A carved garland of fruit and flowers, commonly used in Roman art and its Renaissance and later derivatives.

Taille Directe   Direct cutting in stone of the final statue by the artist himself, instead of the nineteenth-century practice of turning over a plaster model of his work to a stonecutter for conversion into stone by pointing.

T'ao-t'ieh   Ornamental monster mask consisting of animal head with lower jaw missing, China.

Tempera   A technique of painting on a plaster-covered wooden panel. See p. 225.

Terra Cotta   Baked clay. Both architectural and sculptural forms can be molded in clay and then baked to become hardened; they may also be colored and glazed before baking.

Thrust   The lateral pressure of an arch or vault.

Thūpa   Pali for Stūpa.

Tie Rod   A rod of wood or metal whose ends are anchored in the springing of arches or vaults to counteract thrust; Italian architecture resorts to tie rods so regularly that painters introduce them into their paintings, but northern peoples tend to look on them as a subterfuge and to prefer the more structural masonry buttress.

Ting Vessel   Tripod for food offering, China.

Ting Ware   White glazed ceramic ware, China.

Tondo   A circular painting or relief.

Torana   Gateway to Buddhist shrine, India.

Torii   Gateway to Shinto shrine, Japan.

Tracery   The interlocking bars of stone subdividing Gothic windows and supporting the glass.

Transepts   A transverse unit of a church plan projecting beyond the walls of the aisles and usually of the same height as the nave.

Triforium   That gallery in churches between the nave arcade and the clearstory, corresponding in height to the lean-to roof over the aisles.

Triglyph   A group of vertical members alternating with metopes in the frieze of the Doric order.

Triptych   A painting with three panels; the side panels are often one half the size of the central panel and hinged to it so that they may be folded over it like doors.

Trumeau   A post supporting a tympanum within an arch and dividing a doorway into two doors.

Truss   A structure of wood or metal members, based on the rigidity of a triangle, and devised to support a heavier load or cover a wider span than is practicable with beams or girders.

Tympanum   The surface below an arch and above a door, often sculptured.

Ukiyo-e   'Pictures of a floating world'—popular Japanese art.

Ūrnā   Buddhist mark between the eyes, India.

Ushnisha   Buddhist protuberance on top of head, India.

Vajrapani   Thunderbolt-bearers, India.

Vault   A method of roofing an area based on the principle of the arch. See *Barrel Vault, Dome, Groin Vault, Quadripartite Vault, Sexpartite Vault.*

Veneer   A thin layer of material applied as surface decoration for its beauty of color or texture.

Vihāra   Monastic establishment, India.

Volute   A scroll, such as the spirals at the sides of Ionic capitals, or the large scrolls flanking the second-story façades of Italian late sixteenth- and early seventeenth-century churches.

Voussoir   One of the wedge-shaped stones of an arch or vault.

Wainscot   A treatment of an interior wall, especially of its lower part, with paneling.

Web of a Vault   The mass of a vault as distinguished from the ribs.

Woodcut   A graphic process in which the design to be printed is left on the surface of a block of wood by cutting away the portions intended to be left white.

Yaksha   Guardian of mineral treasures of the earth, India.

Yakshi   Nature spirit, tree guardian, India.

Yamato-e   Painting in true Japanese style.

Yang and Yin   Symbols of male and female elements in Chinese art.

Yoni   Symbol of the female in India, a circle.

Yü   Bucket-shaped ritual vessel for carrying liquids, Chinese.

Ziggurat   A Mesopotamian temple tower of stepped form, built of brick.

Zoning Law   A legal restriction on building imposed in many communities to limit the use and size of buildings within specified areas.

Suggested Readings

GENERAL

Chase, G. H. and Post, C. R., *A History of Sculpture*, New York, Harper, 1925.
  The best one volume introduction to the subject.
Cheney, Sheldon, *A World History of Art*, New York, Viking, 1937.
  An exciting, if biased, version of the history of art, brilliantly written by an outspoken advocate of modern art.
Fletcher, B. F., *A History of Architecture on the Comparative Method*, New York, Scribner, 1943.
  Indispensable for reference.
Fry, R., *Transformations*, London, Chatto & Windus, 1926.
———, *Vision and Design*, London, Chatto & Windus, 1920.
  Two volumes of unusually thought-provoking essays on miscellaneous problems in the theory and history of art.
Hamlin, T. F., *Architecture Through the Ages*, New York, Putnam, 1940.
  A splendid interpretation of architecture in civilization by one of the leading American architectural historians.
Post, C. R., *A History of European and American Sculpture from the Early Christian Period to the Present Day*, 2 vols., Cambridge, Harvard University Press, 1921.
  A comprehensive survey, but insufficient illustrations.
Robb, D. M., *The Harper History of Painting: the Occidental Tradition*, New York, Harper, 1951.
  The most recent one-volume introduction to the subject.

PRIMARILY FOR ILLUSTRATIONS

Phaidon Press
  A series of volumes, chiefly of illustrations that are exceptional in quality. Among the periods and personalities covered to date are Ancient Egypt, Roman Portraits, Ghiberti, Donatello, Angelico, Mantegna, Botticelli, Leonardo, Michelangelo, Raphael, Titian, Tintoretto, Dürer, Bruegel, Bernini, El Greco, Velásquez, Rubens, Hals, Rembrandt, Vermeer, The Impressionists, Rodin, Cézanne, Van Gogh, and Chinese Painting.
Propylaean Kunstgeschichte
  A multi-volume work on successive art periods. Although the brief text, captions, and index are in German, the illustrations are copious and of satisfactory quality. The chief defect lies in an over-emphasis on German art.

Skira Books

> *The Great Centuries of Painting*
> *Painting, Colour, History*
> *The Taste of Our Time*
> In these three series, the text has been written by recognized authorities in their fields, but their chief value perhaps lies in their copious color illustrations.

The University Prints

> An extensive and admirable (in view of the very reasonable price) collection of photographs covering architecture, sculpture, painting, and some of the minor arts in Europe, America, and the Orient. The prints may be obtained individually, in sets covering particular art periods, or, in some cases, in bound volumes.

THEORY, ICONOGRAPHY, MISCELLANEOUS

Bulfinch, Thomas, *The Age of Fable*, New York, Crowell, 1947.
> The standard reference book on mythology.

Ducasse, C. J., *The Philosophy of Art*, New York, MacVeagh, 1929.
> A well-balanced and critical discussion.

Greene, Theodore, *The Arts and the Art of Criticism*, Princeton, Princeton University Press, 1940.
> A comprehensive discussion of aesthetics involving literature, music, and the dance as well as the visual arts.

Hamlin, T. F., *Architecture, An Art for All Men*, New York, Columbia University Press, 1947.
> An unimpeachable presentation of the elements and theory of architecture for the layman.

Jameson, Mrs. A., *Legends of the Madonna*, Boston, Houghton Mifflin, 1896.
———, *Legends of the Monastic Orders*, Boston, Houghton Mifflin, 1897.
———, *Sacred and Legendary Art*, 2 vols., Boston, Houghton Mifflin, 1897.
> Indispensable reference works on Christian iconography.

Ruskin, John, *Modern Painters*, new ed., New York, Merrill and Baker, 1873.
> An epoch-making examination of Renaissance and later landscape painting.

———, *The Seven Lamps of Architecture*, Orpington, Allen, 1880.
> A literary classic providing a Victorian moralistic theory of architecture.

Scott, Geoffrey, *The Architecture of Humanism*, 2nd ed., New York, Scribner, 1924.
> A penetrating examination of architectural theory and the fallacies that have crept into the criticism of architecture.

Sullivan, Louis, *The Autobiography of an Idea*, New York, Norton, 1934.
> A picturesque account of Sullivan's life and of his formulation of the functional theory of architecture.

Wittkower, Rudolf, *Architectural Principles in the Age of Humanism*, London, Warburg Institute, 1949.
> A keen critical study of Renaissance and Post-Renaissance theory.

Wolfflin, Heinrich, *Principles of Art History*, 7th ed., trans. by M. D. Hottinger, London, Bell, 1932.
> Hard reading, but widely recognized for its discussion of basic art problems.

PREHISTORIC ART (CHAPTER II)

Breuil, Abbé H., *Four Hundred Centuries of Cave Art*, trans. by M. E. Boyle, Montignac, Centre d'Etudes et de Documenation Préhistorique, 1952.

Brown, G. B., *The Art of the Cave Dweller*, London, John Murray, 1928.

Childe, V. G., *Man Makes Himself*, London, Rationalist Press, 1936.

Howells, W., *Back of History*, New York, Doubleday, 1954.

Maringer, J. and Bandi, H. G., *Art in the Ice Age*, New York, Frederick A. Praeger, 1953.

PRE-CLASSICAL ART (CHAPTER III)

Aldred, Cyril, *Old Kingdom Art in Ancient Egypt*, London, A. Tiranti, 1949.

————, *Middle Kingdom Art in Ancient Egypt*, London, A. Tiranti, 1950.

————, *New Kingdom Art in Ancient Egypt, During the Eighteenth Dynasty*, London, A. Tiranti, 1951.

These three volumes have been printed in one volume.

Frankfort, Henry, *The Art and Architecture of the Ancient Orient*, Harmondsworth, Penguin, 1954.

An up-to-date account of this important field.

Hall, H. R., *Aegean Archaeology*, London, Warner, 1915.

A careful but dry summary of Aegean civilization.

Smith, E. B., *Egyptian Architecture as Cultural Expression*, New York, Appleton-Century, 1938.

A thorough and scholarly presentation of the causes, characteristics, and growth of Egyptian architecture.

GREEK ART (CHAPTERS IV-VI)

Bieber, Marguerite, *The Sculpture of the Hellenistic Age*, New York, Columbia University Press, 1955.

The last word on this period.

Dickinson, G. L., *The Greek View of Life*, 15th ed., New York, Doubleday, 1924.

An admirable commentary on the interrelation in Greek life of religion, the state, the individual, and the various forms of artistic expression. Not illustrated.

Dinsmoor, W. B., *The Architecture of Ancient Greece*, London, Batsford, 1950.

Comprehensive and absolutely reliable.

Richter, G. M. A., *The Sculpture and Sculptors of the Greeks*, New Haven, Yale University Press, 1929.

A scholarly volume on the whole history of Greek sculpture.

ROMAN ART (CHAPTER VII)

Anderson, W. J. and Spiers, R. P., *The Architecture of Ancient Rome*, rev. by T. Ashby, London, Batsford, 1927.

Swift, E. H., *Roman Sources of Christian Art*, New York, Columbia University Press, 1951.

Though savagely attacked, the basic thesis of this book seems sound.

Walters, H. B., *The Art of the Romans*, London, Methuen, 1911.

Satisfactory general account of Roman architecture, sculpture, and painting.

The Arts of the Early Church (Chapter VIII)

Dalton, O. M., *Byzantine Art and Archaeology*, Oxford, Clarendon Press, 1911.
The most satisfactory work in one volume on a field not well covered by publications in English.

Hamilton, G. H., *The Art and Architecture of Russia*, Harmondsworth, Penguin, 1954.
The scholarly standard on a field of growing interest.

Hamilton, J. A., *Byzantine Architecture and Decoration*, New York, Scribner's, 1934.

Lowrie, Walter, *Art in the Early Church*, New York, Pantheon, 1947.
A sound handbook on Early Christian art, covering iconography, architecture, sculpture, painting, and the minor arts.

Rivoira, G. T., *Lombardic Architecture; Its Origins, Development, and Derivatives*, 2 vols., new ed., trans. by G. M. Rushforth, Oxford, Clarendon Press, 1933.
By the outstanding opponent of Strzygowski; this book carries on through the Romanesque period; prejudiced in favor of Italy, especially in dates.

Strzykowski, Josef, *Origin of Christian Church Art*, trans. by O. M. Dalton and H. J. Braunholtz, Oxford, Clarendon Press, 1923.
An attempt to trace the origin of Early Christian art to the eastern Mediterranean and beyond; its thesis finds less favor today than some years ago.

Romanesque and Gothic Art (Chapters IX-XI)

Bond, Francis, *English Church Architecture*, 2 vols., New York, Oxford, 1913.
A scholarly analysis of the development of the several elements of English medieval architecture in the Romanesque and Gothic periods.

Clapham, A. W., *Romanesque Architecture in Western Europe*, Oxford, Clarendon Press, 1936.

Dupont, Jacques and Gnudi, Cesare, *The Great Centuries of Gothic Painting*, Geneva, Skira, 1954.

Evans, Joan, *Art in Medieval France, 987–1498*, New York, Oxford, 1948.
A comprehensive survey of this field.

Mâle, Émile, *Religious Art in France; XIII Century*, 3rd ed., trans. by D. Nussey, New York, Dutton, 1913.
The classic discussion of medieval iconography; two other volumes covering the earlier and later Middle Ages have not been translated.

Meiss, Millard, *Painting in Florence and Siena After the Black Death*, Princeton, Princeton University Press, 1951.
The second half of the 14th century.

Moore, C. H., *Development and Character of Gothic Architecture*, 2nd ed., New York, Macmillan, 1904.
The classic presentation of the thesis that the essence of Gothic architecture lies in its solution of structural problems.

Morey, C. R., *Medieval Art*, New York, Norton, 1942.
Iconography and style from Early Christian times through late Gothic art.

Panofsky, Erwin, *Early Netherlandish Painting, Its Origins and Character*, Cambridge, Harvard University Press, 1953.

Porter, A. K., *Medieval Architecture*, New Haven, Yale University Press, 1912.
The major problems of Carolingian, Lombard, Norman, and French Gothic buildings, with an introduction to the architecture of the early church.

Stone, Lawrence, *Sculpture in Britain; the Middle Ages*, Harmondsworth, Penguin, 1955.

ITALIAN RENAISSANCE ART (CHAPTERS XII, XIII)

Anderson, W. J., *The Architecture of the Renaissance in Italy*, 5th ed., rev. and enl. by A. Stratton, New York, Scribner, 1927.

Burckhardt, Jakob, *Civilization of the Renaissance in Italy*, New York, Oxford, 1944.
> The background and character of the movement; indispensable to both the student and the general reader.

Castiglione, Baldassare, *The Book of the Courtier*, trans. by L. E. Opdycke, New York, Scribner, 1927.
> Imaginary discussions by a contemporary of the characteristics of ladies and gentlemen in the early 16th century.

Cellini, Benvenuto, *The Autobiography of Benvenuto Cellini*, trans. by J. A. Symonds, New York, Macmillan, 1929.
> A highly colored account of his personal prowess and artistic achievements.

Lassaigne, Jacques and Argan, G. C., *The Fifteenth Century from Van Eyck to Botticelli*, Geneva, Skira, 1955.
> Chiefly Flemish, Italian, and French painting.

Maclagan, Eric, *Italian Sculpture of the Renaissance*, Cambridge, Harvard University Press, 1935.

Mather, F. J., *A History of Italian Painting*, New York, Holt, 1923.
> The development and character of Italian painting from Giotto and Duccio through the 16th century, with a brief conclusion on the painting of the 17th and 18th centuries.

Schmeckbier, Lawrence, *A Handbook of Italian Renaissance Painting*, New York, Putnam, 1938.
> Valuable for its concentration on the facts.

Vasari, Giorgio, *Lives of Seventy of the Most Eminent Painters, Sculptors, and Architects*, 10 vols., trans. by G. D. de Vere, London, Macmillan, 1912–14.
> This classic, though often inaccurate, is still worth reading for its gossip about the leaders of Italian art in the late Middle Ages and Renaissance. Many editions and translations are available.

NORTHERN RENAISSANCE ART; POST-RENAISSANCE ART (CHAPTERS XIV-XIX)

Blunt, Anthony, *Art and Architecture in France*, 1500–1700, London, Penguin, 1953.

Fokker, T. H., *Roman Baroque Art*, London, Oxford, 1938.

Hagen, Oskar, *Patterns and Principles of Spanish Art*, Madison, University of Wisconsin Press, 1943.

Kimball, S. F., *The Creation of the Rococo*, Philadelphia, Philadelphia Museum of Art, 1943.

Mather, F. J., *Western European Painting of the Renaissance*, New York, Holt, 1939.
> Painting outside of Italy in the 16th and 17th centuries.

Summerson, John, *Architecture in Britain*, 1530–1830, London, Penguin, 1953.

Traz, Georges de, *The Eighteenth Century, Watteau to Tiepolo*, trans. by S. Gilbert, Geneva, Skira, 1952.
> Chiefly French, English, and Italian.

Waterhouse, E. K., *Painting in Britain, 1530 to 1790*, London, Penguin, 1953.

Wilenski, R. H., *Dutch Painting*, London, Faber & Faber, 1955.

ARTS OF THE AMERICAN INDIAN (CHAPTER XX)

Bennett, W. C., *Ancient Arts of the Andes*, introd. by René d'Harnoncourt, New York, Museum of Modern Art, 1954.

Douglas, F. H. and Harnoncourt, René d', *Indian Art of the United States*, New York, Museum of Modern Art, 1941.

Drucker, Philip, *Indians of the Northwest Coast*, New York, American Museum of Natural History, 1955.

Feuchtwanger, Franz, *The Art of Ancient Mexico*, London, Thames and Hidson, 1945.

Morley, S. G., *The Ancient Maya*, 3rd ed., rev. by G. W. Brainerd, Stanford, Stanford University Press, 1956.

Vaillant, G. C., *Indian Arts in North America*, New York, Harper, 1939.

AMERICAN ART (CHAPTERS XXI AND XXVI)

Andrews, Wayne, *Architecture, Ambition and Americans: History of American Architecture*, New York, Harper, 1955.
> A general account of American architecture.

Barker, Virgil, *American Painting, History and Interpretation*, New York, Macmillan, 1950.
> A thorough and critical discussion of painting down to 1900.

Baur, J. I. H., *Revolution and Tradition in Modern American Art*, Cambridge, Harvard University Press, 1951.
> Painting and sculpture since 1900; well organized.

Burroughs, Alan, *Limners and Likenesses; Three Centuries of American Painting*, Cambridge, Harvard University Press, 1936.
> Brief but stimulating.

Forman, H. C., *The Architecture of the Old South*, Cambridge, Harvard University Press, 1948.

Hamlin, Talbot, *Benjamin Henry Latrobe*, New York, Oxford, 1955.
> The Pulitzer Prize biography.

——, *Greek Revival Architecture in America*, New York, Oxford, 1944.

Kimball, S. F., *Domestic Architecture of the American Colonies and of the Early Republic*, New York, Scribner, 1922.
> The Colonial, Georgian, and Federal periods.

Larkin, O. W., *Art and Life in America*, New York, Rinehart, 1949.
> Painting, sculpture, and architecture from the time of settlement to the present.

Morrison, Hugh, *Early American Architecture*, New York, Oxford, 1952.
> A thorough and up-to-date account down to 1775.

Mujica, Francisco, *History of the Skyscraper*, Paris, Archaeology and Architecture Press, 1929.

Mumford, Louis, *Sticks and Stones*, New York, Norton, 1933.

Richardson, E. P., *Painting in America*, New York, Crowell, 1956.

Taft, Lorado, *History of American Sculpture*, new ed. rev., New York, Macmillan, 1930.
> The only serious and complete work in this field, but the geniality and eclecticism of its author hamper its critical quality.

THE NINETEENTH CENTURY IN EUROPE (CHAPTERS XXII-XXIV)

Clark, Kenneth, *The Gothic Revival*, New York, Scribner, 1929.
> The bases and growth of the movement; hampered by insufficient illustrations.

Fry, R. E., *Characteristics of French Art*, London, Chatto & Windus, 1932.
> Six critical essays covering the story of French painting from the late Middle Ages through the nineteenth century.

Hitchcock, H. R., *Early Victorian Architecture in Britain*, New Haven, Yale University Press, 1954.

Mather, F. J., *Modern Painting, A Study of Tendencies*, New York, Holt, 1927.
> Although unsympathetic in its treatment of the men after Impressionism, its discussion of the earlier movements of the nineteenth century is effective.

Meier-Graefe, Julius, *Modern Art; Being a Contribution to a New System of Aesthetics*, 2 vols., trans. by F. Simmonds and G. W. Chrystal, New York, Putnam, 1908.
> Though spotty and overloaded in the second volume with German painters, its treatment of the Impressionists and Post-Impressionists is excellent.

Rewald, John, *The History of Impressionism*, New York, Museum of Modern Art, 1946.

———, *Post-Impressionism*, New York, Museum of Modern Art, 1956.

THE ART OF PRIMITIVE PEOPLES (CHAPTER XXV)

Linton, R., Wingert, P. S., and Harnoncourt, R. d', *Arts of the South Seas*, New York, Museum of Modern Art, 1946.

Masterpieces of African Art, Brooklyn, Brooklyn Museum, 1954.

Muensterberger, W., in collaboration with W. L. Muensterberger, *The Sculpture of Primitive Man*, New York, Harry N. Abrams, 1955.
> For illustrations.

Radin, P. and Sweeney, J. J., *African Folktales and Sculpture*, New York, Pantheon, 1952.

Tischner, Herbert, *Oceanic Art*, New York, Pantheon, 1954.
> For illustrations.

Trowell, Margaret, *Classical African Sculpture*, London, Faber & Faber, 1954.

Sydow, E. von, *Afrikanische Plastik*, New York, Wittenborn, 1954.
> For illustrations.

Wingert, P. S., *The Sculpture of Negro Africa*, New York, Columbia University Press, 1950.

———, *Art of the South Pacific Islands*, New York, Beechhurst Press, 1953.

TWENTIETH-CENTURY ART (CHAPTER XXVII)

Barr, A. H., *Picasso, Fifty Years of his Art*, New York, Museum of Modern Art, 1946.

———, ed., *Masters of Modern Art*, New York, Museum of Modern Art, 1954.

Giedion, Sigfried, *Space, Time, and Architecture*, Cambridge, Harvard University Press, 1941.
> The growth of modern architecture in structure and aesthetics from the late Baroque style in Europe to the present.

Hamlin, T. F., *Forms and Functions of Twentieth-Century Architecture,* 4 vols., New York, Columbia University Press, 1952.
> Comprehensive discussion of architectural theory and problems in mid-century.

Hitchcock, H. R., *Modern Architecture, Romanticism and Reintegration,* New York, Payson, 1929.
> Thorough account of the growth of modern architecture from the early nineteenth century.

Le Corbusier, *Towards a New Architecture,* trans. from the 13th French ed. by F. Etchells, London, Bodker, 1931.

Museum of Modern Art. Catalogues, especially those on 'Cubism and Abstract Art' (1936), and 'Fantastic Art, Dada, Surrealism' (1936).
> Both the brief introductions and the abundant illustrations are admirable.

The Louise and Walter Arensberg Collection, Twentieth Century Section, Philadelphia, Philadelphia Museum of Art, 1954.

Whittick, Arnold, *European Architecture in the Twentieth Century,* 2 vols., London, Lockwood, 1950–53.

ORIENTAL ART, GENERAL (CHAPTERS XXVIII-XXXI)

Binyon, Lawrence, *The Spirit of Man in Asian Art,* Cambridge, Harvard University Press, 1935.

Finegan, Jack, *The Archaeology of World Religions,* Princeton, Princeton University Press, 1952.
> An illustrated history of Asiatic religious thought.

Grousset, René, *The Civilizations of the East,* trans. by C. A. Phillips, 4 vols., New York, Knopf, 1931–5.
> The arts of Persia, India and Greater India, China, and Japan.

Hackin, J., and others, *Asiatic Mythology,* London, Harrap, 1932.

PERSIA (CHAPTER XXVIII)

Arnold, T. W., *Painting in Islam,* Oxford, Clarendon Press, 1928.

Dimand, M. S., *Handbook of Muhammadan Art,* New York, Metropolitan Museum, 1944.

Ghirshman, Roman, *Iran,* London, Penguin, 1954.
> Excellent on pre-Islamic eras.

Gray, Basil, *Persian Painting,* London, Benn, 1930.
> A good summary, including a discussion of techniques.

Guest, G. D., *Shiraz Painting in the Sixteenth Century,* Washington, Freer Gallery, 1949.

Herzfeld, E. E., *Iran in the Ancient East,* New York, Oxford, 1941.
> Persian art from prehistoric times through early historic periods.

Lane, A., *Early Islamic Pottery,* New York, 1948.

Pope, A. U., ed., *A Survey of Persian Art,* New York, Oxford, 1938–9.

Wilber, D. N., *The Architecture of Islamic Iran,* Princeton, 1952.

INDIA (CHAPTER XXIX)

Anand, M. R., *The Hindu View of Art,* London, Allen & Unwin, 1933.

Binyon, Lawrence, *The Court Painters of the Great Moguls*, New York, Oxford, 1921.
An account of Mogul court and art.

Brown, Percy, *Indian Architecture*, Bombay, 1942.

Codrington, K. de B., *An Introduction to the Study of Mediaeval Indian Sculpture*, London, Goldston, 1929.
Recommended for later Hindu art.

Coomaraswamy, A. K., *History of Indian and Indonesian Art*, London, Goldston, 1927.
———, *Rajput Painting*, 2 vols., New York, Oxford, 1936.

Gordon, A. K., *The Iconography of Tibetan Lamaism*, New York, Columbia University Press, 1939.
Good reference book for beginners.

Khandalavala, K., *Indian Sculpture and Painting*, Bombay, Taraporevala, n. d.

Mackay, E., *The Indus Valley Civilization*, London, 1935.
Résumé of prehistoric art.

Majumdar, R., Raychaudhuri, H., and Datta, K., *An Advanced History of India*, London, 1950.

Mehta, N. C., *Studies in Indian Painting*, Bombay, Taraporevala, 1926.

Rowland, Benjamin, *The Art and Architecture of India*, London, Penguin, 1953.
Except for the omission of Islamic art, a good coverage of India and Greater India.

Zimmer, H. R., *Myths and Symbols in Indian Art and Civilization*, New York, Pantheon, 1946.
———, *The Art of Indian Asia*, ed. by J. Campbell, New York, Pantheon, 1955.

China (Chapter xxx)

Ashton, Leigh, *An Introduction to the Study of Chinese Sculpture*, London, Benn, 1924.

Binyon, Lawrence, *The Flight of the Dragon*, London, Murray, 1943.
———, *Painting in the Far East*, London, Arnold, 1943.

Creel, H. G., *The Birth of China*, New York, Reynal & Hitchcock, 1936.
Recommended for the early arts of China.

Driscoll, L. and Toda, K., *Chinese Calligraphy*, Chicago, University of Chicago, 1935.

Getty, Alice, *The Gods of Northern Buddhism*, Oxford, Clarendon, 1928.

Goodrich, L. C., *A Short History of the Chinese People*, rev. ed., New York, Harper, 1951.
———, and Fenn, H., *A Syllabus of the History of Chinese Civilization and Culture*, New York, Chinese Society of America, 1941.

Grousset, René, *In the Footsteps of the Buddha*, London, Routledge, 1932.
Translations from the diary of a Chinese monk of the seventh century, containing an account of life in China, Central Asia, and India.

Guest, G. D. and Wenley, A. G., *Outlines for the Study of Far Eastern Art—China*, Washington, Freer Gallery, 1946.
Annotated bibliography on China and Japan.

Kuo Hsi, *An Essay on Landscape Painting*, trans. by S. Sakanishi, London, Murray, 1935.

Leach, B., *A Potter's Book*, London, 1940.
Excellent on techniques.

Nourse, M., *A Short History of the Chinese*, Philadelphia, Blakiston, 1944.

Sakanishi, Shio, *The Spirit of the Brush*, London, Murray, 1939.

Sickman, L. C. and Soper, A., *The Art and Architecture of China*, London, Penguin, 1956.

Sirén, Osvald, *Chinese Painting*, 6 vols., London, Lund Humphries, 1956.

JAPAN (CHAPTER XXXI)

Binyon, L. and Sexton, J. J. O., *Japanese Colour Prints*, London, Benn, 1923.

Blaser, Werner, *Japanese Temples and Tea-houses*, New York, Dodge Books, 1956.

Bowie, H. P., *On the Laws of Japanese Painting*, New York, Dover Publications, 1951.

Drexler, A., *The Architecture of Japan*, New York, 1955.

Index of Japanese Painters, Tokyo, The Society of Friends of Eastern Art, 1941.

Koiki, S., *Japan's New Architecture*, Tokyo, 1956.

Ledoux, L. V., *An Essay on Japanese Prints*, New York, privately printed, 1938.

Minamoto, Hoshu, *An Illustrated History of Japanese Art*, trans. by H. G. Henderson, Kyoto, Hoshino, 1935.

Okakura, Kakuzo, *Ideals of the East*, London, Murray, 1905.
> Essays by a man acquainted with both Oriental and Western traditions.

Pageant of Japanese Art, ed. by staff members of the Tokyo National Museum, Tokyo, 1952–54.

Paine, R. T., *Japanese Screen Paintings*, Boston, Museum of Fine Arts, 1935.

—— and Soper, A., *The Art and Architecture of Japan*, London, Penguin, 1955.

Sadler, A. L., *Cha-no-yu*, London, 1934.
> Description of the tea ceremony.

——, *A Short History of Japanese Architecture*, London, 1941.

Sansom, G. B., *Japan, A Short Cultural History*, rev. ed., New York, Appleton, 1943.

Soper, A. C., *The Evolution of Buddhist Architecture in Japan*, Princeton, Princeton University Press, 1942.

Toda, Kenji, *Japanese Scroll Painting*, Chicago, University of Chicago Press, 1935.

Tsuda, N., *Handbook of Japanese Art*, Tokyo, Sanseido, 1935.

Warner, Langdon, *The Craft of the Japanese Sculptor*, New York, McFarlane, 1936.

——, *The Enduring Art of Japan*, Cambridge, Harvard University Press, 1952.
> Methods and media described in a dynamic series of essays.

Index

851

H

Hachiman as a Priest (Kōshun), 808; fig. 647
Haida, Totem Pole, 461-2; fig. 355
Halebid, Temple, 698
Halicarnassus, Mausoleum, sculpture, 101-2, 110; fig. 68
Hals, Frans, 387-8, 523, 525
    Jolly Toper, The, 388; fig. 301
    Officers of St. Andrew's Company, 387; fig. 300
Hamilton, Thomas (High School, Edinburgh), 480
Hampton Court, 343
Hamza-nāmah, illumination from, 710; fig. 549
Harappa, torso from, 676, 680; fig. 511
Hare Chasing a Monkey ('Toba Sōjō), 806-7; fig. 643
Hari-Hara, 717-18; fig. 558
Hartford, Capitol (Richard M. Upjohn), 575
Hartford, Old State House (Bulfinch), 474
Hartley, Marsden (*Portrait of a German Officer*), 605-7, 609; fig. 460
Harunobu (*Crow and the Heron*), 822, 824; fig. 666
Harvesters (Bruegel), 353
Hasta la Muerte (Goya), 495; fig. 374
Hawaiian sculpture, 560-61; fig. 422
Hay Wain (Constable), 503-4; Pl. VIII
Heathfield, Lord, portrait of (Reynolds), 436
Heckel, Erich, 619
Helmholtz, H. L. F., 527
Henri, Robert, 603-4, 613
Hepplewhite, George, 432
Heracles and Antaeus (Euphronius), 70-71, 97; fig. 39
Heracles and Nemean Lion, 687; fig. 524
Hera of Argos (Polyclitus), 98
Hera of Samos, 67, 69, 72; fig. 34
Herculaneum, excavation of, 417
Hercules and Antaeus (Pollaiuolo), 262-3; fig. 204
Hercules Hurling Lichias into the Sea (Canova), 480
Hermes Carrying the Infant Dionysus (Praxiteles), 100-101, 111; fig. 66
Herodotus, 42, 649
High Yaller (Marsh), 610
Hildesheim, Knochenhauerampthaus, 212
Hingham, Old Ship Meeting House, 466
Hireling Shepherd (Bruegel), 354
Hiroshigé (*Shōno*), 828-9; fig. 671
Ho Ch'ü-ping, Tomb of, 733-4; fig. 573
Hogarth, William, 428, 433-4
    Coram, Captain, portrait of, 434
    Marriage à la Mode, 433-4; fig. 337
    Shrimp Girl, 434
Hohokam, 455, 456
Hokusai (*The Wave*), 6, 827, 828; fig. 670

Holabird and Root (Chicago Daily News Building), 9, 591; fig. 447
Holbein, Hans, the Younger, 5, 7, 349-52
    Dance of Death, 349
    Gisze, Georg, portrait of, 351; fig. 277
    Madonna of the Burgomaster Meyer, 349-51
    Seymour, Jane, portrait of, 351-2; fig. 278
Holland, painting, Post-Impressionist, 535-7; figs. 403, 404
    17th century, 384-96; figs. 300-306; Pl. VIII
    20th century, 627-8; fig. 472
Hollywood, Barnsdall Residence (Wright), 598
Homer, 53-4, 64, 65, 105
Homer, Winslow, 573-4, 616
    All's Well, 573
    Northeaster, 574; fig. 433
Honfleurs (Corot), 507; fig. 384
Hooch, Pieter de, 393
Hood and Fouilhoux (Rockefeller Center, New York), 593-5
Hopi art, 459
Hopper, Edward (*Lighthouse at Two Lights*), 610, 616; fig. 463
Hoppner, John, 437
Horace, 278
Horse, The (Duchamp-Villon), 636
Hōryū-ji Temple, Nara, architecture, 785-6; fig. 619
Hōryū-ji Temple, Nara, painting, 791, 793; figs. 626, 629
Hōryū-ji Temple, Nara, sculpture, 787-93; figs. 621-5, 627, 628
Hotī-Mardan, *Buddha,* 682-3; fig. 519
Houdon, Jean Antoine (*Voltaire,* portrait of), 427-8; fig. 333
Howe and Lescaze (Philadelphia Savings Fund Society Building), 593, 595
Howells and Hood (Chicago Tribune Building), 591
Hsia Kuei (*Rain Storm*), 762-3, 776, 815; fig. 599
Hsi-chin Chu-shih (*One of the Ten Kings of Hell*), 768; fig. 606
Hsieh Ho, canons of, 753
Huang Kung-wang, 772
Hui-néng (Liang K'ai), 760; fig. 596
Hui-tsung, 755-7, 758, 764, 772
    Five-Colored Parakeet, 756-7; fig. 592
    Ladies Preparing Newly Woven Silk, 756; fig. 591
Human Concretion (Arp), 640; fig. 479
Hundred Geese Scroll (Ma Fèn), 768; fig. 605
Huntsmen in the Snow (Bruegel), 353

I

Ibibio wood carving, 551
Ibo wood carving, 551; fig. 411